KT-552-292

Also by Jack Nicklaus

My 55 Ways to Lower Your Golf Score

Take a Tip from Me

The Greatest Game of All (with Herbert Warren Wind)

Golf My Way (with Ken Bowden)

Jack Nicklaus' Lesson Tee (with Ken Bowden)

On and Off the Fairway (with Ken Bowden)

Jack Nicklaus' Playing Lessons (with Ken Bowden)

The Full Swing (with Ken Bowden)

My Most Memorable Shots in the Majors (with Ken Bowden)

Paperback
(with Ken Bowden and Jim McQueen)

Play Better Golf: The Swing from A–Z

Play Better Golf: The Short Game and Scoring

Play Better Golf: Short Cuts to Lower Scores

Jack Nicklaus

with Ken Bowden

MY STORY

Ebury Press
London

First published in Great Britain in 1997

1 3 5 7 9 10 8 6 4 2

Copyright © 1997 by Jack Nicklaus

All rights reserved.
No part of this publication may be reproduced, stored in a retrieval system, or transmitted in any form or by any means, electronic, mechanical, photocopying, recording or otherwise, without prior permission from the copyright owners.

Ebury Press
Random House, 20 Vauxhall Bridge Road, London SW1V 2SA

Random House Australia Pty Limited
20 Alfred Street, Milsons Point, Sydney, New South Wales 2061, Australia

Random House New Zealand Limited
18 Poland Road, Glenfield, Auckland 10, New Zealand

Random House South Africa (Pty) Limited
Endulini, 5A Jubilee Road, Parktown 2193, South Africa

Random House UK Limited Reg. No. 954009

A CIP catalogue record for this book is available from the British Library

ISBN 0 09 178631 2

Printed and bound in Great Britain by
Mackays of Chatham PLC, Chatham, Kent

Papers used by Ebury Press are natural, recyclable products made from wood grown in sustainable forests

For all the Nicklauses, past,
present and future, but
especially for Barbara, Jack,
Steve, Nan, Gary, and Michael

Contents

Preface

This book tells, for the first and last time and in detail, from my perspective, the stories of the achievements that have meant and always will mean the most to me. They are, of course, my victories in golf's major championships.

My Story, however, also contains much more than that.

I first began working on this book in the early 1980s and was pretty well into it when I suggested to my longtime collaborator, Ken Bowden, that we take a break. The reason was that while I did not believe that in my early forties I was likely to scale new heights, I had a strong sense I still might enlarge the mountain. The 1986 Masters proved me correct, bringing my total of majors wins to twenty, if you count the U.S. Amateur as such (as it was in my youthful hero Bobby Jones's time), or eighteen, if you include only the Masters, the U.S. and British Opens, and the PGA Championship in that category.

Whether or not I enlarge the mountain still further, as I continue trying to do at the time of writing, that is a record of which I am extremely proud. Unlike most people in golf it seems, I believe my record will one day be surpassed, even if not in my lifetime. But I get immense pleasure out of having made the task so challenging.

When work resumed on the book in the early 1990s, I was pleased to discover that the hundreds more conversations that Barbara and I had had with Ken during the interval, plus the large accumulation of other important resources over that period, had caused the project to grow immensely.

From starting out as primarily a look back at my majors wins, this book now stands as my complete and definitive autobiography. Herein, accordingly, you will find everything I have to say about all that has happened to me in every aspect of my life, from childhood to what I guess is now called late middle age, good and bad, as completely and honestly as I can tell it. And if you are reading the book more for your interest in the game of golf itself than in Jack Nicklaus and his doings, you will, I believe, discover some things you probably didn't know about the game. You will also, I'm sure, enjoy some fresh insights into many of its elements and its personalities.

It would be remiss of me in prefacing the book not to record Barbara's and my thanks to the person who contributed so much to its making. *My Story* is the tenth book Ken Bowden and I have collaborated on in a twenty-five-year association. His commitment, word skills, and golf knowledge have never been more appreciated.

Although what you will read here is as up-to-the-minute as I could make it in terms of my life overall, it ends with the 1986 Masters so far as my tournament play is concerned. You may wonder why. The reason is that, much as I've enjoyed the Senior Tour and value my achievements on it, it is by my record in the open-to-all major championships that I have measured myself since an early age and would like posterity to measure me. If the occasion arises to update this book, perhaps I'll talk more then about golf past the age of fifty.

I hope you enjoy reading *My Story* as much as I have enjoyed living it.

North Palm Beach, Florida, 1997

1

The 1959 United States Amateur Championship

The Real Beginning

EVERYONE's life is scattered with milestones, events that mark a change of course for better or worse. Frequently they go unrecognized for what they were until hindsight produces 20/20 vision.

Late in the afternoon of Sunday, September 19, 1959, I holed an eight-foot putt on the eighteenth green of what was then the East Course of the Broadmoor Golf Club in Colorado Springs, Colorado, to win the fifty-ninth United States Amateur Golf Championship, my first national title. That evening I was on cloud nine, in seventh heaven. But if a fortune-teller with a crystal ball had happened along in the middle of it, and laid bare all that would happen to me over the next three decades, and told me that this victory marked the real beginning, I would certainly have laughed, probably said, "Baloney," and most likely gone off for some celebratory ice cream (double vanilla, heavy on the hot fudge) without another thought.

On that day at the Broadmoor I was nineteen years and eight months old, and had been playing golf for a little over nine years. I'd had a fair degree of success at the game locally, highlighted by a win in the Ohio State Open when I was sixteen. Consequently, as would happen with any seemingly talented youngster in so sports-mad a city as Columbus, Ohio, by the summer of 1959 I was becoming something of a hotshot to the hometown press and golfing fraternity. Nationally, of course, it was a different story. Even after I won for the first time against country-wide adult competition in the Trans-Mississippi tournament in 1958, I don't recall anyone suggesting that Arnold Palmer, then rapidly becoming golf's dominating figure, should start shaking in his spikes.

At the age of eighteen I was certainly a good golfer, and passionately determined to become a better one. But, despite all the flattering talk about natural gifts and precocious maturity, I was also an extremely raw golfer. Essentially, I still did what I'd always done since my father first put a club in my hands on a spring day in 1950 at Scioto Country Club in the northwestern suburbs of Columbus: Hit it hard, go find it, and hit it hard again. If I won, great. If I lost, well, I'd be pretty upset with myself for a few hours, but then on with the show. The hours then were just too full and the years too limitless to live anything but one day at a time.

OFF the course, I guess the same word, raw, fits equally well for young Jack William Nicklaus, circa 1959.

Life in Columbus in my formative years, even for my kind of comfortable middle-class family, was pretty basic Americana. With perhaps one exception, I'm sure I could have played the middle American small-town boy-next-door to an absolute T in all those 1940s and 1950s Hollywood movies about healthy, happy, clean-cut, uncomplicated people. The exception was my nuttiness about sports, all sports, inherited from and tirelessly encouraged by my father.

From the age of six, when my dad first took me to an Ohio State football game, you name it and I played it . . . and watched it . . . and ate and drank and talked and dreamed it. . . . Even as the golf bug began to bite deeper and deeper in my early teens, the game remained just one of a whole range of sports that, given the opportunity, I would play joyfully and exhaustingly from a dawn breakfast to a forced bedtime. Being naturally blessed with a robust physique and good hand-eye coordination, and consequently becoming fairly good fairly quickly at most games, they were all tremendous fun. For a long time even girls came second.

Growing along with the sports mania was a powerful desire to excel, partially inborn perhaps, but also relentlessly encouraged and nurtured by my father. I remember as though it were yesterday Dad bugging me about running when I was in the sixth grade. He would insist on racing me home to dinner, or to the movies, or to wherever we were going, and for a long time he would always beat me despite a slight lameness remaining from an old ankle injury. Finally, he goaded me into going out for track, and by the time I finished seventh grade there wasn't anyone in that grade or the next who could touch me running the 100 yards or the 220. In fact, I recall doing the 100 in eleven seconds flat just after I turned thirteen, which was a pretty respectable time for a kid in those days. That almost satisfied Dad.

This all-sports mania persisted until I was seventeen. Then, in the spring of 1957, suddenly golf began to take first place, although I remained as interested in other sports as I am today. Even now, I don't really know exactly why that happened. Probably simply gaining strength and getting better at the game had a lot to do with it. Certainly an important factor was that I didn't need a group of guys, or even one other person, to go out and play golf. Also, I'm sure the fact that golf is one of the very few sports where your performance depends entirely on you alone had a pretty strong influence on my total commitment to the game. It's also possible that winning my state championship a few months previously was a contributor.

The 1956 Ohio Open was the first tournament I played in that was mainly for professionals. It was held at the Country Club in Marietta on the eastern edge of the state, and it attracted what seemed to me, when I first looked over the pairings, a pretty intimidating field, including a handful of players who were competitive at the national level.

I remember as though it were yesterday how my commitment to play got me all uptight when, out of the blue, came an invitation to join the great Sam Snead for an exhibition in Urbana, some miles west of Columbus, on the Friday of the championship. Desperate not to miss the thrill and experience of playing with one of golf's all-time giants, I could have hugged Bob Kepler, the Ohio State coach, who was involved in running the Open, when he managed to arrange for me to tee off early enough in the second round to be able to reach Urbana by private plane in time for the match with Sam.

I recall shooting a pretty ho-hum 76 in the first round at Marietta, then adding a 70 on Friday morning that left me six or seven shots behind the leader. Flying off in that Beechcraft D-18 on my first private plane ride was quite a thrill. But what a shock I got when I arrived in Urbana and walked out on the practice tee.

At the Open we'd had maybe a couple of hundred spectators, most of them there to watch Frank Stranahan, the muscle-man and one-time top amateur who by then had become quite a factor on the pro circuit. At Urbana there were what looked like thousands of people, all there to see Sam Snead, but who would also be watching young Jackie Nicklaus when they weren't admiring the Slammer. I'd had first-tee jitters plenty of times before, but nothing like the nervousness that struck me this time. But there was nowhere to run and hide, so I stepped out on the tee next to Sam and got ready to hit some warm-up shots.

Still sharp in my mind is how hard I found it to concentrate on my own game during our match. All I really wanted to do was study Sam, watch that big, beautifully flowing golf swing and the wondrous drives and iron shots that poured from it so effortlessly. If memory serves, I shot 72 and Sam 68. Apart from calling me "Junior," he could not have been nicer, and I had a fine old time with him.

And, of course, like everyone else who's played with Sam Snead, I tried to copy him, particularly his tempo. Gradually, as the round progressed, my aggressive lash at the ball became magically transformed into a carbon copy of history's all-time smoothest and most graceful golf swing. At least, that's what happened in my mind. And, in truth, enough of Sam's rhythm rubbed off to make me at least temporarily a better player, because the next morning at Marietta I went out and shot an almost flawless 64, then won the championship with a 72 in the afternoon. It was the first time I'd prevailed over pros, and my first golfing achievement that attracted more than local attention, and there was no doubt who I had to thank for it—so much so, in fact, that I even forgave Sam for all those "Juniors."

Before that win, I had always liked golf a lot, but really not much more than football, baseball, basketball, tennis, track, table tennis, pool—anything I could compete at. By the summer of 1957, I had fallen totally in love with golf. And, as with all great loves, the game from then on consumed me. I like to think I met my responsibilities in other areas at least adequately (my mother might differ on that!), but the passion to play and practice and improve and, above all, *compete* at golf became irresistible. From 1957 on I virtually lived all summer on a golf course, a driving range, or a practice putting green. Ben Hogan probably hit more balls in his peak playing years than I did, but as a youngster I would definitely have given him some serious competition. Several hundred pops on the range, then thirty-six holes, then putting practice until darkness finally drove me home was just a routine day in summertime.

And yet, passionate as I became about the game of golf, it still remained essentially just that—a recreation, an activity to be pursued and enjoyed entirely for its own sake, purely and simply a game.

Like all kids getting better at something, at times I became much too full of myself about my developing skills. But I had no visions in those days of whooping fans and glistening trophies. Basically, I sought three things from the game: to improve at it, to compete at it, and to *win* at it. My competitiveness by then was in full flower, and golf became the primary means by which to feed a persistent craving. But the hunger was still pretty easily satisfied. Even a fifty-cent Nassau around Scioto would do the trick if the opposition was strong and the result favorable, or, if playing alone, simply good numbers on the scorecard.

It was a simple approach, and in that respect very much in keeping with my life generally in those days. Like most teenagers, I rarely thought much about the future, and when I did it seemed pretty clear-cut and, I suppose, also pretty mundane compared with what I've actually experienced: finish high school; go to Ohio State (there was never any question about that); get a job, probably in pharmacy like my dad; get married and build a home and family somewhere around Columbus, meanwhile playing as much golf as those responsibilities properly allowed. In short, even though maybe a little more gifted, hardworking and successful at my chosen game than the average youngster, I was still one of the gang from Upper Arlington in that famously middle American town of Columbus, Ohio—and perfectly happy with the prospect of staying that way for the rest of my life.

ACHIEVEMENT, I have heard it said, is largely the product of steadily raising one's levels of aspiration and expectation. Such profundities were way above my head as I approached my nineteenth birthday in January of 1959, but I was, in fact, just about to have my inner sights raised fairly substantially, at least so far as my golfing abilities were concerned.

The Walker Cup is a biennial match, played alternately home and away, between teams of amateurs representing the United States and Great Britain and Ireland. There is no more prestigious event in amateur golf; thus to represent one's country in the match has long been and remains the dream of any part-time player who can win the war with par pretty regularly.

The Walker Cup of 1959 was to be contested in May in Scotland at Muirfield, the home of the Honourable Company of Edinburgh Golfers, the oldest golf club in the world. Although my prospects of being chosen for the U.S. team seemed fairly remote, the thought of the match had been an extra spur in both practice and tournament play throughout the 1958 season. It often wasn't enough to produce the desired result, but I did make the cut in the U.S. Open at Southern Hills in Tulsa (I'd missed it by ten shots in my first attempt the previous year), win the Trans-Mississippi tournament at Prairie Dunes in Hutchinson, Kansas, and shoot 67-66-76-68 to finish twelfth in the Rubber City Open in Akron, Ohio, in my first encounter with the professional tour.

At the end of the 1958 season, those seemed like pretty slim credentials for a place on a national team, particularly in light of the number of talented and vastly more experienced amateurs in America at that time, and even more particularly when I thought about my loss to one of the best of those golfers, E. Harvie Ward, in the second round of the Amateur at the Olympic Club in San Francisco. Nevertheless, when the team was announced early in 1959 at the annual meeting of the United States Golf Association, it consisted of Charlie Coe (captain), Tommy Aaron, Deane Beman, Bill Hyndman, Billy Joe Patton, Bud Taylor, E. Harvie Ward, Ward Wettlaufer—and, lo and behold, Jack William Nicklaus.

Hopefully, I avoided instantly puffing up like a peacock, but I was extremely excited for quite a long time just by the sheer fact of having made the Walker Cup team. The only problem was that I would have to drop out of school to make the trip. I was not attending Ohio State on a scholarship—not many schools gave scholarships for golf in those days because the game wasn't then all that big a deal at the college level. Nevertheless, I still did not look forward to telling Bob Kepler, "Coach, I made the Walker Cup team and I'll be going on from that to the British Amateur, so I won't be able to play for you this spring." When I did get up enough courage to inform him, Kep was just great about it. "You should definitely go," he told me. "It's a great honor to play for your country, and it will be a fine experience for you." (Can you imagine a college coach reacting that way today?)

As I grew more used to the idea of being a Walker Cupper, I got to thinking about what it meant, and all of a sudden I found myself at a new level in my self-evaluation as a golfer. "This team," I told myself, "is put together by men experienced and wise in the game of golf as the best group of amateurs in America. They've included me, so I must be one of the top players in the country. Wow!"

By far the nicest immediate bonus of the selection was an invitation to the Masters, where would begin my lifelong love affair with the Augusta National club and its legendary springtime rite. Unfortunately, a little of the gloss was taken off that experience by surely the dumbest thing I've ever done in golf—a goof that still makes my cheeks burn half a lifetime later. I tell the story mainly to show how wet behind the ears I still was at age nineteen, no matter how "mature" a golfer I might have appeared to be.

To shake off the cobwebs of the long Ohio winter, I had obtained permission to spend time well ahead of the Masters practicing at the Augusta National. In those days amateur contestants were accommodated for free in the Crow's Nest, a sort of dormitory at the top of the clubhouse. Also, chiefly to protect their amateur status, I suppose, they were charged only a nominal rate for meals—as I recall a dollar for breakfast, a dollar for lunch, and two dollars for dinner. The only person I know who enjoys eating more than I do is Phil Rodgers, and he also had decided to get in some early work on site that year as an amateur Masters invitee. Immediately after golf Phil and I would hasten to the dining room, where we would begin with a double shrimp cocktail, then each polish off a couple of sirloin steaks with all the trimmings, then, if we felt like it, go on to a third steak. This lasted for a couple of days, whereupon someone decided to change the rules. "Fellas," Phil and I were told, "if you're going to eat more than one steak every night, we're going to have to charge you another two dollars apiece for the extra ones." That slowed us down a little bit, but not much. Like everything else about the Augusta National, they were great steaks.

So my first experience of the home of the Masters was wonderful . . . until suddenly I got it into my head that what I really needed as a warm-up for my first encounter with the big guns of golf was more serious competition than was available knocking it around with the other early amateur arrivals. I knew the pro tour wasn't far away that week, and was told when I asked about its exact location that it was in Wilmington, North Carolina, for the Azalea Open. "Gee," I said to myself, "I wonder if they'd let me play?" and got smartly on the telephone to the tournament office. "Sure," said whoever picked up at the other end. "We'll give you an exemption. Come on over."

As soon as I got there I discovered that it would not be as easy as it had sounded. "Sorry, someone made a mistake. We can't let you straight in," I was told. "But you can try to qualify if you want to." This was a little upsetting, but, what the heck, it had been a long drive, and qualifying was a form of competition anyway, so fine.

So I played a practice round, then teed it up on the Monday and made it into the tournament, then went out and shot 73-74 for the first two rounds, which put me in fourteenth place and only six strokes off the lead. But the weather had been terrible, and the course wasn't in very good shape, so after the second round I decided I'd had enough competition and that it was time to get back to those fabulous two-dollar steaks. I found an official and told him thanks, but I'm pulling out, and off I went back to Augusta.

On Monday, when the tour brass arrived at the Augusta National from Wilmington for the Masters, the very first thing they did was come find little old Jackie Nicklaus. And, boy, did they lay it on me. I think it was their then top field official, Joe Black, who did most of the talking. "Jack," he told me, "you just can't *do* what you did. You can't just go and play in a professional golf tournament, and get yourself in a position where you could *win* the darn thing, then just pull out and leave. *You just cannot do that!*"

I tried to explain that, well, the weather had been lousy and the course wasn't very good, and I really felt I'd had enough competition, but it only threw more fuel on the fire. "Do you realize," I remember one of the tour guys asking me, somewhat forcefully, "that if you'd shot a couple of 70s, which you were perfectly capable of doing, you would have *won* the Azalea Open?"

No, I hadn't thought of that. But I thought a lot about the whole mess over the next few days, and my behavior seemed dumber and became more embarrassing to me the more I did so, and it ended up teaching me a lesson that has lasted my entire career—which is that, when you enter a golf tournament, you stay in that golf tournament to its beautiful or bitter end, unless you become physically incapacitated to the point of not being able either to walk or to swing a golf club. Hopefully, my addiction to that philosophy over the intervening years has made up a little for my youthful stupidity.

And my first Masters? The Augusta National greens were exceptionally fast that year, and, although I managed to hit thirty-one of them in regulation in the first two rounds, typically of a first-timer I too often failed to position the ball in the proper areas. That contributed to eight three-putts greens and a missed cut by a stroke. Later, it was eye-opening to learn that the defender, Arnold Palmer, had hit only nineteen greens on his way to the halfway lead. This suggested to me that, if I was going to play big-time golf, I had better learn how to putt fast greens, and particularly how not to leave myself long comeback putts.

Raw as I obviously still was at that point about some golfing niceties, I was smart enough to have learned that you don't hang around after missing cuts, so I wasn't at the Augusta National to see Art Wall make his great stretch run and win the 1959 Masters by a stroke from Cary Middlecoff. By then I was over in Pinehurst, where, a week later, I managed a one-up win in a very tough thirty-six-hole final against Gene Andrews in the much-esteemed North and South tournament. After my Azalea and Masters mishaps, it gave my self-esteem a much-needed boost as I prepared to leave the country for the first time.

Of all the lands in which I have been fortunate to play golf, Scotland is my favorite. That's not just because the game evolved there—historians continue to argue about who actually invented it —or because of its marvelous old links courses, but primarily because of the people. I'll have more to say about this later, and particularly the way the Scots received me in my peak professional years. Right now, my concern is how they felt about me in May of 1959. Frankly, I still shudder to think about it. To many of them I must have seemed like an apparition from another planet.

Crew-cuts were never the rage over the water that they once were stateside, nor, I suspect, were my level of food intake or spit-it-out bullheadedness in public and press relations. Combine my appearance with my verbal directness and all-the-world's-my-oyster demeanor, and the Scots of that era must have believed they were witnessing the epitome of the Ugly American, junior version. At the time, of course, I never gave any of this even a passing thought, but it concerned me quite a bit as a I grew older and hopefully wiser. Subconsciously, at least, I'm pretty sure that it was this initial trip abroad that marked the first glimmerings of a recognition that a certain mellowing of attitude and style might be in order.

Such considerations apart, the 1959 Walker Cup trip was a great success for both the United States team and most of its individual members. We won by 9 points to 3, giving us our fifteenth victory in sixteen official encounters (an imbalance that our transatlantic friends have lately begun correcting).

In the first day's thirty-six-hole alternate-shot foursomes, my good friend Ward Wettlaufer and I edged out Michael Lunt and Alec Shepperson by two up with one to play. Perhaps because of the shock affect my youth, appearance, and surely overconfident demeanor seemed to have had on so many people in Scotland, Captain Coe made me anchorman in the second day's singles. By the time I'd worn down Dick Smith, a scrappy Scot more than double my age, the destination of the Cup had been decided. Nevertheless, the 5-and-4 win over as majestic and fascinatingly different and difficult a golf course as Muirfield was elating, giving me as it did a 100-percent record my first time out for my country.

From Muirfield I traveled down with most of my teammates to the Royal St. George's club in the southeast corner of England to play in the British Amateur, which then as for some years later was scheduled to facilitate the entry of both Walker Cup squads. To help with our fine-tuning, it had been arranged that immediately ahead of the championship we would compete in an old-established thirty-six-hole stroke-play tournament called the Royal St. George's Grand Challenge Cup.

While up at Muirfield, Ward Wettlaufer and I had gone to Ben Sayers's famous old shop in the historic little coastal town of North Berwick and each had made one of the wooden-shafted blade putters that everyone seemed to be using in the old paintings decorating so many of the Scottish clubhouse walls we'd seen. One of the first things I was told about the course when we got to Royal St. George's was how fast the greens were, so it seemed like a good idea to try out the new wand, which was pretty light, in the warm-up tournament.

The weather was terrible, but I managed to hit the first green in two, whereupon I proceeded to use my new acquisition four times before I got the ball into the cup. "Oh, my gosh," I remember asking myself, "what kind of day is *this* going to be?" The answer was a remarkable one, as I proceeded to take only nineteen putts for the next seventeen holes, putt nearly as well the next day, and handily win a lovely little prize, the last of fifty sterling silver replicas of the big Grand Challenge trophy made half a century earlier. (That little memento, by the way, continues to mark the first of only two tournament wins for me in England.)

In the British Amateur proper—the only one I got to play in, unfortunately—Bill Hyndman put me out in the quarterfinals, before losing to Deane Beman in the final. Nevertheless, with my good Walker Cup record and the nice little Royal St. George's cup, I was a pretty happy young golfer on the long journey back to Columbus.

AMATEUR golf was then and remains today easier than professional golf for a whole lot of reasons. One of the biggest in my amateur days was what might be called "spacing."

Playing for much smaller purses than are commonplace these days, the majority of tour pros at that time had to tee it up week after week after week simply to grind out a living. In contrast, there weren't many national-level amateur tournaments, and, even if there had been, few amateurs would have been able to afford either the money or the time to play in more than, say, one a month. That was roughly my schedule from 1957 through 1961, not least because of the expense. My dad once figured it cost him a minimum of $5,000 a year—probably close to $30,000 by today's values—for me to travel and compete even that much outside my home state. Because most of the big events were played in summer during school vacations, time for me was rarely a problem. For the older fellows with jobs and families, it was frequently a bigger headache even than money.

The result of all this was that a good amateur generally had plenty of "space" to work on his game. If you played poorly in one tournament, no sweat. Usually you had weeks—not a couple of days, like the pros—to iron out the bugs. Therefore, you always had the luxury of being able to work yourself back into some sort of form by the time the next important event came around. My 1959 Walker Cup play was a good example of this. With the win in the North and South to boost my confidence, then daily help from my teacher at Scioto, Jack Grout, I had been able to fine-tune myself into top form just at the right time.

My next outing after the British trip was the U.S. Open at Winged Foot in mid-June, and it turned out to be a less happy experience.

In addition to the boost of confidence the Walker Cup had brought me, I believed that it had also taught me a lot about golf course management and self-management, not least from playing so much in practice with all of those experienced "old" guys on the team. In the matches themselves, I felt I'd learned some things about combating pressure: about the art of making yourself plan and execute good shots—or, at least, good scoring shots—when you absolutely had to.

At Winged Foot I found I hadn't learned enough, not by a long shot. A couple of 77s and a missed cut weren't what bothered me the most—sheer tiredness from a long spell away from home inevitably had some bearing on my overall form. Much more troubling was the way I played when I missed those small, hard, elevated A. W. Tillinghast greens compared with the way my partners, Gene Littler and Doug Ford, performed when they failed to find the mark with approach shots. Over those first thirty-six holes, Littler got up and down from bunkers twelve times in thirteen tries and shot 69-74. Believe it or not, Ford did even better—up and down from bunkers eleven times out of eleven for rounds of 72-69.

As observed from my ringside seat, both performances greatly impressed me. On the way home, they somewhat depressed me. Hotshot that I might be with the driver and the 1-iron—the muscle stuff—when it came to the management side of the game, the head stuff, I still wasn't really a contender. I decided then and there that I had better set about truly learning the arts of what the South African champion, Bobby Locke, so aptly called "playing badly well." Beginning the very next day, back at Scioto, I began to spend less time blistering out those 300-yarders and a lot more pitching, chipping, hitting from sand, and putting. Also, because the pros were so obviously the finest exemplars in the world of what I needed to learn, I talked my dad into letting me accelerate the learning curve by playing in three of the tour events staged in the Midwest following the Open.

As the years have passed, golf's analysts seem more and more to have decided that self-management and course management are my strongest competitive weapons. Well, here's where my constant preoccupation with those critical but—by recreational golfers, at least—greatly neglected elements of the game really began.

Out on the pro tour that summer, I wasn't playing with the thought of winning, but simply with the goal of advancing my golfing education. This began by learning to truly "read" courses, beginning at the tee and continuing all the way to the tap-in.

Where was the best position for the tee shot relative to the approach, in terms of distance, of angle of entry, of ground contour, of the location and severity of hazards, of the wind, etc, etc? What type of shot would leave the easiest putt, or, if I missed the green, the simplest recovery shot, and which club would most easily achieve it? When should I belt the drive all-out and when was safety the critical factor, calling for a more controlled swing or less club? What weight should I give to the various hazards along the way, from the worst (out-of-bounds or lost ball) to the least severe (light rough or a slightly angled lie), in mapping the ideal route from tee to cup? How could I master the seemingly infinitely varying textures of sand I encountered, and learn the many techniques the pros seemed to have perfected for slipping the ball within one-putt range from bunkers? On the greens, when should I charge and when should I lag? And so on and on.

Because to answer such questions effectively you must observe and analyze all elements of each course you play acutely and astutely, it was here in the summer of 1959 that my ever-deepening interest in golf course design really took root. In addition to trying to solve the endless shotmaking and strategical problems of tournament competition, I grew increasingly intrigued with how each architect had used the land available to him, and with the seemingly infinite variety, subtlety and beauty of the game's arenas.

Through that came an ever-sharpening awareness that one's true opponent in every golf contest is never another player, or even the entire field, but always the course itself—a realization, I am now sure, that has been common to all great champions and, I believe, a major contributor to their success. It also began to occur to me that, as valuable a competitive weapon as the ability to hit the ball a long way can be, golf at the highest levels is much more a game of precision than of power. I'm sure all of the greats discovered that early in their careers, too.

One of the fastest and finest lessons I learned that summer of 1959 in my encounters with the pros was to quit trying to play "hero" shots from severe trouble situations. I was physically very strong in those days, a consequence of which was an almost irresistible urge to try to mend mistakes with sheer muscle. Frequently, all that did was compound small errors into large disasters. Playing with the pros, I learned that the best of them had progressed far beyond this kind of immaturity. They were able to stay cool, to remain in command of their emotions at all times, to play one shot at a time without getting either wildly excited or deeply depressed about its outcome. Inner self-control, I came to realize, was a much larger factor in winning and losing than ball-striking ability. That was because along with self-control came realism and patience, the only bases from which a golfer can deal effectively with the endless challenges and frustrations that the game of golf has always presented and always will.

Because realism breeds caution, it was also around this time that my essentially conservative approach to scoring began to take shape. I would still do dumb things, but I like to think that both the frequency and the level of stupidity gradually diminished from the summer of 1959 onward. And, in fact, there was an immediate reward. During the third week in August I had a fairly smooth run to the final of the Trans-Mississippi out in Wayzata, Minnesota, where I defended successfully by defeating Deane Beman over thirty-six holes. I'd trailed Deane until the sixteenth hole in the morning round, but then did not lose a hole until the eleventh in the afternoon. I felt I had played much smarter golf than in any other tournament that year, and was pleased with both my physical game and my thinking game as, back home, I worked at keeping everything meshing smoothly in anticipation of the upcoming Amateur Championship.

My record in the Amateur to that point was definitely nothing for anyone to get excited about. Bob Gardner beat me by one hole in the opening round my first time out at the age of fifteen in

1955, about which more later. In 1956, at Knollwood, near Chicago, I'd lost to Ronnie Wenzler, 3 and 2, in the third round. The following year at The Country Club, in Brookline, Dick Yost sent me down the road by the same margin one round later. In 1958, as already mentioned, Harvie Ward, who had won the title in 1955 and 1956, dispatched me at the final hole in the second round after one-putting thirteen greens and chipping in on another. In retrospect, however, the earlier assessment I made of myself during this period must stand: good with the muscles but still pretty wobbly with the mind. I could hit it fine most of the time, but I still couldn't *think* well enough often enough or for long enough.

On the way to the Broadmoor for the 1959 championship, I knew deep down inside that, although the learning curve was by no means completed, there had been definite improvement in that area. Thus, as I went about learning the course, I not only felt good about my physical game, but also enjoyed a comforting sense that there would be fewer mental or emotional lapses than in previous years. In short, as my first match drew near, I experienced more and more that greatest of all sensations for an athlete ahead of an important contest: the feeling of being in every way fully prepared, truly "ready." In previous years, whatever my own failings, there was no question that I had run into some pretty hot golf from the opposition. This time I felt I could handle whatever was thrown at me.

Another important factor was that I liked the golf course and its surroundings and atmosphere. Situated in the foothills of the Rockies, the Broadmoor was then and remains today one of the world's scenically most spectacular golf resorts. But that also makes it the ultimate in mountain golf, and mountain golf is one of the trickiest varieties of the game you will ever encounter. The greater elevation —6,400 feet above sea level in the Broadmoor's case—causes every shot to fly farther, which complicates club selection. Then, although you quickly learn that all putts break away from the mountains (or, as always, in the direction of water flow), the surrounding roller-coaster perspectives make it hard to accurately read the uphill or downhill factors. Finally, the Broadmoor's greens in those days were mostly plateaued, which, combined with their firmness and quickness, presented tricky recoveries from missed approach shots.

To me on this occasion, however—irrepressible youth bolstered by a high level of confidence—these seemed little more than enjoyable extra challenges. I had a fine local caddie to help with the distance adjustments, and had been working my irons nicely from left to right or right to left as circumstances dictated, so saw no reason why I could not hit and hold most of the greens. As for putting . . . well, all you do is walk up and knock it in the hole, isn't that right? What's so difficult about that? (Remember, I was nineteen and still putting very much by instinct, and still of the belief that this was golf's easy part.)

In my first three matches, everything worked out pretty much as planned as I defeated, in sequence, Bobby Jones's son, Bob Jones III, by 7 and 6; North Carolinian Bill Williams by 2 and 1; and Don Massengale, later to become a fine tour player, by 6 and 5. Then came the first hiccup.

Perhaps because of the Pinehurst influence, maybe because they just raise 'em tougher down there, North Carolina has always produced a lot of fine amateurs—good-natured fun-loving guys off the course who turn into street-fighters the moment the bell rings. Our life-and-soul-of-the-party at the Walker Cup, Billy Joe Patton, was probably the supreme example of the breed back in those days. In round five, I ran into a pal of his with the same kind of appetite for an almighty scrap, by the name of Dave Smith.

The day stands out in memory not only for Dave's tenacious golf, but because it was the only time I can remember playing every full shot of a complete round almost totally blind. The reason was fog—fog so thick you could barely see the tee markers when setting up between them for the drives. The conditions were so bad we had to use not only forecaddies, but forecaddies for forecaddies. On every tee shot and approach, judging by the feel of impact, we'd holler "Left!" or "Right!" or "Straight!" then listen for the yell to be repeated on down the line. Amazingly, neither of us lost a ball, but Dave summed it up perfectly with a typical southerner's one-liner: "I wouldn't send my mother-in-law out to plow in weather like this." For the life of me, I still don't know why the United States Golf Association officials didn't postpone play; these days I'm certain they would, whatever the consequences. But we eventually got around, and, at the end of some remarkably fine golf under the circumstances, I managed a tense par on number eighteen to win 1 up and advance to the quarterfinals. If there had been a certain cockiness in my step during the previous matches, I'm sure it was notably diminished by this one.

As I've mentioned, at Brookline two years previously Dick Yost had taken me out of the championship in the fourth round by 3 and 2. I had played the front side in thirty-two strokes but still turned 1 down, and Dick was quick to admit that he'd had one of those delightful days when he could do nothing wrong. This time, using borrowed clubs (his own had been destroyed in a clubhouse fire), he wasn't quite as hot. At three under par, I got my revenge by 3 and 1 and was in the semifinals.

One of the toughest types of golfer to beat in match play is the fellow who seems rarely to produce spectacular shots but who also makes very few mistakes. You know he isn't going to throw a bunch of birdies at you, but you also know he isn't likely to make anything worse than bogeys, and not many of those. If you aren't careful, this can wear down both your concentration and your emotional equilibrium, and particularly over thirty-six holes, which in those days was the distance of both the semifinals and the final (presently only the final is over two rounds). If there had been a worldwide club for this kind of golfer, they would have had to make my semifinal opponent its president in perpetuity.

A sturdily built insurance man from Los Angeles, Gene Andrews had first appeared on the national golf scene by winning the Public Links Championship in 1954 when past the age of forty. In addition to his steadiness as a player, he possessed a number of eccentricities that, if you let them, could further divert your attention from the business at hand. Gene invariably sported a huge planter's-type hat on the course, and, naturally gregarious, liked to converse during play more than is customary in top competition. Perhaps his greatest eccentricity, however, was the painstaking use of notebooks, compiled during practice, containing highly detailed distance charts, plus meticulous contour maps of all the putting surfaces. At the Broadmoor that week, he'd also brought along an oxygen tank to help cope with the rarefied mountain air. As we shook hands and wished each other luck before our semifinal on a bright and sunny Saturday morning, I determined to try to ignore everything about Mr. Andrews except his hole-by-hole scores. I had discovered in our North and South final earlier in the year that, beneath the country-boy folksiness, dwelt one of the fiercest competitors in all of amateur golf. For example, when he'd checked in at Pinehurst for the North and South, he'd asked when the final was, then, when told Saturday, had said, “Fine, register me through Saturday.” My wariness of him proved to be a wise decision.

In the morning round I shot a fairly trouble-free 70 and went to lunch 3 up. Eight holes into the afternoon round, I suddenly found myself 1 down. Gene then gave me the ninth hole with a conceded birdie, but won the tenth and eleventh with a birdie and a par to lead by two again. He should have increased that lead to three on the next hole, but very untypically three-putted from no more than twenty feet to allow me a win. Pumped up by my good fortune and the ever-mounting tension, I drilled a twenty-footer for a winning birdie on thirteen, then almost knocked my approach from the rough into the fourteenth hole for another. We halved the next two holes, so, walking to the seventeenth tee, J.W. Nicklaus led by one with two to play.

At 613 yards, the seventeenth hole on the Broadmoor's then East Course was beyond anyone's reach in two shots short of a helping hurricane. Nevertheless, with the adrenaline flowing and overeager to end the match, I couldn't resist going for all the marbles with the driver. The result, as so often in such circumstances, was a nasty hook into the tall grass. Three hacks later, with Gene certain of his par five, I found myself on the upper tier of a two-level green, with the cup at the foot of a steep and curving slope, staring at a twenty-five-foot putt for a half. As I set up to the ball, I remembered that this green all week had been a little slower than most of the others, so I gave the putt a little extra. Easy as putting then seemed, I still enjoy the memory of the surge of elation that ran through me when the ball dropped into the center of the cup. A few minutes later, after halving the home hole with bogeys, I was in the final.

When the writers asked for a comment about Gene, I told them that what I'd done to him with that par on seventeen shouldn't happen to a dog. I meant it from the heart.

As exemplified by his Walker Cup captaincy a few months previously, my opponent in the final, Charlie Coe, was at that time not only America's leading amateur but, in the opinion of many analysts, one of the finest golfers in the world of any stripe. Unquestionably his greatest achievements among many over the previous decade and more were his victories in the 1949 and 1958 National

Amateurs. In 1959 he had also placed sixth and finished top amateur in the Masters, only four shots back of Art Wall. Two years later at Augusta National he would tie for second with Arnold Palmer, only a stroke behind Gary Player.

A tall, lean, self-contained Oklahoma oil broker, with a look and manner that made me think of western movie heroes, Charlie had treated me nicely at Muirfield, but with a certain reserve that was probably accounted for more by our age difference—sixteen years—than any other factor. From that experience I knew him to be an elegant swinger of the club, with a fully stocked arsenal of shots, and also an extremely determined and disciplined competitor.

Charlie's closest call on the way to the final had been a 2-up victory over Bill Hyndman in the quarterfinals, and his scoring in that match and earlier indicated he was at the top of his game. He knew the course inside-out from vacationing at the Broadmoor. Nonintrospective as I was about my opponents in those days, I couldn't help but be aware how much another Amateur would mean to him; it would make him the first golfer since Bob Jones to win the title more than twice. Falling asleep the night before our meeting, I remember my last thought being that, if I really did want to know exactly what level I had now attained as a golfer, the answer would be supplied the next day.

A healthy if well-concealed respect for one's own capabilities is essential in head-to-head golf, but it should never lead to underestimating those of the opponent. As Charlie and I moved to the fourth tee of the final, I discovered I at least hadn't made that mistake in my previous evening's musings.

After narrowly missing a birdie at number one, I scored a pair of them on the second and third holes. That left me just one down. Charlie had opened with three straight flawless birdies. Thankfully, he slowed down a little after this stunning burst, but not enough for me to have a big smile on my face as we went in to lunch. Driving particularly well, and not doing much else wrong, I'd eased it around in par 71. Charlie had beaten me by two shots on the medal card, and also stood two up in the match.

Commentators were later to describe the entire thirty-six holes of that Amateur final, and particularly the afternoon eighteen, as one of the most exciting finals in the championship's history. I can't speak for Charlie, but I certainly was never involved in as tough and thrilling a battle as an amateur, and very rarely in later years as a professional. Every shot we played is still etched in my memory, and always will be. But, inevitably, a couple of moments from that long-ago afternoon are especially indelible.

Throughout the morning round, the "old" guy had matched me in both placement and distance from the tee with his low, controlled draw, and had not hit a truly poor shot at any point. When he opened after lunch with a badly hooked drive, making me a gift of the hole, my spirits lifted considerably. Then they soared even higher with a two-putt birdie on the 573-yard par-five third hole that brought us even.

Of the next eight holes, only one changed hands when Charlie knocked a lovely approach to within five feet at number six. Apart from that, and a pair of halving birdies at the par-five ninth, both of us covered those eight holes in strict par, leaving me one down with seven to play. Then Charlie suffered what I still believe was a crucial —and very atypical—lapse.

After an elegant tee shot to within twenty-five feet of the cup at the difficult 220-yard par-three twelfth, he three-putted, allowing me to even the match with a scrambled par. Whatever effect this had on his psyche certainly didn't show, but two holes later he missed a relatively easy approach shot, enabling me to get my nose ahead for the first time all day. Two halves followed, meaning that, if I could win the seventeenth, the monster par five that had nearly undone me against Gene Andrews, the title was mine.

Ah, that seventeenth hole! And, oh, the bullheadedness of youth!

Away went my tee shot, hard, low, and left, and even deeper into the boonies than the previous day's pathetic effort—the classic over-the-top "blue darter." Then came a series of even worse hacks, but this time no miracle saving putt. So, a big fat six for the kid and a comfortable five for the defender. Match even with one to play.

Broadmoor's finishing hole then (it later became the sixteenth) was a 430-yard par-four doglegging sharply to the right, and sloping acutely in that direction at about 275 yards from the tee. Drive through the elbow, or let the ball slide right, and an already tricky approach to the hard green would be compounded by heavy rough.

Charlie hit a fine 3-wood from the tee to the ideal position in the left half of the fairway. Using my head despite the adrenaline-inspired urge to try to drive the green, I followed with the same club and an equally good shot that finished about ten feet beyond Charlie's ball.

As it turned out, those ten feet would have a heavy bearing on the outcome.

Playing first, Charlie hit what looked in the air like a perfect 8-iron, beautifully struck and therefore heavy with backspin, and covering the flag all the way. However, when the ball landed about pin high, for some strange reason it took a big first hop, then ran on until it finally trickled over the green and down a small bank into a heavily grassed hollow.

I had been considering the 8-iron also. Now, thinking about what happened to Charlie's ball, I decided to drop to the 9. With it I hit a good if not a great shot that pitched on the front half of the upsloping green and, perhaps a little luckily, continued running until it finally stopped just eight feet short of the hole.

Charlie's predicament now was one every golfer would hate to face in a two-dollar Nassau, never mind when all even on the final hole of a national championship with the opposition looking at a makeable birdie putt. With his ball sitting well down in long grass, he had to pitch sharply up and over a bank, but drop the ball short and softly enough on the fast, downward-sloping rear portion of the green to just trickle the twenty feet to the hole. He did an appropriate amount of studying, then took his sand wedge and played a fabulous little touch shot. Lobbed delicately over the bank, the ball landed gently, then, dead on line for the hole, trickled and trickled for what seemed to me like an hour rather than the ten seconds it probably took. Finally, the ball came to rest no more than a half-turn from dropping in the cup. Charlie looked over and gave me a small grin. I tried to smile back at him as best I could while trying to start my heart and lungs working again.

Then something offbeat happened that is perfectly understandable when you consider the tensions inside a man at moments like this.

In match play, except to clean your ball, you never pick it up when you're on the green until your opponent either asks you to or concedes your putt. The penalty for doing so is loss of hole. Now Charlie walked over and started to pick up his ball. Realizing his error, he immediately mentioned it to me. I told him to forget it—that the putt was obviously conceded. As I did so, suddenly the tension in me began to drain away. Often since I've reflected on how this little break in the pattern of events helped me on what was certainly the most critical stroke of my life up to that point.

As I addressed that eight-foot putt, I just *knew* I could and would make it. I struck the ball firmly, playing about a two-inch left-to-right break. From the moment it left the blade it was never in doubt.

It took me quite a few days to wind down from that momentous match, and to realize that I was not only America's champion amateur golfer but the youngest one in half a century. And it was only after many years that I truly began to realize what a milestone had occurred in my life up there in the Rockies on Sunday, September 19, 1959.

If there is ever really a moment when a man can say a dream began, and he began to try to give it substance, this for me was that moment.

2

The 1961 United States Amateur Championship

The Architect and the Builder

AT the end of every golf season since that first national championship victory in 1959, I've done some serious reflecting on my game in order to get a realistic and precise picture of where and how I should try to improve the following year. Dreams can be great motivators, but I discovered early on that actually achieving them depends mostly on such concrete factors as knowledge and work. Thus I've often been pretty hard on myself, and I remember being particularly self-critical in the winter of 1960–61. The chief reason was an embarrassingly poor defense of my Amateur title at the St. Louis Country Club in mid-September.

I can't blame him entirely, but Phil Rodgers was definitely a contributor to this, even though I nailed him in our actual match. Some people think Phil has always been a little on the aggressive side, but they should have known him in those days. I've never in my life met anyone better than he was as a kid at raising hackles—and, as we were such good friends (and still are), particularly mine. Almost two years older than I am, Philamander's greatest achievement when he arrived in town for the 1960 Amateur was winning the 1958 NCAA title. Once there, he never stopped gabbing on about how deep he was going to bury "that Nicklaus kid" in round three—that being, of course, if "that Nicklaus kid" was "lucky enough" to make it that far.

I was lucky enough, after an admittedly narrow squeak against John Donohue, Jr., in the opening round. I was also eight under par for the twelve holes it took me to launch Master Rodgers on the road back to San Diego—probably the finest short burst of golf I'd played until then. This occurred on the Tuesday morning of the championship. On the Tuesday afternoon, emotionally drained, I three-putted six times, once from near gimme range, and never had a hope against Charlie Lewis, a good golfer from Arkansas.

I learned some more about controlling the psyche and about self-pacing from that experience—and in later years Phil would more than make up for any anguish he caused me with his counsel on technique, particularly about the short game. For months after the 1960 Amateur, though, it really burned me to think of that Tuesday. But I guess time does indeed heal all wounds, because from this distance that season doesn't seem such a bad one for young Jackie Nicklaus, all things considered.

My first warm-up outing that year was a team event in Florida with another very confident little golfer and by then a close friend, Deane Beman. Despite my annoyance at short-hitting Deane for topping me in a long-drive contest with a special drop-kick technique he'd mastered, we won. Next, I made the cut in the Masters, tying for thirteenth and sharing the low amateur award with Billy Joe Patton, as Arnold Palmer won his second green jacket by a stroke from Ken Venturi. In May, I lost the Big Ten Collegiate title by two strokes to John Konsek. A month later, I lost the U.S. Open to Arnie by the same margin at Cherry Hills after leading with six holes to play.

WHEN I think of myself back in those peak amateur days, although I was no match for Philamander Rodgers, I still cringe at how cockily I must have come across to a lot of people. For instance, before leaving Columbus for that U.S. Open I remember telling my college coach, Bob Kepler, "Kep, I'm playing so well I might just win this thing." You might think such things—you *should* think such things—but you should never say them to anyone, or at least not to anyone who isn't extremely close to you like a parent or spouse. I did it all the time, and it embarrasses me now just to remember it.

My past performances in the championship hardly justified such optimism.

I had first attempted to qualify for the U.S. Open in 1956 at Oak Hill, but ended up second alternate and never made it to the championship proper. After I qualified for Inverness the next year, both Dad and Jack Grout did their best to inspire me by talking constantly about how Bob Jones, also at Inverness and a year younger than me, had finished the 1920 Open only four shots behind the winner, England's Ted Ray. It didn't work. I started great—a 3-wood and 7-iron to thirty-five feet and down for birdie at number one, followed by a couple of pars. That got my name on the leader boards, whereupon I double-bogeyed the fourth hole and was on my way to a pair of 80s that easily missed the cut. A year later I managed to tie for forty-first at Southern Hills, nineteen shots back of Tommy Bolt. As previously noted, I missed the cut again at Winged Foot in 1959.

As I'd informed Kep, the condition of my overall game convinced me I would do much better at Cherry Hills. As usual, I played my practice rounds with Deane Beman, and, as usual, we had a five-dollar Nassau going each time, and after a couple of days I'd relieved Deane of forty dollars or so. Our last time out he was looking like he might get a little bit of it back when I hit a 4-iron stiff from deep rough at the last hole to clean him again. "That's it," he growled. "No more bets with you, Nicklaus. You're released."

It was betting that gave rise to another example of what might be called my excessive youthful self-confidence. A couple of days before the championship began, Dad discovered that the odds on me winning were 35 to 1. He said he was going to put a couple of bucks on me, and asked if I wanted to wager on myself. I'd never done anything like that, but, based on how well I was playing, I told him, sure, why not, and said I'd go for twenty dollars to win (it was Beman's money, after all). "Don't you want any place and show?" Dad asked. Although I can't remember exactly what I answered, I'm sure it was something like, "You've got to be kidding!"

After the first thirty-six holes at Cherry Hills, my confidence didn't look too out of place. The leader at that point was Mike Souchak with 68-67–135, a new Open record. With two par-equaling rounds of 71, I had made the cut by five strokes and was only seven shots behind Mike. This being by so much my best performance in the national championship to that point, I was pretty excited as I hustled to the leader board Friday evening to see who I'd be paired with for the next day's double round. The answer was Ben Hogan.

At first I couldn't believe it, but when I checked over the scores again the answer was still Ben Hogan. Big swallow. Although then forty-seven years old, Ben was still a huge force in the game, and obviously now had a great shot at a record fifth Open victory. More gulps. I had not at that point met Mr. Hogan, but had learned enough about him from Jack Grout and other sources to be aware of how intimidating a presence he could be. To say I was a little nervous about spending the next day with him, with both of us battling over thirty-six holes for the world's top golf title, would be an understatement.

In the event, playing with Ben turned out to be, if not what you might call a highly social experience, a perfectly pleasant one. In his normal businesslike, matter-of-fact way he meticulously observed all of the courtesies a golfer is expected to afford his fellows during competitive play, but without ever saying one more word to me than he regarded as essential. Very quickly I realized that this wasn't out of discourtesy, or even an understandable disinterest in a young amateur, but simply a side effect of his own depth of concentration on the task at hand. Ben Hogan had long ago discovered that, to play his best, he had to focus his mind 100 percent on his own golf game, and that's what he did. Once I'd figured this out, his silence was fine with me; in fact, it helped me settle into my own little cocoon, particularly in the morning round.

After the championship, though, Mr. Hogan did express a thought about young Jackie Nicklaus that both gave me pause and made me swell with pride. Talking with writers in the locker room, Ben said: "I guess they'll say I lost it. Well, one more foot and the wedge on seventeen would have been perfect. But I'll tell you something. I played thirty-six holes today with a kid who should have won this Open by ten shots."

• • •

THEY say golf is a game of inches. Before recalling my fumbling and stumbling that afternoon, let me refresh your memory about how a measly dozen of those inches did in the nearest thing there has ever been to a human golfing machine.

Hogan had begun the championship with an indifferent 75, then hit all eighteen greens in regulation in the second round on the way to an immaculate 67. On Saturday morning, I watched him again hit every green in regulation for a 69, then do the same through sixteen holes of the final round. There are no statistics covering such things, but if there were I'm pretty sure this run of fifty-two straight holes under U.S. Open conditions without a single recovery shot would be one of golf's all-time records.

Ben's weakness by then was putting. He would stand over the ball for an eternity, trying to make himself draw the club back. He was always a heavy smoker on the course, and by then Sam Snead used to joke that Ben had one-cigarette and two-cigarette putts, it took him so long. From as little as twelve or fifteen feet, he could knock it in the hole or he could three-putt, and you sensed he never knew which it would be. Hitting so many fairways and greens, and positioning the ball so close to the cup so much of the time, then going through all of that, was clearly agonizing for him.

It was almost certainly his fear of the putter that finally cost Ben Hogan that championship. The cup at the par-five seventeenth that day was cut barely over the pond fronting the green. Figuring he had to make birdie—which in his case meant getting within gimme range—Ben attempted an extremely risky little pitch shot. In the air the ball looked great, but it landed a foot short of perfect and, heavily spun, backed down the bank and into the water. From there he made bogey, then, with all of the steam gone, finished with a triple-bogey for a round of 73 and a share of ninth place. If he had closed with two pars, he would have played off over eighteen holes the next day against Arnold Palmer.

If it was twelve inches of green that cost Ben Hogan a record fifth U.S. Open, it was the six inches between his ears that stopped Jack Nicklaus from becoming only the sixth amateur in history to win the championship that afternoon.

As everyone who has ever swung a golf club with serious intent surely recalls, the hero that day was Arnold Palmer, as a result of perhaps the greatest "charge" of his charge-filled career. What probably only I remember is that, after an outward three-under-par 32, I was two strokes ahead of Arnie, leading the championship, and on a roll with only nine holes to go. A measure of how well I was striking the ball is that I hit over the green with a 4-iron second shot at the 556-yard eleventh hole. Although I failed to get up and down there for a birdie, I made up for it with one at the next hole, a long par three, by holing from twelve feet off a great 2-iron.

Throughout the championship to that point, I had carefully avoided looking at leader boards in order to devote all of my mental energies to my shotmaking. After that birdie at twelve, I just could not resist finding out how I stood. When I peeked at the board it showed that, at five under par, I was leading the Open over four players, including Ben Hogan, by one stroke. Now, remember, I was then still only twenty years old and, despite my good amateur record, pretty green once I moved beyond that league. *Leading the Open! Oh, my gosh!* For the first time all week, it really hit me that I could actually win the world's premier golf championship. Looking at that board was my first mistake. As might be expected, the second one followed quickly.

At that time the green of Cherry Hills' thirteenth hole, a shortish par four, was severely pitched from back to front. I knocked my 9-iron second shot about twelve feet past the flagstick, then stroked what I thought was an excellent putt that barely missed the hole and stopped eighteen inches beyond it. As I marked the ball, I noticed there was an improperly repaired pitch mark dead on my comeback line.

Letting myself think about winning the Open had opened a small crack in my composure. Now another and wider one occurred as I tried to figure out what to do about the ball mark. One part of my mind was telling me that the rules allowed me to fix it, but another part was saying, "Are you absolutely certain about that?" What I should have done is stopped, taken a couple of deep breaths, and asked Ben for clarification, or even requested a rules official. Flustered by my situation and embarrassed by my lack of certainty about the rules, I went ahead and stroked the putt. It hit the pitch mark flush, jumped sideways, and missed the hole.

I three-putted for another bogey at the long par-four fourteenth, made a chip-and-putt par at fifteen, then missed from three feet for a birdie at sixteen. Looking back now, I realize I could probably have gotten home in two at the seventeenth, but, nervous and indecisive,

I laid up short of the water, then left my pitch shot twelve feet from the hole. With the putt came my third and probably biggest mistake. As the ball lipped out, I told myself I'd blown it, that the championship was all over for me. Walking after my drive up eighteen, all I could think of was my bet . . . of how twenty times thirty-five was seven hundred, and what $700 would have meant to Barbara and me on our honeymoon four short weeks away.

When I got to the ball, I hit a 4-iron that finished just to the right of the putting surface, but, being so sure it made no difference, I paid little attention to it. As I got closer to the green, however, I saw Joe Dey, the head of the United States Golf Association and a friend and mentor from my earliest amateur tournaments, come out of the scorer's tent and start picking up hot-dog wrappers and cigarette butts and other trash from around where my ball lay, then all along my line to the green. It occurred to me that this was uncharacteristic of so grand a gentleman, but I didn't take the thought any further before stepping up to my chip shot, knocking it within about five feet, then missing the putt to finish with a bogey. Not asking myself why Mr. Dey was performing clean-up for me was mistake number four.

What Joe knew, of course, and what I in my disappointment and confusion hadn't bothered to work out, was that, if I'd gotten up and down for a par, I would have finished with a four-round total of 281. If Arnold had then missed the twenty-footer he made at eighteen for par a little later, we would have gone into a playoff. But "ifs" never have and never will count in golf. With his fabulous final round of 65, Arnie deservedly achieved one of sport's most famous triumphs.

But, yes, Ben, you were right. Ten shots is stretching it, but if I'd known then what I learned about golf over the next few years, it might have been a different story that long-ago afternoon at Cherry Hills.

SUSTAINING an unpleasant streak, the week after the Open I got dumped out of the NCAA championship in only the second round. Life then took a definite upturn when, on July 23, in Columbus, Ohio, I married Miss Barbara Bash, also of that fair city. In August, things returned—golf-wise, at least—to no better than average as I won my singles in the Americas' Cup match against Canada and Mexico but, again partnered by Beman, lost both foursomes matches. (A contributing factor to one of those defeats taught me a lesson I've never forgotten. Deane had been fiddling around with Charlie Coe's sand wedge as we warmed up before the match. On the par-five fifth hole, as he prepared to play a short pitch shot to the green, Deane asked me, ruefully, "What do you think I should play, Charlie Coe's sand wedge or mine?" Having Charlie's wedge in his bag brought his total of clubs to fifteen, which meant under the rules of that time that we lost every hole played up to that point and were five down. Since then, I've counted my clubs on the first tee before every tournament round, plus my partner's in team events.) Next came the Amateur championship, already discussed—and won, incidentally, by Deane. Then, as summer began turning to autumn, there occurred an unusual chance to at least partially redeem my poor title defense and my near miss in the Open. If I do say so myself, I made what seems all these years later an even better shot at it than I felt at the time.

The World Amateur Team Championship is a golf happening that rarely nowadays attracts much attention in the United States, but that I hope will survive and prosper for a long time to come.

One reason is that the men's competition is played for the Eisenhower Trophy, so in a way is golf's ongoing memorial to the man who, along with Arnold Palmer and television, did so much to popularize the game in America after World War II. I'm talking, of course, about President "Ike" and his widely publicized love of golf as a form of relaxation while running the country for most of the 1950s.

Then there's the actual structure of the event, which makes it by far the most international—and enjoyable—tournament I participated in as an amateur.

Begun in 1958 at the Old Course of St. Andrews in Scotland, the World Amateur is contested every two years in different zones of the world, between four-man teams representing the best amateurs from just about every country where golf is played. What makes it so much fun is the unique mix of cultures, languages, personalities, and skill levels this format produces. Obviously, the principal golfing nations dominate competitively, but the other participants couldn't care less, because the event is generally their only chance to get to know, play with, and learn from the world's best amateurs. Frequently, players from the smallest golfing countries don't break 90, or even 100. Nevertheless, they love every minute of the event, leave it with a lot of new friends, and invariably are stimulated by the experience to keep building and promoting the game back in their own countries.

The 1960 World Amateur was held in late September at Merion on the outskirts of Philadelphia, where teams from thirty-two nations participated. I played on various days with a Finn, a Swiss, a Portuguese, and a Peruvian. They had no chance at the top trophies, but they all had a ball. Barbara will never forget Hans Schweizer, the Swiss, telling her how worried he was about playing in front of a gallery because no one had ever watched him on a golf course before except cows.

I know a lot of people watching good golfers playing with less-skilled shotmakers—as, for instance, in tour pro-ams—feel that all the hacking around is off putting for the big shots. In the majority of cases, that simply is not true. One reason is that anyone who truly loves golf always empathizes with and respects and is eager to help and encourage a fellow addict. Another reason is that, the better the player the better his or her concentration, and the better the concentration the less it's disturbed by what anyone else is doing. In fact, it has always been my impression that, the greater the accomplishments and stature of the tour pro, the more receptive and encouraging he is to pro-am partners, and vice versa.

In the 1960 World Team Championship, you could have fired a cannon between my legs as I stood over a three-foot putt and I would have stroked it right in the heart without missing a beat. My concentration that week was at its peak, and for a very good reason. Every golfer at his or her own level occasionally experiences, usually out of the blue, a spell when everything feels absolutely right—grip, aim, posture, takeaway, backswing, downswing, impact, follow-through . . . the whole enchilada. It's a rare but delightful experience, and that week, for no reason I could think of then or now, it enveloped me for four straight days. The result was a mind totally free of concerns about technique or ball-striking, and therefore a mind applied exclusively to competitive strategy and course management.

This combination of sound mechanics and savvy head work produced scores of 66-67-68-68—269 on a golf course where, ten years previously, Ben Hogan had required eighteen strokes more for seventy-two holes before winning his second U.S. Open in a playoff. My scores assisted the U.S. team—Bob Gardner, Bill Hyndman, and

Deane Beman were its other members—to a forty-two-stroke victory in the main event, and enabled me to win individual honors by thirteen strokes from Deane, and they still represent one of the finest straight seventy-two holes I've played. I remember that the achievement, coming after my second place in that year's U.S. Open, attracted a lot of media attention, and it certainly made me very happy. But honesty obliges me to add a rider.

Merion in any condition is a marvelous golf course, and a testy one, but on this occasion it simply wasn't set up the way it was for U.S. Opens. If it had been, a good proportion of that field of principally weekend golfers might never have completed a round or, if they had, would have felt humiliated by the number of strokes required to do so. Being sensitive to this, the organizing United States Golf Association had taken the course to a point only about halfway in difficulty between how the members normally play it and how it confronts an Open field. We never hit from the back tips of the tees on many holes even though the course at full stretch is less than 6,500 yards, most of the fairway widths were generous, the rough overall was modest, and the hole locations—always the key to Merion as an Open test—were mostly pretty accessible. Additionally, rain and a general all-enveloping dampness the first three days made the greens hold shots that, in an Open, might have finished in downtown Philly.

EVER felt that golf is more of a disease than a game? Here's proof.

On the morning of my wedding day—Saturday, July 23, 1960—I played a full round of golf at Scioto, the reason being that the bridegroom-to-be and three of his friends felt in need of some fresh air and exercise after the previous evening's rehearsal dinner. And it was great fun right up until the final hole, where I announced to the guys, "Well, here she goes, my last tee-shot as a single man. Watch this, because it's going to be the longest drive you'll ever see." Whereupon I cold-topped the ball into the water just off to the left of the tee.

I had a great honeymoon. We spent our wedding night in a motel across town in Columbus, where, just for fun, I registered us as "Mr. and Mrs. Jones." I'd wanted to go to some nice resort where I could play golf, but as neither of us had been to New York, and because

Barbara wanted to go there so badly, our plan was to spend two weeks in the Big Apple. In my white 1959 Buick with the green convertible top, we drove most of the Sunday until we stopped for the night at Hershey, Pennsylvania, the famous chocolate town. I had, of course, heard great things about the country club course there and was friendly with the pro, Jay Weitzel, so naturally couldn't pass up the opportunity to play it on the Monday. Barbara walked around with me.

That night we checked into the now defunct Astor Hotel in New York, and Monday we did some sightseeing, along with some shopping—in fact, a whole lot of shopping. Barbara was a shoe freak in those days—the only thing we had room for in our closet when we first married was what seemed like about four hundred pairs of her shoes. That day in Manhattan we must have visited every shoe store in midtown before she finally ended up with five—yep, five—new pairs of shoes. The first two evenings we went to shows—*Plume de Ma Tante* and *Camelot* with Robert Goulet, as I recall—and ate at Sardi's, the only New York restaurant I'd heard of. By then I was getting pretty restless, and really itchy to play golf. Fortunately, at Eddie Condon's after the theater the second evening, we ran into Pete Peski, the owner of that famous nightspot, who was a member of Winged Foot. Pete kindly invited me to go and play the course, so Wednesday we drove out to Westchester. It bucketed down rain all day but I played anyway and had the place to myself. Barbara walked all eighteen holes again.

On Thursday morning we agreed we'd both had enough of Gotham, and decided to head down to Atlantic City. Its boardwalk was famous and I figured it might be fun to walk it. Driving from New York to that New Jersey spa, you pass right by Pine Valley—well, *almost* right by. I'd never played the course, but figured it was only showing proper respect to stop off and try to do so. Instead of having the sense to call the pro and see what he could do for me, I just drove up to the front door, walked in, and said to the first person I met, "Hello, I'm Jack Nicklaus, and I was wondering if there might be any chance I could play the course? My wife and I are on our way . . ." "Your *what?*" the person I'd approached shot back. "Your *wife?* Where is she now?" When I told him she was sitting right out in front of the clubhouse in the car, a look of horror came over his face. Fortunately, he turned out to be a nice insurance man from

Philadelphia by the name of Dave Newbold, who, after explaining how strictly stag Pine Valley was, both arranged for me to play and took care of Barbara while I did so. The latter was achieved by driving her around the perimeter and maintenance roads, bringing her to the edge of the course periodically to catch glimpses of me as I played around on my own.

Barbara still doesn't believe that anyone who'd been around golf as much as I had by then would not know Pine Valley was for men only, but it was the truth—I didn't. When friends ask what I shot there that first time, I tell them 74, but that it wasn't a fair test because I was on my honeymoon, adding that my second round a year later was eight strokes better. Barbara still talks about how lucky she was to see those three great courses on her honeymoon. (Ha! ha!)

I'm digressing here, but I just have to tell how the honeymoon ended. We were even less excited by Atlantic City than by New York, so, after strolling the boardwalk for an hour or so, we decided to call it quits and go home. However, I adore clams and we were at the seashore, so before we left I bought some nice fresh ones—twelve dozen of them, to be exact. That meant having to stop every few hours on the long drive back to Columbus to look for ice, and I still have memories of driving around Zanesville, Ohio, late that night hunting for an ice-dispenser. When we finally got to my folks' place around one in morning, all of this work had made me hungry, so I decided to have a snack—like, twelve dozen steamed clams. Everything was going beautifully until the smell from the kitchen woke Mom. Down she came, took one look at the clams, and tossed them straight in the garbage can. "Jack," she said, with that long-suffering look unique to mothers of headstrong children, "those are *not* the sort of clams you steam. If you'd eaten those, you'd probably be dead by morning."

I bet your honeymoon wasn't nearly as much fun as ours.

SERIOUSLY, getting married was the big event of 1960 for both of us, but it also produced some challenges in the practicalities of day-to-day living that I don't recall either of us had thought much about.

Until then, almost all of the money I had spent in my life had been provided by my father, including most recently a generous down-payment on a nice little Cape Cod home in Upper Arlington, an attractive northwestern suburb of Columbus. Long before tying the knot, I had vowed that, from my wedding day on, I would stand on my own feet financially. That proved to be not as difficult as I had sometimes imagined it might be.

Thanks to Fred Jones, Sr., and Wayne Lewis, a friend of my dad's and a Scioto member, right after the honeymoon I got a job selling life insurance with the Ohio State Life Insurance Company, owned by Mr. Jones. (Fred's love of golf was such that he later almost single-handedly created one of the Midwest's finest courses, The Golf Club, in New Albany near Columbus. Pete Dye was the architect and I got my first taste of the golf design business when he asked me to help him with a few of the holes.)

A few months later, due largely to Dave Newbold, the Pine Valley member who helped us during our honeymoon, I improved my pay by adding work for Parker and Co., a New York–based insurance firm. Both of the jobs were genuine, requiring me as they did to make regular sales calls and follow-ups, as well as tee it up with customers and prospects—in other words, some fun but plenty of real work and hard work.

To further help with the bills—we had discovered that two definitely cannot live as cheaply as one—I also began doing periodic promotional work for the Hercules Slack Company of Columbus, not endorsing their products, which would have contravened golf's amateur status rules, but playing with department-store buyers and other big customers when I was on the road for tournaments. All told, my earnings from these three jobs totaled about $24,000 a year, a handsome income in those days for a twenty-year-old.

Two big challenges remained, however, and by then they were reaching serious proportions. They were time and energy.

In addition to my three jobs, I was still trying to earn a degree from Ohio State, originally in pharmacy but by then in insurance, as was Barbara, in elementary education. On top of that, we were endeavoring to establish some semblance of a normal married life, which included sprucing up the house. (Making the basement into a recreation room on a budget of five hundred dollars, I recall, became a nighttime and a nightmarish task, as Barbara's father, a schoolteacher, did his best to help me win a war with wall paneling and acoustical ceiling tiles.) Then, on top of all that, I was trying to play amateur golf at the championship level. It was tough, and much as I fought the calendar and the clock and my own periodic exhaustion —my stubbornness can be boundless—deep down inside I knew that sometime, somehow, something would have to give.

In consequence, by the end of that year, much as I was still emotionally committed to remaining an amateur golfer, thoughts about one day playing the game professionally inevitably had arisen from time to time. Deep down I sensed that, living as I was, there was simply no way I could do myself justice at the game. On the other hand, I faced some powerful deterrents to professionalism, not least my father's infrequently stated but very plain and strong hope that I would try to emulate his lifelong hero, Bob Jones, golf's supreme amateur.

My dad, Louis Charles Nicklaus, known to everyone from early boyhood as Charlie, was a remarkable person in many ways and a father in a million throughout his lifetime. He never made headlines at anything—he would have hated even the thought of being any kind of "celebrity"—but to me he exemplified all that is best in the American spirit.

Of solid German workingman stock, Dad was born in Columbus in 1913, the second son of Louis and Arkie Belle Nicklaus, and lived there contentedly all of his life. Imbued early with the work ethic by both ancestral example and immediate need, as a boy and young man he labored hard at whatever would bring the family a few dollars. When in later years he became financially comfortable as the owner of several pharmacies, he continued working hard principally to allow his family and himself to enjoy the fun things of life.

Dad was ample of build, extroverted and gregarious by nature, and almost invariably sunny and upbeat in disposition. He was also strong, independent, capable, responsible, honest, fair, and unfailingly modest and down to earth. So far as I am aware, he never made an enemy in his life, but I know he made and kept a zillion friends. He was certainly my best friend ever, and I have never ceased to miss him since his death from cancer in 1970.

Our deepest bond, from my earliest memory of Dad, was our passionate love of sports, mentioned in the previous chapter. Looking back now, I sometimes wonder how my mother, Helen, and my younger sister, Marilyn, tolerated the pair of us. All of my children have been heavily into sports, and most of their friends—and Barbara's and my friends, too—are sports enthusiasts of one kind or another, so Barb's description of our home as an endless "day camp" is close to the mark. But if she thinks we're bad, she should have known big Charlie and little Jackie back in the late forties and early fifties. Outside of work and school time, sports were just about all that mattered to both of us, seven days a week, three hundred sixty-five days a year. Mom and Sis were hauled along in the wake a good part of the time, but it must have been tough to coexist with such utter and complete sports fanatics as my dad and me.

Although my grandfather Louis wasn't nearly as sports-crazy as his son and grandson, it was he who sparked my dad's interest in sports way back in his kindergarten days. Despite the physical arduousness of Grandpa's work as a railroadman, he somehow found the energy to play catcher in the Columbus industrial baseball league, and would bring home and maintain the team's equipment between games. All of that gear was a heavenly sight to young Charlie, and it started him on a sports career that evolved roughly as follows:

- *High school*—Fullback on the South High football team; guard on the basketball team; left field on the baseball team; co-originator of the tennis and golf teams, including playing number one on the latter squad while shooting in the mid-70s despite no more than one round of golf a week.
- *College*—Freshman football, basketball, and baseball at Ohio State; junior varsity basketball as a sophomore; then, because he wanted to concentrate on getting his pharmacy degree, Sunday semipro ball under assumed names for the Portsmouth Spartans of the NFL (now the Detroit Lions) instead of varsity football; finally, the year he graduated, Columbus Public Courts tennis champion.
- *Postgraduate*—At various stages, golf, tennis, any pickup game involving a ball and lively competition, plus avid support of Ohio State football; then, in later years, hunting, fishing, and gradually less and less golf playing and more and more time watching his son do so.

Early in my career, the story of how my dad first got me onto a golf course became so well known through his constant retelling of it to inquiring writers that he finally gave it a title: "The Famous Ankle Injury." Just for the record, here it is, briefly, once again.

When he was still in his early thirties, Dad severely twisted his left ankle playing volleyball. He was told at the time that he had simply sprained the ankle severely, but a few years later, after periodic trouble with the joint, it was discovered that he'd actually broken a bone. The result by then was arthritis and bone spurs, finally requiring fusion of the ankle in the fall of 1949, followed by three months in a cast. Once the cast was off, Dad was told by his surgeon, Dr. Jud Wilson, that recovery would be speeded by gentle exercise, which to him immediately spelled "golf." He had given up the game after college as too time-consuming for a man trying to build his own business and raise a family, but had joined Scioto Country Club as a social member in 1948. Now, with the perfect excuse, he converted to golf membership. However, after all that time in a cast, he quickly found he couldn't walk more than a couple of holes without resting the ankle, which, in the absence of golf carts, not yet in general usage, prevented him from making regular games. Knowing my readiness to try anything sporting, he invited me to caddie for him. We would amble through a hole or two, then, using a few cut-down clubs, I'd amuse myself on a green or in a bunker while he rested. I enjoyed doing pretty much anything with my father, so this was fine by me. As to the game of golf itself, well, that was okay too—although, you understand, definitely inferior to baseball, long my consuming springtime passion.

What happened next once again proves the truth of the old adage about being in the right place at the right time. If Jack Grout had not arrived as the new pro at Scioto concurrent with my father's convalescence, right now I would probably be selling insurance Monday through Friday and flipping a fishing rod for my weekend fun. Conceivably, I would have continued to play golf, or come back to it in later years. But I am certain that my life overall would have been very different from what it became.

IF my dad was first the catalyst then the architect of my golfing career, Jack Grout was its principal builder and supreme motivator.

Playing with Dad that spring of 1950, we rarely kept accurate scores, but I remember shooting 51 for my first nine holes when seriously "counting," then getting rapidly worse with a 61 the second time and a 71 the third. An instant golfing phenomenon I was not, partly due to the well-known beginner's tendency to swat mostly air, but even more because of a certain casualness at the game not untypical of any normal ten-year-old. Like my own children at around the same age, frogs and other such diversions frequently had a stronger appeal to me than the esthetics of the one-piece takeaway or the subtleties of the double-breaking putt. Then came Jack Grout.

Born in Oklahoma but raised mostly in Texas, Jack at that time was a tall, slender, dark-haired, almost matinee-idol-handsome fellow with the kind of background that, up until a few years ago, traditionally produced golf's finest teachers. He first got into the game professionally in 1930 as an assistant to an older brother, Dick, at the Glen Garden Club in Fort Worth. There, in off-duty hours, Jack would tee it up with a couple of former caddies who had been given junior memberships by the names of Byron Nelson and Ben Hogan. Byron recalled in his autobiography, *How I Played the Game,* that in those days in those parts "Jack was the best pro around, and I had come to be one of the best amateurs, and we won (the local) pro-ams so many times that the other pros got together and made it a rule that a pro could only play with the same amateur once a month." There was obviously a lot of golfing talent in the Grout family, because Dick and Jack had a sister who won the Oklahoma state women's amateur championship, among other achievements.

Like so many of his contemporaries whose primary source of income had to be their club work, Jack never hit it big on tour, but he did win a couple of then-notable events, the 1939 Mid-South Four-ball Championship (with 1938 Masters winner Henry Picard), and the 1947 Spring Lake Invitational, beating the 1941 Masters and U.S. Open champion Craig Wood. Sadly, back trouble eventually forced Jack off the tournament trail and ultimately from any kind of golf playing. Long before then, however, his competitive experience, plus his constant study and analysis of the game's best players, had given him a profound interest in and knowledge of the game's techniques. Very much a people person, he had always enjoyed teaching, and quickly became content to make it the bedrock of his future years in golf. His greatest joy was teaching the game to young people.

Was ever a kid so lucky!

As soon as school finished in June of 1950, Mr. Grout began a two-hour weekly class for juniors at Scioto. My dad asked me if I would like to join, and, eager to get better if I was going to continue with this frustrating game, I jumped at the chance. In fact, in later years Jack liked to claim that I jumped so hard I was the first kid to sign up in his pro shop and the first one ready on the tee at the opening session.

Every Friday morning, about fifty youngsters would show up at Scioto, both boys and girls. Mr. Grout would line us up across one end of the club's huge driving range, give us one simple swing basic to concentrate on, demonstrate it, then let us go at it while moving along the line working briefly with each individual. Almost immediately, this wasn't enough for that impatient perfectionist, J. W. Nicklaus. After only two or three of the group sessions, I talked my father into letting me supplement them with some private lessons from Mr. Grout, and still fondly recall his reaction to the bills that would arrive for those one-on-one sessions, plus the ever-increasing number of practice balls I hit. "Good gracious, Jack," Dad would say to me as he went through the mail. "What's this, *seventeen* buckets of range balls in *one* day? And *another* lesson from Mr. Grout?" He was really just teasing me, of course, because his pleasure in the effort I was putting into golf was so great that he really didn't care how many balls I hit or lessons I took. Then, after a while, as I began to show some potential and Mr. Grout and I came to enjoy each other's company more and more, the bills arrived less and less frequently, until finally they stopped altogether.

Even with all of this coaching, it took most of that first summer for anything to really jell. My mother likes to remember that my first media mention was for winning the ten-year-old flight of the 1950 Scioto juvenile tournament, and by the time school came around again I'd shot 91 from the men's regular tees and was pretty impressed with myself. But it was not until the following summer, when I reduced that "best" by ten strokes, that I began to really get the hang of the game.

Once that happened, the effort to get even better became all-consuming. Daily in the summertime I would arrive at Scioto early in the morning, hit balls for an hour or two, play eighteen holes carrying my clubs, have lunch, hit more balls, go out and play eighteen more, come back and hit more balls or chip and putt until dark —and I mean can't-see-anything dark, so dark that my mother would have to come and haul me home for supper by the ear. In my early and mid teens, weather permitting, I doubt if any summer I missed more than a day or two of doing that. I remember once playing sixty-three holes in a day, and it was nothing for me to hit 500 or more balls a day. I never went to camp, we never went on family vacations. In every other way I was a normal kid—had girlfriends, played other sports, went to the movies, hung out with the guys. But, basically, during the daylight hours in summertime as a teenager, I did what I wanted to do most from the age of eleven, which was practice and play golf.

As I got older, this even carried over to the wintertime. Many were the times when I would take a shovel and a broom and clear the snow off a patch of ground and try to bristle up the turf enough so I could hit practice shots. With my dad's help, Jack Grout eventually installed half a Quonset hut on the Scioto driving range with mats and a little heater inside, with the idea that he could give lessons during the off-season. Well, he didn't give many lessons once I started using the hut, because there were never any golf balls left for anyone else to work with. I'd hit Jack's teaching balls, then my own practice balls, then I'd borrow everyone else's I could find around the club. At snowy times I would wait for the thaw, then go out and pick up all the balls, then go to work all over again. I'm sure some of the older members thought I was mentally impaired, even downright crazy. They probably thought the same about Jack Grout, too, for standing out there in the cold with me.

Much as I liked Jack, it never occurred to me in those days how deep the relationship with my generous, modest, sweet-natured teacher would become, and how much of a contribution it would make both to my game and to my mental and emotional well-being for so many of my adult years. The truth is that we developed a friendship as close and warm and comfortable as two men can, and particularly after my dad's death in 1970, when Jack Grout became a second father to me.

Because they have been so crucial to my career, and also because they will never date and therefore could be helpful to any reader interested in improving at golf, I'll touch later on the swing and shotmaking concepts and techniques that Jack taught me in those early years. For now, I want to mention a noninstructional element of our relationship that has had an equally important bearing on my achievements, and that was particularly crucial in my amateur days. It is one that I believe to be too often overlooked or undervalued in teacher-pupil and coach-athlete relationships.

I'm sure I don't have to remind anyone who plays golf about the huge emotional swings, the massive peaks and valleys of the psyche, that the game produces. One day you're up there in the heavens, and the next you're down where the demons dwell. Everyone needs someone to help him through these peaks and valleys, an individual in the wings who is constantly and totally and genuinely sympathetic and upbeat and encouraging and supportive. From the very first day we met until his death in May of 1989, Jack Grout was that person for me. As such, his contribution to my life and golf game was truly priceless.

My own experiences as a father have shown me how important it is for youngsters involved in sports to have really good coaches. By that I don't mean super teachers or brilliant strategists, but simply people who are genuinely interested in their charges, who will devote serious time to them, and who, through that interest and during that time, are able to motivate and encourage young people regardless of their levels of achievement.

Jack Grout was that kind of man to me. I don't know whether he was the best golf teacher in the world in a technical or mechanical sense; and, frankly, in all the years we were together I never thought or cared about that. When he and I first started out, he was certainly well respected within his profession, but he had no kind of national reputation like the fellows who teach the top pros today seem to so quickly acquire. But I would do anything that Jack Grout wanted me to do because he was so wonderfully supportive of me.

Looking back, the most remarkable thing about those earliest days was how much time Mr. Grout always seemed to have for me. He'd see me coming in off the course and it was always the same: "Well, Jackie boy, how'd you play today? How'd you hit 'em out there, young fella." And I'd tell him my score, a 93 or an 88 or whatever, and he'd say, "Well, let's go out and hit a few, let me take a look." And off we would head once again for the range or the putting green. Certainly he was tickled by my enthusiasm, and in later years he liked to suggest that a certain clairvoyance about where I would go in golf stimulated his efforts to help me. Whatever the reasons, without fail his time was my time.

Equally valuable—especially during my inevitable slumps—was the durability of Jack's conviction about my innate golfing abilities. Come a bad patch and he couldn't wait to start getting me refocused and remotivated by helping to make the game fun for me again. It was like that every single day of his life, even in those terrible times when he was dying of cancer and could barely sit upright in a golf cart. The phone would ring and there he would be . . . the faint voice trying so hard to sound upbeat and cheerful: "Jackie boy, come on, let's go out and hit some balls."

There would be some times as the years passed when Jack's enthusiasm was my *only* motivation, when I would go to the practice tee and hit shots for him that I knew his failing eyes could not even see, simply because he wanted to spend time with me, and because I wanted to be with him just as much. And when I got there it was always fun, and, like as not, without him telling me even one teacherly thing, I'd fall back in love with the game again.

Jack Grout was the most fortunate thing that ever happened to me in terms of golf, and the reason was that he would not, under any circumstances, allow me to get really down on myself. In this respect he was relentless. "Come on, Jackie boy," he'd urge and exhort me, "you'll get it, stay with it, keep at it. You're the best, Jackie boy, you've beaten 'em all before and you'll beat 'em all again. Okay, you lost it for a while, but forget that, put it out of your head. It's another day, and there's another tournament coming up. Now, let's get out there and go to *work*. Come on, let's go hit some balls, there isn't any time to waste. Now, don't you forget, it's right there inside of you and we're going to *find* it. Jackie, young fella, you're going to be unbeatable . . . you hear me . . . *Un-beat-able!* Now, let's get out there and start playing some *real* golf."

It was heady stuff, and there was no way I could not respond to such boundless faith in me. Thank you, Jack, from the bottom of my heart.

ANOTHER advantage I enjoyed during those formative years is that I was never pushed too hard by any of the other people close to me.

With such fond memories of his own semipro football days, plus his great love for the Ohio State program, I'm sure I would have heard no arguments from my father if I had chosen football over golf. But Dad never pressured me on the subject, and he dropped it completely after his good friend Woody Hayes, the legendary OSU coach, offered his views. I discovered years later that Woody had told my father, "Charlie, forget about Jack playing football. I think he'd make a fine quarterback if he stayed with the game, but he could also get hurt, and with the talent he has for golf he'd be crazy to take a chance like that. Just encourage him with his golf, because I think he could have a great career at it."

It was the same with golf. From the time I started competing in tournaments around the age of thirteen, my father always accompanied me, walked with me, watched me, encouraged me, but never pressured me about my play. Much as I loved his company, I remember telling him at one point, "Dad, you sometimes make me awfully nervous out there following me all the time." And he told me, "Well, Jack, you're just going to have get used to it, because I love watching you play and I plan to keep on doing it for a long, long time." And that made me realize how fortunate I was to have such a supportive father, and instead of letting him make me jumpy I decided I was going to use his presence as a stimulus, to perform for him, to try to play better for him. And I did, and it helped me. And the same became true for his pals, for "Charlie's Gang," for Al Johnson and Asa Beavers and Wayne Brown and Bob Daniels and Bill Davis and Ed Coughlin and John Jennings and Howard Hutchinson (whose son of the same name married my sister Marilyn) and my uncle Frank Nicklaus. Some or all of them were there for me time and time again, at the 1959 Walker Cup, and the Amateur championships, then at the Masters and the U.S. Opens, and even a few times at British Opens, never pressuring me but always supportive and encouraging. And their presence added to the specialness of the events for me, and I tried to perform for them too, used the pleasure they got from my excelling to make me work and compete even harder.

The other side of this coin, of course, is the kids you see in sports today who show great potential at fourteen or fifteen or sixteen, but who, by the time they get into their early or mid-twenties, have been driven so hard by parents or teachers or coaches that they're totally burned out. That trap was never set for me. I could always go to my dad and his gang and Jack Grout for help and advice, and they would do anything in their power to provide it, but without ever trying to push me harder or faster than I wanted to go myself.

Which doesn't mean, of course, that I didn't try to go harder or faster than was good for me.

THROUGHOUT my life I've always had a tendency, as the British neatly put it, to squeeze a quart into a pint pot. Maybe this is overconfidence, or maybe it's just a strong desire to live life to the fullest. Whatever the cause, I've always been in the championship flight when it comes to filling up a day. What with marriage, college, three jobs, then, in the fall, impending parenthood, I remember the year 1961 taking on a distinctly blurred character. Nevertheless, it ended up pretty satisfyingly so far as golf was concerned.

In those days, following the weather-enforced winter layoff from sustained practice, I would usually begin working intensively on my game with Jack Grout at Scioto in early February. If it were not too cold or windy, we would hit balls outdoors, if necessary clearing a patch of snow or packing it down and hitting off the top. In really bitter conditions we'd become sissies and work from the aforementioned open-ended Quonset hut. Come the spring break, I would head down either to Pinehurst or Florida for more intensive practice, plus generally a warm-up tournament.

The warm-up tournament in 1961 was the Western Amateur, played in New Orleans. I won it, and soon after took low amateur honors in the Masters, tying for seventh, seven shots behind Gary Player. A month later, I again tried my hand against the professionals via an invitation to play in the old-established Colonial tournament in Fort Worth, but made a hash of the third round and finished well back of winner Doug Sanders. Next came a tie for fourth in the U.S. Open at Oakland Hills, three strokes back of Gene Littler after being only a shot off the lead with seven holes to go. Still burning about a couple of dumb mistakes during that stretch, I played aggressive golf the following week to win the NCAA championship at my second attempt. Then came a couple more unsuccessful encounters with the pros through invitations to the Buick Open and American Golf Classic, followed by a quick end to my defense of the Colonial Invitational (amateur version) in Memphis as Bobby Greenwood eagled the eighteenth and birdied the first extra hole to eliminate me in the opening round. On the first day of September in Seattle, Deane Beman and I easily won our Walker Cup foursome, and the following day I was proud to have maintained a 100-percent record over my two matches following an enjoyable scrap with the legendary Irishman, Joe Carr. Nine days later came the National Amateur at Pebble Beach.

I AM not usually given to snap decisions, but I fell in love with Pebble Beach from the moment I first played it in practice that year. Today, after having played Pebble about three hundred times, along with perhaps six hundred or so other courses around the world, it remains my number one as a championship test. The scenery, of course, has a lot to do with this. Carmel Bay, which Pebble Beach abuts, is the crown jewel of a peninsula purported to have been described by either the writer Robert Louis Stevenson or the artist Frances McComber as either "The most felicitous joining of land and water that nature has composed" or "The greatest meeting of land and water on God's earth." Whichever authored what, I agree.

But there is so much more to Pebble Beach than its superb location. Some of the very finest holes designwise are inland, and not particularly visually dramatic. More than anything, Pebble's appeal to me lies in the head work it forces a golfer to do. As exemplified by the three U.S. Opens played there to date, it is one of the supreme thinking-man's courses in shotmaking terms, and among the most testing I know of a player's grace under fire. Let your game management get away from you or your emotions get the better of you at Pebble Beach and it's sayonara. Invariably, for all of those reasons, the course favors the better golfers, rarely producing fluky winners. I like that also.

"Inspired" is a strong word, but that was the effect Pebble Beach had on me as the 1961 U.S. Amateur championship got under way. Also, the course had provided me with an entirely new golfing weapon, and one that would remain invaluable from this championship on.

In practice, the blustery Pacific winds, combined with firm fairways and greens, had been giving me fits on approach-shot yardages. When I mentioned the problem to friend Deane Beman, he responded, "Then why don't you measure them, like me?" As Gene Andrews had been doing for many years, savvy little Deane by then had ingrained the habit of pacing off and noting down yardages, while I and almost everyone else in the amateur game—and most of the pros, also—continued to rely entirely on visual estimating. Taking Deane's advice, I found that the more yardages I paced off, the more greens I hit and the closer I got to the cups. By the time the championship began, my confidence was as high as my spirits.

If Merion a year previously was among my best ever stroke-play performances, Pebble Beach in the1961 Amateur was by far and away my finest match-play effort. In addition to inspiration and confidence, I enjoyed the same cocoonlike concentration that had been such a factor in the World Amateur Team Championship, and my ball-striking was almost as flawless as on that occasion. Never stronger physically, during that year I had nine times smashed the fiber face insert out of my driver. The club stayed intact that week, but I hit the ball with it consistently between 280 and 300 yards, and mostly to the preferred areas of the fairways (the galleries quickly nicknamed me "The Brute"). Approach shot after approach shot covered the stick, and that lightweight hickory-shafted putter I'd had specially made in North Berwick during the 1959 Walker Cup seemed magically charged.

Pebble Beach that year played at 6,747 yards with a par of 72 but a course rating of 75. In the Crosby the previous winter, only three professionals had beaten par in the final round, each with a 71. In the Amateur, I had a bye in the opening round, then was twenty under par for the 136 holes I played through the final. I made one eagle, thirty-four birdies, nothing higher than a five, lost a total of only nineteen holes, and was below par at the conclusion of every match. In short, as at Merion the previous fall, I enjoyed a week in golfing heaven.

My caddie was a local character by the name of Al "Dede" Gonzalves, who had carried for Harrison "Jimmy" Johnston when he won the first National Amateur played at Pebble Beach in 1929. Dede was a cigar smoker, and you could tell how I was doing by the number of stogies he consumed per round. Basically, it was six to eight for a hard match, four to six for an easy one. Thankfully for his lungs, Dede had only two six-to-eight matches. The first was in the fourth round when, despite being five under par, I eased past old Broadmoor foe, Dave Smith, by only two and one. The other came in the next round when the well-known Long Island veteran, John Humm, led me at the turn and took me to the seventeenth—my longest journey all week.

The final, thankfully, needed only four cigars—three in the morning, one in the afternoon. My opponent was H. Dudley Wysong, Jr., later a tour pro but at that time an advertising salesman from Sherman, Texas, who in earlier years had taken lessons from Byron Nelson, a friend of his father's. Six years previously, Dudley, a year older than I at twenty-two, had suffered a back injury in a train wreck, and he must have felt as though he'd been in another one by the end of this day. Out in 33, I was four up at the turn in the morning round, and maintained that lead at the lunch break with par for the inward nine. In the afternoon, I won the first four holes to go eight up, was whittled back to 6 when Dudley birdied both the front-side par threes, won the ninth, lost the tenth, almost holed my approach to win the eleventh; and became Amateur champion for the second time at the long par-three twelfth hole when Dudley conceded the match after narrowly missing a needed birdie.

My only postscript to the final is that the 8-and-6 margin in the record books doesn't fairly reflect my opponent's true golfing capabilities. I simply played that week the finest golf of my life up to that point.

3

The 1962 United States Open Championship

A Tough Decision and Another World

I SUPPOSE the earliest thoughts I ever had about becoming a professional golfer came after I was chosen for the Walker Cup team in 1959. As I've mentioned, once my selection sunk in I realized that I was a better player than I had up until then considered myself to be. Later that year, after winning my first Amateur title and being named the country's top amateur, I couldn't help again wondering what might happen if I made golf a career, did nothing else but work and compete at the game. But such possibilities continued to be no more than vague musings in the back of my mind for another two years.

Over that time my confidence about my golfing abilities grew steadily, but never to the point where I felt any great degree of certainty about succeeding as a pro. Then, in the late summer of 1961, I worked very hard on my game for three weeks getting ready for the Walker Cup and the National Amateur without letting school or business get in the way. Probably more than anything else I'd achieved, preparing so thoroughly for those two events, then playing as well as I did in them, opened my eyes to how good I might become if I ever totally devoted myself to golf.

During those two years the press must have asked me about turning professional roughly as often as they asked what club I'd hit or the length of putts I'd holed or missed. It was a difficult question, not so much because of its boring repetitiousness, but because, in those days, even the slightest admission by an amateur golfer that the thought of turning professional had entered his head could result in the United States Golf Association immediately ruling him a "non-amateur." This meant, in effect, that he would be ineligible for competitive play on either side of the fence, as an amateur or as a professional. To a guy like me, that was a scary prospect.

Accordingly, through 1959 and 1960, I provided emphatically negative answers to questions about a possible change of status, and, because remaining amateur was still my intention, felt entirely comfortable about that. Following my good showing at Cherry Hills in the 1960 Open, then at Merion in the World Amateur Team Championship—both of which greatly increased this line of questioning—some writers saw fit to appoint me "The next Bobby Jones." When I finally did begin seriously considering professionalism in the second half of 1961, those effusions provided me with a light response that often nicely persuaded all but the most persistent inquisitors to change the subject. "How, if I turned pro," I would ask in return—hopefully with a twinkle in my eye—"could I become the next Bobby Jones?"

It all seems a long time ago now, but I did go through some pretty heavy mental and emotional gymnastics on the question of my golfing future during the latter part of 1961. Basically, I was being pulled by two opposite but equally powerful forces. On one side there was my perception of my parents' wishes and my obligations to them, plus my own desires to be the best player I could become without having the game dominate my life. On the other side were a wife, a first child on the way, an education to complete, and the realities and practicalities of earning a living while still achieving my full potential as a golfer.

My father had worshipped Bob Jones ever since, as a thirteen-year-old, he had watched every shot Jones hit in winning his second U.S. Open at Scioto in 1926. In me, Charlie Nicklaus saw a potential emulator of that greatest of all amateurs, not just in golfing achievement, but, Dad surely hoped, in attitudes to the game and, indeed, to life in the whole. My mother, Helen, shared those sentiments because they were Charlie's, and also because she, too, felt I would be happiest following such a course. As with everything else, I was never pressured on the subject. But my parents' hopes and dreams were nevertheless always crystal clear to me.

Then there was the factor of Dad's and Mom's unstinting and frequently self-sacrificing material support of my golf-playing. My devotion to the game from my early teens until my wedding day at age twenty had been entirely at their expense. It had been made possible by the pharmacy business they had built from scratch, and although neither ever said so, I knew they both hoped my sister, Marilyn, and I would one day take over that business and keep it going and growing.

Added to these concerns were my dad's unwavering support and companionship since I had first begun to compete beyond our immediate locality. His presence and assistance at almost every out-of-town tournament I played from the age of thirteen had given continuity and stability and security to what otherwise could have been a difficult and unsettling experience for a kid of my temperament and background. What sort of response would it be to shove all of that aside seemingly purely for money?

Then there were my own instincts, pulling me through most of my teens just as strongly in the same direction as my parents'. As a golfer, it definitely turned me on to be compared with my longtime hero, Bob Jones, and particularly to think that I might someday approach his record. Obviously, the only way to do that was to remain amateur. Being a homebody and so family-oriented, amateurism was also very appealing temperamentally. From my occasional encounters with the pro tour, I knew it possessed some enjoyable aspects. But the prospect of the endless travel and the superficiality of lifestyle inherent in such a nomadic career was a turnoff, even in those less-than-mature days.

At the other end of the rope the pull was equally powerful and, by late 1961, growing stronger by the day.

Although I was making a decent living while still enjoying sufficient freedom to play plenty of golf, I was sure I would need both more money and more time in the years ahead to give becoming the next Bob Jones my absolute best effort. An equally big concern was whether I still really wanted that, deep down in my heart. After my second Amateur title at Pebble Beach, people had begun expecting me to win every time I teed up, which was making the game less enjoyable for me.

Barbara never complained, but we both wanted the usual comforts, plus a reasonable measure of security, and definitely a large family. Was what I was doing fair to her, and to the child we were expecting, and to the children we hoped for later? And how would its effects on me affect all of them? Was I stretching myself too thin by trying to play top amateur golf in addition to working at three jobs and attempting to complete my college education? Could I sustain the pressures I was inflicting on myself physically and mentally? The more I thought about such questions, the less happy I became with the answers to them.

The resolution of this tug-o'-war really began a couple of weeks after the 1961 Amateur, when I first talked with Mark McCormack about the possibilities of a change in status. We ran across each other in Akron at the American Golf Classic tour event, to which I'd accepted an invitation because of its proximity to home, but where I played indifferently, finishing well back.

A couple of years previously, Mark, then a young Cleveland-based attorney and low-handicap golfer, had begun handling Arnold Palmer's business affairs, then shortly thereafter taken on Gary Player's also. He was, I had heard, doing a fine job for them. There was nothing substantive in our first discussion, but following the Amateur I called Mark and asked him to visit with us in Columbus. There, after a round of golf at Scioto, I asked him to outline what he thought might be my first year's income if and when I decided to become a professional. His answer was $100,000, exclusive of any prize money I won. I realized that the expense of playing professionally would eat heavily into that sum, but it still seemed amazingly high to me. I told Mark I'd think some more about it.

Golf at the top competitive levels is really a very small club, and one in which it seems impossible to keep secrets for more than a few minutes. Just before my last event of the year, the Americas' Cup matches in Mexico in October, one of the wire services, discovering I'd met with McCormack, ran a story that I was turning pro. Being about to represent my country in an international amateur tournament, this greatly concerned and embarrassed me. In Mexico, I talked with my good friend Joe Dey, the United States Golf Association's head man, who convinced me I had broken no rules and need fret no further.

Back from Mexico, the mental and emotional gyrations rapidly accelerated. There were lengthy family conferences. Bob Jones had written me a nice letter encouraging me to remain amateur, but saying he would fully understand the reasons if I chose not to. My dad's sentiments hadn't changed, but his final word on the subject was that I had to make and live with my own decisions. I also talked confidentially with good friends in the game. Finally, early in November, I made the decision to remain amateur.

Then, a few days later, I began thinking about Barbara and little Jackie, who had arrived on the Saturday following the Amateur final. I also again began to wonder, for about the zillionth time, about what amateur golf challenges remained to inspire me, and whether they ever would be sufficient to drive me to reach my full golfing potential. It seemed that I had very little left to prove in the amateur arena. Could I test myself to the limits playing golf as a hobby? Both the world at large and the game of golf had changed so much since Bob Jones's time. Suddenly, I did a mental one-eighty and decided to turn pro. Before I could change my mind again, with Barbara's and my father's help I wrote a letter to Joe Dey informing him of the decision, which Barbara immediately went out and mailed. A couple of days later, on November 8, 1961, after I'd tracked Joe down by phone to be sure he knew of the decision, we made it public at a "press conference" at my home. Present were my two local newspapermen biographers since about the age of eleven, Paul Hornung, the sports editor of the *Columbus Dispatch,* and Kaye Kessler, the star sports columnist of the now defunct *Citizen-Journal,* Barbara, little Jackie, and me.

The die was finally cast.

I remember Joe Dey's response over the phone to this day: "Whatever decision you made, I knew it would be the right one. This changes nothing between you and the USGA. If you have any problems, or anything I can help with, just call me."

Over the next few years, I believe Dad completely reconciled himself to my decision, and eventually even came to believe that it was the correct one. Mom, I'm sure, was mostly just glad I'd stopped dithering. Barbara, as she always was and always has been since, was totally supportive—and definitely relieved that I had at last made up my mind.

• • •

MY single greatest stroke of good fortune in life was meeting Miss Barbara Bash during my first week at Ohio State in September of 1957. We were introduced by a girl whom I was dating at the time, on the steps of the university's Mendenhall Laboratory, and I walked Barbara to the bacteriology building where she was working to help pay her college expenses. I thought she was nice right away —tall, slim, blue eyes, blonde hair, a pleasant and natural manner— so that evening I called and asked her for a date. She suggested an evening three weeks later, and, although after it we both still dated around for a while, we got together more and more from then on.

The relationship went smoothly until the evening before I left for the Walker Cup match in Scotland, when I decided to cut out early from our date in order to enjoy a farewell party with the boys. This was not a popular decision, and to ease my guilt I wrote Barbara seven times from Britain—which, I regret to say, is about seven times more than I have since, although we always talk at least once a day by phone when I'm away from home. Then, for extra insurance, I pinned her immediately when I got back to Columbus, and we became engaged at Christmas that year. We picked July 23, 1960, for our wedding day for what I thought was an excellent reason: it was the Saturday of the PGA Championship, for which, as an amateur, I was, of course, ineligible.

We lived in our first home in Upper Arlington for four years, then moved into the "dream house" we built in the same neighborhood in 1964. We spent as much time there as we could between tour events and other trips during the good weather months, then time in the winter at a place my dad and I bought together in Fort Lauderdale, Florida, mostly so that we could both fish and I could work on my game year-around. In 1965, we decided to live full time in Florida to give ourselves and our children a permanent base and to minimize traveling, finally selling the Columbus home in 1968. We have lived happily in North Palm Beach ever since, although both of us still tend to think of Columbus as our "real" home. For that reason more than any other, we recently built a new summer home and guest house, with enough bedrooms for children and grandchildren, on a lake in a beautifully secluded area of Muirfield Village.

Jack William Nicklaus II arrived on September 23, 1961, Steven Charles Nicklaus came along on April 11, 1963, Nancy Jean Nicklaus (now Mrs. William O'Leary) on May 5, 1965, Gary Thomas Nicklaus on January 15, 1969, and Michael Scott Nicklaus on July 24, 1973. At this writing, we have eight grandchildren: Jack II and his wife Barbara's two sons and two daughters, Jack William III, Christina Marie, Eric Charles, and Casey Grace; and Bill and Nan O'Leary's four sons, William Thomas V, Nicklaus Scott, Christopher Michael, and Robert James.

Ours has been a fine and happy marriage for a number of reasons beyond the fact that we fell and remain in love, or even that we became and remain each other's best friend. Perhaps the single most important is that we share very similar backgrounds and, therefore, essentially the same standards and values.

Both of us come from uncomplicated, hardworking, down-to-earth, closely bonded midwestern families. As a result, despite the millions of miles we travel, the glitzy places we visit, the famous people we know, and the many material comforts that grow from a successful career, we are both at heart still pretty simple-living homebodies who get their greatest joys and satisfactions from within the family unit. The "other lives," the external lives, are fun for both of us in short takes, but we are most comfortable and content in our own tightly knit, informal, unpretentious, at-home normal world with our children and grandchildren at the center.

Because of this, I made a vow very soon after turning pro that, unless I could have Barbara and the children along with me, I would never be away from home for more than fourteen days at a stretch. Over the years, this has caused some traumas for a lot of good people in golf and among my business associates, not to mention the stress I have experienced as a result of the problems I've caused them. Also, I know a certain proportion of the media, along with some of golf's other camp-followers, think I'm overzealous about putting my family first. Be that as it may, the result has been a strong and secure marriage, plus five temperamentally different but basically normal, generally healthy, and—I sincerely hope—reasonably happy children. Case closed.

Another factor in the success of our marriage—and a bigger contributor to my golf career than the world will ever know—is Barbara's intelligence, combined with her strength of character. I knew she was very bright from our earliest dates, and I quickly discovered the source of that intelligence and her unshakable inner strength as I got to know her parents, Stanley and Helen Bash, during our courting days. Barb has never had any pretensions to intellectualism in the academic sense, but she possesses more down-to-earth common sense and what I suppose are called street smarts than any two people I've ever met. There is simply no way anyone can pull the wool over Barbara Nicklaus's eyes—and particularly not Jack Nicklaus. She will put her finger on the heart of a problem, or point to what really makes a person tick, faster than I can swing a driver. In short, she has that special kind of savvy that cuts through flim-flam like a wedge through *Poa annua,* and it has proven a priceless asset in every aspect of both our lives and our children's lives. Despite my long and continuing efforts to destroy the trait, Barbara is also organized—boy, is Barbara ever organized!—thus the big decisions have always been made collectively. However, Barbara is the person the kids and I have to thank most for an awful lot of the better ones, both large and small.

In these times when the attitudes and roles of women have changed or are changing so dramatically from those of our youth, intelligence and character are also what have enabled Barbara not only to survive being the partner of a person in the public eye, but, I truly believe, to thoroughly enjoy it. Very early on Barb recognized that, for better or worse, the spotlight would shine chiefly on me. Being basically a retiring person, that was fine with her—just so long as I didn't expect it to shine on me at home, and also just so long as I totally respected and supported her as an individual in her own right both in public and in private. I have tried my utmost in both directions, and harder and harder as the personal spotlight intensified, and it seems to have worked. In public, without any noticeable effort, my wife has established a clear and strong identity, not as "Mrs. Jack Nicklaus," but as *Barbara* Nicklaus.

In doing so, she has not only forged a million friendships of her own, but saved a lot for me by softening the cutting edge of my seemingly incurable bluntness and abruptness. In private, and more and more over the years as the children have grown, she has developed her own life and interests while still enjoying what most people would regard as a traditional marriage. That she has always been a wife and mother—and, latterly, a grandmother—first and foremost is entirely her own choice.

Barbara's lack of knowledge of golf when we first met was so total as to be laughable. A good example was her reaction to hearing someone say, "No mulligans allowed," as four of us were teeing off at Scioto one day. Barbara told me later she thought that meant, "If you're not good enough to play this course, you can't play here."

Today, I would back Barbara Nicklaus's knowledge of the game of golf against that of any nonplayer in the world. Although she might have to pause a moment before analyzing the pros and cons of, say, the ultra-late hit, her knowledge of the nontechnical elements of the game is pretty encyclopedic. Back in my early days on tour she got a solid grounding from gallerying a lot with Vivienne Player, Gary's wife, who is the daughter of a professional and was a fine amateur golfer in her own right. Since then, Barb's astute intelligence and keen eye, plus the thousands of hours she's spent watching me and, in later years, also our sons in tournament play, have made her a true expert.

A lot of our friends, including some of the writers, will not start out on a round without checking with her on the best walking routes and watching spots. And when anyone in our circle wants to know the state of play, bang up to date and dead accurate, invariably they go in search of Barbara. She will probably be holding a conversation with six people, and worrying about how the grandkids are doing, and thinking about what we'll all have for dinner, but she will rattle off the scores dead to rights, along with, if you like, the shots that made them. If I'm playing poorly, she will most likely also be able to tell you what I'm doing wrong, plus the problems of the other guys in my group (although you'd never get a word from her about that). Sometimes I think she's got at least six pairs of eyes. The truth, though, is that her observational abilities derive from being so genuinely interested and so blessed organized.

For most of our marriage, Barbara played much more tennis than golf, but, since enjoying herself at one of our Nicklaus/Flick Golf Schools a while back, she's teed it up a little more often. Very occasionally she will join me for an evening nine holes, but mostly, if she plays at all, she plays with longtime women friends. She isn't going to set any course records, but her scores are respectable for the amount she gets out, and would be a lot better if she would only get out more often. I'm always urging her to do so, as are her golfing friends, but Barbara's nature has always been to put doing things for other people ahead of whatever she might like to do herself, and I guess that isn't going to change much at this stage of our lives.

With Barbara Nicklaus, the family has always come first, and surely always will.

BEGINNING the first time I played in the Masters in 1959, Dad and I would always spend a little time with Bob Jones during the tournament. The club hosts a Wednesday evening dinner for the amateur contestants, and Mr. Jones—I never called him anything but Mr. Jones—would always look me up there and say, "How about bringing Father down to the cabin for a little visit?" We would spend half an hour or so with him every year until my dad died in 1970. In addition to increasing his specialness for me, plus my good feelings about the Augusta National and the Masters, those sessions taught me a lot about golf. However, the single most important piece of advice I obtained from Mr. Jones came indirectly through my dad. At the 1961 Masters, Bob had been talking to him one day in my absence about the role of a teacher in a golfer's career. Here's what he said:

"I think I was a fairly good young golfer, but I never became what I would call a really good player until I'd been competing for quite a number of seasons. You see, when I started to play in the big tournaments, whenever anything went wrong I'd run home to Stewart Maiden, our pro at East Lake, who taught me the game. Finally, I matured to the point where I understood my game well enough to make my own corrections during the course of a tournament, and *that's* when I'd say I became a *good* golfer."

When Dad passed on those remarks, they really got me thinking. I realized that, from the age of ten, every time I had missed a couple of shots I'd raced back to Jack Grout. From the day Dad reported that conversation, although I still worked assiduously with Jack on refining and honing my game, I made a conscious and ever-increasing effort to figure things out for myself. In the sessions with Jack, I would ask more questions about the "whys" of the various elements of the swing, and fewer about the "hows" of executing them. Like Jones, I recognized the need for the ability, in effect, to teach myself, to have sufficient mental grasp of proper technique to be able to make my own corrections, not just on the practice tee but, so far as is possible, also while actually competing. In short, I had recognized that I'd been playing for too long with crutches, and that the only way to discard them was to gain the independence that comes from truly understanding the game's cause and effect oneself, alone and unaided.

When I started out on the tour in January of 1962, I believed I had progressed a fair distance along this learning curve. Very quickly, I discovered that I had by no means completed it (now I know I probably never will). What brought the lesson home most painfully was the multiplicity of new shotmaking challenges presented by the condition in those days of most of the courses used for professional tournaments. With a few exceptions, they were entirely different from, and generally much inferior, to those of the better private clubs that hosted the important amateur tournaments that had been my principal diet.

And there was, of course, an even bigger challenge: the much larger number of extremely good players one had to beat to ascend to the top of the professional game.

IN order to join the tour back then, you had to be able to prove you had sufficient money in the bank to sustain you through your first year even if you never won a penny. The number involved is a commentary on thirtysome years of inflation—it was $12,000 in 1962. Small a sum as that may sound now, many of the fellows who turned pro around the time I did could not raise it, which meant they had to obtain sponsorship, which sometimes turned as sour on those who succeeded as those who failed. With the first endorsement affiliation arranged for me by Mark McCormack, plus a book deal, enabling me to show the required assets, I was fortunate to be able to play only for myself right from the start.

I had actually first earned a little cash as a professional on December 5, 1961, by giving a talk for the White-Haines Optical Company in Columbus. The check for $75 was nice, but, as I have always hated speech-making, the assignment was tough duty. So was my first paid golf outing. On the next to last day of 1961, I played an exhibition match with Arnold Palmer, Sam Snead and Gary Player at the Country Club of Miami in Florida. I hadn't touched a golf club in a month. I hit my opening drive into a lake. National television coverage began at the sixteenth hole. There, I again drove into water, then on seventeen missed an eighteen-inch putt. On eighteen I dunked another ball. Gary won with a 70 and Arnie and I tied for last with 73s. My chief consolation was that—at least when I stayed dry—I outdrove the others most of the time. Also, the pay had a certain soothing quality: For about five hours' work, it was roughly one-eighth of the amount I'd earned the previous 363 days.

More serious endeavors commenced across the country six days later with the tour's season opener, the Los Angeles Open, then played at the Rancho Park municipal course in the heart of the city. What I remember most about it is that I got a lot of press attention ahead of the tournament, then almost as much after it but for a different reason, namely my unimpressive scores of 74-70-72-73–289. In amateur golf, they probably would have placed me in the top three. In this brave new world, they tied me for fiftieth, twenty-one shots back of Phil Rodgers, who won his first pro event with a final round of 62. I *did* make a check—for $33.33, a one-third share of last-place money. But it was all a far cry from my expectations for myself.

Here's how things then progressed for the new pro whom some of the writers had predicted might "win everything":

San Diego Open—tied fifteenth, won $550
Bing Crosby—tied twenty-third, won $450
Lucky International—tied forty-seventh, won $62.86
Palm Springs Classic—tied thirty-second, won $164.44

Although finding a little consolation in the fact that I had at least won money every time out, I did more heart-searching during those first five weeks of teeing it up with the big boys than I've ever let on to anyone, including even Barbara.

What scared me the most was the inevitability of losing confidence in myself if I went on playing so poorly. For the past two years I had, deep within myself, *expected* to win literally every time out, and I recognized now just how much this high level of self-belief had contributed to my strong 1960–61 amateur record. The I'm-the-best, I'm-unbeatable attitude in athletes, if it shows even slightly, is inevitably interpreted as cockiness or worse. Be that as it may, as I've already pointed out and probably will again, such a mind-set is indispensable to winning at any sport. If you care about how the world perceives you as a person rather than a performer, you try extremely hard not to let it know about your belief in your capabilities. But, at the same time, you must cultivate and nurture the conviction that you are the best.

Now here I was, only just starting on the pro circuit, and already in danger of beginning to doubt myself. That hurt even more than no longer being top banana, which, in itself, wasn't the sweetest medicine to have to swallow.

None of these concerns, of course, was permitted to show publicly. On the surface, I strove to remain as cool and confident as ever —to the point, in fact, of receiving some pretty good media heat at the Crosby for having suggested somewhere along the line that I wouldn't have had a good first year unless I picked up at least $30,000, or about half of what Gary Player had made as top money-winner the previous year. As things turned out, I eventually finished third on the 1962 money list behind Arnold Palmer and Gene Littler with almost $63,000. But suggesting during my less-than-spectacular debut that I would win even half that much was deemed another example of the Nicklaus "brashness" that would rub some people the wrong way for quite a number of years. Of course, as we've seen, it was far from being the first time I'd stuck my foot in my mouth, and it wouldn't be the last.

Internally, I conducted numerous dialogues with myself about patience and fortitude, and the eternally capricious nature of the lifework I had chosen. At the same time, I took some practical steps to try to improve matters. Essentially, my shotmaking problems were at the two most critical ends of the game—driving and putting. I was all over the world from the tee, and had never once bettered thirty-five putts—at least five over tour "par"—in my first twenty tournament rounds.

As an amateur, I had used a driver with an S or moderately stiff shaft. For a reason that now escapes me, I had decided that as a pro I needed a "stronger" club, and had gone to an X or extra-stiff-shafted driver. Trying out various configurations was no problem because in January I'd signed a contract to play MacGregor, then the industry leader, whose clubs I'd used since first taking the game seriously, and that I continued using until I went into the golf equipment business for myself in 1992. During the Lucky International in San Francisco, I went over to the Olympic Club, found a secluded spot, and beat out a few hundred balls with a variety of drivers supplied by the

MacGregor tour rep. By the end of the session I had decided to go back to the S shaft. It would cost me a little distance, but it also would enable me to hit the ball higher and, most importantly, onto short grass. (This rediscovery lasted a long time—I've used basically the same type of shaft almost ever since).

Good a golfer as he was in every department of the game, 1956 Masters and PGA champion Jack Burke, Jr., was specially renowned for his putting ability and savvy. Playing a practice round with him ahead of my next tournament, the Palm Springs Golf Classic, I mentioned how poor my greens work had been—lots of pulls and erratic with distance—and asked what he thought. Jack told me my problems derived mostly from trying to pull the putter head through the ball with my fingers, instead of pushing it through with the palm of my right hand. He suggested that resetting my right hand so that the thumb was on top of the shaft and the palm directly beneath it would help a lot, and he was correct: I began to feel better on the greens almost as soon I made the change. (As in the case of shaft flex, it was a technique I've stuck with ever since.)

Nevertheless, I still was not able to get the ball into the hole with consistency on the many birdie opportunities my improved driving helped me set up. The ninety-hole Palm Springs tournament epitomized the problem. After barely making the cut with a one-under-par fifty-four-hole total, I hit all the par fives in two shots and every other green in regulation at Indian Wells in the fourth round and required only thirty-three putts—my best as a pro—for a 65. Then in the final round I went right back to square one for a 75 and another share of last money. By the end of that tournament I was one frustrated golfer.

Tour course greens now are mostly superb, but back then many of them were poor to mediocre—thinly grassed and bumpy, or overgrassed and deadly slow, or sometimes even newly aerified and/or top-dressed. With the Burke-inspired improvement in technique, I began to suspect that my problem might lie in the tool I was using—that the old Ben Sayers wand I'd stuck with for my last two amateur years, and had seen no reason to change on turning pro, was just too light for most of the surfaces we were encountering.

The next tournament was the Phoenix Open. Just before I was to tee off in its pro-am, George Low came up to me, said he had noticed how much trouble I was having on the greens, and asked if I would like to try another putter. Although I did not know George well, I was aware of his reputation as one of golf's all-time great putters (then and almost up until his death in 1995 he would bet on himself against any tour pro and invariably collect). Also, I had heard that he had recently put out a new line of putters under the Sportsman label. "You betcha," I told him, and off we headed to the pro shop. On the way there, he mentioned to me that the average weight of putters made in the U.S. was around sixteen ounces, which was a good two ounces heavier than my Ben Sayers. In the shop George then pulled off the rack what seemed like the first club he came to, and said, "Try this." It was one of his original Wizard 600 flanged-blade models.

Using the new putter, I shot 64 to tie for first in the pro-am, then tied for second in the tournament proper. Watching Arnie, whom I played with the last day, win by thirteen strokes took a little of the gloss off my performance. But there was no doubting the new putter's contribution to the best four rounds I had strung together as a professional, just as there's no doubt all these years later that that Wizard 600 has contributed more to my overall record than any other single club. (In light of what an original Wizard 600 fetches today on the collectors' market, my only regret is that I didn't buy a dozen of them from George.)

With better putting added to improved driving, things began to pick up a little. I finished seventeenth in New Orleans, then followed a tie with Arnie for ninth place at Baton Rouge with sixteenth at Pensacola. Jack Grout by then had moved from Scioto to the La Gorce club on Miami Beach, and a session with him there produced some really good play for third place in the Doral tournament a couple of shots behind Bill Casper. That week also produced a sharp blip in Barbara's and my life-on-the road learning curve.

Jackie by then had been with us for about six months, which, we decided, was old enough for him to make his first tour appearance. So Barbara and the baby flew down to Miami from Columbus, and naturally I went out to the airport to collect them. I will never forget the sight that greeted me there.

The two of them were to be with me for no more than a couple of weeks, but Barbara had lugged along a port-a-crib, a mattress, and pillows, and blankets, and a huge suitcase full of baby clothes, plus a couple more cases crammed to bursting with her own stuff. Eighty dollars the bill came to . . . eighty dollars for excess baggage for a flight from Columbus to Miami! With first places on tour then mostly paying under three thousand dollars, it seemed like a king's ransom for a new pro to have to fork out for extra space in an airplane hold.

"Barbara," I asked her when we'd finally gotten everything loaded up, "what in the world is this all about? I mean, don't they have beds in Miami? If you needed pillows and blankets and stuff, couldn't you have got them down here?" Well, what dumb questions those were! Certainly not, was the answer. Wherever we went in the world, it appeared, everything Jackie had at home in Ohio was going with him. "No child of mine is going to sleep on any hotel mattress, or hotel pillow, or hotel sheets," his mother announced, with emphasis. And that was that, end of discussion. Looking back, it was one of the funniest things that ever happened to us, and we still chuckle about it to this day.

At the Masters a week later I tied for fourteenth, then shared seventh place at Greensboro and would have notched my first win as a professional in Houston the week after that but for a bizarre occurrence in the final round.

On arriving at Memorial Park, I had hired a local caddie whose real name was Robert Ford, but who was better known, as so many professional loopers seem to be, by a colorful nickname, in this case Four-One—deriving, as I eventually gathered, from his skills with the dice. Four-One was a good guy and a fine caddie, who I would employ on numerous occasions in the future. But I'm sure what happened that week was the most embarrassing experience of his life.

Come the seventh hole and Four-One and I are in the lead, and looking over a putt of some twenty feet for a birdie to increase it. For reasons I don't remember, I decide I'll have a better chance of making the putt with the flagstick left in the hole. Four-One duly attends it, then, as I start the ball rolling, attempts to remove it from the hole in the normal manner, only to find that it won't leave. Finally, in desperation, he gives the flagstick a great heave, whereupon the entire cup comes smartly out of the ground just as the ball arrives, striking the metal cylinder dead center. The rebound plus the penalty turns my almost certain birdie two into a double-bogey five, which puts me into a playoff with Bobby Nichols and Dan Sikes, which I proceed to lose by a substantial margin. Ouch!

The following week, with the past year's winners playing the Tournament of Champions in Las Vegas, I finished third in the Waco Turner Open in Burneyville, Oklahoma. Next came a fourth spot back in Texas at Colonial, followed by a dumb and dismal first trip to Britain as a pro to finish either last or very close to it in awful weather in a tournament sponsored by a cigarette company (dumb because my only motivation was appearance money). Having committed to do so, I played at Indianapolis immediately after getting back, but tiredly and thus poorly. From there I passed up the Memphis event for my first spell of really intensive all-around practice at home in Columbus since joining the tour, plus a look at that year's U.S. Open course. Liking both what I saw at Oakmont and how my game seemed to be coming around picked up my spirits sufficiently to finish second, a couple of shots behind Gene Littler, in the Thunderbird Classic, then the world's richest tournament with a $100,000 purse, at the fine Upper Montclair course in New Jersey the week before the championship.

So . . . half the year gone, sixteen tournaments played, some near misses, but still no victory for the kid who would "win everything." It was all so different from my amateur days, and by now it was really getting my goat. The world of golf still seemed to believe I had the game to win, and I *knew* I did. But when, oh when, was it going to happen?

It was pretty much on the spur of the moment that I had flown over to Oakmont the week before the Open, although it was this trip that launched what from then on became a firm pre-majors reconnoitering/practice ritual. Despite the fact that the course was America's supreme example of the penal school of architecture, the visit invigorated me. Its rugged design challenges and horrendous hazards aside, Oakmont, compared with the majority of regular tour courses in those days, was in superb condition. I particularly liked the superfast and supertrue greens, so different from most of the tour surfaces I'd experienced. Additionally, the championship would be run by the officials of the United States Golf Association, who also administered top amateur golf, which meant that I would be back among old friends. Also, the Open would be run straight, meaning with minimal commercialism and hoopla, which, for me, was equally appealing. Finally, there was the unique thrill of anticipation I've enjoyed before every major championship I've entered since my first Amateur in 1955. I played Oakmont twice, played only fairly, but came away in a much better frame of mind than I had arrived. That stimulus obviously had a lot to do with my good showing in the Thunderbird the following week.

Finishing high and making a big check were then and remain today very satisfying for many tour players, particularly for those struggling to make ends meet. Having earned more than enough from noncompetitive ventures to get by since my first day as a pro, I still had my sights set where they were as an amateur—on first place. Thus, if I could have exchanged the $10,000 check for finishing second in the Thunderbird—my largest to that point—for the number-one position on the leader board and no money, I would have done so without a second's hesitation. In fact, although finishing runner-up was a pleasing measure of my form, it also made me angry at myself. Returning to Oakmont on the Monday morning of championship week, I had never been hungrier. Hopefully, it wasn't too obvious on the outside, but inside I was literally burning with determination—and assurance.

That day I shot 71, then practiced until nine o'clock in the evening. On Tuesday I scored around par while trying to finesse every shot, practiced for an hour, decided simply to belt the ball, went back out and made six birdies in seven holes, then practiced putting in a drizzle until it was too dark to see the head of the club (a member finally appeared and offered me a flashlight!). Wednesday I played a relaxed round making final yardage and positional checks, then took it easy. By Thursday, I felt I was ready.

FOR the first time in years, due to the United States Golf Association's fear of overlong rounds on a course of Oakmont's severity, the 1962 U.S. Open was played throughout in twosomes. As was always the case until the change to a four-day championship in 1965, there would be single rounds Thursday and Friday, then, on Saturday, thirty-six holes with a brief lunch break. When the opening pairings were announced, I had discovered that I would be playing the first two days with Arnold Palmer. United States Golf Association Executive Director Joe Dey had always had a fine sense of theater, and he had made us the feature attraction. The pairing had added some tingle to the excitement of my final preparations.

Arnold Palmer was born and continued to live in Latrobe, a small town about thirty-five miles southeast of Pittsburgh. By the time we teed off that Thursday afternoon, it seemed like the whole population of not only Latrobe and Pittsburgh but the entire state of Pennsylvania had turned out to root him to a second U.S. Open win. The commotion and noise were incredible, and would grow louder and more frenetic throughout the week. Then, as later, it all washed over me like water off a duck's back. Bearing down on my own game as hard as I was, after a couple of holes I had simply blocked the distractions out of my consciousness. I learned later that many in the crowd rooted loudly against me, but nobody talked to me about that at the time and it did not penetrate my intense concentration during play. So far as I was concerned, the noise was just that—noise.

Whatever the appearances, I have always been nervous during the opening holes of major championships—and, indeed, like to be because of the way a little inner turmoil focuses the mind. The butterflies this time resulted in three straight birdies, including a chip-in at number three after driving into the famous "church pews" bunkers. Things cooled down after that, but, apart from a ridiculous double-bogey on the short par-five ninth hole, I eased it around pretty smoothly for a one-over-par 72. On Friday I added a solid 70, then, on Saturday morning, again shot 72. I wasn't playing sensational golf—few ever have or will on a course as penal as Oakmont—but I was doing two very important things very well: driving far and into the fairways, and making the five- and six-footers whenever I fumbled a long approach putt. In fact, over the first fifty-four holes of play, I did not three-putt once, which, on those vast, roller-coaster, superslick greens, seemed to me to be quite an achievement.

Arnold's was a very different story. He had played a little better than I had from tee to green in the first two rounds and, from what I heard, it seemed that he had done so again in the third. He was, however—as I overheard him telling some writers during the Saturday lunch break—going through "absolute agonies" on the greens. "I feel like I'm putting with a wet noodle," was one of his comments. His first round of 71 had included eight threes, but also thirty-five putts. Friday had been better, with thirty-one putts for a 68. But then on Saturday morning he had missed three near tap-ins, and putted in total thirty-eight times—this despite hitting sixteen greens in two shots and eagling the short par-four seventeenth hole. His score was 73. Had he putted even averagely by his standards of that time, he would have been leading the Open by at least three or four strokes. As it was, with a round to play he was tied for the lead with Bobby Nichols, one shot ahead of Phil Rodgers (Philamander had kept on trucking beautifully after a horrendous war with a small pine tree at the seventeenth on Thursday, resulting in a quadruple-bogey).

Leaving the first tee that hot and sultry Saturday afternoon, I trailed Arnold—who would play in the final pairing two behind mine—by two strokes. By the time I left the first green I'd gone three adrift of him, courtesy of missing a comeback putt of seven or eight feet for my first and, as it would turn out, only three-putt of the championship. Thankfully, I shook it off quickly. However, as I followed a good drive off the eleventh tee a couple of hours later, my deficit was still three shots.

At that moment, Arnold was getting ready to play his second shot to nine, the shortish but treacherously tight par five. He was still playing superbly from tee to green, and he hit the shot solidly. However, he pushed it a little, sending the ball into some scraggly rough to the right of the green about fifty feet from the hole. There was plenty of putting surface to work with, though, and I'm sure most people watching thought, "Birdie, and it's all over but the shouting." Arnold took a wedge and flubbed the shot, moving the ball only a few feet. Still in the rough, he then played a fine chip to about seven feet, but missed the putt. He had made a bogey six. When my eight-footer for birdie dropped into the eleventh hole a few moments later, suddenly there was only one shot between us.

I played my next three holes in solid pars. Arnold did likewise, then, at the par-three thirteenth, he bunkered his tee shot to the right of the green. When he failed to get up and down in two, we were tied. Nichols and Rodgers had both begun to fade. More and more it was looking like a two-horse race. (Phil eventually ended with three straight bogeys that cost him the championship. Ever since, he's been fond of telling me, "Nicklaus, if I hadn't gotten tied up in that little pine tree, no one would have ever heard of you.")

Trying to play both carefully and aggressively at the same time, I made a comfortable par at the fifteenth and a less cozy one at the sixteenth by holing a tricky three-footer. Then came the crucial hole of the championship for me—the thought of which still gives me cold shivers.

The seventeenth at Oakmont is a short par four up a curving and slanting hillside to a green almost surrounded by bunkers, except for a little opening on the left. It was extended to 315 yards for the last Open at Oakmont in 1994, but played in 1962 at 292 yards. The smart play then, if you were leading the championship by two or three shots, was a 4-iron off the tee, a pitch, two putts, a par, and a big smile. When you were young, strong, long, racing with adrenaline, and tied with your chief adversary, the only strategy was to drive the green. I gave that my best effort, catching the ball solidly but pushing it a hair. It ended up wedged between grooves of sand in the right side of the big front bunker. The cup was cut in the right center of the green, giving me a tough angle. Had my next shot carried a few inches farther, it would have been one of the finest of my career. Instead, the ball stayed right where it landed—deep in a collar of heavy rough just off the putting surface.

During practice early in the week, the 1959 Masters winner, Art Wall, had given me some tips on how to handle this miserable stuff, and, once again, I salute you, Art. Somehow I stopped the ball four feet from the hole. But what a four-footer! Starting off, if stroked at a speed to die into the cup, it would drift to the left. Then, just before the hole, it would break sharply right. Also, it was fast. I looked it over for a long time, then decided to bite the bullet and try to jam the ball into the hole—to hit it hard enough to eliminate both breaks. If I missed, I would probably be facing at least an eight-footer coming back. I took a couple of deep breaths, tried to stay very still, and fired. Later, Bob Jones, who had been watching at his home on television, told me in a letter that he almost fell out of his chair when he saw the force of the stroke. To have any chance of staying in the cup, the ball had to hit its exact back center. It did so, and somehow rattled to the bottom.

I was so relieved and excited that I hit my best drive of the week down eighteen, enabling me to get home with a 6-iron on the 462-yarder. The resulting twelve-foot putt stayed out, though. As I waited in the scorer's tent with every nerve in my body on fire, Arnold's highly makable putts for birdies on both seventeen and eighteen, either of which would have given him the championship, also failed to drop. And so we tied, and would play off over eighteen holes the next day.

Arnold looked and admitted he was exhausted as we talked with the press and he answered endless questions about his eight or nine three-putts and innumerable missed birdie opportunities over the four rounds. But he was still the same good-hearted guy who had been so nice to a nervous kid from Columbus at the Ohio Amateur eight years previously (see the next chapter). The writers had also been discussing our respective driving distances, and the consensus seemed to be that I had the edge.

"That big, strong dude," Arnie told them, looking at me with what I will always remember as real affection. "I thought I was through with him yesterday. I'd rather be playing somebody else."

I HAVE always needed plenty of sleep, and fortunately have rarely had trouble getting it whatever the next day's events. Frankie Avalon was singing in the hotel where we were staying and his music stopped me getting to sleep as fast as I would have liked, but, once out, I stayed that way for some ten hours, apart from one small interruption around seven in the morning when Jackie woke me. Thoughtful as ever, Barbara decided to take him down to the coffee shop for breakfast. At nine months old Jackie could be a feisty little fellow. Janis Jordan, a *Columbus Dispatch* writer, recorded the following:

"Several hours before his dad won the U.S. Open, Jackie racked up a pretty good score of his own. With true Nicklaus aim he sailed a full jar of baby food across the coffee shop. It hit dead center two tables away to the raves of the gallery of admiring waitresses. Barbara said: 'I took him to the restaurant so Jack could sleep. It was one of those times. He pulled the tablecloth and everything else off the table, howled, and at five after eight I called Jack's dad and hollered for help.' "

Well, I've always sworn the family's a lot more nervous ahead of those big rounds than I am.

The truth is, I wasn't at all nervous getting ready that morning, and the reason is simple: I was hitting the ball from tee to green very well and I was putting very well. There was nothing to be nervous about.

• • •

I HAVE always liked to get to the course an hour ahead of my tee time. I did so that Sunday, went through my usual warm-ups, and arrived at the first tee with time to spare.

I was even more superstitious then about certain things related to golf than I am now, so I had on the same color shirt I'd worn the previous day—an adventurous plain white. I also wore the same pants —a sort of semi-iridescent olive-green $11.95 number that somebody said looked like a special from the work-clothes counter of a discount store, and forever referred to by Barbara as my "Army-refugee pants." Even though Barbara had ironed them overnight the wrinkles were turning into creases, and there were probably sweat marks around the pockets, but the pants were comfortable—and lucky. People used to say that Arnie always looked in disarray the way his shirt flopped out of his pants despite his endless hitching at them, but I can assure you that no one was more sartorially disarrayed than I that Sunday. Nevertheless, as I prepared for the opening drive, I had never felt better.

As we got ready to start the playoff, Arnie came over to me and shook my hand and wished me luck, then asked if I wanted to split the purse. In those days that wasn't uncommon in playoff situations, and I thought it was pretty nice of him—the winner of three Masters and a U.S. Open and British Open—to even consider such a thing against a young tour rookie still looking for his first pro victory. But I told him, "No, Arn, you don't want to do that, that's not fair to you, let's just go play." He agreed, but we did end up sharing the playoff gate receipts with the USGA, each receiving about eleven hundred dollars on top of the advertised prize money.

If I had felt good on the first tee, after six holes I felt better yet. By then I was two under par and four strokes ahead. After opening with three two-putt pars, I'd birdied the par-five fourth hole with a chip and putt, parred the fifth, and holed a six-footer at the par-three sixth for another birdie. Arnold had overhit his approach to the first hole for bogey, parred the next four holes, then three-putted the sixth from fifteen feet.

Counting his chickens any time ahead of the final putt is probably the worst mental mistake a golfer can make. I fought the temptation, and it was good that I did. Of all the many factors that made Arnold Palmer so incredibly popular in those days was his ability to get on a roll and keep it going until, it seemed, he had literally hammered the opposition into the ground. The Charge, his armies of fans called it. I had experienced it—been a victim of it—in the Open two years previously.

Cherry Hills that afternoon in 1960 witnessed what I'm sure every golf historian will agree was Arnold Daniel Palmer's single greatest charge. Heading for the first tee of the final round seven shots off the pace, he had said to his friend Bob Drum, then a Pittsburgh newspaperman, "I may shoot a 65 out there. What'll that do?" "Nothing," Drum told him with his customary bluntness. "You're too far back." Piqued by the write-off, Arnold proceeded to drive the green of the then 346-yard par-four first hole and two-putt for birdie, add five more birdies in the next six holes, turn in 30, come home in 35 for a then Open record of 65, and become at the end of it all the champion of his country and even more of a national hero than when he started.

By the time Oakmont came around, I had been on the receiving end of this kind of thing more than enough to know that it could happen any time. In fact, I *expected* it to begin at any moment.

IT happened on the ninth hole, the short par five back to the clubhouse that had tripped each of us earlier in the week. We had both just bogeyed the very long par-three eighth hole, so my lead was still four shots.

We both hit good drives off the ninth tee, but—overcautiously protecting my advantage, I suppose—I decided to lay up my second shot short of the central fairway bunker. Arnie went for the green with his 3-wood, but again finished in the rough to the right. This time, however, he played a fine recovery to within four feet of the hole. I had wedged to about a foot farther away. Putting first, I missed. Arnold made his putt for birdie. That narrowed my lead to three shots.

We parred number ten in routine fours. On eleven, I missed for birdie from sixteen feet and Arnie holed from seven. Two shots.

Oakmont's twelfth hole played that day at almost exactly 600 yards. I just missed a twenty-footer for birdie after a poor drive. Arnold got within a few yards of the putting surface with two monster woods, chipped to five feet, and holed the putt for his third birdie in four holes.

One shot. *Charge!*

Along with his Army, I really did expect Arnold to go on doing just that, but on the thirteenth tee he seemed unusually indecisive about the club to play. The hole is an uphill par three of about 160 yards. Arnold toyed with his 5-iron, then took the 4 and decided to make what I imagine was intended to be an easy swing for extra control. I thought his ball would finish in the right-hand bunker, but it got a fortunate kick the other way and ended up about forty feet beyond the pin (I can still hear the Army going nuts over that lucky bounce). I hit a 6-iron to twenty feet and two-putted. Arnold three-putted.

With five holes to play in a national championship, a two-shot lead can seem about six times larger than a one-shot lead. Obviously, the cushion isn't that much greater, but it definitely eases the pulse rate. I had just received a gift, and I decided that, if I could now finish with a string of safe pars, there was a very good chance I would win the National Open. I made the first four of them. Arnie matched me.

Pressure can catch you at the oddest times. Addressing the ball on the eighteenth tee, I felt a thousand percent confident I would hit a drive equally as fine as my previous day's beauty. Coming down, my right hand suddenly decreed otherwise. Pull-hooked, the ball finished just off the fairway in a horrible lie, tight to a patch of hard ground and smothered in tangly rough.

Arnold had driven superbly. After what seemed to me surprisingly little thought, he hit his second shot with what I believed was a 3-iron. He said later he hit it fat. The ball landed short of the green and ran into the rough to the right.

That decided me. I took the pitching wedge and carved my ball out of the rhubarb to a spot well short of the big cross-bunker about 130 yards ahead, leaving myself with a full 9-iron. I struck it solidly and felt a surge of adrenaline as I watched the ball stop about twelve feet left of the pin. To force a further playoff, Arnie would now have to chip in and I would have to two-putt.

Arnold surveyed his shot from the rough for a long time, and obviously did not much care for it. When he eventually hit the ball it came out fast, nearly hit the pin, but ran well past the hole and just off the green. After I putted up to about twenty inches, he chipped long, then, after missing his remaining putt, picked up my ball marker as a gesture of concession. As this was stroke play, referee Joe Dey made me put it back and hole out.

It was over. I was the Open champion as well as the Amateur champion. At last I had proved that, playing golf full-time, I could do what I had done when playing only part-time. In my seventeenth tournament as a professional, I had *won*.

It had seemed like a very long road. But now an even longer one would begin to beckon ever more strongly.

4

The 1963 Masters Tournament

Arnold and Augusta

I FIRST saw Arnold Palmer at the Ohio State Amateur, played at the Sylvania Country Club in Toledo in 1954, the year he won the National Amateur. I was a fourteen-year-old contestant in that state championship. Arnie, who was twenty-four, was the defending champion.

As I came off the course one day in heavy rain, I noticed a golfer out on the range all by himself beating balls with a short iron. I went and stood under a tree and watched him for probably an hour. I could hear the balls crack off the clubface, as Gary Player always described it, like thunderclaps. Every swing was flat out. None of the shots flew very high, but they all seemed to go tremendous distances. I could see that the golfer had big hands and wide shoulders and muscular forearms. He didn't notice me, but I was fascinated by him. After a while I asked someone standing nearby who he was.

"That's Arnold Palmer," I was told. "Oh, man, is he *strong,*" was all I could think of to say. Later in the week I was introduced to him, and was impressed with how friendly and natural he was to me, still a kid in short pants. He was exactly the same whenever we ran across each other during all of my amateur years.

The first time Arnold and I played golf together was on Thursday, September 25, 1958, over the 6,382-yard Athens Country Club course in the southeastern part of Ohio. The occasion was an exhibition match in honor of Dow Finsterwald, who was born and raised in Athens and who had just won the PGA Championship. Arnie and I were partnered against Dow and another local amateur, Howard Baker Saunders, whose credentials included six Southeastern Ohio Golf Association championships. Arnie had won his first Masters six months previously and was, I believe, the tour's leading money winner with some forty thousand dollars, a handsome total in those days.

The match was preceded by a long-driving contest at the first hole, a 320-yard par four. I was the only one to reach the green, but this was quickly overshadowed by Arnold almost driving it in the match proper, making three birdies in the first four holes, adding an eagle and five more birdies, and breaking Dow's course record by a stroke with a round of 62. My most noteworthy contribution was driving the 330-yard tenth hole. Other than that, along with the thousand or so spectators, I spent most of the time admiring Arnie's raw strength and his attacking style of play.

Two years later, after Arnold won the U.S. Open at Cherry Hills so sensationally, he was very gracious about my good play in finishing runner-up, and I sensed more than ever that this amiability was not an act, nor even a courtesy, but simply his nature. Then, when I talked with him before turning pro, he was open and supportive in telling me all kinds of things he thought might be helpful. Nevertheless, as I began preparations late in 1961 for my first year on the tour, I couldn't help but wonder if our relationship would remain as cordial once I got out there.

It is hard for me to capture in words the magnitude of Arnold Palmer in golf at that time. He was not only the game's undisputed king, but the emperor-in-chief of contemporary American sports heros—indeed, a national figure as renowned and admired as any man of his generation. In trying to pay adequate tribute to him, writers would sometimes suggest that he had actually invented the game of golf. They were having fun, of course, but a lot of people would have liked to believe them, and some actually may have done so. It is hard to conceive that anyone in history boosted a nation's consciousness of a sport quite as phenomenally as Arnold Daniel Palmer did for golf in America during the late 1950s and early 1960s. Golfing President Dwight D. Eisenhower and the ever-growing affection of the television networks for the game certainly gave Arnie some help, but it was he who mostly launched and sustained that record growth period for both golfers and golf fans with his still-unparalleled combination of superb performance and personal magnetism. For this alone, all those who have come after him who make a living from the game owe him a debt of gratitude that should never be forgotten.

In regard to our personal relationship once I joined the tour, Arnold's enormous stature in golf and as an international celebrity was one side of the coin. The other side was the hullabaloo during my final amateur days about "the kid who can beat the pros." Right after I became a professional, it reached a crescendo, with all kinds of wild predictions leaping from the sports pages. If I had been Arnold—or, for that matter, any successful tour player—I'm sure I would have found it irritating, even though it had no basis in logic.

As soon as I met Arnold at our December exhibition in Miami, and increasingly as the 1962 tour progressed, I knew nothing had changed. He was as friendly and natural and encouraging and helpful as ever. We weren't then the close friends that he and Gary Player and I would become when thrown so much together in the "Big Three" exhibitions and television matches arranged by Mark McCormack through his ever-growing agenting business. But Arnie just could not have been nicer to a guy who about half the sports media seemed to think was going to beat his brains out every week.

And me? What was my attitude toward him? Well, this is a moment for real candor, even though it may cause me to cringe a little.

I liked Arnie a lot as a person—who could not like such an appealing character? Also, having a pretty good idea of what it had taken to compile, I had appropriate respect for his record. Beyond that, however, I guess the best I can say for myself is that I looked on Arnold just the way you would expect of a blinkered youth fixated on bullheading his way to the top of the mountain. In a nutshell, once the whistle had blown, Arnold Palmer was just another player, another guy trying to go my way on a track only wide enough for one. I wanted to *win,* and then win and win and win again—every time I teed it up, now and forever. If that meant not simply beating

Arnold Palmer, but also toppling a legend and throwing half the population into deep depression, well, so long as it was done fairly and squarely, fine and dandy. I respected all the tour players, but I simply did not see any supermen out there, Arnold included. I had no reservations about beating anyone else. Why, then, should I have any about beating him?

Let me now add a couple of thoughts that are the product of a little more maturity.

Whether they would admit it or not, I'm sure this attitude has been precisely that of all successful athletes from the beginning of time. The reason is that you *have* to be this way to ascend the mountain. I'm sure, for example, looking solely at golf, that this was exactly Tom Watson's attitude toward me when he came on the tour, just as it was Lee Trevino's and Johnny Miller's and Seve Ballesteros's and Nick Faldo's and Greg Norman's and Tiger Woods's, and anyone else's who has teed it up with an intense competitive drive and a dream to fulfill. So I make no excuses for what was in my soul all those years ago. However, where I've since seen I could have done a better job is in what I let show on the surface at that time.

In retrospect, if I had to do it all over again, I would still go as hard as I could after the same result, but with more effort to disguise the intensity or rawness of my will to win. At the age of twenty-two, it simply never occurred to me how apparent this was in the way I went about the game, nor that some people might interpret it as coldness of heart or bleakness of spirit. In short, although the goals I set myself probably were acceptable to everyone—maybe, even, to many of Arnie's Army—the fact is I marched toward them along too straight and narrow a path for the majority of observers to want to applaud my passage. My focus was too sharp, too internalized, too locked on where I wanted to go, to recognize and cater to the fact that I was in the entertainment business as much as the golf-playing business. And it was this, I'm sure, that made me such a black hat to so many of the fans for so many of those early years. Sure, I was overweight and crew-cut, and, sure, I dressed like a guy painting a porch, and, sure, I had a squeaky voice and didn't laugh and joke a lot in public, and, sure, I often lacked tact and diplomacy in my public utterances. I believe all of those failings might have been forgiven a young and unsophisticated individual if he had simply papered over the raw intensity of his will to win—including, particularly, trying to knock the game's best-loved idol off his throne. And the best thing I remember about it all was that, hard as I sometimes had to fight Arnold's galleries, the only way I ever had to fight him was with my golf clubs.

It is a tough fact of life that people judge others mostly, or even entirely, by external appearances and mannerisms. Once those judgments are made, they tend to stick. But, as most of us learn over time, appearances and mannerisms can be highly deceptive.

My dad summed up my personality for a newspaperman about as well as anyone ever has a couple of years after Arnie's and my first shootout at Oakmont. "Jack," Dad said, "has a certain shyness. He certainly isn't an extrovert. I am. My wife isn't, and Jack takes after his mother. He doesn't go out of his way to make friends, but he isn't snooty and he very much wants to be liked, just like all of us want to be liked. Jack will never have the flair that Arnie has, but Jack doesn't begrudge Arnie any of the acclaim because he feels he has certainly earned every bit of it. Jack will always be himself. He can't be someone else. He's a little abrupt at times, blunt. He's the same way with me, the same way with everyone. But you know whatever he tells you will be the truth. I've never seen him be anything but kind."

From the moment I began to win at golf, I made many friendships among people whom I could get to know well and who would take the trouble to get to know me, like officials and some of the golf writers. In fact, whenever I happen to look back over press clippings from the late 1950s and early 1960s, I still feel embarrassed by the lavishness of some of the compliments I received. My broader "image" problem was that the public at large simply judged me by externals before it had a chance to get to know what was on the inside. Compounding the problem was the lousy job I did of showing the public what was on the inside. I only got smart enough to begin doing that many years later.

I feel for a lot of the young guys on the tour today in this regard. Seemingly in retaliation for them not becoming instant superstars, a part of the media has taken to branding them as a bunch of zombies. No color, no charisma, no personality, is the accusation. Well, it's baloney. Those writers would find some pretty interesting young men out there if they made the effort to get to know them—to get past the cocoons most of them have to wrap themselves in during their developing years to play their best golf. If we put the shoe on the other foot for a moment and had the players evaluate writers only as they went about earning their livings—as they pounded away en masse on those little word-processors every evening in the tour's media centers—the impression would surely be that they were a pretty dull-seeming group. Join them in a social atmosphere later, though, and some great characters would emerge. The same is true of the tour players. And I think that, like me, the smarter among those players eventually learn to do a better job of showing what's on the inside as they mature and cultivate a more rounded perspective on golf and on life. Good examples of that, I believe, are Freddie Couples, Paul Azinger, and Payne Stewart, just to name three players who began to let their very different, distinctive and appealing personalities show through the older and more experienced and self-assured they became.

Getting back to Arnold for a moment, I'm happy to say that, after drifting apart for a long time as our playing careers and other interests took different paths, the deeper we have gotten into our senior years the more we have found ourselves renewing the old friendship. The rivalry between us will surely exist as long as we live. For instance, I still always look in the newspaper to see what Arnie shot when I'm not in a tournament he's playing, and I know he does the same with me. There is no question we have had our differences along the way. But if Arnold ever were to need anything, I'd be there for him in a flash, both as a friend and as an admirer of the great contributions he has made, not just to golf, but to the advancement and elevation of true sportsmanship. I'm proud to call him my friend.

A COUPLE of weeks after my Oakmont win, Arn and I had at it again in the Western Open at Medinah, and this time he got me by a shot, finishing seventh against my tie for eighth. But his real revenge came in Scotland seven days later.

Arnold had finished second in the centenary year of the British Open at St. Andrews in 1960 by a stroke to the Australian Kel Nagle, then twelve months later had won the title with some phenomenal golf in an incredible gale at Royal Birkdale. With that famous victory he had become as popular in Great Britain as he was at home, not only for his go-for-broke attitude and charismatic personality, but for the immense rejuvenating effect his presence and play were having on the oldest and most historic of golf championships by stimulating other top American players to cross the ocean each July.

Now, three weeks after Oakmont and with his putting brilliantly restored, Arnold romped home at Troon (later Royal Troon) six shots ahead of Nagle amid a frequently out-of-control "army" of golf-crazed Scots. Barbara and I watched his triumphal final two holes from our hotel window, then flew back to New York with him and his wife Winnie, playing bridge most of the way, which helped to keep my mind off how much I still had to learn about links golf. In my first try for the lovely old claret jug trophy, now on its way to a second straight year in Latrobe, I had opened with an 80 and closed with a 79 for a 72-hole total of 305, or a mere twenty-nine strokes more than Arnold's then record 276.

It had been an unhappy week right from the start. On arrival in Troon, I just could not believe how hard the ground was—I mean, burned up and browned out and rock solid, like concrete. "Oh, my gosh," I'd thought to myself after my first practice round. "This is really something new to me and I don't know whether I can handle it." So I was hardly bursting with confidence once we began playing for real.

On top of that, the clubs I had to use under a deal made for me with a British manufacturer didn't fit, and I was uncomfortable with the smaller size ball everyone played in Britain in those days. The long and short of it was that I allowed these added challenges, along with some other irritations, to downgrade my mood from the moment I showed up. That wasn't very smart, but probably unsurprising in a twenty-two-year-old with still an awful lot to learn about the original form of golf.

To really top things off, when the pairings came out I found myself teeing off in the opening round at 3:45 in the afternoon, and not with another contestant but with a marker. Boy, did that raise a head of steam! Thankfully, my good friend Joe Carr, the great amateur, bless his Irish heart, went to the organizing Royal and Ancient and told them it wasn't right to do that to the U.S. Open champion, so they moved me into a threesome. But I was still at the end of the field.

With the exception of the Troon experience, my first few months as national champion were pretty satisfying. I made the cover of *Time* magazine, and was given a parade in Columbus organized by my great friend Bob Barton, with most of my family and friends participating. Following the British Open, I tied for third in the PGA Championship at Aronimink (Gary Player won), then for fifth in the Canadian Open, then for third again in the American Golf Classic at Firestone. Back at big old Firestone over the Labor Day holiday weekend, I got a special kick out of beating Arnie and Gary in the first playing of a thirty-six-hole made-for-television match between the winners of the year's major championships called the World Series of Golf. After that came back-to-back wins in the Seattle World's Fair and Portland Opens. Finally, to round out the season, I made my first trip down under, which I enjoyed immensely despite not playing particularly well—fifth in the Australian Open and the same in the Wills Masters.

Just to keep me from getting too euphoric, however, there were a couple of upsetting occurrences during that period.

My awareness of how deliberately I played golf had been growing, not least because of comments by fellow pros that had gotten back to me. In the playoff at Oakmont I'd been concerned when asked on the tenth hole by an official of the United States Golf Association to try to play faster, and had done my best to comply. Three months later, in the second round of the Portland Open, after allegedly failing to heed an earlier warning to giddy-up, I was penalized for slow play. The person called on to tell me to "add two" was the same fine gentleman who had straightened me out after my brain-dead withdrawal from the Azalea Open in 1959, then PGA tournament supervisor Joe Black.

The Portland penalty infuriated me at the time, chiefly because I felt I was being unfairly singled out from a number of players just as slow as I. However, not long afterward I came to recognize that it was probably justified by my general pace of play, regardless of how fast or slow I was moving on that particular occasion. The trouble was that I have always by nature been deliberate and meticulous and intensely focused about anything that deeply engages me. Thus, when I became engrossed in competing, I tended to immerse myself in a cocoon of concentration that simply precluded awareness of such trivialities as time. I also tended to take more time whenever I was unsure of myself. However, it was clear that none of this justified holding up everyone else, or setting a bad example for golfers in general. Consequently, following the shock of the Portland penalty, I adopted a policy of moving as quickly as I comfortably could between shots, while still not hurrying their planning and execution. To achieve this, I began to do most of my surveying—discreetly, of course—while others were doing the same or playing their shots. I also accelerated my walking speed to a point where other players sometimes had difficulty keeping up with me. And it must have worked, because, from that point on, I incurred only one more slow-play penalty, that being in the Houston Champions International in May 1967, when I still maintain that our group's tardiness was not my fault.

The other upsetting occurrence left an even more bitter aftertaste.

Needing only two more quarters to graduate, I returned to Ohio State following the Portland Open determined to get my degree. When the dean of the College of Commerce found out about my upcoming two-week trip to Australia, he insisted I withdraw from the school, regardless of good grades or anything else. I had spent a good part of five years working for my degree and representing OSU, but, obviously, once I became a professional, I could not simultaneously earn my living and attend school normally. I believed then and do now that the dean's decision was unfair. Not finishing my education is the only significant thing in my life that I've begun and not completed, so the edict still burns me all this time later.

But these really were no more than a couple of hiccups in a very satisfying professional debut, highlighted, of course, by the Open. By winning the national championship for my first victory as a career golfer, I had proven conclusively that I could do my thing with the best in the world, not just with the best part-timers. Excepting the British Open, my record following Oakmont was an indication of what this did for my confidence and strength of purpose. Cliché though it may be, there's no question that winning breeds winning.

Also, both the fact and the nature of that first victory made me more comfortable with the, in some ways, still strange new world to which professionalism had committed me so completely. Like all pro sports roadshows, the tour was then, as it remains now, an exclusive club of which a person becomes a full member only after paying certain dues. Before Oakmont, I wasn't absolutely sure I belonged. Afterward, just by the way the guys congratulated me, I knew I'd been accepted.

• • •

It is hard at this distance to be sure of when I began awakening to what might be called the public relations side of playing golf for a living, but I think it most probably was the evening of December 8 that year as I watched a highlights film of the U.S. Open sent to me by the United States Golf Association.

In common with many college students at that time, I smoked cigarettes all through my OSU years, and continued to do so after I turned professional. I was never a particularly heavy smoker, but there is no doubt I was heavy enough to be hooked, which was what caused me to smoke on the golf course even after dedicating myself to a supposedly athletic career.

That stopped as I watched myself in the film on the thirteenth hole at Oakmont survey a putt for birdie with a cigarette dangling from my lips, throw the cigarette down to putt, then pick it up and stick it back in my mouth and leave it hanging there as I tapped in my second putt and walked off the green. I was appalled. "That's just terrible," I told myself. "Here you are, the national champion, which for kids at least makes you a role model, and there you are doing just about the most unathletic thing a person can do, not only when you're actually playing, but in images that will be part of the game's history." I remember feeling so strongly about it that I phoned Mark McCormack right away and insisted on giving back the money and canceling the endorsement deal he had made for me when I turned pro with one of the top tobacco companies.

After that, I continued to smoke sporadically when traveling or at parties or out fishing or hunting, but never again on the golf course. Then I decided to cut it out at home or wherever else I was around my children, then at the office, until, one fine day shortly after my fortieth birthday, I asked myself, "If you're not going to smoke in all those places, why bother to smoke at all?" and quit totally and for good. And, of course, felt better both physically and mentally as a result.

During my peak years particularly, what got me off the tennis court and the fishing boat and onto the driving range each January was the thought of the Masters. In 1963, golf's great springtime rite had a particularly strong appeal. Since missing the cut on my first visit to Augusta in 1959, I had finished tied for thirteenth, tied for seventh, and tied for fourteenth. As U.S. Open champion, I wanted to redeem myself in America's shrine of golf so badly I could hardly wait to get to the Augusta National again.

It is hard to imagine that there has been a good golfer since the Masters Tournament began in 1934 who hasn't dreamed of winning it. Most readers of this book will know about the event, so I'm not going to waste words describing it. All I want to say is that, for me, it has been a career-long joy. Young as the Augusta National is relative to how long the game of golf has existed, it exudes more history and is home to more ghosts than any other American golfing mecca, to a degree that still pumps me up just driving down Magnolia Lane each April. Part of the appeal is the way the Masters has set the pace in providing the finest quality and condition of golf course and the highest standards of tournament organization and presentation. Many of the refinements and special touches we enjoy today all over the world as players or watchers of top tournament golf derive from the Augusta National and the Masters. It would, for instance, be foolish of me to deny that they were and remain the inspiration and model for the golf club and the competition I started in the mid-1970s, Muirfield Village and the Memorial Tournament.

In 1963, there was another reason, beyond my previous poor showings, for my burning desire to win the Masters. I wanted to win it for the man who had given birth to the club and the tournament, and who had been at the forefront of my golfing consciousness almost from the time I had gone out for the game.

I have talked previously about how, in 1926, Bobby Jones came to Columbus and won the U.S. Open at Scioto, watched the entire way by my then teenaged father, for whom Jones immediately became a lifelong idol. The impact of this on me was that seemingly every time, as a youngster, Dad and I talked seriously about some aspect of golf, Bob Jones would come up in one form or another. Also, Jack Grout had known Jones well and admired him greatly and, like Dad, loved to reminisce about both his wonderful golf and his fine personal qualities. The result was that, by the time I first met Bob Jones, he had become a heroic figure to me. So far as I tried to emulate anyone in my early teens, he was the man.

The occasion of our first meeting was the 1955 National Amateur, played at the James River course of the Country Club of Virginia. Mr. Jones had been invited by the United States Golf Association to speak at the traditional prechampionship players' dinner on this, the twenty-fifth anniversary of his Amateur victory at Merion that completed his 1930 Grand Slam. At fifteen, I was the youngest player in the field. During a practice round, Bob had seen me get home in two at the 460-yard eighteenth hole and asked to meet me. Both Dad and I found him easy and pleasant to talk to. Finally he told me, "Young man, there were only a couple of fellas who got home on that hole today and you were one of them. I'm going to come out and watch you play some more tomorrow."

Did that make me nervous? *N-o-o-o-o,* not a bit. Here I am, a fifteen-year-old, teeing it up in the first round of my first Amateur, against Bob Gardner, one of the best golfers in the country, and all I've ever heard of about golf history is "Bobby Jones this . . ." and "Bobby Jones that . . ." And now Bobby Jones is coming out to watch me play. But what was I going to say, other than, "That'll be just fine, Mr. Jones, sir" ?

All through the first nine the next day I'm looking over my shoulder for Bobby Jones, and finally I see him coming down the tenth fairway in his golf cart as I'm getting ready to tee up at number eleven. At that point I'm one up in the match and feeling pretty good about myself. Half an hour later I'm two down, having gone bogey, bogey, double-bogey. Whereupon Bob Jones turns to Dad, who's walking with us, and says, "I don't believe I'm doing young Jack much good. I think I'd better get out of here." Which he does. Right away I get back to even, but then bogey the last hole to lose the match one down.

As he later explained to my father, Bob felt that his presence might have started me trying too hard, and thus took off as soon as he could without, he hoped, leaving us with the feeling that he had given up on me too quickly. Even at that minimally perceptive age, I was impressed by such sensitivity to and concern for a youngster with whom he had made only the most casual acquaintance. As our friendship deepened over the years, it was for me this kind of thoughtfulness and graciousness to everyone he encountered that continued to shine brightest of his many qualities. As to his golfing achievements, they were stunning to me as a youngster and they have remained that way ever since, particularly when viewed in context with his educational accomplishments, his full family, business, and social lives, and, most of all, how little tournament golf he played even during his finest years.

For Bob Jones by Masters time of 1963, made ever frailer and less mobile by a painful and crippling spinal illness, I think I helped to generate memories of happier years. For me, he was the supreme example of a golfer recognizing, and rising time and again to, the great occasions. The more our paths crossed, the stronger became my determination to show him that I was cut from the same cloth.

In short, what would grow into the dominating force of my golfing career, an endless preoccupation with the game's four modern major championships, was just beginning to crystallize. And there has never been any question in my mind that its chief stimulus was Bobby Jones.

AT the pro-am preceding the Lucky International in San Francisco the last week in January of 1963, I had hit an 8-iron into the final green, then developed so sharp a pain in my left hip that I could barely walk off the course. It turned out to be bursitis, and despite regular treatments—I received numerous cortisone injections over the next few weeks—it troubled me to varying degrees right up until the Friday of the week prior to the Masters. As with so many of the minor ailments of athletes, the only real cure was rest. One of the ways I tried to rest the hip was to reduce the number of full practice shots I hit. This eased the physical pain, but didn't do much for my mental condition.

I tied for second behind Bill Casper in the Crosby that winter, then beat Gary Player with a 65 in an eighteen-hole playoff in Palm Springs. Yet, well as I scored at those and other times, I felt like I was playing only half-prepared. Given my kind of temperament, that is a most unpleasant frame of mind. The frustration was worsened during much of this period by the fact that I was also trying to master a new way of flighting the golf ball.

Up until that time I had faded the majority of my full shots—curved them slightly from left to right. When I absolutely had to move the ball the other way—draw it from right to left—for a strategical or recovery reason, I could usually do so, but never with quite the control and confidence of my long-established bread-and-butter fade. In fact, almost from taking up the game, drawing shots consistently had given me fits. I would feel I had the draw under control for a day or two, but the next time out it would turn into a hook for no apparent reason—that low burner to the left that makes good scoring hard labor if not impossible.

Predominantly fading the ball had never really concerned me until I began thinking so hard about the Masters that winter. I was plenty long enough not to need the extra roll that draw spin produces, and the additional height and softer landing of the faded shot had proven a tremendous scoring weapon, particularly with the long irons, my strongest suit since my midteens. However, reflecting on my previous indifferent showings at the Augusta National, I now experienced three revelations about the course that seemed to demand a change of strategy.

The first of these was that Bob Jones, who helped Alister Mackenzie with the design, was almost exclusively a right-to-left golfer. The second was that, perhaps because of this shotmaking preference of Bob's, at least half of Augusta National's holes either drifted to the left or doglegged that way. The third revelation was that the majority of Masters winners had been essentially right-to-left golfers, notable examples including Arnold Palmer, Sam Snead, and, before his change to the fade, Ben Hogan. The outcome of all this was that I decided I had no option but to finally force myself to learn to draw the ball controllably and consistently.

Now, anyone who reads more than the headlines of the sports pages knows that all professional athletes are champion rationalizers—the reason being, of course, that they will go to almost any lengths to sustain the high levels of confidence necessary to become and remain top performers. What you have just read was one of my all-time classic rationalizations.

Fading the ball reliably had been getting harder and harder for me because, to fade, you have to aggressively lead with and clear the left side of the body swinging down and through, in order to keep the clubface slightly open at impact. For weeks, pain or the threat of pain in my left hip had inhibited such an action, with the result that, quite involuntarily, I was drawing more and more shots purely as the product of an earlier closing clubface. Thus, although I would not have admitted it at the time, what I'm sure I did was cook up those three "revelations" about the Masters course in order to prop up my confidence in the face of a subconsciously unappealing swing change forced on me by injury.

Mentally upbeat about the upcoming Masters as this helped keep me, there remained the problem of hitting sufficient practice shots to become truly confident with the new flight pattern. What it boiled down to was that, in order not to risk compounding the injury, I had to try to learn a new set of tricks on the golf course itself during actual tournament play. That is no-no number one in Golf 101, and it produced erratic performance right up until the Masters. Mostly I was either very good or very bad—high on the leader board or on down the road.

I'm going to digress for a moment here and return to the hip injury, because I think it offers a good example of how important learning your body is for the professional athlete.

Over the weeks following the injury, each of the doctors who administered cortisone injections asked me the same question: Had I heard any kind of popping noise at the time I first felt pain? There had been no audibles from the hip area in San Francisco, but then, in the second round of a tournament in New Orleans in early March, as I whaled a wedge out of heavy rough, something in my hip went "pow" and almost immediately the pain vanished. Back home in Columbus after that tournament, I could hardly wait to see Dr. Jud Wilson, the orthopedic surgeon who had fixed my dad's ankle and given me most of my injections, and tell him what had happened and get his assessment of the situation. His diagnosis was that, in hitting the shot in San Francisco, I had caused a tendon covering the hip bone to slip out of place, and that the "pow" in New Orleans had been the tendon popping back where it belonged as a result of the hard swing I was making.

Given such information, I imagine most people not dependent on their bodies for their living would say thank you very much and quickly put the matter out of mind. What that first incapacitating ailment as a professional golfer did for me was to get me started on what became a lifelong study of how the human body functions in general and of the workings of my own body in particular.

Over the years ahead, that hip tendon problem would recur more often than I have cared to publicly admit. Eventually, I figured out that it was probably caused, or at least aggravated, by my right leg being about a quarter inch shorter than my left, which exerted added pressure on the left hip during the golf swing. By then I had also figured out a stretching maneuver that for many years popped the tendon back in place (if you noticed me contorting myself strangely on the golf course, that's what I was doing).

In the same way—by listening carefully to my body, then searching out ways of making it and keeping it healthy—I was able to play for a long time with very little serious or game-limiting injury. In fact, thanks to my functional anatomist friend Pete Egoscue and the exercise regimens he began tailoring for me in the fall of 1988, I continue to have avoided back surgery despite a couple of herniated discs. Looking back, I am proud that I had the intelligence and discipline to start along that self-care road as early in life as I did.

Getting back to golf, with the hip pain gone a full month ahead of the Masters, I suppose I could have attempted a return to my old left-to-right shot pattern. If that thought occurred at all, it did not survive very long. The relief of being able to play without discomfort, plus the ability to practice hard again, simply increased my confidence in my commitment to the new shape. Passing up the Greensboro tournament, I spent the week before the Masters at home in Ohio, working on confirming to myself one last time that I now really could draw a golf ball consistently with all of the longer clubs. The next Sunday I flew to Augusta in high spirits even though Barbara, imminently expecting our second child, couldn't make the trip (Steve arrived the following week).

Although I had ingrained the habit of pacing off and noting down tournament course yardages everywhere I played following my introduction to the technique by Deane Beman at the 1961 Amateur, I hadn't done so at Augusta the previous year, dumbly assuming I knew the course well enough after playing in four Masters. I corrected this error in practice, as, drawing most full shots nicely from right to left, I scored 69, 70, and 67, then 32 for nine holes of final tuning.

As at Oakmont nine months previously ahead of my U.S. Open victory, on Wednesday night I felt 100-percent ready for action.

ONE thing you can generally bet on at the Masters, in addition to all the scenic beauty and the fabulous atmosphere and the fine organization, is some interesting weather.

This being Georgia in the springtime, everyone hopes for four calm and cloudless days with low humidity and temperatures in the mid-70s. According to the old hands, you'll generally get one day like that, sometimes—if the gods of golf are smiling—two. The other two, the veterans maintain, will be either very windy or very wet or very chilly, or a combination of all three.

In 1963, the final practice day, Wednesday, was perfect. By the first tee time Thursday morning there was a gale blowing—one of the windiest days, some Masters veterans said, in the tournament's history. After thirteen holes, I found myself three over par. What with the wind speed and the dried-out greens, I had plenty of company. But I was still a little surprised, because I had struck the ball much better than this score indicated. The right-to-left pattern was holding up well, and although I'd gotten a couple of bad bounces and missed some makeable putts, I was playing pretty tight golf. The results were disappointing after the practice scores, but then I had long ago learned that practice scores are meaningless beyond whatever they may do for your confidence. But there was a long way to go. I decided to hang cool and keep on trucking.

The reward came immediately with the day's first birdie at the fourteenth hole, followed by another at the par-five fifteenth and a great little chip at sixteen to save my 3. I slipped to another bogey at seventeen, but parred the final hole for a round of 74. I would have liked better, but no one had run away and hidden. Mike Souchak and Bo Wininger shared the lead at 69, with most of the scores in the mid to high 70s.

Friday, typically, was perfect again—warm and sunny with the lightest of breezes. I missed the green at the first hole with a wedge, but made par and never missed another putting surface all day until number eighteen, where I chipped dead from the fringe. From the second through the sixth holes all my first putts were for birdies, and they all looked like they would drop until the last moment. The birdies began on the seventh and eighth, and I added to them on twelve, thirteen, fifteen, and seventeen. With no bogeys, it finally added up to 66, my first round under 70 at Augusta playing for real, and by far the best one I had put together in five Masters. At the end of the day, Souchak still had me by a shot, but I was a pretty contented golfer. What pleased me most was that I had been able to capitalize on the ideal scoring conditions better than any of the other contenders.

It has often been said that most major championships are lost rather than won, and that Jack Nicklaus has claimed a number of his by sailing steady while others were blowing backward. There is some truth in that, and if ever there was a round where the importance of bearing down and hoping for the best in adverse conditions seared itself into my brain, it came on day three of that 1963 Masters.

We had gone from perfect weather in practice, to high winds on Thursday, to perfection again on Friday. On Saturday came the monsoon. The rain fell ceaselessly, totaling more than an inch by the end of the day. A lot of the field felt that the course had become unplayable by late afternoon and that the round should have been canceled. I had little sympathy for that view, having adopted the same philosophy toward rough course and weather conditions as I have to health problems or other personal difficulties: Once the gun has gone off, you keep quiet and get on with the job as best you can. The more you let your mind dwell on negatives, of whatever type, the larger they grow and the greater the risk that you will convert them into excuses. I have preferred to save my energy for finding solutions to problematical conditions, rather than waste it on whining.

I will admit that this round tested that attitude to the limit. On the opening hole I hit a horrible duck hook into the trees separating the first and ninth fairways, but somehow scrambled a par. After ten holes, however, I had missed an eighteen-inch putt and a two-footer, along with several more from under four feet. At the eleventh, the driver slipped in my wet glove—I changed gloves eight times during that round—and the ball flew dead right and smacked a pine tree about 150 yards from the tee. I couldn't see where it finished, and nobody in the gallery had either. Walking down the fairway, I experienced the sick feeling known to all golfers who suspect they will shortly be tramping back up it again, then adding two penalty strokes to the score when they leave the green.

Spectators are not allowed down the left side of the eleventh hole during the Masters, but I had noticed a security guard standing all by himself in the left rough. As I began to look around for my ball off to the right side of the fairway, the guard called out, "Is this yours? A Tourney 6?" *Phew!* Again I scrambled a par, and it lifted my spirits sufficiently to keep on matching the numbers on the scorecard.

The Masters invented the system, now almost universal in golf, of using different colors to indicate under-par and over-par scores on leader boards, in its case respectively red and green. I am red-green color-blind and thus unable to distinguish between the two. Coming up eighteen, I looked over at the big leader board facing the clubhouse and saw a "2" next to my name, which I knew had to be red, along with a whole mess of 1's that could have been either color. My caddie at the Masters for many years was a local character called Willie Peterson. I asked him, "Willie, are we leading this tournament by three strokes or by one?" Willie took a quick look then told me, "Them others is all green numbers. You're leading by three, boss."

By not quitting on myself and keeping my composure, I had somehow struggled around in 74. Normally, a score that high would have dropped me well back into the pack. Because of the awful conditions, it had moved me from one stroke behind into a handsome lead. Nothing like that had happened to me before, but it was a lesson I would never forget. I went home exhausted but happy, dried out, ate, and fell asleep the second my head hit the pillow—and stayed that way for about eleven hours.

A little incident during that round further points up the value of patience and perseverance at golf. I was paired with the leader at the halfway point, Mike Souchak, and I am certain he could have finished a lot better if he had not let himself get trapped into making a false assumption. At the thirteenth hole, the entire fairway in the elbow of the dogleg appeared to be flooded, to a degree permitting neither of us to find a lie for our second shots that wasn't casual water. Mike said to me, "You know, I don't think there's any way we're going to be able to finish today. They're certain to cancel the round." After that, he sort of hockeyed his way through the rest of the hole and made a big number, and finally handed in a 79.

The round was not canceled, of course, and I'm sure Mike's assumption that it would be hurt him more than the shotmaking difficulties he and all the rest of us were experiencing. The lesson is a simple one: Hang in hard until you've holed the final putt or someone in authority has told you to stop. Cliché though it may be, this game is never over until it's over. Keeping that at the front of my mind has been as big a factor in my record as any of the shots I've played.

On Sunday, the gods of golf smiled again, clearing away the clouds about the time I arrived at the course an hour before my 1:25 P.M. tee time. The crowds by then were enormous and would get bigger by the hour—to the point, in fact, where people had to be turned away at the gate for lack of parking space, thereby provoking the decision henceforth to sell only all-tournament admissions.

I felt great—increasingly confident with my right-to-left draw, sure I would play well from tee to green. I hit my first good opening drive of the week and put a 9-iron twelve feet from the cup. I missed that putt, plus real birdie opportunities on each of the next six holes, then bogeyed the par-five eighth hole through stupidly forgetting to check the pin position as I left the adjacent first green. The bogey would have hurt more if anyone had been making a run at me, but at that point no one was. Turning for home, I was still a couple of shots clear.

The rush began on number twelve, that lovely little devil of a par three that surely must have decided more Masters tournaments than any other single hole. As I'd looked over a long putt for birdie on the eleventh green, a huge roar had come from the direction of the fourteenth green. A few moments later, the leader board close to the eleventh green indicated the cause—a birdie by Sam Snead, tying him with me at one under par.

Then in his fifty-first year, Sam had gone on a diet during the winter and, for the umpteenth time, retuned the superb golf swing that had already won for him three times at Augusta, and more times elsewhere around the world than anyone except he could remember. He was playing beautifully despite a sore foot, and, sensing it might be a last hurrah, the fans were giving him their all. Unfortunately, and through no fault of Sam's, some were also inspired to let me know their preference. In those days I was usually far too focused on my own play to hear gallery comments, but these were too loud and pointed to ignore. Because the Augusta National during the Masters was the last place I expected golf fans to root openly against a player, this greatly surprised me, and naturally unnerved me a bit.

When the time came to hit at the twelfth, I watched my playing partner, Julius Boros, float a lovely shot to within about twelve feet of the flagstick, positioned this time at its easiest in the front left of the green. I figured he'd hit a 7-iron, and decided to do the same. My intention was to aim a fraction right and play a quiet little draw. I aimed fine, but failed to stay down on the shot long enough. Caught thin and pushed, the ball looked for a moment as though it wouldn't even clear Rae's Creek, but just made it and landed in casual water in the front bunker. I was allowed a free drop, but there was no way to avoid the ball partially embedding itself in the wet sand. Considering the lie, I thought I hit a pretty good sand shot, but the ball came out fast and ran through the far side of the green. From there I decided to putt rather than chip, but, misjudging the slowing effect of the fringe grass, ended up some eight feet past the hole. It was a gut-wrenching moment. Even if I made the putt for bogey, I would trail Sam by a shot with six holes to play.

The bad news then got worse—fast.

As I watched Boros address his birdie putt, a leader board change indicated that Gary Player had birdied the fifteenth hole. Gary had started five strokes back of me. Now, thanks to a great run of four almost back-to-back birdies, he was a stroke ahead—two if I missed the upcoming eight-footer. Also, Tony Lema, playing brilliantly in his first Masters, was now tied with me. Moments later, Julius joined the club as his birdie putt toppled gently over the front lip. From being out in front alone and seemingly unchallenged half an hour earlier, I now had four of the world's finest golfers tearing at my hide. I studied the eight-footer a long time, told myself to hit it firmly whatever, and did so. A surge of excitement ran through me as the ball dove into the cup. It was a very big putt.

By the time I arrived at the thirteenth tee, Snead had also birdied the fifteenth, so was now two strokes ahead of me. That resolved any doubts about gambling. I hauled out the driver and drew the ball perfectly around the dogleg, then went for the green with the 2-iron, knocking the ball about sixty feet beyond the cup. As always on this tree-shaded, sparsely grassed green, the speed was hard to judge, and I left the first putt about five feet short. Then, surveying the line of that little tester extra carefully, extremely aware of how important a birdie would be, guess what I discovered? . . . Growing dead on my line, was a flower—yes, a *flower.* The Masters greens are cut—generally, almost shaved—every morning and evening, so this was difficult to believe. Closer inspection proved it was just what I'd thought—a dandy little flower, probably a daisy. Golf's rules prohibit interfering with living objects, so there were no options. I would have to bang the ball right over the top of the flower. I did just that and found the hole. The birdie reduced my deficit to Snead to one.

Whether one likes it or not, luck is an enormous factor at every level of golf. Even when the breaks have been against me, I have tried to accept them as part of the game's challenge and charm, because I believe it would be a pretty dull affair if it were entirely predictable. Also, I figure the breaks even out over time. If that's true, I made up for a whole warehouse full of bad ones on the fifteenth hole that afternoon.

After a solid par at fourteen, I had hit a big drive at this long par five. When I got to the ball, however, I found it had settled against the raised front of an old divot. Given a perfect lie, the shot would have called for the 1-iron. To be sure of forcing the ball through the tuft of dried turf, I decided to go with the 3-wood and choke down a little. I made a good swing and impact, but the tuft affected the spin imparted to the ball, because it took off left then hooked—dead on line to bounce and bumble into the pond forming the entire left side of the sixteenth hole. "Oh boy, there goes the 1963 Masters," I said to myself, then aloud to the world at large, "Somebody *please* stop that ball."

Nobody did, and it vanished from sight beyond and to the left of the green. But there wasn't the loud groan that always greets a shot, as Henry Longhurst so graphically liked to put it, gone to a watery grave, and when I got down there, lo and behold, there was the ball —pulled up short of the water by the muddy tracks left by spectators. I took the permitted free drop, blessed Saturday's monsoon, played a great chip from a tight, wet lie, and almost made birdie. About then the adjacent leader board confirmed, as I'd heard leaving the tee, that Snead had bogeyed the sixteenth hole by three-putting. The board also showed that Player had finished his round with two straight bogeys. All was not yet lost.

Sixteen at Augusta National is a 190-yard par three, almost entirely over water. Pumped up, I hit a 6-iron twelve feet short of the hole. As we walked to the green, Willie Peterson, my caddie, glanced at the leader board and immediately got excited. Sam had also bogeyed eighteen. I was in the lead again by a shot. "Boss, all we need is three pars," said Willie. I agreed, but I had a good feeling about the twelve-footer—and it wasn't misplaced. Birdie. A two-stroke cushion with two holes to play.

For some strange reason I felt more nervous setting up on the seventeenth tee than I had been all day, but still managed to hit a solid drive. Climbing the hill after it, I detoured a little left to look at a leader board. Suddenly, I realized we had forgotten all about a gentleman from Oakland, California, by the name of Anthony David Lema. If Tony birdied the final hole and I bogeyed my last two, he would become the first golfer to win the Masters at his first attempt. Then, just as my playing partner, Boros, hit his approach to seventeen, there came an enormous roar from the eighteenth green, indicating that Lema had indeed finished with a birdie. There was no way I was going to play my second shot until I knew for sure whether that was true. I fiddled around until the board changed. Now I *did* know for sure—and also that I must make no worse than two pars to win *my* first Masters that sunny Sunday afternoon.

I hit what felt like a solid 8-iron to the seventeenth green, but heard a fellow in the gallery shout, "Get up! Get up!" even before the ball reached its apex. I sprinted over to the left to see the shot land. It did so on the green. Two putts later, I had the first of those pars.

The entire right side of the eighteenth hole in the driving area at Augusta National is a forest—deadsville. I chickened out a little and drove the ball well to the left. It ended up in spectator territory again, and again I was fortunate and got a free drop onto the fairway because of the mud. However, the lie I gave myself wasn't the best and the green, ten deep with spectators, looked smaller than ever. I did some pacing and some hard thinking. I had 160 yards to the flag, uphill, with the adrenaline on full rush. That computed to a choked 6-iron. I hit the shot exactly as planned, but the ball ran farther than I'd figured it would. The result was a thirty-five-foot downhill putt with a double break, first left, then right. I judged the breaks perfectly, only just missing the hole, but not quite the distance, the ball finishing three feet past. Setting up to that putt, I reminded myself that, even if I missed, I would have another chance to win in a playoff. The thought relaxed me sufficiently to stroke the ball firmly. It broke left faster than I'd expected it to, but slipped into the hole just a millisecond before it caught enough of the lip to spin out.

As I'd walked onto the eighteenth green, the announcer there, Ralph Hutchison, had asked me to save the ball if I won and give it to Bob Jones. When the winning putt dropped, I just had to throw something, so I whipped off my cap and slung it to the crowd.

At the ceremony a little later, Mr. Jones and I made an exchange. After he and the previous year's champion, Arnold Palmer, had presented me with my green jacket, I gave Bob the ball.

It was a small thing, but the look in his eyes remains one of the most emotional memories of my life.

5

The 1963 PGA Championship

Two Surprises

It was said of the great English champion Harry Vardon that he never wanted to play the same course twice in one day because he was so accurate that he would have been hitting in the second round from the divot marks he made in the first.

Harry Vardon died three years before I was born, but I can't believe he was any more accurate than the golfer who gave a clinic during the U.S. Junior Championship at the Los Angeles Country Club in August of 1954. There was a new irrigation system in the fairway where he was hitting, and I'll never forget sitting with other kids watching shot after shot, with all the clubs, drop smack on the line where the center piping was laid. It was incredible . . . awesome, as they say today . . . and still the finest exhibition of golfing accuracy I've ever witnessed.

The golfer was Byron Nelson, then forty-two years of age and seven years retired from regular tournament play. Later, when I got to know Byron, I mentioned that amazing display of accuracy to him, and, typical of his modesty, he changed the subject as soon as he'd thanked me for remembering. Golf has never had a nicer champion.

Back in 1945 Byron Nelson won eighteen tournaments, eleven of them in a row. To me these are two of the game's most stunning records, not least because no one has ever come close to them, and because of the certainty that no one ever will. My best was eight victories in 1971, then seven each in 1972 and 1973, out of about twenty-five tournaments played per year. In recent times, a professional winning three or four times out of twenty to thirty starts in a season is considered to have done exceptionally well.

In other words, golf is a most humbling game.

There are many sports and other activities in life where, once you have reached the top, you lose very rarely. In golf, almost everyone loses a whole lot more than he wins. For instance, even in my peak years I won only about 30 percent of the tournaments I played. Another way to put it would be that I spent 70 percent of my time being humbled!

The infrequency of victory by even golf's top performers is an aspect of the game that puzzles many nonplayers, and perhaps even some who do play to whom the shotmaking capabilities of the big names appear superhuman. I believe there are essentially three reasons for it.

The most obvious of those reasons is surely the huge role luck plays in golf. Another is the ever-intensifying competitive density in professional tournament play worldwide. The third is the difficulty of consistently making a golf ball do what you want it to do.

There is an element of luck in all sports, but in none that I know of does the luck factor play as large a role as it does in golf. As a for instance, every top player through the ages could point to something as seemingly trivial as a spiked-up green or a sudden gust of wind that cost him or her an important victory. Golf's history contains innumerable examples of bad bounces and other tough breaks at critical moments. What they all have in common is that they are inherent to the game and beyond anyone's control. In other words, golf never was intended to be, never has been, and never will be "fair," in the sense that other games either are fair innately or have gradually been made more so for purposes of mass entertainment. The mathematicians might try to convince golfers that, by the law of averages, they enjoy as many good breaks as they suffer bad ones, but it never seems to work out that way to most of us.

Top team sports are very different in this regard. With pro football perhaps the best example, much effort has been and continues to be expended on reducing the luck factor to the smallest possible percentile. This succeeds because both the arenas and procedures of most team games can be so tightly controlled. Because of the standardized court, the luck factor even in a one-on-one game like tennis is relatively small, extending to little more than lets and line calls.

In golf, both the field of play and the playing conditions are ever-changing. In golf, each and every hole is a totally new opponent, posing a completely different set of mental (strategic) and physical (shotmaking) challenges. On top of that, there are the infinite variables of terrain, weather, and bounce. Eliminate them and there's no question that the best players would win more. There's also no question that the game they were winning at would no longer be golf.

The second factor that often gets overlooked by those who can't see how three or four wins a year can make a golfer a star is the depth of talent in the top echelons of the game today. Scores may not be dropping all that fast, but the number of golfers around the world who can consistently shoot lights out has increased at least tenfold in the thirty-plus years I have played professionally. Spawned by golf's constant worldwide growth, and inspired to excel at the game by ever-increasing financial incentives, their number continues to grow, almost, it seems, by the day. As that happens, the difficulty of winning even a single tournament or championship, let alone several, increases dramatically.

To be tops in pro football from 1990 through 1994 required winning an average of fifteen times out of nineteen regular, playoff and Super Bowl games per season, or almost 80 percent of the time. The thought of winning that much would be laughable to any member of today's professional golf tours. After my first few years as a pro, I figured there were maybe thirty guys who might beat me when I was not playing my best, but only about ten when I was on top of my game. If I were out there today with the same hunger and skills, those numbers would be tripled at least. And the players defeating me wouldn't need a lot of lucky breaks, either.

Finally, of course, there's that little old matter of golfing physics to consider. The scientists tell us that it takes only a one-degree deviation from square in a driver's facing at impact when traveling at around a hundred miles an hour to send the ball deep into the tall trees or high weeds—or even, on tighter courses, out of bounds. Think too long about that sort of thing—about how mechanically difficult it is to make a golf ball consistently do what you want it to do—and you begin to wonder why anyone sticks with the game.

Even Ben Hogan, probably golf's most consistently accurate shot-maker, finally admitted, after decades of trying to turn himself into a golfing machine, that the game was imperfectible. Which, of course, is the chief reason why all golfers, at all levels, always lose much more than they win.

And which makes the record of Robert Tyre Jones, Jr., all the more incredible.

IN 1930, Bob Jones won, in order, the British Amateur, the British Open, the United States Open and the United States Amateur, then, with no more mountains to climb, retired at the age of twenty-eight. O. B. Keeler, Bob's writer friend, called it the Grand Slam. To me, the safest bet in all of sports is that it will never be matched.

To equal this greatest of all golfing achievements a golfer would require two rare assets: supreme playing skills plus the resourcefulness and resources to remain amateur. The first of those conditions is a possibility—no, a *probability.* In today's world the second, to my mind, is almost a nonstarter.

In the sixty-some years since Bob's heroic achievement, golf has simply changed too much to permit even a superhumanly gifted player to win its top open-to-all championships in the same year with less than total commitment and devotion to the game—in other words, without playing professionally. Given the high and ever-rising cost of playing top tournament golf, the expense of the effort alone would be a formidable problem for an amateur not blessed with substantial private means. Should that hurdle be cleared, I believe the quantity and quality of talent at the top of golf globally would be an insuperable obstacle.

In 1930 there were perhaps ten golfers, pro or amateur, who might defeat Bob Jones when everything was right with them. (In fact, during his eight peak years from 1923 to 1930, he lost to only nine men in match play, and failed to win only two of the stroke-play tournaments he entered.) I figure standards now have risen to the point where about two-thirds of the contestants in the full-field majors—the U.S. and British Opens and the PGA—have a chance of winning, which means Bob's competition would be multiplied about tenfold. Thus, to me, George Trevor, a well-known golf writer of Jones's time, was correct in calling Bob's greatest achievement "The Impregnable Quadrilateral." I believe it will remain unmatched for all eternity.

Most people knowledgeable about golf have shared that view, which is one of the reasons why, a decade or so after World War II, as the professional game began its first great boom period, a revised version of Bob's crowning achievement began to tickle the sportswriters' fancy, and eventually the golf fans' also. In this, the two Amateur championships were replaced by the Masters (most fittingly, it being a Bob Jones invention) and, once its playing no longer clashed with the British Open, the championship of the Professional Golfers' Association of America, better known as the PGA.

Golf historians generally regard Ben Hogan as becoming the catalyst for this new concept when he made 1953 his finest year by winning the Masters, the U.S. Open, and the British Open. Had he added the PGA, he would have become the only golfer to this day to win what we have now long known as the Grand Slam. Ben has always insisted that the afteraffects of his horrendous 1949 auto smash made the PGA's then weeklong, mostly thirty-six-holes-a-day match-play format too much for him physically, and that he would therefore not have competed in it even if its dates relative to the British championship hadn't made doing so impossible (the 1953 British Open ended July 7 and the PGA began July 6). Be that as it may, Hogan's superb "triple" gave momentum to the concept of a new summit in golfing achievement.

According to a man who can claim to have participated in it, the actual birth of the modern Grand Slam occurred in the form of a conversation on an airplane flying from Denver to New York the day after the 1960 U.S. Open. At some point during that flight, Arnold Palmer, who had just added the Open title to his Masters victory seven weeks previously, asked his friend Bob Drum, then the golf writer for the *Pittsburgh Post,* "What if I win the Open at St. Andrews and then the PGA?" Drum recalled responding that this would indeed be a wonderful accomplishment, whereupon Arn replied, "No, that would be the Grand Slam. Bob Jones did it by winning both Amateurs and both Opens. I plan to copy that feat with the major professional titles." And, of course, Arn certainly came close to taking three of the four when he finished second by a stroke to Kel Nagle in the centennial British Open at St. Andrews, and the same again two years later when he won the Masters, placed second in the U.S. Open, and won his second straight British Open.

REGARDLESS of how the modern Grand Slam evolved, it would be presumptuous of me to claim I was targeting it after winning the Masters for the first time in 1963. Nevertheless, it was impossible not to think about it. For one thing, the writers wouldn't let me not think about it—at least, not until after that year's U.S. Open. For another, there was the Palmer factor. American golf fans seemed to have decided that, if anyone could achieve this supreme pinnacle within the foreseeable future, it would be Arnold or me (other nationalities also gave Gary Player a chance). If that were to prove correct, I wanted it to be me.

I can laugh now about my endeavors in the second leg of the modern Grand Slam in June of that year, but at the time it was difficult to crack even a faint grin. Golf has frequently embarrassed me over the years, but rarely more than at The Country Club in Brookline, Massachusetts, in the 1963 United States Open.

Things had gone well immediately after the Masters. At Houston two weeks later I finished fourth, won my first Tournament of Champions by five strokes from Arnold and Tony Lema in Las Vegas two weeks after that, then hopped back to Texas to place third in the Colonial. After a much-needed week's rest, I played indifferently in Memphis, so decided to take a further two-week break and work on my game. The Open had been heavy on my mind since the Masters, and particularly the small, hard greens, narrow fairways and thick *Poa annua* rough remembered from my encounter with The Country Club in the 1957 Amateur. Now was the time, I decided, to achieve greater control over my golf shots by going back to fading the ball.

ON the day I announced I was turning professional late in 1961, I received a phone call from a man by the name of Joel Gordon, who introduced himself as the president of Revere Knitting Mills of Boston, Massachusetts. After telling me he had just heard about my change of status on the radio, Mr. Gordon asked if I would be interested in endorsing a line of sports shirts and sweaters he manufactured. I told him I would, Mark McCormack negotiated my first commercial involvement with him, and within a month or so everything was going swimmingly with just one little exception: We needed an emblem or logo to put on the shirts but had not been able to think of a suitable one. I'd had plenty of nicknames in college, but neither Barbara nor I felt that "Blobbo" or "Whaleman" would sell many shirts.

Then, sitting around after dinner one evening still trying to come up with something, I recalled a story about me by an Australian golf writer, Don Lawrence, in the *Melbourne Age* newspaper shortly before I turned pro. This had come about through McCormack making a business trip down under soon after he and I had first talked about my prospects if and when I made the switch. Don had interviewed Mark about what was happening in American golf, and my future business agent must have painted quite a picture in describing me—large, strong, blond, and maybe a little growly—because, in the article that followed, Don referred to me as the "Golden Bear."

As I mulled "Golden Bear" over in my mind that evening, it didn't sound too bad, and particularly as I once really was a Golden Bear as a basketball player for my high school team, the Upper Arlington Golden Bears. So I mentioned it to Barbara, who immediately said, "Jack, that's it!" The sportswriters obviously thought so too, because by 1963 I was routinely known by the new moniker.

I don't know about golden, but I sure lived up to the bearish part leading up to my defense of the Open. Even with the best efforts of Jack Grout, recapturing that reliable old power fade turned out to be a lot tougher than I'd figured. For a dozen or so shots I would be certain I had it, then, whammo, along would come a couple of big hooks or some hard pulls, or both. As the days passed, I became increasingly frustrated and irritable. Snippy and snappy around the house, I'm sure Barbara and little Jackie and Stevie were glad to see the back of me as I returned to the drawing board on Scioto's driving range each morning.

The tournament immediately preceding the Open that year was the Thunderbird Classic at Westchester Country Club. I opened there with a 69, and that evening felt I could at least see light at the end of the tunnel. The next morning was cool but humid, not quite sweater weather but shivery when the wind blew. I left the sweater in the bag and must have gotten a chill, because by the end of the round I was experiencing a lot of pain in the left side of my neck and left shoulder. It was severe enough to make me think of withdrawing, but, never having done that, and still needing work on the fade, I decided to live with it. I finished the tournament poorly, and by Sunday night was again a miserable golfer. "Heck," I thought, "a couple of days before the Open, and here I am halfway between two golf swings and with a big pain in my neck. Great way to defend the title and go for the Grand Slam!"

When you depend on your body for your livelihood, you are not inclined to take chances with it, babyish or hypochondriacal as that might sometimes appear to others. Up at Brookline, to be sure I would not compound whatever I had injured by continuing to play, I went for an expert opinion and some X rays. Everything was in order structurally, which indicated the same old problem, the tournament golfer's occupational hazard, muscle strain or spasm. That was a relief. All I needed now was to find a way to swing a golf club that would keep the ball somewhere on the planet.

Looking back, I realize I had no chance that week, principally because of two fundamental mistakes I made. The first was psychological but had a negative physical affect: getting too emotionally pumped up about an event too far ahead of it, which pressured me excessively regarding swing form. The second goof, growing out of the first, was physical, but, in that classic vicious circle so well known to golfers, greatly aggravated the psychological problem: falling between swing methods to the point of never knowing which way the ball was going to fly, than which there is no greater confidence-wrecker.

At Brookline, I hit my opening tee shot dead left, my second tee shot dead right, and my third dead left again. All finished in tall grass and all resulted in bogeys. Walking off the third green, it occurred to me that I was now exactly six shots worse than I had been at the same point at Oakmont twelve months previously. From that moment, I was gone. I had completely lost the feel of how I should be standing to the ball, and I had completely lost the feel of how I should be swinging at it. Sometimes that will happen to a good player for five or six holes, then, if he has the patience to continue searching through his swing keys and the good fortune to avoid disaster while doing so, his game comes partially or even all the way back again.

Never having quit on a golf course in my life, I kept hoping and searching, but there was no way. As I came to the eighteenth hole on the second day, I knew I must par it or miss the cut. I bogeyed the hole and, with 76–77, was out of the championship. Three days later, Julius Boros beat Arnold Palmer and Jacky Cupit handily in a playoff to become, at forty-three, the then oldest American to hold the title (Raymond Floyd relieved him of that distinction by a few weeks at Shinnecock Hills in 1986).

Many years later, Jerry Tarde, the editor of *Golf Digest,* mentioned to me that Frank Hannigan, the golf writer and ABC Sports rules expert who was then working for the United States Golf Association, told him that I went straight to the press room after missing the cut and talked to the writers so openly and honestly that they gave me an ovation at the end of the session. Jerry asked how I had been able to do that.

As with so many things in my makeup, the answer derives from Charlie Nicklaus. My father taught me the single hardest thing a professional athlete has to learn, which is how to lose gracefully. Dad convinced me very early in my involvement with sports that I had to accept the bad with the good; that, however much it hurts inside, you smile and keep a stiff upper lip; that you shake the hand of the man who's beaten you, and tell him congratulations, and mean it.

As I have tried to apply this to fellow competitors, so I've also applied it with the press. After all, it's not their fault that I've played poorly, and there's never been any doubt in my mind that I would never have been able to play golf for a living without them. So, no matter my score, whenever I have been asked to go in the press room, I have gone, and whenever a group of writers or even a single writer has wanted to talk to me about a bad round, I have talked to them or him or her. I try in doing so to answer every question asked of me as fully and honestly as I can, and to give everyone, from well-known columnists to novice reporters, as much time as needed, because, again, they have a job to do, and the only person responsible for my mistakes is me. As a result, writers have told me more than once that I'm a better interview in defeat than in victory, which is a compliment I am extremely proud of.

Despite all of that, though, for a week or more after Brookline that year, I was so mad at myself I could feel my cheeks burn every time I thought about it.

• • •

In the middle of May in 1962, I had done what still has to rate as one of the dumbest things of my professional career. The Carreras tobacco company in Great Britain had launched a new tournament, promoting its Piccadilly cigarette brand, to be played partly on the Southport and Ainsdale course and partly at Hillside, a wild-looking links immediately adjacent to Royal Birkdale, one of the permanent fixtures on the British Open rota. I had received an invitation through Mark McCormack and, still not absolutely sure about my earning capabilities as a pro, had decided that this might be an opportunity for some easy pickings. Oh, yeah?

I flew over directly from the Colonial event in Texas, arriving two days ahead of the tournament. The temperature in Fort Worth had been in the nineties. The weather on the northwest coast of England was what I've since learned to call three-sweater stuff: wet, windy, cold, gray, and thoroughly dismal. The time change between Texas and Britain was seven hours. I spent most of the nights in my hotel reading and most of the days on the golf course yawning. Back then, European tournaments were still played with the British-size ball: 1.62 inches in diameter compared with America's 1.68 inches. You could hit the British ball farther, especially into the wind, but you couldn't hit it as high and you couldn't "work" it from side to side—fade or draw it—as effectively or predictably as you could the U.S. size. Also, for me, because it came off the clubface faster and rolled farther, the small ball was more difficult to chip and putt. What with the weather, the jet-lag, and the smaller pellet, all I picked up was a bright red face. Boy, it was embarrassing—scores of 79-71-70-78, never anywhere near contending, and a miserable ride home all alone, with nothing to think about but what a dummy I was to believe I could just hop across the Atlantic and clean up at a totally different game of golf in completely different conditions.

A couple of months later, just to show how stubborn I could be, I did it all over again, arriving at Troon for my first British Open with insufficient time to prepare thoroughly, and, as mentioned, further compounding all the consequent problems by using an untried set of clubs I had contracted to play with a British manufacturer. I again paid the price, and finally I learned: If you want to play good golf in Britain, Jackie boy, then darn well have the patience and take the time to *prepare* yourself properly. In 1963, I did just that, and it almost worked, and I continued to follow the same regimen for just about every other British Open during my peak years.

The week after Brookline I had finished seventh in the Cleveland Open, then driven home to Columbus and stayed there, passing up the Canadian Open. In Cleveland, I'd felt within a whisker of fully remastering my friendly old fade. Back at Scioto, I switched immediately to the British-size ball on the practice tee, and, following three days of hard work, knew I finally had my swing where I wanted it. On the Wednesday night of the week before the Open I flew to Britain. On Thursday I played my first round at Royal Lytham and St. Annes, the championship site, and, finding the course greener and the holes better defined, liked it better even at first glance than I had Troon the previous year. On Friday I played at a nearby course in an exhibition benefitting a charity headed by the Duke of Edinburgh. Between Saturday morning and the following Tuesday evening, I got in seven rounds at Lytham, this time using my own MacGregor clubs. By Wednesday, when the championship began, I was sleeping civilized hours, was comfortable with the small ball, and felt I knew Royal Lytham and St. Annes inside out. I told myself over breakfast that morning that, win or lose, I was certain this time I at least would not humiliate myself. Deep down inside, the sense of swinging well, plus the memories of the two previous British failures along with the missed cut at Brookline, produced an even more positive feeling. Not to beat about the bush, I secretly believed there was no way I could lose.

FOR seventy of that championship's seventy-two holes, this belief never waned. An opening 71 left me four shots adrift of friend Phil Rodgers and the Australian Peter Thomson, then a four-time winner of the championship who would add a fifth title a couple of years later. But I was still brimming with confidence, and particularly after reducing my deficit on the pair to three strokes with a 67 in the second round. In the third round on Saturday morning, a 70 pulled me within two shots of the new leader, the left-hander from New Zealand, Bob Charles. In the fourth and final round on Saturday afternoon I quickly picked up another shot on Charles, then eagled the 551-yard seventh hole with a 350-yard drive, a 200-yard 5-iron, and a three-foot putt. That gave me the lead all alone, which I figured was about in sync with my game plan.

Some distance from the sea and surrounded by rows of red-brick houses, Royal Lytham to me is the least visually appealing of all the British Open courses, but my favorite among those used in England for the quality of its design. I think the par-three twelfth is a superb golf hole, and I rank quite a number of Lytham's other holes good to excellent in architectural terms. The strongest feature of the course as a championship test, however, is its finish: five par-fours then measuring respectively 448, 456, 354, 428, and 379 yards (the eighteenth has since been lengthened to 412 yards). When I birdied the first of this powerful quintet, I opened up a two-shot lead over Charles and Rodgers. I had never felt more relaxed and confident on a golf course. It was as good as over. Ha!

At the fifteenth hole off a fine drive I hit as solid a 2-iron as I've struck in my life, and for an exhilarating moment thought I'd holed it. Apparently the ball barely missed the cup on the roll, but it ended fifteen feet past. "Another birdie," I thought as I surveyed the putt, "and it's a lock." Somehow the green looked faster than the others. It wasn't. I left the fifteen-footer two feet short, then gut-wrenchingly missed what was really no more than a tap-in. Nevertheless, my sense of invincibility remained, and was reinforced a few minutes later when I holed from fifteen feet for birdie at the drive-and-pitch sixteenth hole. I figured all I needed now were two solid pars.

Seventeen at Royal Lytham is a fairly sharp dogleg to the left, famed as the site of a spectacular 175-yard mashie-iron (4-iron) shot by Bob Jones from a sandy lie in 1926 that contributed to his first British Open victory. To be sure of not hitting through the elbow, I drove with the 3-wood. The ball ended on the right side of the fairway about ten yards short of where I had driven in the morning round. Then I'd played a 3-iron and come up about twenty-five feet short of the pin. I decided to go now with the 2-iron, and I must have caught it exceptionally pure, because the ball landed beyond the hole and raced into some wiry rough on the beginning of the upslope of a bank behind the green. From there I played a poor wedge chip and two-putted. Bogey.

In reaction to some wild mob scenes at Troon the previous year, the organizers of the British Open, the Royal and Ancient Golf Club of St. Andrews, had this time not simply roped off the course as we do in the States, but surrounded many of the playing areas with chest-high wood-paling fences. These had given me a strange feeling all week—almost like being in a cage—but they certainly did the job of keeping the patrons away from the performers. Unfortunately, the fences also made it extremely difficult to discover how you stood in the championship, by preventing you from getting close enough to the tiny leader boards to read them clearly. Also, I had discovered in earlier rounds that the boards were often out of date or faulty in their information, or both. The only other method of determining how one stood was to ask a "steward" (British for marshal) or a spectator, but, if there's one place in the world where you can be certain of misinformation, it's on a golf course as any close-fought tournament comes down to the wire.

Waiting on the eighteenth tee and feeling less invincible than I had a short while before, I did my best to figure out how I stood in relation to Rodgers and Charles. There was no way to see reliably, and I did not feel like opening up a guessing game with the gallery. After a lot of mental gymnastics, I decided I must still have a two-stroke lead. This meant that, assuming neither Phil nor Bob birdied any of the last three holes, I could win even with a concluding bogey.

That was mistake number one, because my lead over both Rodgers and Charles had, in truth, by then been cut to a single stroke. My second goof followed right along. Because I heard no applause as Phil and Bob putted on the sixteenth green as I waited to drive at eighteen, I decided that neither of them had birdied the hole. In fact, both of them did just that, but the wind blowing in my face as I stood on the tee prevented me from hearing the applause. Thus the reality was that I had to *par* the final hole to *tie,* again assuming neither Bob or Phil birdied seventeen or eighteen.

But it was mistake number three that physically cost me the championship. Huge clumps of gorse bushes bordering the right side of Lytham's finishing hole make the region a deathtrap. Determined to avoid it at all cost, I decide to aim for the farthest bunker on the left edge of the fairway and let the left-to-right breeze and my foolproof fade ease the ball back to its center. And what do I then produce? Yup, a dead straight shot, probably my straightest drive of the week. It thumps into the bunker, there's no way out but semisideways, after which I pitch too strongly then two-putt for a big fat bogey five.

And so Charles and Rodgers both par in to finish at 277, with that great mathematician, Jack William Nicklaus, at 278.

By the time Bob made history the next day in the last of the British Open's thirty-six-hole playoffs by becoming the first left-hander to win a major championship (still a unique achievement), I was well on my way to Dallas, Texas, for the PGA Championship. It would be extremely hot in Dallas, but not as hot as I was for most of that five-thousand-mile airplane ride. More than thirty years later, the assumptions I made that day remain the biggest mental blunders of my career.

ONE of the Royal and Ancient's many neat touches in running the British Open is having the winner's name engraved on the trophy by the time it's handed to him at the prize presentation immediately following the end of play. I'm not a gambler, but if I had been I would have bet a tidy sum as the final round began at Royal Lytham and St. Annes that, at its end, the letters flowing from the engraver's needle would end up spelling Jack Nicklaus. When I arrived in Dallas late the next day, I would have bet twice as much that the PGA would not be adding that name to its silverware a week later.

I was depressed, tired, stale, and angry. Somewhere in the recesses of my mind lay a faint awareness that we were about to play another major championship, but the pictures in my head were of getting it over with as painlessly as possible, then going home and going fishing. My mental errors in England were, of course, responsible for the down mood, and the long journey to Texas for the tiredness. The feeling of staleness came from the heavy schedule of both tournament and exhibition play I'd been following for more than eighteen months, and was, of course, entirely my own fault. What made me so angry—in addition to recurring memories of that final tee shot at Lytham—was the seeming inability of the game's governing bodies in golf's two leading nations to work together to schedule championships in a way that permitted maximum performance by the top players.

As I mentioned earlier, even if Ben Hogan in 1953 had wanted to attempt completing the modern Grand Slam, he would have been prevented from doing so by the British Open/PGA dates clash. That nonsensical situation was changed shortly afterward, but the improvement was for some years at best marginal. There we were one week in forty- or fifty-degree weather playing with a small ball on bumpy, baked-out linksland, and here we were a few days and many thousands of miles later teeing it up in twice that temperature with a large ball on steamy, soggy parkland. I survived somehow on this occasion, but Phil Rodgers, who had almost won in England the previous week, failed to make the cut, and Bob Charles, Arnold Palmer, Gary Player, and Doug Sanders were among those who couldn't get over the transition in time to do themselves and the championship justice in Dallas.

It just did not make sense, at least not to the more internationally minded and ambitious players, and I'm sure speaking our piece on the subject ever more loudly was what finally produced the present adequate separation of golf's last two major championships. Both have benefitted greatly from standing clear of each other, the British by attracting ever stronger American entries, and the PGA by having fields of relatively fresh and rested golfers. As I write, golf's tournament chieftains appear to have been provoked by an abortive attempt to launch a "World Tour" outside their jurisdiction into taking a less insular or more visionary look at the many other scheduling problems deriving from the game's huge and continuing international growth. Our most pressing need is for a collaboratively arranged worldwide yearly tournament schedule, and hopefully this will emerge from the new attitude of the professional tournament game's various governing entities. If not, I believe it will eventually be forced on them by top player pressure, regardless of the deeply embedded isolationist attitudes that have to be overcome.

IF it is possible to set criteria for major championship status, it seems to me that the vital ingredients are these: all of the world's best players always in the field; mature and well-established golf courses that rigorously test the players' mental and emotional capabilities as well as their physical skills; and a strong sense of occasion created by superb presentation.

The PGA Championship was begun in 1916, and until 1958 was decided at match play. It was an important event from the start for the home players who were members of the Association, and was won more often than not by the best of them—including Walter

Hagen five times, Gene Sarazen and Sam Snead three times each, and Byron Nelson and Ben Hogan twice apiece. Nevertheless, to much of the golfing press and public the PGA during my early years seemed not to carry quite the weight of the Masters and the two Opens. The fact that it was the last of the "Big Four" obviously had some bearing on this, about which more in a moment. Its biggest problems, however, were its lack of internationalism and the indifferent quality of many of the courses it was played on. The first seemed to derive from the association's leaders at one time being more concerned with providing an opportunity for fellow club pros to participate alongside the full-time home-bred tour players than with attracting the top foreigners. The second was rooted in venues being determined more by political considerations than golfing sophistication.

Thankfully, recent years have brought major improvements in all aspects of the championship. Through better qualifying criteria and an internationalist invitation policy, the PGA fields of recent years have been at least equal to and sometimes superior in strength and depth to those of the other three majors. With occasional exceptions, the championship has also been played on courses befitting the stature to which it aspires. And its presentation has also steadily improved.

As to the PGA's largest remaining problem, falling so late on the calendar, I've nursed an idea since way back in 1971 that would offer at least a partial solution. When I won the championship that year, it was played, for purely political reasons, in February just up the street from my Florida home. Winning for the first time in that state and on Bermuda greens added to the specialness of the week for me, but so did the excitement among fans, media, and most of the players flowing from the championship being the year's first rather than last major. To always play it first would be too geographically limiting, even if today's scheduling complexities and rivalries so permitted, which they don't. What I would like the PGA powers that be to consider, though, is *occasionally* playing the championship early in the year—say, once every five years. After all, there are always thirteen weeks between New Year's Day and the beginning of the Masters. And there surely would be a long line of fine courses from Florida to California, and even Hawaii, ready to bid for the event, should the scheduling hurdles be surmountable. If the PGA still needs a boost, I can't think of a better one.

All of the above apart, though, for certainly the past decade I have rated the PGA right up there alongside the other majors in all departments. I still think the Masters is the most glamorous, the U.S. Open the toughest, and the British the most fun, but I have gone into the PGA every bit as excited as for the others. And, of course, been equally thrilled to win it.

BEYOND those I've enumerated, there was another factor working against great excitement at the Dallas Athletic Club course in 1963: heat. The only word for it was unbearable. From the moment we arrived until the moment we left, I doubt the temperature ever fell below one hundred degrees. By the early afternoons it would have risen to one hundred ten or more. The second you walked out of the motel room your shirt was soaked, and by the time you came off the golf course you could literally wring out every article of clothing—shirt, pants, underwear, socks, the lot. At least three players were forced out of the championship by heat exhaustion, and fans keeled over like ninepins every day. Gary Player even laid aside his "strength-giving" all-black outfit for an all-white ensemble. Apart from playing and eating, I spent almost the entire time in our motel room, praying the air-conditioning wouldn't go kaput. Everyone was dripping all week.

Being forced to stay inside so much helped in one regard: I got in a solid ten hours of sleep every night, so had beaten off the jet-lag and most of the fatigue of the British expedition by the opening round. That perked up my spirits some, as did my mother-in-law, Helen Bash, on the phone one evening. She knew absolutely zilch about golf, but she was just as sure I would win in Dallas as I had been the previous week at Royal Lytham. Here was her reasoning: "Jack, you lost by two strokes at Cleveland and by one stroke in England, so I just *know* you're going to win the PGA." Her confidence tickled me, and Barbara and I got a much-needed laugh out of the interesting logic behind it.

Because of the heat, there was no way I could drive myself in practice the way I had before the British. I hit a few balls and played one round each day and let it go at that. However, as I caught up on rest I was pleased to find that my swing seemed just as solid as in England, and the long-driving contest on the final practice afternoon indicated no loss of strength: I won with 341 yards and 17 inches, still my longest officially-recorded belt, the prize for which was a solid gold money-clip that I've used ever since. By the time the gun sounded, where the question mark hung was over my putting.

I suppose it's a terrible admission for a guy in my business, but ever since my early teens I have found practicing putting immensely boring. It's a necessary chore, of course, but I generally have to push myself to do it and, when at home, have frequently failed in that effort. I've always tried to make up for that with time on the practice greens at tournament sites; but, whether because of lack of work or not, the fact is that my putting in competition throughout much of my career has been what you might call inspirational, meaning either I've had it or I haven't. Prior to the 1963 PGA, I suspected I would not have it, and I was correct.

THE Dallas Athletic Club course we played in the 1963 PGA was built in 1955, and like so many layouts of that era, it's chief features were length—7,046 yards—and large greens (a few years ago I was commissioned to redesign both the club's courses). However, the course was nicely groomed, and this, combined with the need to keep the greens damp to prevent them dying of heat, made for comparatively easy scoring conditions in the opening round. I played extremely well from tee to green but made very few putts, and was disappointed at being able to hand in no better than a two-under-par 69. That left me in a small group three shots back of Dick Hart, an assistant club pro from Massachusetts, who had been helped to a 66 by a hole-in-one on the 216-yard sixteenth hole.

Friday I drove and approached even better, needing only thirty-four strokes to reach all eighteen greens. Once there, I performed abysmally, three-putting three times and two-putting the rest for a total of thirty-nine putts—the most I'd needed in a single tournament round since turning professional. It added up to an infuriating 73, which left me four strokes back of Hart and two back of Tony Lema, Julius Boros, and another club pro, Shelley Mayfield. I felt I could partly blame the poor putting on the seeming millions of spike marks kicked up by the traditionally huge field (167 players this time). But that evening, heat or no heat, I did do some putting practice, and no one had to push me to do it.

The PGA in its first forty-four years had never been won by a foreign golfer, perhaps chiefly because so few foreigners had been able to play in it. Gary Player had fixed that at Aronimink twelve months previously, beating Bob Goalby by a stroke and George Bayer and me by four. Sixteen months before that, the little South African had become the first foreigner to win the Masters, but his victory in what so many people then still regarded as the "home pro" championship created quite a stir in the sports pages. So did Australian Bruce Crampton's performance in the third round in Dallas.

In those days, quite a number of the American players did not go out of their way to welcome foreigners on the tour, and a few were distinctly unpleasant to them. In recent years the trend toward globalization in golf, as in most other things, appears on the surface to have softened such attitudes. I didn't understand the insularity and small-mindedness back in 1963, and I still don't today so far as they still exist. As I see it, if a fellow has the game to make a living on our tour, plus the moxie to get along happily in a foreign country, then good luck to him. If he is also a good guy and fun to be with off the course and wants to make friends, then I'm delighted to reciprocate. I am sure being treated so well when I played overseas as a youngster underlies this attitude; but, whatever the reason, I've hit it off just fine with most of our visitors—guys like Gary Player, Bruce Crampton, Bruce Devlin, Bob Charles, Tony Jacklin, David Graham, and Greg Norman.

Early in the 1950s, Crampton had decided to make golf his career after being left off an Australian national amateur team because, in the view of some officials, he was too young at seventeen to meet the "social requirements" of the trip. The inference obviously was insulting, and Bruce decided not to sit still for it. At the PGA in Dallas he told the press: "I decided to show them they were wrong by arranging a trip of my own, so I turned pro." To me, that showed a great attitude (and a typically Australian one), and there was no question it had proven a sound decision. Playing in a prodigious number of tournaments each year—the writers nicknamed him "Iron Man"—Crampton had already won a couple of times in his four years in the States, and would go on to build a fine record in his adopted country until he finally grew tired of the gypsy lifestyle and retired early to become a successful businessman. After turning fifty, he then came back for a successful career on the Senior Tour.

With no wind and fewer spike marks after the halfway cut, and needing only twenty-eight putts, Bruce eased it around on Saturday in a then PGA single-round-record-tying 65, to lead at day's end by two strokes from Dow Finsterwald. Although I had not approached that standard, I had putted considerably better than the previous day for another 69, leaving me three strokes behind Bruce with eighteen holes to play.

Because there's usually such heavy television and press focus on the final nine holes of major championships, to the public the first three and a half rounds must often seem like nothing more than warm-ups for a final sprint. If only because of the mounting nervous tension—when you're in contention, pressure mounts in direct ratio to the number of holes remaining on which to win or lose—those same holes can sometimes seem just as critical to the players as they appear to the fans. However, the intelligent golfer tries never to look at the game this way. He knows that every one of the seventy-two holes is as important as all the others, and that he had better therefore put the pedal to the metal right from the opening tee shot. No one has ever done it, of course, and I'm pretty sure no one ever will, but the best attitude standing on the first tee is that you are about to make eagles or birdies on every hole, starting right now. At least, that's been my goal ever since I first broke 70 way back at the age of thirteen.

The opening hole at the Dallas Athletic Club course in those days was a 521-yard par five. I had struck the ball superbly warming up for the final round, and I carried it over to the first tee, whaling out a drive of some 350 yards. I chose the 5-iron for my second shot, put it fifteen feet from the pin, and holed the putt for an eagle. Crampton and I were playing together, and, although he birdied, the eagle suddenly brought me within two strokes of him. It also produced a surge of confidence. I remember that, for the first time all week, I started to think seriously about fulfilling my mother-in-law's prediction as I walked off the green.

I generally have excellent recall of my play in the majors, but the murderous heat of that final day in Dallas turned much of the round into a blur. Beyond the opening eagle, I can clearly remember only three holes. The first of them was the fourth, a 573-yard par five.

After another big drive, I found my ball had rolled into a gorgeous lie—sitting up pretty as a picture and just begging to be nailed.

Even with a fine lie, though, in the days when all drivers were wooden-headed, playing them from the fairway was a hard and risky shot, much more so than with most modern metal-headed drivers. Consequently, I never once had tried to do that in my twenty months as a pro. Probably because I was swinging so well, the temptation here was irresistible. Out came the big stick and away went the ball —pushed miles to the right and behind a stand of trees close to the green. Walking after it, I anticipated the worst, and I anticipated correctly.

The lie was awful, there was water behind the green, and the trees were thick and high and much too close for comfort. Miss the shot and there was no limit to the number I might compile. On the other hand, there was no safe recovery route that added up to less than a bogey 6. After much thought, I decided to try to nip the ball over the trees with the sand wedge but, in my effort not to contact the ground first, caught the shot thin. I couldn't see the flight clearly, but was still convinced the ball would reach the water when I saw it drop in some rough behind the green and stay there. Later I was told it had caught a tree that deflected it back to dry land. I pitched up to six feet and missed the putt, but still felt most fortunate to have made no more than a bogey. I also there and then made a decision I basically adhered to until the metal-headers came along: No more drivers from the fairway.

The next hole that sticks in memory is the fifteenth, and it does so for the same reasons as number four: a hefty helping of luck. After a bad drive I found a perfect lie in the rough, hit an easy 9-iron to the green, and holed the longest putt I made all week, from about thirty-five feet, for birdie. This put me two shots ahead of Crampton and one ahead of Dave Ragan. My lead then increased to three and two strokes respectively when Bruce three-putted the sixteenth and Dave bogeyed the seventeenth after a wild drive. We remained that way as, arriving on the final tee, I toweled myself down for what seemed the zillionth time that afternoon.

The last hole at the DAC was then a 420-yard par four with a creek crossing the fairway out around 290 yards. Needing only a par for the title, I figured the smart tee shot was to lay up with a club that could not possibly get me to the water, such as the 3-iron. Hot, tired, and tense, I made one of my few really poor swings of the week and pulled the ball into the thick Bermuda rough. Immediately, thoughts of the final drive at Royal Lytham flashed through my mind, but this time I had made sure of the arithmetic. I pitched out safely short of the creek, then hit an easy 9-iron to the green. The ball landed about twenty feet past the cup and sucked back to within four feet. Then, even though I was certain of my calculations, I got a sudden attack of nerves over the putt. I took my time, along with some deep breaths, and somehow squeezed the ball into the hole for a 68 and a two-shot victory over Dave, with Bruce and Dow Finsterwald tied for third a stroke further back.

The rest of that day is even fuzzier than the golf, but I do remember two things that nicely summed up the week. As the security man appointed to help me get through the crowds to the clubhouse reached the door, he passed out cold with heat prostration. Then, at the prize presentation, there was no way I could do the traditional thing and hug the trophy. It had been standing out in the sun all day and was red hot.

A couple of days later, over a fishing rod in Zanesfield, Ohio, reflecting on the previous two weeks, I could not help but wonder at the sheer contrariness of this mystifying, aggravating, wonderful game that had become my life's work. There I was one week, certain of winning and just as surely losing, and there I was the next with never really any serious thoughts of winning, and doing just that.

As the years ahead would continue to prove, the only certainty about golf is its uncertainty.

6

The 1965 Masters Tournament

Everyone Likes to Be Liked

WHATEVER my competitive peaks and valleys, one thing I felt reasonably confident about by the end of 1963 was my ability to earn a decent living from golf.

In my first year as a professional I had finished third on the official PGA money list to Arnold Palmer and Gene Littler with a little over $60,000 from twenty-six events, an amount I more than doubled in nontournament earnings. In my second year I moved up a notch in official earnings, finishing second to Arnold with $100,040—big money in those days. I also did well financially in "unofficial" events in the States, such as the World Series where I defended successfully, and in the four overseas tournaments I played—namely, the British Open, the Canada Cup in Paris (Arnie and I won and I took individual honors), the Australian Open, and the Wills Masters. Additionally, I was earning handsomely from the exhibitions and television matches and product endorsements arranged by Mark McCormack.

Because we traveled so much as a family and liked to live as comfortably as possible on the road—"Live on hamburger and you'll play like hamburger," somebody once said, correctly—expenses were high, at least a thousand dollars a week, as was the tax bite. But, when I looked at the bottom line, it was clearly considerably better than I could have achieved as a young pharmacist or insurance salesman. In fact, it was so much better that, in the middle of the year, I was able to alleviate a nagging problem by making a large but, as I saw it, vitally important business investment.

My single toughest challenge off the golf course during my first couple of years as a pro was moving from A to B to C and back again without losing my luggage, my temper, my sanity, or all three. I learned how to pack for long spells on the road after a while, and also got to know U.S. and world geography better than I had in high school. But my wars with the airlines seemed more and more unwinnable. After six years of struggling with the same problems (like muscle spasms, it's an occupational hazard), Arnold Palmer had greatly reduced them by acquiring and learning to pilot his own airplane in 1960. Arnie had been interested in flying all his life, often as a teenager, he once told me, hanging out with fliers at his local airport, and eventually becoming so adept a pilot himself as to set an around-the-world record in a Lear jet. Barbara and I rode with Arnold and Winnie once or twice early in 1964 in the twin-engined prop plane they then owned and quickly bought his argument about the importance of reducing the stress and fatigue of the endless travel that is an inescapable part of the tournament golfer's life. The downside was the scary cost of buying and running one's own aircraft. But eventually I decided that where there is a will there has to be a way, and began to make inquiries. The upshot was that in July of 1964 I bought a twin-engined Aero Commander 680 FL, generally known as the Grand Commander. It had a cruising speed of 220 miles per hour, a range of about a thousand miles, and seven passenger seats, and it quickly became my pride and joy.

So began what has come to be known among my friends and business associates as "Air Bear." Since that big initial step I have rarely been without an airplane of some sort, either owned or leased. Presently, I operate a Gulfstream IV-SP with a cruising speed of around 520 miles per hour, a range of almost five thousand miles, and seating for sixteen passengers and three crew. In my early prejet days, influenced by how much Arnie loved piloting, I reached a fairly advanced stage with flying lessons, logging about 800 hours at the controls as a student and copilot, before finally deciding to leave the work to professional pilots and be a passenger. From day one I have loved my peaceful hours in the air, relaxing, watching movies, listening to music, catching up on paperwork, napping—and also doing some of my best thinking.

Business associates sometimes remark on my ability to carry what seems to them a heavy load of varied activities without becoming overly fatigued. Well, along with the fact that I do not abuse myself and try always to stay in good physical shape, Air Bear is a big part of the answer. It has taken enormous pressure off me, not only in easing travel hassles, but in greatly increasing my productivity, particularly in the golf course design work that has been such a big part of my life since the early 1980s. With the jet, I can make almost as many stops around the United States in a day as I could in a week flying commercially, and still often eat breakfast or dinner in my own home. Also, thanks to Air Bear, I'm able to get twice the amount of work done in half the time on trips to Europe, Asia and Africa. Thus I look on the cost not as a personal indulgence but as a totally necessary and justifiable business expense. In fact, my airplane is my most essential and efficient business tool.

WHILE on the subject of money, I'd like to touch on its place in professional golf relative to other sports. I have strong feelings about that, and also about the most productive perspective from which to view money as a player.

In America's top team sports nowadays, keeping body and soul together is the last concern of any truly talented beginning professional. That's because, from the moment he shows serious talent in high school or college, a long line of agents and owners will be fighting for the right to hand him hundreds of thousands or even millions of dollars.

With the single exception lately of Tiger Woods, whose endorsement deals made him a multimillionaire before he even struck a shot as a pro, golf has never been that way, and I hope it does not take that route. In professional golf, a player's earnings have been directly proportionate to the quality of his or her performance. I believe it is this factor above all others that has made and keeps golf what, for want of a better word, I would call the "cleanest" of all the major professional sports. Sponsorship of beginning tour players by syndicates has become increasingly commonplace during my years in the game, but such groups generally have comprised mostly affluent friends or well-wishers getting a kick out of giving a kid a chance, then simply enjoying the association with a successful professional athlete if and when he or she makes good. Accordingly, in America, professional tournament golfers are unowned, unbossed, and, most important, unbuyable individual entrepreneurs. They are playing for profit, for sure, but entirely for their own profit, not for some guy whose greater wealth or ego gratification rests on their performance. At base, that's why there aren't the problems in golf that are now so routine, and so destructive, in other big-time professional sports.

Those are the upsides of the money factor for the game of golf overall. The downside for the individual player is that, unless he is already unusually well fixed, he cannot help but worry about money when he first decides to play the game for a living.

Being no exception to that, I did some hard thinking on the subject before joining the tour early in 1962. Partly out of pride, but mostly because I could not stand the thought of being answerable to anyone but myself for my golf game and my life, it took me very little time to reject the idea of sponsorship or any other form of external support. There was some comfort in Mark McCormack's assurances about nontournament earnings, but I was smart enough even at twenty-one to know just how long those would last if I did not win and keep on winning. Probably it was dwelling on this last factor that produced the attitude to money I've had ever since.

"Jack," I eventually told myself, "the more you think about money, the less you're going to think about performance, so forget it. Just get out there and play your hardest. If you play well, the money will follow automatically. If you play so badly you can't meet the bills, you can always go back to selling insurance—as you should, anyway, in that situation. The only way you can influence the money factor one way or the other is by your scores. The less you pressure yourself by thinking about it, the better those scores are likely to be."

The great benefit of this attitude was, of course, that it allowed me to continue treating golf the same way I had as an amateur, simply as a game, with my achievements deriving solely from my competitive spirit and will to win. Today, I am proud of the fact that I was able to stick with the philosophy through my most productive years, and I am sure it will prevail as long as I keep playing. And I am certain it is why I love what I do so much.

Inevitably but unfortunately, dollars are the supreme yardstick of athletic performance to many sportswriters and much of the public. Also, we have become increasingly guilty of promoting that notion on the PGA Tour with our ever-increasing emphasis on week-to-week purse size and first-place payouts and cumulative money-winnings. I don't much care for all of that. I happened to top the money list eight times during my peak years, but to me that was one of the least noteworthy statistics in my record. Number of major championship victories is far and away my top yardstick, followed by wins in other events, followed by high placings, followed by scoring average. Don't get me wrong: I like winning money at golf and earning money in other ways, and I absolutely *love* spending money—there, Barbara, I've admitted it publicly! What I have never done is use money as a measure of performance. And I strongly advise anyone starting out as a tournament golfer to adopt the same mind-set.

As I've said, I believe I did a fine job of sticking to this attitude right from the start of my professional career. Nevertheless, I have to admit that, with a total of eleven victories and five "majors" under my belt—seven if you count my two U.S. Amateurs—doing so became much easier from 1963 onward.

I HAVE met some people along the way who have made many millions of dollars but who will never have enough money. I feel sorry for them, because, when money becomes such a dominating force in life, it invariably produces misery in one form or another. What most sane people discover as they become materially successful is that there is another commodity in this world even more valuable—and certainly more elusive—than money. That commodity is time, and particularly the time to do what *you* want to do, rather than what you are obligated or are made to feel obligated to do.

As the years passed, I attempted to apply this discovery to my own life ever more resolutely. It was frequently interpreted as selfishness, and it definitely cost me dollars; it may even have cost me some victories. None of that matters alongside the fact that it brought my family and me more emotional fulfillment and enjoyment of each other than any amount of money or entries in the win column ever could have done. However, it has never been an easy battle, and it was particularly tough during my early pro years. Looking back, I can identify a number of periods where I came within the proverbial whisker of severe burnout. Late 1963 was one such time, and I suspect now that it had some bearing on my failure to win a major championship the following year.

Prior to the 1963 PGA Championship in July, I had played in fifteen tournaments in the following locations: Los Angeles, Monterey, Palm Springs, Phoenix, New Orleans, Miami, Augusta, Houston, Las Vegas, Fort Worth, Memphis, New York, Brookline, Cleveland, and Lytham St. Annes in England. Here's my schedule over the eighteen-week period immediately following the PGA: The Western Open in Chicago, eight exhibition matches in ten days with Gary Player, the Insurance City Open in Hartford, a two-day match with Arnold and Gary in Chicago, the World Series in Akron, the Seattle Open, the Portland Open, a hop over to Japan for some customer golf with businessmen, the Whitemarsh Open in Philadelphia, a two-day pro-am in Cincinnati with old friend Pandel Savic, the Sahara Invitational in Las Vegas, the Canada Cup with Arnie in Paris, two tournaments in Australia, and—because I badly wanted to top $100,000 in official prize money for the year just for the sake of having done so—the Cajun Classic in Lafayette, Louisiana, in late November.

To the golfer restricted by family or business obligations from playing more than a round or two a week, the idea of teeing it up this much probably seems little short of paradise. For the tour pro, it has its problems.

The first of them is fatigue. Tournament golf may not be an athletic sport compared with, say, basketball or tennis; but at the highest levels, if only because of the amount and intensity of concentration demanded, it can be extremely tiring mentally and emotionally. When you are not frequently in contention, I suppose the game becomes more frustrating than wearying—although that in itself can be pretty fatiguing. When you are fighting for the top spot most times you tee up, as the best players generally are, both the mental and physical exhaustion become enormous. Add to the fatigue of competing the energy expended on practice and the game is also much more physically taxing than it may look from the outside. Then there is the nonstop travel, plus the stress of interminably living out of a suitcase. As every corporate executive knows, the more one is on the road, the harder and more taxing become even the simplest day-to-day chores, so easily taken in stride at home. Successful tour players try to minimize the snafus and irritations of constant "away-from-homeness" with private planes, automobiles always at hand, room service in the suite, caddies who will handle nongolf-related chores, and the like. But after a while, no matter how comfortably you can afford to go, just having to go in itself breeds both physical and mental exhaustion.

During my best years I found the "sameness" of the PGA Tour, with its endless string of identical seventy-two-hole stroke-play tournaments, an exacerbating factor in this regard, making me glad our authorities have lately become more receptive to offbeat formats like skins games and team matches and mixed events in what has become known as a "second season." Tour purses long ago reached levels enabling the best players to quickly achieve sufficient financial independence to compete less than they otherwise might. There is a lot of print press criticism of offbeat formats and made-for-television events, but it seems to me that—especially when contested on fine courses—they help keep the big guns from hibernation by alleviating boredom and staleness.

Legend has it that golf was a magnificent obsession for Ben Hogan, to the point where he could never get enough of it. I know from observation that Arnold Palmer is much the same, never tiring of the game, or, if he does, able to call on some deep resource that enables him to go on practicing and competing despite his fatigue. Even in his late fifties, Lee Trevino candidly admits that all he wants to do, and all he really does do, is practice and play golf, seemingly tirelessly. Much as I admire the achievements deriving from this single-mindedness, I could never have equaled it. That's because, when fatigue or boredom with the game produced staleness, I simply could not give it my best. And I believe there are a lot more golfers like that than not.

History shows that, man not being a machine, even the Hogans, Palmers and Trevinos could not sustain peak mechanical form for more than a few weeks at a time, indicating that physical variations in swing and stroke always play the primary role in golfing performance. For most pros, however, the battle against staleness is almost as critical as the struggle to achieve and sustain mechanical excellence.

The first sign of this insidious and often unrecognized invader is an inability to concentrate fully on anything, but particularly on making a golf score. If not tended to, the symptoms escalate to include irritability, inertia, and finally an almost irresistible urge to do just about anything except practice and play golf. Most players' chances of excelling at the game when in this mood—they should ask their wives if they're in doubt about it!—range from slim to none, meaning they would be better off packing their bags and heading home.

That was exactly my frame of mind during the late fall of 1963, and fortunately I was smart enough to take the appropriate action. After the Louisiana tournament, I went home, barely touched a club for the better part of two months, and didn't miss golf for a single second.

THE foregoing notwithstanding, and despite four victories at home and wins in the World Cup (the Canada Cup renamed) and the Australian Open, my 1964 season indicated that I still had not figured out my ideal pacing.

During that year I finished second in the Masters, the British Open and the PGA Championship, missed winning four other tournaments by one stroke, and finished third, fourth or fifth seven times. To a lot of people that might have seemed a pretty fair season. I was not happy with it. "Nicklaus," I told myself at the end of the year, "this isn't good enough. Here you are, after only three years as a pro and only twenty-four years old, and already you're going backward." The majors performances were what troubled me the most, and particularly my Masters play.

After the long winter break, I had felt strong and ready as I rejoined the tour at the Crosby tournament. In the first round there I made a triple-bogey 6 at Cypress Point's infamous over-the-ocean sixteenth hole, then opened my second round with a double-bogey. Missing the cut gave us the chance to fly up to Chicago and pick out furniture at the Merchandise Mart for our new "California Traditional" eight-thousand-square-foot ranch house, by then almost completed in Upper Arlington. I would much rather have been teeing up at Pebble Beach, mostly because I really felt like playing golf, but also so I could have blamed Barbara for what I didn't like when all the furniture arrived.

Things improved after that, with a win in Phoenix followed by a run of second, fourth, second and fourth at New Orleans, St. Petersburg, Doral, and Greensboro, boosting my confidence going into the Masters even higher than at the same time the previous year. In fact, dining with my dad and his pals the evening before the opening round, I raised my glass of Coke to join enthusiastically in their martini-inspired toast to "Jack Nicklaus, the first golfer to win back-to-back Masters and the modern Grand Slam."

It did not work out that way, and largely for the same reason it hadn't in 1962: I had gotten myself way too pumped up about the tournament, with the result that I tried to force good scores instead of being patient enough to let them happen.

In the opening round I was awesome with the big clubs, never missing a fairway or green and placing most tee shots perfectly for the approaches. But, with thirty-seven putts, it added up to a highly frustrating 71, and from then on I was pressing. I finished the tournament with a 67, but there was little joy in tying Dave Marr for second place, six shots adrift of Arnie, whose four solid rounds made him the first four-time Masters champion. I was glad for Arn because by then we had become truly good friends, frequently dining and playing bridge together with our wives, while still, of course, trying to outneedle each other as hard as we tried to outplay each other. But, on the inside, I was pretty despondent—to the point, in fact, of even briefly considering not playing any more tournament golf for the rest of the year.

Contributing to that mood was a shot that continues to rate high on my most-embarrassing list. Because of the eagle possibilities at thirteen and fifteen, I figured I was still not totally out of the tournament as I arrived on the twelfth tee in the final round, even though Arnie was well ahead of me. Sitting there in a cart were Bob Jones and his cofounder of the Augusta National and the Masters, Clifford Roberts. I pulled out the 8-iron and made what felt like a decent swing, only to watch in shock and horror as the ball flew low and hard to the right. It wasn't the only shank I've hit in competition, but it was definitely the most humiliating.

The despondency of that Masters failure passed quickly enough for me to finish second yet again in Houston the following week, then win the Tournament of Champions a week after that. But the Masters had definitely taken something out of the year for me. In the

U.S. Open at Congressional in Washington, won so heroically by Ken Venturi in his famous battle with heat exhaustion, I finished a pathetic seventeen strokes back, not as embarrassing as missing the cut at Brookline the previous year, but barely less so. I perked up sufficiently to tie for third in Cleveland a week later, then managed with a struggle to hold off Gary Player by a stroke and Arnie by two to win the Whitemarsh Open in Philly, from where the three of us departed for Scotland and the British Open along with a handful of other American players.

After the embarrassment of my 1962 debut in the world's oldest golf championship at Troon, then my costly mental lapse the next year at Royal Lytham, I had been greatly looking forward to playing "The" Open for the first time at the home of golf, St. Andrews. I had frequently heard that golfers either loved or loathed the Old Course at their first encounter with it, and very much wanted it to be the former in my case. After overcoming my initial shock at its tightness, blindness and boniness, I did indeed fall in love with the course during my practice rounds, and particularly the sense of living history I got from the way it began and ended in the heart of the charming old town, almost as the focal point of the community. In fact, those good feelings, combined with the buzz of the Whitemarsh win, lifted me into probably my best competitive frame of mind of the year.

I played as well as I expected to that week, but, as can so easily happen with Britain's helter-skelter climate and its championship's large starting fields and thus long opening days, I was unlucky with the weather. In the first round I had a late starting time and in the second round an early one, which exactly coincided with the worst winds I have experienced in more than thirty British Opens. With gusts exceeding sixty miles per hour, it was sometimes a struggle to remain standing, never mind swing a golf club. Two players reported having bunker shots blown back over their heads, and, with the wind moving balls around on the greens, all of us had to play catch as catch can with the putter to avoid being penalized for hitting a ball in motion. In the U.S. we might have postponed the round, but the Scots are so used to big winds and rain that the thought probably never entered their heads ("If its nae windy, it's nae goff," one old boy fighting to hang onto his hat confided to me). I worked my tail off those first thirty-six holes, but, with 77 putts in rounds of 76-74, ended up nine strokes adrift of Tony Lema, who, with exactly opposite starting times to mine, had been fortunate to miss the worst of the wind.

To have any chance after that I needed a fast start in the third round, and got one in much improved conditions with birdies at the first, fourth, seventh, ninth, and twelfth holes. Scores in those days were posted in Britain showing the player's relationship to "level fours." As I walked down the thirteenth fairway, Tony was coming up number six. Looking at his scoreboard, I saw that he was two over fours to my seven under fours, meaning my hot streak had pulled us even at that point. I went on to finish well with six pars and a birdie for a then course record of 66, but seeing how we stood as we passed obviously inspired Tony, because he proceeded to make seven straight threes around "The Loop" on his way to an impressive 68. I matched that in the final round, but was no threat to him as he locked up a famous victory with a solid 70.

This was Lema's first visit to Scotland and his first experience of links golf, and he had arrived in St. Andrews with time enough for only one and a half practice rounds over the Old Course, then as now regarded as golf's toughest to learn. Those factors made his victory one of the most stunning in the championship's history to most British fans. What they perhaps failed to take into account was how superbly Tony was playing at that time, and how confident he had become in his game as the result of winning three of his last five tournaments back home.

Most U.S. analysts believed this run of successes, culminating with a major championship, was the beginning of Lema's rise to the superstar status that had seemed within his grasp for some time, and his likableness as a person and overcoming of humble origins made most golf fans hope they were correct. A native of Oakland, California, a notoriously tough town, Tony had shown up in his caddying days for his first tournament at a local muni in a pair of sneakers so full of holes that Ethel Venturi, Ken's mother, took up a collection to buy him his first pair of golf shoes. A marine in the Korean War, he developed a taste for the high life once golf brought him the wherewithal, as exemplified by his practice of treating writers to champagne following victories. Although we never became close, I enjoyed Tony a lot whenever we played together, and agree with the general consensus that his death in July of 1966 at age thirty-two, in a private plane that crashed while attempting an emergency landing on a golf course in Lansing, Illinois, robbed golf of one of its finest self-made players and most colorful characters.

DISAPPOINTED by a second straight near miss in this, for me, the most elusive of the four major championships, I rushed home from Scotland determined to have it all together for family and friends in the PGA, being played the following week almost in my backyard at the Columbus Country Club. All these years later, I recall how being able to defend out of my own home conjured up a memory of my first encounter with the championship fourteen years previously.

The 1950 PGA had come to Scioto a few months after I began playing golf there. As a ten-year-old, it seemed like a great idea to get some autographs from the stars of my new sport, and Jack Grout was able to arrange for me to spend a little time in the locker room for that purpose with one of the players he knew well, Skip Alexander. After I'd gotten Sam Snead and Bob Hamilton and a few others to sign, Skip walked me over to Lloyd Mangrum, who had won the U.S. Open four years previously and was among the favorites that week. More than forty years on, I can still see that slim, dark figure sitting at a table with a fan of cards in one hand and a glass of hooch in the other and a cigarette dangling from his lips, and recall how intimidated I was when he turned to me and gave me that famous tough look of his and snarled, "Whattya want, kid?" But he signed my autograph book, and I remember being extremely proud of my courage in standing up to such a fearsome character.

Enjoying home cooking and my own bed, I started well in the 1964 PGA with a 67, and finished even better with a 64, but my middle two rounds were not good enough. Arnie and I tied, which was nice, but we were both in second place, three strokes back of Bobby Nichols. It was, of course, the first of three occasions when Arnold came close to the one title he needed to have won all four of the major championships.

And so this first year of no major victories and so many near misses continued: third in the Western, fourth in the American Golf Classic, a win again in Portland, tied for third in the Sahara Invitational. As in the previous year, my last outing was the Cajun Classic in Louisiana. I'm sure I played down there as much for the Creole cooking I loved as the competition, but, with Arnie finishing fourth, it was fun to nip him by $83.13 for year's top money winner. Yet that final tournament really made me hot under the collar. Yeah, you've got it. Runner-up for the seventh time that year.

I WOULD finish second an awful lot more times over the years ahead—in fact, I recall someone telling me right after the 1984 Doral-Eastern Open that I had just done so for the fifty-fifth time. What I remember more clearly about that Doral is how much it reminded me of the period immediately ahead of the 1965 Masters. That's because, although I scored pretty well in losing at Doral to Tom Kite by two strokes, every day I felt like some new little fault had crept into my swing, sending me three evenings out of the four in search of help from Jack Grout.

Does Jack Nicklaus taking lessons during a tournament surprise you? You thought only high-handicappers did things like that? Well, spend some time at the driving range at any tour event and you will quickly learn that the pros, at their level of golf, do as much searching for swing magic as Joe Blow does at his. In fact, as purses have climbed and competition intensified over recent years, an intriguing phenomenon of the tour is how many of its members have acquired personal instructors for both swing mechanics and mind-work, to a point where it sometimes seems there are more "gurus" than golfers on the driving ranges these days. The reason for the swing instructors, of course, is the same one that sends you to the local pro: just when a fellow thinks he's finally "got it," along comes another problem, and there he is, scrambling around for the "secret" yet again. (There isn't a secret to golf, of course, but no real player will ever believe that.) As for the psychologists, well, never having had one myself, I'm not sure of what they do or how they do it. What does seem certain is that they have helped many players better handle pressure, particularly when "coming down the stretch," and in that regard I say more power to them.

Generally, the little mechanical hitches that afflict tour players are minor compared with those of the average golfer, but they have to be attended to for three reasons. First, of course, is their immediate effect: Even the tiniest flaw can be the difference between a 65 and a 75 on any given day. Second is their long-term effect: If you let a minor swing problem go unfixed for too long, it usually turns into a major one. Third is their impact on confidence: However small a mechanical problem, once you know it exists, it will always inject doubt into your shotmaking.

For much of the winter and spring ahead of the 1964 Masters I had fought a tension problem in my right wrist and forearm that did not abate until the middle of the summer, when, desperate after my sad showing in the U.S. Open at Congressional, I finally strengthened my right hand grip a little—moved my right hand a little more to the right on the club. Although this eased the sense of restriction in my wrist action, I never really liked the new positioning because I suspected that, sooner or later, it would cause me to start hooking shots. Sure enough, two weeks ahead of the 1965 Masters, at Jacksonville (second again!), I began doing just that, particularly on tee shots. Up in Augusta, where I had immediately gone for my customary on-site practice, the hook got worse, so I decided to fly down to Miami and see Jack Grout. He appeared to have fixed the problem on the La Gorce practice tee by having me swing my hands higher on the backswing. However, when I returned to the golf course at Augusta the next day, there she was again, the blue-flamer way off to the left. Then, as happened so many times during those early years, along came salvation in the shape of Deane Beman.

As a small and not particularly strong individual, Deane early on in his golfing endeavors had recognized that he needed to develop a deep understanding of cause and effect in the swing in order to get the most out of what physical resources he possessed. The knowledge so acquired enabled him to fix his own problems faster than most players I have known, and it also gave him a fine eye for other players' flaws. "Jack," he told me, after we'd hunted for yet another of my drives in the left boonies, "you're doing something I've never seen you do before. Your feet are lined up perfectly, but just before you start back you're closing your shoulders and hips. Coming down, that's forcing you to either block out with your body or roll the club over too fast with your hands."

Bingo! Right on the nose. By the end of that round, every shot I hit felt sweet off the clubface and flew to the target with the gentlest of fades. Riding on cloud nine, I went home to Columbus for two days, hit balls for only an hour on each of them, then returned to Augusta on the Monday evening. The next day I played my last complete practice round with Ben Hogan and, if memory serves, relieved him of a few dollars—an achievement generally regarded by tour regulars of that time as equivalent to winning the Grand Slam. I had shot an almost error-free 67. On Wednesday for my final tune-up I played nine holes in 33 strokes.

Alive to the lessons of 1964 regarding becoming excessively excited by the prospect of the Masters, I had tried all of that spring simply to let it sit in the back of my mind as just another week to take in stride. Now, with Lady Luck sending her blessing so opportunely via Mr. Beman, on the eve of the tournament I felt calm, relaxed, and about as prepared physically as I ever had before a major championship.

IN the nearly forty years I have competed in the Masters, I can't remember the Augusta National course playing quite as benignly, condition- and weather-wise, as it did for three out of four days in 1965. We had a strong breeze on the Friday, but apart from that, conditions were flawless. The fairways were immaculate, the greens like pool tables, the thousands of trees and shrubs that make the course golf's loveliest arboretum all in peak leaf and bloom. It was simply gorgeous.

My opening shot was not in harmony with the setting: The Nervous Nicklaus Masters First Tee Howling Left-to-Left Blue Darter away into the tall timber. However, I had a clear line to the green and stuck an 8-iron eight feet from the flagstick. Then, as I got down over the putt, my nerves played up again—badly. I just did not want to stroke the ball. I stepped back and regrouped, trying to force myself into a positive frame of mind. When the putt dropped dead center, suddenly all the fear and tension evaporated. From then on, the closest I came to a mistake from tee to green was a slightly pulled short-iron to the seventeenth hole that finished barely off the putting surface. It all added up to a 67, which left me two shots behind Gary Player and tied with Dan Sikes, Tony Lema and Tommy Aaron. Easy hole locations combined with the ideal scoring conditions had enabled the boys to make mincemeat of the course. There were ten scores under 70 and thirty-one under par—a then unprecedented happening at Augusta National.

Although Bob Jones was the inspiration for and, until his death in 1971, the dominating presence at the Masters, the man who did most of the work that built the tournament into golf's most glamorous occasion was Clifford Roberts. Once he had attained what he regarded as a reasonable measure of financial security as a New York investment banker, Mr. Roberts—very few people called him "Cliff"—devoted himself to the Masters and the Augusta National club with a passion and a perfectionism probably unique in the history of sports. The all-time supremo of the "benevolent dictators" who have been the force behind so many of America's finest pure golf clubs, Mr. Roberts liked to have things his own way, and one of the things he was always adamant about was the positioning of the holes during the Masters. There were, Mr. Roberts insisted, only four different cup locations on each green consistent with the original Alister Mackenzie/Bob Jones design plus later modifications. Although these surely were mixed up from round to round, they were never ever toughened or eased relative to what the fellows had shot the previous day.

Well, not to take issue with a good friend long gone to his reward, all I can say is that Mr. Roberts never convinced the players or the more knowledgeable members of the press on this point, and certainly not on the Friday of the 1965 Masters. The wind was a factor in the high scoring that day, but the hole locations were much the bigger one. They were night and day tougher than in the opening round—I'd have said brutally "tucked" at any other tournament—and they took a heavy toll. Only one golfer—Arnold Palmer, with a 68—broke 70, and only three others beat the par of 72. They were the Australian Kel Nagle, the PGA champion Bobby Nichols, and that beefy young guy from Ohio, Jack William Nicklaus.

Things had gone reasonably well for me until the eleventh green, where I arrived two under par for the day, making me seven under for the tournament and alone in the lead. There at eleven I looked up on a chip shot, and did the same on the twelfth hole for a second straight bogey. With steam jetting from my ears, I then attempted a stupid second shot at the thirteenth, trying to hit the ball 230 yards with the 3-wood off pine needles and an acute sidehill lie. It plopped into the creek to complete a trio of bogeys. That got my brain functioning again, and I was able to finish strongly with birdies at fifteen and sixteen for a 71 and joint leadership with Arnold and Gary. But, having literally split the fairways and hit the ball exceptionally long and felt good with the putter, the sting of that sloppy patch around what the dean of American golf writers, Herbert Warren Wind, so aptly christened "Amen Corner" stayed with me long into the evening.

And yet, deep down inside, I also felt upbeat that evening—exhilarated even. The reason had nothing to do with my golf game or scores, but everything to do with the atmosphere in which I had played the first two rounds. For no reason that I could perceive, suddenly at this 1965 Masters I was no longer golf's Black Hat. For the first time in my career, right from the opening drive on Thursday, entire galleries had rooted for me. "Go get 'em, Jack!" and "Attaboy, big fella!" and "Birdie every hole!" people had yelled all the way around, and the same on Friday.

At first, I could hardly believe it, especially with Arnie so much in contention, and I was sure it wouldn't last. When it did, I became as charged up as I ever had been on a golf course to that point in my career. I wanted to play well for those wonderful people, to tear the place apart for them. The more they encouraged me, the more relaxed and responsive I became, and the harder they then rooted for me. By Friday evening, some of the more reserved types among those huge crowds must have thought I'd turned into a grinning, nodding, waving, chuckling, babbling idiot, but I just had to show how much I appreciated this sudden and unexpected about-face. It was a most moving experience, and, I now realize, one of the great turning points in my career.

There is no question about the impact all this had on my performance in the final two rounds of that Masters. I was on my stick, for sure: Only in the World Team Championship at Merion and the Amateur Championship at Pebble Beach five and four years previously had I felt as absolutely "right" with my swing and as infallibly sharp in my strategical decisions. But now the galleries had added an extra dimension, and it lifted my desire to an all-time peak. Now I knew how Arnie had felt through all those years as four-star general of his clamoring "Army," and why he could raise his game so high on the biggest occasions, and it made me want to reward these newfound friends of mine with the same sort of show.

I had never before and have never since played quite as fine a complete round of golf in a major championship as I did on Saturday, April 10, in the third round of the 1965 Masters. There were a couple of small slips early on, and one particularly lucky break, but all in all I drove the ball great distances, hit it virtually dead straight with the irons, putted the eyes out of it, never fumbled a strategy decision, never was nervous, felt all the while as though golf were the simplest of human activities, wanted to go on murdering par for ever and a day, and had an absolute ball. My final score was 64, eight under par, which tied the then course record set by Lloyd Mangrum in the Masters twenty-five years previously. Conditions were perfect, of course. I'm so proud of that round even all this time later that I can't resist recalling it blow-by-blow:

1. *400 yards, par four.* Perfect drive, sand wedge blown too far by the wind, fifty-foot putt to six inches. Par.

2. *555 yards, par five.* Worst drive of tournament, pushed into trees right, but found an opening—luckiest break of tournament. Three-iron to within 110 yards of green, pitching wedge to twenty-five feet, one putt. Birdie, one under par.

3. *355 yards, par four.* 250-yard 3-wood, pitching wedge to ten feet, two putts. Par.

4. *220 yards, par three.* Four-iron caught slightly fat, eight-foot putt. Birdie, two under.

5. *450 yards, par four.* Perfect drive, 175-yard 6-iron (would normally have been a 5-iron but the adrenaline was rising), two putts from twenty feet. Par.

6. *190 yards, par three.* Six-iron to twenty feet, one putt. Birdie, three under.

7. *365 yards, par four.* Super drive, even better wedge to two feet. Tap-in birdie, four under.

8. *530 yards, par five.* Big drive (320 yards), 3-iron, eighty-foot putt to eighteen inches. Birdie, five under.

9. *420 yards, par four.* Another 320-yard drive, over trees to bottom of hill. Pitching wedge to twenty feet, two putts. Par. Out in 31, five under par.

10. *480 yards, par four.* Another big drive, 8-iron to twenty feet (I'd have needed a 6-iron but for the adrenaline), two putts. Par.

11. *445 yards, par four.* Big drive again, and another 8-iron, hit deliberately to right side of green to be certain of no water trouble. Two putts from fifty feet. Par.

12. *155 yards, par three.* Perfect 8-iron to five feet, then too excited on the putt, which had no chance. Par.

13. *475 yards, par five.* Super drive drawn around corner of dogleg, 5-iron, two putts from forty-five feet. Birdie, six under.

14. *420 yards, par four.* Drive kicked right into rough. Seven-iron punched under tree limb and bounced onto green. Two putts from twenty-two feet. Par.

15. *520 yards, par five.* Killed the driver (330 yards), but pulled it left a fraction, finishing behind stand of trees. Hooked 5-iron to just off right side of green, pitching-wedge chip to eight inches. Tap-in birdie, seven under.

16. *190 yards, par three.* Six-iron to eight feet short of pin, putt dead in the heart. Birdie, eight under.

17. *400 yards, par four.* Solid drive, 8-iron that spun back to seventy feet from cup, two putts. Par.

18. *420 yards, par four.* My longest tee shot ever on this hole, faded 320 yards around the dogleg. Pulled pitching wedge to left side of green after backing off for fan in a low-flying airplane. Two putts from twenty-five feet for par. Back in 33 for a record-tying 64.

The stats are as follows. Ten pars and eight birdies. Three twos, two threes, thirteen fours, and no fives. Thirty-four tee-to-green shots, missing only two fairways and one green. One chip, no pitches, no bunker or other recovery shots. Thirty putts, the longest holed from twenty-five feet. Six-iron the biggest club used on par-four approach shots, and 3-iron the longest to reach a par five.

Somebody said after the round that I had played the 6,900-yard Augusta National course about the way you'd expect a good pro to handle an undemanding 5,900-yard country club layout on a perfect day. It certainly felt that way, and, with the adrenaline flowing like a gusher and the crowds rooting me on as never before, I loved every moment of it.

IN the Masters official record book the following words appear for the year 1953: "Ben Hogan believes that in the 1953 Masters he played the best golf of his career. Masters Tournament officials are of the opinion that Ben achieved the best seventy-two-hole stretch of golf ever played by anyone anywhere. Ideal weather and favorable scoring conditions on greens and fairways, plus a perfection brand of golf on each one of the four days of play, enabled Ben to break the tournament record by five shots. At the time it was questioned if such a combination of favorable factors would ever again be experienced during the whole of a tournament. Ben's record of 274 appeared to be difficult to better."

You just know, from the understatement in the last sentence, that this could only have been authored by one person—Clifford Roberts. I quote it because of the subject matter, the seventy-two-hole Masters record, which seemed about the only topic of conversation around Augusta National that Saturday night.

My 64 had given me a lead of five strokes over Player and eight over Palmer, and the mood immediately following the round seemed to be that I had already won the 1965 Masters, leaving Ben's record as the only issue to be resolved. I did not share those sentiments, and I did my best in the media interviews—without much success, I'm afraid to dispel them. As I have mentioned before, and probably will again, counting your chickens at golf ahead of the final stroke is always foolish and frequently dangerous in that, almost without fail, it produces defensive play. On top of that was the fact that I have always been win-conscious, not scoring-record-conscious. It's certainly nice to have the asterisk against your name as the course or tournament record-holder, but the reality is that in a game like golf, involving such huge variations in playing arenas and conditions, the total number of shots struck, beyond where it places you, is of academic interest only. Nobody but the stats nuts really remembers who scored the lowest, any more than the man in the street remembers who finished second. That's why I will always play conservatively if necessary to win, even though by so doing I'll miss breaking a record.

This was my thinking beginning the final round of the 1965 Masters. I knew a 71 would give me the asterisk, and reflected for a moment while loosening up that the conditions were certainly conducive to such a score—warm and sunny again with only the lightest of breezes. Much more prominent in my mind, however, was the number I needed to be absolutely sure of winning. With Gary and Arnold leading the pursuers, I figured it might have to be better than 70. If I could shoot 64, so could they. That was fine, because having something in the sixties as a target would force me to play "intelligently aggressively" from my opening shot. That it would also break the Masters record was an incidental bonus.

This thought process paid off handsomely. I birdied the first hole, followed up with two pars, then slipped down a tricky fifteen-footer for another birdie at the always dangerous long par-three fourth hole. A bogey followed, but, with solid pars after that, I reached the turn in 35. Then, checking the huge leader board off to the side of the eighteenth fairway as I walked to the tenth tee, I got some excellent news. No one was making any kind of a run at me. Short of breaking a leg, it would now be pretty difficult to lose.

In the 1963 Masters, I had tried my darndest to do just that at the twelfth hole, and the following year on the Saturday had, as mentioned, ruined a little tilt at Arnold by embarrassingly shanking my tee shot there. Now, following careful pars at ten and eleven, I decided as I stood on the twelfth tee looking at the flagstick, tucked tight behind the right bunker, that another unheroic par would do just fine. "Heart of the green, fella," I told myself as I set up over the 8-iron, and dropped the ball right there, about twenty-five feet from the hole. Surveying the putt, I felt good about the line I'd chosen, and there was that lovely solid feeling as the ball came off the putt-erface. Plop.

It occurred to me as I picked the ball out of the cup that I had now birdied seven times in fifteen attempts on the par threes. "Nicklaus," I said to myself, "this is blasphemous. People are simply not supposed to do things like that at Augusta National." The excitement was almost uncontainable, and especially as this seventh birdie two had increased my lead to eight strokes. Walking to the thirteenth tee, for the first time I felt 100-percent confident that I would win, and for the first time allowed myself to think seriously about the seventy-two-hole record. I was now sixteen under par, which meant that regulation scores on the remaining holes would improve on Ben's total by two strokes.

Two of the pars came routinely at thirteen and fourteen. At fifteen, probably now a little too conscious of the record, I overhit my first putt going for eagle from twenty-five feet, and missed the five-footer coming back for my only three-putt of the week. Sixteen I parred, then at seventeen came an unexpected bonus when I almost holed my 9-iron approach. After that, anything worse than a par at the final hole, seemingly twenty-deep in people from tee to green, would have been anticlimactic and embarrassing, and once again the butterflies began fluttering in my stomach. But the par came safely for a round of 69, giving me the record by three strokes with a four-round total of 271 (which Ray Floyd would equal in 1976).

A little later, waiting for the televised green jacket presentation ceremony in the Butler Cabin, I watched a replay of my final approach shot, and realized from the time I took to hit it just how nervous I'd been. I wiggled and waggled, and adjusted my cap, and hitched my pants, and studied the lie and the green and the wind, and looked generally as though this was the most critical golf shot I had ever confronted. Watching myself go through all of this on television was unbearable. "Holy cow," I remember saying, "I wish I'd just go ahead and hit the ball!"

EVERY major championship victory remains indelible for me, but there was a special joy in this second success at Augusta National. For one thing, I had beaten Gary and Arnold, the two golfers who gave me the most trouble in those days, and by nine strokes (their 280s would have won the Masters seventeen out of the previous twenty-eight times). Secondly, I had had a sense after the 1963 Masters that I'd sort of backed into it with some not particularly good golf, rather than gone out and flat won it. There could be no doubts in that regard this time. Most important, there were Bob Jones's many flattering, widely quoted, and inspiring remarks, including a line that seems to have stuck in the game's lore: "Jack is playing an entirely different game—a game I'm not even familiar with."

Then, back home relaxing and preparing for our third child (Nan was born May 5 that year), for the first time I genuinely felt that I had "arrived"—that at last I had utilized to their fullest capacity the golfing gifts I had been given, and in so doing had fulfilled both my own expectations and those of the many friends who had so faithfully supported and encouraged me over the years.

Most of all, though, there were the fans. It was obvious from their treatment of me that I was at last beginning to emerge from the shadow of Arnold, and was becoming a golfer people could enjoyably follow and yell and holler and whoop for. I had hit the shots in Augusta that week, but the ten or twenty or thirty thousand people who had watched them were more responsible for the way those shots came out than they will ever know. Each time I thought about it all for weeks afterward, a lump formed in my throat.

As my dad said, everyone likes to be liked.

7

The 1966 Masters Tournament

Winning at Its Hardest

I HAVE argued many times over the years that golf for the ambitious player is a continual learning process. The older I've gotten, the more convinced I've become about that. The reason lies in the almost infinite spectrum of knowledge and skills the game demands to be played expertly.

Most recreational golfers see mastering the full swing as golf's supreme challenge, and there can be no questioning its importance. I never have stopped developing new insights on the full swing, and I'm sure I will continue discovering different ways to finesse the short shots and get out of trouble and fine-tune a putting stroke as long as I keep playing.

Once a golfer has developed and ingrained a fundamentally sound method, however, by far the biggest mountain he has left to climb is learning how to win. Thankfully, I had gotten an excellent grounding in this department of the game as an amateur. Nevertheless, with the extra pressure of playing for my living and against stiffer competition, I quickly found I was still some distance from becoming a Ph.D. in the art of winning when I first joined the professional tour.

The ability to win is not easy to describe. The more obvious attributes are certainly major contributors: confidence, concentration, desire, discipline, willpower, patience, love of competition, lack of fear (of success, perhaps, even more than of failure). Yet the fact that many athletes who appear to possess these qualities in spades, plus all of the necessary physical skills, still do not win consistently suggests that they aren't quite the whole story. If more is involved, precisely what is it? With the benefit these days of perfect hindsight, I would pinpoint four qualities that seem to be shared by all consistent winners, at least insofar as golf is concerned.

Number one is the ability to think clearly under pressure. Stress and tension tend to fuzz up the mental machinery, which leads to errors in shotmaking strategy and/or execution, generally as the result of impaired observation or muddled analysis, or both. A mind that can focus more sharply and exclusively on the tasks and routines required in the playing of the game under the greatest competitive heat is a mighty asset to a golfer. If I had to pick the attribute that contributed most heavily to my golfing successes, this would be it.

Number two is patience. Impatience breeds hastiness, and the hastier you get the less clearly and coolly you are able to think. I have seen a lot of tournaments given away, not because the giver was innately stupid, but because he played dumbly as the result of becoming impatient. And, of course, I have done that myself a few times. Like so many cliches, the ones about the impossibility of forcing golf scores or victories are also truisms. The moment you begin pushing too hard at golf is the moment the game nails you to the mast. To avoid that, you must have the patience to wait for your true scoring opportunities.

Number three is self-centeredness. The only thing a player can control at golf is his own game, so concern about what other competitors may or may not be doing is both a useless distraction and a waste of energy. The biggest winners in my time in golf have invariably competed with blinders on about everything other than making their own best possible numbers. The supreme example of this has to be Ben Hogan commenting to Claude Harmon, as they walked off number twelve at Augusta National in a Masters after Claude had aced it, that the birdie he, Hogan, had made there was his first on the hole—in other words, Ben was too self-absorbed to notice even a hole-in-one. Not far behind might be Jack Nicklaus becoming so self-focused in the final round on the way to his 1966 British Open win that he forgot to mark down any scores for his playing partner, his good friend Phil Rodgers. Although I've rarely been able to get quite that deep in my shell, there have been many occasions when I have deliberately avoided looking at leader boards, or, if I did glance at them, took in only the numbers without connecting them to names. A lot of people might call this sort of thing selfishness rather than self-centeredness or self-absorbedness or self-focusedness, and especially when it happens beyond the competitive arena. Be that as it may, it is a major factor in finishing first.

The fourth and final quality on my list of essentials for winning is simply working harder at all of the above when you are playing poorly than when you are playing well.

Meeting such challenges is never easy, but to me the urge and the struggle to do so are what competing at sports is all about. That's because, when I succeeded, excepting the birth of my children, the emotional high was my single biggest thrill in life—certainly way beyond anything I could ever hope for from money or any other form of material reward. And the reason, of course, is not—as many might believe—that I have whipped up on all those other people, but that I have conquered the toughest opponent of all: Myself.

IN the 1965 Masters I was never hard pressed and won easily. In 1966, after a good opening round, I rarely looked like winning, but finally managed to do so, making me the first and, until Nick Faldo's victories in 1989–90, the only golfer to successfully defend at the Augusta National. I believe this was one of the times when I was best able to meet the mental and emotional challenges I have just described.

The 1966 Masters was a troubled tournament for me in quite a number of ways.

To begin with, having played only four tour events since the beginning of the year, I was far from sure that I was adequately prepared. This lack of competitive play had its roots in the staleness with golf I had again experienced at the end of the 1965 season, accentuated as it was by memories of poor performances in the other three majors after the euphoria of a second Masters victory. Following Augusta, I had won four more times, at Memphis, Westchester, Philadelphia and Portland, and completed the season as top money winner again. But I had also finished tied for thirty-first in the U.S. Open at Bellerive in St. Louis, seventeen strokes behind Gary Player; tied for twelfth in the British Open at baked-out, bone-hard, self-igniting (truly—the course caught fire one day) Royal Birkdale, nine strokes back of Peter Thomson; and tied for second in the PGA at Laurel Valley, two strokes adrift of Dave Marr. All in all, I had played tournament golf more than half the weeks of the year, and rushed hither and yon for other engagements seemingly most other weeks. By the end of the year Barbara had convinced me—without much effort—that, if I hoped to be a factor in golf past my midtwenties, I had better start thinking about getting some rest and an occasional complete change of scenery.

Gary Player and his wife, Vivienne, and Barbara and I had become close friends by then, and the Players had been suggesting for some time that we visit with them in their native South Africa. When Gary raised the subject again, I needed no further persuasion. With my father and mother and Barbara's parents, we spent most of February in that beautiful country, sightseeing, fishing, and hunting, and generally taking our ease at the Players' lovely home in Johannesburg. There was golf in the shape of six challenge matches between Gary and me, in which he cleaned my clock. But, overall, it was a relaxing and therapeutic trip that did much to restore my enthusiasm for tournament play. It left, however, a couple of residual problems.

Because of its frequency of use and role in setting up the play of most par-four and par-five holes, the driver is, after the putter, the most "personal" club in the bag for every good golfer. In a practice round before the first challenge match with Gary at the Zwartkop Country Club in Pretoria, the head of the driver I had been using since my fifth pro tournament in 1962 split in half as I hit the ball off the eighth tee. (It was an unlucky spot, because the next day there in the match proper we were attacked by a swarm of bees that stung both of us a number of times.) By the time the Masters came along I had tried more than twenty drivers with supposedly identical specifications, but without finding one with precisely the feel of my old faithful. The final replacement was "okay," but I wanted my tools to be a little more than that going into the year's first major championship.

The other problem was the limited amount of competition I had been able to get in ahead of the Masters.

I am sure there are plenty of golfers who can prepare adequately for big events by beating a lot of balls on driving ranges and playing regularly at their home courses, but that sort of regimen has never worked for me. I have certainly needed adequate practice-tee time for eliminating faults or fine-tuning my swing or mastering special flight patterns, but knowing I can tee up again without penalty when I've missed a shot makes heavy ball-beating of little value in my case as preparation for competitive play. The same applies to rounds of golf at home: "There she goes, deep in the woods again, darn it, so let's just drop another ball. . ." There is simply not enough incentive in that kind of golf, not enough challenge, not enough pressure, to prepare me for the real thing. To be able to compete at my best, I have to have competed. In 1966, although I'd practiced amply from the new year on, I had teed up for real only at the Crosby, Doral, the Florida Citrus Open, and in Jacksonville. That sent me on my way to Augusta the week ahead of the Masters with a distinct unease about my readiness.

As was by then becoming customary, before heading for Georgia I had gone down to Miami Beach for a session with Jack Grout at La Gorce. There, we felt we had once again corrected the problem Deane Beman had spotted the previous year, and that I would eventually have to learn to continually guard against: setting my feet correctly parallel to the target line, but then involuntarily closing my shoulders to that line just before starting the club back. It became apparent after only a few holes in Augusta, however, that my tee-to-green game was far from healthy.

Following the 1965 Masters, someone had computed that I had played my last fourteen rounds at Augusta National in fifty-five strokes under par (composed of concluding tournament rounds in 1964 of 71-67, then 1965 practice rounds of 67-69-71-69-67-70-67-64, then tournament rounds of 67-71-64-69). I was proud of that string and would have dearly loved to sustain it, but it died on my first 1966 outing with a 73 born of a bunch of pull-hooked tee shots. And then, just in the nick of time, yet again came help—yes, you've guessed it—from Deane Beman. Playing the eighth hole in my second practice round, I dragged another drive badly left into the trees. "Here's your problem," pronounced old eagle-eyes. "You're taking the club back nice and slowly—fine tempo. But then you're speeding up too much starting down, with the result that your shoulders are coming out and over way too fast. Just try to feel that you're starting down to the ball with the same nice easy tempo that you started back from it." Bingo! Bye-bye pull, bye-bye hook. I completed that round in 69, added another 69 the next day, then flew home to Columbus for the weekend much happier and more relaxed than when I'd arrived.

SINCE my amateur days, when, courtesy of the Augusta National club, I hung out with the rest of the amateurs in the Crow's Nest, the dormitory at the top of the clubhouse just below its famous cupola, it has been our custom to rent a private home close to the course for the week of the Masters. Because this arrangement allows me to relax and rest more by getting entirely away from the frenetic extracurricular activities of the big events, while permitting us to live as we do at home, I have also preferred it for most other major championship weeks. Another reason for this preference is that it facilitates the company of close friends in an informal, relaxed atmosphere. Both Barbara and I enjoy company, especially that of people we can be entirely ourselves and at ease with. Thus, from the beginning, Pandel Savic and his late wife Janice, two of our closest friends from Columbus, regularly shared the Augusta house with us and in more recent years were joined by John and Nancy Montgomery, two of our best Florida friends.

Pandel, who was born in Macedonia and came to the States at the age of ten, was a star quarterback at Ohio State, leading the team to a famous Rose Bowl victory in 1950. We first became acquainted around that time when, seeing me help myself to candy in Dad's drugstore and not knowing I was the owner's son, he snitched on me to my dad. "Sav"—his given name is Pandelis Michailo Bogosavlevich, about which I love to tease him—has long been a fine amateur golfer, and since its inception has served outstandingly as General Chairman of the Memorial Tournament. He's also the guy who, earlier in 1966, on account of my highly vocal expertise about a whole slew of sports techniques on a vacation in Baja California, gave me a nickname that unfortunately has stuck with other friends exposed to my Carnac tendencies, namely "La Boca Grande." Knowing me so well has contributed a lot to the friendship we've enjoyed for more than forty years.

Big John Montgomery is the founder and nowadays the chairman of Executive Sports, Inc., the leading concern in the staging of professional golf tournaments around the world, which in 1995 became a part of Golden Bear International. "Senior," as we mostly call him, probably knows as many people in golf, particularly the pros, as anyone on this planet, and there isn't a more down-to-earth, genuine and popular individual in the game. He, too, was once a football star, at Duke, followed by a stint in the FBI, but his great joys today are fishing and hunting; in fact, he's the most passionate outdoorsman I've ever encountered, which has contributed to the close bond between us. He's also the most offbeat and extravagant gift-giver I have ever met, to the point where Barbara and I have learned to dread his frequently off-the-wall remembrances of our birthdays.

For most of the years I've played in the Masters, another friend from my earliest golfing days at Scioto, Bob Hoag, has made the pilgrimage, a few times with his wife, Louise, but usually as the leader of a somewhat boisterous stag group of mutual friends from Columbus, which explains why he doesn't stay with us. Bob is one of those people who always marches to his own drummer, but, once you get past his eccentricities, you find a fellow who never has and never will fail a friend in need. Like Pandel with the Memorial, Bob is a strong force in the affairs of Muirfield Village Golf Club, of which he is the long-serving chairman. Like Pandel also, he has never forgotten his first encounter with me.

As Hoagy tells it, he had just played his second shot to the par-five sixteenth hole at Scioto one summer day back in 1953 and was walking toward the green when a golf ball bounced between his legs. A past champion of the club, Bob was then one of the longest hitters in the state of Ohio, and maybe the entire Midwest. "Who in the world was that?" he asked one of the fellows he was playing with. When told it was the Nicklaus kid, Hoagy asked how old I was. "Thirteen," his friend told him.

Bob says his response was "No way," because he just did not believe anyone so young could hit a golf ball that far. He discovered someone could when he came and talked to me after I completed the round, following which we played a lot of golf together, frequently ruining our scores by trying to outslug each other. We have sparred off the course, too, which has led to Hoagy cracking some funny lines about me. I guess his best one comes from our years of pairing up in the Crosby pro-am without ever making the team cut.

"If Nicklaus would only get his game in shape," he used to tell everybody, "we'd kill 'em in the team tournament." Well, I want the whole world to know that when I finally did "get my game in shape" and won the Crosby for the first time in 1967, we still missed the cut in the team event—about which Hoagy ever since, of course, has taken merciless ragging.

Ivor Young and his wife, Carol, whom I had also met in my teens through golf at Scioto, were other frequent Masters attendees, and it was from a conversation between Ivor and me in 1966 in Augusta that Muirfield Village Golf Club and the Memorial Tournament took shape. The lore is that Ivor and I were sitting chatting under the famous old oak tree behind the Augusta National clubhouse or on its veranda. The truth is that, after drifting off by ourselves one evening after dinner at our rented house, we began talking about how great the Masters was, and how terrific it would be if something similar could be created in Columbus. I mentioned how the success of the PGA Championship played at the Columbus Country Club a couple of years previously had exceeded everyone's expectations, and Ivor made the point that the city had only one major sports attraction, Ohio State football six times each fall, despite its constant population and industrial growth. Finally, we became so enthusiastic about the idea of doing something with golf in Columbus that I asked Ivor if he would be willing to look for a site for a really fine course in or around the city, which he agreed to do. Although the idea of staging a professional golf event in my hometown had crossed my mind before—in fact, had come up the previous Christmas in Pandel and Janice's kitchen—it was Ivor beginning to hunt down the land that really got us going.

That conversation between Ivor and me is typical of our Masters week evenings. We'll sometimes talk peripherally around golf, but rarely about the playing of it, and almost never about my game. These days, Sav and Senior will take a "shooter" or two, and other friends and members of my business team will stop by to do the same or join us for dinner. No one stands on ceremony, the needles usually flash a lot in an amiable way, everyone hits the sack early and usually in good spirits, and the sociability makes the week one of the most pleasant of the year for Barbara and me, regardless of my golf scores.

We had enjoyed just such an evening on Wednesday, April 6, 1966, and were about to go to bed when the telephone rang and we received devastating news. Flying down from Columbus to watch their first Masters, two of our dearest friends, Bob and Linda Barton, along with some friends of theirs, Jim and Jeretta Long, had been killed when their private plane crashed near Johnson City, Tennessee. An air force reserve pilot with over four thousand cockpit hours, Bob had been flying the plane, a leased Beach Travelair. Apparently ice had formed on the wings over the Great Smokies, then an engine had cut out. As Bob tried to get down on the remaining engine, the plane had suddenly nose-dived, perhaps as a result of further power loss. It then hit a car, cartwheeled, and burst into flames.

After first meeting at Scioto, Bob Barton and I by 1966 had played so much golf and done so much fishing and hunting and other fun things together that we had become the closest of friends, to a point where in the summer of 1962 he had organized a Jack Nicklaus Day in Columbus following my U.S. Open win. He was an outstanding individual, a person I admired without reservation and in many ways tried to emulate. I had been untouched by true tragedy until the moment of that phone call, and I did not know how to handle it. Neither Barbara nor I were able to sleep much that night, and we talked about a lot of things, including whether I should withdraw from the Masters. Suddenly, golf had lost a great deal of its importance. Finally, at Barbara's urging, I decided to go ahead and play. She felt that Bob would have wanted me to, and I am sure she was right. Inevitably, there was much media commotion about the tragedy and its effects on me, but I tried to say as little as possible consistent with expressing my deep distress. I felt strongly that this was a personal matter, and, having decided to play, I wanted to minimize exploitation of the accident should I perform badly. However, much as I tried to downplay the tragedy publicly, it was continually on my mind during the tournament, and for a long time thereafter.

The final problem that week was the Augusta National golf course. If it had been at its best and easiest in 1965, it was at its worst and toughest in 1966.

Despite some heroic efforts by the greens staff, an unusually cold and dry winter had left the Augusta National's fairways as sparsely grassed as I had ever encountered them. Because of strong drying winds immediately ahead of and going into the tournament, the club decided it dare not mow as tightly as normal for fear of losing them entirely. This made for "fliers," shots carrying less backspin due to

1

At my first birthday party.

Five years old and
golf still five years away.

2

3

An extremely proud moment for a sixteen-year-old Ohioan after winning his state's Open Championship in 1956. On the right is the low professional, Earl Christiansen.

4

My dad, Charlie, and me with the Walker Cup in his pharmacy in Columbus in 1959.

My longtime teacher, motivator, and great friend Jack Grout wishes me luck as I leave Columbus for the 1959 Walker Cup match in Scotland. It was my first overseas trip.

5

6

Just married to Barbara Jean Bash—
Saturday, July 23, 1960.

Playing the last two rounds of the 1960 U.S. Open with Ben Hogan while still an amateur was an honor and a pleasure. Either of us could have won, but it was Arnold Palmer who "charged" to victory.

7

8

With two of my biggest supporters: my uncle Frank Nicklaus and my dad, in the early 1960s.

9

Despite trying to beat each other's brains out for more than thirty years, Arnold Palmer and I have remained firm friends. Here we are before our 1962 U.S. Open playoff.

10

With my father-in-law, Stanley Bash, and my father, Charlie Nicklaus, at my first World Series of Golf at Firestone in 1962. Both loved to watch me compete.

Entertaining son Steve at age two.
Our facial expressions suggest he wanted to stay and I wanted to leave.

Nothing like getting 'em started early! Son Jackie goes fishing with me—a favorite activity since my teens.

12

Am I teaching or being taught? With son Gary on our backyard putting green.

13

14

Practicing for the 1971 PGA Championship in Florida with three good friends: from the left, Gary Player, Deane Beman (later to become PGA Tour commissioner), and Tony Jacklin.

15

With daughter Nan at Carnoustie for the 1975 British Open. Nice bonnet, wee lassie!

What an athlete! Tennis has become a great love and a big part of my life outside of golf.

16

17

Barbara's and my great friend and mentor, Joe Dey, the first commissioner of what became the PGA Tour, congratulates me on winning the first Tournament Players Championship (now Players Championship) in 1974. Joe's many contributions to the game include his longtime service as executive director of the U.S. Golf Association.

18

Enjoying a laugh with two pals, Gary Player and Arnold Palmer. As fiercely as we competed, we always remained friends.

19

Time-out, final round of the 1977 British Open at Turnberry, due to a sudden storm. Always a tough adversary, Tom Watson went on to beat me by a stroke in our great head-to-head match.

20

I was so emotional about my first Memorial Tournament win in 1977 in my hometown of Columbus that I almost retired from tournament golf. Thankfully, Barbara talked me out of it before I could blab to the press.

21

With our youngest, Michael—one of my favorite photos.

22

With daughter Nan and wife Barbara after receiving an honorary doctorate at St. Andrews University, Scotland, in 1984—one of my proudest moments.

23

With my mother, Helen Nicklaus, and my sister, Marilyn Hutchinson, at the 1986 Masters. I sometimes wonder how they survived my childhood!

24

Quite a foursome at the "Golfer of the Century" award banquet in New York in 1988. With me are Patty Berg, Ben Hogan, and Arnold Palmer.

25

Daughter Nan marries Bill O'Leary in 1989. From left to right, Gary, Jack II and his wife Barbara, Dad, the happy couple, Mom, Steve, and Michael.

26

Three of my sons are involved in golf course design with me—from the left, Gary, Jackie, and Steve.

27

Jim Flick, one of golf's greatest teachers, has been a big help to me since my first instructor, Jack Grout, passed on.

28

Grandpa and Grandma Nicklaus, Christmas 1996.
The children are, from left to right, Jackie Nicklaus holding sister Casey, Nick O'Leary holding brother Bobby, Christopher O'Leary, Christie Nicklaus, Charlie Nicklaus, and Billy O'Leary.

grass intervening between clubface and ball at impact, and thus given to unpredictable behavior in terms of both trajectory and distance. Compounding this problem was the condition of the greens. They, too, were hard, dry and unreceptive, and they too had been mown less tightly than normal. In consequence, although the ball rolled a long way on tee shots, getting approaches close to the toughly located cups and putts into the hole set, for me at least, a new kind of Masters examination. One thing was certain as we wound up practice: There would be no record scores this year.

Despite my troubles, plus the seemingly standard right-to-left blue darter off number one tee, I opened my defense of the title strongly. Luckily, that opening drive somehow wiggled through the trees between the first and ninth fairways, enabling me to hit a 4-iron twenty-five feet from the hole. I got a charge when the putt dropped, then another with a six-footer for birdie at the long and always difficult par-three fourth, then an even bigger charge with a birdie at the tricky ninth hole to be out in 33. I enjoyed a second lucky break at thirteen, where my pulled drive nicked a tree but was deflected into ideal fairway position, from where I capitalized with the 4-iron again and two putts. That was it for birdies, but I had made ten routine pars and four with chips and one-putts, so the total came to 68. Under the course conditions I've described, and with the wind gusting up to thirty miles an hour, I felt it was a notable round of golf. "That's one for you, Mr. Jones," I said to myself as I went to wind down on the practice tee. No one else broke 70, so that at the end of the day I led Don January and Bill Casper by three strokes.

What a crazy, unpredictable game golf is. In the second round I played better from tee to green than I had on Thursday, but was obliged at the end of the day to hand in my highest Masters score as a pro to that point, an infuriating 76. The chief problem was putting. My touch had evaporated overnight. I missed seven times from under five feet, three-putted five times—three times from under fifteen feet—and totaled in all thirty-eight putts, the most since a round at St. Andrews in a gale in the 1964 British Open.

What really drove me nuts was that, over the ball, I had felt like I would make every one of those putts. Probably it was the frustration of this that produced the second problem: poor concentration. By the middle of the round, I was having great difficulty keeping my mind on the job at hand. The result, as always when one's focus falters, was poor judgment in shot planning. Thus, from believing at the start of the round that I might be able to run away from the field and hide, at the end of it I was tied for second with three other players, a stroke adrift of Paul Harney and the English golfer Peter Butler. Deciding that I could at least do something about the putting, I worked for two hours that evening with Bruce Devlin, the fine Australian player who had become a good friend. Bruce did his best, but they still weren't dropping as often as I would have liked when I finally dragged a weary body home for a late dinner.

RECALLING that untimely and seemingly inexplicable loss of putting touch inspires me to reflect a little on what Ben Hogan insisted was both a game unto itself and a game unrelated to true golfing skills.

Par allows for two putts per hole, and, as par is normally 72, that means putting theoretically is half the game. In actuality, it's a little less than that for both tour players and the majority of amateurs, the former because they average fewer than two putts per hole, and the latter because they take proportionately more strokes reaching greens.

Either way, though, putting has a bigger impact on scoring than most golfers are inclined to admit to themselves. It is an overstatement to say the tours are nothing more than putting contests, but it's equally true that if you can't get the ball in the hole, you will not be much of a contestant on any of them. And I guess that's true, too, of all those Saturday morning Nassaus.

The attitudes toward putting among both top golfers and nongolfers are interesting. They range all the way from Hogan's conviction that rolling the ball along the ground is not really golf, to Bobby Locke's assertion that putting is the most critical part of the game. I guess the in-between attitude is nicely typified by the comment of a high-handicapper friend of mine after following me during a tournament in Florida some years ago. I hit every fairway and green in regulation or better, and had the ball within a dozen feet of the cup eight or nine times, yet could score no better than a 68. "Boy," said my friend afterward, "that must have been frustrating. If only you could have putted, you'd have shot 62 or 63."

If only I could have putted . . . ? Well, I made five birdies by holing sizable putts, and three-putted only once from a difficult position.

But, to my average-golfer friend, all that was by the way. What impressed him was not how fortunate I had been on those five birdie putts, but how "unlucky" I'd been not to make five or six more. This mind-set explained to me why he himself was such an awful putter. His expectations were way too high.

At tournaments with many nongolfers or occasional players in the galleries, you can tell from the stunned silence when you miss anything under about twenty feet that a lot of people have unrealistic ideas about the difficulty of rolling a 1.68-inch-diameter ball into a four-and-one-quarter-inch-diameter hole over a surface of tightly mown but always slightly irregular grass. They just can't see what can be so difficult about something that looks so easy. Powder a drive 280 or more yards but deep into the weeds and these folks will "Oooh" and "Aaah" and "Yeah!" and "Wowee!" Miss from six feet and they'll look at you as though you should be in a padded cell.

What's even more intriguing is how even the best putters have a tough time looking upon this facet of the game realistically, particularly in regard to their own ability at it.

(I should explain that by "best putters" I don't mean wonderful-looking strokers of the ball, of whom there are many among nonwinners on the world's tours, but guys who can get the ball in the hole time after time when it matters the most, which is when they are going to either win or lose *right now.* Germany's Bernhard Langer is a fine example of the difference between a "wonderful putter" in a technical or esthetic sense and a golfer with tremendous ability to get the ball in the hole under maximum pressure. Two or three times Bernhard has suffered from the yips about as badly as a golfer can. The result was an ungainly looking technique worked out by and unique unto himself, but one that made him a consistent winner for a number of years.)

The best putter I have encountered in more than forty years of golf was Arnold Palmer in the late 1950s and early 1960s. To this day, however, there is no way Arnie would concede that he was ever more than half-decent on the greens. Whenever I've tried to tell him differently, his response has always been, "Boy, if I could only have putted *half* as well as *you* did . . ."

I guess the reason Arnold is so hard on himself about putting is that during his best years, when to everyone else he seemed to hole almost everything he looked at, he came to see great putting as never missing. If that's true, then he has a lot of company among tour golfers. In all the years I've been out there, I can't remember one player—myself included—admitting he was a "great" putter, and not too many who would go along even with "very good." Gardner Dickinson, who admitted after his retirement from competition that he lost tournaments purely as a result of convincing himself he was not a good putter, believes ego or "macho" plays a big part in this. Whereas, he explains, it's manly to crush out huge drives, hit towering long-irons and spin wedges tight to the pin, it's somehow a bit nerdy or wimpy to be good at rolling a ball along the ground into a hole.

Whatever the source of the I-can't-really-putt mind-set, the truth is, of course, that just to obtain, then hold onto, a tour card a golfer has to be an excellent putter. To win consistently, he has to rank—by realistic standards—much of the time in the "great" category. What, then, makes us all so reluctant to admit such skills? Gardner's reason has some validity, I think, but there are other factors as well.

I know from my own experience that, the better a golfer putts, the better he expects to putt, until, like Arnold at his peak, it can become inconceivable to him that he should ever miss. In other words, the greater one's success, the harder it becomes to accept the realities of the difficulty of putting and the luck factors involved in it (as illustrated by even a putting machine missing two or three times out of ten from a distance of ten or so feet).

Another reason for the reluctance to admit skill with the short stick may be the seemingly overwhelming significance of putting in winning and losing at golf. I am sure there are players on the tour now, as there were in my day, who believe they never would lose if only they could putt all the time like Ben Crenshaw or Nick Price or Greg Norman, or whoever currently heads the putting stats. That is obviously baloney, yet it is also understandable that a guy whose living depends on birdies and eagles would equate his achievements primarily with his performance on the greens. It's just hard to get your mind past the fact that putting is the final determinant of your score on every hole, as well as the one element of the game where, unlike a missed drive or approach, a missed putt is a mistake from which you cannot recover—in short, a stroke gone forever.

There are a lot of people in the golf commentating business who regard the "I-should-hole-everything" mind-set as the ideal attitude on putting. Having made a lifelong habit of favoring the positive over the negative, I would have sided with them for much of my career. In later years, I have become a little less sure.

The longer I have played, the clearer it has become to me that putting is mostly a matter of eyesight, touch and nerve, all of which, fight the process as we may, steadily decline with age. As I approached senior status, I could still see the ball and the line just fine, still feel the stroke well, and still execute without my nerves playing up. Nevertheless, I was not as sharp on the greens as I was twenty years previously, and there is no denying this hurt my overall game. As fewer putts dropped, the closer I felt I must hit my approach shots, which meant the straighter and farther I needed to drive the ball. That's a trap I had seen a lot of in my peak years on the tour. Eventually, it struck me that avoiding it required some revision of my expectations.

Now, don't get me wrong on this. When I am putting poorly, I don't just tell myself to heck with it and start hockeying the ball around, as seems to be a tendency among some of my higher-handicap friends. While on the course, I continue to give every element of the game my best effort, and keep on doing that regardless of immediate results. On the greens I may fiddle around even during competition with some element of my setup or stroke if I think that might help. Afterward, if there has been no improvement, invariably I will head for the practice putting green to look even harder for an answer.

What I have learned to avoid in my senior years is increasing the pressure on the rest of my game by believing Planet Earth will stop rotating if I shoot 68 when I "could have, should have" shot 62 "if only" I'd putted better. The latter happens to be my best score in competition, and I putted superbly on each of the five occasions I have recorded it to date. However, what maturity has taught me is that to seriously *expect* to putt that well more than periodically is not only unrealistic but counterproductive. That's because, unpalatable as it may be, the truth is that you and I both, and all who follow us into this great game, are always going to miss far more seemingly makeable putts than we hole.

The biggest lesson I have learned from all of this is that putting is the element of golf that rears up and bites you hardest when you try to force success. There have been occasions when consciousness of this has made me too conservative on the greens, defensive when I should have been aggressive, and some of them have cost me dearly. But there have been even more times when, through getting mad at myself, I have tried to force the ball into the hole, and all that's happened is that I've gotten madder still because it wouldn't go in, until eventually I was caught up in that vicious circle of ever-increasing self-imposed pressure I described a moment ago.

The essence of putting to me, then, is that it is far more difficult and much more dependent on luck than most of us can easily accept, but, the better we learn to accept this truth about it, the less risk we run of sabotaging our entire game.

Keep this in mind the next time you sense the wheels are about to fly off in one of those "could have, should have" or "if only" rounds.

GETTING back to Augusta National and the Masters in the spring of 1966, there is no doubt that judgmental failings hurt me again in the third round on Saturday. With the wind dropping to a balmy breeze, conditions had become much easier, enabling me after eleven holes played in three under par to regain the lead by a stroke. By the time I left the twelfth green, I was back in the pack again.

I could go on for a long time about the many factors that make that storied little par-three so tough—it's only 155 yards from tee to center of green—but will stick to the main one, which is wind swirl. The teeing area is protected rear and right by a thick stand of tall pine trees, so that, even in a stiff wind, you are often hitting from a pocket of comparative calm. The problem is that the trees end about halfway to the green, which is the point where any wind that happens to be around begins to affect the flight of the ball. Perhaps because this is the lowest section of the course, the further and larger problem is that the wind here swirls a lot. You can glance up at the tops of those big old pine trees to your right and note that they are blowing one way, then flick your eyes over to the green and watch the flag blowing in the exactly opposite direction. Picking the correct club and shot at this hole on anything but a dead calm day is, therefore, always something of a guessing game. However, due to the narrow and diagonally angled green, and all the water and sand and other unpleasantness that surround it, if you guess wrong there is no limit to the score you can make—as witness Tom Weiskopf's famed thirteen there in the 1980 Masters.

On this attempt I figured the club correctly, the 7-iron, but guessed wrongly about how to hit it. "Be sure to get over the creek," I said to myself, which is a much more negative thought than, say, "Be sure to land on the green." As a result, I swung too hard, flew the creek and the putting surface, and half-buried the ball in the downslope at the back of the bunker behind the green. Now I had a real lulu: Firing back directly toward the water from a downhill, partially buried lie. To have put myself in such a predicament by sloppy thinking made me angry, and the anger, as it so often does in golf, compounded the original mistake. I underhit the bunker shot, left the ball in the sand, and walked off the hole with a double-bogey 5.

Fortunately, the shock of making two mental errors on the shortest hole of the golf course settled me down sufficiently to birdie thirteen and follow up with three solid pars. But my mind still would not remain in high gear for more than short spells. I followed a careless bogey at seventeen with another at the final hole, thereby turning a potential 68 into a par 72. It was good enough to tie for the lead with Tommy Jacobs, who had capitalized on an eagle at thirteen for a fine 70, but my back-nine sloppiness made me disgusted with myself. Chances two days running to open some serious daylight on the field, and I had tossed away both with muddy thinking. "What's happened to your *brain,* dummy?" I kept asking myself as I tried to cool off on the driving range.

THE standings as the leaders began the final round the next day were Jacobs and Nicklaus at 216 (through 1984 the highest fifty-four-hole leading total in Masters history, incidentally); Don January at 217; and Ben Hogan, Arnold Palmer, and Gay Brewer at 218. The pairings were Brewer and Palmer, followed by Jacobs and January, followed by Hogan and Nicklaus.

As was our custom, I had joined Ben for a practice round earlier in the week, during which it became clear that, although then half-way into his fifty-fourth year, he was playing as solidly as ever from tee to green. It was also obvious that the only thing that had kept him from winning since his last victory seven years previously—in the Colonial in his hometown of Fort Worth—was putting. Compared with the authority of his long game Ben had to some extent always struggled on the greens, but he was now undergoing terrible agonies with the putter in hand. I found it hard—and sad—to watch this otherwise machinelike golfer of such great accomplishment torture himself over the short ones, knowing that an involuntary nervous spasm in his right arm would time and again disrupt the sure stroke his mind was demanding. In fact, it was so bad that the previous evening Ben had said to Arnold Palmer during a rare press interview: "I want to apologize to you for having to watch me go through the jitters out there on the greens. I am very sorry, I really am."

Ben Hogan had been nice to me ever since we had first met at the U.S. Open at Cherry Hills in 1960, and, regardless of how he played, it was for me an honor and a pleasure to be paired with him. Normally, it would also have been inspiring, but, hard as I ground, inspiration was hard to come by that day. Ben soon putted himself out of the picture. With an ailing stroke and a balky mind, I was afraid sooner or later I would do the same.

For openers I bogeyed after plugging my approach in a bunker, then went two over par for the round at the fourth hole when I again hit sand from the tee. On seven, I drove into the trees, knocked the recovery into another bunker, blasted to four feet, then missed the putt for a third bogey. At ten, I three-putted for a fourth. These were all judgmental errors, mental mistakes, the kind that most infuriate me, and with eight holes to play they had put me three shots behind Brewer and seemingly out of the tournament. Walking to the eleventh tee, I told myself: "Okay, there's no way you're going to win with intelligent golf, because you're not capable of playing intelligent golf this week. So from now on, just let it hang out. Just go for it."

The pep talk bore little immediate fruit. I missed for birdies from around twelve feet at both twelve and thirteen, three-putting the latter from the fringe for the third time that week. This kept me three shots behind Brewer, who appeared to be playing the most solid golf of the contenders. Arnie had also put together a fair front nine, but, I later learned, had then begun to miss short putts. He was two back of Gay and tied with Tommy Jacobs. The odds at that point seemed heavily against a repeat winner at Augusta National.

At the fourteenth hole I hit an awful drive, the classic over-the-top hard pull. The ball caught a tree trunk flush and rebounded back toward the tee, stopping some forty yards behind Hogan's fairway-splitter. The approach for me at this 420-yard par four is normally an 8- or 9-iron. Now I needed a 3-iron, and, with steam coming out of my ears in high-pressure jets, go for it I did. The shot was my best of the entire tournament. The ball landed on the front apron and rolled perfectly up to the top plateau of the severely terraced green, leaving a straight-in seven-footer. When I made the putt I got a huge lift. I had turned what on the tee had all the makings of a bogey into a birdie.

The leader boards showed that Jacobs had just birdied the par-five fifteenth to pull within a shot of Brewer. If I could do the same, I felt there was still a chance of at least getting into a playoff. I powdered the driver but drew it a little too much, stymieing myself behind the pine trees to the left of the fairway. Laying up short of the water—the intelligent strategy from such a situation at this hole any time you're in the driver's seat—simply would not get the job done. I took the 2-iron and hooked the ball around the tree to the back of the green. That was my second finest shot of the tournament. Two putts later, my deficit was down to one stroke.

As I walked to the sixteenth green after a fine tee shot, Brewer and Palmer were moving to the eighteenth green. Following a birdie at the ninth, Gay had made eight straight pars, and there was an excellent chance that a final one would win him the 1966 Masters. There was also an excellent chance that he would make the par. Gay had joined the tour ten years previously, and, despite the little twirl at the top of his swing, proved himself a fine striker of the ball. That he hadn't won more than a handful of times was due to his putting, and this, he had said all week, had recently improved. I learned later that at the eighteenth he had gotten the ball in two shots about sixty feet beyond the cup, which was set in its customary Sunday position toward the bottom of the slope in the front left of the green. He judged the weight of the stroke almost perfectly, which is the tough part from such a distance downhill on a fast surface, but didn't quite get the line. This left him a nasty sidehill putt of about seven feet, which he missed on the low side. That meant Jacobs and I now had to par in to tie him.

Tommy made his par routinely on seventeen, but, he said later, caught his final drive weakly on the toe of the club and pushed it off to the right. The ball came out of the trees but left him with about 220 yards to the green. He took his 4-wood and hit a superb shot to within twenty feet of the cup. Two putts later he was in a playoff.

Although there was no way for me to know it at the time, a third straight birdie at the sixteenth would have won this Masters for me outright. I had a real chance, too, from twelve feet, but never touched the hole. Then, on seventeen, after an exciting 9-iron, I had an even better chance from three and a half feet, and again never touched the hole. I misread the break a little, but I also made yet another poor stroke.

Bursting with adrenaline, I hit a big drive off the eighteenth tee into gallery territory to the left, then a 7-iron to the green. With the surface so firm, there was no way to stop the ball close, and it finished about forty feet above the hole—a shorter version of Brewer's putt. I studied it for a long time, then made what for once felt like pure contact—delicate but solid. The ball seemed to trickle down the hill for about a week. When it got to within two feet of the hole, I was certain it was in. At the last second the ball dribbled to the left, stopping a couple of inches away. Somehow, after slopping around for three straight days, I had gotten myself into a playoff.

I'VE had my share of lucky breaks over the years, and one of the biggest arrived that Sunday evening. Just happening to catch a television replay of my pathetic effort on the seventeenth green, I saw immediately what was wrong with my putting. After missing that three-and-a-half-footer, I had asked myself if it was because of nerves and decided it wasn't: I'd been excited but not the least bit fearful. The reason had to be mechanics. But what was wrong with my mechanics?

CBS Sports provided the answer. I was lined up incorrectly. My head was inclined too far forward, so that I was actually looking backward or inward at the ball and the putter blade. I thought I was squaring the blade to the line along which I wanted to start the ball, but this was an illusion. In reality, I was lining the blade up to the left. That evening I went to the practice putting green and, with my eyes in the proper position dead over the line, stayed there until it was too dark to see. What a difference! To celebrate, I went home and polished off four tenderloins. No, make that three and a half—I remember giving most of the last one to someone else.

In the playoff on Monday I did not hit a single bad putt, although I made some mental mistakes that would have cost me dearly if Tommy and Gay had been a little sharper. At the third hole, for instance, I underhit my pitching-wedge approach and was lucky to make par with a chip and putt. On the fourth hole, I forgot to allow enough safety margin in club selection to be sure of clearing the bunker fronting the green, buried the ball almost out of sight, and was fortunate to make even a bogey. Then, at nine, where the severely sloping green will invariably roll an underhit approach back toward you, I again forgot to apply enough muscle and took another dumb bogey.

Thankfully, that last lapse in concentration jolted me sufficiently to get a grip on myself. From then on I hit a few mediocre shots, but no more stupid ones. At ten I missed the green but almost holed the chip, then birdied eleven with a twenty-five-foot putt. That put me two strokes ahead of Tommy and five ahead of Gay, who by then was having an unhappy day. Tommy gave me a scare at fifteen, but I scrambled a matching birdie with a fifteen-foot putt and was still two ahead walking off the eighteenth tee. There I got another fright when I pulled my 7-iron approach down the bank to the left of the green. The lie was bare and there was no room to pitch to the pin, and to play a bump-and-run risked thinning the ball over the green or leaving it short and having it roll back to me. After much deliberation, I decided to use the putter, judged both break and weight perfectly, and stopped the ball five feet from the cup. With the pressure off after Tommy had missed his birdie putt from about thirty feet, I knocked the five-footer in the heart of the hole.

With about fifteen thousand people watching a single group and scrambling for the best vantage points on every hole, the round had taken five hours and four minutes, and we were all pretty tired. For the record, the playoff scores were Nicklaus 70, Jacobs 72, Brewer 78 —and I'm glad to be able to note that Gay came back from what must have been a painful experience to win a green jacket the following year.

THE custom at the Masters prize-giving had always been for the previous year's winner to help the new champion into his green jacket, so my successful defense necessitated a little conference between Bob Jones and Cliff Roberts. Their decision was that I should help myself into the jacket, which was fine by me. As I did so, I couldn't help but think that the week just past had moved me another lengthy stride along the curve of learning how to win.

Above all, it had taught me the two most important factors in that art: patience and determination in adversity.

8

The 1966 British Open Championship

The Most Elusive One—Finally

THE week after winning my second U.S. Amateur at Pebble Beach in September of 1961, I was scheduled to defend a pro-am title with Bob Kepler, my Ohio State golf coach, in Cincinnati. Barbara was then overdue with our first child, so as I kissed her good-bye I restated for about the fiftieth time that, as soon as something happened, she was to let me know and I would come back as fast as I could. Typical of her strength and greater concern for others than herself, what she didn't tell me, because she knew I wouldn't have left if she had, was that she had already begun labor.

So Bob and I went down to Cincinnati and played a practice round. The next morning around eight o'clock the phone rings in my room and it's Mrs. Nicklaus. Still half-asleep, I ask her why in the world she's calling me so early. "Well," comes the answer, "I thought I'd better let you know you are a father. You have a beautiful baby boy." I say wonderful and fantastic, and that I'll leave for home immediately. "No, no, no," she tells me. "Go play the round and come this evening, because there's nothing you can do back here right now."

So I drive far too fast straight to the hospital as soon as I get off the course, rush into the maternity ward and over to where all the babies are, and ask the nurses which is mine. They point out little Jackie to me, I take one look at him—and, whammo, down I go, backward onto the tile floor, in a dead faint, out cold. Then, nineteen months later, I give a repeat performance with our second son, Steve. "You know," says Barbara when I come around that second time, "you won't ever let me have even a single moment in the spotlight, will you?"

Golf included, the happiest event of the year 1965 for both of us was the arrival of our daughter, Nancy Jean, on May 5. And, once again, I required an embarrassing amount of medical attention.

The day before Nan arrived, Bob Hope, Jim Garner, Scioto pro Walker Inman and I played an exhibition in Columbus for the American Cancer Society, following which I invited them and a few other friends over to the house. Despite her advanced stage of pregnancy, Barbara agreed to make some dinner for us while we shot a little pool in the game room. After a while Barbara yelled to me to fix the charcoal on the barbecue, and I yelled back that I would do it after one more game. Then a little while later she asked me to put the steaks on to grill, and I said I'd be right there but somehow forgot about it and kept on playing. Finally, we all sat down to dinner around nine o'clock, but had only been eating for a couple of minutes when Barbara excused herself and disappeared. With Hope and Garner making us laugh so much, I didn't really register her absence until about forty-five minutes later. When it finally struck home, I got up and went into our bedroom. She had packed her bag, called the doctor, and was putting on her coat. She said, "Are you going to take me to the hospital or should I call a cab?" When I went back and told the guys where we were going—like *now*—you've never seen a group clear out of a place faster.

Barbara and I left the house at eleven o'clock, and Nan came along at ten past midnight, which I thought was nice timing. When they wheeled my wife and new daughter out to where I could see them, down I went again in a dead faint. Fortunately, a couple of the nurses caught me and hauled me off to the recovery room, where I came around about fifteen minutes later. To be sure I got home safely, Barbara's doctor, Bill Copeland, insisted on following me in his car. When I argued with him about the necessity for that, he told me, "I think I'd better, Jack. After all, you spent more time in the recovery room than your wife did."

Single-mindedness about whatever is at hand has been one of my greatest assets in golf and other areas of endeavor, but there is no question that it became harder to sustain as my joy in our family increased with its size. Looking back, I am sure it was soon after Nan arrived that my unhappiness whenever Barbara and the kids weren't with me on the road really started to grow, even though, with the additional workload and responsibility, I sometimes found I had less energy for golf when they were. There were other reasons, too, for not being able to lock my mind as totally on the game in the late spring and early summer of 1966 as I had been used to doing when I had only myself to think of.

The tragic deaths of the Bartons and the Longs on their way to the 1966 Masters began the first period in our lives where Barbara and I had to face and deal with the emotional stress that mortality and illness among family and friends creates. Within a matter of weeks, one of Barb's uncles died suddenly of a heart attack, Steve had to be rushed to the hospital for an emergency tonsillectomy, and we were deeply concerned that Jackie would need major surgery on both legs to correct a toeing-in problem that special shoes did not seem to be helping. Then our baby daughter began choking and passing out, which the doctors discovered had been caused by her inhaling a piece of crayon. Delicate surgery was necessary, a bronchoscopy, following which she contracted pneumonia and, during the week of the U.S. Open, became seriously ill. As she was beginning to recover, my dad was ordered into the hospital for abdominal surgery.

FOLLOWING the customary winner's dinner with top officials after my third Masters win, we had arrived back home in the middle of the night. The next morning, as I took Jackie to school still a little groggy from lack of sleep, the thought that kept recurring was how lucky I had been to defend successfully.

Sure, I'd been patient and determined, and thus able to grasp the opportunity when it arose. But the deeper truth was that it had been one of those rare occasions when no one had played really great: when no one had been able to hold every element of his game in top gear for four straight days. Had that happened, it was difficult to imagine the same outcome.

Thankful as I was, there was no escaping the fact that, Masters or no Masters, if the Nicklaus golf game didn't perk up soon—or, rather, if Nicklaus didn't find a way to perk it up—this wasn't going to be one of those seasons that ended with a sense of contentment and a can't-wait attitude to the next one. For the first time at all seriously, I even briefly wondered that morning about retirement. Much as I enjoyed my chosen profession, after five years on tour I kept finding myself more and more concerned about the stresses the lifestyle imposes on the family unit. Also, I had been growing increasingly uneasy in a vague sort of way about the shortage of mental stimulus inherent in doing little more than, as a nongolfing friend once put it, "chasing a small white ball around a big green field"—concerned that I wasn't challenging or using my brain sufficiently. It certainly was a strange time for such musings, but, by that point in my career, although always enjoying a great sense of satisfaction after a win, I was past the days of prolonged euphoria.

As the season progressed, my game continued to disappoint me. I finished tied for fifth at the Tournament of Champions, tied for third at New Orleans, third alone in Oklahoma City, and tied for fourth at Memphis. I felt as though I could, and should, have won at least two out of the four, but had blown them through poor concentration, exemplified by erratic scoring—shooting lights out one day and barely glimmering the next. The U.S. Open at Olympic in San Francisco did not improve my mood. Excited as ever by a major, and conscious inevitably of a second grand slam leg, I ground my way at the end of the third day to within a stroke of leader Bill Casper (who would go on to defeat Arnie in an historic playoff), only to compile a mentally sloppy 74 in the final round to finish third again.

As the family crises gradually eased with the onset of midsummer, I hoped this state of affairs would be rectified by the stimulus of the year's third major—for me the most elusive of all the great championships, the British Open.

A MARK of their graciousness is that the Scottish people have never seemed to hold the young and raw Jack Nicklaus of the 1959 Walker Cup against the older and hopefully more polished and perceptive one. For that I am most thankful, because, of all the countries where I have been fortunate enough to play golf, theirs is my favorite. That's not just because the game evolved in Scotland (some historians claim it originated elsewhere), or the wonderful linksland courses, or the country's unspoiled quality, or even because of how well the Scots understand the subtleties of golf. Much as I enjoy those and other elements of this lovely land, my affection for Scotland derives mostly from my affection for its people. Increasingly during my years as a professional the Scots, for whatever reasons, seemed to take to me more than any other nationality. It would be emotionally impossible for any normal human being not to reciprocate such feelings.

To me, the Scottish people share many of the characteristics and values of the midwesterners I grew up with. In the main, they are honest, independent, uncomplicated, hospitable, hardworking, and exceptionally friendly and open in a quiet and unpushy sort of way once you show that you would like to get to know them. In a word, they are singularly unphony, very "real." I don't know how they got the "dourness" tag, unless it's because they don't babble and bubble and get wildly excited about something or other every minute or two. Whatever, my experience of the Scots, both on and off the golf course, is the exact opposite of dourness. I've swallowed more lumps in my throat and gotten damp-eyed more often in response to Scottish galleries than to any others, and I have made more good friends in Scotland than in any country except my own.

In consequence, I have always greatly enjoyed visiting and playing golf in Scotland, and that holds as true now as for the years when I generally seemed to be a contender. Even though it probably marked the beginning of my indifferent British Open play, 1984 at St. Andrews will always be particularly memorable because of what happened on the Tuesday of the championship week. At a most impressive and moving ceremony in an elegant and history-soaked collegiate hall, I was made an Honorary Doctor of Law of the University of St. Andrews, Scotland's oldest and one of the world's most renowned establishments of higher learning. I was the first sportsman to be so honored, and, despite my concerns about having to speak formally and at length in black gown and white tie to an audience consisting mainly of eminent academicians and intellectuals, there has been no prouder moment since I first picked up a golf club.

Wherever it is played, in Scotland or in England, the sheer stature of what the local purists insist on calling *The* Open is another reason I have always so much looked forward to each July. The U.S. Open began in 1895, the PGA Championship in 1916, and the Masters in 1934. The British Open began in 1860, and therefore is the undisputed grandfather of golf championships worldwide. It has had, inevitably, some ups and downs over all those years; but, since Arnie gave it such a shot of adrenaline in the early 1960s, the organizers, the Royal and Ancient Golf Club of St. Andrews, have built it into a great spectacle and a grand convocation of the game, as well as a primary golfing examination. As with the Masters, its only real rival for color and atmosphere, although in a much different way, anyone who is anyone in the world of golf—and I mean the *entire* world—always attends *The* Open. This, along with the huge tented village and the enormous crowds, gives it a flavor somewhere between a United Nations assemblage and an American state fair. In short, the modern British Open not only is firmly entrenched as one of golf's four major championships, but serves simultaneously as a celebration of the game's history, its most massive gathering of fans, and a huge week-long trade fair. That's a pretty zesty mix, and there's nothing else even a little bit like it in golf.

Yet another reason the more ambitious or history-conscious American players have become so devoted to the event is the refreshingly different challenges set by the great oceanside courses over which it is traditionally played. The rota presently includes, in Scotland, the Old Course of St. Andrews, the Honourable Company of Edinburgh Golfers at Muirfield, Royal Troon, and the Ailsa Course at Turnberry; and, in England, Royal Lytham and St. Annes, Royal Birkdale, and Royal St. George's at Sandwich. I have also played Opens at Carnoustie in Scotland, where the championship is slated to return in 1999 after a long absence thanks to a new hotel, and at Royal Liverpool, equally well-known as Hoylake on the northwest coast of England, which had to be dropped due to inadequate support facilities.

To the best of my knowledge, only Prince Andrew of the British royal family—an exceptionally intense competitor, as I discovered when partnering him at Gleneagles—has played golf since his great uncle, the Duke of Windsor. Nevertheless, as their names imply, most of the Open-hosting clubs enjoy royal patronage, and all of them except Turnberry are, at least by American standards, genuinely ancient and therefore oozing with history, tradition and "atmosphere." The courses are also, to a greater or lesser degree, all true links, the name deriving from the sandy terrain inadequate for agriculture left by the receding ocean and "linking" it to more fertile inshore land. That means they are virtually treeless, invariably windswept, rich in tough and tangly grasses and even tougher gorse, broom, bracken, and heather, and always severely 'umped and 'ollowed, as the late Henry Longhurst loved to put it.

Because the British like their golf to be as economical and as natural as possible, American-style super-grooming is unknown, and manicuring even of tees, fairways and greens is kept to a minimum (this being made possible, of course, by the hardy indigenous strain of grass known as fescue, plus a much damper and cooler climate than ours). The net result is a different game from what we know in the States—or in most other parts of the world, come to think of it—and one that presents a different set of strategical and shotmaking challenges. Thus yet another element of *The* Open's appeal for a fellow like me: a refreshing change of style, look, feel, and shotmaking from those offered week after week on the PGA Tour.

Any one of those reasons should be enough to make any red-blooded golfer play in as many British Opens as possible, but I have left until last the reason why, ever since my first attempt in 1962, I wanted to win this championship so badly.

Almost from the moment I began playing golf I had heard a message, first from history-conscious Scioto members, then from my dad and Jack Grout, then from Bob Jones and many other friends in the upper echelons of the game. It was that, if you want to be remembered as a complete champion, you must win all of the great championships. That meant there would always be a question mark against your name unless you crossed the water and added the British Open to your record. Walter Hagen had been the first native-born American to do that in 1922, and he had then gone over and won the championship three more times. Gene Sarazen had won it twice, Bob Jones four times, Sam Snead once, and Arnold Palmer twice. Even the reclusive Ben Hogan, after much persuasion by friends with a sense of history, had made his one famous expedition to Carnoustie in 1953 to become *The* Open champion.

I had decided after my disastrous first performance in 1962 that I was going to make the trip until I, too, could sit that beautiful little silver claret jug Open trophy on my mantel for a year. Then, when that finally came to pass, it was so much fun I knew I could never allow myself to miss this championship just as long as my game was respectable enough for public display.

YET another excitement of going to the British Open is never knowing what sort of golf course you will be playing until you actually get there. In the States, with our hefty maintenance budgets and love of the highly cosmeticized, emerald-green-all-over look, the condition of top tournament courses from year to year has become more and more predictable. In Britain, where a much more natural brand of the game is traditional and weather is the major arbiter, that is never the case. If it has rained a lot, the course will be green and holding and the rough lush and heavy; if it hasn't, everything will be shades of yellow and tan and brown, with little or no tall grass problem but endless difficulties in stopping the ball on baked-out fairways and greens. In other words, British Open conditions are always something of a lottery, which is fine with me because of the endless variety of mental and shotmaking challenges thereby presented. As a kid, I used to think golf should be a fair game and would tend to go bananas if I felt the condition of courses didn't properly reward proper shots. British golf gradually taught me differently (which, incidentally, has helped me better handle unlucky breaks anywhere in the world) and also helped make me a better shotmaker. As the old Scotsman said when an American spectator registered dismay as a perfect-looking Arnie Palmer long iron bounced sideways off a knoll and buried in the face of a bunker: "Well, tha' mon's a professional, is he nae? So let's forget about luck, laddie, and see wa' he can dae wi' this wee shottie." In short, if you can't keep your wits about you when the ball bounces "unfairly," and/or learn what over there they call the art of "manufacturing" shots, then you are much better off staying home.

With Nan finally on the mend, some productive time spent with Jack Grout, and the prospect of sitting the links golf exam again at much-loved Muirfield, my spirits lifted as I prepared to leave for Scotland. I would fly to London for a one-day television match against Peter Alliss at Wentworth, then go directly to the lovely little Greywalls Hotel next to the Honourable Company's clubhouse, leaving me almost a full week for on-the-spot fine tuning. So much time was not necessary to relearn the course, which I remembered vividly from 1959, but I had discovered the hard way that I needed at least five days to completely shake the effects of time change, adjust to the different climatic and living conditions, and become comfortable with the smaller British ball. Memories of my joint twelfth place finish, nine shots adrift of Peter Thomson at Royal Birkdale the previous July, had encouraged me to add one more day for insurance, as had my overall Open record. After four unsuccessful tries, including two near misses, it had occurred to me that this might be a championship that would always elude me. I believed I had a better chance at Muirfield to prove such thoughts groundless than anywhere else I had yet played an Open. Thus I was determined to do everything possible to be 101-percent prepared.

The chief reason for these high hopes was my happy memories of Muirfield as a great golf course well suited to my game. I recalled it as basically mellow and receptive, treeless, but only moderately undulating, with generous fairways, ample and finely conditioned greens, lovely springy turf, reasonable rough, and the trouble—consisting chiefly of some 170 bunkers—largely visible from wherever one was hitting. It seemed to lack the harshness or bleakness of most of the other major links I'd played: a challenging course, certainly, but also an inviting one. Above all, I remembered Muirfield as being "fair" almost in the sense of the word as we use it to describe the best American courses. Indeed, I could well imagine Donald Ross or Alister Mackenzie building something like Muirfield in the U.S., given a comparable piece of land.

Even at this distance in time, the shock I got when I walked out the back door of Greywalls for my first glance at Muirfield in seven years remains a sharp memory. This was not my beloved Walker Cup playground at all. What lay before me was a huge rolling, waving, dun-colored hay field. I remember a momentary sense of disorientation, as though I had mistaken a turn and ended up at the wrong location. The only thing anyone could compete for here was a harvesting championship. There had to be some mistake.

It quickly transpired that, if there had been a mistake, it was strictly a judgmental one by the organizing Royal and Ancient's Championship Committee. At 6,887 yards (it has since been stretched a little), Muirfield in those days was the shortest course on the Open rota. Although no one had come close to tearing it apart in the nine

Opens previously played there, the Championship Committee had decided that these hallowed acres needed defending against the ever stronger American entry attracted by the Palmer-initiated renaissance of the early 1960s. To achieve this, a lead had been taken from the United States Golf Association, which for years had lined squeezed-down fairways with notoriously luxuriant rough for U.S. Opens. But the R and A had gone way beyond anything their American counterparts would have dared. Perhaps forty yards wide at their starting point, most of the fairways gradually tapered down to where, in the areas a reasonably powerful hitter would hope to land his drives, they were at most twenty yards across. And the stuff immediately bordering them . . . ? United States Golf Association-doctored U.S. Open courses generally feature about a six-foot collar of two-inch "secondary" rough, then a few yards of five-inch "primary" rough, and only then—where nobody should drive if he hopes to win a national championship—sometimes real jungle. At Muirfield that year, the fairways gave way immediately to acres of thick, thigh-deep, billowing (and frequently seeding) fescue, in which, even with the army of white-smocked forecaddies provided, simply finding a golf ball, let alone hitting it, would be little short of a miracle.

It soon became clear that the man most responsible for all of this was the chairman of the championship committee, Gerald Micklem, a fine amateur golfer who had been the nonplaying captain of the home team in the 1959 Walker Cup match at Muirfield. I knew him to be one of the all-time great servants of golf in Britain, and we had also become friends, so I tried not to show my feelings as he explained the rationale behind what, during the playing of the championship, the less establishment-minded sections of the press referred to as "Micklem's Folly." But I was sorely disappointed. First, this simply wasn't the golf course I had enjoyed so much on my first trip abroad seven years previously. Second, and of more practical concern, was the fact that dear old Gerald had totally negated one of my strongest golfing weapons: power. As long drivers go, I was pretty straight, but in these wheat fields there was no way anyone could hit full bore from the tees for four rounds and not meet disaster. Even if the muscles were up to it, the nerves certainly would not be, and particularly in any kind of close finish. In a pointless and probably vain attempt to prohibit low scoring, the R and A had virtually eliminated the most exciting element of the game—the big tee shot.

Standing on the first tee of my first practice round, I wanted very much to hate the new Muirfield. Then, thankfully, two things sank home. The first was that this was exactly the kind of reaction that would have killed the chances of at least half the possible contenders a week from now. The second was that I had plenty of time to learn how to play this new style of thread-the-needle golf. There and then, before striking a blow, I decided to behave like the professional I prided myself on having become. Distasteful as they were, I would find a way to accommodate myself to the conditions.

IN order to avoid the attention of religious pressure groups, the British Open had for many years begun on a Thursday and concluded with the traditional double round of thirty-six holes on the Saturday. It would be another fourteen years before the R and A would risk completing the championship on Sunday (it didn't appear to cause much fuss), but, like most of the players, I was pleased with the decision to extend it to four days beginning in 1966. The official reasons were to increase gate revenues, television exposure, and size of field. I was in good enough shape physically to easily handle thirty-six holes in a day and, as a traditionalist, had always enjoyed the marathon conclusions of the U.S. and British Opens. On the other hand, I had never enjoyed the rushing and commotion between completing the third round and beginning the fourth when both were crammed into one day. I believed that having more time and space to prepare for the final push could only help me.

The change meant starting on the Wednesday. By then, with Nan rapidly recuperating at home and Barbara thus able to join me, I was feeling pretty perky about my prospects. A general players' outcry had resulted in a little hay mowing and fairway widening, but, to me, after six practice rounds, the condition of the course had become almost immaterial. I had begun by hitting the driver experimentally at all of the par fives and most of the par fours, then had clubbed progressively down in succeeding rounds depending on the outcome in the previous one. By the Tuesday evening I had a firm game plan. I would play the driver for sure on one par five, and possibly, depending on the wind, at three or four of the par fours. Everywhere else I would hit either the 3-wood or a long iron from the tee, again depending on the wind and also, perhaps, on the state of play.

Helping this plan formulate through the practice days was a growing consciousness that, with my length advantage through the bag, using these clubs from the tee would cost me little in distance relative to shorter players forced to hit driver to set up manageable approach shots. The prospect of the extra control I would enjoy, without giving up excessive yardage, helped in dispelling my initial disappointment with my old Scottish friend. Also, my game was finally 100 percent solid again: The fade seemed locked in, "manufactured" shots such as low-liners were generally coming off as planned, and my putting stroke felt better than it had for most of the year.

In all of my previous British Opens the bookies had made me the favorite, which, as I had never won the championship, had seemed somewhat dumb to me. Now they had done so again, at odds of seven to two. Reflecting over dinner on the Tuesday evening that this was my most thorough preparation ever for a major championship, I decided they might be smarter than I figured.

MUIRFIELD's par is 71—36 out, 35 in. In the opening round I bettered it by one stroke. Although not much more than a breeze, the wind had about-faced from the prevailing westerly direction of the practice days, which persuaded me to hit the driver more than I had planned on doing—six times. I caught the hay with it once, which cost me a bogey, and dropped two more strokes with other mistakes, but offset them with four solid birdies—the one on seventeen, set up by a thrilling 1-iron off a badly angled lie (the ball was a foot above my feet), being particularly pleasing. The longest putt I holed also came at a good point for the morale—a twenty-foot par-saver at eighteen after carving a 6-iron into the bleachers from just off the fairway. Remembering clubs I had used in an east wind during the Walker Cup helped me on a number of occasions. The wheat and the wind combined seemed to have produced somewhat tentative play among most of the field, to the point where at day's end only London pro Jimmy Hitchcock and I had broken par. We were tied for the lead.

Because of Britain's long summer days, the Open starting fields are larger than ours, which often means a very early tee time and a very late one the first two days. I dislike the late ones—going off when normally your thoughts would be turning to dinner plans—but tried all day Thursday not to let my 3:22 P.M. start bug me too much. It did, but I soon shook off any effects, shooting an almost error-free 67 in a mild west wind to lead alone—for the first time in Britain—at the halfway mark by one shot over Peter Butler, who broke the course record with a 65, and by two from Harold Henning, 1960 Centenary Open winner Kel Nagle, and Phil Rodgers. (Good old Philamander, always seeking new secrets, was using a long-shafted putter—thirty-nine inches—with the top end anchored in his ample midriff. With only twenty-seven putts in a 66, he seemed to have found one.) I had used my driver only four times but my 1-iron six, so the plan seemed to be working. I decided that night to stick with it, whatever the temptations of the next two days.

Ahead of my arrival at Muirfield there had been a lot of rain, and the moisture had remained in the ground sufficiently through practice and the first two days of the championship to permit almost American-style hit-and-stick target golf—exactly my cup of tea. That changed dramatically as the wind from the west more than doubled in strength during the early hours of Friday morning. By the time I teed off in round three at 1:40 P.M., we were playing a totally different golf course. Muirfield had become the ultimate form of links golf, fast, slippery, bouncy, unpredictable, and growing ever more so by the minute.

For thirteen holes I handled those conditions as well as I ever had, matching par and increasing my lead over the nearest challenger, Butler, to four strokes. Then, trouble. Irritated at hitting through the fourteenth green, I played a poor chip back and missed from twelve feet for a sloppy bogey, then almost duplicated the performance at the next hole. Suddenly, all of the confidence I had been so carefully building for the past nine days evaporated.

If you play competitive golf, I'm sure you are only too familiar with the nervy, jittery feeling in which the game can envelop and imprison you, almost, it sometimes seems, in less than the blink of an eye. Well, the jailhouse door had just slammed shut on me. At the par-three sixteenth I three-putted for the first time in the championship, from under forty feet, for a third straight bogey, then mishit a pitch from the rough and barely scrambled a par at the long seventeenth, the easiest birdie hole on the course when played downwind. Finally, dry-mouthed and dying to get out of there, I made it four bogeys in five holes with an awful second shot to eighteen, for an inward score of 39 and a big fat 75. Meanwhile, tired of what he called "pitty-pattying around" and letting it all hang out with the driver, Arnold had come home in 32 to pull to within two strokes of me. Even more impressive, friend Rodgers had covered the same territory in 30 strokes to make up nine shots on me in nine holes, giving him the lead by two strokes. If I hadn't given this championship away, I had sure made one heck of a try. For most of that evening, I'm sorry to say, I wasn't much fun to be around.

As mentioned earlier, I am always nervous at the beginning of an important round, but have learned to welcome the sharpened concentration this produces when it doesn't become excessive. The butterflies must have been buzzing at the perfect pitch on Saturday afternoon, because I opened with a gorgeous 3-wood dead into the wind, followed it with an equally fine 3-iron, and knocked the resulting twenty-five-footer cleanly into the heart of the hole. A birdie on such a tough hole so early in the round felt like a bonus, and particularly after it tied me with Phil—we were the final pairing—when he could only scramble a bogey after hay trouble from the tee. It also gave me a great lift, which I capitalized on with a tap-in birdie after a bunkered 7-iron to the 516-yard fifth, and a 9-iron to three feet for another birdie at the 451-yard eighth. Rodgers was hanging in, as I expected him to, so, when I missed from under three feet at the ninth hole for a second straight birdie to be out in 33, I hoped it would not prove to be a decisive slip.

By the time we both completed number ten, all such thoughts had vanished. At 475 yards and with the wind dead across from the right, this was probably the scariest hole on the course, and it nailed Phil as it had Arnie a few minutes earlier. After lengthy wars with the wheat, each took triple-bogey sevens. I had made a cautious four—1-iron, 3-iron, two putts from fifteen feet. Suddenly I was leading *The* Open by three strokes. Finally, *finally,* this most elusive championship was mine for the taking.

Oh, boy!

At the eleventh hole I hit an excellent 1-iron from the tee and followed it with a super pitching wedge to within seven feet of the cup. "Jack," I told myself, "you're playing one of the finest rounds of your life. Just be sure you keep it going." As I walked to the green, I could tell that the huge galleries, pulling for me all week, believed it was all over but for the prize presentation. Had that seven-footer dropped, they might have been right. What happened is that I never touched the hole with the first putt, then, despite giving it all the care in the world, also missed the second from fifteen inches. As I watched that miserable little nothing of a putt rim out, I experienced one of the most severe mental jolts I've suffered on a golf course. Immediately, thoughts of the previous afternoon's collapse swamped my mind. Jittery is not a strong enough word to describe my feelings as I walked to the twelfth tee.

And, of course, this had the inevitable effect. With the hole playing dead into the wind, I needed the driver. It flew left to left and away into the boonies. But then I got one of those breaks that every winner at golf must acknowledge as critical if he has an honest soul. The shot was so bad that it cleared "Micklem's Folly" and landed where the spectators had been trampling the stuff down all week. From an almost perfect lie I hit a 9-iron to twenty-five feet and two-putted for par.

But still the fires of doubt were burning, and still I could not douse them. The thirteenth hole at Muirfield is its shortest and easiest par three. I hit a weak 9-iron and a jabby chip that scuttled twenty feet past the cup, then never had a hope with the first putt. Bogey. At fourteen I pulled my drive into a bunker, could only go at the ball with the 8-iron, then hit a poor sand wedge thirty-five feet past the hole and two-putted. Bogey again. Three bogeys in four holes.

In 1966 fifteen years had passed since a British golfer had won the Open—Max Faulkner at Royal Portrush, the one time the championship was played in Northern Ireland. In 1958 at Royal Lytham, however, Dave Thomas, a large and amiable Welshman, had come close, tying the event's then dominating figure, the Australian Peter Thomson, only to lose in the playoff. Big Dave had again been what the locals called "thereabouts" all week at Muirfield, and was popular with the fans, not only for his pleasant personality but for his power: He was at that time by far and away Europe's longest straight driver. Only a weakness with short pitch shots—actually, as he freely admitted, a terrifying phobia about them—had prevented him from becoming a major factor in world golf. But, pitch shot problems or not, I knew him to be a fine player, and had figured him as one of the men most likely to give me trouble in the final round.

As I walked from the fourteenth green to the fifteenth tee, word came that Dave had done exactly that, finishing with a fine 69 for a seventy-two-hole total of 283. Also, I learned that Doug Sanders—

he of the phone-booth-size swing and colorful outfits, but a superb shotmaker—was on the eighteenth fairway needing a par for the same total (he got it). That meant I must par in to tie them. It was not a happy thought. Not to beat about the bush, I doubted my ability to do so.

At fifteen I managed a par, but shakily, somehow squeezing the ball in from four feet after three indifferent shots. At sixteen, 198 yards downwind, I hit the green with the 7-iron, but thirty feet short of the hole. Looking over the putt, the first thing that occurred to me was that if I was a little too strong with it I would be looking at a nasty down-hiller coming back. "Nicklaus," I told myself, "with what you've just done to yourself there's no way you're going to win this thing thinking and playing defensively, so for goodness sake go ahead and *hit* it. Get a grip on yourself, man." Hit the ball I did, squarely and solidly and dead on line for the first time since the tenth green, and only missed holing it by a couple of turns.

And then, just as suddenly as I had gone to pieces at the eleventh hole, I came together again. That one firm, positive stroke restored my confidence in my shot-making abilities. Walking to the seventeenth tee, I told myself to forget about playoffs. "This is a birdie hole," I reminded myself. "Make one, and then a par, and let's all go home."

Seventeen at Muirfield is a par five of 528 yards that swings to the left a couple of hundred yards from the tee, with all kinds of scrubby and sandy eruptions along the way, particularly over the last hundred or so yards. Downwind, it is easily reachable in two, but both shots must be purely struck and precisely flighted to find the ridge-protected green. Preventing the tee shot from running through the fairway is the first challenge. Even though I had hit one-iron all three previous days, after considerable thought I decided to eliminate the risk by going down two clubs. I struck that 3-iron almost too well, the ball finishing no more than six feet from some knee-high rough. But it was on the short grass, which was all that mattered.

My yardage references told me I was now 238 yards from the hole, which at that time would normally have called for the 1-iron. After even more deliberation than on the tee, I decided on the 5-iron. Here's the computation that resulted in that possibly surprising-sounding decision: one club less for the small ball, one and a half clubs less for the wind, one less for extra roll resulting from firm ground, and half a club less for the effects of adrenaline, equaling four clubs less than normal.

I hit the shot as well as I am capable of doing, and watched it land on the fairway about twenty feet short of the green, exactly as planned. Then, not being able to see the ball's roll, I waited for what seemed an agonizingly long time for a crowd reaction. Finally, there came a big roar. Tingling with excitement, I almost jogged to the green, to find the ball fifteen feet short and left of the cup. Suddenly, I felt calm as well as confident, a great sensation at a time like this because of the assurance it provides that your nerves are not going to inject any flinches into the putting stroke. Nevertheless, I told myself, "No heroics," and lagged the putt a few inches short of the hole. Birdie, and half the task accomplished.

Muirfield's 429-yard eighteenth is a better finishing hole than it appears visually: level and straightaway from tee to cup, but requiring pinpoint accuracy all the way to avoid the severe fairway and greenside bunkering. Blessing the west wind coming dead from the right, I decided on the tee shot that had worked the previous three days—the 1-iron with a touch of fade. Banked against the wind, the ball landed in the middle of the fairway, leaving me 208 yards from the hole. For a moment I thought of the 4-iron, then, reminding myself of the dangers of trying to force a shot under pressure, chose the 3. I struck it perfectly, and enjoyed a huge thrill as I watched the wind counteract the fade just as planned, drifting the ball back to the right rear portion of the green, twenty-two feet from the cup. Again, it was no time for superman stuff. Not even thinking of making the putt, I lagged it eight inches to the left of the hole, then, after Phil had holed out, tapped in very carefully.

When you have dreamed of achieving something for what seems forever, and it finally happens, and it's been as hard a grind as that week was, so many emotions tumble around in your mind that you're sort of pleasurably confused and light-headed for a little while. I thought I was over that by the time of the prize presentation. By then it had occurred to me that I was only the fourth golfer to win all four of golf's major championships, joining Gene Sarazen, Ben Hogan, and Gary Player in that select group. Counting up how many times I'd used the driver during the four rounds—seventeen—I was also forcibly struck with how much more precision counts in golf than power, a realization that has stayed with me ever since, and that hopefully is reflected in my course design work. Also, I had begun to realize how exhausted I was beneath my happiness.

When the moment came to accept the trophy, the tears began welling up and I couldn't get any words out. Being about to receive something that even I, never much of a self-doubter, had genuinely doubted would ever be mine was extremely emotional. Finally, I asked the people to excuse me and to let me just stand there and enjoy myself for a moment.

It's a moment I still enjoy recalling as much as any in my career.

If I had to put a date on the beginning of my "second" career, that of golf course designer, it would be a few weeks before that first British Open victory.

Like so many golfers, I became an "armchair architect" at an early age, constantly visualizing ways to improve my home course, Scioto, in Columbus, along with, as my wings spread, many of the others I played. By the late 1950s I had become convinced, along with other members, that Scioto had deteriorated badly, particularly in greens growing away from bunkers and bunkers filling in, along with an overall erosion of charm. Eventually, in response to our ever more persistent lobbying, the club decided to hire a top architect to do some rejuvenation, and brought in Dick Wilson, whose credentials by then included a well-regarded revamping of Shinnecock Hills. I immediately appointed myself Mr. Wilson's unsolicited, unpaid and probably unwanted assistant, following him around the course and listening to his ideas and his rationale for them. Unfortunately, it wasn't until later—too much later, sadly—that I recognized what he was doing, particularly in bringing in two design associates, Bob Von Hagge to redo the front nine and Joe Lee for the back. Both would become renowned designers in their own right, but the result of their work on Scioto, in my estimation, was that one great eighteen-hole course became two unrelated nines. The only good thing about it was that it taught me the difference between rejuvenation and redesign.

My interest in architecture naturally broadened during my early years on the tour, as I met and enjoyed the challenge of figuring how best to play the holes I encountered and of identifying the design factors behind the shot values that made golf so appealing to me. However, as my observation and analysis grew, I found myself becoming increasingly disenchanted with the giant fairways, the huge "turf-nurseries" for greens, and the general lack of character of so many of the courses we played, particularly in the exhibition matches that were so popular in those days. More and more, I began to ask myself whether it was possible to create something more interesting and inviting, particularly on a nice piece of property. And then came Pete Dye.

A fine amateur golfer from Indianapolis, Pete decided after a successful spell in the insurance business that he wanted more fulfillment from life, and decided to look for it in creating innovative golf courses. He and I had become friends on the amateur circuit, so, when he started building The Golf Club on the outskirts of Columbus early in 1966, he asked me to take a look at it and used some of the suggestions I made, particularly regarding the third and thirteenth holes. Seeing my ideas come to fruition whetted my appetite for the work even more, and, recognizing this, Pete about a year later invited me to formally consult with him on further projects. The first course we worked fully on together was Harbour Town Links on Hilton Head Island in South Carolina. I made twenty-three visits there between mid-1967 and the opening of the course in the fall of 1969, and enjoyed the assignment so much I consulted with Pete on a few more courses. Eventually, I decided I wanted to try designing on my own, which I did with Pete's blessing and good wishes.

Although by then—the early 1970s—I felt I had acquired a sufficiently good grasp of the technicalities of course design not to need a partner, I discovered that the complexities of land planning with some of the projects that began coming my way required more expertise than I possessed. The result was a teaming up with an internationally renowned land-planner, the U.S.-based Englishman Desmond Muirhead, on about half a dozen projects, including Muirfield Village in Dublin, Ohio. From Desmond I learned a lot about environmental factors, and also how to conceptualize land use on a grand as well as a detailed scale. By the time Muirfield Village opened to fine reviews in 1974, I had worked on a total of nine courses with Pete and Desmond, which I decided was sufficient schooling. Since then, I have taken the leadership role in expressing my design ideas, although always working with highly qualified associates, particularly in the many technical disciplines required to turn a mental concept for a golf course into a finished product.

As more and more tournament golfers have gotten involved in

design in recent years, skepticism has grown as to their actual contributions to the courses carrying their signatures. Hopefully, the following look at my design philosophies and methods will satisfy any remaining skeptics as to my personal commitment levels, while also shedding some light on what may seem a mystifying process to many outside the business.

The first step in creating a golf course is always to determine if the proposed site is large enough, drainable enough, irrigable enough, and "buildable" enough to meet the objectives of the developer within the ever more stringent environmental restraints imposed both by law and by the esthetic concerns of all interested parties. Step two is to be sure that adequate funding is solidly in place to fulfill the objectives of all interested parties.

With affirmatives in those areas, our next step is to prepare in our North Palm Beach design offices, using an assemblage of all available topographical information, a first draft of a basic layout for the holes, known as a "routing." Before seeing the actual land, I will have studied that routing sufficiently to have imprinted a clear picture of it in my mind.

My top priority as I walk the land on my first visit is to establish both the playing potential and the engineering feasibility of each hole. I'm particularly on the lookout for any characteristics that would enhance either shot values or the "framing" of holes, such as attractive grade variations, specimen trees, and interesting wetlands. At the same time, I also begin to mentally evolve a theme for the course, usually drawn from one or more of the principal land characteristics, such as grade patterns, tree density and quality, water availability, and background setting. Because these days they impact so heavily on what is doable and what isn't, I am always highly conscious of certain or potential environmental factors. For both esthetic and commercial considerations, I am also concerned with the overall land-planning—where the homesites or the hotel or the clubhouse is to go, along with all the other necessary amenities. When a draft routing works for me in all of these areas, fine. When it doesn't, I change it. Rarely are the original and the final routings the same.

The hardest thing for me to accept in my early days as a designer was that every routing ends up as a compromise between golfing purity, environmental requirements, and commercial necessity. On real estate-related projects particularly, all golf course designers increasingly have become mandated to work with the least desirable portions of the available property. I disliked that trend intensely and fought it hard, until, of late, I have learned to accept it as simply a greater challenge to my creativity and ingenuity. The same goes for the environmental obstacles that all designers increasingly must surmount, particularly in the United States. In the golf course design business today, either you accept the conditions as they exist and do your best, or you get out.

Once we have decided that the routing is feasible developmentally, environmentally and "golfingly," our next step is to clear the site, working outward from the center lines of the fairways. In order to preserve as much of whatever nature has put there as possible, I like to clear more narrowly than the finished width of the holes, then open up gradually as the rough grading turns to fine grading. It breaks my heart to have to cut down mature trees, and by phasing our land clearing we lose the minimum number of them.

Grading all elements of the holes at both the rough and fine stages proceeds according to plans created by my design team, using in every case these days highly sophisticated multidimensional computer-created images of what we are trying to achieve. I visit and walk sites at various stages of the grading processes, ideally accompanied by the developer plus a representative of whoever is building the course, as well as one or more of my senior design associates. Because of the efficiencies and economies it provides, as well as the quality it assures, the actual building more and more is handled by our own construction affiliates.

In all of my work, I try to let the character and flow of the original land determine shot values as much as possible. When a need arises to change things substantially at a grading stage, natural drainage patterns are mostly the determining factor. That's because there is no future in creating wonderfully challenging or beautiful golf courses of which large portions are under water much of the time.

There is no question that it was my boyhood love of what he achieved at Scioto that made Donald Ross my favorite among the old master golf architects. I am a big fan, too, of Alister Mackenzie's work, particularly his genius in creating Augusta National in such a way that turning it from one of the world's top tournament tests into an enjoyable members' course requires nothing more than moving up tee markers and cutting cups in gentler green areas. Because they are so mentally as well as physically demanding, I have also been influenced by the great British seaside courses—if you can't or won't think your way through a round over there, you might as well save yourself the trip.

Despite this fairly broad canvas, early in my design career I was sometimes accused of producing stereotypical holes. That hurt, because the quality I have striven hardest to achieve from day one in my design efforts is variety. I intensely dislike the idea of a golfer walking off a course of mine without knowing I created it and saying, "Well, Jack Nicklaus obviously did that." Consequently, I have only some broad rules of thumb about what any course should consist of when I begin work on it.

To me, a well-balanced golf course should have one long par five rarely reachable by anyone in two shots, a par five definitely reachable with two *excellent* shots under almost any circumstances, and two par fives that may or may not be reachable depending on the conditions. There should be one short par three of around 150 yards, one long one of 200 or more yards, and two of medium length, and ideally they should go in different directions to vary the wind factor. The par fours should range in length on each nine from a drive and a flip wedge shot to a drive and a long iron or even a fairway wood, and both their direction and the look and "feel" of the approach shots they call for should vary as much as possible. Ideally, I like to include water as a hazard on about a third of the holes—say, two of the par fives, two of the par threes, and two of the par fours.

There is no question that Scioto, with all of the out-of-bounds on the right, contributed to my preference for a fade as my game evolved as a youngster. There is also no question that some of my early designs received criticism for having too many holes calling for left-to-right tee shots or approaches, or both. That spurred me to more consciously seek balance between straightaway, left-to-right and right-to-left patterns in creating par fours and par fives, so as not favor a particular type of player.

As to overall distance, I am happiest—because I know most golfers also are—when the blue tees present a course of between 6,500 and 6,700 yards, the whites 6,000–6,200 yards, and the reds 5,400–5,600 yards with no forced carries of more than sixty yards. In a nutshell, what I try to do at each of those distances is create facsimiles of the shots that I would most enjoy hitting. From the gold or championship tees such a course would generally play between 6,900 and 7,100 yards, and it is my assumption that only professionals and strong low-handicap amateurs will hit from back there. I have zero time for others who try to do so, then complain that the course is too tough or the designer screwed up.

On the subject of distance, I am fully aware that more and more golfers have come to intensely dislike the stretching of seemingly all modern courses to seven thousand or more yards, not only because they can't handle such length, but because of the higher construction and maintenance costs involved. There are two answers to that.

The first and simplest answer is that, to my knowledge, no one in golf forces anyone else to bite off more than he can comfortably chew. The second and more complex answer lies in the developer mind-set that has evolved from the massive overuse of perhaps the single emptiest phrase in the entire history of golf, namely, "Championship Course." Whatever my personal inclinations and arguments, nine out of ten of the developers I have worked with over the years all around the world have insisted I create something that they can instantly label "Championship Course." Consequently, almost every course I do has to be seven thousand or more yards from the back tips. In Japan particularly, there is also the factor that, if you don't have a course with a par of 72, you "lose face."

Another cost factor that is often overlooked by armchair critics is the demand that every new course these days instantly look both beautiful and mature—sufficiently esthetically "finished" to seem like it has existed since the Dutch or Scots first invented golf. In the old days, it was accepted that time would produce maturity, chiefly through tree importation and growth, and that maturity would add or increase beauty. Now, with real estate sales, hotel occupancy or fast recoupment of investment through high green fees on the line from opening day, and the interest meter always running, there simply is not time for that. Consequently, the esthetics have to be part of the overall design plan, and obviously that adds to the cost, often substantially. At one course I did, the expense of adding mature trees and moving others around ran into millions of dollars, but was perceived by the developer to be well justified by how much more they enabled him to ask for membership fees and homesites.

Getting back to the distance factor, an interesting statistic to me is that the average length of a dozen of my favorite American major championship courses—Augusta National, Baltusrol, Inverness, Medinah, Merion, Oak Hill, Oakland Hills, Oakmont, Olympic, Pebble Beach, Shinnecock Hills, and Southern Hills—is only 6,880 yards. One reason why, of course, lies in their average age of around three quarters of a century. Shoving large quantities of dirt around back then was a difficult and arduous undertaking, whereas these days designers can just roll in an army of earth-moving machines and remake nature virtually overnight. Add to that the huge improvements in golf equipment since the golden oldies were built, plus the developer syndrome that big yardage denotes "championship" quality, and you have the answers to why the game becomes ever more power-oriented.

Although in my peak competitive years I enjoyed power aplenty, the only major championship in which it gave me a big advantage, because of the openness of the Augusta National course, was the Masters. As the stories herein of my wins and losses clearly illustrate, the severe penalties for missing fairways and greens in most U.S. and British Opens would cause me to throttle back many more times than I would let out shaft. This fit comfortably with my philosophy, particularly since the 1966 British Open, that golf is principally a game of precision: that you will score your best when you map and then play your way through each hole most intelligently. For many years now, that is how I have designed my courses.

My number-one goal, then, in terms of creating individual shot values, is to make the player use his mind ahead of his muscles—to control his emotions sufficiently to really think through his options before drawing a club from the bag. Beyond that, I want to make well-thought-out shots look interesting and inviting, and I want the ball to be collected rather than repelled whenever it is properly played or only slightly missed. Also, I always prefer a downhill shot to an uphill one, and particularly from the tee.

To achieve all of this, I need to actually see my holes evolve, which is why I have often made many more site visits than most of the developers I've worked with believed I would before we got involved. Depending on the experience of the design associate I am working with—a number of my people have become accomplished architects in their own right—I will make at least six and sometimes twice that many visits to my courses in the U.S. during the center-lining and construction processes. I naturally make fewer visits to jobs outside the U.S. purely because of distance. However, both at home and abroad, one of our firmest rules is that work is never taken to the next stage of construction before I have signed off on it. That enables us, when I feel something is not quite right, to make adjustments for the minimum expenditures of time and money.

The greatest challenges in designing golf courses, and the greatest rewards, lie in situating and creating greens. The joy of a fine piece of land is that wonderful green sites often suggest themselves, in relation to natural water, or wetlands, or woodlands, or hills, or valleys, or simply the general flow of the land. The top challenge with a poor piece of land is to create varied and enticing greens out of next to nothing, or sometimes even nothing at all. As a rule of thumb, the prettier or more rugged the land, the less movement the greens need, whereas the duller or flatter the site the more I need to create undulation. Frankly, I have never been 100 percent happy with how I've responded to the greens challenge on really bad land, and I'm sure no other golf course designer has either.

Because I personally dislike playing golf in a cart, my pet peeve as a designer is being forced by land-planning considerations to locate greens so far from tees that golfers can't comfortably walk the course. I have gone to the mat many times with developers over compromising the flow of a course just to accommodate a few more homesites. I don't always win, but we usually manage to strike a compromise that makes the course walkable, even if in a few instances marginally. In that regard, I always push hard with developers for caddie programs, and particularly for using youngsters during the summer months, giving them the opportunity to make some money, to learn the game, and to absorb important lessons about life by being around intelligent, successful adults.

It has often been said that there are only three types of golf course: strategic, heroic, and penal. Although heroic is often perceived and criticized as penal by the golfer who continually tries to exceed his capabilities, if I had to categorize myself it would be as mostly a heroic designer—although tempered by a strong desire always to offer strategic alternative routes. For instance, I like par fives that require a heroic effort under risk of severe penalty to get home in two for an eagle chance, but that also offer one or more safer but still appealing routes to a possible birdie or a sure par.

The thing I take the greatest pride in as a designer is honesty—

not tricking up holes, trying to keep everything out in the open. I don't want to play with the golfer's mind, just make him or her use it fully. I go to great lengths to avoid deception—making a shot look one way when actually it plays another way. Although, as I have said, I may have been overinclined to favor my own left-to-right flighting preference in shaping doglegs in my early days, for many years now I have striven to achieve complete balance in all aspects of the courses I've created. That has frequently meant including shots that are more appealing to a middle-handicap player than they are to me.

At the time of writing, more than 130 of my designs are in play in the U.S. and some twenty-three other countries around the world, and I am extremely proud of the large number that have made various "best" listings and/or been used for top amateur and professional tournament play. It is still a great adventure for me to be invited to take a piece of raw land and try to create on it something that will give enjoyment to people for many years after I'm gone, and I hope the opportunities to do so will keep coming as long as I am able to commit fully to meeting them. Beyond that point, I am delighted to say that my oldest son, Jack II, has both fallen in love with designing courses and become extremely adept at it. Also, in 1995 two other sons, Steve and Gary, made their first design efforts with the help of our ever more skilled in-house team of specialists, which includes my son-in-law, Bill O'Leary.

There is no question that I am handsomely capitalizing in my design business on the reputation I have built and the knowledge I have acquired over my forty-plus years in golf. At the same time, however, I feel I am contributing something of value and permanence to the game that has been so good to me.

9

The 1967 United States Open Championship

"What's Wrong With Jack Nicklaus?"—Round 1

In my first four years as a professional golfer, I averaged more than twenty-four tournaments a year in the U.S., plus the British Open and a number of other overseas trips for the Canada Cup (the World Cup from 1967), various other tournaments, and television and exhibition matches. Add made-for-television events and corporate outings in the States and I traveled and competed at golf more than forty weeks each year.

My love of competition was partly responsible for this busy schedule, as was the difficulty of saying no to friends: Then as now, when a friend tells me he needs me I find it hard not to respond, even when I know it's not doing me any good. Also, it would be foolish to deny the significance of money in those early days. No matter how confident an individual may be of his or her abilities, everyone who plays a game for a living is always at least subconsciously aware that it can't go on forever, and that injury or illness could end it overnight. Although I believe such thoughts are more a positive recognition of reality than a product of insecurity, they tend to make you want to get yours while you can, even though, as in my case, you may never think about money while actually competing.

Looking back over my entire career reminds me of how fortunate I am to possess the kind of mind that allows me to leave my golf game at the golf course. Then as now, how I played on any given day was rarely a topic of conversation once I arrived home. One reason was that all of the Nicklauses were always too busy with their own activities to want to help dissect Pop's wobbly wedge play or jerky putting stroke. (Wherein lies a great tip: If golf is driving you crazy, get involved in so many other things that you simply don't have time to think about it.) Another reason was that I have never thought it proper for a spouse or parent to impose his or her workaday trials and tribulations on the rest of the family. Does a plumber bore his closest and dearest by going on about faucets or a broker about derivatives? When decisions affecting the entire family had to be made on which my golf had a bearing, it received the appropriate consideration. Otherwise, my game as a conversational topic ceased as I closed the trunk lid on the clubs.

I believe this ability to compartmentalize activities contributed importantly to a happy household whenever I was home during my early pro years. What had become evident by the end of 1965, however, was that I wasn't home as much as I needed to be. With a four-year-old, a two-year-old and a less-than-year-old baby, it was increasingly difficult for Barbara to travel with me as much as we both desired. That being the case, the only way for me to spend more time with her and the children was to cut back my schedule. Although we were then far from attaining lifelong financial security, I would shortly top half a million dollars in total prize winnings, so paying the grocery bills was no reason to keep pushing myself so hard. I had vowed when I turned pro that I would never spend more than two weeks on the road without my family accompanying me, and the only time I had broken that vow was by leaving the kids home during our South African trip the previous winter. Over the year-end holidays of 1965 I reaffirmed the vow to myself, and told the media that henceforth I would be playing fewer tournaments.

THOSE good intentions survived 1966 pretty much intact. I had played only ten tournaments ahead of the British Open, and disciplined myself to the same number thereafter, partially making up for a tired performance in the PGA immediately following the Muirfield victory with second places in the Thunderbird and Philadelphia Classics, then wins in the Sahara tournament and, both times with Arnie, the Canada Cup in Tokyo and the PGA National Team Championship played in mid-December on my doorstep in Palm Beach Gardens. It had been a fulfilling year, and it seemed reasonable to assume that the less hectic pace had some bearing on that. Beginning work on my game with Jack Grout after the holidays, I saw no reason why 1967, if similarly well paced, should not be likewise.

One slight hiccup in the pacing was right at hand. For years the Bing Crosby National Pro-Am had been the third tournament on the schedule late in January, which suited me just fine. Now it had become the second, which, if I were to play, meant a break of only five weeks between the end of one season and the start of the next. For a while I was tempted to pass up the Crosby, but Bing had become a good friend and I loved Pebble Beach and Cypress Point. Finally, beginning with the Crosby, I decided to play three tournaments in a row in California with the family along, take a break until the tour hit Florida where I could play everything while still spending a couple of days at home each week, then follow pretty much my usual summer schedule with some pruning in the fall if necessary.

In one way, it was a fortuitous decision. Out of the blue on the back nine at Pebble on the Sunday, after trailing playing partners Palmer and Casper by a couple of strokes, suddenly golf became a piece of cake and I birdied five of the last seven holes to win my first Crosby by five shots. As things turned out, however, the cake would leave an unpleasant aftertaste.

The morning of that final round, I had experienced pain in my back and left side while doing my exercises. I had taken a long hot shower, and Barbara had done her best as a masseuse, but trying to swing forcefully on the range had been difficult, and the cold sweat that hit me on the first couple of passes for real almost made me withdraw. Instead, I decided to try going at the ball predominantly with my arms and hands, which worked well enough for me to go out in 37 then return in 31 as warming weather and adrenaline buildup reduced the pain to little more than a dull ache.

The problem was that restricting body motion in the swing required me to hit extra hard with my right hand, which, as it generally will for most golfers, resulted in most of my full shots drawing from right to left. Gone was the gentle fade that had served me so well during most of the second half of 1966. As always before when I had chosen to draw or accidentally fallen into drawing the ball, getting my left-to-right game back would prove extremely difficult.

At the Los Angeles Open the week after the Crosby, although my back had improved, I finished well out of the money. I played a little better from tee to green in the Bob Hope Classic the week after that, but putted like a comedian. Impatient for the opportunity a three-week break would give me to recover my trusty fade, I was glad to be going home.

During the first three days of the Doral Open, the beginning of the Florida swing, I felt sure the homework I had done had done the trick. Over the last seven holes of the final round I discovered otherwise, giving up the lead to eventually finish tied for fourth, two strokes behind Doug Sanders. Pressure will always tell you the truth about your game, and it told me that I still could not move the ball consistently, not just from left to right, but in any direction. Increasingly painful confirmation came in my other Florida tournaments: tied seventh in the Florida Citrus, tied thirty-fourth at Jacksonville, tied thirty-first at Pensacola.

By then, with the Masters only eleven days away, to say I was worried would have been quite an understatement. The previous June I had at long last become a Class A member of the Professional Golfers Association of America, thanks largely to Leo Fraser, a vice-president of the organization who managed to slice through a morass of red tape for me. That gave me eligibility for the Ryder Cup, and I badly wanted to make the 1967 squad. With only nine months to win sufficient points, instead of the then usual two years, plus my poor start to the season, I figured a great Masters was critical to my chances.

They say problems generally arrive in multiples, and this was certainly true that spring. Following Jacksonville, I had given fellow tour player Gardner Dickinson, who lived a few doors from us, a ride home in my plane, and stopped by his house to be friendly. When I discovered his kids had mumps it had turned into a short visit. Even so, as I had never had them, the next day, just for insurance, I visited our children's doctor, who suggested some vaccine shots. Within hours of getting the first one, my neck and middle back became stiff as a board. This did not help any at Pensacola, and another shot immediately after that tournament produced the same reaction. However, with the discomfort gone after three days of practice up at Augusta the week ahead of the Masters, I probably would never have given the shots another thought but for something my own doctor had told me when I went to him about the stiffness.

One of the vaccine's side effects was a period of poor coordination, and I can't think of two words to better sum up my performance that year at Augusta. After an opening 72, I was hopeless on the Friday, particularly around and on the greens. The result was a 79, still my highest Augusta National score. It not only took me out of the Masters, but also out of the 1967 Ryder Cup. Then, the following week, I added to the embarrassment of missing the cut at Augusta as the defender by giving away the Tournament of Champions over the final holes. Once again, I could not call on a consistent flight pattern —either fade or draw—when the screws tightened all the way down.

By then, virtually everyone I met had only one question: "What's wrong with you?" The short answer was that I had entered the worst slump of my career up to that point. Flying gloomily home from the T of C in Las Vegas, there was no escaping the fact that I was on the brink of completely losing confidence in myself and that, unless I found a way to fix things quickly, I could slide all the way down into the abyss. But find *what?* And *how?*

And then, as so often happens with golf at all levels, inexplicably things began to turn around. During the next three weeks, off the tour but playing some relaxed exhibition rounds, I began to sense the return of, first, a setup and then a swing pattern that would allow me to fade the ball consistently. Toward the end of that period, I found myself going at the full shots freely for the first time all year. With that, my driving power began to come back and my approaches to land where they were supposed to. But—wouldn't you just know it —now my putting was going all to pot.

At the Houston Champions International early in May, needing a good second round to make the cut, I hit virtually every fairway and green on the Friday, but never made a putt of more than five feet and missed one from fifteen inches. (Then, along with playing partners Al Geiberger and Cary Middlecoff, was slapped with an infuriating two-stroke penalty for slow play, turning a 69 into a 71.) A week later at New Orleans, the same miseries on the greens turned what should have been an easy win into second place behind George Knudson. Things then got progressively worse at the Colonial, where I tied for eighth, and—in what supposedly was my warm-up tournament for the U.S. Open—in Memphis with a tie for twentieth.

For the life of me, I just could not get the ball into the hole whatever I tried—and I must have tried everything anyone has ever dreamed up about putting since the days of Old Tom Morris. While playing with a fine seventeen-year-old amateur by the name of Tom Watson, I remember hitting rock bottom in an exhibition in Topeka, Kansas, by requiring twenty-one putts on the front nine, the most since my frog-chasing days with my father at Scioto. There was just no way.

Not helping my frame of mind was waking every morning to yet another "Is Nicklaus Finished?" column. At first they had simply been irritating. As the weeks passed, I almost reached the point of asking the same question.

I MUST have been asked a thousand times over the years for my rating of golf's four major championships. Here's how I feel about them.

It is sometimes argued that the Masters should not be included among the majors because it is not the championship of anything, and I know that its founder, Bob Jones, was sympathetic to that viewpoint. The truth is that Bob had no intention when he started the tournament of it being anything but an enjoyable springtime outing for his friends. His modesty was such that he insisted the inaugural event be called the "Augusta National Invitation Tournament," and in the years I knew him he disliked any reference to his creation as a "championship." As he invariably pointed out when such matters came up, it was the media that named his tournament "The Masters" and elected it a major.

For all of those reasons, even though the Masters is the major I enjoy playing the most, I have always placed it fourth, behind the U.S. Open, the British Open, and the PGA Championship, when pressured to rate the big four.

I rate the U.S. Open first for numerous reasons that I will get to in a moment. Heading them is the fact that, as an American, it is the championship of my country. I also believe it is the toughest of the four to win.

To me, the British Open earns its number-two rating as the world's oldest golf championship, as the championship of the country where the game began, and as the most international of the majors. The unique challenge of the big links courses it is traditionally played on makes it for me the second most enjoyable of the four, only slightly behind the Masters.

The PGA is third in my ranking because of its age, and because, when American players dominated golf, it often enjoyed the strongest fields of all tournaments worldwide.

Largely, I suppose, because they had played the game the longest, the British and their Open championship dominated the scene until about twenty years after the game had taken solid root on this side of the Atlantic. In 1913, however, American players received a boost that in a relatively short time led to a superiority that lasted for more than half a century. This was, of course, the victory in our Open of a nineteen-year-old, virtually unheard-of Boston amateur and ex-caddie by the name of Francis Ouimet over the legendary English golfers Harry Vardon and Ted Ray, in a playoff at The Country Club of Brookline on the outskirts of Boston.

Before Ouimet's victory, only one native-born golfer had won the U.S. Open, Johnny McDermott in 1911 and 1912, to twelve victories by players emigrating from Scotland and four from England. After Ouimet's sensational achievement, foreigners would win our championship only four times in the next sixty-seven years. Also, over that period, Americans, with previously zero victories in the British Open, would capture twenty-four out of fifty-six, along with all but five of the sixty PGA Championships and the forty-two Masters played. Although the best foreign players in recent years have become the equals and sometimes the betters of the top Americans, it was obviously this long U.S. dominance of golf that, most of all, gave our national championship its preeminence. There are, however, some additional reasons for its stature.

Number one is the quality of the courses over which it is generally played. The better the course, the more enjoyable the playing and the greater the fulfillment in winning. Throughout most of its history, and certainly in my time, U.S. Open courses have generally been the finest in the nation. Excepting the fixed-location Masters, this is true of no other old-established tournament.

Number two is the condition of those courses. The traditionally narrow fairways, heavy rough and firm ground conditions of U.S. Open courses annually present players with their most severe mental and physical examinations. Win the U.S. Open and you know you have survived golf at its most demanding.

Number three is the field. Any golfer with fire in his belly dreams of winning the championship of the world's largest golfing nation, which means the best players of every era almost always participate. This again is not true of any other event, including even, I'm sad to say, because of its limited invitational field, the Masters.

Fourth is a factor you rarely hear much about but which I think is an important contributor. More than any other top event, the U.S. Open is still pure, straight golf, with a minimum of commercial hoopla. In an age where money increasingly dominates all sport, and despite the corporate tents of recent years, the U.S. Open's single objective remains identifying the best player. For me, that gives it an aura and a flavor unattained by any other championship. Over the years there have been some justifiable criticisms of the Open's organizational standards, but, if less than operational perfection is the price to be paid for minimal commercialism, then fine and dandy with me. If money ever becomes more of a factor in the U.S. Open than generating enough to stage it decently, that will be the day it begins to slide off its peak among the world's great golfing occasions.

You can probably tell from these sentiments that the U.S. Open has always been extra special for me, and it was never more so than in the spring and early summer of 1967. As in the past, I felt a thrill of anticipation every time I thought about the championship. Unfortunately, though, that feeling tended to get wrestled aside by another emotion that was both unfamiliar and unpleasant: anxiety. Not only was I coming into the Open off the worst six months of my career, but also with my weakest record in a major since turning pro. In 1963 at Brookline I had missed the cut. Twelve months later, at Congressional, I had tied for twenty-third, seventeen shots behind Ken Venturi. In 1965, at Bellerive, after an exceptionally thorough study of the course with friend Gary Player, he had won and I had tied for thirty-first, again seventeen strokes off the pace. Then, at Olympic, in my last try, I had fumbled at least a slim chance of victory with a sloppy final round to finish third behind Casper and Palmer.

I had heard it said by old hands about the U.S. Open that any half-decent golfer on a hot streak might luck out in it once, but that it took a real champion to win it a second time. As I flew north from Florida the week ahead of the championship for my first look at Baltusrol, I let my mind dwell on that thought as an extra stimulus.

BALTUSROL Golf Club is located in Springfield, in the rolling hills of central New Jersey, about twenty miles southwest of Manhattan. Founded in 1895, it played a prominent role in the formative years of American golf, and today is rivaled by only one other old-timer, Oakmont, as our leading host of national championships.

In 1967 we would play the Lower Course, designed by one of America's finest golf architects, A. W. Tillinghast, and opened in 1922. In most respects I liked it immediately. To begin with, the course had the same settled, mature feeling as the one where I grew up, Scioto, opened in 1916 and thus one of the older clubs in the Midwest. Additionally, the layout had a natural, uncontrived, un-prettied-up quality, particularly on the less wooded stretches from the seventh through the sixteenth holes, that reminded me a little of the great British links courses. I decided this more than made up for the handful of semiblind drives and eight or nine approaches where you couldn't see the bottom of the flagstick.

What I liked most about Baltusrol, though, was its condition. For a reason I never discovered, the United States Golf Association had not narrowed the fairways to a point where they eliminated or severely limited the use of the game's most exciting club, the driver. Here we generally had between thirty-five and forty yards of short grass to aim at from the tees. And what fine grass it was. Composed of bent and *Poa annua* cut very low, the fairways were the best I had encountered for playing iron shots, the ball sitting cleanly on top of them, enabling you to get all the way down to its bottom with no risk of trapping grass between blade and ball. There would be few if any "fliers" here, which was excellent news. Equally good, due to a long spell of dry weather, was the reasonable height and consistency of the rough. Miss those gorgeous fairways and you generally had a chance of advancing the ball with something more than a sand wedge and a prayer. All in all, I felt this was the best balanced U.S. Open course I had yet encountered: consistently demanding from the tee, invariably challenging on approach shots, never a cinch if you missed a green, but, taken in the round, a fair and enjoyable test of golf.

Liking a course always increases one's desire to play well, and Baltusrol added to mine. But, in one respect, it also worried me. The less penalizing the conditions, the better the chances of a larger number of players, and the more contenders, the greater the impact of putting on the outcome. After two days of practice, I was certain that putting would be a critical factor in the 1967 U.S. Open. Considering my recent efforts in that department, this was not good news.

Well, it sure is great to have friends! I had played both of those days with Deane Beman, and—surprise, surprise—here comes little Deano to my rescue yet again.

For most of the previous year I had used a Ping putter, and had persevered with it on the well-known principle that poor putting invariably derives from the "puttee," not from his implement. Nevertheless, I had brought half a dozen other putters to Baltusrol. Following our Friday round, still trying to figure out which one to use (and how), on the spur of the moment I picked up a spare center-shafted Bull's Eye of Deane's, and decided immediately that it might be the answer to my prayers. Seeing the covetous look in my eye, Deane, one of golf's all-time great putters, quickly reclaimed his trusty weapon, but the next morning dug a selection of similar clubs from the trunk of his car and invited me to take my pick. Naturally, none of them felt as good as Deane's second-string putter, and I was about to return to my Ping when Fred Mueller, a pal of Deane's from Washington who was on the green with us, told me that Deane had worked on his Bull's Eye, and that I was welcome to try it if I cared to. I accepted the offer, and knew on the first stroke that it was identical with Deane's with the exception of having an all-white head (Fred had painted the brass to prevent sun glare). Recognizing how much I liked it—and probably how much I *needed* it—Fred offered to let me keep it. I thanked him, promised him some MacGregor putters in return, and took the club home to Florida and practiced with it over the weekend. By Sunday night, I couldn't wait for the Open to begin.

By Tuesday evening, back at Baltusrol and back on the putting green after my practice round, I was at square one again. I had struck the ball beautifully getting to the greens, then performed on them like a beginner with a hangover. "White Fang," as the putter came to be known, still felt good—but there was still something seriously wrong with the fellow using it.

Like everyone who has enjoyed any success at this game, I have had the good fortune on more occasions than I can recall to just happen across a tip at a moment of extreme need that fixed a seemingly insoluble problem. In this instance, the bearer of good tidings was Gordon Jones, an old friend from Ohio and a periodic tour player with a fine knowledge of technique. After watching me for a while not even hit the hole from no more than ten feet, Gordie suddenly said, "Jack, why don't you try taking a shorter stroke and hitting the ball harder?" For months I had been trying to do exactly the opposite, taking the club back long and flowingly in an effort to obtain the necessary distance by a free-swinging pendulum-type motion rather than by force of strike. But what the heck . . . as an amateur, I'd mostly swung relatively short and popped the ball . . .

The moment I tried Gordon's suggestion, orchestras began to play and angels to sing. I have never believed in miracles, but this was close. I worked on the shorter backswing for an hour or so, and couldn't get the silly grin off my face all through the rest of the evening. The next day, in my final practice round, despite closing with two par fives, I holed almost everything I hit for a round of 62.

PRACTICE round scores are, of course, meaningless beyond whatever they may—or may not—do for your confidence, but low ones always seem to make headlines, so Thursday morning I got a big share of the sports section's large type. However, Friday's papers had a very different slant.

During my peak years, it became almost commonplace for an "unknown" to lead the U.S. Open after the first round. The 1967 championship was no exception, but this time there was an extra dimension to further excite the fans and the media. Marty Fleckman, who had opened with a smooth 67, was not only a new name to almost everyone at Baltusrol, but an amateur barely out of college. With the last victory by an amateur in the U.S. Open being Johnny Goodman's in 1933, for the three days that Marty remained in the thick of this one he received enormous attention. Unfortunately, all the fuss, along with his inexperience, finally exacted a price: an unhappy final round and a slide to a tie for eighteenth place. But it was a valiant effort by the young Texan, and one that increased the excitement of the championship for all involved.

I excited nobody that first day, and particularly not J. W. Nicklaus. The full shots were not coming off the clubface quite as easily and sharply as the day before, but basically I had arrived on the greens in decent numbers. Also, I was pleased not to have hit one hook or even a draw. My problem, yet again, was on the greens: a complete reversal of the previous day. Then, I had drained everything. Now, I could make nothing. The result was a one-over-par 71. What annoyed me as much as the thirty-five putts was the missed opportunity in such fine scoring conditions. It had become and would remain stiflingly hot and humid. ("Hot?" commented Ben Hogan. "Hell can't be any hotter, and I'll check that out one of these days.") Nevertheless, nine men had broken 70, including Arnold Palmer, Bill Casper, Gary Player, and Deane Beman. Working on my putting after the round, it was tough not to get despondent. I heard that Arnie had canned a monster for a birdie after two poor shots, then, pumped up, immediately made a couple more snakes. I would have given a lot for one of those morale-builders.

It arrived on the fourth green early the next morning.

After opening with a bogey and two pars, I had not been in the best of spirits sizing up the tee shot. Number four is generally regarded as Baltusrol's prettiest hole, but it is also one of the trickiest: 190 yards with a stone-walled pond immediately fronting the shallow green and four bunkers in back. Distance is thus the critical factor, and I had gotten that part right in choosing the 3-iron. But overanxious and hurried (the two are synonymous), instead of fading the ball, I'd drawn it into light rough to the left of the green, then fallen asleep on the chip. Now I had an eleven-foot putt for par. Studying it, the predominant thought in my head was that if I missed and went three over for the championship, I could almost certainly wave it good-bye. There were simply too many fine players firing low for me to be able to bridge a big gap.

It is probably kind of dumb to suggest that a single stroke can win a championship, but this one still sticks in my mind that way. When that putt dropped, everything changed. Despondency turned into elation, doubt into confidence, sluggishness into momentum. I birdied the next hole from four feet, the eighth from twelve feet, the twelfth from fifteen, the sixteenth from twenty-five, and the 545-yard eighteenth with two putts from forty feet after a great drive and 1-iron, for my then-lowest round in a U.S. Open of 67. At the end of the day there was only one golfer ahead of me: Arnold Palmer.

• • •

In one respect, this was excellent news, because nothing then more inspired me than doing battle with Arnie. That evening, however, I also had some less positive thoughts on a couple of counts, neither of them relating to his one-stroke advantage.

The United States Golf Association's pairing system for the last two rounds of the Open was then and is still strictly arithmetical: first plays with second, third with fourth, and so on. This meant that Arn and I would be paired together for Saturday's third round. My first concern was the extra burden this imposed on us of focusing on besting the course and the field rather than just each other. Not since the Open of 1962 had we been paired in a major championship with both of us contending, but it had happened on numerous occasions in regular tour events. No matter how strong our resolve—and we had discussed the problem candidly—with so intense a rivalry it had proven impossible for us not to end up going at each other head-to-head, which invariably had cost us both. I knew I would have to fight hard to prevent it happening again the next day.

My second concern was speed of play. When I got behind in those days it made me try to hurry, which led to mistakes, which compounded the problem by making me take even more time over shots. Being overtly timed by officials in the previous year's Open at Olympic had made me fretful, and, as mentioned, I had been penalized for slow play only a few weeks earlier in Houston. Thus I had made a vow on the eve of this championship to keep myself moving along, to, if necessary, force myself to stay up with the group ahead. However, while Arnie himself certainly would not interfere with that—he was always a fast player—we now had to contend with the large and boisterous New York/New Jersey battalion of his famed Army. Inevitably, the bigger and more excited the crowds accompanying them, the harder it is for players to giddyup. All I could do was hope the officials would take this factor into account if we began falling behind.

I had one more thing to dislike that evening: television. This was about the time that the networks began to exert the pressure on golf's administrators that today has given them almost total control over the timing of weekend tournament rounds. The broadcaster had decreed seven o'clock finishes for the 1967 Open, which meant that Arnie and I would not tee off until three in the afternoon. It was a challenging prospect and it proved a challenging reality. I remember Barb and I yawned through *Casper the Friendly Ghost,* then *The Winsome Witch,* then a Bob Hope movie, then most of Randolph Scott in *Riding Shotgun* before it was even time to leave for the course. B-o-r-i-n-g, not to mention the impact on the nervous system.

As things turned out, thanks largely to fine crowd control, the slow-play problem never materialized. Both of us striding as fast as we could between shots, we got around on Saturday in three hours forty minutes (spurred toward the end by a threatening storm, we would improve on that by fifteen minutes the next day when we also played together). But, whether subconsciously or not, that old head-banging bugaboo got to both of us yet again in round three. On the eighth tee, Arnold finally suggested we stop playing each other and start playing for the championship, and I agreed wholeheartedly. By then, though, it was too late for either of us to change the mind-set. Compounding the problem, perhaps for him almost as much as for me, was the size and volatility of the "Army." It was the biggest and noisiest I had ever played before, and also by miles the most blatantly partisan. I knew I had some fans out there, too, because they had been rooting for me the first couple of rounds, but on Saturday they were mostly invisible and inaudible. Conceivably that's because I could give them so little to get excited about. Birdies on seventeen and eighteen kept my final tally out of total disaster range at 72, which bettered Arnie by a stroke. But both of us had produced basically miserable displays of golf.

The only consolation was that Casper, who had carved himself a four-stroke lead leaving the fourteenth green, had backpedaled into a tie with us by the time he left the eighteenth. But all this was inside-page stuff. The big news once again was the Byron Nelson protégé, Marty Fleckman. Most people had been expecting him to follow his opening 67 with an 80-something, and, when that didn't happen in the second round, were sure it would in the third. Instead, Marty, with a fine 69, had ended up in the lead.

REGARDLESS of how I have played, throughout my career I have almost always spent some time on the driving range following tournament rounds. One reason is simply to "wind down" my nervous system—to let off steam, if you will. Another is to seek a solution while the memory and senses are sharp if something is off kilter, or to reaffirm and reinforce the good moves or feelings if I'm swinging well. In fact, I've generally been able to achieve more with my swing following tournament rounds than at any other time.

By the time we got through the interviews and other postround chores that Saturday evening at Baltusrol, there was not much daylight left, but I was determined to get in a solid session. Sloppily as I'd played, I still believed I had some fine golf in me, and I wanted to prove that to myself before going to bed. As on the course, the first few swings did not feel right—okay, but a little forced. After a few more shots reviewing my basics, I discovered why. To fade the ball, you need to align the body a little left of target. As so often over the years, I had been creeping to the right in my setup. With a slight change in shoulder alignment, everything suddenly fell in place. I went through the entire bag just to be sure, then moved over to the putting green. On the course I had sensed I was quitting with my left hand through impact. I worked on that until I lost the hesitant feeling, then wended my way back to the motel to wait out another challenging starting time—3:08 P.M.

ONE of the great moments of anticipation in golf occurs when you walk onto the practice tee before the final round of a major championship when fully in contention. That's because within a minute or two you will have a pretty accurate idea of your chances from the feel of your golf swing. The Sunday of the 1967 U.S. Open is still one of my happiest warm-up memories. The first few wedges were perfect. So were the other short irons, then the medium irons, then the long irons, then the driver. On to the putting green and, there again, a great feel. Down they went, easy as shelling peas. "Well, Nicklaus," I said to myself, "maybe you can finally play golf again. Let's go find out."

No doubt helped by the good practice session, my qualms of the previous day about playing with Arnold had evaporated. As always in those days, when he was in contention I saw him as the man to beat. That being the case, I was now happy to be playing alongside him. His presence would heighten my concentration, force me to keep my mind 100 percent on the task at hand. The Army was in full force and song again, but I resolved to have it serve as a spur rather than a distraction.

By the time we arrived at the fourth tee, my anticipation of a two-horse race appeared to be materializing. Fleckman and Casper, playing immediately behind us as the final pairing, had both begun poorly. Following a steady opening par, I had bogeyed number two, but then sneaked a twelve-footer in the side door at the third hole for birdie. That had tied me with Arnie again, and given me the kind of lift I'd gotten the previous day with the saving putt on number four. Now I enjoyed a couple more boosts, with a perfect 3-iron to four feet for a second straight bird, then a fifteen-footer at the fifth hole for a third. That put me two ahead of Arnie and alone in the lead.

I will always believe that the next three holes decided this Open.

At the first of them, number six, Arnie made his sixth solid par in a row while I bogeyed, missing from seven feet. It was a tricky putt and I fretted less over missing it than about reopening the door for my toughest adversary. Arnold's drive at the rugged 470-yard seventh hole confirmed the boost he had received: Dead straight and absolutely nailed. I hit a solid one, too, and when we got to the balls was delighted to find mine a couple of steps ahead.

Even off a good drive, the second shot to this hole is one of Baltusrol's most challenging (the members play it as a par five but it's a four on the Open card). The green is oval-shaped and drops away at the back, and the bunkers fronting it hide the bottom of the flagstick. Arnie hit what he would later describe as one of the best shots of his life, a superb 1-iron that came to rest no more than twelve feet behind the cup. I followed with a high, faded 2-iron that ended up about twice as far away.

The Army had gone nuts over Arnold's great shot, and became even wilder as he strode onto the green. My thoughts as I followed him were very much on the psychological impact of what would happen next. If I missed and he made, we would be tied again, and he would be all set for another of those legendary "charges." I decided this was not a moment for playing safe. "Whatever else, get it there," I told myself, and stroked the ball firmly. As soon as it took off I thought, "That's in," and as the ball got to within five feet I started to walk after it, certain I'd made it. The look Arn gave me as I picked the ball out of the cup is one I will never forget, and he told me later that this putt "absolutely crushed" him. When he missed his own birdie effort by a whisker, suddenly I was again leading by two strokes.

The perfect tee shot at number eight on Baltusrol's Lower Course is a driver started down the left side of the fairway with a slight fade. Now, really pumped, I could not have played a better one in a hundred tries. And then came another opening. Obviously reacting to the unexpected turnaround on the previous hole, Arnie hit what he later described as his only bad tee shot of the championship, overcutting the ball into the right rough, where it stopped behind the trunk of a tree. He had no option but to pitch out sideways, and from there was unlucky to trickle off the fringe of the green into a bunker. Thus he now had played three strokes to my one, and would have his work cut out to make better than a bogey five.

The shot facing me was a pitch of eighty-five yards, definitely not my strongest suit. However, while trying to refind a golf game during those miserable weeks after the Masters, I had discovered that my chief problem on short pitch shots was an insufficiently firm left arm both swinging back and swinging through. By doing some strengthening exercises and keeping the arm almost rigid, I'd found I could keep the clubhead on a consistent path. Applying that technique now with the sand wedge, I stopped my ball almost where it landed four feet from the hole. When the putt dropped, I'd picked up another two strokes on Arnold and was leading the Open by four.

It had happened before and it has happened since, and it will probably happen again. Despite my good golf and large lead, all of a sudden on the back nine I could not shift my mind off the possibility of a disaster. The trigger, unquestionably, was number ten. The hole is a long par four with a tight driving zone, particularly for a fader of the ball, and the previous two days I had blocked myself out from the tee and bogeyed it. Now it cost me three putts, and, walking down the eleventh fairway, even though I'd hit a fine drive, I experienced a bad burst of jitters. Two solid pars helped to reduce them somewhat. Finally, after a pitching wedge to three feet at thirteen and a 7-iron to five feet at the next hole for a pair of easy birdies and a five-stroke lead, self-doubt became idiotic and was dispelled.

Baltusrol's Lower Course par for Opens is 70, and the birdie at fourteen had taken me to four under for both the round and the championship. Leaving the green, it occurred to me that Ben Hogan's seventy-two-hole record for the Open, set at Riviera in 1948, was 276, and that I could break it with three pars and one more birdie. I told myself to resist any impulse to try to force the birdie. Arnold had told me that the real reason for his stumbling golf over the final nine holes at Olympic the previous year was focusing too much on breaking the record, rather than on winning the title (he finally tied with Casper and lost in their playoff). With that in mind, I decided four pars in for 276 and the title would do just fine, and resolved to work on them speedily enough to beat an imminent and nasty-looking thunderstorm.

The first three of those pars came safely enough. On the 542-yard par-five closing hole, even though a good drive would have set me up to reach the green in two (I'd done so with a drive and 4-iron the previous day), for safety's sake I decided on the 1-iron for the tee shot. I felt a little foolish about it, but Arnie had birdied seventeen to cut my lead to four, and there was big trouble down the left side. Most of all, I knew I had a better chance of making six, which would still give me the championship even if Arnie eagled, off a missed 1-iron than a missed driver.

Miss the 1-iron I did, at least a little bit. Started straight rather than left, and faded too much, the ball finished just in the right rough close to a television cable drum. I was permitted a free drop clear of that obstruction, and knew as soon as I'd taken it I could forget the heroic option. The only intelligent shot from a lie as bare and tight as the one I had given myself was a punch out short of the water hazard 120 yards ahead. I took the 8-iron, choked down, made a nice compact three-quarter backswing, looked up halfway through the downswing, hit the ground about three inches behind the ball, and dribbled it all of fifty yards. Trying to relieve my embarrassment, I walked over and said to Arnie: "That was stupid, wasn't it?" Diplomatic as ever, all he offered was, "You said it, I didn't."

I guess if you have enough of it, pride will sometimes come to your rescue. I figured I now had 238 yards to the pin, uphill, all carry, and against the wind. Mathematically, that indicated the 3-wood. Emotionally, because of the greater confidence I've always had in it, I chose the 1-iron. The swing felt perfect, and, absolutely nailed, the ball carried the bunker, landed a few feet short of the green, and ran up onto it to finish twenty-two feet from the hole. It was certainly the longest 1-iron I've ever hit in competition, and quite likely the best.

Walking up the hill, knowing I had won the Open, there was now no reason not to let myself think about the record. This putt would do it, and I decided to be bold on it. When it dropped, giving me a 65 and 275 total, I let go with a mighty kick—the biggest spontaneous burst of emotion I had shown in a moment of victory. It was my lowest and best-played round in the Open, but the big thing was I had won the championship for that critical second time.

At last I could stop asking myself, "What's wrong with Jack Nicklaus?"

10

The 1970 British Open Championship

"What's Wrong With Jack Nicklaus?"—Round 2

BORN with a silver spoon in his mouth; had things too easy. Came up too quickly as a kid; didn't know how hard the game was. Made too much money too fast; no incentive left. Overweight and out of shape; lacks stamina now the years are adding up. Has a flying right elbow; bound to get him in the end. Is burned out and bored with golf except for the majors; can't stay competitively sharp. Doesn't practice hard enough. Spends too much time playing with his kids . . . working on business deals . . . going fishing . . .

After the 1967 U.S. Open at Baltusrol, I did not win a major championship until the British Open at St. Andrews in 1970. Above are some of the reasons offered in explanation of that long "slump" by various experts, singly or in combination, in print and elsewhere, and with ever-growing intensity over that three-year period. And the fact is, of course, that all through the later years of what some analysts chose to call my domination of golf, any time I went more than a season without winning a major, there was an encore to that chorus. Then, beginning in the late 1980s, it appears that everyone eventually decided I really was "finished" so far as the big four were concerned and pretty much stopped the inquests, usually after penning one last obituary.

This, therefore, might be an appropriate time to identify the real reasons for the dry spells during my peak years. First, though, let's quickly review those hypotheses so favored by my friends in the sportswriting business:

• The "poor little rich kid" articles of my late amateur and early pro years were bull. When my dad had only his first pharmacy on the Ohio State campus, he never made more than fifteen thousand dollars a year. Joining Scioto when he hurt his ankle wasn't easy for him financially. Things got better as his business grew, but he was never what most people would think of as a rich man. So, although I certainly never knew any kind of deprivation in my youth, it was always clear to me that hard work was the only way to preserve that situation.

• I did come along fast in golf, and did not fully learn how difficult the game is until after I turned professional. More on that in a moment.

• I'm no genius, but I was smart enough at twenty-one to know you cannot excel at sport by using money for motivation. As I said previously, if you play well enough, the money follows automatically, and if you play very well, there is soon enough of it to allow you to forget all about it as a performance factor. That happened to me long before 1967.

• I was overweight between my late teens and late twenties, chiefly because I was too young to worry about what I thought was heredity. My father and his family were all heavy, so I figured heavy was normal for me too. But I was also physically strong and full of energy, as exemplified by my tee shots and hectic schedule.

• I never had a flying right elbow in the true sense of that term, and I felt then as I do now that my high elbow position at the top of the backswing was the correct position. My hands swung so high and so deep that tucking the right elbow would have resulted in the club not remaining between my arms throughout the swing, as it always should.

• Continually improving at anything demands constantly escalating goals—that's basic to the human spirit. I made the major championships my spur and my goal for all the reasons I've enumerated.

Over the years that inevitably took some of the shine off the regular tournaments, but I was never stupid enough to believe I could win majors by competing in them alone. Also, out of sheer pride, I have never played a competitive round of golf without wanting to win and trying my best to do so.

• The supreme practicers in my time who were also great champions were Ben Hogan, Sam Snead, Arnold Palmer, Gary Player, Lee Trevino, Tom Watson, Seve Ballesteros, Greg Norman, and Nick Faldo. Building a golf game as a kid, I was certainly in their league. As I've described, every day in the summertime I would hit balls for an hour or two, play eighteen holes, grab a sandwich, hit more balls, play another eighteen, then hit balls or work on my short game until dark, and sometimes after dark. Some days I'd play fifty-four holes—once even sixty-three—carrying my own clubs. Or I'd hit balls all day long, five hundred, six hundred, seven hundred . . . We never took family vacations and I never went to camp as a kid. From my late teens on, what I did was work on building a golf game, every minute of every day I could get out there. Once I had built it, however, I practiced only enough to keep it tuned, or, if a problem arose, to fix it. Anything beyond that by then seemed like wasting time and energy. But, although I've always practiced more than people may have been led or chosen to believe, there have been times when I have become a little mentally lazy in certain departments. More on that in due course.

• My priorities have never changed since the day I got married: family first, then golf, then business, then my own amusement. If golf had ever seriously jeopardized our family life, I would have quit the game cold. I enjoy business, particularly the business of designing golf courses, as a change from golf and as a means of stimulating and exercising my brain more than is possible through any form of game-playing. Once I have a clear conscience about meeting my family, golf and business responsibilities and obligations, I have no hang-ups about enjoying myself with fishing tackle or hunting equipment or a tennis racket or a pair of skis, or in any other way. I figure I've earned the fun, and I find it a great change of pace and scenery and thus highly rejuvenating.

If all of this is true, then why the "slumps"?

Later, I will comment on some intrinsic qualities of the game of golf that are either little understood or too easily overlooked by many fans and writers, but that can make a good player seem to be "slumping" when he actually isn't. For now, though, let's stay with just this one golfer's genuine decline.

Mental laziness or complacency, or both, were contributors to my poor 1968–69 record, as they were again toward the end of the 1970s. There were a couple of other factors also.

Possessing the kind of mind that says nothing is impossible, and having progressed so rapidly at golf as a youngster, I eventually reached a point as an amateur where my ball-striking and shotmaking potentialities seemed limitless. As a result I sort of believed when I turned pro that, now that I could practice and play nonstop, I should be able to attain optimum form then hold onto it for long periods, maybe forever. Reality gradually hit home once I joined the tour, forcing me to recognize and accept golf's eternal inconstancy. Looking back, I believe that this had a certain demoralizing effect on me around the mid-1960s that reduced my drive to work at the game.

Compounding that problem was becoming so busy in so many other areas that I lacked the opportunity and energy to work as intensely at golf as I by then needed to do. I still practiced, but had fallen into the habit of not practicing either thoughtfully or thoroughly enough. Instead of returning to the basics and rebuilding from there, I made do with Band-Aids. As a result, when the wheels began wobbling in early 1967, I continued to try to live on my natural talent until, finally, the impact of the lean years on my pride, plus a traumatic event in my life, forced a different perspective, new priorities, and a return to the grindstone. Much the same pattern, minus the tragedy, would occur again some ten years later.

It would be tedious to go into a lot of detail about the results of my mid-1960s decline in terms of tournament performances, but a quick survey indicates its progressive severity:

Second half of 1967. Runner-up to Roberto De Vicenzo in the British Open at Hoylake—he simply played better to beat my not unsatisfying 71-69-71-69 by two strokes, and I was happy for him because he's one of the nicest people in the game. Missed a playoff in the PGA in Denver by a stroke due to a poor second round and an indifferent final one (Don January beat Don Massengale). Then, one of my hottest-ever streaks: won the Western Open, tied third in the

American Golf Classic, won Westchester and the World Series, tied second at Thunderbird, won the Sahara Invitational, teamed with Arnie to win the World Cup in Mexico City (our fourth victory), and led the money list with a record $188,988. The PGA voted me Player of the Year. What an easy game golf is!

1968. Oh, yeah? Tied fourth at Augusta, four strokes back of Bob Goalby, after closing the third round three-putt par, bogey, bogey, par, par, bogey. Second in the U.S. Open at Oak Hill with strong tee-to-green golf but awful putting, four back of a funny little guy I had never heard of when he'd finished fifth at Baltusrol the previous year, but would get to know well from then on—Lee Trevino. Second in the British Open at Carnoustie to Gary Player after a repeat of Oak Hill—fine from tee-to-green, unhappy with the putter. Watched at home on TV as Julius Boros became the oldest winner of the PGA at forty-eight after I missed the cut at Pecan Valley with an ugly second round 79. Then a spark: Reverting to an old putting stance and the putter I'd used in winning the 1966 British Open, I defended successfully in the Western Open, won the American Golf Classic and captured a third Australian Open in late October despite going five over par in my opening six holes. Can the man still play a little bit after all?

1969. Who's he trying to kid? Sixth in the Crosby and first in San Diego, then forget it until the fall. Tied sixteenth, tied fourth, tied tenth, tied twenty-eighth, tied twenty-third (ten shots behind George Archer in the Masters), tied sixteenth, tied fourth, tied forty-seventh, tied thirty-seventh (defending the Western), tied twenty-third (in the U.S. Open at Champions in Houston, eight strokes back of Orville Moody), tied fifty-second, tied fifth (in the British Open at Royal Lytham five back of new British hero Tony Jacklin), tied sixth, tied fourteenth, tied eleventh (in the PGA at NCR in Dayton, seven back of Ray Floyd). Then, after a Ryder Cup debut leading to a personal metamorphosis, first in the Sahara and Kaiser Invitationals and second in Hawai, before closing out the year with a sixteenth-place finish behind Arnold in the first Heritage Classic on a course I'd helped design.

I recognize now that the effect of my unwillingness during those years to go back to square one with my game was to make me weakest where once I had been strongest. The power that won me the reputation of golf's longest straight driver in my early pro years remained, but my directional problems grew. From being a consistently good putter, I became erratic on the greens—awful one round, okay the next, then bad again, then fine, then okay, then lousy again. I regarded my strongest competitive weapon as the ability to focus exclusively on the task at hand, enabling me to think my way around a golf course hole by hole and shot by shot with few errors. Now I made more and dumber mental mistakes, born mostly of poor concentration and insufficient patience, particularly under pressure. The mental lapses especially would make me mad, which escalated the other problems into a vicious circle.

All in all, the game of golf over most of that period was not a whole lot of fun. Then came an event that made it all seem pretty inconsequential.

I AM a little biased, of course, but it would be hard to convince me that any football team in the nation, amateur or pro, could exceed Ohio State for fan loyalty. Equally, nobody will ever persuade me that my dad wasn't the all-time grand champion OSU fan and booster. It's fortunate the college football and championship golf seasons didn't conflict, because, if they had, Charlie Nicklaus would have been faced with a terrible dilemma. As the years rolled by, due to illness or other matters beyond his control, he would occasionally have to miss following his son in one of the major golf championships. To the best of my recollection, he never missed an Ohio State home game until the fall of 1969.

Around the middle of October that year, Dad was at the stadium with his regular gang, but not behaving quite as robustly as usual. One of his pals noticed he looked a little yellow and suggested it might be a good idea to check with the doctor. Dad did so, and the diagnosis was hepatitis. He began a course of treatment, but over the next six weeks got sicker and sicker. Barbara and I became really concerned when he and my mother were unable to join us at Hilton Head Island for the Heritage tournament, being played over Thanksgiving. Then, on December 1, we got a call saying we had better come right away. We immediately flew to Columbus, and they opened Dad up the next day. He had inoperable cancer of the pancreas and liver. They told us he had between six and twelve weeks to live. He died February 19, 1970. He was fifty-six.

My father's death was a traumatic experience for me. Ever since I could remember he had been so much more than just a father: My guide, my companion, my mentor, my supporter, my defender, but always most of all my closest and surest friend. As I grew older and in my opinion wiser, we would sometimes squabble over trivialities, but always knowing in our hearts that nothing could ever change how we felt about each other and, in my case, that here was the rock I could always turn to whenever the need arose.

On top of the shattering sense of loss was the shock of my first experience of family tragedy. Apart from the deaths of the Bartons and the Longs prior to the 1966 Masters, there had been none at all in my life until this point, and I was ill-equipped emotionally to handle it. Still a young man, and always moving too fast in too many directions for much introspection, I had not developed the awareness and acceptance of mortality that can help a more rounded person better cope with this kind of experience. In other words, I still had a lot of growing up to do, in the real world as opposed to the golf world.

Barbara, in fact, has always believed that I only came to full maturity after my father's death, and I know now that she is right. I would hardly ever make any kind of decision without talking to my dad, phoning him day and night for his thoughts on even the most minor personal or family or golfing matters. With most of my business decisions then being made by Mark McCormack, there had never been much call on me for analysis or decisiveness; everything was laid out almost too easily. Then, boom, Dad was gone and suddenly I had to grow up.

It may seem a strange thing to say, but all these years later there is no reason not to face the truth. Even in his final days my father did me one last great service. As his decline continued, and knowing there was no hope, the emotion that surfaced more and more as I thought about our lives together was guilt. It hit me hardest after losing a playoff in San Diego a few weeks before he passed on. Here was a father who had done so much for his son, who had seen what he believed to be a rare potential and who had struggled and sacrificed so selflessly to help make that vision come true, and here now was the son, grown complacent, faltering, taking the easy way out, accepting second best, trying to get by on God-given talent alone.

By the time Dad died, I had decided those days were over. I might never fulfill it, but now at least I had recovered the will to do everything in my power to live up to his dream.

I HAD made my first acquaintance with St. Andrews in 1964, the year of Tony Lema's superb British Open victory in gale-force winds after only twenty-seven holes of practice. Within hours of arriving there that year, I had learned three things about the cradle of golf. First, as I've said before, I really loved the place. Second, reckoning the locals knew best, the correct pronunciation was "Sint Andrews," not "Saint" as we colonials want to call it. Third, assuming I ever could completely "learn" the Old Course, it would take me a lot of rounds to do so.

As more of the world's golfers have played the Old Course of St. Andrews than any other, and as more has been written about it than any other stretch of golfing terrain, I'm not going to take a lot of time describing all of the many factors that make it so difficult and perplexing.

As a tournament golfer, two stand tallest in my mind. The first is that even though, contrary to popular wisdom, the Old Course as we now know it was designed mostly by man rather than by nature, there is nothing remotely like it anywhere else, visually or architecturally. The second difficulty factor is the wind, and not just its strength, which can be mighty, but its unpredictability. As the compass has 360 degrees, so there are that many wind directions at St. Andrews. Worse yet, they frequently seem to change every few minutes.

Accordingly, to have any hope of winning over the Old Course, a golfer must meet two special conditions. First, he must become acclimatized to and comfortable with playing the game on what much of the time—and particularly if he's an American—doesn't look or feel like a golf course at all. Second, he must learn what those ever-changing winds will do to his ball, relative to a seemingly infinite number of invisible or partially hidden hazards, on each and every shot he might be called upon to play—including, sometimes, putts. To me, those two factors in combination make a British Open at the home of golf the most intriguing and maybe the most demanding challenge in the entire game.

These factors contributed heavily to our arriving in St. Andrews in 1970 the Friday morning of the week before the championship. A third and perhaps even sharper spur was the intensity of my desire to win the British Open in that place. Not every great golfer was able to do that, but, almost without exception, they admitted how badly they wanted to, and some even regarded the failure as a gap in their record. The thought of such a gap in mine depressed me. A lot of people I respected in golf believed that winning at St. Andrews was the only certain way for a golfer to forestall questions about his standing in the game's honor roll. After the experience of the 1964 championship, I had become caught up with that idea hook, line and sinker.

There were a couple more incentives as I settled in for five days of solid practice over the Old Course. Due to the Open's rotation around Britain's top links, I was unlikely to have many more opportunities—perhaps only one, two at the most—to win it at St. Andrews. There was also my performance to that point in 1970, particularly the previous week.

As had happened a number of times after a winter's rest followed by some intensive practice, I had come out fairly fast that season, finishing second in the Crosby (Bert Yancey fired a final 65 to beat me by a stroke), then only a shot adrift of Pete Brown and Tony Jacklin the following week in San Diego (Pete won their playoff). Thereafter, my only high spot had been defeating Arnie at our first playoff hole in the Byron Nelson Classic in Dallas in late April. In the Masters, thanks mostly to two awful putting days, I had never been a factor as Bill Casper tied with Gene Littler then won the playoff. In the U.S. Open at Hazeltine, won so handily by Jacklin for the first British victory in fifty years, I could not stop myself from disliking the course and played it accordingly: 81 in the opening gale and, short of missed cuts, my worst performance in a major to that point, tied for forty-ninth.

I recall experiencing only two emotions as I traveled home from Minnesota, then almost immediately over to Scotland: embarrassment and anger. By the time we arrived at St. Andrews, I was about as mad at myself as I ever had been, but in a positive sort of way. The following week, I was going to provide an answer to that boring old question now following me everywhere I went: "What's wrong with Jack Nicklaus?"

Nothing. *Not one darn thing*!

• • •

The Old Course is the hardest I know on which to align yourself correctly for both drives and approach shots. Its legendary undulations make the majority of its landing areas invisible as the ball is addressed, and there are no trees and relatively few other landmarks to serve as guideposts. This is particularly true of the first seven holes, where you are heading for the featureless expanse of the Eden Estuary with its backdrop of low hills. Correctly targeting myself had been tough in 1964, and it was again in practice this time until one of the guys I was playing with happened to mention the concept of using a short marker as an aiming aid. "Gee," I said to myself, "it's obviously a darn sight easier to align yourself on a spot a few feet ahead of the ball than on something a couple of hundred yards away. What a great idea!" Thereupon, having identified the distant target, I began on every shot to draw an imaginary line back from it through the ball, then to look for a bit of debris or grass discoloration on that line three or four feet ahead of the ball, and to use that as my key setup reference point. This system, which is followed today by many tour players, helped enormously not only in that championship but for the rest of my career.

The prevailing wind at St. Andrews is from the southwest, or from left to right on the first seven plus the tenth and eleventh holes. As a fader of the ball, this had troubled me in 1964 by forcing me to aim farther left than I was comfortable doing, then pray that the wind would swing the ball back on target. When the wind eased suddenly or gusted extra strongly, as it frequently did, that would not happen, and I had been left with some nasty recoveries.

Confronting the problem in practice this time, I decided to try something I had mostly resisted over the years: applying draw-spin to the ball by toeing-in the clubface at address, rather than through setup and swing variations. The technique worked beautifully immediately, enabling me to hold the ball against the wind and fire straight for my targets, and reminding me yet again that, no matter how long or well you play, there's always something new to learn about the game of golf.

Having spent five days practicing for gales, Wednesday's opening round conditions were, of course, exactly what you might have predicted: southern California by the North Sea . . . brilliant blue skies without even a zephyr of breeze. I shot 68, hitting every fairway and green in regulation, birdieing both par fives, and requiring thirty-two putts. It was a nice confidence-building beginning, but, with a third of the field beating par in some of the most benign conditions ever in an Open at the home of golf, it attracted minimal attention. What did cause a fuss was the defending champion, Tony Jacklin, now even more of a hero to British golf fans after adding the U.S. Open at Hazeltine a month earlier.

As recognition of Tony's contribution to European golf may have faded more than it should have over the years, I would like to digress here a moment with the hope of putting it in perspective.

Late on a sticky Sunday afternoon in October of 1983, at the PGA National complex in South Florida, America scraped home in the twenty-fifth Ryder Cup match against the European team by a single point. I was the nonplaying captain of the home squad, and I had never been as nervous on a golf course in my life as I was during the final hours of that memorable battle. Along with every member of our team, I was aware that the standards of European professional golf had been rising steadily for some years. Until that 1983 encounter, though, I don't think anyone over here fully appreciated how good our friends across the pond had become. For me, and I'm sure for a lot of others, that event marked the burial of any notion that Europe's best golfers were less than world-class.

Their play over the next decade in both major championships and Ryder Cup matches proved us right, of course. By 1983, Seve Ballesteros had already won two Masters and the first of his, through 1996, three British Opens. By the spring of 1994, Nick Faldo, Sandy Lyle, Bernhard Langer, Ian Woosnam, and José María Olazabal had joined him in lifting the tally of European big-four victories to sixteen, while also serving as the nucleus for back-to-back European Ryder Cup victories in 1985 and 1987, followed by a tie in 1989, the narrowest possible last-green, last-putt, single-point loss in 1991, a two-point loss in 1993, then a famous triumph in 1995.

There is no question that this grand renaissance was inspired, motivated and dynamically spearheaded during its most critical early years by Ballesteros, the mercurial Montanese from northern Spain. Nevertheless, I believe it was seeded well before that, back in the fall of 1967, when the man who happened to be my opposite number as European captain in the 1983 and 1987 Ryder Cup encounters,

Tony Jacklin, qualified for the U.S. tour and decided to make a 100-percent commitment to it.

Although then only twenty-three, Tony realized that to beat the best you had to learn directly from the best, and the only way to do that was by competing regularly with and against them. An outgoing and adventurous type, he made up his mind not only to do that, but to accept and enjoy the American lifestyle, historically the biggest challenge for European players. Accordingly, he was able to fit in quickly and comfortably in the States, which gave him the ease of mind to work diligently at and master our style of play. Following a win in the Jacksonville Open and a number of high placings in 1968, he had acquired by July of 1969 not only the techniques but the confidence and assurance to beat anyone in the world. As we know, the result was the first victory by a native in the British Open in eighteen years, then, eleven months later, the first in our Open in half a century by a Briton who had not immigrated to the United States.

Although Tony did not sustain this pace for long, I believe it was his two major championship victories that stirred European golf from its long slumber. Further, I believe that the respect shown for Jacklin by Seve Ballesteros when playing under his captaincy in Ryder Cup matches indicates that the Spanish champion feels the same way. Ballesteros certainly picked up the reins and ran with them, but they were first cracked by an Englishman while the young Spaniard was banging around with an old 3-iron on a beach at Pedrena. Jacklin of late has shown decent form on the Senior Tour after once again boldly committing to America and its ways.

As Barbara and I were preparing to go to dinner on Wednesday in St. Andrews in 1970, a huge storm swept in, swamping the course and forcing seven golfers, including Tony, to mark their balls and complete their rounds early the next morning. At that point, after a record-tying outward 29 including an eagle two at the driveable par-four ninth, Jacklin was eight under par and looked set for a 62 or 63. The Open authorities had often privately fretted about the susceptibility of the Old Course to a super-hot golfer in ideal scoring conditions, and Tony must have added to that concern overnight. Unfortunately for him, the magic cooled the next morning as he bogeyed three of his remaining five holes to finish with a 67.

Nevertheless, with Neil Coles setting a new course record of 65, and so many players beating par, the importance of wind in an Open at St. Andrews had never been more clearly demonstrated. I am sure there was also a little mumbling in the Royal and Ancient clubhouse that evening about the watering system installed on the Old Course the previous year. Controversial from the day it was installed, it had taken, I suspect, considerably more fire out of the auld sod than anyone had anticipated. Whereas traditionally, wind or no wind, a player facing an approach shot would be forced to stretch both his imagination and his striking ability to get the ball somewhere near the hole, on this day he could make simply a standard swing with complete assurance that the ball, if fully spun, would stick close to where it landed. Also, the lusher and slower greens had taken a good deal of the fire, and thus the fear, out of putting, and particularly on the three- and four-footers that are inevitable on such huge and severely undulating surfaces. In a nutshell, something akin to the American brand of golf had arrived at St. Andrews.

Thankfully for the traditionalists, it would not stay long. The locals had sworn that Wednesday's storm was the trailer for, as they saw it, more appropriate conditions, and they were correct.

By Thursday morning, the purring pussycat had become a roaring tiger that would grow meaner by the day through the remainder of the championship. Temperatures dropped as the wind rose, making you want to run after approach shots not only to mark the ball before it blew farther from the hole, but—despite, in my case, eventually three layers of sweaters—just to stay warm. At its peak in the playoff, the wind was officially clocked at 53 knots: gale force and close to hurricane strength. It ripped at the muscles and plucked at the nerves, and scared the daylights out of everyone, particularly on the greens, for fear of incurring a penalty through the ball blowing against the putter blade before it could be stroked.

I remember that on the more exposed greens out around The Loop—holes seven through twelve—it took a considerable effort of will for me just to ground the putter, never mind draw it back. The amount of break sometimes doubled, even on what would normally have been tap-ins, and players talked of stabbing the tops of balls and leaving putts halfway to the hole through their inability to anchor themselves. Whatever you had shot, good or bad, the feeling once you got off the course was of having been in a wrestling match rather than a golf tournament. "Not too bad a day for golf," I heard one old lady remark to her friend as she clung to her bonnet for dear life out by the eleventh tee. Ma'am, let me tell you, it was *exhausting.*

With my new clubface alignment and draw-spin techniques, I survived these challenges extremely well, going out in par, then eagling the 316-yard twelfth hole after driving to within ten feet of the pin, and closing with a birdie from twenty-five feet for a 69. As in the first round, I hit every fairway and green in regulation or better and never came close to a bogey, both of which I regarded as no small achievements. At day's end, I found myself tied for second place with Jacklin, one stroke behind Lee Trevino, who had shot a second straight 68. With his Texas-honed, low-ball wind game and unquenchable confidence, Lee was obviously the principal threat. Also, although the scoring overall had risen dramatically, there were a number of other fine wind players still within range, most notably Doug Sanders and Arnold Palmer. However, for two straight days, in wildly differing conditions, I had concentrated well, strategized intelligently, struck the ball immaculately, and putted at least adequately, so there was nothing to fear.

Easy of mind for the first time in a major for longer than I could remember, I retired early for ten hours of much-needed sleep.

THE most distinctive features of the Old Course are its seven enormous roller-coaster double greens, serving every hole except the first, ninth, seventeenth, and eighteenth. I like the concept of two greens in one to the point of including quite a few "doubles" in the courses I've designed, and also copied all six acres or so of the Old Course's greens contour for contour in creating the New Course at Grand Cypress in Orlando, Florida.

What I'm getting at in a roundabout way is that, although every golf tournament is to some degree a putting contest, the premium on the short stick at St. Andrews is greater than anywhere else in the championship game. If your stroke—or, even more, your nerve—begins to falter on those vast combinations of usually crusty and brown-tinged bent grass, fescue, *Poa annua* and whatever else will grow, you might as well pack up your sticks and go sightseeing.

I wasn't, therefore, quite as upbeat checking my card after the third round as I had been starting it. I had holed a putt of six feet, two of about ten, and one from twenty feet for birdies, and was duly grateful for them. On the other hand, I had missed three birdie chances from under twelve feet and the same number of times from less than twenty feet. Also, I had made five bogeys, three of them with three putts, including two back-to-back at eleven and twelve. My 73 kept me in joint second place with Jacklin and Sanders, and only two strokes back of Trevino, who had again played beautifully in equaling par. But, because I had handled the wind so well from tee to green, it was a disappointing round. After signing my scorecard and talking with the media, I went to the practice putting green and remained there for some time.

Trying to win golf tournaments has taken every bit of energy and concentration I can muster, so I have never been big on speculating about what other players may or may not do. Nevertheless, warming up on the Saturday, I was certain that only an excellent round would win this championship for me. There was no questioning Lee's mastery of the Scottish brand of golf—low to and/or along the ground —and Tony was still playing off the high of being the first golfer since Max Faulkner to whip those bloody Yanks. Both were obviously in top form in every department of the game, and Jacklin particularly had, along with enormous pressure, the exceptional incentive of knowing he would be set for life if he could repeat his Royal Lytham triumph at St. Andrews. Being from modest circumstances but with an admitted taste for the better things of life, Tony made no bones about how much winning majors meant financially to a British golfer.

Doug Sanders, too, was popular in Britain, as much for his obvious appreciation of the stature of *The* Open as for his rainbow get-ups and playboy lifestyle. I knew Doug well enough to believe that, even if he had started out the week partying, he would have been doing very little of that the past couple of nights, and I did not need to be reminded how close he had come to winning the Open at Muirfield four years previously. Doug had had to prequalify this time, was 37 years old, and had not won since 1967, but you don't capture the Canadian Open as an amateur and almost twenty tournaments on the U.S. tour without plenty of talent and heart. That splay-legged, ultra-abbreviated swing and wobbly follow-through may have offended the style purists, but the truth was that the Georgia Peacock had two of the finest hands ever attached to a golfer. When he was "on," no one in the game could better figure out and then execute the best shot for any given situation, particularly in tough conditions. I also knew that Doug was where he was despite beginning the championship by pitching into the Swilcan Burn and making double-bogey ("I guess my game isn't built around early-morning starts," he'd quipped). When you do something like that and are still only a couple of shots off the pace with a round to go, there's a mighty fine chance that this is your week.

I was paired for the final round with Jacklin immediately ahead of Trevino and Sanders. As I tacked through the howling left-to-right gale after a solid opening drive, I decided two things: first, that I would almost certainly win, or at least get into a playoff, if I could score no worse than par; and, second, that the key to doing so would be great patience. In these conditions, bogeys would be inevitable. My task was to put them instantly out of my head so as to keep my mind 100 percent sharp for every possible offsetting birdie opportunity.

For nine holes, this plan worked like a dream. I made birdies at two, five, and nine, and bogeys at six and seven for an outward 35, which would turn out to be the day's low. The only disconcerting thing about it was the nature of the bogeys—back-to-back three-putts from around thirty-five feet. But, with Trevino beginning to three-putt himself out of the picture, and Jacklin and Sanders making no headway, and the wind beginning to blow from right to left against my natural fade, I decided I was in excellent shape.

The eleventh hole of the Old Course, the 172-yard par three called "High-In," is one of St. Andrews's most famous, not least for having in 1921 provoked nineteen-year-old Bob Jones, after going out in 46, to pick up his ball and retire from the Open in fury following a battle with the notorious Strath bunker. I hit my tee shot into Strath, but managed not only to get out of the fearsome sandpit with one stroke but to stop the ball eight feet from the hole, only to miss the putt. So, bogey and back to even par for the day. Okay, no cause for panic. Just hang in there, Jack.

Two putts for par at twelve, then two more at thirteen from ten feet for another. Now the fourteenth, the par five. Driver and 3-wood to front of green, forty feet away, birdie time again. Three putts later, what a dummy! Par at fifteen. Sixteen, super drive, nailed 5-iron too strong, and again three putts. That's right, Nicklaus, just go ahead and give it away. Seventeen, the Road Hole, the scariest par four in golf. Driver, 5-iron, two putts from twelve feet. *Phew!* Eighteen. Reachable from the tee? Not quite. But the tee shot is in the Valley of Sin, only forty-five feet from the hole, and puttable. Oh yeah? Three putts, par. A round of 73, one over par, and one more than the number I had believed all along would win for me.

As I was walking up the eighteenth fairway, the huge crowd jammed around the seventeenth green had let out an enormous roar. It signified one of the greatest shots of Doug Sanders's career, from out of the infamous pot bunker to within a few inches of the hole. That superb recovery meant he could win the 1970 British Open by finishing with a par.

After miserably checking and signing my scorecard, I decided to do my initial suffering in as much privacy as possible and headed for a Royal and Ancient trailer office to watch Doug finish on television. By the time I got there, he had hit a fine drive to within about seventy yards of the flag. There was no question in my mind that he would make par, but he seemed to take a lot longer than usual in deciding on the shot to play. I had heard that he had gone all week whenever possible with the Scottish specialty, the bump and run, and obviously it had worked for him. Now I was a little surprised to see him take out a pitching club. He hit what looked like a nice shot, but the ball failed to grip on the wind-dried green and finished about thirty-five feet above the hole. The putt was downhill with a tricky left-to-right swing, and he left it about two and a half feet short of the hole. As the ball stopped, Tony Jacklin, standing next to me, said, "Hey, Jack, you're still alive." At the same time Royal and Ancient official Gerald Micklem was saying to Barbara, "I chose the hole positions this morning and that's a very difficult putt. It looks straight but it breaks to the right. You can't read it. More to the right and he could read it, but not there."

I had been thinking of heading out so I could be among the first to congratulate Doug on his first major championship victory. Now I decided to stay and watch. Doug looked over the putt carefully, then took his stance and seemed all ready to stroke the ball when he suddenly bent down to pick up a loose blade of brown grass that, he said later, he thought might have been a tiny pebble. Then he took his stance again, took his time getting set against the wind, and stroked. Almost as it seemed in the hole, the ball trickled away to the right.

• • •

No golfer ever really enjoys another's misfortune, and I felt bad for Doug and told him so as best I could right away. He had played superbly and had deserved to win. Whether he would have done so that Saturday if he had played a Scottish-style run-up approach to the eighteenth green, or hit that putt the first time he addressed it, no one will ever know. Those are the breaks in this game, and everyone who plays seriously has suffered plenty of them. There is never any point or satisfaction in second-guessing them.

Nevertheless, it would be foolish to deny that Doug's misfortune was one of the luckiest breaks of my career. I had done a lot of things right all week, for sure, but I had also three-putted what seemed an awful lot of times, including a pathetic effort after nearly driving the eighteenth green when a two-putt would have won for me. Getting a second chance after that many mistakes seemed little short of miraculous, and I resolved that night to make the most of it.

For the first thirteen holes of the playoff on Sunday, this did not seem like particularly hard work. I had gone two strokes ahead of Doug when he three-putted the third green then drove badly at the next hole. I picked up another shot when he took two to get out of Strath bunker, and extended my lead to four when he half-shanked his approach to the thirteenth green. By then you could tell from the demeanor of the crowd that, in their opinion, it was all over except for the prize presentation. Savvy as the Scots are about their national game, they should have known better.

Doug had done very little with the putter until that point. Now, suddenly, he found the touch, holing from six feet for birdie at fourteen after a great sand shot, then from triple that distance on the next two holes, first for another birdie then for par. I hadn't exactly cheered those birdies, but, coinciding with my first bogey of the day, his long par-saver on sixteen to take back three strokes in as many holes certainly eliminated any slight vestige of complacency that might have remained. I was delighted the Road Hole was playing downwind, and thus a little less dangerously than usual. Both of us handled it nicely but missed birdie putts, so I remained one stroke ahead with one hole to play. Okay, come on now, Nicklaus. Nail it down, fella.

Doug had the honor, and, with the wind at our backs so strong,

I'm sure he knew I had a chance of driving the ball the 348 yards to the eighteenth green, because he hurled himself into his tee shot like a whirling dervish. This produced a fine hit, the ball coming to rest only about thirty yards short of the flag, from where I had to assume he would get down in two more.

I took my time and thought hard about the correct club. In 1964, in similar conditions, I had driven the green three times with the 3-wood, but this week had been short three times with the driver and barely reached the front on the fourth attempt with the same club. Also, I was six years older, not to mention twenty or so pounds lighter. It had to be the driver. I decided it would do no harm to remove one of my sweaters, which, later on, caused a writer to suggest an effort to intimidate Sanders. That was not the case. All I was looking for was a little more swing freedom

I caught the ball very solidly and started it exactly where I'd aimed —at the flag. I could not be sure what happened when the ball landed, but was told it touched down just short of the putting surface and almost hit the flagstick. Whatever, I'd given it a little too much, rolling it through the green and into some tall, heavy grass about halfway up the bank, and only about three or four feet from the out-of-bounds perimeter fence.

Doug now played a nice little pitch-and-run with his 4-iron to within five feet of the hole. In view of the way he had putted over the last five holes, I was certain he would not miss this time. That meant I must get down in two to avoid going into sudden-death. Once again, luck was on my side.

When I got to my ball, I found it lying better than I had anticipated, with the grass slanting toward the green, reducing the chance that it would snag the club. I pulled out the sand wedge and made a number of careful practice swings, feeling out the slope and the weight of stroke necessary. Then, standing with my feet well ahead of the ball to give me room to swing the club parallel to the downslope, I got into the address position . . . and suddenly remembered an almost identical shot at the seventeenth hole at Muirfield in 1966, when I'd moved the ball three feet. "Forget it," I told myself. "Just concentrate on the weight of the stroke."

The ball came out almost perfectly and rolled down eight feet short of the cup. I was still away, and it occurred to me that my putt, although longer, was on the exact same line as Doug's the previous day, thus would break more to the right than it appeared to. I lined up accordingly and made a positive stroke. About three feet from the hole, the ball started to break across the cup, and I felt the beginning of a tightening in my stomach. Then the ball caught the right side of the cup, wavered, and fell in.

I had won the British Open at St. Andrews! I had won a major championship after three long, hard, lean years! The excitement was uncontainable. I leapt straight up in the air, and up with me went my putter—for what seemed about forty feet. Doug ducked, but I told him "You're all right," meaning the club wasn't about to bean him. I was almost in tears, as was my long-time British Open caddie, Jimmy Dickinson. I had never shown emotion like that before, and it was totally out of character. But then I had never before won the oldest golf championship in the world at the cradle and home of the game.

At the prize presentation, I told Doug I wanted him to win a major championship as much as he did, and I meant it from the bottom of my heart. Later that evening, I told Barbara, "They've all been for Dad in a way, but never quite like this one." I feel the same today, and am sure I will for the rest of my days.

11

The 1971 PGA Championship

Twice Around

FROM 1962 through 1967, I won thirty-four times at home and abroad, including seven major championships, topped the money-list three times, and averaged 70.34 strokes in U.S. tournaments. From 1970 through 1975 I won seven majors out of thirty-five victories, led in prize money four times, and reduced my stroke average to 70.13. Those stats point to the latter period as the best of my career, and the interesting thing to me now is what that says about the impact of a person's overall attitude to life on his achievements.

It is all too easy for the successful athlete to become so accustomed to taking that the concept of giving never enters the mind. I hope I wasn't only a taker during my early years in golf, but there is no doubt that my desire to put something back into the game grew with the maturing process that followed my father's death. The form it took was my ever-increasing interest in golf architecture. Designing courses was a sound business proposition, as well as an enjoyable creative challenge. No less a motivation was the feeling of making a more lasting contribution to golf than I ever could as a player.

My principal stimulus in that regard was what would become Muirfield Village Golf Club and the Memorial Tournament. As I have related, I had first gotten excited about the idea of giving Columbus a fine new club and a first-class golf tournament back at the 1966 Masters. Once we had taken the plunge, however, progress had been slow and increasingly stressful, until, by the early 1970s, the financial pressures on me personally were scaring the daylights out of most of my associates. A few years previously, I might have compromised my vision of how it should be done. Now, the faith and will to do it right, whatever the personal consequences, never wavered.

Although in this case there were no altruistic motives, the same sort of thing happened in a personal area that had been troubling me for some time, that of my business representation.

In my deliberations about turning professional late in 1961, the prospect of being represented by the same person who handled Arnold Palmer's business affairs was a major factor in my joining Mark McCormack. As the top golfer of the day, Palmer was the player I needed both to measure myself against and to learn from if I wanted to become a successful professional. Participating with him in exhibitions and other activities as the result of being a fellow client of Mark's would present enjoyable—and profitable—opportunities in both regards. Additionally, I figured getting to know Arnie better through those endeavors would probably lead to us practicing together at tournaments, and perhaps also sharing travel or social time. Even though he was also the guy I would be taking aim at, as a rookie pro the prospect of having such a man as a friend was most appealing.

And, of course, that's how it worked out. I learned a lot from Arnie my first few years on the tour, much of it through his generosity with advice, some by observing how he went about things. An example is a tip he offered about the smart play from the fringe of the green. I'd been practicing little chip shots from two or three feet off the putting surface, and not doing too well with them. After watching me for a while, Arn told me I would get better results by putting rather than chipping the ball. He said, "I've found over the years that my worst putt from the fringe is at least as good as my best chip." I tried it, and he was right, and I have used that tip ever since.

So, as hard as we tried to whip each other in competition and relentlessly as we needled each other—"Seventy-five today, huh? Where'd you get all your birdies?"—Arnie and I became friends, our wives became friends, we traveled together, we ate dinner together, we played cards together, we won four Canada/World Cups and three national team championships together. In short, we established a bond that has lasted for many years.

I should add that much the same thing happened with Gary Player. As other passages herein indicate, the Player and Nicklaus families became great friends during my early professional years, and have remained so ever since.

As time passed, however, despite the great relationships that our common link of being represented by Mark McCormack and his International Management Company had helped me form with Arnie and Gary, it became steadily more apparent to me that I had to make a change in my business life. Finally, the desire to control my own destiny became irresistible.

One reason for this was the professional athlete's inevitable uncertainty about career longevity—what you might call the one-injury-and-it's-over fear. Another was the recognition that learning and growing as a businessman necessitated such a step. A third factor was a growing awareness that my makeup was such that I would never be content until I was completely in command of every element of my life; that peace of mind depended on making my own judgment calls.

Until my father's death, although I often thought about these things, I could never quite summon the will to make the leap. Soon after Dad passed on I found that will, leading to an amicable parting with Mark McCormack in July of 1970 and the assemblage of my own business team. This, of course, imposed new strains on me as it alleviated others, but it was fun—a new set of mental stimuli and challenges. It was particularly gratifying to discover that I possessed the resources to face each challenge squarely and with more resolve than I would have been capable of in earlier years.

Looking back, I realize that there was nothing unusual or remarkable in any of this. All I was doing was what every man eventually must do when he loses his father: growing up to the point of finally assuming full control of his own life. I have chosen to reflect on it here because of the impact it had on how I played golf in the years ahead.

Perhaps the most important single change in attitude, so far as golf was concerned, involved a new perspective on the major championships.

If you include the U.S. Amateurs, I had averaged one major win a year between the ages of nineteen and twenty-six. Fast and frequent success can give a young athlete so strong a sense of invulnerability that he begins to harbor unrealistic expectations of his capabilities. I realized around this time that I had fallen into that trap. For instance, I had done things like blab off one week about bettering Bob Jones's majors record, then only a few days later about retiring from golf before I was thirty. Such talk—such thinking—was nonsensical. Instead of expecting to win at least one of the big four each year and getting upset with myself if I didn't, I should have been thankful for possessing the health and the skills to be able to try to do so.

It was this more philosophical approach to golf that underpinned my happy six-year run in the 1970s. While desiring and trying to win as hard as ever, I became more realistic about so-called failure, which allowed me to become more patient in my playing of the game, which increased my success at it.

I realized that for much of the time from 1967 through 1969 I had been attempting to win by forcing good scores. So often during that period I would follow a minor error with a more costly mistake by taking a dumb risk or pressing my swing to produce an improbable shot. Reflecting on this, it dawned on me that there was still plenty of time. Bob Jones may have won his thirteen majors in only eight years then retired at twenty-eight, but Ben Hogan had won all nine of his in his thirties and forties . . . and look at Sam Snead for longevity. Everyone with an ounce of common sense knew golf required patience above all else. "Jack," I told myself, "just back off a little and enjoy your life in the round, and let the chips fall where they may. You will always give golf your best shot, because that's your nature. But if it doesn't work sometimes, well, so be it. The sun will continue to rise each morning, and you are still young enough to have plenty more opportunities."

The most valuable product of those turbulent emotional times was a greater psychological stability that would enable me to handle the inevitable ups and downs of life and golf with more equanimity, or a better sense of proportion, over the years ahead. Undoubtedly contributing to this was a more stable physical pattern of living from 1971 onward.

• • •

In 1964, believing we would never permanently leave Ohio, Barbara and I had moved to our dream home in the Upper Arlington suburb of Columbus. Anticipating a large family, we had built big—eighty-eight hundred square feet—and furnished with all the care appropriate to a principal residence. However, with northern winters necessitating time spent farther south in order to work on my game, we decided eventually to build a second home at the Lost Tree Village community in North Palm Beach. There we chose a medium-sized ranch-style model pleasantly situated not far from the golf course on Little Lake Worth, and next door to our good friends Cary and Edie Middlecoff. The plan initially was to live nine months in Columbus and three in Florida. However, after spending the entire winter of 1965–66 in a rented home at Lost Tree while ours was being built, this, to me at least, no longer seemed like a great idea.

By then, I had fallen totally in love with the easygoing Florida lifestyle: Outdoors most of the daylight hours, rarely needing to dress in more than shorts and golf shirt, fabulous fishing right on the doorstep, a pool to cool off in and laze by whenever you felt like it, and none of the pressures and hassles inescapable in and around all big cities. Barbara liked Florida okay, but, with family and so many friends in Ohio, she was reluctant about living there full-time. However, as so often in our decisions, large and small, she was willing to go along with what she believed would make me happiest. Also, and really the decisive factor for both of us, there was Jackie, who would begin kindergarten in the fall of 1966. Bringing our children up normally was obviously going to be more difficult than for most families, and a vital factor would be not constantly disrupting schooling and friendships. Finally, the decision was made to reverse the original plan and live most of the time in Florida, with some part of each summer spent in Columbus.

On January 15, 1969, Gary Thomas Nicklaus had joined Jack, Steve and Nan. With a new baby added to three highly active children of seven, five and three, plus their friends, plus Barbara's and my liking for company, we were bursting at the seams. Also, we had sold our Columbus home in 1968 and were concerned about leaving its contents too long in storage. Consequently, in the fall of 1969 we broke ground on our present home, across the road from the Lost Tree clubhouse and looking out over the northern end of Lake Worth, and again in the single-level ranch style but this time with six bedrooms. We moved into it in mid-December of 1970, just in time for a nice disorganized Christmas! Since then, like so many well-loved homes, this one has grown and evolved, to now encompass one of my greatest joys, a garden containing a wide assortment of native and exotic trees, shrubs and flowering plants. Our home is spacious, informal and comfortable without, I hope, being ostentatious; ideal for entertaining family and friends in both large and small groups; and just perfect in every way for a sports-mad family like ours. Most important, it is the one place in the world where we can completely relax and be totally ourselves. Although you never know what life will bring, the way things are today I do not see us relocating.

I HAVE stood back from the politics of golf for most of my career, with one notable exception some six years after I joined the tour. I am still proud of what was achieved for my profession at that time.

From the earliest days of American golf professionals (that is, club pros) becoming professional golfers by playing tournaments for prize money on a more or less regular basis, they had periodically talked about breaking away from the Professional Golfers Association of America in order to own and operate their own road show. Of the many arguments offered for such a move, the principal one was that the club professionals who constituted most of the PGA's membership, and thus controlled the unionlike organization, neither empathized sufficiently with nor properly served the interests of the tournament specialists. The bottom line was money. In a nutshell, as the rewards of the tour grew, the players saw less and less reason why noncompetitors should profit from it.

Through all the periods of unrest, the PGA's chief rationale for retaining ownership and command of the tour was that it had earned that right by first spawning the tournaments, then helping to service and grow them through many years of providing financial and administrative support.

With the backing of Ben Hogan, Sam Snead, and other top performers, talk among the players had almost escalated into a breakaway effort in the mid-1950s. What finally turned words into action in the summer of 1968 was television.

By then, the tour had become a stand-alone and firmly established entity, with a membership almost unanimously desirous of controlling its own destiny. When it was discovered that the PGA had negotiated contracts for the television rights to the World Series of Golf and Shell's Wonderful World of Golf without consulting the players, and had decided to put all of the proceeds into its general fund, action to free ourselves from the association became imperative.

Gardner Dickinson, then the chairman of the players' representatives on the PGA's tournament committee, spearheaded the effort, with the other three representatives—Frank Beard, Doug Ford and myself—in full and voluble support. Perhaps largely because of Mark McCormack, who wanted us to remain with the PGA, Arnie offered up something less than a complete rupture as a compromise plan. But the die was cast, and, recognizing that, he came fully on board with us.

The new entity we formed was called the Association of Professional Golfers, or APG. One of its first acts was to make Doug Ford's New York–based lawyer and our valued counselor, Sam Gates, its acting commissioner, in which capacity he would serve as our front man in the inevitable battle with the PGA. When, to our great delight, ex-FBI agent Jack Tuthill, who had been doing a fine job of running the tour in the field for the PGA, decided to side with us, he was hired as tournament director and provided a small office in a Manhattan hotel. No one, including Jack, knew how and when he would get paid, but we all knew that his first and most critical job was to bring aboard the sponsors of the tournaments then being played under PGA auspices. I tried to help by writing an article for *Sports Illustrated* explaining what the players were attempting to achieve, and why. By December of 1968, twenty-eight AGP tournaments had been lined up for the winter, spring and early summer of 1969, with only four holdouts among the existing sponsors. We made a schedule for the year and arranged a qualifying school at Doral in Miami.

Thanks mostly to a gentleman by the name of Leo Fraser, those APG tournaments never materialized. A bright, outgoing and highly regarded lifelong club professional, Fraser ascended late in 1968 from the treasurership to the presidency of the PGA. That proved most fortuitous for us, because, after starting out backing the PGA's position, he gradually became more and more sympathetic to our case. Simultaneously, he came to realize that the PGA had no means of thwarting or competing with the players' new organization. The upshot was that—initially against the wishes of many of his fellow officers—Fraser finally managed to shut down the months of verbal artillery on both sides by instigating and leading an official dialogue with the "rebels." There were many often difficult meetings, and there is no question in my mind as a participant in most of them that Leo's honesty, openness and goodwill toward all involved, plus his clear disinterest in personal advancement, were major contributors to the settlement that was finally achieved. The clincher was surely the agreement of our old friend Joe Dey, the longtime head man at the United States Golf Association, and the most highly regarded golf official in the country, to become commissioner of the new organization.

Thus was born the Tournament Players Division of the PGA, from which soon evolved today's PGA Tour, with player control assured in both cases via a majority of player-directors on the policy boards. It is common knowledge that the PGA and the PGA Tour have had a few disagreements since, but, all in all, they nowadays seem to sustain an amicable relationship, as certainly do the great majority of club professionals and playing professionals when encountering each other one to one. What is for sure, and still in my view for the best, is that neither organization has an effective voice in the other's affairs.

WHAT brings that club pros/tour pros conflict to mind is another highly politicized situation involving the PGA of America that also had a happy outcome, and for me in particular.

Throughout much of the time the PGA was warring with the tour players, it was also embroiled in a battle with its landlord, John D. MacArthur, the supersuccessful but eccentric and strong-willed insurance and real-estate magnate.

MacArthur had financed the PGA's new headquarters and two adjoining golf courses, called PGA National, in return for the promotional value of having the association based at a development he owned in Palm Beach Gardens. Ultimately, as part of a deal to get MacArthur to drop a proposed lawsuit, the PGA had to commit to play its championship one time at the PGA National. This would mean either enduring great heat and humidity that might detract from the championship, or changing the traditional late summer date.

The PGA stalled on that issue as long as it could, but finally had to bite the bullet. In 1971, the last major of the year became the first. The PGA Championship was played in late February over the East Course of the then PGA National.

Being so much a traditionalist about golf, at first I did not much care for this situation. The more I thought about it, however, the more appealing it became, for a number of reasons.

To begin with, the PGA National—now the John D. MacArthur Golf Club—was only about five miles from our new home, which would allow me to commute to a major championship for only the second time (I'd been able to do so to the 1964 PGA in Columbus). That would be fun, and should help keep me relaxed and rested.

Second, although Arnie and I had won the 1966 National Team Championship in Florida—on the PGA National East Course—I had never won an individual tournament in my adopted home state. Setting that right would, I figured, add even more to the fun, by answering those experts who insisted I could neither play in the wind nor putt Bermuda greens.

Third, the PGA National's East Course, designed by Dick Wilson, considered by many to be America's finest "flat land" architect, was a superior challenge: long and heavily bunkered, with many dangerous lateral water hazards, some monster par threes, and not one straight-away par four or par five. There would be a premium on strategy, stamina, nerve, and, above all, patience, which suited me just fine.

Finally, and most important, here was a great incentive to get seriously down to work immediately after the holidays. Unrealistic though it may be, the Grand Slam has always been in the back of my mind every season at least through the end of the first major championship. Normally, that was the Masters in April, allowing me a leisurely fourteen weeks to prepare. Now I had just half that time. Along with all the other stimuli, this became a great prod. That December, January and February, I worked as hard and consistently at golf as at any time since my teens.

From the outset, I felt confident about my tee-to-green game. The British Open victory had done wonders for my morale, and this had led to some pretty fair golf for much of the rest of the 1970 season.

Following a second win with Arnie in the National Team Championship at Laurel Valley, I had tied for second two weeks running at

Westchester and in the American Golf Classic at Firestone, and liked my chances the next week in the PGA at Southern Hills after an opening 68, only to putt myself out of contention with poor second and third rounds (Dave Stockton won handily). After an indifferent performance in the then richest tournament in golf, a $300,000 event sponsored by Dow Jones at the Montclair club in New Jersey, I'd won the World Series for a fourth time, then hopped over to England for the Mark McCormack-created World Match-play event at Wentworth, edging Lee Trevino in the thirty-six-hole final. After almost a month's break from the game, little had gone right at the Sahara in Las Vegas in October, and not much better at the Heritage Classic at Hilton Head a month later. But by then I was overgolfed and therefore not too concerned. All in all, and particularly compared with the previous two years, it had been a gratifying season.

By the Sunday night before the PGA, despite all of the hard work, I was in a somewhat less upbeat frame of mind. I had played the East Course that day in a cool 80 strokes. It had been windy, and I was concentrating on yardages and shot placement, but that was no excuse for the way I'd putted. Here I was, about as ready as I'd ever been from tee to green, but yet again having trouble with the short stick. It had been that way in the Crosby, then, after an improvement to finish third in San Diego, bothersome again in Hawaii. Back home, I had worked on putting for two straight weeks, but with no real improvement.

Then, guess what?

I had played that practice round with Deane Beman, after which he and his wife joined us at home for steaks and bridge. During the card game we got to talking about how sluggish the East Course greens were and the problems I'd always had on slow greens, particularly slow Bermuda greens. Deane told me he thought I wasn't completing my backswing, not swinging the putter back far enough to start the ball rolling smoothly, which is the key to holding the line on heavily grained grass. "You're tickling the ball," said Deane. "You've got to whack it on Bermuda, and you don't have enough backswing to do that."

With my mind now much more on putting than bridge, the Bemans murdered us; but before they left I got my putter and a couple of balls and went out to the Astroturf surrounding our pool and tried stroking the ball with a longer backswing, making a little pause at the end of it before swinging the putter forward. It felt great and Deane approved, but would it work on grass? The answer next day was yes. And, while working on the longer backswing, I hit upon another aid.

Years previously, I had filed two notches in the top of my putter blade about an eighth of an inch apart, to mark the sweet spot. Now I started using the notches as an aiming aid, by aligning them square to the starting line of the putt. Why it had taken me almost ten years to think of doing this when it had been staring me in the face every day, I don't know. What I do know is that it immediately took the guesswork out of accurately setting the blade behind the ball. Suddenly, magically, I knew I could putt again.

I LIKE to think I've enjoyed good relationships with most of my contemporaries on the tour over the years, but the closest friendship I formed with a fellow intent on defeating me at every opportunity was with Gary Player. As time passed and Gary played less in the States, and we both got busier with nongolf activities, inevitably we saw less of each other. But our feelings persisted, and the Senior Tour of late has given us opportunities to enjoy each other's company again.

Gary Player's story is one of the most remarkable in golf. Born and raised in modest circumstances near Johannesburg, chiefly by his father and elder brother, Ian, after losing his mother when he was eight, Gary came to the game at fifteen, a comparatively advanced age for a future world-beater. Within a short time he was totally consumed by golf. Four years later, in 1956, after a daily workload rivaling that of his hero, Ben Hogan, and helped by the man who would become his father-in-law, club pro Jock Verwey, he decided to make a learning visit to Britain's pro circuit.

Gary readily admits that he had an awful golf swing in those days, and the story is that he drove Britain's top players crazy with his endless questions about technique, and particularly with his insistence on addressing everyone as "Mister." Whatever, the following year he won the first of his innumerable South African Opens, then, straight off the boat from Jo'burg, a big tournament at the famed Sunningdale course near London. Three years after that, at Muirfield in 1959, Gary became at twenty-three the youngest winner of the British

Open since Willie Auchterlonie in 1893, then, in 1961, the first non-American Masters champion and top money-winner on the U.S. tour and, in 1962, the first foreign PGA champion. In 1965, with his U.S. Open victory at Bellerive (where he donated half of his purse for American junior golf promotion), he joined Gene Sarazen and Ben Hogan as the only golfers then to have won all four of the modern major championships. His current total of majors is nine, and, as he's proud to keep telling the world, he's flown more miles than any golfer in history, to win more tournaments in more countries than any player in history.

Throughout the 1960s, Gary Player, along with Arnold Palmer, was my favorite and toughest opponent, and the success of the three of us, together with the fact that we were all represented by Mark McCormack, quickly led to "The Big Three" as a collective media moniker. We naturally spent a great deal of time together, at home and abroad, in tournaments and exhibitions and TV matches, and we all became great buddies. But the friendship between Gary and me, and also between Barbara and Gary's wife, Vivienne, was particularly close.

To begin with, we possessed similar values, all having a deep commitment to family—the Players have six children—and to a clean and healthy way of life. Then, in Gary's and my case, there was a commonality of non-golf interests: fishing, hunting, sports, and the outdoor life in general. Also, we both liked to leave the subject of our golf games at the course, and we laughed at the same sorts of things, and each of us got great joy from inserting and twisting the needle at every opportunity—he by interminably reminding me that my thighs were nearly as big as his thirty-one-inch waist.

Then as now, I had great admiration for this feisty little South African as a golfer and a man. Only 5′7½″ in his spikes and 150 pounds soaking wet, Gary had taken a minimum of natural talent and, through rigorous physical and mental conditioning, endless practice and incredible competitive drive, made himself into one of the world's all-time great golfers. Also, he had done it while spending more time traveling, and farther from his home, and—because of his nationality—frequently under greater psychological duress than any athlete I could think of. People could not help but respect and enjoy a fellow like that, and I am sure Gary has made and nurtured more genuine friendships around the world than any golf professional in history. Back in those days, Barbara and I used to kid him about all the gifts he kept receiving, but the reason for them was simply that people who got to know him well grew to love the guy, particularly those big brown eyes and ultra-expressive eyebrows that would hop up and down with each inflection of his voice whenever he got excited.

Gary's one peccadillo was then and is still today a certain boyish theatrical quality, a sort of hyper enthusiasm, that can lead him to get carried away and exaggerate things a little bit. I guess it's a means of pumping himself up, of building his confidence. Whatever the sources, I can recall endless instances, but will recount just one for the amusement of our mutual friends.

In 1967, I ran into Gary before the U.S. Open at Baltusrol and we decided to play a practice round together, and all the way around he rattled on about these fantastic new exercises he was doing. "Jack, you wouldn't believe it, they're just *fabulous.* I never—really, I mean *never*—miss doing them every morning, and they're just sensational. Jack you just won't *believe* what they're going to do for my golf . . ." And so on, and on.

Well, after the round I was thinking of leaving, but Gary talked me into staying over and invited me to share his hotel room, and the first thing he did when we got up there is show me all his new exercise equipment, the weights and the stretchers and the this and the that, and it was all very impressive. Then came morning, and we got up and went down and ate some breakfast, and then went back up to the room and talked for a while, then decided to head out to the golf course. I waited until we were almost there before saying, as innocently as I could, "Gary, I saw you eat six pancakes for breakfast this morning, but I didn't see you lift any weights or anything like that. When exactly did you do all those exercises you were telling me about?" Well, he gave me a look as though one of the weights had just fallen on his head. "Oh, golly!" he said. "Oh, golly! I forgot. Would you believe it. I *forgot.*" And, I mean, the darn exercises he never, *ever* missed doing *every* morning had never even entered his head! I love you, Gary, and I know you *have* exercised a ton, but if you'd exercised half as much as you've talked about exercising, you'd never have had any time left to win all of those golf championships that have made you so famous.

The thing is that Gary's "embroidery" is all guileless and therefore harmless, and never gets in the way of his warmth and his ability to laugh at himself. He is a superb golfer, and just a great guy.

What brings Gary so much to mind at this point is that he was our first houseguest at our new Florida home. The Players had shown Barbara and me and our parents great hospitality five years previously when we had spent seventeen days in South Africa. Now, with ample space to have people stay for the first time, we thought it would be nice to put Gary up for the week of the PGA. As things worked out, we would both be in contention every day, but, as always between us, the mood stayed light, as Dan Jenkins recorded in his *Sports Illustrated* report of the championship:

> On Sunday, Player and Nicklaus entered the locker room separately, about a moment apart, as if they were strangers . . .
>
> "Gary will answer any of my questions," Jack said.
>
> Someone dutifully asked Gary what they had enjoyed for breakfast in the Nicklaus household.
>
> "It doesn't matter," said Jack. "He puts catsup on everything, anyhow."
>
> "Barbara's getting a complex," Nicklaus went on. "She gives him a cheese omelet, he pours catsup all over it. A couple of fried eggs, catsup all over it."
>
> Player broke in. "So would you if you had a catsup contract."
>
> "I didn't know you had a catsup contract," said Jack.
>
> "I will when these fellows get through writing it," said Gary—fast on the draw as always.

My joviality at that point was well justified. With eighteen holes to go I was sitting on a handsome lead and fairly certain that, short of an exceptional round by one of my closer pursuers, I would not be caught. The reason was putting. Yet again, Deane Beman had hit the nail flush on the head.

WITHOUT Deane's tip, I can't imagine what I would have shot in the first round of that championship. On a golf course as brutal as the then PGA National's East Course, you expect to have at least one scrambling round. My play that Thursday has to be the wildest I've experienced in winning a major championship.

Tee to green, it was a joke. Afterward, I remember I described it to the writers as a "terrible, great, awful, beautiful" round. I was paired with Gene Sarazen and Mike Hill, and afterward Gene talked flatteringly to the press about my power. I certainly drove a long way, but I also drove off the world much of the time. Of the fourteen fairways, I hit five. I also hit four bunkers with approach shots and got two free drops after ending up in television equipment. Every hole seemed to threaten some kind of disaster that would blow me out before I had really begun. You are always fighting a hard golf course to some extent, but this round was eighteen successive knock-down drag-outs.

I will spare you the details except for the last three holes, which typify the performance. Sixteen, 193 yards par three: 4-iron buried in bunker, out to twelve feet, one putt, par. Seventeen, 588 yards, par five: drive into TV gear, free drop, 6 iron, 8-iron through green into more TV equipment, free drop, pitch to six feet, one putt, par. Eighteen, 431 yards, par four: drive into fairway for a change, 4-iron bunkered, out to eight feet, one putt, par.

When I added up the scorecard, I found I had shot 35-34–69. What I'm proud of at this distance is how well I managed to hold myself together emotionally. With me, there has always been a fine line between properly preparing for a major and becoming too keyed up. This time, I had let myself get so pumped it resulted in excessive nervousness—my stomach flopped around all through that first round, and I simply could not quiet it. But somehow I willed myself to hang tough. When the ball will not go even approximately where you intend it to, the most difficult thing in the world is to sustain your concentration: to grind it out, to make yourself keep on bearing down. Eventually, you just ache to relax and say, "To heck with it," whereupon, of course, you immediately start playing even worse.

Somehow this day I managed despite the jitters to force myself to continue concentrating hard. "Don't get desperate," I remember telling myself, "don't start trying for miracles." Helping me, no doubt, was the conviction that I had gotten my long game in good shape, so that at any moment it would come around. Also, the scoreboards showed that no one else was having a particularly happy time. Then, of course, it was early: Whatever the numbers that evening, there were still fifty-four more holes to be played.

But none of this was what really saved me. What did was putting. Boy, could I *putt* that day. Afterward, sitting in the press tent, I figured my total at twenty-three putts, including one-putting eight of the last ten greens. I have never kept putting stats, but twenty-three putts is almost certainly my lowest number in a major-championship round. I said a short prayer for Deane, and ran to the practice tee at Lost Tree to see if I could find a way to keep the ball somewhere in Florida the next three days.

With the wind adding to the severity of the course, I had expected 69 to put me in the picture at the end of the day, but was surprised that evening to find myself leading. Three Bobs—Charles, Goalby and Mitchell—had scored 70, and there were about a dozen golfers on 71, including my houseguest, the famous exerciser from Johannesburg.

Gary has a good appetite, and the previous evening had put away four pieces of fried chicken, a big salad, and a couple of slices of homemade prune cake. He said he hadn't felt good for most of the round, and I told him it was the prune cake. By dinnertime, judging by the way he tucked in the meatloaf, he was clearly feeling better, and he kidded me about my putting, calling me a "lucky dog." I agreed 100 percent, but I gave him back one of his own favorite lines whenever anyone suggests he's lucky: "Yes, I was lucky, and the harder I work, the luckier I get." The lengthy practice session at Lost Tree after my round had convinced me that the day had simply been one of those temporary aberrations that, for no identifiable reason, suddenly spring themselves on all golfers.

By Sunday morning, this seemed the correct diagnosis. With another 69 on Friday, followed by a 70 on Saturday, I was leading by four strokes. Both my driving and iron game had been night and day better than in the opening round, and I had continued to putt exceptionally well, if not quite as sensationally as on Thursday. There had been some jitters after beginning the second round at the tenth hole with a bogey, but a nailed 1-iron to the 232-yard eleventh, followed by two putts from sixty feet, calmed me down, after which I played the front side in four under par. Then, on Saturday, I'd made the round with five birdies in six holes from the ninth through the fourteenth holes, with putts of respectively twenty-five, forty, two, three, and twenty-five feet.

Gary had informed the press that, after switching plates with me each mealtime when I wasn't looking, he had felt fine Friday and Saturday, which helped him to shoot 73-68 and become my closest pursuer. That evening he told us he was going to dinner with some business associates in Miami. "Not taking any chances, huh?" said Barbara. The Bemans came over again, along with some other friends, and once again I thanked Deane for the putting lesson.

YOU never let on about such things, but after surviving the opening round's awful tee-to-green play with such a good score, I had felt all along that this was my championship: that the gods of golf were smiling on me. After eleven holes of the final round, I wondered what I'd done to suddenly get them so mad at me. There had been some indifferent shots, but there had also been some cruel bounces, especially at the eleventh hole where a 1-iron nailed dead on line into the wind kicked way off the green. The result was four bogeys to one birdie, allowing a whole gang of very fine golfers to pull within striking distance. Was this going to be the great giveaway?

At the 510-yard par-five twelfth hole, I hit a solid drive then a 1-iron to the green and two-putted for birdie, which settled me sufficiently to follow with three solid pars. When I looked at a leader board coming off the fifteenth green, the jitters returned. An unlucky bounce out-of-bounds off a cart-path at that hole had taken Gary out of it, but Bill Casper, Tommy Bolt and Miller Barber had by then each made up five shots on me. A strong finish by any one of them, along with just one more slip by me, could cook my goose.

The sixteenth hole was a 193-yard par three. I needed a 4-iron to reach the green, but, with the putting surfaces now so wind-dried, there was no way I could stop the ball and it finished in a spectator's blanket. I received a free drop, chipped to five feet, and made the putt for par.

I had gotten a nasty scare the previous afternoon at the seventeenth hole, a par five of 588 yards with water all along the left side and a heavily bunkered green. After a fine drive I'd tried to get home with a big 3-wood but, as so often happens when you swing with 100 percent of your strength, had hooked the ball badly and been fortunate to have it stop inches short of the water down the bank to the left of the green. Now, knowing Casper had birdied the hole to draw within two strokes of me, I told myself, "No gambles," and hit the tee shot with the 3-wood. It was a good one, but just as I began walking after it, there was a big roar from the eighteenth green, signifying that Casper had closed with a second straight birdie. That meant he was in at five under par to my six under. It also meant that, if I failed to birdie seventeen, I would have to par eighteen to win outright.

This was not a pleasant prospect. Due to its long right-to-left curve around close-up water, plus its heavy rough and awkwardly placed green, the eighteenth hole, although only 421 yards long, had played by far the toughest for the entire field all week. I had scrambled one-putt pars there the first two days and bogeyed the third. A birdie now at seventeen would let an awful lot of pressure out of the Nicklaus cooker.

If I had known how Bill was going to finish, I believe I might have hit the driver off the seventeenth tee in the hope once again of being able to get home in two. As it was, I had no hope of doing so, and I'm still glad about that. What I did was lay the ball up short of the bunkers guarding the front of the green with the 1-iron, and from there cut a nice soft little wedge pitch to within five feet of the hole. When the putt dropped, leaving me with a bogey to win, all the pressure evaporated. On the final hole I hit 1-iron off the tee for safety, then 2-iron to just off the green left, then a good chip to four feet and a relaxed putt dead in the heart. The score wasn't anything to shout about at 73, but it was good enough to win and that was all that mattered.

Bob Hope, at that time a PGA Advisory Committee member, was on hand to present the trophy, but it had been standing in the sun all day and was too hot to handle. That raised a laugh, and as we joked around, I tried unsuccessfully to recall a stranger week.

I had started out totally unable to putt, then, thanks to my old sidekick Beman, had putted better than I ever had in a major—just 117 times for an average of 29.25 putts per round, or twenty-seven under putting par. I had finally won in Florida and on Bermuda greens, and I had led alone from start to finish for the first time in a major. I had commuted from home, and had one of my chief rivals as the first guest in our new home, and, with all the needling between us, never stayed looser off the course. Barbara had enjoyed having Gary with us, too, and now she could celebrate a unique double—a major championship on her birthday.

But the longest lasting thrill was the other "double."

This victory made me the first golfer to win each of the major championships at least twice. The possibility of that had been in my mind from the time I began preparing for the event in December, and there had been a lot of press hoopla about it all week. I had tried to downplay it as much as possible, but, now that it had happened, it was wonderfully satisfying. I had long ago recognized that setting records must one day become my primary goal and motivation if I hoped to go on being truly competitive.

This was a record to savor and be proud of.

12

The 1972 Masters Tournament

A Metamorphosis

FASHIONS come and go in golf apparel as in everything else, but for a number of years most golfers played in shirts with open half-sleeves, a crisp polo-style collar, and a weighty enough placket to hold the collar in position. I thought those shirts just perfect for golf, and also liked the fact that they were dressy enough for evening wear under a jacket. Which is as it should be, because I had a hand in bringing that type of shirt into being, as well as helping to establish it in the marketplace.

I got the idea back in the late 1960s from an old friend, Sockeye Davis (E. Hugh Davis, to be formal about it), who had managed Scioto Country Club in Columbus before retiring to Florida, where he worked for me on a part-time basis. Sockeye was over at our home one day wearing one of those short-sleeved Oxford cloth dress shirts with buttons about halfway down the chest that you pulled over your head. I was wearing what pretty much everyone wore for golf at that time, a close-fitting, tight-sleeved, soft-collared knit shirt designed originally for tennis. Sockeye knew I had a contract with what was then the Peerless-Hathaway shirt company. Suddenly he

My favorite collection. From left to right, the trophies are U.S. Open, British Open, Masters (below), U.S. Amateur, and PGA Championship.

This father-son embrace with caddie Jackie, after tapping in my last putt in the 1986 Masters, will always be one of my fondest memories.

53

The only winners through 1996 of all four of golf's major championships: Gene Sarazen, Ben Hogan, Gary Player, and Jack Nicklaus.

54

52

The six birdie putts I made on the back nine the last day of the 1986 Masters were all thrilling, but this twelve-footer for eagle at number fifteen produced the biggest charge.

51

Michael Nicklaus, our youngest, gets in the act at the 1980 PGA Championship presentation.

Baltusrol, U.S. Open, 1980, and Jack comes back. Barbara said about this photo, "The look on his face as that putt dropped, so relieved, so ecstatic, showed the world how much golf mattered to him."

49

I enjoyed playing all four rounds of the 1980 U.S. Open with Japan's top golfer, Isao Aoki.

50

My last tee shot in the 1978 British Open at St. Andrews. Like many before it that week, it was a good one.

47

Barbara's favorite photo of me—with the British Open trophy at St. Andrews in 1978.

48

45

Made it! On my way to victory in the 1975 PGA Championship at Firestone.

Wife Barbara and sons Steve and Jackie help me celebrate my fourth PGA Championship win in 1975. It came after the riskiest shot of my career in the third round.

46

More antics at Augusta National's sixteenth hole, as a long birdie putt drops in a thrilling last-round battle with Johnny Miller and Tom Weiskopf. That 1975 Masters win was my fifth.

43

44

42

This shot of son Gary leaping into my arms as I completed round two of the 1973 PGA Championship won a national sports-photo award. The win raised my total of majors past Bob Jones's record.

Caddie Willie Peterson joins me in a dance as a birdie putt falls at sixteen in the opening round of the 1972 Masters.

For once I came out ahead of my toughest opponent. Leaving the last green at Pebble Beach in 1972 with Lee Trevino after winning my third U.S. Open and the second leg of the Grand Slam.

38

Saying, "This is the nearest I got to it," Doug Sanders reaches out to touch the old claret-jug trophy after losing the British Open to me in a down-to-the-wire playoff. St. Andrews, 1970.

Opening tee shot, final round of the 1971 PGA Championship. Playing out of my Florida home made the win extra sweet.

36

After secretly fearing I might never capture it, I won my first British Open at much-loved Muirfield in 1966. My longtime British caddie, Jimmy Dickinson, looks on.

37

U.S. Open, Baltusrol, 1967. Holing for birdie from twenty-two feet after a thrilling 1-iron to the final hole gave me the seventy-two-hole championship record. Friend and mentor Joe Dey applauds.

34

An eight-footer for birdie at sixteen contributes to one of my best rounds ever, a 64 on Saturday at the 1965 Masters. I won by nine strokes.

35

A forty-footer for birdie and victory just misses in the 1966 Masters. I won a playoff the next day to become the tournament's first successful defender.

32

The hero of my youth, Bob Jones, watches as the previous year's winner, Arnold Palmer, helps me into the famous green jacket after my first Masters victory in 1963.

Runner-up Dave Ragan looks on as I receive the Wanamaker Trophy for my first PGA Championship win in 1963. Standing in the blazing sun all day, the cup was almost too hot to hold.

33

30

On my way to a second U.S. Amateur win at Pebble Beach in 1961. I fell, and remain, in love with that course.

31

My opening tee shot in the 1962 U.S. Open at Oakmont. I was still the amateur champion at that time, and four days later had won for the first time as a professional.

Being congratulated by runner-up Charlie Coe
after winning my first national title in the 1959 U.S. Amateur.

said, "Jack, why don't you get your shirt people to make a shirt like this with open sleeves and a looser fit and a decent collar. It would give more freedom for golf and also look better."

What a great idea, I thought, and immediately got busy trying to persuade Peerless-Hathaway to make such a shirt, using lisle cotton and also adding a little buttoned pocket on the left side. I was not in those days quite the right shape to have much credibility as a fashion expert, so it was a while before they would take the risk. Eventually, though, they began making the shirts in plain colors, and I began wearing them, and pretty soon they were all the vogue. Then came the 1971 PGA—which is what brings this whole thing to mind—and patterns began to take off as well. The company gave me some snazzy experimental numbers ahead of the championship, but had decided not to market them because its sales force believed they would never sell. "Baloney," I said, and wore one every day except the last. Within a week, the sales guys had received a couple of hundred calls from retailers around the country demanding patterns. These days, patterned golf shirts outsell plain in just about every manufacturer's line.

As you can see, it was utility rather than "image" that involved me in shirt designing. There is no doubt, however, that a different wardrobe, along with a loss of weight and a new hairstyle, were big contributors to a new public perception of me that evolved during the early 1970s.

I freely admit that throughout my first eight years on the tour I was a heavy man. My weight never topped 215 pounds during that time, but it also never fell below 205. The reason, of course, was that I just loved to eat, and rarely made any effort to discipline myself either during or between meals. I don't know the precise definition of a compulsive eater, but if it is a person who has to exert tremendous willpower not to pig out all the time, then I have been a compulsive eater all my life.

Another reason I stayed heavy in my early pro years was the medical attitude toward being a bit overweight in those days. Every year when I went for a physical, my doctor, O. F. "Rosie" Rosenow, would tell me, "Jack, don't worry about it. You're young, you're strong, you're playing great golf. You can handle the extra weight." But Rosie would also tell me that there would come a time in my life when I would know that I should lose some poundage. I remember asking him what he really meant by that on more than one occasion, but all he would say was, "Believe me, you'll know when the time comes." Well, he was right.

Because of PGA of America restrictions when I turned pro, it wasn't until 1969 that I became eligible to play in my first Ryder Cup, at Royal Birkdale in England in the fall of that year. Because the U.S. captain, Sam Snead, wanted me to be in good shape to anchor the final day's two series of singles matches, he gave me only one foursome and one four-ball match the first two days of the event. Even so, playing thirty-six holes on the last day, I became seriously tired on a golf course for the first time in my life.

Part of that could be ascribed to pressure.

Tony Jacklin, still on top of the world from his British Open win a couple of months previously, had defeated me in the last of the morning singles to give the British and Irish a one-point lead with eight more singles to play. Tony had then holed a putt clear across the seventeenth green for an eagle to tie our afternoon match, meaning that the entire contest rode on our final hole. To try to ease the tension as we followed our drives down the eighteenth fairway, I asked Tony if he was nervous. "Bloody petrified," he told me, and we laughed, and I admitted to him that I was also feeling the squeeze.

We both hit good second shots, Tony to about thirty feet from the cup, and me to within half that distance. Tony then left his putt a couple of feet short, after which I knocked mine about five feet too far. After I had holed the comeback putt and was picking my ball out of the hole, I also picked up Tony's marker, conceding his putt. As I handed it to him, I said, "I don't think you would have missed that putt, but under these circumstances I would never give you the opportunity." The reason, of course, was that I believed good sportsmanship should be as much a part of the Ryder Cup as great competition. With the match thus ending in a tie for the first time in its forty-two-year history, we walked happily off the green arm-in-arm. But it had been a draining experience for both of us.

As we flew home the next day I began to reflect on how I'd felt over the final holes, and became concerned to the point where I raised it with Barbara. "Do you think this is what Rosie meant, that my body's telling me it's time to lose weight?" I asked her. When she said she thought it was a probability, I decided then and there to go on a diet. "Okay," I told her, "I'm going to be home for a while, and if I eat the way I normally do I'll gain twenty pounds. Instead, I'm going to lose twenty pounds."

The only diet I had heard much about was Weight Watchers, so as soon as we arrived home I got a book about it. There was a deal where you could go on a program and attend meetings, but I figured I could handle the discipline part without that, so I simply asked Barbara to prepare our meals as closely as she could to the recipes in the book. After three days of that regimen, to help keep me motivated, I called Hart Schaffner & Marx, the Chicago-based apparel company whose products I wore and endorsed, and asked them to arrange for one of their tailors to visit with me in two weeks' time. When they asked why, I told them, "Because I'm on a diet, and in two weeks I'm not going to have one pair of pants that fit me." They chuckled over that, and ten days later called me back to ask, "Are you sure?" And I said, "You'd better believe I'm sure, because I've lost ten pounds already." So down came the tailor, and off came another ten pounds, and eventually along came the beginnings of a svelte new wardrobe for a proud 190-pounder. And the best thing of all was where I lost most of the weight: only an inch off my waist, but seven inches from around the hips.

To be sure of being able to follow my diet, I had rearranged my schedule to spend the entire three weeks at home. I played no golf for the first few days, but when I got back to the game I decided to jog rather than walk the course, both to help in losing weight and to improve my overall condition. Fortunately, it was still out of season for Florida, so there were not many golfers at Lost Tree. Instead of taking my big tournament bag and a caddie, I would carry five or six clubs in my hands, trot to the ball, set the clubs down, hit the shot, pick up the clubs, and trot to the ball again. I remember it took me only about an hour to play eighteen holes, and that it was a lot of fun.

And the payoff?

My first tournament when I rejoined the tour was the Sahara Invitational in Las Vegas. I won that. A week later came the Kaiser International in Napa, California. I won that. From there I flew to Hawaii where I shot 63 in the first round but slipped a bit the last two days to finish second to Bruce Crampton. Two weeks later I wrapped up my season by tying for sixth in the first Heritage Classic on the first golf course I had had a hand in designing, Harbour Town Links on Hilton Head Island (Arnie won going away).

I had been careful about what I ate on the road, and when I got home and stepped on the scale I found I'd lost another five pounds. That was good news, but even more pleasing was not once becoming tired during all of that tournament play. Another bonus was no longer having Hart's photograph me in the latest fashions, then show only my top half, or an artist's rendering of my complete figure in more pleasing proportions; it's been the real Jack in all advertisements since that time.

I have to admit, though, that keeping my weight at a reasonable level remains a tough challenge. I still diet most days, although of late in a way that lets me splurge sometimes. I will eat very carefully for a week, then over a couple of days gobble down cake and ice cream, or whatever. Then the next day, because I feel fat, I'll be good for another week or so, then indulge myself again. This causes my weight to fluctuate, usually between 180 and 190 pounds. Barbara, who stays slender whatever she eats, laughs at my diet-splurge-diet-splurge routine, but indulges me because she knows it keeps me happy.

Other than the weight loss, there was nothing deliberate about the metamorphosis in my appearance that began with the 1969 Ryder Cup. What happened was simply a gradual keeping up with the times that I'm sure happened to millions of other men. As a youngster, it was not manly—macho, in today's lingo—for guys of my background and interests to be much concerned with how they looked or what they wore. Even if it had been, I was too busy with sports in general and golf in particular to have time for such stuff. Basically, I just grabbed what was clean and handy when I climbed out of the shower each morning and got on with the true priorities of life, such as my backswing or putting stroke.

Even after Gardner Dickinson told me, as nicely as he could, how awful I looked one day and I began buying more expensive pants, there was not a whole lot of improvement. I kept my hair so short it made my head look like it came to a point, which got me wearing floppy hats. Later, when I let my hair grow, the hat left a ridge around my head until I finally discarded it. One way or another, I guess it took quite a while for people to discover I even had hair.

What sharpened my dress sense was Hart's sending me wider ranges of outfits once they could show me in totality in photographs. Gradually I began to enjoy clothes, and thus to think more carefully about looking good in public (I was then and still am pretty casual around the house and office). Because I am partially color-blind this took some help from Barbara, and, having such great clothes flair herself, she naturally encouraged my new interest, even though she stuck the needle in pretty deep at times with stuff like, "My husband the sex symbol. You wouldn't believe how much he's enjoying the new fans, the swooning galleries. . . . And now, of course, he's after everyone about weight." Despite that and more, pretty soon I had a larger wardrobe, and was working more with my clothiers in expanding the lines I endorsed, and in promoting them through professionally coordinated outfits for advertising and for televised tournament play.

The longer hair followed much the same pattern.

From the then fashionable near-scalped look of my late teens, my hair had gradually lengthened through the 1960s, evolving into a big slicked-back wave in keeping with the general male trend. In the early 1970s, youngsters all over the country began adopting what a few years previously would have been regarded as hippie hairstyles, until eventually there was no way for parents to fight it any longer. I remember kidding friends about letting their sons walk around looking like girls, but pretty soon Jackie and Stevie had joined the club. Once we got used to it, both Barb and I liked the way they looked, so I thought "Why not?" and started going to the barber less often myself. Soon people were telling me I looked younger and less Teutonic and all kinds of nice things, and from then on I just kept up with the times in what I wore and how I had my hair cut.

The positive impact my new "image" made on the fans is an interesting insight into the importance of what are really superficialities in people's judgment of others. What I can assure you is that, however radical the exterior metamorphosis, it was not accompanied by any significant interior changes. I may have looked different, but I did not feel different. And I sure hope I didn't act differently.

CLOTHES and hairstyles were the last things on my mind following my PGA Championship victory in 1971. My thoughts focused mostly on, in order of importance, the Grand Slam, my business affairs, and the development in Dublin, Ohio, that would eventually become Muirfield Village Golf Club.

In those days I was constantly interrogated by the media about why I did not play in more tournaments to ready myself for the majors. I would often answer with a basketball analogy. If you followed pro basketball at that time, you would have noted that, in most regular-season games, the play became all-out only in the last seven or eight minutes. That was because the players, with such heavy competitive schedules, could not make themselves give 100 percent for the entire duration of all those games. I had become the same way in golf. When I played too many tournaments, I got tired and sloppy both physically and mentally. When I was tired and sloppy in regular tournaments, there was no way I could produce my best in the majors.

Thus I now had an interesting new challenge. With the Masters as the first major, for ten years I had begun working in January to elevate my game to peak in early April. This year, I had been required to begin in December to peak in late February. How could I best raise myself again five weeks later? I decided to follow the formula I had adopted between the Masters and U.S. Open, which was to compete just enough to stay sharp and hungry, but not so much as to become fatigued or bored. That translated into playing only at Doral and Jacksonville, where I did well enough to remain encouraged but without ever threatening to win.

This gave me plenty of time to work at golf as I had always preferred, peacefully and privately at home, and also for the business activities that were increasingly requiring my personal attention. Golden Bear, Inc. (later to become Golden Bear International, Inc.), was firmly in place as a main holding company, with a management team of six people.

Heading the group was a fellow with an agile mind and a strong personality, and an even more powerful moniker—Putnam Sandals Pierman. Put ran his family-owned heavy-construction company in Bryan, Ohio, but lived in Columbus. He and I had known each other slightly in high school, and were brought together as adults at the 1967 Masters by mutual friend Ivor Young in relation to the Muirfield Village project. Despite everyone's continuing enthusiasm, this had been in limbo for a couple of years, mainly for want of strong leadership. At a meeting in Las Vegas in October of 1968, Put, who had become an investor in the project, agreed to take charge of it. Then, in 1970, he assisted me with my separation from Mark McCormack, which quickly led to him becoming involved in all of my business activities.

Put quickly brought on stream two business associates and personal friends, Tom Peterson and David Sherman, both solid midwesterners like himself and myself. Tom, Golden Bear's first full-time executive after our controller, Esther Fink, was a banker from Fort Wayne, Indiana, with particular expertise in investment strategy; he would serve as our chief operating officer. David, an attorney practicing in New York, was already involved in the Muirfield Village project. He would shortly accept a partnership with a renowned Columbus law firm, from where he would handle our legal affairs. To provide general financial counsel and tax advice, Tom brought aboard a friend from his Detroit banking days, Jerry Halperin, a CPA and a lawyer as well as a senior partner with Coopers & Lybrand. To this accomplished team I added Bill Sansing, an experienced marketing and advertising man from Austin, Texas, whom I had gotten to know when he was with Hart Schaffner & Marx in Chicago. A little later, after a desire for a more entrepreneurial lifestyle caused him to relinquish the editorial directorship of *Golf Digest* magazine, the group was rounded out by my collaborator on this and other books, Ken Bowden, to look after publishing and other communications interests.

Put and I agreed to be partners in most of our endeavors. We had many goals, but the most pressing on the Golden Bear front was strengthening my associations with the major corporations for whom I worked as an advertising spokesman. Our explorations had confirmed my belief that they needed more personal input from me, plus better coordination of the collective effort. Mark McCormack's policy had been to keep each company at arm's length. Put believed there would be a lot more mileage—and fun—for all concerned if we brought everyone together, and soon after he came aboard he asked me to call the heads of the businesses whose products and services I endorsed with that objective. "I can't do that," I told him. "I don't know any of those guys." He persuaded me to go ahead anyway, and his predictions proved correct when we instituted the first of many Golden Bear–hosted yearly seminars (in the spirit of the associations we called them "partnership meetings") for the senior executives of the companies with whom I was involved. Synergism immediately took over, as everyone began working directly with everyone else on both existing projects and new opportunities involving me.

With this group in place—we actually called it "The Group"—

there were soon some additions to my corporate associations. My instincts had always told me to associate myself only with top-quality products and services that I believed in sufficiently to use personally, and then only as many as I could properly service without hurting my family or my golf career, and that was the policy we followed.

For quite a while I greatly enjoyed this new dimension of my life. Golf being such a lonesome endeavor, it was stimulating and pleasurable to work closely for the first time on an almost daily basis with bright and compatible people all dedicated to a common cause. Having had no formal training for business, I enjoyed delving into its complexities, and particularly after I fairly quickly figured out that succeeding at it depended mostly on two qualities which hopefully I possessed: common sense and decisiveness.

Regarding the latter, Barbara summed me up pretty well when she told a reporter one day, "Jack is a man who doesn't mind making decisions. A lot of people are scared of making them. He's always enjoyed it. Of course, few things are black and white in any business decision, but the thing about Jack is that he's not afraid to try. He'll dive right in, then give it 110 percent, as he does everything else. He's not a man to be on the outside watching other people make things happen. He wants to be the man who does it. He is extremely focused and can he ever concentrate. I tease him that he could be watching television and be so intent on it that he wouldn't know if the house burned down around him."

Put and I made some mistakes, as is inevitable in any business, but they were outnumbered in our early years by successes. It was satisfying to know I could take direct credit for part of that, while also building something more substantial than a golf swing for my large family. Accordingly, I became as happy going to the office each day as I was spending part of it at the golf course, particularly after discovering that I could handle both without shortchanging either. In fact, looking back, I believe that plunging into totally different disciplines was more helpful than hurtful to my primary career.

In a nutshell, I did not get bored with golf nearly as quickly as when it was my only real challenge in life.

ON February 11, 1968, I announced publicly that I was going to build a golf course in the Columbus area and host a tournament on it. We broke ground for the course July 28, 1972. The first "official unofficial" round, consisting of thirteen holes in a downpour by Bob Hoag, Pandel Savic, Ivor Young, and the designer, was played on October 1, 1973. Tom Weiskopf and I "officially officially" opened the course for member play with an exhibition round on May 27, 1974. The first Memorial Tournament began on May 24, 1976. Today, the success of the club, the large primary-home development surrounding it, and the tournament, plus the community benefits they have generated, exceed my wildest dreams. Getting to that point, however, took as much willpower and generated as much anxiety as anything I have ever attempted.

The complete story of the evolution of Muirfield Village Golf Club and the Memorial Tournament has been well told in a book by Paul Hornung, the onetime *Columbus Dispatch* sports editor and golf and football writer who knew and wrote about me since I was knee-high to a grasshopper, so I don't intend to retell it here. What does merit acknowledgement, though, is my naivete in those days about the size of the mountains to be scaled in an enterprise of that magnitude, and particularly the financial Everests that keep knocking the wind out of you. If you would like a primer in how not to become a golf course and real-estate developer, talk to any of the guys involved in the early days of that project. If we had known what we were getting ourselves into, there is a good chance there never would have been a Muirfield Village or a Memorial Tournament. It was a painful learning experience.

What finally carried the day was blind, pigheaded, cloth-eared, head-in-the-sand, Teutonic stubbornness, plus large amounts of thought, sweat and salesmanship along with many sleepless nights. The stubbornness was my contribution. The rest came from the friends and business associates I dragged into the nightmare. Paul captured it well in his book:

"Late in one of the all-time marathon (solution-seeking) sessions, the Nicklaus/Pierman 'group' got around to an open discussion of name suggestions for the golf course. 'Finally, Put said, "We ought to call it 'The Anvil,' " ' Young recalls, ' "because it's such a weight on all our backs." '

"That lifted the tension of the moment, but not the troublesome burden. No one had quite reached the panic stage, but Nicklaus associates and friends like Young, Savic and Hoag began to have grave fears for him financially. But Jack remained remarkably unconcerned.

" 'It was only frustrating to the people trying to handle my finances,' he chuckled in recollection. 'A lot of people wanted me to abandon the project even before we got started, but I never thought of abandoning it. Never! It was just a case of a stubborn kid deciding he wanted to do something and just blindly going ahead with it.' "

In all seriousness, the project did come awfully close to taking me down the tubes. My financial position then was nowhere near as strong as it would become later, but by 1971 I was personally carrying more than fifteen hundred acres of prime development property, every square inch of it nonproductive. But I would not give up the dream, which meant that we just had to find a way to make it materialize. Thanks to the efforts of a lot of good people, and particularly Put Pierman and the other members of my original business group, we eventually did so, and today Muirfield Village and the Memorial Tournament are among my proudest accomplishments.

Despite the pain stubbornness can bring, as I have found on the golf course, it often pays off in the end.

DURING my best years, whenever I went a few weeks without winning, a golf writer somewhere would resurrect the tired old theory that I was putting commerce ahead of golf. How did my plunge into business, plus the problems in Columbus, affect my game in 1971? The answer is, "Beautifully." I could have won the Masters, I should have won the U.S. Open, and by the end of the year I had won eight tournaments, my highest one-year total as a pro. And my game would get better yet in 1972.

At Augusta in 1971 the Grand Slam was still alive—at least in my head—until the final hole. Probably as a result of thinking and blabbing about it too much, I had been exceptionally nervous during the first two rounds, playing much of the time with a churning stomach, and I performed accordingly for scores of 72 and 73. However, a 68 on Saturday not only tied me for the lead with Charlie Coody but boosted my confidence about putting together a strong final round. With the exception of the twelfth hole, where I tangled with Rae's Creek, I did so from tee to green, but gave it away with the short stick, shooting even par with four three-putts.

Charlie finally finished two shots ahead of Johnny Miller and me, but Miller particularly gave him a scare. At age twenty-four, Johnny then had been only three years on tour and had yet to win, but this was where he made headlines for the first time with seven birdies over the first fourteen holes to lead Charlie and me at that point by two strokes. Overboldness at the sixteenth hole finally did him in, but from then on he would become one of the game's dominant players.

I was happy for Charlie and Johnny, but my disappointment was acute. When you have gotten yourself as primed as I had for that week, then beaten yourself as I did, the psychic pain is extreme. In fact, it was so bad that, by the time we got home that Sunday night, I was really down in the dumps. The next day I told Barbara, "That's it, I'm not playing any more until the Open," which meant I would be passing up the Tournament of Champions. "Oh, no," she said firmly. "That's all you need, for everybody to call you a quitter." And she got on the phone and scheduled my flight to California that afternoon. She had never done anything like that before and it really surprised me. "Taking over, eh?" I asked her. But she was right, because when I got out to La Costa all of the work I had done for the Masters finally paid off and I won my third T of C by eight strokes.

That victory, thanks to my wife, put me on one of those shotmaking highs where for a while you feel you can do nothing wrong, enabling me to add the Byron Nelson Classic by two strokes, and only lose the Atlanta Classic to Gardner Dickinson in a sudden-death playoff. With two wins and a near miss under my belt I was pretty optimistic about my chances in the U.S. Open at Merion as we settled in there for the week. The Grand Slam would have to wait, but it had been five years since I had won two majors in a single season, and Merion was where I had played probably my best four rounds ever in the World Amateur Team Championship of 1960. Also, I loved the golf course. Let the battle commence.

I guess it's kind of dumb when you've played ninety holes and made a bunch of mistakes along the way to pick out one hole as having cost you a championship. But that's how my memory works, so the eleventh at Merion that year remains indelible for me. This is the 370-yard par four, with the small green guarded on three sides by the Baffling Brook, that Bob Jones made famous when he completed the Grand Slam on it by defeating Gene Homans in the final of the 1930 U.S. Amateur. I believe there is a commemorative plaque on the hole.

By major championship standards, Merion is a very short golf course; it played at only 6,544 yards that year. Accordingly, with precision so much more important than power, I decided to adopt the strategy that had worked so well at Muirfield in the British Open five years previously and leave the driver in the bag most of the time. It worked well enough in the opening round to keep me close to the lead, and in the second I looked all set to improve my position as I set up with the 1-iron on the eleventh tee. My intention was to play a nice soft little fade to the center of the fairway, leaving a straight-in pitch to the pin. The result was a slice into heavy rough, followed by an 8-iron deep into woods short of the green as the tangly grass turned the clubface over, followed by a poor effort with the wedge, followed by an even poorer chip that almost reached the Baffling Brook, followed by another chip to four feet, followed by a shaky putt. Six. Double-bogey.

I have sometimes thought, as you might have also, that a better name for golf would be "If only." If only I had made par at that hole, or even bogey . . . or if only I hadn't double-bogeyed the fifth hole in the fourth round by yanking a drive left into a creek . . . I never would have been in a playoff that June with Lee Trevino. But I did make those mistakes and Lee and I did tie, and he did beat me in the eighteen-hole playoff with some superb golf after I had taken two to get out of bunkers on both the second and third holes. And that, friends, is the nature of this game, and all you can do about it is lick your wounds and go on and wait for another day, hopefully with at least a wry smile on your face.

For a long time after that Open I was asked a lot about leaving those two bunker shots in the sand, and also about chunking a wedge at the tenth hole in the playoff. All I could say was that I hit them fat. I did not know why then and I do not know why now. All three of those shots totally surprised me. I still shot 71 that day, but Lee beat me by three strokes—those three. Things like that just happen in golf for no reason you can figure, but that does not make them less infuriating.

Trevino, of course, used the high of his second U.S. Open title to win the Canadian Open the following week, which I passed up to prepare for the British Open. Lee then continued his streak at Royal Birkdale for a wonderful triple, with no threat from me after I completed the first round with a pair of bogey sixes due to some ugly chipping. It was clear that, much as I tried to put them out of mind, the disappointments of the Masters and U.S. Open had taken some starch out of me.

Back from Britain, I trailed Arnie by ten strokes at Westchester, then paired with him to win another National Team Championship at Laurel Valley, followed by fourth and third places in the American Golf and Philadelphia Classics. The tour that summer staged its first medal match-play tournament in my time as a pro at the Country Club of North Carolina in Pinehurst, but I saw little of it as Ray Floyd eased me out in the first round. In the World Series I lost to Charlie Coody by a shot, then helped Uncle Sam retain the Ryder Cup in St. Louis, after which I hopped "down under" for a third Australian Open win by eight shots from Bruce Crampton at the Royal Hobart Golf Club in Tasmania, followed by a seven-stroke victory the next week in the Dunlop International in Sydney. Back home, I finished third in the Heritage, captured a fifth World Cup title in partnership with Lee Trevino at the PGA National, and rounded out the year by winning the first Disney World tournament in Orlando.

I had played a lot of golf and worked hard in numerous other areas, but had never ended a season feeling fitter or happier. "Roll on 1972," I thought as I grabbed fishing rods and piled the kids in the boat most days over the holidays.

PUT Pierman decided after six years of our partnership that it was time for him to do other things, but he left us with memories of a lot of enjoyable times plus a number of legacies. One was "Amazing Grace" as a group song, mostly to be heard, badly out of tune, late at night around the house the senior Golden Bear guys rented each year at the Masters. Another was a couple of mottoes: "No amount of self-sacrifice is sufficient," and "Self-doubt stinks." I've cleaned the second up a little, but what brings it to mind is the degree of quiet confidence I had about golf early in 1972.

Fear of any kind is the number-one enemy of all golfers, regardless of ball-striking and shotmaking capabilities. For most, fear of winning is even harder to overcome than fear of losing. Psychologists will tell you that's because, however much such players may believe and tell themselves they want to win, having become so familiar with losing makes them, deep down, comfortable with only that experience. Not knowing what winning is like, they simply are not sure they can handle it, are frightened of what it might do to them. This happened to me before my early successes enabled me to control that kind of fear. That's why I've always said that winning breeds winning: The more you win, the less you fear winning again, or the less frightening success becomes.

The other kind of fear everyone has to fight is the kind where, when you seem to have a tournament won, a couple of strokes slip away or something negative about your game creeps into your mind, and suddenly you are eaten up by thoughts of losing. You begin thinking about bad things that might happen, instead of focusing solely on the good things you need to do to win. In my experience, the only answer to this kind of fear is preparation. The better prepared you are, the more confident you become; and the more confident you become, the less room there is in your mind for negative thoughts, and the better your chance of getting them out if they do manage to sneak in. Which, of course, is why I have always worked so hard at preparing myself for golf's major championships.

Another little understood factor in conquering fear is patience. Tournament golf is a waiting game, a game of easing quietly along and waiting for scoring opportunities to evolve. When you try to push too hard you usually start making mistakes, which opens the mind to fear.

There is, however, a difference between fear and nervousness.

Whatever the appearances and regardless of my inner confidence level, I have always gotten nervous at golf. I have played 90 percent of my rounds in major championships with a touch of tremor. Every time I have gone to the first tee when it has truly mattered, there has been some floppiness in my stomach. Moreover, I have always welcomed those feelings in that, so long as I am playing well enough to have genuine confidence in my game, they will get me "up," keep me alert, prime me for maximum effort.

If nervousness hurt me over the years, it was on the greens. I believe I won most of my majors by thinking out the shots through the air, then playing them effectively, rather than by making miles of putts. Perhaps because of a back-of-the-mind sense that my stroke was not quite sound enough, there were times when nervousness prevented me from being as aggressive with the putter as I needed to be. I was a fine two-putter, but sometimes too defensive—too concerned about three-putting—to go for putts that I probably should have gone for. Looking back, I'm pretty certain this conservatism cost me some wins, including major championships—just as it probably won me some, too.

Over the years, though, nervousness has done me more good than harm, if only by helping me never to take the game for granted, no matter how well I was playing or how big a lead I had built in the final stages of a tournament. Another reason I have never taken anything for granted competitively is that I'm a little bit superstitious, so am not inclined to risk invoking the wrath of whatever force wields that giant hammer on overly cocky or complacent golfers. A third reason for taking nothing for granted is that, having caught and passed players with seemingly insurmountable leads, sometimes in just a few holes, I am acutely aware of how fast the tables can turn. Double-bogeys and eagles are about equally common in pro tournaments. If you make the former while your opponent makes the latter, you are staring at a four-stroke swing. It can happen anywhere, at any time, and in the blink of an eye.

In the final analysis, however, there is no question that a genuine belief in yourself is the top requirement for winning golf tournaments. There have been many players in my time who have possessed all of the attributes necessary to win with the single exception of sufficient confidence in themselves. Whether this is a matter of ancestry and genes, or upbringing and environment, or a combination of those things and more, I do not know. What I do know is that inner certitude about one's abilities is a golfer's primary weapon, if only because it's the strongest defense against the enormous pressures the game imposes once a player is in a position to win. Golf's gentlemanly code requires that you always hide self-assuredness very carefully. But, hide it or not, you will never go very far without it.

By 1972, many factors had come together to restore the high level of confidence I had enjoyed through 1967, but one proved more important than the rest. Deriving from my dad's conversation with Bob Jones already discussed, by then I had developed an arsenal of shots that I could play reliably most of the time without running back to Jack Grout, and that I was confident I could recover whenever they seemed to be departing. This did wonders for my secret belief that there just wasn't any reason why I should not win every time I played.

AMERICA's dean of golf writers, Herbert Warren Wind, described the 1972 Masters in his *New Yorker* report as "the least exciting running of that tournament in a good many years." I knew what he meant, but, for me, particularly over the final nine holes, it was a lot more exciting than it should have been. I have made some gifts to opponents over the years, but I can't recall opening the door in a major quite as persistently as I did in the final stages of that one.

To be honest, though, this was not entirely my fault—perhaps only about 50 percent. Apart from the 1966 Masters, I don't remember Augusta National playing harder than it did that April.

As everyone in golf knows, the efforts made to have this magnificent course in perfect shape for the Masters are unequaled in the world. Cliff Roberts, the man behind the scenes in creating the club and the tournament for Bob Jones, was still running the show then, and there were no limits to how far he would go in terms of money, time and labor to get things right as he saw them. Unfortunately, although he seemed able to control pretty much everything else, the one thing Roberts couldn't orchestrate was nature.

When we got to Augusta that year, we found the course infested with the green superintendent's nightmare, the annual bluegrass called *Poa annua*. The conditions were favorable for excessive seeding that spring, and the whitish blotches this produced on the greens made them highly inconsistent. Because it grows so fast, you have to mow *Poa annua*–infested greens very tightly to make putting surfaces even passably uniform, and the Augusta crew had been, and would continue, doing that throughout the tournament. Combined with the wind ahead of and during play, this made the greens more bony, bumpy, slippery and unpredictable than I had ever known them. You needed large complements of luck, as well as patience and skill, to get the ball close on approaches. When you missed a green, the challenge frequently was to get down in three more shots, not two. Putting was extremely difficult all four days. There were twenty-four scores in the 80s that year, which may be a Masters record. That *Poa annua* drove everyone crazy by the end of the week.

I was already a little frustrated when I got there, for a couple of reasons.

The first was my full swing. Things had gone well for most of the winter and spring, with victory at the Crosby over Johnny Miller on the first hole of a playoff, a one-shot loss to Tom Weiskopf in Jackie Gleason's Inverrary Classic, then first place the following week at Doral and second to Gary Player in New Orleans, my last outing before the Masters. (The Doral win, incidentally, nudged me ahead of Arnie in career money winnings, after he'd occupied the number-one spot for a decade.) I had also played, but less well, in San Diego, Hawaii, Palm Springs, and Jacksonville. All in all, though, I believed my game to be pretty solid.

However, while practicing the week before Augusta, I suddenly began having problems with hooked iron shots. I knew what was wrong: Poor leg action on the downswing, caused by the old bugaboo of closing my shoulders and hips as I initiated the backswing, resulting in my hands coming in too fast and closing the clubface prematurely. It was a tempo problem as much as anything, and not really a big one. I just wished it had picked another time to appear.

The heaviest media focus in golf is inevitably on the players at the top of the game, and this was a time of change in that area. Arnold was still the magic man for his loyal millions, but not by the record the dominating player he had been in the 1960s. My old friend Gary Player was still right up there, and Johnny Miller was on his way, and a lot of people expected great things of Tom Weiskopf. But Tom Watson had just turned professional, while over in Spain Seve Ballesteros, age fourteen, was still wearing out his hand-me-down 3-iron on the beach by the Bay of Biscay. To much of the press and public, therefore, every tournament was now a duel between Lee Trevino and Jack Nicklaus.

Lee and I knew better, of course, and I should have known better than to say more about the Grand Slam than "It's improbable." Instead, I had kept adding, "but not impossible." Also, figuring his game was unsuited to Augusta National, Lee had missed the Masters the previous two years and was thus not regarded as a Grand Slam candidate. The upshot of all this was that, by the spring of 1972, the burning question in every press room and every interview seemed to have become not, "Will Jack Nicklaus win all four?" but "How soon?"

As this continued through the early 1970s, I became sufficiently acclimated to it to be able to put it out of mind. In 1972, however, there was so much clamor as the Masters approached that I could not get the darn thing out of my head. What bugged me was that it was a needless addition to the already heavy self-inflicted pressure of the year's first major championship.

Such selfish concerns apart, there was also a different mood about this Masters for me and for many of the other players. A week before

Christmas the previous year, Bob Jones had died at his home in Atlanta of the rare spinal disease, syringomyelia, that had crippled him so cruelly for so much of his life. Bob had been too sick to get to Augusta after 1968, and all of his friends had known during 1971 that it was just a matter of time. But his death was still a shock. I had missed my visits with him in his cabin at the club, and now, back for the Masters for the first time since his passing, I wondered what affect it might have on this, his greatest legacy to the game. I wondered, too, how my own life might have differed without Mr. Jones's inspiration and friendship during my early years, and decided I would surely have been a lesser golfer and possibly a lesser man.

I BEGAN my first round of the 1972 Masters at the eleventh hole. I had, of course, been playing in the tournament for a couple of hours by then, but not what I would call golf. Tentativeness bred of nervousness, combined with the scary course conditions, had produced three bogeys to one birdie, plus only two nonscrambled pars.

Following a good drive at eleven, I decided enough was enough. Normally on this hole, with the pond guarding almost the entire front of the green, I would deliberately play to the right side for a safe two-putt par. All I had now was a 5-iron, and I hit it directly at the flag. The ball stopped ten feet away, and when the putt dropped, followed by another from twice that distance at twelve, I began to feel a lot better. A nice little bunker shot to three feet at thirteen made it three birds in a row, then, after a solid par at fourteen, I hit a drive and 1-iron to within thirty feet at fifteen and holed the putt for an eagle. My playing partner that day was Eddie Pearce, a prominent amateur, and he told me he knew the putt was in as soon as I struck it, adding, "That's when I lost my concentration and became just another spectator." At the sixteenth I put a 6-iron about twenty feet from the hole and again rolled it home. Two over for ten holes, then six under for the next six—how's that for consistency? Two routine pars got me home in 68, and, after going to the press room and the practice tee, I joined my business group on the terrace and enjoyed some good laughs. Turning a round of golf around like I had that day does wonders for one's sense of humor.

Only four other players had broken par, led by Sam Snead, just a few weeks short of his sixtieth birthday, with 69, followed by Arnold

Palmer with a 70. Sam told the press he did not expect to maintain that pace, which led to much discussion about some fresh Palmer-Nicklaus fireworks. That was fine by me, but what interested me equally were the scores of some other top golfers: Player 73, Weiskopf 74, Trevino and Casper 75, Miller and Floyd 76. My back-nine turnaround had set up a golden opportunity. All I had to do now was capitalize on it.

And that, of course, became my problem.

One of the toughest challenges in golf is not to play defensively once you have gotten yourself into a strong position. Even though you know they are potentially lethal, your instincts keep on insisting, "Preserve, preserve. Be careful. Go easy. Don't do anything dumb." Especially when you move ahead early, playing to extend your lead rather than sitting back on your haunches and hoping the others won't come after you becomes quite a challenge. When you are behind, you *know* you have to make a fine score to win, which fuels your mind to both strategize and execute the shots that will do it. Although I would never pass up a tournament-long lead, with rare exceptions throughout my career I have played better golf when coming from behind. I have also had the most fun winning that way.

The weather for the opening round had been warm but breezy. For the second it was chilly and windy, making the greens even bonier and more skittish. I handled the conditions reasonably well until the fifteenth hole, where I hit a 3-wood second shot when a 3-iron would have done. The ball finished in the lake fronting the sixteenth tee, and by the time I got back there to play the par three I was writing down a big fat double-bogey seven. At the end of the day, with 71, I was leading by three strokes, but the mistake at fifteen really upset me. With a par there I would have been ahead by five, which, given a decent third round, might have locked it up. The one consolation was that only Weiskopf and Casper among the "names" had held their ground.

As was my custom, on the Thursday and Friday evenings I had gone directly to the practice tee after talking to the press. On Saturday, following a 73, I went to the practice tee first, then had to apologize to the writers for keeping them waiting so long. I had played too defensively and started hooking irons again, and was so hot with myself that I needed extra cool-down time before the media session. After increasing my lead at one point in the round to five strokes, I had ended up one ahead of Jim Jamieson. Exacerbating matters was that, despite working on my swing until dark, I was still not sure I had licked the hooking problem. I was not much fun at dinner that evening.

I pride myself on honesty, so am not going to beat about the bush. Giveaway golf is the only way to describe my performance in the final round on Sunday. I did just about everything in my power to hand the Masters on a platter to anyone who could come and get it.

Here's a summary. Front side: bogey on seven, birdies on the two par-fives, the second and eighth holes. Back side: three putts for bogey at eleven, three putts for par at thirteen, three putts for bogey at fourteen, bogey at fifteen after a pulled second shot and two weak chips, single-putt par from eleven feet at seventeen after a fat 8-iron into the front bunker. Total: 74, tying the second highest fourth-round score by a Masters winner since Arnie's 75 to get into a playoff with Gary Player and Dow Finsterwald in 1962.

Afterward, I tried to kid myself that I hadn't played all that badly, and said something along those lines to the writers. The truth is that my saving factor that day—indeed, all that week—was having sufficient patience not to quit on myself. Other than that, my golf was defensive and inconsistent, and I was extremely lucky to win.

Of all the major championships, the Masters is reputed to enjoy the most dramatic finishes. As Herb Wind so rightly recorded, the 1972 tournament was an exception. In the end, I finished three strokes ahead of Tom Weiskopf, Bruce Crampton, and Bobby Mitchell. But the fact is that, if they or anyone else had been able to make any kind of run at me in that final round, it could well have been a different story. My luck lay in the difficult condition of the course, which simply precluded "attacking" golf.

And so there I was, stumbling and bumbling all day, but with a twelfth major championship under my belt, tied with Arnie as the only four-time Masters winner, and with another chance at the Grand Slam.

Gentlemen, I am still grateful to you all.

13

The 1972 United States Open Championship

Halfway There—Then Muirfield

If golf had not become my career, I like to think I would have been successful at whatever line of work I turned my hand to—with one major exception. I would have made a terrible diplomat.

First of all, I'm hopeless at keeping secrets; my friends insist that telling me something on the Q.T. is worse than putting it on the wire service or the Internet. Even harder for me is not instantly saying whatever comes into my head, usually pretty bluntly. I get a burn on about something and I just have to talk it out. The urge to let everyone know where I stand seems to be irresistible. Although I rarely intend them that way, sometimes my sentiments come across a little too sharply.

Barbara's irritation over these traits, plus her frequent suggestions about engaging brain before operating mouth, has slowed me down and smoothed me out some over the years, but there are still too many lapses for the comfort of either of us. I have tried to explain that the cause is really a most admirable trait—honesty. Unfortunately, this doesn't make much of an impression when your mouth is filled with your foot.

One phone goof that still makes us both cringe—and easily my most embarrassing at a golf event—happened way back at the old Crosby Tournament, now the AT&T Pebble Beach National Pro-Am. In those days my birthday, January 21, usually fell during the tournament, and this particular year John Swanson, a golfing friend from San Francisco, called our room at The Lodge at Pebble Beach pretty late in the evening to see how I had enjoyed the day. I could tell from the background noise that he was in the cocktail bar and that there was a pretty good party going on. Just as he was about to hang up, he asked me to hold on, because there was someone with him who wanted to say hello.

Well, on comes this voice, and it's singing to me. Yeah, *singing* . . . "Happy birthday . . . happy birthday to you . . ." And on and on it goes, through the entire song. I'm sitting there asking myself, "Now, who in the heck is this, standing there in a bar singing this whole song to me at this time of night?" When the singing finishes, I say into the phone, shall we say a little brusquely, "To whom am I speaking, please?" There is a pause, then back comes the answer: "Bing Crosby here. Happy birthday, Jack. Sorry you didn't recognize my voice. I guess I must have been a little hoarse. Good-night now."

Oh, boy! Where's the nearest crack in the ground I can slide into and disappear for the next year or two?

Face-flushing as that was, it was nothing to the embarrassment I suffered during another stay at The Lodge. The perpetrator was Louise Hoag, wife of old friend and longtime Crosby amateur partner Bob Hoag. Boy, did she tie one on me.

In my early days of staying at The Lodge there had always been a newspaper outside the room each morning. But that nice little gesture had been dropped by the time Bob and Louise and Barbara and I had eaten breakfast this particular morning. Afterward I picked up a paper from a pile by the front door and took it back to our room with me. As I did so I sort of half-noticed a sign saying please pay fifteen cents per copy at the reception desk. Considering I was forking out around six hundred dollars a night for two rooms—by then son Jackie was partnering me in the tournament—I figured it would not put the place deep in the red to let me have a newspaper gratis, as in the old days.

Well, that night when we got back to the room after dinner, there was a note under our door saying as follows: "Dear Mr. Nicklaus. It was noticed this morning when you picked up a newspaper in the lobby that you failed to pay for same. Please on the next occasion be sure to leave your fifteen cents at the desk. Thank you. The Management."

Wow! *Hot?* Within about two seconds twin jets of steam were whistling out of my ears, even before Barbara started in about how *embarrassing* it was for me to steal a newspaper like that, and how could I have *done* such a thing, and what would the people running the hotel *think* of us, and, boy, I had better be sure to pay for my newspaper the *next morning* . . . By which time I was fit to be tied, absolutely livid.

Well, Barbara finally wound down, and as she headed off to take a shower I told her, "I'll be back in a minute," and stormed down to the front desk, where I asked, quite forcibly, to see the manager. And, of course, it was late and the manager wasn't around, and wouldn't be until the next morning. But I just had to unload on someone, and the only someone available was the young woman behind the desk, who obviously hadn't a clue—not an inkling, poor soul—of what I was yelling about as I told her about this crappy little note I found under my door, and what an insult it was, and here was a twenty-dollar bill, and that twenty-dollar bill would take care of all of the newspapers I'd taken in the past, and all of the newspapers I would take in the future, that being, of course, if I ever again stayed in this hotel. . . . And would she now, please, tell her bosses that I had *taken care* of this problem, once and for all, and that *I never wanted to hear about it again*. Okay? *Okay?*

The next night a group of us were going over to a local friend's house for dinner, and as soon as we picked up Louise and Bob I launched into the story, going on and on about this crappy little note, and what an insult it was, and how I'd gone down and given them a piece of my mind and twenty bucks for the darn newspapers, and on and on some more, until eventually Louise said something from the back seat of the car. But I was still so steamed up I didn't hear her, and not even when she said it again. When she said it for the third time, the words finally registered. What she said was, "Jack, *I* wrote that crappy little note."

Well, it was the greatest "gotcha" of my life. And to cap it off, the moment Barbara and I arrived back in our room that night there was a knock on the door and a newspaper arrived courtesy of the Hoags

—with a stack more of them knee-high outside the door when we went to breakfast the next morning, courtesy of a couple of business associates who'd heard the story. And to *really* cap it off, I have to admit that it was years before I plucked up the courage to stop by that front desk again and risk encountering that unfortunate desk clerk, who, I'm sure, is as bewildered to this day about my behavior as she was at the time. If she happens to read this, I hope she will accept my heartfelt apology.

Yes, Louise, you really nailed me that time.

IT has been my custom for most of my career to make final preparations for three of the four majors the week before the championships at the courses where they will be played.

In the case of the Masters I have usually flown up to Augusta for two or three days, then returned home for the weekend and gone back again on the Monday evening or early Tuesday morning of tournament week. When a U.S. Open or PGA venue has been within reasonable flying distance, I've normally followed the same pattern. However, with the 1972 U.S. Open being played all the way across the country at Pebble Beach, I decided to do what I do for the British Open, which is get there early and settle in for the duration.

By following this regimen I have, of course, had to miss the regular tour events immediately prior to the majors, and in 1972 I received some press criticism on that score. It was not the first time and it wouldn't be the last, so I would like to offer my perspective on the matter to those who felt I was being selfish.

As the crown jewels of golf, I believe the major championships merit a special effort by any player who wants to see them remain at the pinnacle of the game. Throughout my career I have tried to go into every tournament well prepared, but have felt a responsibility to do a little bit extra for the majors, not only for my own competitive interests but because of the occasion and the people who contribute so selflessly to it. If I were to perform poorly in a major through lack of preparation, I would feel I had let down not only Jack Nicklaus, but the game of golf in its entirety.

There are also, of course, some more selfish motivations.

Practicing on site the week ahead of a major allowed me to work more intensively on my game, and with greater privacy and fewer distractions than anywhere else. There was not the lure of family activities or the office as there always is when I am at home, nor the attentions of the media and the fans. I could practice and play peacefully, as much as I wanted to and with whom I wanted. Beginning with Jackie at Pebble Beach in 1972, I have often taken one or more of my children along, and on other occasions close friends have joined me, resulting in some of my most enjoyable times on a golf course.

Then there is my need to feel fully prepared. Possessing the kind of temperament that hates surprises of any kind, I simply cannot rest easy in my head if I am not able to assure myself that I have learned everything there is to know about a major championship golf course before the gun goes. But wait a minute, you say. You'd played Pebble Beach probably a hundred times before the 1972 U.S. Open. What was there new to learn about it? Aside from that not being the point in terms of satisfying myself psychologically, the answer is, "A great deal." Since the 1961 U.S. Amateur, I had played Pebble only in the Crosby tournament in wintertime. I suspected it would be a different course under summer conditions, particularly when the United States Golf Association got through toughening it. And I was right. There was no comparison. If I had not spent those eight days there ahead of the championship, I am pretty certain there would have been a different result.

The other side of this argument is that I and other leading players who follow similar routines damage the tour and its sponsors by not supporting other well-established events. For instance, someone asked me at Pebble Beach that year, "What if everyone skipped the tournament before the Open?" The answer is that, if they did—and, of course, they don't and never will—we simply would not schedule a tournament that week.

Because golfers on America's tours are not paid salaries, or even expenses, attempting to mandate which tournaments they play never has worked and never will. Under this structure, a player's schedule is solely a matter of what he believes works best for him and what jibes with his conscience. My conscience would be a lot more troubled if every holder of a tour card did not have the opportunity to prepare for the majors as I customarily have done, but that is not the case. Those who choose otherwise are simply exercising their option, which is no more my business than how I prepare is theirs.

What I do know is that many of the truly great players in the game—particularly Bob Jones and Ben Hogan—frequently made their final preparations for their most important events at the sites, beginning well ahead of the actual contest. Did their absence ruin the tournaments they missed? If so, then Bob Jones's Grand Slam year must have been a pretty miserable one for everyone else, because he played in only six tournaments that whole season. The fact is that today, with such a depth of talent in golf, the absence of any one player, no matter how big a "name," never hurts a finely staged tournament on a challenging course.

Writers and other players have expressed curiosity about what I do with myself the week ahead of a major; what the fine-tuning consists of. Pebble Beach in 1972 is a good example.

Beginning on the Wednesday, I basically practiced in the morning, played eighteen holes in the middle of the day with Jackie and my longtime Crosby partner Bob Hoag, then went off and spent three or four hours with my caddie—Angelo Argea at that time—studying and replaying selected holes on the course. Once official practice rounds begin, players are not allowed to hit more than one ball. Until then they can hit as many as they like. Covering five or six holes at a time, I would hit two or three shots from various areas of the tees, then four or five second shots from different locations in the fairways and rough. Additionally, I would hit shots from various lies in the bunkers, and pitch and chip from the fringes and rough on all sides of the greens. And, of course, I would putt from many distances and angles—I must have putted those greens for five or six hours over those eight days.

What I was looking for was an intimacy with every nook and cranny of the course that can only be achieved through intensive study and direct experience. Particularly, I wanted to know where to try to position the ball on every tee shot and approach shot in all wind conditions. For instance, I reaffirmed that it was death to miss the first green to the left—double-bogey territory for sure. In the championship, I missed that green long, short and to the right the first three days, but never left. Also, despite the burying tendencies of the new sand in the bunkers, I only failed to get "up and down" once.

As it so happened, young Jack Nicklaus II also learned something about golf that week that has stayed with him ever since. Jackie was only ten at the time but really falling in love with the game, so one day we decided to go over and play Spyglass Hill. It is an exceptionally difficult course and I knew it would be hard on him, but it got to him at the very first hole. Really mad at himself after missing a shot, he started pounding the club on the ground and sulking, and I told him pretty sharply to stop it or else.

Playing the fifteenth hole at Scioto one day when I was eleven years old, I hit a super drive, leaving myself an easy 8-iron to the green. I fanned the ball into a bunker, then slung the club after it. My dad came over to me and said quietly, "Young man, that will be the last club I'll see you throw or hear of you throwing, or you will not be playing this game anymore."

When Jackie and I got down to the first green at Spyglass and his temper had not improved, I walked over and picked up his bag and we drove back to the hotel. When we next played Spyglass together twelve years later he reminded me of his previous one-hole encounter with it, and thanked me for the lesson.

By the time most of the other players arrived on the Monterey Peninsula on Monday of championship week, I had completed my preparation for the Open and felt most content with it. I believed I now knew Pebble Beach, in its summer and USGA garb, inside out. On Monday I played a relaxed eighteen holes, hit balls for a short time on Tuesday, and wound up with another leisurely round on Wednesday. By then I felt as calm and relaxed and ready as I ever had.

Arnold Palmer followed pretty much the same regimen as I had for that championship, and he would play well that week also.

THERE was a special reason why the Grand Slam so dominated my thoughts during the first half of 1972.

You play your best on the courses you like the most, and for me there never had and has not since been quite as appealing a combination for the major championships as there was that year. Augusta National is Augusta National—enough said. Pebble Beach had been my favorite American course since my first practice round there for the U.S. Amateur in 1961. The British Open would be played at Muirfield, the finest course I had encountered outside the United States. Oakland Hills, near Detroit, the site of the PGA, was the only one of the four I had not won on, but I remembered it from the 1961 Open, where I finished fourth and top amateur, as a fine test. Someone had been smiling on me when this quartet fell together in a single season.

Although Pebble Beach had been the site of three Amateurs, it had not been used for our national championship, the chief reason being its distance from the nearest major population center, San Francisco, and the resulting concern about selling sufficient tickets to cover costs. After some 14,000 all-week admissions had been snapped up at more than thirty dollars a pop four months ahead of the championship, the USGA discovered there were no problems in that direction, and thereafter put the course on the regular Open rota, hopefully forever. Tom Watson pulled off a sensational victory there in 1982 before a sellout crowd (about which more later), as did Tom Kite in 1992.

Another reason for the USGA's nervousness about going to Pebble Beach before 1972 was that it is essentially a public golf course, and, due to its worldwide fame and great scenic beauty, one of the most heavily played by what might least harshly be called casual or occasional golfers. Staging an Open at a public facility would be a first, but of more concern than this break with tradition was the condition of the course. Pebble Beach had been known to become badly chewed up in the normal run of things. Could it be brought to the condition necessary for the national championship?

As I discovered during my first practice round, thanks to much hard work by many people, the answer was yes. I also discovered that the USGA had not gone overboard in what it calls "Open preparations." Apart from a few new bunkers, the layout was essentially unchanged beyond narrowed fairways and increased rough, and even the rough was reasonable by USGA standards. The course was designed around the time of the First World War by Jack Neville, a California amateur champion and real-estate salesman, for its owner and his employer, Del Monte Properties, with the help of a friend who had also won the state amateur, Donald Grant. Everyone in golf with whom I had discussed Pebble Beach felt Neville and Grant, amateur designers though they were, had created a masterpiece, and now even the USGA appeared to agree. Perhaps they were intimidated by the thought of the uproar that would have ensued if they had tried to improve the Mona Lisa.

At this distance I am sure the USGA would agree it was a good thing they were restrained in their prechampionship preparations, but they orchestrated the condition of the greens each day. Pebble Beach was tough enough for all of us just the way Jack Neville and Donald Grant built it, but when those small, sharply contoured greens got some USGA-ordered rolling and triple-cutting before the final round, then high winds evaporated every drop of moisture out of them, it turned into Godzilla. Normally, par there is a hard 72. If you go by the average scores of the low twenty finishers that year, who supposedly represented the world's best golfers, par from June 15 to 18 was 76.6. Bill Casper, who had won a couple of Opens and been around for a lot more, said, "It was the first time you had to absolutely plan the perfect shot, shot after shot, then execute the perfect shot, then be lucky." Arnie called it the toughest Open course he had ever played.

On the first day of the championship there was little wind and the greens were still reasonably soft and holding. I played much as I had expected to and handed in a satisfying 71. It comprised birdies on the second and fifth holes, a three-putt bogey at the eighth, and fifteen basically routine pars.

At first that evening I was surprised to be a coleader with such a score, but then I figured that, as usual in the first round of the Open, the better golfers had played fairly cautiously, as I basically had, there being nothing worse than a disaster before you are fully in stride. Only five others had beaten par: Kermit Zarley, Orville Moody, Mason Rudolph, Tom Shaw, and Chi Chi Rodriguez. Arnold had started with three straight bogeys and shot 77. The defender, Lee Trevino, was just out of hospital following a bout of bronchial pneumonia, and should not, according to his doctors, have been playing. Lee shot 74 and said he never would have survived but for the seventeen pills he'd taken.

The big news on Friday was Arnie. Then in his forty-third year and without a major championship win since his fourth Masters in 1964, old Arn had finally gotten the putter going again and, finishing with a brace of birdies, eased it around in 68. This brought him fully back into contention and was a fine round of golf, particularly compared with mine.

Everything had gone fine for me until the par-five fourteenth hole, that always-awkward dogleg, where for my second shot I had feathered a 4-iron from some high fescue to one foot beyond the out-of-bounds line. I went back and hit another ball into the fairway, then pitched to twenty feet. When I made the putt for a bogey it felt like an eagle and I was thrilled. However, by the time I walked off the eighteenth green I was pretty upset with myself.

At fifteen, through not stopping for a gust of wind, I had semi-topped my first putt from twenty-five feet, then missed the resulting six-footer. At sixteen I had hit a simple 5-iron approach into the rough well wide of the green, chipped to under twenty feet, then missed for a third straight bogey. At the par-three seventeenth I had hit the 3-iron to five feet and lipped out, and at the final hole my fifteen-footer for birdie was in all the way until it suddenly broke off about six inches from the hole. What should have been a score under 70 had become a one-over-par 73. My only consolation was that I retained a share of the lead, along with Bruce Crampton, Homero Blancas, Cesar Sanudo, and Lanny Wadkins. Palmer was now one stroke back of me and Trevino two.

On Saturday in the third round I played my best golf of the championship from tee to green but had a cold putter. Nevertheless, my even-par 72 gave me the lead alone for the first time by one stroke from Trevino, Crampton, and Zarley, with Arnie a shot farther back. My total of 216 for fifty-four holes was even par, and I told the writers I was pleased but somewhat surprised to be leading the Open without being in red numbers. I meant it, too. With the increasing wind off the Pacific—the reverse of the prevailing Crosby wind—making the inward holes the toughest, the course had been growing harder by the day. But, even so, this was the national championship. What were those guys up to while I was missing all those birdie putts? Somebody said they were doing the same. That did not stop me from announcing, and really believing, that I would have to shoot better than par in the final round in order to win.

Next morning, I wished I had never had that thought.

I normally sleep as well as ever—which is like a log—before the last round of any tournament. Not this time. On Sunday morning I awoke about seven o'clock, which was at least two hours too early relative to my starting time. Then, trying to go back to sleep, I tossed and turned for what seemed like a week in that awful half-asleep, half-awake state that generally produces the worst kind of dreams. From seven to nine that morning I must have played the seventeenth and eighteenth holes a hundred or more times in my subconscious. And, for the life of me, I just could not play them.

I arrived at the seventeenth tee every time with a comfortable three-stroke lead, but there was no way I could make par there with the cup cut left of the hump in the green. Finally, I decided to take the bogey and go on to eighteen. There, now leading by only two shots, all I could do was hit the tee shot either into the ocean on the left or out of bounds to the right. I tried the driver, then the 3-wood, then the 1-iron, then went through them all again, and either dunked the ball or knocked it OB every time. Finally, I couldn't stand it any longer and leaped out of bed. "What's the matter?" Barbara asked. I told her, "I've played the seventeenth and eighteenth holes for two hours, and I can't play them. I don't know what I'm going to do if I get there this afternoon with a three-stroke lead, but I'm sure not going to play them again right now." It was the worst dream I've ever had about golf—just awful.

The three final pairings for the last round were Crampton and Zarley, Palmer and Johnny Miller, then Trevino and me. After what he had done to me at Oak Hill in 1968 and at Merion the previous year, I expected the most fireworks from Lee, and was glad I was playing with him, because I have always found it useful to be able to sense the mood of the man you have to beat.

Pneumonia or not, Lee was as chipper as ever before we began. At Merion, as we were getting ready for the playoff on the first tee, he had dug a toy rubber snake out of his golf bag and tossed it over to me. This time, as we were warming up on the range, he began topping 3-wood shots. "Look at that, Jack," he said. "Can't even get 'em in the air." It got a big gallery laugh, but there would not be many more for the Merry Mex that day. After bogeying the second and third holes, he made a bogey at six by missing from three feet and was pretty much out of it thereafter.

There were not a lot of leader boards at Pebble Beach that year, so I was unaware when I reached the turn that I was three strokes ahead of Blancas and four better than Palmer, Crampton, and Zarley at that point. In the conditions by then prevailing, however, it was a fair assumption that going out in par had kept me ahead, probably by a shot or two. The wind had gotten up to around thirty knots, and those rolled and triple-cut greens had become as firm and fast as skating rinks. It was hard to visualize anyone scoring much better than I had.

Thanks to my intensive practice and a lot of patience, I had handled the conditions extremely well, offsetting a three-putt at the fourth hole with a twenty-five-footer for birdie at the seventh, the lovely little par three out on a spit of land in the ocean. That had given me a rush of confidence, which had been further boosted by perfect pars at eight and nine, two scenically spectacular holes but, at 431 and 464 yards with the Pacific tight on the right, both potential disaster territory.

The tenth at Pebble Beach is the last of the ocean holes until you get back to seventeen and, at 421 yards, also the last of what may be the greatest trio of consecutive par fours anywhere in golf. Sitting more across the wind than its two predecessors, it was playing that Sunday as tough as any hole on the course—in fact, I learned later, so hard that only one of the top ten finishers made even a par there. Because the cup was cut in the left side of the green and the right-to-left route offered the only hazard-free approach, I needed to land my ball in the right side of the fairway, which meant flirting with the ocean. I had been driving well all week, so I stood up to the ball now with complete confidence. About halfway into the backswing—too late to stop—a gust of wind hit me and forced me slightly off balance. The result was a mighty slice that landed on a neck of beach down in Carmel Bay.

As regular Crosby/AT&T watchers will know, the Pacific is not out-of-bounds at Pebble Beach, so, walking onto the cliff overlooking the beach about a hundred feet below, I hoped I would be able to climb down and play the ball. Some chance. It was on the beach all right, but also in the beach—badly plugged. One look and I decided there was no way I could get the ball back onto short grass with one swing. The best alternative was to drop another ball up on the clifftop and take the one-shot penalty for a lateral water-hazard. I did so, then walked ahead to check the yardage. It was 221 yards, spelling 2-iron. "Knock it on," I told myself, "and take your two putts for bogey, then run for the next tee." The impact felt good and for a moment I thought the ball would reach the green. But the 2-iron was insufficient club to make the carry. I was over the cliff again.

What counts most at times like this is self-control. If you panic or get too angry at yourself, you're dead—particularly on an eat-'em-alive course like Pebble Beach in rough weather. I told myself I was certainly not the only golfer making mistakes, and that up until then I had made very few, and that there was no reason why I should make any more so long as I remained calm. And I was lucky. The ball was sitting up nicely in some sandy rough not far below the edge of the cliff. I hit a pretty good shot with the sand wedge that ended up about ten feet short of the cup. I thought I'd hit an even better putt, but right at the hole the ball broke left—away from the ocean, contrary to all the theories. Double-bogey—my first of the championship. I told myself to forget it, and did so, and made a routine par at eleven.

Normally, I pay little attention to leader boards when playing tournaments. For one thing, they are often out of date or plain wrong. For another, I figure the only thing I can do anything about is my own game, so there is no point in concerning myself with anyone else's. Even when I do glance at boards, for the latter reason all I usually look for are numbers, rarely names. However, as I walked to the twelfth tee, probably as a hangover from the double-bogey at ten, I had a burst of curiosity. It would be nice to know exactly how I stood. I decided to check the leader board by the green when I got there.

The twelfth hole is a 205-yard par three with a plateaued green set diagonally to the tee, a big bunker in front, and a sharp drop-off behind. On this day it was a devil. The wind was howling dead across from the ocean on the left, and I knew that the green, if anything like those I'd played so far, would be rock-hard. The ideal play in calm weather is a high, faded, feathering-in long iron, but it was not the shot for this day. I finally decided on the 3-iron, drawing the ball slightly to hold it against the wind.

I did exactly what I had visualized—in fact, if I had fired balls there all day I would never have hit a better shot. The ball landed dead on line ten feet short of the pin, but from there it just kept going, through the green, and down the steep bank behind it. Standing there was P. J. Boatwright, Jr., the USGA official who had set up the course and was now refereeing the final pairing. P.J. was a good friend, but as I walked by I gave him a hard look and said, "What did you do with all the grass?" It was a less harsh comment than I was tempted to make.

As I had walked onto the green I'd looked at the leader board, which showed I was still ahead by two strokes. Nevertheless, my heart sank when I got to my ball. It was in the worst lie imaginable, deeply buried in thick, tangled grass. After inspecting the lie every which way, I decided I had to be conservative. If I tried for too much with the shot but hit it a little too hard, or thin, it would end up in the bunker on the far side of the green. Using the sand wedge, I attempted to pop the ball barely onto the putting surface, and missed hitting a perfect shot by about two inches, the ball hanging up in the short rough atop the embankment. I pitched it from there as delicately as I knew how, but it was like hitting to a glass-top table. The ball finally stopped eight feet past the cup.

This was now Trouble with a capital T. Surveying the putt, it occurred to me for the first time all day that I might lose this championship. "Look," I told myself, "you've just made one double-bogey and you are not going to make another. Forget what's just happened and bear down on this shot." I took a long time over the reading, and finally decided to play the putt about a half inch above the hole. That made me feel a little better because, for me as for most right-handed golfers, a right-to-left-breaking putt is easier than a left-to-righter. Having determined the line, I told myself not to start the putter back until I was good and ready. I'd had problems getting totally comfortable over putts all week, but this time I waited and wiggled until the feeling of readiness finally arrived. I stroked the ball very gently. As it got about halfway to the hole—just as Trevino supportively yelled, "Get in there!"—I knew I had made it.

After two near disasters I still had the lead, and it did wonders for my psyche. If I had known what I discovered later, I would have gotten an even bigger boost. As I dropped that putt on twelve, Arnie, playing fourteen, was over a putt of the same length for birdie. If I had missed and he had holed, instead of the other way around, we would have been tied.

I hit a big hook off the tee at thirteen, but got another lucky break when the ball finished in a clean lie on a dirt service road. Nine-iron, two putts, par. At fourteen, yet more good fortune. Trying to cut the corner of the dogleg to get home in two—the hole is a 555-yard par five—I pushed my drive to within six feet of the out-of-bounds stakes, from where I barely missed making birdie.

But this was living too dangerously, so on the fifteenth tee I treated myself to another pep talk, then settled for the 1-iron over the driver or 3-wood. I hit it solidly and straight, followed with an even better 9-iron to twelve feet, and knew the putt was in from the moment the ball left the clubface. Birdie . . . which just had to give me a cushion. Although I had not looked at any leader boards after the twelfth hole, I figured there was no way anyone could have caught me. After hitting my approach to the sixteenth green, that was confirmed by a man in the gallery. "Don't worry, Jack," he called out. "You're ahead by three." He seemed pretty confident about it, and that relaxed me even more. The pressure of fighting this by now close to unplayable golf course just for pars had eased. I could afford a bogey, or even two, and still win. The two putts for par at sixteen became that much easier.

And so there I was, at the tee of the first of the two holes I simply could not play, and leading by three strokes, just as I'd dreamed. The pin was where my subconscious had seen it, on the right side of the green's left rear section, making it virtually impossible to get up and down from a miss to the right. But close up on the left was the Pacific Ocean. Bale out to the right side and take a sure bogey? To heck with it. "Give me the one-iron," I told Angelo, and took dead aim at the flag. Swinging back, I felt myself closing the clubface and working the club too much to the inside. But my tempo and timing had been outstanding all week, and now it produced one of the most memorable shots of my career.

Frequently when you get closed and too much to the inside going back, the clubface will remain closed through impact and you will hook the ball badly. Now, thanks to my fine sense of pace, coming down I was able to block or delay the release just sufficiently to catch the ball with the face square. The result was a low, boring flight dead on the stick. I could not see the ball after it cleared the front bunker, but there was a huge roar from the gallery. When I got up there, I found the ball about two inches from the hole. It had struck the flagstick and almost dropped in for an ace.

Despite my early-morning bad dream, I hit the eighteenth fairway from the tee with the 3-wood, laid up with the 4-iron, and pitched onto the green some thirty feet from the hole. Then, before putting, I decided to check the scoring with someone I could totally trust. Since the 1963 British Open I had been extremely reluctant to rely on leader boards, or even well-meaning fans. I *thought* I was four strokes ahead, but it *might* have been only two—or one. Overhearing me, Bruce Crampton, the "leader in the clubhouse" at five over par, held up five fingers. That meant I could six-putt and still tie, and I guess it made me a little casual because I three-putted to win from Bruce by three, with Arnie third a stroke farther back.

Son Steve was playing in a Little League championship game right after that Open, so we wanted to get home fast and took a "red-eye" out of San Francisco that Sunday night. After those twelve straight days of concentrated effort, I was bone-tired by the time we arrived in Florida on Monday morning. However, it had become a habit by then to have Sockeye Davis videotape tournament telecasts, chiefly so I could review them for faulty technique. This time, even before unpacking, I flopped down and watched the entire five and a half hours of ABC's weekend coverage of the championship. I spotted a flaw almost immediately—in my putting setup—but that wasn't what kept me glued to the screen.

Exhausted or not, this was something I had to savor. A third national title, and on the most demanding course I had ever encountered. A thirteenth major championship, tying me with Bob Jones's record total. And, of course, halfway to the Grand Slam. . . .

What really kept my droopy eyelids apart all that time was a strange sense of disbelief. When I had glanced in the mirror that Monday morning, some questions I'd asked myself many times before but had always thrust aside out of self-consciousness had finally stopped me cold. "Am I that good? Do I really deserve all this? Is it true?

I guess you could say I needed those pictures to assure me it wasn't all just a beautiful dream.

OVER the nine weeks between the Masters and the U.S. Open I had played in three events, losing the Tournament of Champions on the first hole of sudden-death to Bobby Mitchell, and placing in the middle of the field in the Byron Nelson and Atlanta Classics. Pebble Beach was thus my thirteenth outing in six months, and, with the British Open only three weeks away, I decided that what would do me a lot more good than more competition was a rest.

In those days we owned a house on Great Harbour Cay in the Bahamas. As soon as we'd watched Steve in his Little League championship game, I gathered up the family and we flew over there for a few days. The smaller ball was then still optional in the British Open (the American 1.68-inch-diameter ball became mandatory two years later), and I took along a practice bag of the 1.62-inch pellets, together with the Slazenger clubs I then endorsed outside of the U.S. Mostly, we fished and lazed, but I worked some on the driving range with the smaller ball each day, and used it on the course when playing with Jackie and Steve. Back home again, feeling relaxed and rested, I gradually increased the intensity of my work with this equipment until we left for Scotland nine days ahead of the start of *The* Open.

I had been thinking about Muirfield a lot since leaving Pebble Beach, and it was a delight to get there and settle into the lovely Greywalls Hotel and renew my acquaintance with the magnificent golf course just beyond its grounds. So far as I could tell without actually competing, my game had lost nothing that had been present in California, in addition to which I was pleasantly surprised by the condition of the golf course.

There was some horrendous rough, to be sure, but nothing like the hay fields of 1966. Also, the expanses of semirough between fairways and tall fescue were more generous this time, giving the course more the character of my first encounter with it in the 1959 Walker Cup: tough but basically as fair as a big links course ever will be. However, accuracy being so much more a factor than distance at Muirfield in any condition, I'd imagined right after the U.S. Open that I would probably stick with the strategy that had been so successful six years previously. As the early practice days passed productively and enjoyably, this became a firm resolve. All these years later I can admit that it may have been the most costly mistake of my career.

I DO not believe anyone who knew me as a young golfer would question my aggressiveness in those days. As an amateur, and even on occasion during my early pro years, fearlessness—or what some might prefer to call blinkered stupidity combined with blind luck—was frequently my greatest strength. Often I would go for everything simply because it never occurred to me that (a) I would not pull it off, or (b) I wouldn't be able to find a way to recover if I didn't. Cocky? I suppose so. But typical of immaturity and inexperience—and, I submit, not a bad attitude for any youngster to start out with.

But time and the hard knocks that go with it breed greater caution in most of us, and by 1972 they had moved me to the other end of the competitive spectrum: analytic, careful, conservative—particularly in the major championships. I had learned by then that far more golf tournaments are lost than are won, and particularly the most important among them, where the pressure squeezes the hardest. Thus, although I would not say I went about golf fearfully, I had become averse to chancing high-risk shots or to gambling unless circumstances forced me to. Also, due to that slight touch of stubbornness mentioned before, playing attacking golf had become even more difficult for me once I had mapped out and locked in an essentially conservative game plan. Inevitably, the success of my conservatism at Muirfield in 1966, plus the enormous importance of the British Open to me in 1972, made it even more difficult to deviate from the blueprint.

Then, two days before the championship began, I suddenly had little choice in the matter. Through sleeping awkwardly, I awoke on the Monday morning with a pain in my neck that I immediately knew would limit if not prohibit aggressive play from tee to green whether I liked it or not. The same thing would happen to me again at the U.S. Open at Oakmont the following year, in the same area of my neck, after which I carried my own pillow on the road just about everywhere I went. If the injury occurred today, thanks to what I've learned from Pete Egoscue, I would do four or five exercises and the pain would be gone. Back then, all I could do was grin and bear it. I told Barbara and a few close friends about it, but no one else. As I've said before, once the game is on I hate to make or hear excuses.

I will spare you a blow-by-blow account of the golf this irritating injury produced in the first three rounds that year at Muirfield, except to record them as unexceptional: 70-72-71. That left me six shots back of Lee Trevino and five behind Tony Jacklin with eighteen holes to play. At the halfway point I had trailed them by only a stroke, but Lee had performed a series of miracles on the back nine in the third round to come home in 30 for a record-tying 66. Neck-and-neck (no pun intended) with me at the thirteenth, he'd birdied fourteen from twenty feet, fifteen from fifteen feet, sixteen by clattering the pin with a thinned bunker shot that dropped into the hole, the par-five seventeenth by reaching the green in two, and eighteen by chipping in from beyond the green. Despite having to watch all of this, Jacklin had put together a fine and more orthodox 67. If I was going to retain my chance of the Grand Slam, I now had a problem of some magnitude—like, say, shooting no worse than 65 in the final round.

When I awoke on Saturday morning the pain had gone and I knew I would again be able to make the swings required to have a shot at such a score. The weather had been good all week and looked like continuing that way. Although troubled on the big shots, I had putted well for fifty-four holes. The time had come to change the game plan. Having regained the ability to attack the golf course, I had everything to gain and nothing to lose by doing so. It might not work, but I was going to give it my best try. Over breakfast, I told Barbara I was going to win the 1972 British Open. Charge!

My popularity had been growing in Scotland ever since my 1966 win at Muirfield, and I sensed as soon as I teed off that afternoon that a great part of the crowd was pulling for me, even though Jacklin, a British player, was in the thick of it. There appeared to be tens of thousands of fans on every hole, and they seemed more demonstrative than the Scots usually are, and it got my adrenaline flowing right from the start.

On the front nine, going for everything, I played almost flawless golf, birdieing the second and third holes off fine pitches, then both of the par fives, and parring the rest for an outward 32. When I then birdied the difficult tenth hole and added another at eleven to go six under par and into the lead, the running and the roaring became incredible, sending shivers down my back and putting a lump in my throat and tears on my cheeks. And, of course, the applause and encouragement continued to fuel my by now soaring confidence. Never in doubt that I would keep the lead now that I'd grabbed it, I narrowly missed a third consecutive birdie at twelve, then made solid pars at the next three holes. Still six under par, and still the leader. And just listen to those folks holler!

The sixteenth hole at Muirfield is a 188-yard uphill par three to a long, slim plateaued green. Standing on the tee I had a flashback. In the final round in 1966 I had been tied at this point with Dave Thomas and Doug Sanders. "Okay," I had said to myself, "all you need to do is go three, four, four and you'll win the championship," which is what happened. Now I told myself that all I had to do was finish the same way and I would win again.

In 1966, both sixteen and seventeen had played downwind, making the tee shot to the par three relatively easy and the par five an almost cinch birdie hole. With the wind now dead against, both holes were playing much harder.

I made a good swing with the 4-iron at sixteen, but pulled the ball just enough for it to trickle a little way off the green into some thick rough. I worked hard at the pitch and stopped the ball six feet beyond the cup, then worked even harder at the downhill putt, judging the break at one and a half inches from right to left. The ball broke down the slope much faster than I had figured and never even touched the hole. Bogey.

At seventeen, the par five, I hooked the driver into an awful lie, bunted the ball back to the fairway, knocked it onto the green, and never looked like making the birdie that I was beginning to sense I would almost certainly need. At the eighteenth hole I made a routine par. I had shot 66, one stroke shy of my morning target. But would it be good enough? All I could do was wait and see. It was up to Trevino and Jacklin. All either of them now needed to beat me was two pars.

As I was finishing on eighteen and checking and signing my card, Lee and Tony were playing seventeen. Thus I could not watch them on that hole on television, and, in fact, have never to this day seen a replay of what became one of golf's most storied moments. But I'm only too aware of what happened.

The farther he got down the long seventeenth, the more it seemed as though Trevino could kiss the title good-bye. He had hooked into a bunker off the tee, then, after barely knocking the ball out, hit a fairway wood into rough short of the green and put his fourth shot up on the bank to the left rear of the putting surface. Friends of mine watching said you could tell from his body language that he believed it was all over. I'm told he said to no one in particular after the fourth stroke, "That's it. I've thrown it away." Jacklin, on the other hand, was about eighteen feet from the hole in three shots and looked all set to win a second Open.

Trevino then came walking up to his ball, grabbed a wedge, took a perfunctory glance at the hole, and hit the shot the moment he'd assumed his address position. To anyone who knows anything about golf it looked like one of those "get-me-out-of-here" efforts, and Lee admitted afterward that he did not give the shot the appropriate amount of study or time. Nevertheless, the ball came bumbling straight for the hole, then, when it got there, fell in. Trevino had turned what seemed a certain bogey, maybe even a double-bogey, into a par. Badly shaken, Jacklin three-putted.

Trevino was too good a player with too much experience, and too strong in the heart and gut, not to capitalize on that jumbo helping of good fortune. He made his par at eighteen easily, hurrying to the tee and nailing the drive before he could become tense, then drilling an iron to within ten feet of the hole. Jacklin, probably still in shock, again took three putts, which moved him into third place. Trevino had successfully defended his title with a total of 278 strokes. I finished second with 279.

My reactions?

I congratulated Lee as soon as he came off the course. I told him he was a great champion and deserved the victory, then added, "But why don't you go back to Mexico? You've done this too many times!" We both laughed, then he told me how bad he felt for me. I believed then and believe now that he meant it sincerely.

As soon as we were done with the ceremonies, I headed off to the hotel for my sneakers and got out on the Greywalls tennis court with Jim Fitzgibbon, an old friend from Ireland. He was a former Davis Cup player and I got a strong workout, and that eased some of the immediate sting. But the frustration and disappointment were more intense than I care to remember even now, a quarter of a century later.

I had shot five under par for a 66 on a difficult golf course, which, nineteen times out of twenty, would have been good enough to win. But I had not won, and that was that. You could say it simply wasn't fated to happen, just wasn't in the cards, but I'd had my chances and failed to take them. In 1966 I had finished as I believed I needed to, with 3-4-4, and won by a shot. In 1972, I finished 4-5-4 and lost by a shot. It had nothing to do with Trevino chipping in. As always in golf, I had controlled my own destiny. It hurt, but life would go on. There was nothing I could do but get on with living it, and that's what I did as I'd done after all the other disappointments along the way, and would again in the future.

As we have discussed, at golf you will always lose a lot more than you win, and if you want to retain your sanity—and protect the sanity of those around you—you just have to conjure up enough fatalism to live peacefully with that fact.

• • •

LOOKING back now, I realize I took a lot away from that championship, despite the immediate hurt. During that final round at Muirfield in 1972, it became clear to me that something had changed.

The Scots are the most knowledgeable golf watchers in the world, and accordingly the most sparing with applause. That day there was a wildness about them that was out of character. Even with the third leg of the Grand Slam on the line, the ovations that greeted me as I moved more and more into contention were stunning. When at the eleventh hole all those thousands of people just would not stop cheering and applauding after I hit my 7-iron close, I could hardly see my way down the fairway for the tears.

I would cry tears of joy again in the years ahead, but the memories of how those Scots made me feel in 1972 will never fade.

14

The 1973 PGA Championship

Trevino and Others—And a New Record

I WOULD like to think I had a small hand in Lee Trevino's decision to play in the Masters in 1972 after passing up the tournament the previous two years.

I had developed great respect for Lee Buck Trevino as I got to know him better following his 1968 U.S. Open win, and somewhere along the line—probably when we teamed together to win the World Cup in November of 1971—I told him I thought it a shame that a player of his caliber did not give himself a chance to win all of the major championships. Lee responded that his game simply wasn't suited to the Augusta National course, first, because he wasn't long enough, and second, because the course was built for right-to-left shots and he was a left-to-right player. I told him that was baloney. "Lee," I said, "your game is good enough to win anywhere you believe you can win, and if it's good enough to win the U.S. and Canadian and British Opens back-to-back, then it's certainly good enough to win the Masters." Trevino never came close to winning at Augusta, but I am glad he played in the Masters a number of times after we talked. His record and his personality were such that his absence took something away from any great golf tournament.

As I mentioned earlier, I had never heard of Lee Trevino when he finished fifth in the U.S. Open at Baltusrol in 1967, but he made a large impression on me from then on. Of all my contemporaries, he has been the hardest to beat.

If you are a purist about swing technique that statement may surprise you, because you probably believe Trevino has a strange-looking way of playing golf. Well, it isn't a method I would be inclined to copy if I were just starting out or would recommend to anyone else. But that goes by the wayside when it comes to results.

What Trevino achieved technically is what every golfing great has done since the game began, and what everyone who hopes to become a consistently fine player must strive his utmost to do. That is discover what works best for him or her, then stick with it through hell and high water.

In Lee's case, this process began when he quit school in the eighth grade and took a job at a Dallas driving range and par-three course; then his skill was honed when he played for folding money without a nickel in his pocket. Essentially, he learned golf by instinct, mimicry, experience and hard work, which is exactly the way the old champions who began as caddies mastered the game. But the key to the player Lee became is that, once he moved into a world of more esthetically "correct" or orthodox ways of playing, he had the intelligence and the strength of will not to abandon his own self-taught techniques for what so easily could have seemed "better" ones. In other words, he was smart and secure enough to put scores ahead of style. And what that did is make him the most consistent shotmaker since Ben Hogan. When Lee Trevino at his best stands up to the golf ball, he knows exactly what he wants to and can do with it, and most of the time he does exactly that. And it is your knowledge of his great confidence in himself and his shotmaking consistency that makes him such a tough opponent. You just know Lee Trevino is going to make very few mistakes. In my estimation, he and Hogan were about as close to golfing machines as we have so far seen.

I have sometimes wondered if the Merry Mex would have achieved all he has in golf if he had come to the game via a more advantageous route, like the one I was so fortunate to follow. Trevino was dirt poor as a youngster, which instilled in him a hunger for success and a capacity for work and perseverance that have never dimmed, and those remain the key forces behind his tireless competitive drive. But there is a technical factor here that is also interesting.

Golfers who grow up in more affluent circumstances have the advantage of being able to afford plenty of coaching. While this sounds great, it can sometimes be a double-edged sword. Take me, for example. It is unlikely that I would be where I am today without the teachings of Jack Grout. On the other hand, I could have gone on relying on Jack forever, or made the even bigger mistake that you see so much of in the game today, with its ever-growing supply of swing "gurus," of becoming a "professional pupil"—of running endlessly from one teacher to another in the vain hope that somebody, somewhere, somehow would deliver me a fine golf game on a platter.

Lee Trevino never had the wherewithal to fall into either of those traps, which may have been a blessing in disguise, as it was for so many of the game's earlier champions who had to haul themselves up by their bootstraps. Even though it may take longer, as it did Lee, when a golfer eventually *himself* discovers and ingrains his best way to play, alone and unaided, he gains a depth of confidence that produces a powerful competitive edge. The time it takes to "arrive" may be extended by the need for one real success to dispel any lingering doubts about what he has created, but, after that, watch out! This is what happened to Lee, with, first, a strong performance in the U.S. Open in 1967 at the age of twenty-seven, then the title just twelve months later—and superstardom ever since.

Beyond my respect for his game, my admiration for Lee Trevino increased the better I got to know the man behind the public persona.

If you think Lee's swing compared to his record is a paradox, it's a tiny one compared to his public and private personalities. More than anyone I know, Trevino is two completely different people. On the course or elsewhere in public when he's on top of his game, he's invariably the Merry Mex, the lolloping, laughing, wisecracking, love-everybody, life's-a-bowl-of-cherries entertainer. As you get to know him better, you begin to realize that this side of him is a carefully and cleverly cultivated facade: a deliberate and skillful way of fighting pressure by letting off steam while also keeping the customers happy. Some of the fellows find the self-preoccupation and noise inherent in this performance tough to play against, but Lee generally tries to hold it to a level where no one gets too upset.

Even harder for some players to deal with is the touch of psyching or needling in some of Lee's chatter. For instance, over the years he must have told both the media and me personally hundreds of times what a great player Jack Nicklaus is . . . the best, tops of all time, never been anyone so good . . . almost unbeatable . . . certainly more than a match for a little ol' Tex-Mex just trying to make an honest dollar . . . de dah, de dah, de dah. I remember Gary Player once commenting to me about how strange he found all of this, in that he could never openly admit that a golfer he was trying to beat was better than him. What Gary had not then grasped was Lee's cleverness at the mind games. The theory in my case was that, by beating me after giving me all that you're-the-greatest guff, he would boost his own confidence while eating into mine. The latter never happened, of course, because I always knew exactly what he was about and could quickly laugh it off. But, judging by the record, it did wonders for him.

But back to the seemingly split Trevino personality.

Although innately I am a pretty private guy, I have tried hard throughout my career to avoid letting being well known force me into an abnormal lifestyle. Unless I am in a hurry, I make no attempt to get away from people, at the golf course or anywhere else. For instance, when I go out to dinner, I don't ask for private rooms or places where no one can see me or find me. I figure that, by and large, people desire and expect their own privacy sufficiently to respect mine. What I do try to avoid are places where there will be a lot of drinking, because drunks have no respect for anyone, including themselves.

Many years ago, Lee Trevino had a bad experience with a drunk in a restaurant, which, added to the powerful self-preservatory instincts deriving from his background, has made him one of the most private people outside of working hours I have ever encountered. The moment Lee leaves the public arena, click goes the switch. Unless you are family or an old and close friend, you will never get to know, or even see, this other person: quiet, serious, introspective, analytical, totally self-sufficient, and as savvy and shrewd as all get out.

What feeds the disparities between the public and private man is surely Lee's acute awareness of how most of the golfing world would react to and treat a guy of his background if he were not a champion. That recognition probably also underpins the qualities I most admire about him, which are integrity and independence. If Lee Trevino says he will do something, you can rely upon him absolutely. Beyond that, he participates in a particular facet of the world in order to satisfy his immense competitive drive and make a fine living, but without accepting a lot of its social systems and imperatives. I believe he has become a little less reclusive since his present marriage, but he will always be true to himself first, and that's what I like most about him.

All I wish is that he hadn't hit that darn time-to-go-home chip shot at Muirfield back in 1972.

IF things had gone a little differently for me in the 1972 British Open, what would have been my chances of completing the modern Grand Slam by winning the PGA Championship at Oakland Hills three weeks later? This is really a pointless question, but, as I am still sometimes asked it, I guess there is no harm in playing the famous game of "If only" one more time.

Soon after returning home from Britain I went for a haircut and, for some unknown reason, decided to get a manicure at the same time. I had never had one before, and I wish I had not had one then, and you can bet I will never have another one. That's because a few days after the manicure, which seemed fine at the time, an infection developed under the cuticle of the forefinger of my right hand. I ignored it at first, but it quickly became so painful that I decided I had better get it checked out. The next thing I knew was that I had spent a couple of hours on the operating table, had a bandage the size of a fist on the finger, and would be lucky even to be able to play at Oakland Hills, let alone win. Thankfully the injury healed fast and I did play, holding the finger off the club throughout, and finishing tied for thirteenth, six strokes behind Gary Player. (I have a constant reminder of that time in a grip change it triggered. Ever since the 1972 PGA, I've played with my right forefinger just barely resting on the club, rather than snuggling it firmly around the shaft as before.)

Even at this distance it is hard for me to offer much more about my chances of winning that PGA. Had I prevailed at Muirfield, the pressure at Oakland Hills obviously would have been tremendous, almost certainly the greatest I would ever have experienced. But the fact is I thrive on pressure: The higher the mountain and the harder it is to climb, the better I respond—given, of course, that my game is in appropriate shape. Competition to me is truly the "spice of life." So the answer is simply that I do not know what would have happened, and particularly if I had not had that manicure.

Apart from the little grip change I just mentioned, the one legacy of the 1972 season was an even greater reluctance to talk to the media about the Grand Slam. The 1972 British Open taught me just how much of an improbability it really is, and, as a consequence, made me less inclined to call it even a possibility. As the days passed following the PGA, I took some consolation from the idea that half a Slam was better than no part of one, and decided simply to try to finish the year as well as I had begun it. When that worked out pretty well, my policy became and has remained to take one tournament at a time—to compete in the present and let the future take care of itself.

The week after the PGA, I won at Westchester, then, two weeks later, defeated Frank Beard on the last hole of the final of the U.S. Professional Match-play Championship in Pinehurst. Gary Player edged me by two in the World Series, but I finished in the top ten in the Kaiser and Sahara Invitationals in October, then rounded the year off nicely by tying my biggest winning margin of nine strokes in defending successfully at Disney World. With two majors and five other wins, along with a record amount in prize money and a second PGA Player of the Year award, the holidays that year were a happy time around the Nicklaus home, Grand Slam or no Grand Slam.

IN 1973, I did something I had never done before, which was pack my bags and leave for the tour on New Year's Day. There were three reasons for that.

The first was that the Los Angeles Open had moved from the Rancho Park municipal course to the Riviera Country Club. That was where Ben Hogan had won three times in eighteen months in 1947 and 1948, including his first U.S. Open, then tied Sam Snead in the 1950 Open less than a year after his car smash, only to lose in a playoff. I could not resist the challenge of what the old hands referred to as "Hogan's Alley." A great golf course was sometimes all it took to get me out of hibernation.

The second reason was that, as I am sure you know from your own experience, playing golf well makes you want to go on playing golf. At Disney World a month previously I had shot 68-68-67-64, or twenty-one under par. I wanted to find out if my game was still in that groove.

The third reason was the new mountain on my mind. The U.S. Open win at Pebble Beach had given me my thirteenth major championship. One more and I would have bettered Bob Jones's record total. I was determined to talk about this as little as possible publicly, but that did not mean I couldn't use it as a private motivator.

Of all the records in golf, this was the one I had become the most attuned to almost from the time my dad introduced me to the game. At first it had been like the North Star—always there, always glittering, but so remote as to be forever out of reach. Then, slowly but steadily year by year, it had drawn closer and closer. Now, at what must surely be the peak of my powers, I could reach out and touch it. Moreover, if my record was not a mirage, this goal, unlike the Grand Slam, was no pipe dream. If I could win thirteen major championships there was no reason why I could not win fourteen.

Not surprisingly after a month's layoff, I was not as sharp at Riviera as I had been at Disney World, finishing sixth, four shots behind Rod Funseth. But I played decently and continued working enthusiastically on my game after returning home. Out west again three weeks later, I defended successfully in the Crosby in a playoff against Orville Moody and Ray Floyd, then finished joint second with Johnny Miller in the Bob Hope Classic, two strokes behind Arnie (his last win on the regular tour, incidentally). Things cooled somewhat on the Florida swing, where Trevino won back-to-back, but my game came together again in New Orleans, my last tournament before the Masters, with a win over Miller Barber in sudden-death. That made a tally of two firsts, a second, and a couple of sixth places out of seven tournaments played, plus, between times, my only (so far!) score of 59 in an exhibition at the short Breakers Hotel course in Palm Beach. Was I ready for that fourteenth major? You had better believe it.

The 1973 Masters was won by Tommy Aaron by one stroke from J. C. Snead. I tied for third with Jim Jamieson and Peter Oosterhuis, another shot back. Tommy had turned professional around the time I did, and we had played on our first Walker and Ryder Cup teams together, and I was happy for him. I was also pretty disgusted with myself. After trailing Tommy by a stroke in the opening round with a 69, an acceptable score in cold and clammy conditions, I had three-putted six times for a 77 in the second. Then, on Sunday, following a day of idleness due to Saturday's play being washed out, I had gotten myself back in the hunt until a triple-bogey eight at fifteen, resulting from two shots in the water, knocked the wind out of me. The resulting 73 left me with eight strokes to make up over the final eighteen holes. I made a pretty good stab at it, with eight birdies for a 66 on Monday. But, in the end, it was yet another case of "If only . . ."

My problem in the second and third rounds had been putting. I lost my confidence with the short stick and was awful with it both days. The only reason I can think of for that lapse is self-inflicted pressure. Yet again, with a fourteenth major so much on my mind, I had let the Masters become too important for my own good. Then, of course, when I had shot myself out of it to all intents and purposes, the pressure lifted and I regained my confidence and my putting touch with it.

Don't ever try to tell me golf is not 99.9 percent a mental game.

THE Tournament of Champions is not a major, but, open only to the previous year's tour winners, it is one of the more satisfying tournaments to win. A week after the Masters letdown I got a double kick out of doing so: a fourth victory in the event and, finally, a win over Trevino. Following a month off for business activities, including preparations for the Muirfield Village ground-breaking, I added the Atlanta Classic, then, the week before the U.S. Open at Oakmont, tied for fifth in Philadelphia. This was a break in my custom of making final preparations at the championship site, but, knowing Oakmont so well and having played only two tournaments since the Masters, I felt in need of extra competition.

When you make a change like that, then come up empty, it is easy to second-guess yourself. I came up empty at Oakmont by three shots to Johnny Miller, but I doubt if even a month's preparation at the course would have made much difference.

After winning the Heritage Classic the previous November for his second tour victory, Miller had placed eight times in the top ten during the first half of 1973, and was building a reputation for bursts of inspired golf. There would be many more of those in the years ahead, but his play in the final round at Oakmont that year has to be the most inspired of his career. After a third-round 76 to fall six strokes back of the leaders, he closed with a sensational single-round Open record 63, made up of nine birdies, eight pars and a three-putt bogey, to win by a stroke from John Schlee. Tom Weiskopf was third and I tied for fourth with Palmer and Trevino.

It is common knowledge that Oakmont's members pride themselves on having a gorilla of a golf course, and there is no doubt Johnny's performance traumatized some of them—to the point of noting on his scorecard on display in the clubhouse that the greens were wet and holding that day. This was true, but incidental to his performance. A 63 is a 63, period. The measurement of the quality of Miller's play at Oakmont is that, although Lanny Wadkins shot a 65 and a couple of players 68 the last day, only four others beat the par of 71. I had one of the 68s, and I know I played exceptionally well for it, and in my estimation Johnny Miller's 63 to win the 1973 U.S. Open is one of the finest rounds of championship golf ever played.

JOHNNY Miller's achievement at Oakmont naturally launched a spate of "new superstar" predictions, and it left no question in my mind that he would become a major factor in the game. I had seen enough of him following the 1971 Masters, where we tied for second, to know he possessed all of the necessary physical skills, and Oakmont answered any questions about how his heart and stomach behaved when it mattered most. When asked about his long-term prospects, I told the writers I believed he could become as good a golfer as he wanted to be, and so it proved. John won nine times in 1974, including the first three tournaments he played in the United States and one in Japan. In 1975 he won four times, then three times in 1976 including the British Open at Royal Birkdale. It was a wonderful run, and only when John talked to me about it years later did I realize it was launched by more than the Oakmont boost.

John told me that, even after the Oakmont triumph, he still did not totally believe in his golfing abilities. What finally convinced him was he and I, as respectively the U.S. Open and the PGA champions, winning the team title in the 1973 World Cup as he took the individual prize. He told me he discovered as we played together in Spain that, while I might have had the edge on him with the longer clubs, he was better than I was with the short irons, and that there was little difference so far as the rest of our games were concerned. It was these realizations, he said, that finally convinced him he had what it took to beat the best. "It was playing with you in the World Cup that turned my career around," he assured me. Naturally, I was pleased by the compliment.

If Miller's achievements in 1973 did not surprise most analysts, those of another player making at least as many headlines, namely my fellow Buckeye and longtime friend Tom Weiskopf, certainly did.

By the start of that golf season, Tom Weiskopf had become professional golf's greatest enigma. Even if you barely knew a sand wedge from a sand dredge, just to catch a glimpse of his majestic swing was to recognize an immensely gifted athlete. Here was a golfer who appeared to have a game sent from heaven, but who in eight years on tour had won only six tournaments. No one could understand it, and no self-respecting golf writer could resist trying—and failing—to provide answers. All everyone agreed about was that someday six-foot three-inch "Big T" or "The Towering Inferno"—Tom had great trouble controlling his anger when he felt he'd done something dumb on a golf course—must surely become a dominating player. In 1973, he would finally fulfill that prediction.

Early that May, Weiskopf won the Colonial in Fort Worth, then, after a week off, finished second to me in Atlanta. A week later he won the Kemper Open in Charlotte by three strokes from Lanny Wadkins, and the week after that the 1VB Philadelphia Classic by four from Jim Barber. Next came third place in the U.S. Open two strokes behind Miller, then a tie for fifth in the American Golf Classic at Firestone. Following a break back home in Columbus, Tom headed for the west coast of Scotland, arriving sufficiently far ahead of the British Open to get in eight practice rounds over Royal Troon with his great buddy Tony Jacklin. At the end of the championship, after leading all the way, his 276 had tied Arnold Palmer's seventy-two-hole record set eleven years previously over the same course, and had defeated Miller and Neil Coles by three strokes. Two weeks later, Tom added a second national championship, winning the Canadian Open at Richelieu Valley in Quebec—his fifth victory in eight tournaments played. By the end of the year he had added two more, in the World Series at Firestone and the South African PGA Championship, placed third at Westchester and in the Ohio

King's Island Open, been a factor in the PGA Championship, made a strong contribution to America's Ryder Cup victory at Muirfield in Scotland, placed third in a European tour event, and gotten to the semifinals of both the U.S. Professional Match-play Championship at Pinehurst and the World Match-play in England.

What it all added up to was seven wins including a major championship, one second place, six thirds, and a fifth and a sixth in sixteen events over a seven-month period, plus a share of a Ryder Cup victory. The critics designated it one of the hottest runs by a male professional since Byron Nelson's incredible eleven wins in a row and eighteen in a season in 1945.

After a year like that, the consensus was that Tom Weiskopf was finally on his way to a rightful place among the game's all-time greats. As a friend of his, I certainly hoped that was true. Unfortunately, it did not happen. After that one superb season, Tom reverted to his former periodic flashes of brilliance, and particularly in the Masters, adding two more second places to the two he had already achieved. But his victory total over the next decade was below most people's expectations. As he began to compete less and less in the early 1980s in favor of television work and course designing, Big T had once again become tournament golf's principal puzzle.

Because of our shared associations and friendship, I have often been asked for my thoughts about Tom's ability relative to his record. I do have a couple.

It has always seemed to me that the root of the problem was that Tom's priorities for life in the round never jelled with his immense golfing talent. All of the skills were there in abundance, but it was impossible for him to sustain the amount of desire necessary to totally capitalize on them. As time passed, he simply found that he got more contentment from spending time with his wife, Jeanne, and his children, Heidi and Eric, or from going hunting or having a few beers with friends, than he ever could from winning golf tournaments. He tried for a long time to put golf first, and in 1973, spurred by the death of his father, he succeeded for one whole year. But, over the long haul, the game just could not offer enough for him to make the sacrifices it demands in order to both scale and remain at its summit.

Tom Weiskopf is one of the least selfish people I know, and in relation to golf this might have been his greatest handicap. A part of him wanted to ride his immense talent to the top of the mountain, while the rest ached for all of the things that would mean missing or shortchanging. My guess is that the temper and self-disgust he displayed over relatively minor mistakes in tournaments, along with what the world saw as moodiness, was the product of this conflict. Finally, as he matured, Tom developed the self-knowledge and emotional strength to quit feeling guilty and thus stop tearing himself apart, and as a result became much happier. As a friend, I believe this was the correct decision for him, and as a player I admire the willpower required to make it and stick with it. I also think it contributed greatly to his success as a senior, and particularly in winning the 1995 Senior Open, where his composure was even more impressive than his wonderful shotmaking.

Although they are night and day different in most aspects of their personalities, I believe Johnny Miller has a lot in common with Tom Weiskopf in this one regard. After his three years at golf's pinnacle, John's priorities swung more toward his family (he has six children), his faith (he's a devout Mormon), and the pleasures and contentments of a free and easy western lifestyle in and around his home. In other words, golf to him became a means to an end rather than the center of his existence. Having first developed the self-knowledge to recognize that fact, he then had the guts to live happily with it. In light of this, plus his success at golf television commentary, it will be interesting to see what he does on the Senior Tour.

Both of these men have frequently been criticized for not being "more dedicated to golf" or "true to their talent." In my opinion, what they really deserve is applause for being true to themselves.

APART from another brief chorus of "If only" following a closing 65, I stayed pretty much in the shadows as the year's two hot hands, Weiskopf and Miller, battled for the 1973 British Open at what was then just Troon Golf Club but later became Royal Troon. I had played what I call "okay but not okay" to finish tied for ninth in the American Golf Classic at Firestone the week after Oakmont, then had gone over early to Britain for some much-needed fine-tuning.

Due to the imminent arrival of our fifth child—Michael Scott was born a few days after I returned home—Barbara could not be present. It was the only one of my British Opens she has missed, and, as always, her absence did nothing for my mood. Then, just to round things out, my back began acting up in practice, necessitating frequent trips for treatment from my hotel to a private home some business associates were renting so that the press did not discover the problem (sorry about the deviousness, guys, but I hate excuses).

Troon that year was back on the British Open rota for the first time since I had begun playing in the championship in 1962, and the thought of redeeming my pathetic initial effort there was an added incentive to play well. Despite my back problems, I did so with 69-70 for the first two rounds, which put me four strokes behind Weiskopf. Then, in the third round, after a bad shot and a dumb one early on, and in such hot and clammy weather that even the natives were complaining, I totally lost my concentration and could do no better than 76.

Now nine strokes back of Tom and eight behind John, I told myself I was out of it and joined my business group for dinner that evening. It turned into the kind of party to which I would definitely not have gone if I had considered myself in contention. Although I limited myself to a couple of glasses of wine, as a nondrinker they were sufficient for me to awake with a headache the next morning. Despite the blahs, however, I managed to ease it around in 65 for a new course record and fourth place.

As Big T said as we helped him celebrate that evening, "Maybe you should live it up with the boys more often."

INCENTIVE is the fuel of success in sports, and I had a full tank of it going into the PGA Championship at the Canterbury Golf Club in the Beachwood suburb of Cleveland that August.

I had won one or more of the big four each season since my "comeback" in 1970, and I badly wanted to extend that string. This was my final opportunity for 1973. On top of that, Canterbury would be another chance to win a major in my home state, with all of my immediate family, most of our relatives, and a great many of my oldest friends and most loyal supporters present. Then, of course, there was the lure of the majors record.

Not surprisingly, the favorite that week was Tom Weiskopf. Although then a longtime resident of Columbus (from where he moved some years ago to Arizona), Tom was born in Massillon, Ohio, and raised in the Bedford section of Cleveland, which naturally made him the sentimental choice. After a couple of practice rounds scoring in the mid-60s, it was clear he was still in the groove that had begun in May, which made him number one in form also. For me, that worked as yet another incentive. As with Arnie and Gary, and most lately Lee, the stiffer the competition the sharper my focus on the job at hand. There would be some press comments that week about how grim and self-contained I seemed. When a person is concentrating as hard as I was, it is bound to show in his demeanor.

Canterbury played that year at 6,852 yards, with a par of 71. I took one more than that in the first round, which put me five strokes behind Al Geiberger and Don Iverson, a former club pro from Wisconsin playing in his first major championship. The 72 did not please me, but it didn't concern me a whole lot either. In the earlier majors that year my swing pattern had felt somewhere between 80 and 90 percent of ideal. In the last round of the Westchester Classic the week before the PGA, it began to feel close to 100 percent. On Thursday at Canterbury, although not threatening the hole much, I had struck the ball very solidly. I was sure I would do even better as the week progressed.

Although a little cramped for space, Canterbury is a fine golf course of the older genre, which means that, in order to maximize natural drainage, most of the greens are elevated above fairway level and sloped from back to front. That would have been fine in normal conditions, but, like so many of its northern contemporaries, the course had become almost entirely *Poa annua,* necessitating heavy nightly watering to keep it alive through the daytime heat and humidity. Also, with the constant threat of thunderstorms, the cups were cut mainly in the most flood-resistant or highest back portions of the greens, which areas naturally dried out fastest in the hot sun each day.

What it all added up to was that, in playing from a lot of wet "flier" lies, you could choose between hitting the front parts of the greens and chancing three-putts, or going for the dried-out back portions where the holes were situated and risking a tough recovery from heavy rough or worse. This tested the nerves, and it cost some of the less patient players dearly as the week wore on. I took the attitude, as I always had, that, like it or not, you do the best you can with what confronts you. A golfer fights enough frustrations without getting all out of sorts about something that is beyond his power to remedy.

In the second round on Friday I put together a 68, which brought me to within a stroke of Iverson and his new coleader, Mason Rudolph. I drove well, approached well and putted well without doing anything spectacular, and had a similar round the next day for another 68. This gave me the lead by one from Mason, with Bruce Crampton the next closest three strokes back. Of the "names," present and future, Weiskopf was four strokes behind, Player eight, Miller and Tom Watson nine, and Trevino eleven. Gary, the defending champion, had had bladder surgery and a cyst removed from a leg the previous January and was not fully back in stride. Arnie, for the first time in a PGA, had missed the cut.

Some of the writers later described this as a dull championship, and I guess for many of the people following me the most exciting thing that happened the second day was young Gary Nicklaus's race onto the green and leap into his father's arms at the eighteenth hole. This was the first time the four eldest of our five children had attended a major championship together (two-week-old Michael stayed home), the chief reason for that being Barbara's and my doubts about handling them as a group on such occasions. The solemnity deemed proper to golf was definitely not their style in those days, but, with so many relatives around to lend a hand, we had decided to take a chance.

Jackie was the one who beat the odds. He was standing behind the eighteenth green with brother Gary, who had just turned four. As I holed out Jackie said, "Look, there's your dad, go on out and give him a big hug." And, of course, Gary did just that. A photographer from Akron caught the moment and won an award for best sports picture of the year. But Gary previously had also somehow wriggled past a security guard and jumped into my lap during my postround press interview, and this second adventure displeased Mom to the point where he was grounded the next day. "Missed the cut," says Barbara, when anyone recalls the incident.

That evening one of my business associates, in reviewing the state of play, mentioned how close I had come at Augusta, Oakmont and Troon, where three golfers had won their first majors, and wondered if that was what was written in the cards again. I refrained from commenting, until we got to talking about a hunting trip to New Mexico some of us were considering for the autumn. Nothing had been firmed up, and it occurred to me that it was time to do so, and I said as much. "Well," said Put Pierman, "wouldn't it be better to wait until tomorrow and see what happens? If you don't win you may feel the need to play a few more tournaments in the fall." I thought that over for all of two seconds before telling him, "Book the hunt." Swinging as I was, putting as I was, and thinking as I was, there was no way I was going to lose.

Warming up Sunday, the figure in my mind was 70. "Shoot that," I told myself, "and it's yours." On the final green, under no pressure and winding down, I missed a tap-in for par to finish with a 69, giving me a four-stroke victory over Bruce Crampton. My driving had been less than a thing of beauty, and I had done some heavy recovering on the back nine, but I had never been seriously threatened and thus never became tight or nervous. Consequently, once the butterflies had settled after the first few holes, it had been as easy a final round as I could recall in winning a major. I remember my biggest immediate reaction was relief at finally having taken my majors total to fourteen.

Somebody dug up a cake at the club with that many candles, then most of the family and friends came over to our rented house, where the business guys broke out champagne. The next day I worked until dark in ankle-deep mud on the routing of Muirfield Village, then flew home to Florida. On Tuesday the kids helped me pick about two hundred key limes off our trees; then I cut down a spare driver for Jackie and watched him hit balls, and was as tickled as he was that it added about twenty yards to his drives. In the afternoon I did a whirlwind catch-up at the office, during which I changed the Muirfield Village clubhouse plans, giving the architect and builder fits by shifting its site. Then I took the kids for a boat ride and came home and spent a quiet evening with them and Barbara.

I remember we used some of the fruit for a key-lime pie. To a guy like me, that was as good a way of celebrating as any.

IN Bob Jones's day, golf's major championships consisted of four events: The U.S. and British Open and Amateur championships. Bob's thirteen victories in them comprised five U.S. Amateurs, four

U.S. Opens, three British Opens, and one British Amateur. He won those championships over a period of eight years from 1923 to 1930, playing strictly as a part-timer while first obtaining three college degrees, then raising a young family and launching a career as an attorney.

The major victories credited to me at this point in my career were two U.S. Amateurs, four Masters, three U.S. Opens, two British Opens, and three PGA Championships. That is five events, not four. Had I also played each year in the British Amateur until I turned professional, my total of available majors would have become six, meaning that I enjoyed a considerably greater opportunity to win majors than Bob did. Also, even though I probably faced stiffer competition than he did, it took me from 1959 to 1973, or seven years longer than Jones, to total fourteen victories—and that while devoting as much time as I wished to golf.

Those are a few of the reasons why I felt that some of the comparisons made between Jones and me following my Canterbury win reflected unfairly on Bob's achievements. The differences in the designation of the major championships, the differences in course and equipment quality, the differences in incentives and opportunities, and the differences in so many other areas of his time and mine are too vast to permit valid comparisons between us. I guess professional historians are the only people who can put these things in their proper perspective, but I wished then and I wish now that the writers and television pundits would be a little less fast and free with their "finests" and "mostests" and "greatests."

After Canterbury, I received all kinds of fanciful accolades, including a lot more of "the greatest of all time." I know it was meant genuinely and complimentarily, and it was obviously flattering. But it was also a little unsettling to me at times because of the shadow it seemed to cast on those who had gone before.

What Bob Jones did, just as Harry Vardon before him and Ben Hogan after him, was to become the best golfer of his time. That's all any man can do, and it is what I have been trying to do all through my career. If when my playing days are finally over I am judged to have succeeded, that will do just fine for an epitaph.

15

The 1975 Masters Tournament

Fun Time at Augusta

In 1945 Byron Nelson won eighteen tournaments, eleven of them in a row, a record that most experts are convinced will never be broken. The following year Ben Hogan won thirteen times. From then on, as the nation recovered from the Second World War and professional golf entered its greatest boom years, it would become increasingly harder for one player to dominate the American tournament game.

Ben won eleven U.S. tournaments in 1948, and Sam Snead ten in 1950, but the highest total for the next quarter of a century would be seven, achieved by Arnold Palmer in 1962 and 1963 and equaled by me in 1972 and 1973. The modern record is now eight, and here, just for you to wonder at, are the scores that produced it, as compiled by Johnny Miller in 1974:

Bing Crosby Pro-Am	68-70-70*
Phoenix Open	69-69-70-67
Dean Martin Tucson Open	62-71-71-68**
Sea Pines Heritage Classic	67-67-72-70

Tournament of Champions	75-69-67-69
Westchester Classic	69-69-65-67
World Open	73-63-73-72
Kaiser International	69-69-67-66

* *Reduced to three rounds by bad weather*
***Third straight victory*

Six years later, in 1980, Tom Watson won six American tournaments. As I write, the best anyone has been able to do since then on the PGA Tour is five victories, by Nick Price in 1994, including the PGA Championship (just prior to which he had also won the British Open). With three wins in his first nine pro outings, Tiger Woods would seem likely to match or better such numbers, but it is hard to imagine even a player of his incredible talent matching the Nelson-Hogan-Snead numbers.

I am often asked to comment on the causes of this "decline of the superstar," as many writers have chosen to call it. To my mind there are essentially three. Although it may not be the most critical, the first is golf equipment.

Throughout my career I have been against anything that changed the essential nature of golf. That is why I was so strongly opposed to square grooves during the controversy they created some years ago. I could change the nature of the game with square-grooved short-irons by spinning the ball more from rough. I change it, too, by driving the ball straighter and sometimes farther with a metal wood, and I worry about that effect on the game also, even though I play with and promote the metal woods made by my equipment company.

But my biggest concern about the impact of equipment "improvements" on the nature of golf, as both a player and a course designer, is how far the modern ball travels.

Through 1996 the United States Golf Association, based upon its ongoing research into equipment technology, continued to insist that modern balls go only minimally farther than older ones—eight to ten yards, according to the association's longtime technical director Frank Thomas.

With all due respect to that stance, direct experience convinces me that the ball I use now goes substantially farther for the same quality of hit than the ones I used thirty years ago. Also, I can't think of a player on any of the tours old enough to make the comparison who would tell you differently. Certainly Arnold Palmer, Gary Player, Raymond Floyd, and Tom Watson are among those who feel as strongly as I do on this subject—not least in Raymond's and Tom's case because they were hitting their drives at respectively fifty-three and forty-six years of age farther than they did when in their twenties and thirties.

Let me quickly emphasize that I support maximum-yardage balls for average golfers, who generally need every bit of distance they can generate. Where such balls impact negatively is at the top levels of the game, in two ways.

As equipment overall has improved, but particularly the ball, most of our great old courses have become less challenging or less interesting to play, or both. Merion is perhaps the best example. Merion is a wonderfully designed golf course, a real gem, but at under 6,500 yards, it must be tricked up in terms of fairway width, rough density and green speed to guard it against being savaged. As a result, after hosting fourteen national championships and a World Amateur Team Championship, it has not been used for an important competition since the 1981 U.S. Open.

Perhaps even more distressing is what is happening at Augusta National. The course over which I won my first five Masters was definitely easier than the present one, to the point where, if I had been playing under today's conditions in 1965, it is very unlikely that I would have set a new seventy-two-hole record of 271. The toughening factors are lengthening of holes with new tees, tighter mowing of banks sloping into water hazards, and faster-paced bent-grass greens. And the sole objective of these changes is, of course, to protect against the distances virtually every player in a Masters field now hits the ball.

Even more unfortunate to my mind than the impact of equipment advances on our finest courses is their contribution to the homogenizing of the players. Simply put, the more forgiving the tools, the tougher it becomes for the best to rise above the rest. Much as Seve Ballesteros and Nick Faldo, for example, stood out from the crowd in their peak years, I believe their talent and dedication would have separated them even more had all the players still competed with the equipment of my early professional years. As Herbert Warren Wind, America's leading golf historian and a man not given to hyperbole, was quoted as saying in the summer of 1995, "We want to produce players who can play the ideal shot, who can play different shots, and that's now out of the game. The United States Golf Association has been lax in allowing all those special balls and clubs to come in. The quality of golf has changed in the wrong way."

Is there a solution to these problems?

I am convinced that at least a partial answer would be to have all top tournaments worldwide played with a uniform ball, a "competition" ball if you like, manufactured with say a 5-to-10–percent reduction in distance capacity. This ball would be made by all existing manufacturers to the best of their ability, with the single exception that they must use standard and identical molds provided by the USGA. Such conditions would not, of course, in any way prevent manufacturers from advertising and otherwise promoting their balls in the customary fashion.

If we need a precedent for such uniformity, all we have to do is look at other sports. I can't think of one that doesn't use standardized balls at the highest levels of competition. Golf remains the only game where a top performer can take his pick from fifty or so supposedly different missiles every time he plays.

Getting back to my starting point, I believe the greatest benefit of such a system would be the return of the superstar, and perhaps even the dominating player, to professional tournament golf. This would happen as the hungriest and most talented players separated themselves from the rest by making up for what they lost in distance through better self- and course-management, improved shotmaking skills, and greater competitive intensity. A bonus would be the continued use of Merion and the like for championship play.

Will this ever happen?

Because of how much reduced-distance balls would show up their weaknesses, it is hard to imagine less successful players voting for such a change, which means that the tours would have to mandate it against the will of the majority. That is obviously unlikely to happen in the present climate of professional golf.

A stronger possibility is a brave step by the USGA for, say, the U.S. Open and Amateur championships, perhaps in parallel with the Royal and Ancient for the British equivalents. There is no question this would create uproar among the ball-makers, who hate the idea of distance restriction and standardization for many reasons, among them the invalidation of the "ours-is-longest" sales pitch (which is baloney anyway), and the frustration of the average golfer's desire to play the same ball his or her hero uses. Be that as it may, I am 100 percent certain that no manufacturer, if faced with a *fait accompli,* would refuse to supply the required balls.

Sadly, we will probably have to come close to emasculating all of our old championship courses before the people most directly impacted—the players—wake up to the consequences of not making such a change. Nevertheless, I believe it will happen one day.

IMPROVED equipment is, of course, not the only reason for golf's lack of dominating performers in recent years.

One of the biggest changes in professional golf during my time in the game has been the physical fitness of the players. Thirty years ago, with a few exceptions like Gary Player, nobody did anything to increase his athleticism or improve his physical condition. Some guys after they had played might hit balls for a while—most notably Ben Hogan—but the majority would just sit around and tell each other stories while having a few beers.

Those days are long gone. For years now, the fitness trailers on all of the tours have been full of players almost all of the time, truly working out, really taking care of themselves. Most players eat more healthily than they used to, and they smoke and drink less, too. With a few exceptions like Greg Norman, who for years has trained strenuously under professional supervision, their athleticism might not compare with pro basketball players or marathon runners. Nevertheless, it is way beyond the standards of my early years. And, of course, the fitter the mass of golfers, the harder standing out becomes for any one of them.

Then there is the incentive factor.

Except for the Masters, the biggest purse on tour in my first year as a professional in 1962 was the Thunderbird Classic's $100,000, with most tournaments offering between one third and one half that amount, to be divided between thirty-five or forty players. Win and you generally took home between $5,000 and $9,000. Finish last and you hardly made bus fare to the next event—usually well under $100.

Thirty-four years later, in 1996, the *average* purse on tour was $1,400,000, with highs of $3,000,000 (Players and Tour Championships). The average winner's check was just under $252,000, with highs of $540,000 (Players and Tour Championships again). Around seventy players received a check each week, with the last of them never making less than $2,000.

In evaluating those numbers, consider if you will how many more contenders your business would have attracted, and how much more competitive it would have become, given comparably huge increases in financial incentive over a similar time span. By then imagining how much harder it would have become for you to remain a market dominator, you will get a sense what it takes to become a dominating golf champion as we approach the second millennium.

Whether for the above reasons or any others, the fact is that, to be able to hold onto their cards and earn a decent living, the golfers in the middle of the pack today have had to become as good as the players at the top were when I started out thirty and more years ago, while those at the top have become the equals of the superstars of my generation.

To further illustrate how much the standards of play have improved during my time in the game, let me offer a couple of personal statistics.

Beyond major-championship victories, the best measurement to me of any golfer's long-term capabilities is his scoring average: all of his tournament rounds added together, then divided by the total number played. If I relate my scoring averages to high tournament placings, I think the picture will become pretty clear.

During my first eleven years on tour, I won forty-four tournaments, finished second thirty-three times, and placed third on twenty-four occasions. Excluding an exceptionally bad year in 1979, during my next eleven years I achieved twenty-six victories, twenty-two seconds, and nine thirds, or barely half the previous total of top-three placings. And yet, compare my scoring averages for those two periods. From 1962 through 1972, I averaged 70.40 in U.S. tournaments, and from 1973 through 1984, again excluding 1979, 70.49. That's a difference of less than a tenth of a stroke per tournament, or, let's say, one missed three-footer per event.

If I tried for a week, I could not think of a better way to illustrate how much better equipment, better physical conditioning and greater incentives elevated playing standards during my first two decades as a professional. And, of course, they have continued rising ever since—and, I believe, will continue to do so.

I took time out for the above because it obviously has a bearing on my record over the years following my fourteenth major victory in the PGA Championship of 1973. But there was another factor, too, that had to do only with Jack William Nicklaus . . .

A COUPLE of weeks after my Canterbury high, Lee Trevino once more brought me down to earth by easing me out of the U.S. Professional Match-play Championship in the second round, and a week later Tom Weiskopf provided another dose of humility by defeating me in the World Series at Firestone. But the season ended nicely with wins in my two final outings, at the King's Island course outside Cincinnati that Desmond Muirhead and I had designed for the Taft organization, followed by a third straight Disney World title.

Looking back, there is little doubt that 1972 and 1973 were standout years for me, and particularly if you rate consistency as highly as I do in measuring golfing achievement. Adding those two seasons together, I won more than a third of the tournaments I contested, fourteen out of thirty-nine, including three major championships; only once placed worse than fourth in the other five majors; finished second seven times and out of the top ten only seven times; took top money and PGA Player of the Year awards in both years; and, in 1973, achieved my lowest-ever stroke average of 69.81. There would be some good years ahead, particularly 1975, but nothing to quite touch the 1972–73 period. From that time on I would play well in spurts, but never again contend quite as consistently as I had at age thirty-two and thirty-three.

For much of that time I did not really know what it was that caused this to happen. Now I do. There were two reasons, one mental, one physical, and the first led to the second.

Of all the qualities needed to become and remain successful, the one that always stands the highest is desire. The greater your desire, the greater your capacity for work, your willingness to sacrifice, your will to win, and your zest for battle. As desire wanes, so inevitably do all of those other qualities. And the fundamental problem therein, of course, is that success and desire work both ways in inverse ratio: the more of one and the less of the other. The corollary problem is that you do not usually recognize a decrease in desire until after it has happened—and, even if you do, human nature being what it is, probably are not able to do much about it anyway.

I did not notice any decrease in my desire to excel at golf after I had reached the landmark of fourteen major championship wins, and I certainly did not make any drastic changes in my habits or lifestyle. But I'm sure it happened, even if only a little bit, because I realize now that the fatalism that had been building in me with increasing maturity took a definite upturn after 1973.

I continued to pride myself on my game, felt like I wanted to win as intensely as ever, and believed I suffered just as much embarrassment when I played poorly. But the key to what was really going on lies in my attitude when I did not win: I simply burned less on the inside. In short, as time passed I became more and more philosophical in accepting less than first place. And that was what gave life to the physical problem. For the next six years I would play golf with a swing that, in my heart, I knew was becoming more and more flawed.

BUT I am getting ahead of myself.

The major-championship winners of 1974 were by now a fully rejuvenated Gary Player with a great Masters and British Open double, an overdue Hale Irwin in the U.S. Open, and that old nemesis of mine, Lee Trevino, in the PGA Championship.

A lot of guys had had their chances at Augusta until Gary finally put it away by almost making an eagle two on the par-four seventy-first hole. The U.S. Open at Winged Foot had been very much Tom Watson's until he opened the door for Hale with a 79 in the final round. The only thing I remember about that championship is my start—a good drive and approach to twenty feet beyond the cup, followed by four putts after rolling my first attempt almost off the fast, sharply canted green, followed by two more three-putts in the next three holes. From New York we went to Royal Lytham and St. Annes for the British Open, where Player led for the first three days then sewed it up with a birdie-birdie start and an eagle at the sixth hole in the final round.

I had finished respectively tied fourth, tied tenth and third, and endured some frustration at not being able to lift my game that little bit higher at Augusta and Lytham. However, it was nothing to the frustration of the PGA at Tanglewood in Clemmons, North Carolina, after a twenty-foot putt on the final green that would have tied

Lee missed dropping by half a turn of the ball. This was the fourth time in seven seasons Trevino had beaten me in majors, not to mention the other defeats he had handed out. I had played close to my best every time, which always helps you feel a little better about yourself than when you've tossed a tournament away. But there could be no question by now that Lee Trevino was the player who had given me the most trouble up to this point of my career.

So 1974 was a disappointing season. And yet at the end of it I did have a nice memento, plus the consolation of winning an important new event originated by one of my oldest friends in the game.

After a poor job of defending the Crosby in awful weather the first week of the new year, I had decided not to compete again until the Los Angeles Open a month and a half later. However, both Barbara and I are great lovers of wildlife art, and particularly the work of two world-renowned artists who specialize in that field, the Englishman David Shepherd and the American Guy Coheleach. Shepherd was then offering to sell a wonderful painting of three elephants, and I was eager to own it.

The mistake I made was to mention this desire in a business group meeting, plus the price. The general consensus was: Forget it, you can't afford it. "Oh, no?" I told the guys. "Well, just you watch." I had rarely played in the Hawaiian Open, but there was still time to enter. I did so, won by three strokes from Eddie Pearce, and still get pleasure every time I look at David's magnificent elephants hanging in our living room. I call the painting my "Hawaiian Elephant."

The Hawaii victory came at the beginning of February. Seven months later, I won the first championship of the then Tournament Players Division of the Professional Golfers Association of America, or, in short, the Tournament Players Championship, by two strokes from J. C. Snead at the Atlanta Country Club. This was a pleasing victory, not only because of the long gap between wins, but because of how the event had come into being. It represented the culmination of that critical interlude I discussed back in chapter 11 when the tournament players finally separated from the club professionals and Joe Dey came aboard as commissioner.

Although I am frequently late for just about everything else, I have never missed a tournament tee time. The reason dates back to 1953, when, at age thirteen, I was the youngest player in the field at the U.S. Junior championship at Southern Hills in Tulsa, my first national event. Scheduled to play a New York youngster, Stanley Ziobrowski, in the leadoff match in the first round, I wandered nonchalantly onto the first tee with about thirty seconds to spare. Standing there glaring at me were Joe Dey, then the Executive Director of the United States Golf Association, and the championship starter, a white-suited and goateed colonel from Kentucky by the name of Lee S. Reed. "Mr. Nicklaus," said the colonel as Joe nodded his frowning head for emphasis, "half a minute more getting here and you would be on the second tee, one down."

From that inauspicious beginning, I developed not only a friendship with Joe Dey that became deeper by the year, but an ever-growing admiration and respect for his encyclopedic knowledge of golf, his administrative capabilities, and, most of all, his unshakable integrity and commitment to nurturing the game in all its elements. Back in those troubled times of 1969, Joe was a godsend, a man we could rely on, with absolute confidence that he would protect and advance our interests while we got on with the job of competing. And so it proved.

By the time Joe, then well past normal retirement age, decided to step down and hand over the commissionership to his chosen successor, Deane Beman, on March 1, 1974, the tour as we know it today was solidly in place, running smoothly, and almost twice as rich as the day Joe joined us. All I wish is that the trophy for the Tournament Players Championship still bore his name, as it did for its first few years. It was Joe Dey's idea to create a championship exclusively for the members of the organization, and the Players Championship, as it is now known, has taken on a special stature, and I believe it was wrong not to continue to honor Joe Dey by associating his name with the trophy for what is surely his greatest legacy to professional golf.

WHILE on the subject of the tour's administration, a thought or two about developments since Joe's time might be in order.

Let me say right away that Deane Beman, who held the commissionership of what has long been known as the PGA Tour from 1974 through the middle of 1994, is an old and dear friend of mine. Let me also say that, even if I had never laid eyes on him before he took it, I would consider him to have done an outstanding job. That is particularly true when you consider the conflicts he faced on a daily basis between the interests of the tournament sponsors and the television broadcasters, those of the rank-and-file players, and those of what I suppose can most conveniently be called the "name" golfers. The more the tour grew, the more acute these conflicts became.

The sponsors and broadcasters wanted the best dates, plus all of the "names" in their fields every year. The rank-and-file players mostly recognized that pleasing sponsors and broadcasters by having the stars play was in their best interests also, and thus favored strong fields. Only a few shortsightedly saw better earning opportunities for themselves in the absence of top performers.

The "name" players saw things very differently. The more financial independence their achievements won them, the less they became inclined to compete, and the more selectively they did so. To them, the very essence of professional tournament golf was that every player was and should remain an individual entrepreneur. They believed no one is owed a living just because he can manipulate a small white ball around a large green field in a low number, and they believed very strongly that this situation should never change.

Deane, as commissioner, was highly ambitious, an extremely hard worker, and an astute and at times exceedingly tough businessman. He was also possessed of a mind that was almost impossible to change once he had made it up, which sometimes served him well and sometimes not so well. There was no doubt he saw generating cash and other benefits for the players *collectively* not only as his principal mission but as the best way of establishing and sustaining his power base. As this strengthened, he used it to exert ever greater control over every component of the tour. The one fly in the ointment was that the more this happened, the more uncomfortable the better players became with what they saw as the one-for-all-and-all-for-one "trade-union" approach from which Deane drew his authority.

Throughout his reign I applauded his efforts to increase purses, lock in solid sponsors and cut rich television deals as much as I applauded his predecessors' work in those areas. The resulting funds were the traditional and legitimate lifeblood of the pro game. So long as they were all put up as prize money after deducting operating expenses, then dispersed strictly according to playing ability—and we did not push the funders so hard as to kill the golden goose, as other sports had done—I had no quibbles. Where I balked was at open-ended franchising of PGA Tour–designed courses, aggressive pursuit of PGA Tour product and service endorsements, and other entries into collectivized earning beyond the tournament arena: in short, at operating the tour as an ever-growing profit center in its own right.

As I see it, the more PGA Tour courses there are, the more formalized and/or standardized the pro game is likely to become, not to mention the fewer opportunities for its individual members to make *individual* contributions to golf's style and flavor. That second concern may sound selfish coming from a person whose principal business activity is course design, but, if you follow golf closely, you will surely have noticed the ever-increasing number of tour players entering this field. I welcome that, not only for their pocketbooks relative to a sometimes short peak-competitive-earning period, but for the lasting contribution they are making to the game through their experience and imagination. On the other hand, every design job going to the PGA Tour is one less for individual designers laboring entirely for their own accounts, whether they be professional architects or professional golfers turned architects.

Returning to that first concern about regimentation and standardization, there is a feeling within golf's inner circles that, if the tour has any problems, they lie in the "sameness" of its tournaments, along with, some believe, its players. If that is true, it follows that our greatest needs are "different" tournament formats and more "colorful" performers. If that in turn is true, then it seems to me the last thing we should be doing is adding yet another element of standardization to what is already perceived as a cookie-cutter game.

In the area of PGA Tour endorsement of products and services, my concern is certainly not for myself, because for years now I have turned down many more opportunities in those areas than I have chosen to accept. But, like many other players, I have sons who sought to play the tour, and one day might have grandsons doing the same. Whether they would excel sufficiently to serve as advertising spokesmen is unknown, but, assuming that happened, how would they feel about competing for opportunities with their own organization? I know that in my early years such a situation would have disturbed me greatly, and I do not imagine it will please the better players of future generations.

If I feel so strongly about all this, why haven't I done something about it?

In the early 1980s, a number of the leading players, including

Arnold Palmer and Tom Watson and myself, got together at the Memorial Tournament to brainstorm these and asssociated issues, then wrote a long letter to Deane expressing the depth and detail of our concerns and requesting a number of policy changes. They were not only never made but, if memory serves, never submitted to the tour's policy board. Why? We believed one reason was that the makeup of the board was such that Deane could be certain it would not be sympathetic to our suggestions. The bigger reason was the degree of support he had by then won from the tour's rank-and-file members. It was clear that, if push came to shove, the collective as represented by the commissioner would easily defeat the "names" as represented by Palmer, Watson, Nicklaus, etc.

While on the subject of tour politics, I would like to air my views on another matter that has concerned me greatly for a number of years.

In common with most of the better American players, I have always deeply disliked and regretted the efforts of our tour to limit the participation of top foreign golfers in our tournaments. I recognize that the rank-and-file members of the "union" will forever favor rules that keep outsiders from biting into their pie. Nevertheless, I believe that the tour's top administrators should long ago have been big and brave enough to ignore that petty attitude in favor of the broader interests involved.

What we have here, of course, is another example of the tour brass listening harder and catering more to those who constitute its power base, the "collective," than to its "names." Every top American golfer with whom I have discussed this issue has an open-door mind-set. That's because he desires to play against his peers as often as possible, first, for the competitive stimulus so provided and, second, for the greater fulfillment in victory so afforded. In other words, the stronger the fields, the more our best players are likely to show up, the harder they will compete, and the more winning will mean to them.

Even stronger reasons for easing or eliminating the restrictions imposed on top foreigners by the Beman administration are the interests of the tournament sponsors and the fans, both at tournaments and through television.

During the 1980s and 1990s, as overexpansion of the tour's all-exempt category allowed U.S. players to earn more money for less risk and effort, non-Americans became the world's best golfers, with

Seve Ballesteros being followed by Nick Faldo, Bernhard Langer, Greg Norman, and Nick Price. It seems to me that, by restricting such players' appearances in U.S. tournaments, we shortchange all of the people without whom there wouldn't even be a tour, by providing them with less than the best possible product. In fact, it has always surprised me that the sponsors have not gotten together and forced the tour to fully open its doors, which is certainly within their power should they decide to pursue such action. It had appeared possible that the Federal Trade Commission might do that job for them. However, after a number of years investigating restraint of trade issues regarding the tour, the government authority, without giving reasons, decided against forcing policy changes.

Despite the abortive effort of early 1995 to launch a "World Tour," my guess is that the final resolution of the closed door issue will accompany the evolution of just such an entity in one form or another. That's because some kind of world golf circuit is such a logical end-product of golf's ever-growing internationalization. Hopefully, having read what the 1995 shenanigans wrote so clearly on the wall, this entity will derive from the existing tours summoning the will to put the universal good ahead of their insular imperatives. If not, here's a possible alternative scenario:

A giant international corporation, deciding that golf has grown big enough around the world to be used as its major promotional tool regardless of cost, decides to sponsor each year for, say, five years a twenty-player, champions-only tournament in each of say a dozen major markets. To justify the enormous costs involved, however, it must be certain that the planet's best twenty golfers will play in every event. To entice them, this monolithic new sponsor sets purses at five million dollars per tournament, while also irrevocably guaranteeing each of its targeted golfers two million dollars against winnings for each of the five years. The players remain free, of course, to contest the four major championships, along with any other nonconflicting events that tickle their fancy.

The biggest mistake of the 1995 world tour promoters was not quietly signing up the top players ahead of publicizing their efforts, almost certainly because they did not concretely possess the necessary funds. Would the world's top twenty golfers sign for a two-million-dollar-per-year-per-head guarantee against a total purse of three hundred million dollars over a twelve-tournaments-a-year five-year schedule? Would the top broadcasters assemble worldwide networks for such contests? Would the top print media send their top sportswriters? Would the golf fanatics of the various territories turn out to spectate? Given that there was no conflict with the major championships, which is achievable in that none of the four is controlled by a tour, I believe the answer to all of those questions, regardless of how hard the tours might fight, is yes. The reason is that both the competitive challenge and the dollars involved would have become irresistible.

Unless the game's established authorities seal off the opportunity by themselves creating some form of collaborative world tour, I believe there is an excllent chance of this, or something like it, happening in my lifetime.

What our administrators tend to overlook is that, as the 1968–69 players' rebellion proved, there is ultimately a limit to how far the people most responsible for the success of any given tour will put themselves out for the benefit of those whom they perceive as making a lesser contribution. That may sound selfish, but it is the nature of the true entrepreneur and also the law of the marketplace. And, thankfully, it is not going to go away in America under our present political and social systems.

I must add as a footnote that, as this book goes to press, the world's major tours appear to have taken the first steps toward collaboratively creating some sort of world circuit. That was the best news I had heard on golf's "political" front in a long time.

ON January 21, 1975, I reached the halfway point of man's Biblically allotted span of three score years and ten. Although I had talked less about retirement in the recent past than in my twenties, writers raised the subject, and here's what one of them quoted me as saying about it: "If I were to win all four majors this year, I probably wouldn't play nearly as much on the tour as I have in recent years. But if I were to win one major this year, and one next year, and go on like that, then my guess is I'd still be playing a pretty full schedule ten years from now."

That proved to be a good piece of crystal-gazing, but the reason I recall it is for what it reveals about the mountain still looming in the back of my mind. Possibility or probability, there was no escaping the lure of the Grand Slam. And, if the condition of my game that spring was any guide, it had to be more than just wishful thinking coming into the Masters. Almost from the time I began working on golf early in January, things began clicking into place in every department, but particularly in the most important area of all, my setup to the ball.

In clinics and magazine articles I have talked and written endlessly over the years about the importance of aim, alignment and posture to all golfers. I've also acknowledged that sometimes, no matter how hard they try, even the best players cannot get themselves 100 percent comfortable in all those areas, causing them to play a little bit stressed, sort of aware that the wheels could fly off. The opposite of this, the can't-miss feeling sometimes deriving from a perfect setup, makes the game not only simple physically but a stroll in the park mentally. Then, you just *know* you can swing your best time and again, and your confidence zooms into the stratosphere.

I guess this is what keeps us endlessly pondering the mechanics of golf and pounding those balls so persistently, and for me in the month before the 1975 Masters it all paid off.

I had opened the year with a tie for sixth in the Crosby and a tie for fourteenth defending in Hawaii, then third place in Los Angeles and the same at Inverrary after blowing a three-stroke lead with seven holes to go. The problem at Inverrary had been sprayed tee shots, and it occurred to me, fiddling around at home the following week, that in ten years of searching I had never found a driver quite as good as the one that had broken in South Africa in 1966.

Although not much of a fiddler with golf clubs—Arnie's the champion at that—I have always kept a few spares in my club room, and now I decided to look them over. Among them was a driver I had originally gotten from David Graham, another great equipment guru, then loaned to Eddie Pearce. Eddie had told me what a great club it was, but for some reason I had never given it a thorough trial. Now I went and hit some shots with it, then had it kinked a bit to reduce the loft by a degree or so, then hit some more shots. Wow! What a beauty!

The club cost me a few yards in the forward direction, but it also saved me a lot more in the sideways directions. I won by three shots using it a week later at Doral, then two weeks after that beat Tom Weiskopf by the same margin in the Heritage Classic. It was the best

I had played immediately ahead of the Masters, and I was as excited as a puppy with a new bone. I could hardly wait to get to grips with the Augusta National.

WRITERS have to put something in the papers ahead of the majors, and their favorite standby, if no headliner breaks a leg or the greens don't turn to mud, is predicting winners. With my two recent successes I got my share of votes, but the two guys getting even more were Johnny Miller and Tom Weiskopf.

Johnny had repeated his early-season desert-golf heroics of 1974 with victories at Phoenix, Tucson and Palm Springs, but had been taking a little flak about his majors performances since the Open at Oakmont. From his comments, he clearly intended to put an end to that at Augusta. Tom had followed his second place at the Heritage Classic with first in the Greensboro tournament immediately preceding the Masters, where, having finished three times second at Augusta, he made no bones to the writers about how much a victory there would mean to him.

What concerned me more than either of them was the condition of the course. That year it was as lovely to look at as I had seen it, brilliantly green and so flawlessly manicured as to seem like a golf club had never touched it. As a result of an exceptionally rainy spring in the southeast, however, it was also extremely wet. Not being exceptionally long and with so much room off the tees and so little rough, what had traditionally sorted the men from the boys at Augusta National were firm and fast greens. Playing as well as I was, I would have greatly preferred those conditions. As it was, I told myself I had better set the thermostat on high right from the gun or have a lot of catching up to do later.

Apart from a chilly putter on Thursday, it worked out beautifully. In the first round, I hit every fairway but one and all the greens in regulation or better, one-putted the fourth for a birdie, and two-putted three of the par fives for three more and a 68. If I had putted even half as well as I played from tee to green, it could have been a lot less. But, only a shot behind Bobby Nichols at day's end, I was happy with my position, then even happier on Friday after adding a six-birdie 67.

I had missed a lot of makeable putts in those thirty-six holes but only one full shot, a hooked 4-iron to eighteen the second day that resulted in a single bogey. My 135 total was a new Masters halfway record, but better yet was the size of lead it established: five strokes over Arnold Palmer, Bill Casper, and Tom Watson. Weiskopf was in a group including Trevino a further stroke back. Miller, then eleven shots off the pace with 75-71, seemed entirely out of it.

When I called the club to check my tee time for Saturday's third round, I discovered I would be playing with Arnold Palmer. I could have been paired with any one of the three players closest to me, but I guess it was inevitable that those in charge of such things, looking for as much "theater" as possible, chose to put Arnie and me together.

This did not please me, and I knew it would displease Arnie equally. Friendly as we were off the course, on it together we still could not prevent ourselves from playing each other, always to the detriment of our scoring. Beyond the extra commotion of bringing two huge galleries together, this was not a matter of "Arnie's Army" versus "Jack's Pack." The fault lay in ourselves, and we knew it. But we couldn't stop it and so, particularly when in contention in a major, were always unsettled by such a pairing.

And, yet again, neither of us played well. Arnie had recently quit smoking, and at forty-five was making a maximum effort to restore the old order of things, but only some hard recovery work got him around in 75. I fared a little better with a 73, but three-putted three times and played generally blah golf, and came off the course mad at myself for having gone backward when a good round might have locked it up for me.

As things were, at the end of that exhausting afternoon I was in second place, one stroke behind Tom Weiskopf. Tom had smoothed it around in 66, which was strong. Even stronger was Johnny Miller's 65, featuring six consecutive birdies from the second through the seventh holes. They had contributed to a new front-nine record of 30, but, more important, had brought John back to within four strokes of the lead. No one who had watched him in this kind of mood doubted he would have more to say the next day.

I RECALL that the 1975 Masters was a memorable one in a number of ways. As a result of having qualified by winning the previous year's Monsanto Open in Pensacola, Lee Elder became the first black golfer to play in the tournament, and Lee Trevino returned to it after a lengthy absence. Sixty-two-year-old Sam Snead shot an opening 71, and Hale Irwin tied the single-round record with a closing 64. But what has really stuck in the golfing consciousness was the Sunday climax.

In the opinion of many expert watchers of the game, the final round of that Masters was the most exciting in the tournament's history, and, in the opinion of some, the most exciting conclusion to a major championship ever. I am not qualified to make a judgment on either of those propositions, but one thing is for sure: I have never been involved in a more thrilling shoot-out than occurred that crisp and sunny day among the springtime splendors of America's best-known golf course.

The reign of Tom Watson as a dominating player would really begin two years later, but he had won the Western Open the previous season, and, then only twenty-five, clearly had the most potential of the young lions. Although Tom would not be in at the kill this time, the fact that he and I were paired together, immediately ahead of Weiskopf and Miller, added to the tension for all present. As a British writer neatly put it, "So . . . the king and the three princes. Here's where we find out how firm that crown is."

A traditional part of Masters Sunday, until the creation of a private locker room for winners of the tournament, was a large gathering of writers in the main locker room, there to observe the protagonists preparing for battle, much, I imagine, as the newshounds of Roman times eagle-eyed the gladiators before they stepped into the Coliseum. Its mood was usually fairly laid back in deference to the nervous systems of those about to face the lions, but amid the banter there was invariably a serious question or two, to which, as was my custom, I would try to give serious answers. I can't remember what the inquiries were about that time, but they must have been distracting because, when I got to the practice tee, I noticed my caddie, Willie Peterson, giving me a strange look. "What's up, Willie?" I said, then watched his eyes go to my feet. I was still wearing my street shoes.

Those around us got a good laugh, and it was a nice lightener too for Mr. Organized. But it was also for him a most positive sign. My concentration on golf the previous three days had been total. To have made such a slip indicated that nothing had changed.

With trees lining both sides of the fairway and a large and deep bunker narrowing it at the top of the hill on the right, the opening tee shot at Augusta always gave me butterflies, the result of which invariably was too short a swing. That happened now, and, as I walked into the woods after the ball, I told myself to slow down and to make my number-one thought for the day, "Complete the backswing." On the par-five second hole I hit two super woods into the greenside bunker, then splashed out to three feet and holed for birdie. "Okay, you're back where you started," I said to myself. "Now go for it."

At the third hole I spun a wedge to within three feet of the cup and made the putt for birdie, parred the tricky fourth hole, then hit a 5-iron to four feet at five and made that. After three solid pars, an 8-iron to six feet at the ninth hole produced a fourth birdie. I was out in 33 and eleven under par for the tournament.

Although I could see something of Weiskopf and Miller in the final pairing immediately behind me, I had kept my focus strictly on my own game, and so was unaware of how they were scoring. Walking from the ninth green to the tenth tee, I decided to check the large leader board off to the side of the eighteenth hole. With two birdies and six pars through eight holes, Weiskopf was tied with me at eleven under par. With four birdies and one bogey, Miller had pulled to within three strokes of both of us.

There is always debate during Masters tournaments as to whether the front or back is the tougher side of the Augusta National. What is beyond argument to me is that the home stretch, with five water holes against none going out, is the most dangerous, especially what Herb Wind so aptly labeled "Amen Corner"—holes eleven, twelve, and thirteen. More Masters have been lost in the liquid around that lovely little stretch of real estate than anywhere else. Despite a poor chip from a tough lie when well positioned for a birdie at thirteen, I was content as I walked off its green to have completed the trio in par.

On my way to the twelfth green I had seen both Weiskopf and Miller bogey the eleventh hole, Tom with a pitch stone dead after hitting his second shot in the lake, and Johnny when he missed what looked like little more than a tap-in. That had put me one ahead of Tom. However, Johnny had birdied the ninth hole, so was still only three back of me. The door remained open for them.

After three-putting from the front fringe off a poor approach to the fourteenth green, I knew I had opened it even wider. A birdie or better at the par-five fifteenth was now mandatory. After busting my drive I found the ball lying slightly uphill on a little nob between a couple of chocolate-drop mounds. I carefully checked and rechecked my yardages, finally deciding I had 246 yards to the pin, which was set back right. This meant I could miss slightly to the right without going into the bunker, and to the left without scooting down the hill behind the green. Normally the distance would have called for 3-wood, but I was striking the ball solidly and oozing adrenaline. It had to be the 1-iron. And with some margin for error to either side, I was going straight for the flagstick.

Until then, the best 1-iron I had hit when it mattered was the shot to the final hole in the 1967 U.S. Open at Baltusrol, and the second-best the shot to the seventeenth hole at Pebble Beach in the last round of the 1972 championship. The one I played now capped both of them—in fact, may just have been the best full shot under extreme pressure I have ever hit. Absolutely nailed, the ball took off dead on the flagstick and stayed that way, and for a thrilling moment I thought it might go in the hole on the fly for a double-eagle. It actually landed about fifteen feet short of the cup and stopped about ten feet beyond it. Perhaps still too excited about the shot as I stroked the putt, I never came close to the eagle. But there was no doubt about the birdie. And, boy, did I need it.

As I walked to the sixteenth tee, the leader board showed that Miller had birdied thirteen and Weiskopf fourteen. That meant Tom was now even with me, with Johnny only two behind. Seeing where they had driven, I expected them both to at least birdie fifteen. As I walked after my tee shot at the par-three sixteenth hole, I could tell from the crowd reaction that each had safely carried the lake fronting the green. It was now match play for the three of us. Having always loved that form of golf, that was fine with me.

I hit my tee shot to sixteen with the 5-iron, plenty of club to get all the way back to the hole, which was cut close to the front of the small, elevated plateau that forms the rear right portion of the green. But I had not gotten all of it, and the ball finished about forty feet short and left of the cup, making par a tricky proposition. And now came a delay of several minutes as my playing partner, Tom Watson, went back to the tee after finding his first effort unplayable in the edge of the lake. This gave me a chance to watch Weiskopf and

Miller back on the fifteenth green. To huge crowd reactions, both birdied, Johnny with a two-putt and Tom from about fifteen feet after chipping from behind the green. That put Weiskopf one ahead of me and Miller one behind.

By then Watson had also hit his second tee shot in the water, but had gotten his third on the green a little farther from the hole than mine and on almost the same line. I watched his putt carefully, and particularly as it twisted off to the left soon after cresting the final slope. Also, I remembered that final break from a twelve-footer I had made for birdie in winning my first Masters back in 1963. As I looked over my putt, the thought in my mind at first was "Make par." Then, as I stood up after a last look at the line, I realized it was crystal clear in my mind's eye. I told myself, "Make it."

I stroked the ball solidly, starting it exactly where I intended to. As the ball got within about twelve feet of the hole, I was so certain it was going in I thrust my putter high in the air. As the ball actually fell in the cup, both Willie and I went into what can only be described as war dances. It was an unforgettable moment for both of us. Holing a putt of that length over that difficult a line at that moment was just a humongous break. The excitement was almost unbearable. After hustling to the seventeenth tee, surrounded ten-deep with still-hollering fans, I had to give myself a little calming-down talk before setting up to the drive.

Because of the delay caused by Tom Watson's misadventures, Miller and Weiskopf had been watching all of this from the sixteenth tee, and I knew it could not have helped their states of mind. Johnny made par routinely, but Tom caught his 5-iron shot heavy, leaving the ball about twice as far from the hole as I had, from where he three-putted. I now led him by one stroke and John by two.

I made a careful par at the seventeenth hole, then played two equally careful shots to eighteen, stopping the ball about twelve feet to the right of the hole, set on the left side of the green's lower tier. As I began sizing up the putt, a huge roar erupted from the seventeenth green. Someone had birdied.

There was no way I was going to stroke my putt until I knew who. I fiddled around looking at the line until the scores came up on the big leader board off to the side. It had been Miller. That meant I did not have to make my twelve-footer to gain a playoff should either he or Weiskopf birdie the final hole, and I decided to play conservatively. Somebody later commented quizzically about me missing on the low side of the cup, the "amateur side," but let me assure you that this was deliberate. The reason is that I left myself a straight uphill tap-in, which, on that wickedly slanted final green, is the most work a body needs at such a moment.

After checking and signing my card, I stayed around the scorers' tent to watch Tom and Johnny finish. Johnny hit a good drive and Tom a monster, one of the longest I'd ever seen at that hole. Playing first, John's approach stopped about twenty feet beyond and a little to the right of the hole. Tom's 9-iron sat down like a butterfly about seven feet past it.

They talk about cutting tension with a knife, but you would have needed an atom bomb to make any impression on the enormous crowd ringing almost the entire hole as Tom and Johnny came up on the green and started surveying their putts. Even though I knew I would have another chance in a playoff if either of them holed for birdie, I was as tight as the rest of the onlookers. That was because I expected at least one of them to make his putt. "If Johnny doesn't make it, then Tom will, or if Tom doesn't, then Johnny will," I told myself. After a battle like we had had, I really believed this would happen.

In an atmosphere so quiet as to be eerie, Johnny finally stroked a putt that looked good for the first half of its roll but was plainly not in the rest of the way. I guessed Tom would play his putt for the right lip of the cup, allowing just a whisker of break, and he confirmed this later. I thought he had judged the speed perfectly, but the ball, not seeming to break at all, trickled agonizingly slowly past the edge of the cup. Later Tom said he had stroked it a little too firmly.

After his poor start, then a sensational final thirty-six-hole record 65-66–131 finish, Johnny did not seem too unhappy. For a long time afterward, Tom looked to be in a state of shock, and I don't blame him one bit.

WINNING at Augusta in 1975 brought my total of Masters victories to five, which was the record until I was able to add another eleven years later. To have held that record so long is pleasing, but nothing to the memories of that final day.

Even the hardest-nosed members of the media seemed to have

gotten exceptionally wound up by the day's events, and one of the topics they kept coming back to long into the evening was what such a shootout felt like to the participants. Some of them seemed to think of it as being agonizing, an ordeal, a trial by fire, four or more hours of nothing but dry mouth and churning gut. I still don't know if they really believed me or not, but here's what I told them:

"It was *fun*. To be out there in the middle of that is just the greatest fun. You're inspired, you're eager, you're excited. You almost want to break into a dead run when you hit a good shot. It's what you've prepared yourself for, what you've waited for, what keeps you ticking. To know you can look back someday and recall you were a part of something like that, well, that's just the greatest. I've never had more fun in my life."

And, win or lose, I still feel that way whenever I am in that kind of situation.

16

The 1975 PGA Championship

Miracle at the Monster

By the end of 1975, I had been put to the test a couple of times in regard to that attitude.

I had won the Masters in April, and in August I won the PGA Championship. In between, I missed playoffs by two shots and one shot in the U.S. and British Opens, so it could be argued that I had lost the Grand Slam by a total of three strokes. If you buy that hypothesis, then this is the closest anyone has yet come to scaling golf's present Everest since Ben Hogan's triple crown of 1953.

Oh, my . . . "If only, if only . . ."

The U.S. Open that year was played over the rugged No. 3 course of the Medinah Country Club on the outskirts of Chicago. The big news early in the week, as at Winged Foot the previous year, was Tom Watson, with a new Open thirty-six-hole record of 67-68. But Tom faded in the third round, and as I came to the sixteenth tee in the fourth, so, pretty much, had everyone else. "Three pars," I told myself, "and either it's yours outright or you're in a playoff."

Playing that year at 452 yards, the sixteenth was Medinah No. 3's toughest hole. However, curving gently from left to right, it appeared made to order for the patented Nicklaus fade. The problem was that I had been drawing the ball all day due to difficulty in getting onto my left side in the downswing. Deciding I now just had to play the correct shot, I set up on the tee for a fade, then, accustomed to a draw swing feel, failed to clear my lower body correctly and closed the clubface through the ball, pull-hooking it deep into the trees. That was the first bogey. The next came as a 4-iron flew two feet too far and ran through the green of the par-three seventeenth, following which I closed with a third straight bogey. So the final reckoning was Lou Graham and John Mahaffey 287, Jack Nicklaus 289. Lou won the Monday playoff by two strokes.

Solid putting was mostly what had kept me in the hunt at Medinah, and it did the same three weeks later in the British Open at Carnoustie. After going over as usual with ample time for acclimatization, helped by a hot putter I shot 67-65-67-65 in four practice rounds on the longest and supposedly the toughest of all the British Open courses. In the championship proper I putted equally well until the long par-three sixteenth in the fourth round, where I missed from eight feet after bunkering my 1-iron tee shot. I sensed this miss would be crucial at the time, and an hour later was proven correct. Tom Watson and the Australian Jack Newton completed the seventy-two holes in 279 to my 280. Tom, who was playing in his first British Open, won the playoff by a stroke the next day.

During my post-round press session someone pointed out that my record in this championship over the previous nine years was first-second-second-sixth-first-fifth-second-fourth-third, and asked how I felt about that. "Lousy," I responded. "Nine times right there with a chance and only twice a winner. What a dope!"

Infuriating as the Medinah and Carnoustie near-misses were at the time, I have to admit now that they should not have been any great surprise, considering the condition of my golf swing. Between Augusta and Medinah I had thrown away chances at both Memphis and Atlanta by having to make artificial moves in order to get the clubhead on the ball half-decently, and those contrived maneuvers were still Band-Aiding me in both of the Opens. At the time, and particularly after my excellent swing pattern of the spring, I could not figure out why such things kept becoming necessary. Later, of course, it became clear that the reason lay in the basic flaw I mentioned in the previous chapter.

• • •

THE 1975 PGA Championship was held over the South Course of the Firestone Country Club in Akron, Ohio, a layout that had been exceptionally kind to me over the years.

Firestone was where I first became acquainted with the professional tournament game, at the age of eighteen, in the Rubber City Open of 1958, before the course was redesigned into its present form for the 1960 PGA Championship. The impression I took from finishing twelfth, with 66-67-76-68, was that I could probably survive in that arena if I wanted to, and that I would probably enjoy it if I ever made such a decision.

Four years later, now very much part of that world, I won the first World Series of Golf at Firestone, a thirty-six-hole made-for-television match between the year's major championship winners, then went on to take three more World Series along with, in 1968, the successor to the Rubber City Open, the American Golf Classic. Thus, in terms of total prize money earned at one location, Firestone was far and away my top of the bill.

However, as has often happened at Firestone, questions arose in a press session about the esthetic quality of the golf course, and I responded a little too glibly. What I said was, "This is a great golf course, but it's a boring golf course because, although each hole is outstanding on its own, when you put them all together it seems like you're playing the same one over and over, and so you have to be careful not to fall asleep." This got heavy ink, and for the rest of the week a part of each of my press conferences was taken up with qualifying the comment. I did so by explaining that it becomes harder to concentrate, and thus easier to make mental errors, when you are playing either a lot of similar shots, or a course where many of the holes run in the same direction (sixteen of Firestone South's run either north or south).

That had always been a special challenge for me at Firestone, and perhaps a significant factor in my record there: Knowing I needed to concentrate extra hard helped keep me mentally alert. Another challenge had been the sheer size of the golf course. Firestone South extends 7,200 yards overall, with seven par fours of between 440 and 470 yards and three monster par threes, requiring virtually every player to hit flat out from the tees, then bust long irons or fairway woods on all but three or four holes. That's hard on the mechanics as well as the mind.

I knew rain would have made the course play even longer for the PGA, and it was the distance factor in particular that made me decide to play only a couple of practice rounds, hopping over from Muirfield Village with Jackie one day the week before the championship, then making a final check on yardages the day before it began. I was concerned that, if I took on the gorilla more than that, whaling at the ball all the time would have me seeking a new golf swing by the time we teed up for real.

Firestone South's par is a hard 70. I equaled it in the first round to lie three strokes back of Mark Hayes and two behind Larry Hinson and club pro Bobby Benson. I had driven well, hit my irons well and putted well, and was a little surprised at the overall quality of the scoring. The next day, after compiling an almost error-free 68, I was even more surprised to find it bettered by five strokes. With an eagle and six birdies to one bogey, Bruce Crampton had eased around in 63, a new course and PGA Championship record, to lead at the halfway point by three strokes from Hale Irwin. Almost as surprising as Bruce's record was Johnny Miller missing the cut, but Tom Weiskopf was still in good shape at one over par. Lee Trevino, the defender, seemed to have convinced himself the course was too long for him and was at five over.

I know a lot of people who watched this championship either in the flesh or on television would swear I won it at the sixteenth hole in the third round, and it's hard for me to argue.

The sixteenth is, of course, Firestone South's signature hole and one of the more infamous in golf. Known as "The Monster," it runs downhill and doglegs slightly from right to left, with a total distance of 625 yards. Despite that yardage, however, except for one element, it would be no big deal for any touring pro—just a driver and a lay-up 99 percent of the time. What makes the hole one of the scariest we play anywhere is a large lake immediately abutting the front of the green. No matter how long your drive or how fine your swing groove, the water makes going for this green in two one of the riskiest shots in tournament golf. In fact, when the pin is tucked only a few feet beyond the lake, as it frequently is for the professionals, there is a tendency for the nerves to speak up even with just a wedge in hand and a perfect angle from which to hit it. In sum, then, the sixteenth hole on the South Course at Firestone is a difficult and dangerous one under any and all circumstances.

By the time I arrived there in the third round on that hot and humid Saturday, my position had improved dramatically. Bruce and I were playing together, and, with four bogeys going out including three consecutively, it was apparent that the magic of the previous day had deserted him. With three birdies to one bogey, I had gone from four strokes back of him to two ahead at the turn, and by the time we left the fifteenth green my lead had increased to five. No one else seemed to be making a move, and I guess I must have started feeling a little too pleased with myself, because now I got downright sloppy.

As we walked off the fifteenth green, Angelo Argea, my longtime caddie, had handed me my driver and headed on down the sixteenth fairway. Out of habit, I had taken the club without a thought and let him go. However, when I reached the tee I found that the markers had been moved about thirty yards forward of their regular position, meaning that I needed the 3-wood rather than the driver if I was going to position the ball where I preferred it for my second shot. I deliberated briefly about calling Angie back, then told myself to heck with that on such a hot and tiring afternoon and decided to hit an "easy" driver.

I have made some dumb decisions over the years, but this was one of the dumbest, and I got what I deserved. Geared by the size of the course to swinging the driver pretty much all-out all week, I eased off on the way back, never completed the swing, and pulled the ball far to the left and into a water hazard. After surveying the situation for a while, I finally decided the only way I could get enough distance to be sure of reaching the green in four was to drop about fifty yards back of where the drive had landed. I did so, into a flier lie, then decided to go with 6-iron as the longest club I could play that would not take me through the fairway. Hit solidly but pushed, the ball traveled about 230 yards, clearing the fairway on the fly and ending up in the rough, directly behind a large tree.

I was now faced with some interesting options. The ball was in long grass, the tree was about thirty feet high and dead ahead of me, the pin was 137 yards distant, the lake was in front of the green, and the ball, the tree, the lake and the pin were all in line. I could punch out sideways, then hopefully pitch safely to the green and two-putt. That would be 7. Alternatively, if I went for it and landed in the water, then dropped under penalty behind the lake and pitched on and two-putted, that would be 8. Alternatively again, if I went for it and made the green, then one-putted, that would be *5*.

Of all golf's television commentators, my good friend Bob Rosburg is the most decisive—some would say dogmatic—in assessing players' chances in trouble situations. I learned later that Rossie's take on my predicament was, "Jack's absolutely stone dead. No chance at all of making the green. Got to come out sideways." Which, I guess, is why some twenty years later in a magazine interview he recalled the shot he then witnessed as the greatest he had ever seen.

After looking at the lie and the tree and the lake and the green a few times, I reached for my 9-iron, laid back the face, told myself, "Stay still," and swung as hard as I could. The ball cleared the top of the tree by about three inches, and the lake by a couple of paces, and stopped thirty feet beyond the pin. And now, of course, it would have been just too anticlimactic not to make the putt. So it was that I walked off with a 5, which I followed with a par at seventeen and a three-putt bogey at eighteen for a 67 and a four-stroke lead over Crampton with one round to go. "Nothing to it, fellas," I told the press afterward. "Just your routine miracle par."

As I prepared for the final round the next day, a writer suggested that this PGA so far had been an "unsuspenseful" major championship, and asked if I thought I might provide a thrilling climax. I inquired as to where he had been hiding while I was playing sixteen the previous day, and suggested he should position himself there in a couple of hours or so. Then I commented that, seriously, things should only change if someone else played exceptionally well or if I played poorly. As I said that, thoughts of Medinah a couple of months previously flitted through my mind. Also, it occurred to me that spending the previous evening up at Muirfield Village hauling furniture around helping ready the place for a Monday event was a pretty stupid thing to do with such an important round ahead of me. But again I was lucky as no one within reach got hot that afternoon, allowing me never to come close to giving the championship away. Bruce pulled to within two strokes of me at one point, but in the end my 71, including a double-bogey on the final hole that was by then of no consequence, was good enough to win by two from him, with Tom Weiskopf third a further shot back. All in all, it was a relaxed round considering what was at stake.

And what now about that "Miracle at the Monster"?

The fact is, of course, that I could very easily have made 8 or 9 or more as a result of my sloppy-mindedness at the tee; and, in the emotional downer that inevitably would have followed such a stupid mistake, there is no telling what might have happened on Sunday. That 9-iron shot over the tree and the water was then and remains now my biggest gamble in a major when not at a point where a high-risk effort offered my only chance to win. Because the longer I had played golf the more conservative I had become in my strategizing, the shot was out of character, to a point where, when reminded of it, I have wondered whether I would have attempted it in a repeat of the situation. The answer is I don't know, and the reason I don't know is, of course, that what decides all golfers on gambles of this magnitude is a little inner voice that sometimes says "Yes" and sometimes says "No."

This time the little voice said "Yes," and it is my great good fortune that I didn't argue.

NOT that I needed it, but I had an extra incentive to play well that long-ago Sunday at Firestone. On the following day I was scheduled to host an event at Muirfield Village of great importance to the future Memorial Tournament.

As I have mentioned, the forerunner of the Memorial was the Columbus Pro-Am, co-sponsored by the *Columbus Dispatch* and the Columbus Children's Hospital, with all proceeds going to the newspaper's and the hospital's charities. Begun in 1966, this event had become one of the most successful of its type in the nation, with excellent fields and, in my view, unparalleled community and volunteer support. In 1975, its last year, the pro-am was to be staged as a sort of dress rehearsal for the first Memorial Tournament the following May, which naturally put extra pressure on everyone involved, including the future host. With ties in the PGA Championship then settled by eighteen-hole playoffs on the Monday (sudden-death was adopted two years later), all week at Akron I had not dared let myself think about what would happen if I should become involved in such a situation. However, a decade later I recall this additional pressure as just one of many extra burdens I subjected myself to that year. The truth is that, well as I played, I let myself get awfully close to the edge in energy expenditure and mental stress in 1975.

Muirfield Village and the Memorial Tournament were obviously high among my priorities that year. Financial concerns apart (and those would continue in relation to both the club and the tournament for some years), I found myself living with an ongoing compulsion to achieve instant perfection in every element of both of them. We had made a major commitment to our club members; another to the PGA Tour in persuading its administrators not only to accept the Memorial, but to allocate it a prime date; another to the players who would participate; and the biggest of all to the many hundreds of my fellow Buckeyes and Columbus townsfolk who were giving up their successful charity pro-am in order to help with the new event. A great many people had come to place a great deal of faith in Jack W. Nicklaus and his team out there in Dublin, Ohio. Any thought of letting them down even a little bit was most unpleasant to me.

I am not normally a fretful kind of guy, but I became like a hen with new chicks about Muirfield Village and the Memorial Tournament. If I would not be there charging around trying to do twenty things at once, I was on the phone checking about other people doing them, or writing myself and others notes about things to take care of when I next called or visited. Frankly, I don't know how our original manager and tournament director, my old friend from Las Vegas, Herb McDonald, or his staff stood me. I did my best to drive everyone nuts.

The other and increasingly major concern as spring turned to summer that year was my business life. Putnam Pierman had done a fine job as my partner and was and would remain a friend. But he had always possessed a strong entrepreneurial streak, and now, after nearly six years in the golf world, he began to find it harder and harder to disguise a growing restlessness. Finally, around midsummer, we started to drift apart on a day-to-day as well as on a policy basis, to the point where, as the golf season wound down, I discovered I was not only chairman and chief executive of Golden Bear, Inc., but for all practical purposes also its president and chief operating officer. This pleased me in the sense of being totally independent in business activities for the first time since I had turned professional, and particularly as the rest of the outstanding team we had built remained in place to handle most of the routine. But, inevitably, I had to find ways to cope with both a greater workload and added mental stress. In a nutshell, in 1975 I was one busy fellow.

Being so much in the eye of the media, it was impossible to

pretend otherwise, and inevitably this resurrected the old broken record: Nicklaus would win 'em all if he'd just quit all that other stuff and work at the game like Ben Hogan did. We've touched on this issue before in these pages, but let's try to put it to rest once and for all.

After the PGA that year I competed six more times, winning the World Open at Pinehurst and a fourth Australian Open, finishing second to Tom Watson back at Firestone in the World Series, and assisting in America's Ryder Cup victory at Laurel Valley. Thus in twenty 1975 outings I achieved six individual wins including two major championship victories, a team win, two seconds, four thirds, sixteen finishes in the top ten, a scoring average of 69.87, plus top money-winner and PGA Player of the Year honors. Also, if you will forgive a little fantasizing, I missed the Grand Slam by a total of just three strokes.

If, as I have indicated, 1972 and 1973 were my best years, then the above stats have to make 1975 a close runner-up. Overextended or not, the truth is that I was a factor almost every time I teed up, which means I competed *consistently* well, which is my prime measurement beyond major victories of golfing success or failure. How do I explain such a record relative to all the other preoccupations I have outlined?

The simple fact is that inactivity has always bored me, and, when I get bored off the golf course, I get bored on it as well. Throughout my life I have needed to stimulate myself to be productive, because, if I am not happy with myself in one area, I won't be happy in any other. When I get excited about things outside golf, I get excited about the game as well. Barbara has always said that the busier I am the better I play, and she is correct.

That's one factor in my ability to juggle a lot of activities at once. The even bigger factor is as follows.

Beyond good hand-eye coordination, perhaps my greatest inherent gift in regard to golf is the ability to compartmentalize my mind, to switch it at will totally from one activity or concern to another, then, for the required duration of the new focus, blank everything else out 100 percent. I am that way with pretty much everything in life, and it has a limiting effect in not allowing me to operate on more than one level at a time, as many bright people I admire seem capable of doing. Generally, once on any particular track of strong interest to me, I remain on it exclusively to the bright or bitter end, totally blinkered and traveling dead ahead, oblivious to and thus unconcerned about anything else. This explains, of course, why I am so often late for everything except tee times.

At golf, then, and particularly when I am playing well in an event that means much to me, I can wrap myself in a cocoon that is virtually impregnable until the round ends and it becomes time to click the switch to another activity. Sometimes the cocoon becomes so all-enveloping that it takes quite a period of winding down for me to break free of it, which is one reason I so often go to the practice tee after a round, and why I welcome and enjoy visiting what used to be press tents and are now called media centers.

I am told that this characteristic is very much of a Teutonic nature, and my heritage is, of course, German through and through. Whatever, I believe it is a wonderful gift for a golfer to possess because of the depth of concentration it permits over the large amounts of time the game consumes relative to other sports. The only other golfer I have played with who seemed to share it to the same degree is Ben Hogan, and I am sure it was as big a factor in his career as it has been in mine.

And, for me, it surely was at an all-time peak in the year nineteen hundred and seventy-five.

I GUESS you could say my first tournament of 1976, the Bing Crosby Pro-Am, was something of an omen for the entire season to come.

After three rounds I was leading by a stroke, and was still very much in the thick of things with nine holes to play on Sunday. I then proceeded to come home in forty-five strokes, by quite a margin my highest-ever nine-hole score since my earliest days of golf with my father at Scioto. I was so terrible it was laughable, and I ended up laughing along with everyone else—which, of course, was the only alternative to crying.

The debacle began when I hit through the green then chipped poorly and two-putted for a bogey at the par-three twelfth hole at Pebble Beach. Suddenly, all of that marvelous concentration I've just described disappeared, and my golf game with it. I triple-bogeyed the thirteenth hole, bogeyed sixteen, double-bogeyed seventeen, and rounded out with a cool "snowman" or triple-bogey 8 at eighteen. I then raced for a helicopter to San Francisco; shredded what was left of my nerves waiting for a friend to arrive with my passport so we could fly to Japan on Pan-Am and made it by about five seconds; arrived in Tokyo seemingly in the middle of the next century to a reception committee of hundreds of pressmen hollering, "Mister Nickraus, Mister Nickraus, why you shoot 82?"; went straight to work on a new golf course I was designing; and turned around a few hours later and flew home, where I fell into bed for the first time in three days.

Why *did* I shoot that 82? The short answer is that I just was not ready to play tournament golf. After my final 1975 tournament the previous October, it had been family, business and tennis time. Then, over the holidays, I had said to heck with the risk, life is to be lived, and had done something I'd wanted to do for years and had taken Barbara and the children skiing for the first time. I had entered the Crosby only because I enjoyed the location and the courses so much, and because doing so would get me partway to Japan. Having hardly touched a club in three months, and being forced to play with an artificial swing, it was a miracle I contended for three and a half rounds. But I was waiting all the way for the wheels to fly off, and eventually they did—big time.

During the rest of that year I played eighteen tournaments, and out of them managed to win a second Tournament Players Championship at Inverrary in Florida in late February and the first of a new-style World Series at Firestone in early September, then a fifth Australian Open in the fall. Between those successes, I had my chances but came up empty-handed. Ray Floyd waltzed home in the Masters by eight strokes after opening with 65-66, and Jerry Pate hit a famous 5-iron shot almost into the final hole at the Atlanta Athletic Club to win the U.S. Open, and I offered no resistance on either occasion. At the British Open at Royal Birkdale I was more of a factor, but in the end tied for second with a nineteen-year-old Spanish prodigy by the name of Severiano Ballesteros, six shots behind an inspired Johnny Miller. In the PGA at Congressional an uncomfortable four-over-par 74 on Sunday squelched my hopes of defending successfully, finally dropping me to a tie for fourth, two shots back of winner Dave Stockton.

Although I took top money and another PGA Player of the Year award, all in all 1976 was a pretty blah season, and by the end of it I believed I knew why. Although not as badly as at the Crosby, I had never felt totally "ready," never had that vital sense of being completely prepared, thus never enjoyed complete confidence in my game when under the gun or required to play boldly in order to win. My lowest tournament round in the U.S. all year was 67, which is indicative of what I call "hang-back-and-hope" golf, and for most of the time that phrase exactly summed up my play. So why didn't I just haul off and take the time to get in top gear?

I tried, but there were a couple of obstacles besides business, and the Memorial Tournament, and my ever-increasing golf course design work. One was that ever-so-gradually worsening swing flaw I mentioned earlier, but that I still did not have sufficient motivation to set about permanently fixing. The other was something I have recogized only in recent years, which is the greater amount of time required, as one gets older, to accomplish the stressful workload of preparing properly for tournament golf, plus the increased time necessary for recuperation.

In my early twenties, working nonstop from dawn to dusk, I could sometimes raise my game from ground zero to its zenith in just two or three days. By the time I reached my late forties, because my body would no longer take the abuse of such marathon practice sessions, the same process required two or three weeks, and necessitated far more rest along the way. This indicates that, in my mid-thirties, my preparation time should have been halfway between a few days and a few weeks. Through either not being smart enough to recognize that need or too stubborn to accept it, I continued trying to do what had worked in my twenties and early thirties. It was not in the cards, and 1976 was the year this began to show in my record. In short, I was beginning the period of my career where only my innate talent kept me competitive.

Competition apart, however, the year did bring one great fulfillment, plus an important decision that I have never since regretted.

THE first Memorial Tournament was played at Muirfield Village Golf Club in Dublin, Ohio, from May 27 through May 30, 1976, and in every way it was a grand success.

We had long previously established four objectives for the tournament: to further the game of golf, to salute its great past champions, to provide a fine sporting entertainment for the fans, and to benefit local charities. We would continue to improve in all of those areas as the years passed (and will continue trying to do so as long as I am involved), but essentially we met all four of the goals better the first year than any of us had dared hope.

In preparation for the tournament I had prevailed on friends who had served golf notably in one or another capacity to become members of an entity we named the Captains Club, principally to select our honoree each year, but also to provide general counsel on tournament policy and operations. Much to my delight, they had selected Bob Jones as our first honoree; and the first of what has become a popular pretournament ceremony, beautifully emceed by Joe Dey, went off gracefully in a lovely setting behind the eighteenth green. Bob's grandson and daughter-in-law attended, along with his partner in the creation of Augusta National and the Masters, Clifford Roberts, wearing the gray blazer of a Captains Club member. Mr. Roberts had paid a first visit to Muirfield Village in the fall of 1974, then written me a letter in which he said, "You have a chance to do there in five years what it took us forty years to accomplish in Augusta." He mentioned this again the day we honored Bob, and it was a personal highlight of an altogether happy week.

In designing the course I had done everything in my power to make it not only challenging for tournament professionals, but accessible and enjoyable for everyone watching them. This involved either laying the holes through existing valleys or producing valley effects by creating elevation along the perimeters of the playing areas. We called it "amphitheatering," and it was obvious from the easy trafficflow and relaxed mood of the large crowds that it had worked out well. I watched our patrons watching golf a lot that week, and everyone seemed to be having a good time.

As I have said before, what makes one golf tournament more successful than another is principally the quality of the course and the organization. We have been blessed all along in the latter regard —indeed, in my view our community and volunteer support over the Memorial's first twenty years has been unparalleled anywhere in the world. Even so, I was amazed by its strength that first year. Everyone I talked to—and I made it a point to talk to a lot of the committee members and volunteers—seemed just as dedicated as the professional staff and myself to making the Memorial a special event.

At our Executive Committee inquest on the Monday following the tournament we identified numerous ways in which we could improve, but with the knowledge that we already possessed all the people-power and enthusiasm necessary to achieve everything we aspired to. It was tremendously gratifying to all who had been involved in the long and often arduous building process, particularly to my three loyal and tolerant friends from way back at Scioto, Bob Hoag, Pandel Savic and Ivor Young.

Competitively—although a future two-time winner of the event surely didn't see it this way—we could hardly have gotten off to a finer start. With a round to go Roger Maltbie led by two strokes, but, by the time he got to the eighteenth green on Sunday, Hale Irwin had made up seven shots on him with a fine 69 and was in the clubhouse at even-par 288. Roger then missed winning outright from twelve feet, which sent the pair back to the fifteenth tee to begin the four-hole stroke-play decider I had persuaded the tour authorities to approve (they later insisted we adopt the standard sudden-death procedure). After the two matched birdies and pars, Hale knocked his second shot safely on the green at seventeen, then stood aside to watch Roger play. Little did he know he was about to experience one of the worst moments of his career.

Badly hooked, Maltbie's 4-iron approach shot was heading way left and long into deep trouble when suddenly it changed direction by 90 degrees or more and ended up on the green some twenty feet from the cup. Amazingly, the ball had been deflected there by a half-inch-thick metal gallery-rope stake. The shock of that incredible break obviously affected Hale because, now in effect playing sudden-death, he double-bogeyed the eighteenth hole. Maltbie was the winner with an easy birdie, and for a long time he carried that metal stake around in his golf bag. Heartbreaking as all this was for Irwin, who came back to win in 1983 and 1985, for the fans and television viewers it was one of the thrillers of the year, and it remains a conversation point come Memorial time all these years later.

So the Memorial Tournament at long last was off and running, which was a great relief. But now there was another sizable challenge to be met beyond the realm of competitive golf. As the spring of 1976 turned to summer, I plunged into the thick of it.

Following Put Pierman's departure and almost a year alone at the helm of Golden Bear, Inc., it had become plain to me that, if I wanted to regain the peace of mind essential to successfully continuing my playing career, I could not go on captaining the ship without the help of a top business professional.

Whether admitted or not, every successful person has a hard time with ego. When you have excelled in one area, it becomes all too easy to believe you will automatically do equally well at anything else you try. This has caused the decline of numerous large American corporations, and it finally came home to me that my small one could easily go the same way. Good as I believed my business instincts generally were, our activities were growing too fast and too diversely for my level of practical experience. On top of that, the work had become too time-consuming to enable me to properly handle all of it without compromising either my golf game or my family responsibilities, or both. Then there was the fact of being personally on the line financially in too many endeavors. Last but not least, there was the mass of daily decisions to be made involving detail as well as policy, immersing me so deeply in the minutiae of the business that there wasn't enough space in my head for the activity that made it all possible in the first place, namely winning golf tournaments. Capping it all off came the gradual realization that I had no idea where I was going in this area of my life, where the whirl of activity would or should finally land me.

The result of all this was some conversation with an old friend from Lost Tree by the name of George Chane, who had enjoyed a distinguished career both running large companies and consulting on their management and operation. George took a hard look at where we were, then recommended we employ a leading "head-hunting" organization, Heidrick and Struggles, of Chicago, to find Golden Bear, Inc., a president and chief operating officer. Gardner Heidrick himself orchestrated the search, and through him we began to look at candidates. On September 15, 1976, after Barbara and I had interviewed him during the PGA Championship in Washington the previous month, we hired a man by the name of Charles Edward Perry.

Chuck Perry came to us with an interesting background. Then age thirty-nine, he was a West Virginian by birth and an Ohioan by upbringing. He had recently been based in New York as the president and publisher of *Family Weekly* magazine, then the nation's fourth largest circulation periodical, and it was the sale of this property that gave him the opportunity to join Golden Bear. However, where Chuck had really made his mark was in the educational field. As we got to know each other better I needled him a lot about being way overschooled, what with his string of MAs and BAs and BSs and certificates in this, that and the other. Kidding apart, his academic achievements obviously well qualified him to work professionally in education, and he made a notable contribution to it as the chief founding officer and for some years the president of Florida International University in Miami.

Chuck and I at the outset agreed on some things that I had learned from my experiences with Mark McCormack and Put Pierman would be critical to both his peace of mind and mine. Number one, he would run the business and I would run the golf. Number two, he would handle the detail, but he and I would jointly set the policies that produced the detail. Number three, I would never apply myself to business as hard as he would like me to, and certainly not on the regular businessman's normal nine-to-five-and-more basis. Number four, there would be no surprises in either direction, meaning that, if there were problems, they would be raised and addressed the instant they surfaced.

Chuck was obviously a take-charge guy, and he took charge with a vengeance from the moment he signed on. With his passion for structure and orderliness, he immediately made a strong impression as an administrator. He was also clearly a workaholic, at his happiest behind a desk or on the phone or in a meeting or out somewhere trying to make a deal. He was highly ambitious and growth-oriented, with the nerve as well as the drive to go hard after whatever he wanted. Most importantly, he swore that my interests and my family's interests came first and always would. He wanted me to make money and he wanted to make plenty along with me, but he appeared to recognize and accept that this could only happen in tandem. For the better part of almost ten years we enjoyed a fine professional and personal relationship, during which his loyalty was beyond question.

WITHOUT some comprehension of how prominent athletes capitalize on their success beyond the playing field, it could be difficult for anyone not involved with them to fully appreciate what caused Chuck and me to finally separate.

Along with exhibitions and the like, the principal noncompetitive earnings opportunities for top sports performers lie in the endorsement of products and services. To put it as simply as possible, someone comes to you with an item of merchandise or a commercial service and you make a deal to help publicize and promote it, in most cases chiefly through television and/or print advertising, plus perhaps some help with customer entertaining. This type of deal, largely in the fields of golf equipment and leisure apparel, was an underpinning of my association with McCormack in the early 1960s. However, it had become apparent to me by the time I hooked up with Pierman that there were some strong reasons not to go overboard as a pitchman. The principal one was credibility.

Spokesman opportunities flooded in during my peak 1970s playing years, and there was a natural temptation to jump at many of them. What stopped us was the recognition that, the more of this work I did, the less credibly I would come across in the marketplace and therefore the shorter my long-term validity and appeal as a spokesman. By then we had also come to understand the factor of market segmentation: Namely that, tempting as it is for an athlete to believe he can simultaneously promote top-drawer and lower-level products and services, over the long haul that not only never works but will cost him in both credibility and dollars. Thirdly, there was my lifelong dislike of promoting anything I felt less than 100-percent comfortable about using personally. Finally, there were the time and energy negatives of overextending myself at this type of work.

After adding it all up, our best strategy had become clear: a handful of long-term associations with outstanding companies marketing top-quality products or services, plus a maximum ongoing effort to assist in growing and cementing those associations. My original team member most involved in this area, marketing and advertising expert Bill Sansing, came up with the phrase "partnership companies" as encapsulating this concept, and over time we found that it did, indeed, nicely reflect both the style and substance of the relationships we sought and developed. By the time Chuck Perry arrived, this philosophy of business was well established and the associations it spawned were all thriving.

By then I was also deeply committed to designing golf courses, and enjoying the work not only for its creativity and artistry but, as I have said, for the permanent legacy the courses represent to the game I love so deeply. I had done a fair amount of designing in Japan and Europe as well as North America. However, recognizing that we had hardly begun tapping the full potential for new courses, Chuck aggressively set about expanding our marketing efforts, to a point where we became under his direction not only a world design leader, but able to provide whatever ancilliary services clients required. And, of course, since that time, through our largest operating division, we have planned, designed, redesigned, built, maintained, staffed and managed just about every conceivable type of golf facility in most of the major countries where the game is played, along with quite a number of the smaller ones.

ALTHOUGH Chuck and I inevitably differed periodically on minor issues, I had no serious problems with the way he conducted the business for almost nine years. Then, in the summer of 1985, at the age of forty-five, and with the belief that twenty-three years of building one of the best records in the history of golf had brought me a comfortable measure of financial security, came a severe shock. Out of the blue I was informed by my longtime legal counsel, David Sherman, and a young accountant by the name of Dick Bellinger, who would eventually become the next president of Golden Bear, that both the company and I personally were so deeply in debt and at risk in real-estate and other non-golf-related projects as to face imminent financial disaster.

This was obviously a tremendous blow, and it triggered a period of great stress and distress for Barbara as much as for me. It became clear as the full scenario was revealed to us that the root of the problem was overambitious commitment of capital to projects we should never have been involved with in the first place. Deeply believing it was the right course of action for growing the business, Chuck had worked hard and long at these deals, so it was difficult to fault him. Now as then, I blame myself for allowing myself to become involved in projects about which I had little knowledge or expertise. We should have concentrated on our strong suits, those being golf-course design and endorsement of quality products and services.

With no way to bail myself out of a mess of that magnitude with my golf clubs alone, what saved me, as it had so many times over the years, was my innate optimism, along with my ability to concentrate on a single goal to the exclusion of all else. As the shock eased, I rolled up my sleeves and looked hard for solutions. In addition to resolving some fundamental issues with Chuck, it quickly became apparent that the best solution, and maybe the only one, lay in negotiating with the bankers. After some of the toughest meetings I have ever experienced, we finally settled with them at a high personal cost to me. Long before then, my discussions with Chuck had produced joint recognition that our different visions of Golden Bear Inc.'s future required us to go our separate ways, which we did reasonably amicably.

To sum up this episode, let me say that my first twenty-three years of business taught me many things, some of them painfully. Among the most important was to involve myself only in ventures about which I possessed true expertise, and never again to enter into anything requiring that I guarantee loans or losses.

The most important lesson of all, however, was to move from the periphery of my business activities to the center and stay there.

WITH the help of a growing number of design commissions accompanying the late-1980s worldwide boom in golf course development, it took about five years for me to recover from those traumas. By that time, I had learned something else about my business activities that, come the summer of 1996, resulted in radical changes to Golden Bear International's structure and goals.

What became ever more clear to me over those five hard years was that the business as constituted depended far too much on Jack Nicklaus personally. Much as we sometimes tried to rationalize otherwise in our strategizing sessions, the reality remained: Should I wish to slow down or retire, as much as 90 percent of what we were doing would almost certainly decline or disappear. As a young man at the peak of his powers, such indispensability might have been acceptable, and surely ego-gratifying. But as I approached and then entered my fifties, it was a situation that disturbed me more and more. One reason was a personal workload greater than I wished to carry. A bigger concern was what would be left for my family.

The solution clearly lay in diversification. To fund that, instead of salting away money for Barbara's and my retirement, I invested heavily in enterprises that required little if any of my time but that were within our orbit of expertise, among them golf schools, golf centers, public-course golf, television production, and the marketing and management of golf tournaments. And it worked. Some five years after we headed down that road, only about 30 percent of our activities required significant time from me on a day-to-day basis. This permitted us finally to do something that had been in the back of my mind for many years.

As GBI's diversification grew, its executive team had spent more and more time on and around Wall Street, exploring debt-financing arrangements and venture-capital propositions. When we got to the nitty-gritty, however, the downsides invariably outweighed the upsides. Finally, late in 1995, after much internal evaluation and some valuable outside counsel, it was decided that our best possible course was to take the parts of the business not dependent on me public.

The market at that point was booming, with a seemingly insatiable appetite for initial public offerings (IPOs). Also, it contained by then numerous excellent golf-oriented models, led by Callaway and the merger of Cobra with Titleist following Cobra's purchase by American Brands that paid off so handsomely for Greg Norman. As 1996 progressed, my executive team worked ever more intensively on putting together a public offering with the help of Merrill Lynch (a big customer of our golf schools), Dean Witter (our long-time Memorial Tournament title sponsor), and William Blair and Co.

The workload involved in an IPO, including two weeks of super-intensive selling to hard-nosed institutional investment managers nationwide—the infamous "road show"—is stupendous and accompanied by ever-increasing emotional tension as the offering date draws closer. After not really looking forward to the process, I found myself enjoying it immensely, not least because of how much more I learned about business in general, our business in particular, and the capabilities of my people. It turned out to be a lot of fun.

Our big day was August 1, 1996. With the market becoming highly volatile over the previous two weeks, it gave my four top executives, Dick Bellinger, Mark Hesemann, Tom Hislop, and Jack Bates, an emotional roller-coaster ride they will never forget as they huddled with the underwriting team at Merrill Lynch's New York headquarters. Having been advised that my presence on the trading floor might be too distracting, I spent the better part of the day not far from home playing Hammock Creek, a daily-fee course I own and operate. Young tour pro Glen Day joined me for the round, and after nine holes he called his broker to see how his order for some of our stock was doing. A weight lifted off my shoulders when Glen told me it was trading above the issuing price.

The proceeds from the IPO—$36.9 million—provided us with the capital to quickly grow the new company's core business, the ownership and operation of family-oriented golf centers nationwide and eventually internationally. Nine were purchased quickly to join the three already operating, putting us well on the road to our target of twenty-two such establishments across the United States by the end of 1997.

The new company, trading on the NASDAQ exchange (symbol: JACK), is called Golden Bear Golf, Inc. In addition to Golden Bear Golf Centers, it embraces six former GBI divisions: Paragon Construction Company, a leading builder of golf courses worldwide; Golden Bear Club Services, a management entity; the Jack Nicklaus International Club; the high-profile Nicklaus-Flick Golf Schools; all of my clothing endorsements under Nicklaus Apparel; and the worldwide licensing of Nicklaus and Golden Bear trademarks.

Remaining under private control within Golden Bear International, Inc., are my sons' and my golf-course designing activities; the golf-equipment company I co-own with Nelson Doubleday; Executive Sports, golf's leading tournament marketing/management company; community real-estate development in North America and overseas; a West Coast–based television production business co-owned with Terry Jastrow and Ken Bowden; and various publishing and other communications interests.

At the time of writing, four members of my family are engaged in the private business: Jack II as a course designer, Steve as vice-chairman of Executive Sports, Nan as director of clubhouse design, and her husband, Bill O'Leary, as a senior officer of my design division. Gary was still pursuing a career as a touring professional, but had indicated he would get involved once his playing days were over, with a particular leaning towards some type of cyberspace enterprise. Michael was still at Georgia Tech, but also anticipated coming aboard.

As this is written, both the public and private businesses are headquartered in North Palm Beach, Florida, about a drive and 3-wood from my home, with representation across the U.S. and also in Europe, the Far East, Mexico, and South Africa. I serve as chairman of both entities and chief executive officer of the private company. The president and chief excecutive officer of the public company and chief operating officer of the private business is Richard Bellinger, a Florida born-and-raised CPA and University of Miami (Florida) Business School graduate who joined GBI in late 1979 as controller of our course-design and real-estate divisions.

As I mentioned, Dick played an important role in informing me of and evaluating my business problems in the summer of 1985, following which he took the lead in solving them as Golden Bear's president and chief operating officer. He is intelligent, energetic and ambitious, but the quality I prize most in him, as in all of my business associates and associations, is loyalty. Wherever we may be in the world, Dick and I remain in constant and invariably extended communication. He understands that businesses do not work for anyone —shareholders, private owners, management personnel, other employees—unless they are consistently profitable. Our personal relationship is strengthened by the fact that he is a good and passionate enough golfer to have an innate feel for as well as intellectual mastery of everything we are doing on all fronts.

In discussing my business life, it would be remiss of me not to mention my ever-gracious and super-efficient chief administrative assistant, Marilyn Keough. Marilyn joined us early in 1981 and I hate to think of her ever wanting to leave, because I can't imagine getting through even a fraction of my workload without her knowledge, energy, and cool under fire.

The word I like best to describe Golden Bear Golf and Golden Bear International at the beginning of 1997 is vibrant. That's because it connotes to me the quality, not just of our executive team, but of all the people the company has attracted, along with the conditions under which they work. Numbering almost three hundred at our North Palm Beach headquarters alone, they are, of course, too many for me to name here. I assure you, however, that both Barbara and I try to know every member of both staffs, to understand what they are doing and why, and to properly value their contributions. I think what most of them like best about their employment is that, having been hired on the basis of strong credentials to do a particular job, they are encouraged and trusted to get on with it pretty much in their own way. Our experience is that the relaxed atmosphere this breeds—helped by an anti-formality policy exemplified by our dislike of suits and ties in the office—leads to maximum productivity.

The good news, then, is that my businesses today are soundly constituted and profitable for all concerned. The even better news is that they are also a lot of fun.

17

The 1978 British Open

"It's Only a Game"

OVER the Labor Day weekend of 1975, Tom Watson beat me by two strokes in the last of the old-style four-man World Series of Golf at Firestone. Afterward, when the writers asked for a comment about him, I told them: "Tom knows exactly where he's going—straight ahead. Nothing distracts him. He has great abilities, super confidence, and just enough cockiness. He's not a comer—he's arrived."

If anyone had any doubts then about that last remark, they would be dispelled two years later.

Tom Watson joined the tour in 1972 after graduating the previous year from Stanford with a degree in psychology. Despite a strong amateur record and plenty of talent and competitive drive, it took him a while to rise from the pack. In his first five years he won twice in the United States and added a British Open, but also did not win when a lot of folks felt he should have, particularly in the 1974 and 1975 U.S. Opens at Winged Foot and Medinah. As a result, there were questions about his ability to finish when under the gun. Despite his back-to-back victories in the Crosby and San Diego tournaments at the beginning of 1977, those questions were resurrected two weeks ahead of that year's Masters when Tom stumbled in the final round of the Heritage Classic to lose by a stroke to the Australian, Graham Marsh.

Any writer or television commentator who applies or implies the word "choke" to an individual of Watson's character and ability is demonstrating his ignorance of both golf and human nature, and I'm sure it was Tom's recognition of this that enabled him to handle the barbs and insinuations so intelligently and gracefully on the outside. On the inside, I'm equally sure that all they did was fire up his determination to win the Masters. He is like I am in that, the more I'm doubted, the greater my motivation. By the time the first of the majors began that year, I guarantee Tom Watson was about as charged up mentally as he ever had been.

I, too, was eager for the arrival of that Thursday in Georgia that more and more had come to mark the real beginning of my golf season. With the success of the first Memorial and the installation of Chuck Perry, my mind had become freer for the game. Also, I was in excellent form. Beginning with the Crosby, I had played five tournaments, winning at Inverrary and finishing no worse than eleventh in the others. Driving up Magnolia Lane each practice day, I was as excited about my Masters prospects as I ever had been.

By the middle of the final round on Sunday afternoon, the anticipation had turned into a river of adrenaline.

Paired with his fifty-four-hole co-leader, Ben Crenshaw, Tom Watson was playing immediately behind me, and I had seen or heard him make four consecutive birdies from the fifth through the eighth holes. That left me four strokes back despite some excellent golf, and the message had become crystal clear: if I wanted this one, I would have to reach out and take it the hard way. Whatever some of the writers might feel, Mr. Watson was not going to keel over this day and hand anyone the 1977 Masters.

I had looked into Tom's eyes sufficiently by then to know such a day would surely come. Now it was here, and recognizing what I was up against served as a spur. I birdied the tenth, saved par from fifteen feet at eleven, birdied twelve and thirteen, parred fourteen, and birdied fifteen. Walking to the sixteenth tee, I looked carefully at the leader board. I was now a stroke ahead of Watson and three clear of the best of the other twelve players who had started the round within five shots of him and Ben.

I expected Tom to birdie fifteen, and he did so with a fine long iron to the back fringe and two putts as I played the sixteenth hole in par. We were tied. As I walked after my approach shot up the seventeenth fairway, the crowd reaction back at sixteen told me that Tom had also made a par there. Still tied. I two-putted for my par at seventeen and went to the eighteenth tee and hit a solid 3-wood exactly where I'd planned in the left side of the fairway. And then I made a fatal mental mistake.

Standing by the ball on the eighteenth fairway, I had a strong sense that one more par would at least get me into a playoff. That translated into a solid 6-iron into the heart of the green. However, as I finished programming myself for the shot, there was an enormous roar from back down the hill. Tom had obviously birdied seventeen.

For whatever reason, the possibility of him doing so had never entered my mind, and it jolted me. I backed off from my shot and began refiguring, trying to regather myself mentally at the same time. It was highly unlikely that Tom would bogey eighteen, and he might well birdie it, but the odds were that he would make par. That meant I now must birdie simply to have a chance of tying him. This created a clubbing predicament. I couldn't be sure of reaching the putting surface with a hard 7-iron, but would almost certainly finish beyond reasonable one-putt range with a solid 6. Finally, I decided I had only one option: a soft 6-iron.

While getting set at the ball I tried my hardest to relax, but the adrenaline flow and the previous programming were just too strong. I made a bad swing, caught the ball slightly fat, and knew immediately it would not clear the left front bunker. I splashed my sand shot to within about twelve feet of the cup, but, when the putt just slid by, I had provided Tom with a two-stroke cushion and knew my hopes were history.

I waited for Tom to finish and congratulated him as he came to the scorers' tent, and I meant it from the heart when I told him he had played great. I'd given it all I had on that back nine, and finished with one of my finest Masters rounds, a 66, but had run into a fellow who just wouldn't crack and who matched me shot for shot before, in the end, pulling out that little extra something he needed to win.

And I had no doubt it would not be the last time.

• • •

TOM Watson's victory in the 1977 Masters marked the beginning of his rise to golfing greatness. The more I saw of him along the way, the more certain I became of his eventual place in the game's record books.

In some ways, it was like watching a documentary of my own early professional years. The self-containment and self-assuredness, the depth of commitment and the blinkered determination, the combination of reserve and forthrightness, the marching in a straight line toward some lofty privately determined destination, gave me a fresh insight into my early impact on golf and its supporters. "Heavens," I thought, "no wonder everyone yelled so hard for Arnie Palmer when I started bulling my way up the mountain. This guy knows where he's going and to heck with who gets wounded on the way. Winning is the only thing, just as it was with me."

Tom and I naturally developed a healthy respect for each other as golfers, and as people I believe he has felt as friendly toward me as I have toward him. But what became apparent as we spent increasing time together on and off the course is that all-around buddyism just isn't his style. Many of our mutual acquaintances have found Tom hard to get to know as a man, and that includes a large percentage of tour players from the best to the also-rans. There is a depth of reserve there that creates a shell that is difficult to penetrate. You can be talking to Tom and have the sense that, although he's listening on the surface, on the inside he's not really with you. In short, he's a very private individual, very much his own man, and he knows it and never tries to be someone else. And I admire and respect him for remaining so true to himself through the temptations that always accompany fame and fortune.

As time passed, a perception grew that Tom's record was built largely around a magnificent short game. I felt at the time that this sold him short, and still do. There is no question that at his peak he was one of the finest pressure putters there has ever been, and his imagination, dexterity, touch and confidence on all the little shots around the green were equally impressive. But Watson was and remains a superb iron player. As time has passed he has also become a tremendous driver of the ball, as witness his famous comeback in the 1996 Memorial Tournament, when he consistently outdrove the huge-hitting South African, Ernie Els, in the final round.

For a man of medium size—5 feet 9 inches, 160 pounds—Tom

has always been long off the tee, and he seems to have lost nothing with age in that regard while gaining in accuracy. This indicates strength, and if you look at his arms you'll see where much of it lies. Always a hard practicer, after all those early years of endless ball-beating his forearms became just like Popeye's. Also, as is obvious when you watch him swing, he has strong legs that he uses to maximum advantage. If he has a weakness in the physical or technical sense, it's the same as mine: a dissatisfaction with less than perfection, and thus a tendency to overadjust in searching for it. Like Ben Hogan and Gary Player, we're always looking for a better way, and sometimes when we overdo the search it hurts us for a while.

Accomplished all-around shotmaker that Tom Watson is, however, there have been plenty of guys as the tour statistics prove, equally good at moving the ball from A to B and getting it into the hole. So what raised Tom to his higher plateau? The answer, as always in sport, is his mind. I've heard it said that to play great golf you have to be either very bright or very dumb. Tom Watson is the former. I've always considered course management and self-management my strongest suits, and I believe they have been Tom's also. He has a fine brain that he uses powerfully in navigating his way around a golf course. Also, the greater the pressure, the better it has usually worked.

And then, of course, there is the ultimate arbiter of success or failure, the will. As with so many athletes, Watson's strength here showed in his best years in the incisive, decisive way he both talked about and actually played the game. The man simply burned to *win* and, within the rules, was prepared to pay whatever price was necessary to do so, and that quality just oozed from his body language whenever he was at full bore. Where it shone through mostly, though, was during his nine dry years, from the 1987 Tour Championship to the 1996 Memorial, and most notably in his persistence and self-control throughout an agonizing and endlessly media-hyped war with short putts. I never doubted that his strength of will would one day bring him back, and was as happy for another golfer as I have ever been when he proved me correct at Muirfield Village.

THERE was no way to obliterate the ache of the 1977 Masters loss to Tom, but a week later I eased it a little with victory in the Tournament of Champions in a tense playoff with Bruce Lietzke.

Then, a month after that, I enjoyed the most emotional moment of my entire career, resulting from what I still think of as my most difficult victory, when I won the second Memorial Tournament at Muirfield Village.

The Memorial, unfortunately, has become famous for foul weather over its first twenty years. If memory serves, this began in 1977 with a deluge on Sunday afternoon that forced completion of the final round the next morning, obliging me to sleep on a two-stroke lead over Hubert Green and three over Watson. That resulted in one extremely nervous golfer teeing up on Muirfield Village's sixteenth hole at nine A.M. on Monday. Columbus was my hometown, its people were my friends, I had created the course, the Memorial was my tournament. Never in all my years of wanting to succeed at golf had I ached as badly to win as I did that morning. When it happened, I was so far up in the clouds that my first reaction was simply to retire, to hang up the sticks and quit then and there. Fortunately, I mentioned this to Barbara before I got the chance to blab off at the presentation, and her wise counsel prevailed. But it was a close-run thing.

Four weeks later, Hubert Green made up for his disappointment in Ohio by winning the U.S. Open at Southern Hills in Tulsa. Unable to catch any momentum, I finished tied tenth, seven shots back, and began immediately to think about the year's third major.

The British Open would be staged less than three weeks later on a new entry into the established rota, the Ailsa course at Turnberry on the southwest coast of Scotland. Years previously I had hopped down and played the Ailsa ahead of a British Open at Troon, and enjoyed both the course and the place. There is only one Pebble Beach in the world, but, with five or six holes bordering the Irish Sea, along with its spectacular mountain and ocean views and dramatically situated hotel, Turnberry possesses a similar scenic quality, as well as some comparably challenging golf. Thinking about the upcoming British Open there, I was pretty certain Turnberry would help stimulate the necessary mood for a fellow who had now gone almost two years without a major.

There are those in golf who would argue into next month that the final two rounds of the 1977 British Open were the greatest head-to-head golf match ever played. Not having been around for the first five hundred or so years of the game, I'm not qualified to speak on such matters. What's for sure, however, is that it was the most thrilling one-on-one battle of my career.

Memories of Tom Watson's and my Masters battle were still fresh among the fans, and the rivalry had been further spiced by my Tournament of Champions and Memorial victories, then Tom's win in the Western Open two weeks before Turnberry. On his way to Scotland, Tom had then won a tournament in Spain by eleven strokes, including a round of 63. Not surprisingly, the British fans had convinced themselves that another round in golf's new Gunfight at the OK Corral was imminent. I'm happy to say we didn't disappoint them.

Following a period of southern California–type weather that would persist throughout the championship, Turnberry was pretty much burned out except for the greens, and, with its defenses so low, scoring washot right from the start. John Schroeder, son of Ted, the onetime tennis champion, led after the first round with 66, and our first Memorial winner, Roger Maltbie, put himself on top halfway with 71-66. Tom and I were both one off that pace with identical scores of 68-70, which got us paired together for the third round. We were still tied at its conclusion, each having shot 65, and now jointly in the lead by three strokes over Ben Crenshaw, with the next closest players five shots back. And, of course, we were paired again for Saturday's final round, as the final twosome.

I've written previously about playing badly well, and that most difficult form of golf sums up my game over those first three days. The driver particularly gave me problems, but, with the rough sparse and dry and the greens well watered against the heat, there were usually opportunities to recover. Concentrating and putting well, I'd been able to grab most of them. Tom, on the other hand, judging by the practice rounds we'd played together, was doing everything beautifully, and there was no reason to believe this would suddenly change. An exceptional round of golf would be required to defeat him.

An early lift in a situation like this can be valuable. After missing the fairway at the second hole, I got one with a birdie there as Tom bogeyed, then another with a birdie at the fourth to his par to go three strokes ahead. Four holes later, after three immaculate Watson birdies, we were tied again.

So the encounter was, indeed, turning out to be just what the fans had anticipated—but unfortunately to the point where their enthusiasm, combined with marshaling inadequacies, began giving us problems. There was a lot of yelling and running and raising of dust, which was only to be expected and tolerable. What wasn't acceptable was the way people were crowding us, particularly when it got to the point where we could not properly see our approach-shot markers. As we played the ninth hole, I walked over to Tom and said, "Let's not go on until they get these people under control." He agreed, and so we paused while the police and marshals did their best, although not very successfully, to restore order. When we resumed I went a stroke ahead with a par at the ninth, then increased my lead to two strokes with a good birdie at the twelfth hole. Tom then came right back at me again with a birdie at thirteen. On the fourteenth tee our glances happened to coincide for a moment and he said, "This is what it's all about, isn't it, Jack?" He couldn't have put it better, and I told him, "You're darn right."

After we both parred that difficult fourteenth, Tom still had the honor. When he hit his 4-iron considerably left of the green at fifteen, a par three of 209 yards that was playing downwind, I felt he might have given me a crucial opening. Using the same club and playing for the heart of the green, I put my ball about twenty feet below the cup. When we got down there, Tom's ball was sitting on hard-pan about pin-high, but a good ten feet off the putting surface and at least fifty feet from the hole, and sharply downhill most of the way.

Tom took his time assessing the shot, finally deciding to putt the ball. Watching him set up, I figured he would be fortunate to get down in two. And, of course, he did not. He got down in one. Always on line but going too fast, the ball slammed against the flagstick and dove into the hole. When I missed my twenty-footer, we were tied yet again.

Both of us narrowly missed birdies at sixteen, then hit good drives at the par-five seventeenth. Playing first, Tom put a 3-iron about twenty-five feet above the hole. I felt I made an excellent swing with my 4-iron, but the ball hung out a little, finishing in a fluffy lie just off the green to the right and short of the pin, leaving an awkward little chip. I played it well, to within just under six feet. As I marked the ball, I knew, of course, that the putt was an absolute must. After Tom had two-putted for his birdie I did some careful studying, then produced what I will always believe was a fine stroke. The problem was I had fractionally misread the break, probably as a result of being overly influenced by the behavior of Tom's ball on his first putt on almost the same line. Whatever, I was now one stroke back with one hole to play.

From the tee used for the Open, the eighteenth fairway of the Ailsa course is one of Turnberry's tightest and most awkwardly angled. Intelligently in his position, Tom went with his 1-iron and hit a perfect shot. If I had been ahead, or even tied, the 1-iron would have been my choice also. But now there was nothing to lose and everything to gain. I took the driver and tried to hit it hard, and got a typical result when you force a shot under extreme pressure. Pushed and semiballooned, the ball finished in the right rough just a few inches from unplayable in a bank of gorse bushes.

By the time I got to the ball through what can only be described as a churning mob, Tom had hit his second shot and, judging by the reaction from the packed bleachers, had almost holed it. I took the 7-iron and somehow managed to force my ball to the front edge of the green about thirty-five feet short of the cup. Some of the spectators were so impressed with the shot they threw coins in the divot, apparently a Scottish gesture intended to bring the recipient good luck.

After finally bulldozing my way through a now virtually uncontrollable crowd, I walked directly to the cup to see exactly how long a putt Tom had left himself. His marker was no more than two and a half feet away, and I said to him, "You're really close, aren't you?" and he nodded. It was obviously not much more than a tap-in, but, if I had learned anything about golf in twenty-seven years of playing, it was that it is never over for sure until you've seen the putt that beats you actually fall into the hole. I went back and did my reading, and made an excellent stroke, and got a nice little charge when the long putt dropped for a birdie three and a round of 66.

I had not expected Tom to miss and he didn't, dispatching that winning putt with speed and authority for his 65. My immediate reaction was that it had at least been nice to force him to birdie the final hole to win.

Before the round, Barbara and I had made plans to entertain some friends, including Ken and Jean Bowden, at dinner in the hotel. After the presentation and the press conferences and television interviews and all the rest, Ken came to me and suggested I might like to cancel the arrangement in favor of Barbara and me spending a quiet evening together. "What's the matter?" I asked him. "Don't you want to eat?" Ken said he did, but was simply thinking of our feelings. I proposed that we go right ahead with the plans as made, and told him that if he was going to join in, it was time he ran along and got washed up. And he's never since failed, whenever this championship comes up in conversation, to remind me of my parting comment: "After all, Kenny, it's only a game."

If there's one thing I'm proud of about that famous shoot-out at Turnberry, it is that I was able to say something like that at such a time and really mean it. As Tom had remarked on the fourteenth tee, our battle had been a superb example of what golf at its best is really all about, so that, regardless of the outcome, the actual doing of it had been tremendous fun.

The standing ovation I received when I walked into the crowded Turnberry dining-room that evening was also as pleasing as it was unexpected.

MANY people were surprised when, after missing what's been called the most pressured putt in golf history to allow the U.S. to defeat Europe in the 1991 Ryder Cup match at Kiawah Island, Bernhard Langer bounced right back to win a tournament in Europe the following week. I wasn't. The balanced life that Langer enjoys through his faith and his family enabled him to keep what others might have found deeply traumatic in the proper perspective, that being the "it's-only-a-game" perspective. I'm sure golf is incredibly important to Bernhard Langer, as it was and is to me. But we retain our sanity and our balance because it remains for us just a single component of life, not all of life.

Losing big as I did to Tom Watson twice in 1977, and Langer did at Kiawah, can also be a blessing in disguise. Bernhard was a fine putter in that Ryder Cup match, but he was an even better putter when he won his second Masters two years later. What made him that way, just as it spurred him to repeatedly overcome the yips in earlier times, was the challenge of failure. To a certain type of personality, it's by far the sharpest spur.

My strongest motivation through all my best years wasn't the championships I won and the golfers I defeated, but those I lost and the players who beat me. If Arnold Palmer hadn't been there when I turned pro, or Johnny Miller or Lee Trevino or Tom Watson hadn't come along and whipped me as often as they did, I'm certain my record would have been a shadow of what I'm proud to have achieved. Losing to them simply increased the challenge, made me hungrier, pushed me to practice and play harder. But my perspective on it all never changed. Win or lose, golf was a game and nothing more.

A month after Turnberry, I got more of this type of motivation when at Pebble Beach I failed to join Lanny Wadkins and Gene Littler in the first sudden-death playoff for the PGA Championship, missing by a stroke after an uninspired final round of 73 (Lanny won at the third extra hole). This meant that in six of the eight major championships since my 1975 PGA victory I had finished either second, third or fourth, and, in the last four, had lost twice by two shots and twice by a single stroke. Looking back, I recall it as a particularly painful run of near misses, although I did my best never to show how much I burned inside. Occasionally I've been asked by writers about what is really going through a player's mind at such times. Well, let's talk about that for a moment.

I am proud to say I have never wished that an opponent miss a shot or a putt at any time in all the years I've competed at golf. Rather, I have preferred to focus exclusively on giving my absolute best effort to whatever I needed to do to win, thereby allowing me to live comfortably with myself whatever the outcome. Also, I have never seen or heard of a really good player rooting for an opponent to fail, and particularly not on the professional tours. There are a number of reasons why, if this happens at all, it's such a rarity.

In the first place, there's the camaraderie of golf itself. The best players in every phase of the game, pro and amateur, surely are trying their utmost to beat each other at every opportunity. But they also have to live with one another while doing so, and that produces a bond among them that seems to override the darker sides of even the most competitive types of personality. When you have been there yourself, you know only too well how much it hurts to play badly and lose, and that does not incline you to wish such anguish on a person who, if not always a friend in the full sense of the word, is at least a person sharing the same experiences and challenges as you.

On top of that there is the respect the players hold for each other as technical practitioners. You don't get the opportunity to win in modern professional golf without having learned to play the game extremely well. Once you have been through the mill of that process, you are inclined to respect others who have done the same. Because everyone recognizes how seldom fluky victories occur in top tournament golf, there is little appetite for envy or second-guessing. When a player has won—especially when he's won a lot—you know just how hard he has worked for that success, mentally, physically and emotionally. Thus the instinctive reaction becomes: "Good luck to you, fella. Maybe it'll be my turn next week." To see this, just watch how any pro greets a recent winner the first time he runs into him after his victory. He will never be effusive, but he will always be quick with a good word and a pat on the back, and you can tell from the way they are offered that they are sincerely meant.

The third factor, and the one that makes the "My-turn-will-come" attitude so easy, is the scale of the reward in modern tournament golf. In the old days of fewer tournaments and far smaller purses, the pros got along with each other because cooperation and mutual assistance were the only ways to prosper as a group and survive financially as individuals. Nowadays, there is so much money in the game that, if you can play at all, paying the bills should never be a problem. The only guys I know who show real jealousy are the ones who don't have enough skill or stomach to be out there anyway.

A fourth reason for the player-to-player congeniality that is such an attractive feature of tournament golf is, very simply, its self-governing structure. Goodwill as well as honesty and integrity grow out of and are protected by our collective rules-making.

The biggest reason why tour pros enjoy such a good atmosphere and interrelationship, however, is the manner in which they must play their game to play it successfully. The American public, so used to violent contact sports and media-hyped antagonisms between athletes, would surely like golf to be much more of a head-to-head encounter—an endless succession of Turnberrys, you might say. Be that as it may, the truth is that the professional tournament game is exactly the opposite and always will be (which, of course, is a principal reason why it will never rival top team sports as mass entertainment). Here's why.

Even if you don't start out on tour seeing things this way, you very soon learn that your opponents aren't really the other players, but yourself and the golf course, in that order. As in all competitive situations, this was Tom Watson's and my attitude at the Augusta National and Turnberry in 1977, and the reason why should be quite obvious. As golf involves no physical interaction between participants, yourself and the playing field are the only two things you can do anything about. Smart players, therefore, quickly achieve the habit of putting personalities out of mind from the moment they tee off until the moment they sink their final putt. As I said earlier, I see numbers when I look at leader boards, but rarely do I connect them to names. I have enough trouble not beating myself, let alone worrying about a hundred or more other guys.

Add up all of these factors and you have the answer to why professional tournament golf is such a clean and wholesome sport. In no other does the nature of the contest allow the players to be so free of jealousy and enmity, so willing to help and support each other, and so sincere in their acceptance of each other's successes.

TWELVE months after Turnberry's debut, the British Open returned to its most traditional and my favorite location, the Old Course of St. Andrews on the other side of Scotland. By then, most of my writer friends were deep into yet another round of identifying what one rather grandiosely labeled "Golf's new royalty."

Tom Watson had begun 1978 with a bang, winning our season opener at Tucson, following up a couple of weeks later at the Crosby, then in early May adding the Byron Nelson Classic. Owning now two British Open titles and a Masters green jacket, he naturally was the scribes' favorite for kingship, although Ben Crenshaw, after a fine year in 1976, also got some votes. Then, for the locals, there was the most exciting threat to America's domination of the game in decades in the form of Severiano Ballesteros.

Following his heroics in the Open at Royal Birkdale in 1976 at age nineteen, Seve had won the Dutch Open, then in 1977 the championships of France, Switzerland and Japan. Even more impressive to the many British fans who had begun to adopt him as a semi-native was his first victory in the United States three months previously, in which he made up a ten-stroke deficit after two rounds to win the Greater Greensboro Open by a stroke from Fuzzy Zoeller the week before the Masters. Although he was then still only twenty-one, everything about Seve gave off an aura of potential greatness—his big, self-taught swing, his power, his magical short game, his dark good looks, his undisguised raw hunger for victory, and, most of all, his gutsiness as a go-for-everything player. Thus there were many at St. Andrews who could foresee no other name being inscribed on the old claret jug trophy after the one-hundred-and-ninth playing of the Open than this exciting young Spaniard's.

With a couple of exceptions, 1978 had not been all that bad a year for the "old man" either, at least early on.

Toward the end of February I had finished with five straight birdies, including a couple of chip-ins, to win at Inverrary by a stroke over Grier Jones, placed second by the same margin to Tom Weiskopf at Doral two weeks later, then the week after that won a third Tournament Players Championship in some rough weather at Sawgrass. The couple of exceptions were, unfortunately, the ones that mattered most to me, the Masters and the U.S. Open.

The former had been won by Gary Player with a sensational closing nine of thirty strokes, and the latter, at Cherry Hills, by Andy North in a rugged battle with J. C. Snead and Dave Stockton. I'd had my chances but finally trailed by four shots on both occasions. This meant, as I arrived early at St. Andrews after some time in Germany and Paris with daughter Nan, that I had now gone almost three years without winning a major. As I was in my twenties during a comparable dry spell in the late 1960s, the commentaries then had chiefly been of a "What's-wrong-and-when-will-he-fix-it?" nature. Now I was thirty-eight, and had given extra weight to the advance of time by a well-publicized schedule reduction early in the year. Now the questions were more along the lines of "Is the Bear too old?" Once again, they added to my resolve as I went about the work of final preparations.

My warm-up tournament back in late May for the U.S. Open had been the Atlanta Classic, but by then the swing problems I'd been experiencing since before the Masters had escalated severely and I'd missed the cut. Then, the week after forcing and straining to no avail at Cherry Hills, in playing the Canadian Open at the Glen Abbey course I'd designed as its permanent home, I'd found myself hitting 1- and 2-irons where everyone else was hitting 3s and 4s.

"That's it," I told myself. "You've been trying to work it out on your own now for almost three months and you've failed, so quit being a stubborn German and go find Jack Grout." Jack by then had become professional emeritus at Muirfield Village. I flew directly down there from Toronto. After silently watching me hit about ten shots on the driving range, my old friend said, "Try strengthening your left-hand grip a little." Magic! Suddenly the man could play something resembling golf again.

When a thing like this happens, you're always worried that it's just a Band-Aid and won't last. But I had struck the ball well in an exhibition in Germany, and I continued to do so during practice over the Old Course. The grip change was fractional, but it put both the shaft of the club and its face in a much better position at the top, which gave me the freedom and confidence to release completely through the ball. The excitement of the restored length and accuracy, combined with the long hours of Scottish daylight, tempted me to play more than one round each day, but I talked myself out of it ("Remember you're *thirty-eight,* fella"), sticking with eighteen holes plus modest practice-tee sessions, and getting plenty of rest and relaxation. I had watched son Jackie try unsuccessfully to prequalify for the championship for the first time, and that had been a disappointment for all of us. But by the evening before the opening round I'd gotten to feeling pretty chipper about my own prospects, and quietly said so to Barbara over dinner.

A HAPPY memory of that week was the news, delivered after the second round, that I had been elected an hononary member of the Royal and Ancient Golf Club, a rare honor for a professional, and one I still treasure. The measure of my golf those first two rounds was the composition of my score in the second: an even-par 72 with thirty-six putts. I was almost flawless from tee to green on both the Wednesday and the Thursday, and also, with six-inch tap-in after six-inch tap-in, not all that much worse with the putter. But nothing of consequence had dropped either day, leaving me at the halfway point four strokes back of the leaders: Seve Ballesteros, Ben Crenshaw, and—for the first time in a British Open—a golfer from Japan, by the name of Isao Aoki.

Aoki since then has become famous around the world for his handsy swing, toe-in-the-air putting style and expressive facial reactions to shots. His putting style in particular had generated much interest that week, and on Thursday evening a friend suggested that maybe I ought to give it a try. Instead, I gave him a smile and just a two-word reply: "Patience, patience." When you're hitting the ball as close to the hole as I'd been doing, at some point the putts are going to start dropping. I was confident they would if only I didn't let myself become too restless, and I didn't, and it happened in the third round.

With a 69 and a fifty-four-hole total of four-under-par, by Friday evening I had narrowed the gap to one stroke. Ahead of me were Tom Watson and Peter Oosterhuis, then the best of the British players. Sharing my total were Aoki, Crenshaw, and a new name from New Zealand, Simon Owen. We had planned to leave St. Andrews for home immediately after the championship ended on Saturday, but during dinner I had a word with Barbara, then went to the phone and made arrangements for us not to leave until Sunday morning. Apart from the possibility of a tie and a Sunday playoff, I wanted no distractions of any kind the next day.

If I had to guess at the two most famous—or infamous, take your pick—holes in the world I'd point to the sixteenth at Cypress Point in California and the seventeenth at the Old Course at the home of golf. I probably don't have to remind you that the latter is the Road Hole, a 461-yard par four doglegging severely from left to right in the driving area, with a rough-surfaced road bordering the right edge of the long, skinny, diagonally angled green, and a terrifying pit bunker eating deep into the green's left side. This little baby has inflicted serious hurt on both golf scores and golfers' psyches in the twenty-three Opens and countless other tournaments played at St. Andrews over the years, but it's hard to believe it ever wreaked as much carnage in one week as in the championship of 1978.

After going out in 31 in the first round, Tom Weiskopf made 6 at the seventeenth and was never again a factor. The brawny Briton, Brian Barnes, made the same score the same day after putting for a birdie—into the pot bunker. Three under and very much a contender, Arnie Palmer took 7 at the Road Hole in round two, and encored there the next day. If Seve Ballesteros had played the hole in even par, as he would six years later in winning at St. Andrews, he would have lost the championship by only a single stroke. Instead, he played it in 5-6-6-5.

However, the champion 1978 victim of St. Andrews's most famous piece of real estate, by a good margin, was Tommy Nakajima, then little known outside Japan but thereafter periodically a contender on the PGA Tour. In the third round, when only a stroke or two off the pace, Tommy, with an outside chance at a birdie, underhit his putt, then could only watch in dismay as it curled slowly away and trickled ever so gently into the pot bunker. Now, to keep from going over the green and into the road—from where, of course, you nightmarishly see yourself hitting back into the bunker, then back to the road, then back to the bunker, and to and fro forever and ever—he had to get the ball up very high very quickly, but with only enough forward momentum to barely clear the bunker's front bank. It was the shot that Doug Sanders had executed so superbly for a vital par on the seventy-first hole of the 1970 Open, and that John Daly and Constantino Rocca would match as they battled for the 1995 championship. Unfortunately, Tommy's touch must have been affected by the shock of what had just happened to him, because he tried once, then a second time, then a third, then a fourth, until finally with his fifth attempt got the ball out of the sand and back onto the green. Two putts later he completed the hole in 9, leading the writers to rechristen it for the rest of the week "The Sands of Nakajima." If Tommy had made the birdie he was trying for originally, he, too, would have finished second in the championship.

These antics at the Road Hole come to mind because of how critically the seventeenth would figure in my final-round play, along with its two predecessors. But I'm getting ahead of myself.

The moment I had walked out of Rufflet's Hotel that Saturday morning my spirits soared. For three days we had played with the wind at our backs on the first seven and the tenth and eleventh holes, and in our faces on the eighth and ninth holes and from thirteen in. Now the wind had swung through 180 degrees, and I believed this would give me a considerable edge over most of the other contenders. These were the conditions I had won in eight years previously. Even more important, thanks to those initial practice rounds in the same conditions, I had been able to fully refamiliarize myself with the radical changes in target areas and club selection necessitated by the wind reversal. "Boy," I thought, "am I glad I didn't shortchange my preparation time." I'm sure Ray Floyd, who had arrived equally early, felt the same.

Paired with Simon Owen immediately ahead of the last twosome, Watson and Oosterhuis, I made a solid start into the wind, parring the first two holes and birdieing the third. At the long par-four fourth, my one slightly missed drive thus far all week threatened trouble for a while, but I scrambled a par and another at the par-five fifth. Then, after a solid par at six, I looked at a leader board for the first time. It showed that Watson had bogeyed the second and fourth holes, and that the wind reversal was also giving everyone else problems. I now held the lead for the first time.

The only knowledge I had of Simon Owen's game was what I'd observed as we started out: a big, freewheeling swing that moved the ball a long way, and a demeanor that showed no sign of being fazed by contending for the world's oldest golf championship. After he bogeyed the fourth and sixth holes to give me a three-stroke advantage, there was no call to pay him any special attention beyond the normal courtesies, and I became even more intensely locked into my own game. That changed after he birdied nine and ten, and even more after he added another birdie at twelve to cut my lead to a single stroke.

Both of us parred thirteen, then, on the long par-five fourteenth hole, Simon hit a big drive and another wood close to the green, from where he chipped to six feet and holed the putt for a fourth birdie in six holes. Suddenly we were tied. The rest of the field was making no headway, but Mr. Owen had definitely gained my attention. He was obviously a fine golfer, with no intestinal or cardiac weaknesses under extreme pressure, and he proved it again at the very next hole when he sank an eighty-foot chip shot from behind the green for yet another birdie to go one ahead of me. As we walked to the sixteenth tee, a vision of Tom Watson's putt on the same number hole a year previously at Turnberry flashed into my head, and I thought, "Oh, no, not *again*." But my next thoughts were good ones indeed: "Well, Jack, that's up to you, isn't it? Let's get back to work."

Simon Owen was obviously an attacking kind of golfer, which is often the best strategy for a fellow who still has a lot of winning to do, and I admired him more for it the farther the round progressed. What did puzzle me, however, was his persistence in hitting the driver off of every tee after we turned permanently downwind at the thirteenth hole. That had obviously worked beautifully for him thus far. But I've never met a golfer who could control a driver as well as a 3-wood or long iron, and if there's one need greater than all others at St. Andrews, wind helping or wind hurting, it's maximum control over tee-shot placement.

With the honor at the sixteenth tee, Simon laced a superb drive seemingly not very far short of the green, following which I hit my 3-wood well to the left of the Principal's Nose and its companion bunkers. I took plenty of time deciding on the second shot, then played a perfect little 9-iron that came softly to rest about seven feet from the cup. Simon's shot was no more than a flip wedge, and I still don't know what happened to it, but the ball cleared the green on the fly, ending up beyond the seventeenth tee and leaving him a testy touch shot. He finally decided to putt the ball, but left it short of the green, meaning he would have his work cut out to make no worse than bogey. "Okay, no mistakes," I told myself over my putt, and made none. Birdie three. When Simon took two more to get down, it was a two-stroke swing. I led by a shot with two holes to go.

Hitting dead into the wind at seventeen the previous three days, I had been forced to use the driver simply to get enough distance to set up some sort of shot to the green. Thinking as always of the hole as a par four-and-a-half when played into a headwind, I had not been unhappy with three fives. Now, with the eighteenth such a birdieable hole, not only for Simon but for Oosterhuis behind us still with a chance, four was an absolute must.

For a moment I was tempted to take the driver again, then recalled the horror stories I mentioned earlier and put the thought out of mind. I hit the 3-wood exactly over my aiming point, and knew I'd find the ball in the center of the fairway. And now, going with the driver again, Simon finally severely penalized himself, hooking away into the rough. To hit for the pin and hold the green wasn't even a possibility from there, but he decided to try and found the road. Short of a miracle, that meant the best he could do was a bogey five. That being the case, with the pin set way back on the narrow little shelf only a few feet from the bunker, there was no way I was going to try to get even part of the way back to it. I took the 6-iron, swung easily, put the ball in the tightly mown hollow fronting the green, then stroked maybe the best sixty-foot putt of my life that didn't actually drop to within less than a foot of the cup. Leader by two with one hole to play.

Golf has left me with a vast store of rich memories, but the scene as I walked to my second shot at that most famous of all golf's finishing holes late that Saturday afternoon, after hitting a solid 3-wood safely left toward the first fairway, is as vivid today as it was then.

Packed in those huge bleachers, crammed in all the windows, filling every inch of the pathways above and to the right of the hole—even, it seemed, dangling from rooftops—some thirty thousand people simply let it all hang out. I had never received such a huge ovation, and haven't since, and don't expect I ever will again. A lump started to grow in my throat and my eyes began to tear up, and when I looked over at my loyal and faithful caddie through almost all the years of playing in the British Open, good old Jimmy Dickinson, it was obvious that he was totally choked up too.

"Wait a minute now, Jack, it's not over yet, we've still got some work to do," he finally got out, which brought me sufficiently back to earth to stroke a pitch-and-run safely well beyond the Valley of Sin to about thirty-five feet above the hole, from where I carefully two-putted. And then, finally, it was over, and, as so often on such occasions, the emotions were so strong I really don't have any idea how to even begin describing them.

Once again I had come back after nearly three years of failing to meet my own lifelong goal, and with the finest four days of tee-to-green golf I had produced in a major championship, even including the 1965 Masters, to win a third British Open and become the only golfer to capture all four of the game's top titles at least three times. And I had done it at St. Andrews, my favorite place on earth to play golf.

For once there had to be more than a Coke to ease my throat before the prize presentation. George Simms, the Open's press chieftain, looked a little stunned when I asked him for a beer, but one duly arrived. It was the best I ever tasted.

18

The 1980 United States Open Championship

"Jack's Back"

I SAID at the time, and still believe, that in winning that 1978 British Open I played as well from tee to green as I had in any major championship. The confidence in my swing carried into the following week to produce a one-stroke victory over Gil Morgan in the IVB-Philadelphia Classic at Whitemarsh Valley, and I enjoyed another spell of good form in mid-November at the Australian Club in Sydney to win my sixth Australian Open. Equally enjoyable, not least because it was so unexpected after a good but hardly my best year, was being named Sportsman of the Year by *Sports Illustrated*. Maybe they figured it was my last chance!

In one respect they weren't too far off the mark, because, mulling over that period now, it's clear to me that 1978 was the last year in which I could still periodically produce winning golf fairly effortlessly. From that time on, giving of my best demanded harder work, certainly physically and usually also mentally. In short, being able to depend mostly on raw talent ended in my thirty-ninth year.

Much as I still tried to do that in 1979, a look back as it drew to a close forced me to accept reality. I had competed twelve times in the

United States, with chances of winning only in the Masters and in defending at Philadelphia. On all but one of the other occasions I hadn't even made the top ten. Although I'd tied for second with Ben Crenshaw in defending my British Open title at Royal Lytham and St. Annes, I had never really looked like catching Seve Ballesteros. It was my first winless year since turning pro. Even more indicative of the condition of my game was plunging to seventy-first on the money list after never previously finishing lower than fourth.

A common theme of the heavy media analysis that followed this performance—or, rather, lack of performance—was that much if not all of it derived from reducing my U.S. tournament schedule to only twelve events. Well, as I'm afraid they were at other times in deciding what ailed Jack Nicklaus, the analysts were wrong about that.

Most fans of golf probably are not aware of the tremendous pressures applied to the game's top performers to play in virtually every tournament on the calendar in their own countries. As Tiger Woods is now discovering with a vengeance, sponsors deeply concerned with their gate numbers and television ratings go to exteme lengths to capture the "name" players. When the people doing the persuading are friends, as they frequently have become over the years, it's especially difficult to say no. There is also the factor that, if you have taken heavily from the game of golf, you have an obligation to put something back into it, and the best way of doing that is simply by playing in tournaments as often as possible.

The other side of the coin in my case was that golf alone could never give me everything I wanted from life; that I needed complete breaks from the game in order to be "hungry" about it when I did compete; and, more and more over time, that the only tournaments that truly motivated me were those that had come to mean the most to me personally, and increasingly to the game generally, namely the major championships.

After wrestling with these conflicts through most of the 1970s, at the end of 1978 I came to a decision about them. It was that I could only be true to golf, and all of the people and institutions in it, if I were first true to myself. I expected excellence of myself, and golf had come to expect—and deserved—excellence of me. Therefore, I should only play when I could give my best. An inner voice had long been telling me that the only events that really mattered to me anymore were the four majors plus my own tournament, the Memorial. Henceforth, therefore, I would compete only enough elsewhere to prepare myself for those five.

The problem in my first year of putting that policy into effect wasn't that I did not play enough preparative tournaments, but that my game had deteriorated beyond being preparable. Glibly as I'd talked about quitting golf over the years, as 1979 drew to a close I had to face the fact that it had truly become one of just two options. The other was to remake my swing.

This was one of the more difficult decisions I have faced over the years. I was forty years old, financially secure, a successful golf course designer and businessman, and deeply immersed in an ever-growing range of family activities. I had not worked really hard at golf for many years. I had established an energetic but enjoyable lifestyle in my off-seasons in which the game was of low priority, mentally as well as physically. Above all, there was the disturbing prospect of making radical swing changes. The more I thought about what that would take in time, effort and frustration, the less appealing the task became.

That was the downside.

Heading the upside was the certainty that Barbara would support whatever decision I made, although I had a sense whenever we talked on the subject—which we did a lot that fall and early winter—that her secret hope was that I would continue playing. Another important upside factor was the growing interest and involvement of our children in the game; if they played I wanted to be able to play, and play well, with them. A third was my excellent physical condition —I was probably fitter then than at any time in my life to that point. A fourth was the availability of Jack Grout, who was wintering in south Florida for the first time in many years. Last but far from least, there was my old stubborn perfectionism, plus a sense that my record wasn't yet quite the one I wanted to leave behind for all the strong young comers to shoot at, that even though I might not scale new heights, the mountain could still be enlarged.

Right after the new year celebrations, it suddenly hit me that the upside in all of this outweighed the downside. I decided to go and get myself something resembling my old golf swing.

• • •

THE best thing about Jack Grout in those long-ago times when he actually taught me, rather than simply encouraged and enthused me, was his fundamentalism and his minimalism.

Jack believed in the simplest possible approach to the game of golf, and also in a broad approach. He would give you the bare bones of a basic, then encourage you to figure out the details for yourself. He did that, first, so that you would use what came most naturally to you in learning and mastering the fundamental and, second, so that you would learn and remember the cause-and-effect factors through feel, not words. Rather than direct, he would suggest and guide. "Gee, Jackie," he'd say, as something began to take hold, "that looks just great. Doesn't it *feel* just great? Let's do it some more." All the rest of the time would then be devoted to enthusing you about whatever it was you were now doing so splendidly—or, in other words, to building your confidence. Jack always wanted you to do it *your* way, the most natural way you could, which made him the polar opposite of all those pros who want you to do it their way, or to adopt some "method" they believe they've invented for the salvation of golfers everywhere.

Jack's simplicity or minimalism derived from his background. Like most professionals who learned the game via the youthful mimicry that comes from hanging around caddie yards, he never saw the golf swing as a particularly complex maneuver to start with. Then, as he studied good players in the tournaments he entered and elsewhere, an already simple approach became even simpler. By the time I happened along in 1950, at least as far as juniors were concerned, he had refined the golf swing down in his mind to just a handful of fundamentals.

There was less than the usual amount of attrition in Jack's junior classes at Scioto, and I think it was this lack of complexity that kept so many of us coming back. His instructions were clear and easily comprehensible, and you sensed from his great conviction and enthusiasm that, if you could just master these three or four simple things, then you would have an awful lot of fun at a game that at first might not have seemed like any fun at all.

The first and always the most important of Jack's fundamentals concerned your head. You had to keep it in the same place throughout the swing, not rigidly anchored but *steady.* It wasn't good enough to "keep your eye on the ball," because you could keep your eye on the ball and still move your head around quite a lot, and when you did that you changed your body angles, which messed up your arc, and upset your balance, and wrecked your timing.

Like most healthy youngsters, I wanted to go after that little white pellet with every muscle fiber in my body, which made my legs way too active, and put a dip in my swing, and, worst of all, caused my head to bob around all over the place. Despite constant appeals, I got away with it for almost a year before Mr. Grout decided the time had arrived for desperate measures.

Jack had an assistant then by the name of Larry Glosser, and I'll never forget the day he had Larry come out and stand in front of me and stick out his arm and grab my hair as I was addressing a shot. Like most midwestern boys of that period I sported a crew-cut, so, to be sure he would keep me still, Larry had to hold on to my little bit of hair pretty tightly. "Okay, Jackie boy," said Mr. Grout, "now just you go ahead and hit that ball for me." *Ouch!* And ouch again, and again, and plenty more times during the next few weeks, until little Jackie finally learned to keep his head *steady, every time,* on *every* shot, until the ball was well on its way. And, of course, doing that has been my number-one golfing fundamental ever since.

The second of Jack's basics concerned the other end of the anatomy, the feet. Here, he believed, lay the source of balance and of full, free coiling and uncoiling of the body, both indispensable to good golf. The way you achieved them was through your ankles. You didn't go at it stiff-legged like a stork, or jump up on your toes like a ballerina. What you did was roll your left ankle inward on the backswing and your right ankle inward on the through-swing. "But that's hard to do, Mr. Grout!" "Well, then, Jackie boy, let's see you hit those three buckets of balls without letting your heels come off the ground *even a little bit.*" I must have practiced and played at least one whole season with my heels glued to mother earth. And I'll still keep them grounded even to this day when I'm working on things like balance and complete clubhead release.

Number three in Jack's order of priorities was to hit the ball as hard and far as you possibly could from the moment you first picked up a golf club. Even a hint of laziness in this regard would bring stern disapproval. Although Deacon Palmer had taught his son, Arnold, the same way, it was a somewhat heretical approach in those days, but Jack believed in it for three reasons. First, raw distance was the number-one weapon in a golfer's armory. Second, height with the longer clubs—a product of great clubhead speed—came a close second. Third, if you didn't fully extend and stretch and strengthen your golfing muscles when you were young, you would never do so when you got older.

The encouragement to belt the ball was endless and exciting. "Go on, Jackie boy, hit it harder. Give it hell. Whack the daylights out of that ball. Don't worry about where it goes. We can fix that later. Go ahead, knock the *devil* out of this one!"

And, of course, I did, with joyful abandon. And right off the bat it made me long for my age, although much of the time at first I'd be longer sideways than forward. But then, as my technique steadily improved and matured, it became easier to find the foul balls. From being a hundred yards or more wide, I'd find I'd cut the spraying down to only seventy or so yards, which inspired yet more work on control. Then it became fifty yards, then thirty, then twenty, then ten, until finally I was finding the fairway more often than not but without giving up any length. Which, of course, is when I also began to find a score.

When necessary and without becoming overfinicky, Jack paid appropriate attention to a youngster's grip and stance and aim and posture, but he really had only one more fundamental. This was the size of the clubhead's arc in the backswing. For him, it could never be too big. "And there's only one way to make it as big as I want to see it, Jackie boy. You've got to *turn* that body of yours around until it just won't go any farther, and you've got to *extend* those arms until they reach right on up through the clouds." *Phew!* Did I sweat and spray—and ache—in those days! But coil and extend I did, and eventually *almost* enough to satisfy the man with the eagle eye. And now I know, of course, that, without the freedom and fullness of swing Jack Grout insisted on, I would never have played as well as I have for as long as I have.

I guess it took about six years of almost daily toiling and grinding to put it all together, then refine it sufficiently to begin scoring consistently well. As this book and particularly this chapter illustrate, the honing and tuning process has never ended, and probably never will. But, by the time I won the Ohio Open at the age of sixteen, the basic pattern was well set.

By then I had ingrained an extremely full golf swing based mostly on big-muscle work—body and leg as opposed to hand and wrist action. Also, because the largest possible arc is only achievable that way, I had built an exceptionally "tall" or upright golf swing. In other words, seen from behind me looking down the target line, the path of my clubhead was closer to the perpendicular than to the horizontal plane, with my hands swinging at the top well above the level of my head.

As I began spreading my wings competitively in my late teens, this pronounced uprightness raised eyebrows among some of the arbiters of golfing style. They pointed out that most of the great champions of the game had swung the club on a flatter or shallower plane, and particularly the golfer then considered to be the finest shotmaker of them all, Ben Hogan. Another argument involved a question of physics; that is, the shallower the path of the clubhead as it approaches the ball, the more forward rather than downward its force is directed, and thus the more solid and powerful the hit. By coming into the ball so steeply, the critics suggested, I was risking catching it an oblique or glancing blow, which could cost me both power and accuracy. This would become progressively more injurious, they suggested, as age gradually ate away at my strength and flexibility.

Well, much as I hate to admit it, those critics were basically correct.

Up to and through my early thirties, I possessed the strength and flexibility to swing the club not only wide and high, but also *deep* enough—sufficiently behind me at the top of the swing—to deliver it traveling from far enough inside the target line and low enough to the ground to meet the ball solidly. I really did hit it a very long way up to that time—often 300 and more yards with the driver—despite slightly fading most shots. And I assure you that no one has ever achieved that much yardage with that kind of flight without striking the ball solidly in the rear.

It was in the mid-1970s that things began to change. As time steadily exacted its inevitable physical toll, the depth of my swing began to diminish as the plane remained upright. For about five more years I could still play, and well enough to win a fair amount of the time. Then, gradually—in fact, so slowly that at first I was barely conscious of it—my full shots began to fly both shorter and less accurately. As season followed season, this steadily increased the pressure on my recovery game and putting, and, through that, on my composure and patience.

Jack Grout watched the decline with increasing concern and repeated urging of me to go all the way back to the drawing-board and, with his help, fix my full swing once and for all. What he said, always in his even-mannered way but ever more bluntly, was: "You have let yourself get way too upright. You are high, which is good, but you have lost your depth, which is very bad. If you don't do something about that, your career will be a lot shorter than both of us would like."

I realize now that, although I heard Jack, I never really listened to him. Periodically we would work a little on trying to deepen my swing, but there was no way I could make it happen quickly and reliably. Fearful of falling between an old method and a new one, fearful of losing whatever game I had left, I simply wasn't ready to make the commitment in time and effort necessary to, as I saw it, master a new golf swing. Instead, I continued to fiddle around and make do, basically applying one useless Band-Aid after another, until the only alternative to quitting became starting over again.

THIS book is not the place for elaborating on golf technique, but a little more discussion of particular swing mechanics is probably necessary for readers to fully appreciate the need for the changes I made.

Unconventionally "steep" or upright as my swing may have looked in my teens and twenties, it was in those days also exceptionally "deep." What this means is that, although my shoulders tilted considerably as the backswing progressed, which is essential to swing on an upright plane, they also turned or rotated or coiled very fully. Additionally, although my hands and arms extended well away from my body early in the backswing and rose unusually high by its completion, they also finished well to the inside or around behind my body as I reached the top. The net result was that I set the club not only high, or upright, but well behind my body, or deep.

Looking at me then, down the line at the top of the swing with a driver or other long club, you would have seen the shaft positioned directly above or even slightly behind my right shoulder. That may not be as deep as a flatter swinger might get, but it was plenty deep enough to give me immense power with a high degree of accuracy.

To achieve such depth with height in the golf swing requires both strength and flexibility. As an all-around sports addict from an early age, I had developed enough of both to get the job done perfectly well at least into my early thirties, particularly with Jack Grout always on hand to assist with the fine tuning. Although it took more than a decade to remove me from the winner's circle, I'm convinced that what initiated my eventual loss of depth was our move in 1965 from central Ohio, where there is little wind, to the southeast coast of Florida, where there rarely isn't wind.

The more wind a golfer is exposed to, the harder it becomes to build and maintain a big, high, and particularly a deep golf swing. Constant wind saws at your nerves and seems always to be threatening your stability. The effect is that you want to get the action over with as fast as possible. Inevitably over time that will in some way restrict your backswing. (This could explain why Ben Hogan and Lee Trevino, teaching themselves golf in windy Texas, developed relatively flat swings.)

The effects of constantly practicing and playing in wind after moving full time to Florida were exacerbated by the fact that, although I still periodically spent time with Jack Grout, he wasn't on hand almost daily, as during my Ohio-based years. Because you can't see yourself swing a golf club, and because feel alone is so fickle, you can never be sure you are actually doing what you want to do, and are even mentally convinced you are doing, without the help of an observer who knows your game. If I had been able to work with Jack more frequently in the late sixties and early seventies, the problems that peaked in 1979 likely would have been less severe. Which is why, of course, since Jack's passing, I have depended so much on a couple of highly regarded teachers who have also become my good friends, Jim Flick and Rick Smith, for regular feedback on my game.

When I finally committed myself to trying to rejuvenate my game at the beginning of 1980, the effort did not begin on the practice tee. With the willing cooperation of my business associates, I first arranged to reduce my nongolf activities to a minimum, at least through the Masters. Second, I made it a rule that, instead of going to the office in the morning and to the golf course in the afternoon —maybe—I would go to the golf course in the morning and the office—maybe—in the afternoon. Third, I persuaded Jack Grout not only to reside for some months about a drive and 3-wood from my home, but to be on hand every day, including weekends.

To understand the changes we then set about trying to make, it helps to understand the type of impact created by an over-upright swing plane, plus the effect on clubhead speed of lack of backswing depth.

The more upright the swing, the more downward or less level the arc of the clubhead through impact. The steeper or more downward the clubhead arc, the tougher it becomes to strike the ball squarely in its rear. Instead, you get what I call, from its feel, an oblique kind of hit—a sense of catching the ball a slightly glancing blow, rather than that great meaty sensation that comes from socking it solidly in back. I had become very familiar with bad-feeling golf shots during the late 1970s.

Distance in golf is the product of clubhead speed squarely applied. One of the lessons I relearned in 1980 was that squareness depends just as much on the clubhead's downward angle of approach to the ball as it does on the path of the clubhead relative to the target line. I was losing some distance, plus some directional control, by delivering the clubhead to the ball too steeply—by hitting it too obliquely. However, that same steepness was causing me to lose even more distance by decreasing my clubhead speed.

Clubhead speed in the golf swing is ultimately the product of centrifugal force, which in turn is largely generated by torque or leverage. To oversimplify a little for the sake of clarity, the deeper your backswing, the more torque or leverage you are able to generate to release in the form of centrifugal force on the through-swing. To put this another and even simpler way, the less you turn or coil your upper body, while also swinging your arms and hands *behind* your upper body going back, the less clubhead speed you generate and thus the shorter you hit the ball.

The degree to which a golfer turns or rotates or coils his torso going back is heavily influenced by his arm swing. The more directly upward, rather than upward *and rearward,* the arms swing, the sooner the body will stop turning or rotating or coiling. This is an involuntary reaction caused by a false sense of having made a complete backswing created by high-swinging arms. It's a lazy, lift-and-chop way to play, common among recreational golfers, and a principal reason why they hit the ball so lifelessly and short. If not quite to the degree of your average weekender, that was what was hurting me.

The challenge then, as Jack and I began work in January 1980, was in essence to deepen or flatten my swing sufficiently to produce a shallower or more level clubhead arc through impact. Sounds simple? Well, if you've ever had a long-ingrained golf fault, then made a mental commitment to fix it, I don't have to spell out how difficult doing so can be when you actually begin trying.

What we focused on principally were two setup changes and one backswing adjustment that in combination, Jack assured me, would deepen my swing arc by the necessary few inches. At address I needed both to stand taller and to position my head "where God put it"—Jack's phrase—centrally in relation to my body, and thus more over rather than canted behind the ball at address. Combined with those seemingly minor but at first amazingly uncomfortable changes, I had to learn to let my right arm fold earlier and more easily at the elbow as I swung the club back. This was even more difficult than the setup modifications. Time and again I would be convinced I had it all down pat, only to watch Grout and others who happened to be on hand and knew my game somberly shake their heads. It was *tough*. And, as we'll see later, it wasn't until the U.S. Open in June of that year that I proved conclusively to myself that it was the correct medicine.

When not laboring on those full-swing modifications with Jack Grout, I began working equally hard on other elements of my game as winter turned to spring that year. I had happened to read some theories that intrigued me in a *Golf Digest* magazine excerpt from a book by Paul Runyan, widely regarded as one of the all-time short-game masters. I obtained a copy of the book and began working with its chipping recommendations. My old pal Phil Rodgers, a lifelong Runyan disciple, was by then spending much of his time teaching, and a few weeks before the Masters I persuaded him to come and stay with us for a spell and teach me more about pitching and bunker techniques as well as chipping. We also spent some time on my putting, trying to get me back more to my 1960s style with my head well behind the ball at address, from where I could better see the line, and also recapture the feeling of giving the ball a distinct push with my right hand while keeping the left hand firm.

All in all, it was the hardest I had worked at golf since my teen years. But the big question remained: would it pay off?

• • •

RIGHT up to the week of the U.S. Open, the answer to anyone aware of my efforts must have appeared to be no.

My first three outings resulted in ties for eleventh, sixteenth and fifty-third places. Despite losing to Raymond Floyd in the playoff, a tie over the regulation distance at Doral was encouraging, only to be followed by more mediocre scoring in my next three tournaments, including a particularly disappointing tie for thirty-third in the Masters, sixteen shots back of Seve Ballesteros as he launched the European golfing renaissance that we're still witnessing.

My next tournament was the Byron Nelson Classic in Dallas in early May, where I finished tied for forty-third, fifteen strokes behind Tom Watson as he achieved his third consecutive victory in the event. The frustration at that point suddenly became overpowering, sinking me into as depressed a mood as I can recall suffering. Barbara told me, "Quit if you want to. I don't mind. You have so many other things to do. But golf is such a big part of your life I don't think you can be happy without it." Just talking things over with her seemed to make them better, and after a while the depression lifted and I decided to hang in.

It was a good decision, because, by the time of the Memorial Tournament a couple of weeks later, I began for the first time to feel that all of the work I had put in might finally be coming together. A week before the Memorial I had hit the ball well enough in a casual round at Muirfield Village to have scored in the low 60s with any kind of putting. Also, despite making little on the greens then and other times I played, I felt close to beginning to putt well. In fact, I was so chipper about it all that I told a friend I might just be ready the following week.

That proved premature. Then, on the Saturday evening following the third round of the Memorial, Jack Grout came up with what proved to be the finishing touch. Typical of his great diagnostic eye and his minimalism, he watched me stroking for only a minute or two before saying, "Stop dragging the putter through the ball, stop blocking the hit. Take the thing back inside and release it—*hit* the damn ball!" I rolled a few more putts and something clicked.

The U.S. Open was then eighteen days away. For years I had foregone competing the weeks before majors, but, because I felt the new stroke needed tournament-testing, I entered the Atlanta

Classic. Concentrating so heavily on putting, I hit too many loose approach shots the first day for a 78. But the 67 in the second round, despite missing the cut by a stroke, told me that I'd found what I came for.

When I mentioned to Barbara how I felt despite what seemed like just another failure, she said, "You know, Jack, if that's true, then you have a chance to become the first person to win a U.S. Open in three decades." It was a nice thought, but I restated it. "No, Barbara," I responded, "what I have is a chance of becoming the first golfer to win major championships over four decades." And I really meant it, because for the first time in at least two years I felt truly confident about every element of my game.

It was clear from my first practice round at Baltusrol that scoring likely would be unusually low for a U.S. Open. One reason was that, although the Lower Course had been altered slightly, the decision had been made to set it up as closely as possible to its 1967 condition, which, to my memory, had been about seven on a USGA one-to-ten Open difficulty scale. Perhaps even more important, the twenty-plus inches of rain that had fallen on New Jersey over the previous six months had softened the bases of the greens, ensuring that a lot of the moisture deposited by Monday and Tuesday night storms of Open week itself would remain in their upper areas. In short, as is rarely the case in our national championship, approach shots of just about any length would mostly hit and stick, at least early on.

My optimism coming in proved justified in my three practice rounds, to the point where Tom Weiskopf, with whom I'd played one of them, told the writers he had never seen me so sharp. Sometimes practicing exceptionally well can take a little shine off your game when the gun goes off for real, but that did not happen to me this time. Partly inspired by watching and trying to match Weiskopf's scoring as he proceeded from an opening bogey to an Open record-tying 63, I eased it around in the same number, to join him as co-leader at the end of the day. With a single bogey at number two off a poor tee shot to eight birdies, three of them in a row from the eleventh through the thirteenth holes, it was as close to a flawless round of golf as I had played in a very long time, not to mention my best ever start in a major championship. The only disappointment was missing a three-footer for birdie at eighteen that would have given me a new Open single-round record. But, as I told the writers after breaking the thirty-six-hole record on Friday and the fifty-four-hole record on Saturday, scores were of importance only in where they placed you on Sunday night.

Our 63s gave Tom and me a three-stroke lead over Keith Fergus, Mark Hayes, and Lon Hinkle, with fourteen more golfers breaking the par of 70. My attitude as I began the second round was to play aggressively, with the objective of leaving as many of them as far behind me as I could as fast as I could. The plan seemed to be working after birdies at the first and third holes, but soured soon after I turned for home at one under par for the day.

The eleventh hole on Baltusrol's Lower Course is a medium-length par four doglegging sharply around some large pine trees with a bunker cut into the elbow. That's where I drove, settling for a two-putt bogey after pitching short out of the sand. The next hole is one of the trickiest on the course at 193 yards with a tightly guarded green. Irritated at myself, I caught my 4-iron fat, burying the ball in the face of a bunker, from where it took most of my strength simply to dig it out into rough short of the green. This left me with a lie calling for a bladed wedge, always a dangerous shot. I missed it so badly that the ball would probably have gone through the green if hitting the hole hadn't slowed it down. But two putts later it added up to a double-bogey five, putting me at two over par with six holes to play. I needed to settle down.

Rolling my tee shot through a bunker at the short par-four thirteenth was a lucky break, and I thought I'd capitalized on it when I pitched nicely to within about twenty feet of the hole. Then, still a little jittery, I babied the putt, leaving a nasty downhill eight-footer for par. Disgusted, I willed myself to make it, and did, and it definitely saved the round and possibly the championship, because, as I told the writers later, I don't know what I might have shot if that putt hadn't dropped. Feeling better, I parred the next three holes, birdied the monster seventeenth from five feet after three solid shots, then saved par at eighteen by lobbing a Phil Rodgers–type super-wristy little pitch stone dead. Bob Rosburg had walked the round with us commentating for television, and as I walked past him to the green he told me, "People don't know how good that shot was." "No, but I do," I responded, with a big grin on my face.

So the total was 71, which meant that I hadn't run away and hidden as I'd hoped to, but that, at the end of the day, with a two-stroke lead over Fergus, Hinkle, Isao Aoki, and Mike Reid, it was still very much my championship to win.

Aoki, who had been one of my playing partners those first two days, was at that time far and away Japan's premier golfer. He and I would also play the last two rounds together, making this as good a time as any to mention his superb putting during that championship. As all golf fans surely know after Isao's sensational 1983 Hawaiian Open win and many recent successes on the Senior Tour, he putts with the toe of the club high in the air, relying almost entirely on his wrists to rap the ball smartly with the heel of the club, rather like he was driving a tack into a post with a hammer. It's one of the most unusual techniques ever employed by a world-class player but, as I witnessed at Baltusrol for four days in 1980, also one of the most effective.

On Thursday Isao's 68 included just twenty-three putts, and on Friday he needed one less to record the same score—including, if memory serves, only nine or ten of them on the back nine. He fell off a little on the weekend, with thirty-one putts each day, but his seventy-two-hole total of 112 was awfully impressive, as was his demeanor with the short stick in hand: he knew, and you knew he knew, that he was going to make most of what he looked at. His English then was minimal, so most of our conversation consisted of me saying "Good putt" and him saying "Thanks, Jack." I remember after the third round telling the writers that there would be much thunder and lightning if Isao Aoki ever three-putted a hole. But he was then, and still is, an easy golfer to play with, intensely focused on competing while never getting in anyone else's way, and demonstrating in his manner and occasional comments a nice sense of balance and humor about the game. Scare me as he did toward the end, I very much enjoyed playing with Isao Aoki those four days in New Jersey.

Despite the second-round slips, I decided, based on my confidence in my game overall, that there was no reason not to try again to distance myself from the field in the third round. Once more I got off to a fast start, making one bogey but holing three twenty-plus-footers for birdies at the fourth, fifth, and seventh holes to turn in 32 with only fourteen putts. And, once again, I faltered coming home: bogey at fourteen off a sloppy approach, a three-putt bogey at fifteen, a fight for par at seventeen after half-topping my 3-wood second shot, then three putts at eighteen going too boldly for eagle after a fine drive and an even better 1-iron.

You will usually take a par round uncomplainingly in a U.S. Open, but this one irritated me as I later played the "if only" game that golf so often inspires—if only I'd shot two under instead of two over coming home, which wasn't an unreasonable expectation, I'd have a four-stroke lead instead of being tied with Aoki, with at least six or seven other guys still well within range. . . . In short, I had twice set myself up to make this Open a very dull one by running away and hiding, but could not pull it off. So now I was vulnerable, and particularly to my friend from Japan.

Isao that day had gone out in 33 to drop three strokes back of me. Coming home he cut the deficit to two with a birdie at thirteen, reduced it to one when I bogeyed fourteen, raised it to two again by bogeying sixteen (the ground shook when he missed from seven feet!), then tied us up by birdieing seventeen with a putt that hit the hole hard enough to jump inches in the air before falling back in, followed by a fifteen-footer for another birdie at eighteen. The one thing I knew for sure was that neither his putting stroke nor his confidence in it was going to evaporate overnight.

I HUSTLED to our rented house after my wind-down practice and media sessions that Saturday night because I wanted to see the James Bond movie *Dr. No* on television. Barbara and I watched it as we ate the veal piccata she'd cooked, the same meal she'd fixed before my 63 . . . ("Can't hurt," she said.) After that we watched another film before going to bed around midnight. As usual, I was asleep a couple of seconds after my head hit the pillow. The next morning—Father's Day, I won each of my four U.S. Opens on Father's Day—I killed some time by watching Tom and Jerry cartoons and playing catch with Michael, our youngest, who at age six was attending his first tournament, then reviewing some chapters of a book I was working on. I mention this simply to show how relaxed a guy can be coming to the final round of his national championship as a co-leader when he hasn't won anything in a couple of years.

The chief reason for my happy frame of mind was my high level of confidence in my golf game, but there was another one, too.

By 1980 I had enjoyed wonderful receptions in Augusta and Scotland, but never anything quite like what was happening at Baltusrol: an essentially New York crowd, supposedly the toughest there is, going increasingly nuts about Jack Nicklaus, as one writer later put it, "arising from the dead." From the moment I'd dipped into red scoreboard numbers on Thursday, both the size of the galleries accompanying our groups and their encouragement and applause seemed to have grown continuously. By Saturday some entrepreneur had sold hundreds of yellow tee shirts to young fans announcing "The Bear Is Back," and that message seemed to have become the theme of the championship. The applause and encouragement had thrilled and inspired me for the better part of three rounds, and I expected it to do the same on Sunday.

Although Keith Fergus and Lon Hinkle hung on for quite a time, and might have threatened more with hotter putters, my feeling right from warming up that memorable Sunday afternoon was of a match-play contest against Isao Aoki. Even though we both knew that, as always, the golf course remained our primary opponent, I'm pretty sure he felt the same. Whatever, I went one up when, to my astonishment and everyone else's, he three-putted the second hole, then two up at number three. He won a stroke back with a birdie at eight, but bogeyed nine to put me in front by two again. Thanks to a critical self-correction, that was the closest he would get.

Deep down inside, I suppose because it had happened so often over the previous two years, a little voice had periodically inquired, "Are the wheels going to come off again?" When it spoke up on the eighth hole, following a third straight drive into rough, I was able to quiet it for good with a precise diagnosis. Due to a touch of overanxiety, I had allowed my head to move forward and up a smidgeon too soon. From that moment on, using "Head steady" as my swing key, I never missed a shot, hitting every fairway and green in regulation or better, and gauging the distance of my approaches almost perfectly. There could well have been more birdies after the one at ten, but, walking to the seventeenth tee, I was content with the string of solid pars I'd put behind me. What did concern me, though, in light of his short-game wizardry and with two par-fives to close, was that I still led Aoki by only two strokes. I was certain I needed to birdie either seventeen or eighteen to avoid a playoff.

Corroboration came in the form of Isao's pitch to the green nestling down five feet from the hole at seventeen—a gimme, as I saw it —as I looked over a pitch of eighty-eight yards. When the pressure is greatest there is a strong urge to relieve it by rushing. I forced myself to think the shot through methodically, finally deciding to play to the right of the hole, both to protect against the trouble to the left and to leave myself an uphill putt. But which club? A three-quarter pitching wedge or a full sand wedge?

The greater the adrenaline flow, the tougher finesse or "part" shots become. Pumped up, you tend to take too long a backswing, then either hit the ball too far with a reciprocating through-swing or slow down through impact and leave the shot short or drag it off line, or both. You are better off, consequently, with whatever club you can swing most fully and freely, which in this case was the sand wedge. I made a nice pass with it, hitting the ball pin-high twenty-two feet to the right of the cup.

As I walked onto the green and began looking over my putt, I became even more certain than when watching Aoki's ball arrive there that he would make his five-footer, meaning that, if I missed, I would have to birdie eighteen to be sure of avoiding a playoff. It occurred to me that my putt was the kind I had made for many years when I really needed to, and also that I had not done this over the past two years. Determined to correct that, I continued my surveying until I felt certainty about both line and speed, then stood over the ball until I felt completely ready, then stroked. The ball rolled exactly as I'd planned and dead into the heart of the hole. The huge crowd roared crazily as I thrust my putter high and smiled a smile that Barbara for one will never forget. Afterward, she would say, "The look on his face as that putt dropped, eyes squeezed tight shut, so relieved, so ecstatic, showed the world just how much golf mattered to him, and how wonderful it was to know that winning wasn't over." In fact, she kept running the sequence through our video player because, she said, she'd never seen a look like that on my face before and never wanted to forget it. And, of course, Isao did make his putt.

That birdie at seventeen remains one of my sweetest memories. But there was, of course, still one hole to play. And for a moment, as

Isao's third shot, a little pitch from the right and short of the eighteenth green, rolled dead for the cup and an eagle three, it looked as though the two of us might have to go eighteen more holes on Monday. But the ball missed by an inch and rolled three feet by, and things eventually quieted down enough for me to stand over my ten-footer and, with two putts to win and a sharp drop in pressure, watch it dive into darkness for another birdie.

It finally was over. And Jack truly was back.

All through the back nine the crowd had been yelling and screaming at and for me, with hundreds of people trying to shake my hand or pat me on the back as the marshals and police struggled to escort me safely from the greens to the tees. After screaming "Jack! Jack! Jack!" all the way up eighteen, the fans had broken through the gallery ropes and past the marshals to encircle the green seemingly about fifty deep. The moment my putt dropped, those in the front began a wild charge toward me. I turned to face them and stuck up my hands like a traffic cop, and thankfully they stopped long enough for Isao to hole his putt for birdie. But bedlam broke out again the second his ball vanished, to a point where it became quite scary as well as thrilling, particularly after I was accidentally kicked hard in the shin and could do no better than limp along as the police and officials fought to clear our passage to the scorers' tent. It was by far the most emotional and warmest reaction to any of my wins in my own country, and it remains as sharp and wonderful in my memory all these years later as the day it happened.

Late that night after we finished with the presentation and the congratulations and the interviews, Michael's choice for dinner was McDonald's, so we celebrated there with hamburgers and milkshakes. In my case, not too many meals have tasted better.

By the summer of 1988, Jack Grout had become seriously ill and debilitated with the cancer that would end his life less than a year later. Even when feeling his lowest, though, he would drag himself out to the Loxahatchee Club in Jupiter whenever I was there, to watch me hit balls or simply to say hello. Frequently I had such a lump in my throat I could hardly respond adequately.

There was nothing I would have loved more than for Jack to have been able to join the party of friends and Memorial Tournament staff that attended *Golf Magazine*'s "Golfer of the Century" award celebration in New York that June, but it was clearly out of the question. By then, though, it had become my habit to call Jack regularly and shoot the breeze and generally try to cheer him up, and I did so right after getting home from receiving the award. A few days later I received this letter from him:

Dear Jack:

I appreciated your call more than I can tell you. As you might have guessed from my voice, I don't have a lot of pep these days. If I had had a little more energy, I would have told you a couple of things. Since I didn't, or couldn't, I have asked Bonnie [Jack's wife] *to help me write this letter.*

What I wanted to tell you is this. I know you have had so many honors over the years that they are becoming old hat. I think, nevertheless, that you ought to pay some attention to this latest "Player of the Century" honor. Don't go get a big head or anything like that, but at the same time don't shrug it off either. Those people must have given a lot of thought about it. I can tell you from personal experience that you won over a bunch of real good players. I haven't lived the entire hundred years, so I haven't known them all. But for you to have placed ahead of Jones, Hogan, Nelson, Hagen, Snead and Sarazen—to mention a few I did know—was some kind of an accomplishment.

I think I know how you did it, Jack. I used to think that the greatest thing in the world was high achievement in sport. Now that I have more time to sit around and think about things, I have decided that even greater than high achievement in sport is high achievement in sportsmanship. Your dad and your mother taught you about the second one, and I think that's why you won.

Whether I taught you anything about golf or not is not for me to say. In your own heart you know whether I did or not, and I'll take my chances on that. If your development had stopped with your understanding of the mechanics of the game, Jack, it is possible that some of those other great players would have beat you out. I can tell you that several of them know just about all there is to know about golf.

What you have going for you, however, was born into you and then nurtured by your home life. When Charlie told you you couldn't play anymore if you threw another club, he did you a great favor, Jack.

Don't get me wrong. You wouldn't be the "Player of the Century" if you weren't a heckuva player. But so is Arnold a heckuva player, and Byron, and the rest of them. And they are all great sports. After the judges gave it a lot of thought, though, they gave the honor to the guy who is a great sport and a great sportsman. As far as I am concerned you are the greatest golfer who ever swung a club in the entire history of the game.

I wish you the very best in the coming years. Needless to say, I'd like to be some thirty years younger, so I could share some more of the good times.

All things considered, however, I don't think I have any reason to complain.

Sincerely,
Jack

Great teacher that he was, Jack Grout was an even greater human being. I miss my friend still, and am sure I always will.

19

The 1980 PGA Championship

An Unbelievable Year

THE week following the U.S. Open in 1980, Bob Gilder won the Canadian Open over the course of the oldest club in North America, Royal Montreal, by two strokes from Jerry Pate and Leonard Thompson. Considering my upbeat mood, I finished disappointingly in a tie for thirteenth, eight strokes off the pace. Then, following a much-needed rest from tournament play, came another disappointment in the shape of a tie for fourth in the British Open at much-loved Muirfield, nine strokes back of a red-hot Tom Watson. Two weeks later I won the PGA Championship at the Oak Hill Country Club in Rochester, New York, by seven strokes from Andy Bean.

I've never been a heavy reader of press reports of my achievements, but you won't need to ask why I got a kick out of Dan Jenkins's lead in his *Sports Illustrated* story the following week:

> With that flying right elbow on his backswing and those small hands that force him to use the unorthodox interlocking grip and all of that time he takes standing over his putts, the chances are that Jack

Nicklaus never will win thirty major championships. It has to catch up with him sooner or later, any golfing expert can see that.

Yeah, sure. Jack won his nineteenth major—six more than Bobby Jones or anyone else, ever—last week by turning the PGA Championship into a hunting expedition in which you were supposed to find the rest of the field. But you could see that because of Nicklaus' age, which is forty, his desire and the mechanics of his game were deteriorating at the finish.

He made a bogey on the next-to-last hole and won his fifth PGA by seven strokes, not eight. Oak Hill was definitely the beginning of the end because the course had been made tougher to prevent anyone from shooting an embarrassing 275, five under par, as Lee Trevino had back in 1968 when he won the U.S. Open. And on this tree-infested, rough-gnarled, water-patrolled layout, which had been carefully, even evilly, doctored, the best Jack could do was fire rounds of 70, 69, 66 and 69 for a total of 274.

Dan went on to suggest that, a few days before the championship began, I would probably have taken 274 for three rounds of Oak Hill, and he wasn't far off. That's because, over the nine weeks since Baltusrol, my putting stroke had steadily deteriorated until it finally vanished off the face of the earth.

The lowest points were forty putts in an exhibition round with Tom Watson in Lake Tahoe and four three-putts each day in President Ford's tournament in Vail the week before the PGA. On the theory that my faithful old George Low blade might finally have lost its magic, I obtained half a dozen different putters, and began working with them immediately on arrival at Muirfield Village for my final PGA tuning. A Ping A-Blade similar to the one then being used so successfully by Watson—his British Open win that July was his third in five years—raised my hopes for a couple of rounds, but died on me the next time out. I'd abandoned White-Fang, the center-shafted Bull's Eye that had helped me win the 1967 U.S. Open, after putting poorly with it in defending at Oak Hill a year later. Now, I retrieved it from the trophy case at Muirfield Village and stuck it in my bag. In a word, I was desperate. And then, as happened so often over my career when it was most urgently needed, along came salvation.

The Monday before the PGA was Jack Nicklaus Day in Columbus, a tribute from my hometown folks that I greatly appreciated. With the festivities concluded, however, I felt compelled to head yet again for the practice putting green and more searching. Our eldest, Jackie, by then a solid player and a longtime observer of my game, decided to join me. After watching me putt for a minute or two, he asked, "Dad, why do you keep breaking off your stroke?" Click! As we worked together on improving my setup and getting me to swing the head of the club fully through the ball, instead of quitting at impact and pulling it left, putts began to drop one after another. By the time we got home the sky was black, but in my head light had replaced dark.

FOLLOWING Lee Trevino's record-tying score of 275 in winning the 1968 U.S. Open at Oak Hill—the first time anyone broke 70 for all four rounds of the championship—the United States Golf Association, when asked by the club about hosting future Opens, suggested that it might no longer be difficult enough to merit that honor. The result was some doctoring of the old Donald Ross course by George and Tom Fazio that provoked much complaining by the players during practice for the 1980 PGA Championship. Tom Weiskopf, for instance, told the press, "I'm going to start an organization called the Classic Golf Course Preservation Society. Members get to carry loaded guns in case they see anybody touching a Donald Ross course." Lee Trevino commented: "I just feel sorry for the members. They have to play Oak Hill all year long."

Having long ago learned how disliking a course can hurt your performance on it, I kept my thoughts on the design changes and the brutal rough to myself, particularly as I thought Oak Hill generally was in fine condition, and especially after shooting 65 in my final practice round, including an ace at perhaps the most criticized of the new holes, the fifteenth. Putting by then probably as well as I ever had, all I wanted was for the championship to begin.

There's little to say about my par-matching opening round of 70, except that, with strong tee-to-green play and thirty-two putts, I didn't hole as much as the quality of my stroke kept leading me to expect. The reverse occurred the second day, when I struggled much of the time getting to the greens, but kept one-putting from sizable distances, once to save bogey and five times for par, before dropping a long putt for birdie at eighteen and a round of 69. The scrambling was tiring, but also satisfying in that it left me only a stroke behind the leader, Gil Morgan, tied in second place with Lon Hinkle.

Dull as it may be for fans, the greatest feeling for a contender in an important tournament is that of running away and hiding—of forging so far ahead of the field that only a major mishap could steal away victory. For the first fourteen holes of the third round of the 1980 PGA, that feeling enveloped me as strongly as it ever had in a major championship. It was fed by an opening birdie from fifty feet, a 1-iron that almost went in the hole at the par-three third, then five more birdies off putts ranging from five to twenty feet that dropped me to six under par for the day and into a seven-stroke lead. By the end of the round, however, my euphoria had evaporated.

It began to disappear with a three-putt from under thirty feet for a bogey at fifteen, the hole I'd aced four days previously. More departed as I scrambled for par at sixteen after hooking so badly from the tee that the ball would have gone out of bounds but for catching a snow fence, then failing to capitalize on my luck by bunkering the approach. The little that was left vanished with a bogey at the long and difficult par-four seventeenth off a bunkered 3-wood second shot. My predominant feeling walking from the eighteenth green after holing from ten feet for a hard par was relief. I had shot 66, an excellent score that would give me a three-stroke lead over Hinkle and six over Morgan and Andy Bean at the end of the day, and prove to be the low round of the championship. But the way I'd played those final four holes was unsettling to say the least. After managing to joke with the writers that I'd wanted to come in after those fabulous first fourteen holes, but had been made to play the last four against my will, I hurried to the practice tee to work on my hand action. Basically, I had stopped using my hands after my second shot to fourteen.

Despite the quality of my game and the size of my lead, I was nervous much of the morning before the final round, and welcomed the feeling for the same reason I had so many times before: it would stop me from becoming complacent. Three cleanly made pars to open settled me nicely, and by the time I reached the turn after six more, putting me five strokes ahead of Lon and Andy, with everyone else eight or more adrift, it was time to just enjoy the day. Both swinging and putting as well as I ever had in a major, I even started thinking about the PGA seventy-two-hole record of 271 after birdieing the eleventh and twelfth holes, but dropped the thought after missing for birdie at fourteen. The final tally of one of the easiest competitive rounds I've ever played was 69, giving me a seven-stroke win over Andy Bean and the biggest victory margin in the championship since it changed from match to stroke play in 1958.

The win produced many other satisfying statistics: my nineteenth major championship (if you count the Amateurs); tied with Rochester-born-and-bred Walter Hagen for most PGA wins at five apiece; two majors in a year for the fifth time; only the third golfer to win the U.S. Open and PGA in the same year (Gene Sarazen and Ben Hogan were the others).

It also produced some amusing comments from other players: "They redid a course so only one guy could break par on it, and he did." "Why did anyone start saying he was over the hill? It only made him mad." "Doesn't he know he's middle-aged?" "The field averaged 74.6 strokes, he averaged 68.5. Does that mean he's six strokes better than anyone else in the world?" And my favorite, from Ed Sneed: "Who does he think he is, Jack Nicklaus again?"

With the help of my old friends Jack Grout and Phil Rodgers, and finally a timely tip from son Jackie, plus my own stubbornness, the answer had become yes. And it resulted in what I still think of as the most unbelievable year of my career.

I HAVE tried to tell my story to this point more or less chronologically. However, looking so deeply back into my life brought more to mind than could be comfortably fitted into that structure. Pretty much at random, here are some of those memories, thoughts and happenings:

Competitive Stimulus

Charlie Nicklaus, my father, was extremely competitive all his life, which made him a great needler. Even when he had a bad ankle, he would race me to the movies or wherever and still beat me. Then he'd say something like, "You must be the slowest kid in town. How do you expect to be an athlete?" It was a way of goading me to do better. And it worked, because, after a while, I joined the track team without any pushing from him. And pretty soon he was coming in second.

There's no doubting where I got my love of needling.

Advice to Barbara

Barbara will never forget the day she was sitting on the porch at the Augusta National during my first Masters as a professional in 1962, bemoaning the fact that she missed her baby, Jackie, who was eight months old at that time and whom we had left at home. The challenge she was still dealing with at that time was the lack of routine in the life I'd led her into. As she said later, "It was such a different way of living. My father was a teacher. He left at eight in the morning, and if he wasn't home by three o'clock, my mother panicked. I'd never traveled farther than the next state, and I'd taken a month to prepare for that."

Although Barbara didn't know it, because they had never met, the woman sitting next to her on the porch at Augusta was Aleta Mangrum, the wife of the 1946 U.S. Open champion, Lloyd Mangrum. Suddenly this lady turned around and looked hard at Barbara and pointed her finger at her and said, "Listen, little girl. You had Jack a long time before that baby was born, and you hope to have him a long time after that baby is gone. So you just grow up now and *be a wife.*"

Not knowing the woman, this little homily really shocked Barbara. But it registered, too. Years later she would tell me that, every time I called from some place on the tour and wanted her to come out for the weekend, she would see Aleta's finger pointing at her, and would pack a bag and get on a plane. What Aleta made her realize, she says, is that, despite its appearance of glamour to some people, the life of the tour pro, just going from a golf course to an empty hotel room and back again, is a limited and lonely one, and that she had better help alleviate that situation even when it would have been much easier to say, "Oh, thanks for asking, but I've got a couple of kids in diapers here, so I'll see you Sunday night."

About ten years after that incident, Barbara was able to tell Aleta how much she appreciated her speaking up. I never had the opportunity, so, Aleta, thanks from me too.

Study the tour and I think you will find that guys whose marriages haven't been too great have either had a lot of ups and downs in their careers or never achieved their full potential. Barbara's supportiveness and selflessness made it possible for me to escape that trap. For the benefit of the entire family unit, she put her aspirations and wishes second to mine so that I could do what I wanted and needed to do to make myself into the best golfer I could become, without domestic turmoil. Without that, I would probably have been just another tour golfer. In fact, I think Barbara deserves credit for a lot of my major championship wins.

Barbara has told and continues to tell her Aleta Mangrum story to many of the young wives on the tour. Then she'll tell them, "If you're married to a golfer who's a family man and really enjoys being with his wife and kids, it's impossible for you to have a career because you just have to be always available if the marriage is going to work. You've got to be where he is when he is, and not worry about your own deal. If you look around on the golf tour, you'll find that very few bachelors have been successful. The successful ones are married with a stable family that travels with them as much as possible."

I hope the young wives listen hard, because, selfish as it sounds coming from me, she is right.

Barbara's Parents

Barbara Bash, as she was when I married her, grew up the daughter of a mathematics teacher in Clintonville, Ohio. Here's how she once described her folks:

"My father never made more than seven thousand dollars a year, yet my brother Ray and I never wanted for anything. I look back on it now and just don't know how they did it. Stanley and Helen Bash were good people, solid people. I can't think of anything they ever did that wasn't good."

Barbara, by Her Friends

Barbara Nicklaus is an anchor for more than her family. Says one of her closest friends, Lee Neal, "I'll call her up and ask, 'Got a little couch time?' She has such a gentle spirit. She's always so caring. I tease her about being Florence Nightingale. She's the best nurse in town."

Tim Rosaforte once wrote about these qualities of hers in a magazine profile:

"Lee Neal had surgery once in Miami. Who drove her down and back twice? Barbara Nicklaus. Lee Neal once broke her arm in four places. Who drove her to the hospital? Barbara Nicklaus.

"When young Jackie was four, he cut off half of his finger in an ice-crusher. Who saved the finger by not panicking and getting him to the doctor so it could be sewn back on? Barbara Nicklaus. When (tour golfer) Bruce Fleischer's wife was in the hospital recovering from surgery, Barbara Nicklaus drove down to Miami regularly with home-cooked meals. When her great friend from Columbus, Janice Savic, was dying of cancer, she entrusted Barbara Nicklaus to give everyone their marching orders before passing on. When Laura Norman needed someone to lean on when her husband Greg was getting ripped in the press, she sought the advice of . . . Barbara Nicklaus.

" 'You can't really compare her to anybody,' says Mrs. Shark. 'With Barbara, you can't say, "Gee, I'd like to be like her as a wife." She's beyond that, just like Jack is as a golfer. In his field, no one has ever done what Jack has done. I think the wives feel the same way about Barbara.'

"She was a Brownie leader for daughter Nan. She was scorekeeper for her sons' basketball teams at the Benjamin School. Somebody had to keep coach Mickey Neal organized. 'Remember, Mickey,' she would say, 'you have two time-outs left . . .'

"She's the real Jack-of-all-trades in the Nicklaus household. On the kitchen counter, the center of the Nicklaus universe, is a golf ball box with a Golden Bear on it. 'Open it up,' she says. Inside are nails and screws and staples and tacks. Picture-hanging supplies. It belongs to Barbara Nicklaus, the handyperson of the house.

" 'If I can't fix it, we call a repairman,' she says. 'Right after we got married, I asked Jack to put up a cup rack for me. Mind you, it was three screws. Forty-five minutes and a few choice words later, his shirt was wringing wet and he still didn't have the screws in. . . .'

"When they were putting the finishing touches on the clubhouse at Muirfield Village, it was Barbara Nicklaus who wielded the hammer and hung the pictures. She had her initials on that hammer. She was proud of it.

"Most people probably think the Nicklauses have a cast of helpers to do the cooking and cleaning, a butler to answer the door, a chauffeur to ride them around town. Wrong. One year Barbara felt bad because she had to have the office Christmas party catered. Of course, there were only two hundred and twenty guests over at the house. Five days prior to that, however, the Nicklauses had the Benjamin School football team over. With the players' parents, that made for a casual get-together of eighty-five. Barbara did the cooking for them, although Jack did pitch in by firing up the grill and barbecuing tenderloins.

" 'The amazing thing is she does her own clean-up,' says Lee Neal. 'She never leaves the kitchen until everything is picked up and out of the way.'

"Amazing is the best adjective to describe her. . . . She can remember somebody's name she met once twenty years ago on a golf course in Scotland. She can find time for charity work and not let it interfere with her family. She convinced Jack to go up and down eighteen times in one day in a helicopter to benefit the Center for Family Services. She has donated his cars to charity auctions. She more than tithes at her church—Trinity United Methodist in Palm Beach Gardens can thank Barbara Nicklaus for its van. The Fellowship of Christian Athletes golf ministry can thank her for more than a million dollars. . . ."

What can a fellow say? Barbara is the way she's always been, which is just like her mother: always doing things for other people before she does anything for herself.

What a wife! What a woman! What a lucky guy!

Barbara on My True Nature

Particularly when I've stuck my foot in my mouth about something, Barbara will sometimes get asked about my true nature—like, am I more of a grizzly bear than a golden bear? Her answer is that I'm just a big old teddy bear at heart. "He intimidates people with that blunt manner and those steely blue eyes of his," she will say, "but there's a teddy bear behind them." I'm not as sure about that as she is, but it's true that my bark is usually worse than my bite.

Big Catch

I've always loved fishing and hunting. Perhaps the most fun I've had at either was catching a 1,358-pound black marlin in a six-hour twenty-five-minute battle off the Great Barrier Reef right before the 1978 Australian Open at the Australian Golf Club in Sydney, which I'd recently redesigned. Some of the pros and other friends and I had spent a week fishing out of Cairns on the north coast of Queensland with my old friend Kerry Packer, the Australian media magnate, who was involved in sponsoring the Open. With tired arms and back, I shot 73 in the first round, but then a course record 66, followed by

74 in a big wind and 71 in an even bigger wind and rain the last day to beat Ben Crenshaw by six shots for my sixth victory in the event..

Bill Casper

When I first went out on tour in 1962, I would always look over the lists of who was playing in the tournaments I entered to see who my chief competition was likely to be. Arnold Palmer obviously ranked highly, as did the other member of the so-called "Big Three," Gary Player. Many people who knew golf at that time felt that the trio should really have been a quartet—"The Big Four," if you will. I certainly would not have argued with them, because the name Bill Casper stood right up there alongside Arnie's and Gary's as far as I was concerned.

Mostly, I believe, because of his conservative playing style and unassuming manner, Bill Casper never enjoyed the recognition his record deserves, but there is no question that he is one of golf's all-time greats. Even today, thirty years past his peak, his fifty-one victories, including two U.S. Opens and a Masters, rank sixth on the all-time PGA Tour win list, and only Arnold Palmer among American players comes close to his points total in a record-equaling eight Ryder Cup appearances. He won at least once every year on tour between 1956 and 1971, was year-long low scorer five times and Player of the Year twice. Among his nine victories as a senior are a Senior Open and a Tournament Players Championship.

I believe Bill achieved most of his successes fading the ball from left to right, but recall him handling courses that favored a draw just as easily and effectively. Either way, what stands out about him in my mind was his mastery of both ends of the game—highly efficient driving and a magnificent short game. If he had a weakness it was the long irons, chiefly because he liked to keep the ball down, to hit most shots relatively low—which made him, of course, a fine wind player. Accepting this weakness, he had the intelligence and discipline in winning the 1970 Masters to play to the par-five greens in three shots except on a couple of occasions, despite knowing that many of his adversaries would be getting home in two at least half the time. That is a great example of one of the least appreciated qualities of the great players, the will and the smarts not to beat one's self, as well as the supreme testimonial to his short game.

There has probably never been a better wedge player than Bill

Casper, and he was also magnificent from bunkers and a great chipper. And what took the pressure off all those shots, of course, was his putting. Knowing you are rarely going to miss from inside ten feet, as he did in his prime, does wonders for your confidence about the little recovery shots. Bill's greens-in-regulation stats may not have been the greatest, but I doubt if anyone topped him in getting the ball up and down.

If too few fans recognized how great a golfer was Billy Casper, even fewer, I am sure, have gotten to know how fine a man he is. Family and his deep religious faith have been his top priorities, and no one in the game holds more dearly to enjoying life off the course, generally in the company of treasured old friends.

When we played the Memorial Tournament in tribute to Bill Casper in 1996, we honored him as is traditional on the Wednesday. Knowing he would be in the area, he volunteered to return on the Sunday to be part of our closing ceremonies. This gesture typifies one of golf's all-time nicest champions.

Greg Norman

I liked Greg Norman from the moment we first met, which was on the first tee of the opening round of the Australian Open at the Australian Golf Club in Sydney in 1976.

Then age twenty-one and only four months a professional, this big strong Queenslander with the blond good looks of a surfing star had stunned his countrymen the previous week by winning an important tournament in Adelaide by five strokes from two of the nation's top players, David Graham and Graham Marsh. Greg told me later that he had begun golf when he was sixteen and dropped from twenty-seven handicap to zero in two years, largely with the help of two of my instructional books given to him by his mother, *Golf My Way* and *My 55 Ways to Lower Your Golf Score.* Perhaps that increased his nervousness about being paired with me, because he cold-topped his opening tee shot and ended up with an embarrassing 80. But he'd calmed down sufficiently by the second round to show me his real potential in matching par, and he eventually finished in the middle of the pack.

After his unhappy first round I sat and talked with Greg for a while in the locker room, trying to help him pick up his spirits. Then, as we talked again after the second round, I told him I thought he was already a good enough player to come to America, and offered to help in any way I could if he decided to do so. The upshot was that he made his U.S. debut in the 1977 Memorial Tournament, missing the cut by three shots but, as I understand it, looking from then on to the PGA Tour as his ultimate goal.

Over the next fifteen years, and particularly after he and his family moved for a while to within a couple of wood shots of our Florida home, Greg and I became close enough friends for me to feel comfortable with offering him a little unsolicited advice the night before the final round of the 1986 British Open, in which he held a one-stroke lead.

I should probably mention that this is not a common occurrence among professional tournament golfers, if for no other reason than how bad the adviser feels if the advisee listens and nods but then goes out and loses. However, Greg had taken a lot of media heat for costing himself the chance of playing off with me for the Masters three months previously with a poor shot to the final green, and I did not want to see that situation exacerbated. So, at what seemed an appropriate moment, I got up from our dinner table in the Turnberry Hotel and walked over to his and asked if I could talk with him for a moment. He said "Sure," and pulled his chair away from the table, and I grabbed a spare chair and told him that what I wanted to talk about was the thing I believed had caused his miscue at Augusta, quickly adding that if he didn't want me to mention it I would be happy to simply get up and leave. "No, fire away," he said. "It doesn't bother me. I'll see whether it works."

What I then told Greg was that, as had happened to me with the adrenaline gushing, his left hand grip pressure had become too strong. This made him lift the club and extend it away from him going back, rather than swinging it around his body as he normally did, resulting in the shot being blocked to the right. We talked a little more about why that sort of thing happens, and how to counter it, then he thanked me and I returned to my table. He has never told me whether my thoughts helped him or not, but it was clear that they did him no harm as he put together a fine 69 the next day to win his first major going away.

Greg would win another British Open in 1993, and enjoy periods as the world's top-rated golfer following remakes of his swing, his physical condition, and his mental attitude. But he would also suffer too many more near misses in the majors for a golfer of his talent and dedication to the game, including an infamous collapse in the 1996

Masters after leading by six shots entering the final round. Much as I've been asked for one by the media, I don't have the answer to why these things happened, except to say that there are times when aggressiveness will achieve wonders on the golf course, and other times when it will kill you stone dead.

You have to admire Greg Norman, though, for what he has achieved, and also for his contribution to the fans' enjoyment of tournament golf worldwide. Win or lose, he possesses a quality that allowed another aggressive golfer by the name of Arnold Palmer to make a great contribution to the game: charisma.

Tiger Woods

I got a close-up view of Tiger Woods's capabilities when Arnie and I played a practice round with him at the 1996 Masters. Afterwards I told the media that he was not only the most fundamentally sound golfer I'd ever seen but an exceptionally composed individual for his years, as well as a most pleasant and appealing young man.

It has been suggested that I went overboard in saying that Tiger had the talent to win more Masters than the ten Arnie and I captured together, but after what happened a few months later—a third straight U.S. Amateur followed by three victories in his first nine tour events—it may not have appeared so far out. Tiger clearly possesses all of the physical tools and seemingly the mental qualities to rewrite the record books, which leaves only the questions of desire and physical well-being. He did get awfully rich awfully fast once he turned pro, but if he can put that aside sufficiently to retain his competitive hunger, along with handling fame, his long-term impact on the game could be awesome.

I'm often asked since Tiger hit the headlines how such a slightly built person can generate so much power. Beyond fine physical conditioning and superb swing fundamentals, the key lies in the speed with which Tiger releases the immense torque he creates in the backswing by winding his upper body so forcefully against the resistance of his lower half. A friend of a friend of mine who owns professional videotape-editing equipment that measures motion in thousandths of seconds compared the speed of Tiger's hips unwinding from the completion of the backswing to impact with a dozen or so other top tour players. Tiger was 20 percent faster than anyone else, and as much as 50 percent quicker than some players.

It's great to see such a talented and attractive figure enlivening the game.

Gambling at Golf

In the old days, many professionals used to figure on making some part of their living by betting on themselves against wealthy amateurs, or even against fellow pros in tournament practice rounds. With so much prize money available, only a handful of today's tour golfers seem to enjoy playing for high stakes, more, I imagine, for the fun of competing hard than the cash itself.

Gambling big at golf has never appealed to me. My limit is a twenty-dollar bet, and then only when I'm up against players I know can easily afford any losses they may incur. Most of the golf I play outside of tournaments is with family or close friends. If I beat them, I feel I've hustled them on strokes, or that, if I give them enough strokes to beat me, I don't really have a game. So my limit with friends is usually a five-dollar bet.

Speechmaking

Like everyone else, I lack confidence in my ability to do certain things. Speechmaking is perhaps the best example. If I'm going to make a speech I want it to be a good one—as good as my golf game. But I've never had the time nor inclination to make the effort to achieve that. As a result, when I've agreed to make a formal speech, I've always fretted about it for days in advance. That lack of confidence is the chief reason I go out of my way to avoid making speeches.

Superstition

If continuing to do things that have worked for me in the past is superstition, then I'm superstitious. Certainly friends who know about things like my three-pennies habit think that's the case.

I never play a round of competitive golf without three pennies in my pocket. This dates from years ago when some incident I don't remember got me figuring that, if I carried only one penny and lost it, I'd be without a ball-marker, and that if I had two pennies and lost one and a fellow player needed to borrow one to mark his ball, I'd still be out of ball-markers. So, logical or not, three pennies it has been ever since. Also, I always mark the ball with the tails side of the penny up.

Horticulture

As a course designer, I've always been a tree and plant nut, hating to have to cut down whatever nature has put there. Over the years this led to an ever-growing interest in cultivating tropical trees and exotic plants at our Florida home. For years now I've greatly enjoyed being able to pick all kinds of fruits and flowers from our garden for our family table and those of friends, or just wander through what has become, I'm told, one of the most extensive and representative private gardens in our part of the country.

I've also picked up just enough horticultural knowledge to drive the good people who care for our grounds to deeply wish I would stick to the picking and admiring.

Children Challenges

One of the most difficult challenges Barbara and I have had to meet over the years has been protecting our children from the wrong kind of media exposure, which means attention deriving purely from their name rather than from their achievements. All of them have had more than their share of this at various times, and, I'm sorry to say, will probably never be entirely free from it.

A classic example of the kind of thing I'm talking about occurred when Gary was fourteen and playing in an age-group golf tournament. An ESPN reporter stuck a microphone in his face and asked, "Are you going to follow in your father's footsteps?" I thought Gary's answer was perfect. "How do I know?" he said. "I'm only in the ninth grade." A few years before that, his brother Jackie told a reporter at a junior tournament who was pestering him, "You know, I wish you'd wait and talk to me when I've done something for myself, and not just because I'm my father's son."

After *Sports Illustrated* imposed huge pressure on Gary by featuring him in a lead story and putting him on its cover, he actually quit playing golf for a while. But his innate toughness eventually pulled him through that spell, as it would later when he experienced some difficult times as a neophyte professional. Also, as he got older and better at the game, and wise enough to recognize that the attention wasn't going away, he decided to try to enjoy it rather than fighting it.

Because he had all of the names, Jack William Nicklaus II probably suffered more difficult questions and thoughtless remarks than any of the others, and, as the above instance illustrates, he also handled it extremely well. For instance, if he was playing in a high-school tournament and way off the lead, but people were still taking his picture, he'd just smile quietly and go about his business. In college, where he was endlessly quizzed on how it felt to be Jack Nicklaus's son, his answer was always the same: "I really don't know because I've never been anyone else."

Aware that things would only get worse in this regard if he chose golf as a career, we actually tried to steer Jackie away from playing professionally. Then, when he decided that he wanted to try it, and we talked about what he would have to endure off the course, he assured us he could handle it. And he did, extremely well, with answers like "I'm out here for myself, not for anyone else," and "All I can do is try to become the best golfer I can become," and "My name doesn't make the game any harder or any easier for me. I'm thankful for the opportunities to play that I wouldn't otherwise have, but after that it doesn't hit the shots for me—I still have to do that."

Despite never being into golf as much as his brothers, our second son, Steve, has also had his share of tough name-related situations, and has handled them well. Most occurred during his football days at Florida State, but he was always able to put them out of mind and get on with his life.

Because she also never really got into golf, our daughter, Nan, experienced less of this kind of treatment. However, as this is written, our youngest, Michael, has gotten his golf game to a point where he's beginning to go through the media mill. Thankfully, he's taking his cue, both mentally and response-wise, from his brothers.

Barbara believes that the strong relationships I was able to form with all of our children helped them greatly in getting through what otherwise might have been troubling experiences. A little while back she told a writer:

> Jack was always there for them, to the point even of flying across the country to watch their Little League or basketball or football games. As they got older they recognized what an expression of love and caring that was, and how tremendously proud of them he was, and they became equally caring about and proud of him in return. They always behaved like pals, really good friends who are totally comfortable with each other.

> Also, because Jack had to be apart from the children so much, he was never able to make himself into much of a disciplinarian when he was with them. As Stevie once put it, "He's not The Great Santini," referring to the marine colonel in the movie of that name who treated his kids like they were members of his platoon. Most of the reprimanding that needed to be done around our place came from me. Gary summed it up pretty well one Mother's Day when he gave me a coffee mug that said, "Thanks for getting me through my teenage years and for remembering those three little words 'Don't tell Dad.' After I'd admired it and thanked him, he said, "You know, what it really should have said is 'Don't tell Mom'."

"I'm sure all of this made brushing off the negative stuff much easier for them than if their father's feelings for them, and theirs for him, had been less solid."

Few words of hers have given me greater pleasure.

Happy Times at Pinehurst

It's natural for golfers to favor courses where they've won, but Pinehurst No. 2 will always be extra special for me for more than my victories in the North and South Amateur there in 1959 and the World Open in 1975.

Although the course was hard, fast and badly browned-out, the more I played it in that long ago North and South tournament, the more impressed I became with the way it constantly challenged both my mind and my muscles, despite rarely looking all that difficult. The first thing that struck me was the premium both on figuring the correct line for the tee shot, then achieving it: most drives just slightly misdirected, even if they landed in the fairway, would end up skittering into the woods. Then there was the demand for carefully figured bump-and-run shots from tight lies almost every time you missed a green. The scoring that week reflected Donald Ross's genius at creating these and other subtle difficulties. Bill Campbell and Gene Andrews and I tied for the qualifying medal with four-over-par 76s. Then, even though I enjoyed a couple of hot rounds, I was over par in squeezing past Gene, one up, on the thirty-sixth hole of the final, and a lot over for the tournament overall.

The next time I saw the course, on arriving for the 1974 World Open, I was shocked. Four years previously a development company had bought what was America's first golf resort from its creators and longtime guardians, the Tufts family. In the course of "modernizing" No. 2, the new owners had grassed in the famous sandy waste areas bordering the fairways, converted the greens from Bermuda to bent grass, and poured what must have been oceans of water on everything. The old lady was now wall-to-wall green and lush. You hit the ball from the tee and it went splat. You hit the ball to the green and it went splat. It was a completely different golf course. Nevertheless, Ross's genius still shone through, and particularly to me, in the absence of water and trees as strategic hazards. After losing in a playoff, I remember telling Dan Jenkins, then of *Sports Illustrated,* "So, I lost another golf tournament. But I never enjoyed playing a golf course more. I learned at least five things about design this week, and on a course more than fifty years old." Coming back the following year and winning the World Open in another playoff, against Bill Casper, was even more fun.

But my most memorable visit to Pinehurst came ten years after that, by which time the No. 2 course had largely been restored to its traditional condition by more golf-knowledgeable and history-conscious owners.

Having heard me so often extol Donald Ross courses, and this most famous of them being only a little over an hour's drive from Chapel Hill, it was no surprise when, in 1980, Jackie made Pinehurst No. 2 a factor in his decision to accept a golf scholarship to the University of North Carolina. Once there, he and other squad members would ride over and play Ross's masterpiece whenever they got a free weekend, which surely was a factor in what happened five years later.

Prior to him teeing up in the 1985 North and South, the squad had won seven of eight of the tournaments it played, with strong contributions from Jackie mostly due to improvements in his chipping and putting. That fine form continued as, following a 4-and-3 win over Peter Persons in the semifinal, he defeated former pro Tom McKnight in the final by 2 and 1 with the help of eight birdies.

Before this I had tended to get very nervous watching Jackie play tournaments, mostly because I was worried about where he would hit the ball next. He had a tendency to play a stretch of holes well, then hit one bad shot and go to pieces. For quite a while I had been trying to impress on him that a round of golf takes a lot of time, and therefore requires a lot of patience. Along with strong iron play and putting, his self-management that week was the key to his victory. There were some tense moments in his six matches, but he never needed to go to the eighteenth hole. The longer I'd watched him, the less concerned I'd become about the eventual outcome.

His mother told the new champion as we started out that evening for Ohio and the Memorial Tournament that I had been so excited I'd stepped on her feet all day without realizing it, and I admitted to him that it wasn't easy being the father of a famous golfer. In truth, as my lackluster performance at Muirfield Village proved, I was emotionally drained by the whole experience. But also the proudest dad on planet Earth.

President Ford

Former President Gerald Ford is one of the nicest people you could ever meet, and Barbara and I treasure the friendship that evolved as we came to spend time with him and his family at golf events, then on skiing vacations in the Vail area. Both of us feel that, if people could have gotten to know him a little better, he would have been elected to a second term in the White House.

Typical of his selflessness and thoughtfulness was his response to a letter I wrote him when, after partnering each other in the Crosby for a number of years, I got a sense that he wasn't enjoying the tournament as much as he once had, due to the effect of so much walking and a knee problem that was increasingly troubling him. In the letter I basically told him that, if he wanted to go on playing with me that would be great, but that he wouldn't be letting me down if he decided it was time to call it quits. I said that someday I would like to partner with my son Jackie, but that Jackie had a lot of years of golf ahead of him so there was no hurry on that score.

A few days later I got a call from the President—I've never called him anything else—in which he told me right off the bat to go ahead and play with Jackie, and then why I should do so. "When I was in Congress," he said, "I went years and years without being able to do things with my sons, and I deeply regret that. The demands of public life stopped me from enjoying and helping my boys grow up, and that was a mistake. So there is no way in the world I'm going to contribute to you making the same mistake. You just go ahead and play with Jackie and don't give it another thought."

Funny?

One of the great honors in golf is to be invited to serve as a ceremonial starter for the Masters Tournament. Scots-born Freddie McLeod and Jock Hutchinson were the dew-sweepers during most of my best years at Augusta National, followed by Gene Sarazen, Byron Nelson and Sam Snead.

As that distinguished trio reached the age where they limited their efforts to an opening drive, the writers started conjecturing about Arnie and me eventually taking over the task. This led Bev Norwood, whose dry wit is much appreciated in golf's media centers, to come up with a joke that I still don't think is particularly funny but that others have found hilarious.

Within golf's inner circles, Arnold's hardness of hearing and my less than perfect vision have been well known for years. According to Bev, here's the scenario when we come together for the first time early in the morning of a Masters Thursday.

I get up on the tee first and give the ball a good smack, then squint anxiously down the fairway. "Where'd it go?" I ask my old sparring partner. Looking at me blankly, then cupping his hand to his ear, Arnie replies, "What'd you say?"

May we both stick around long enough for this to actually happen!

Enhancing the Ryder Cup

The United States won eighteen of the first twenty-two Ryder Cup matches, mostly by lopsided margins. By the time of the 1977 contest at Royal Lytham and St. Annes in England—my fifth time on the squad and another easy victory for the U.S.—it had become clear to me that the imbalance inherent in pitting a nation that then possessed about fifteen million golfers against two countries, Britain and Ireland, with barely a million between them was turning the match into a nonevent, at least so far as the American public was concerned, and also to some extent for its top players.

I had enjoyed a friendly relationship with Lord Derby, the long-time president of the British PGA, for many years. During the 1977 match, I asked him if we could talk, as a result of which we sat down together one evening at the Clifton Arms Hotel, where both of the teams were staying.

"John," I told his lordship, "please don't think me presumptuous, but I want to be honest about this. The American players love to get on the Ryder Cup team, because there is no greater honor in sport than representing one's country. But the matches just aren't competitive enough." Also, I told him I thought the British and Irish players must be frustrated too, if only by the futility of the results. We talked about the players' attitudes a while, then he asked me how I thought we could fix things. I told him the best way I could think of would be to match the U.S.A. against a team from the entire European Tour, which by then had brought all the countries of the Continent together with Great Britain and Ireland.

A proud traditionalist among a nation of traditionalists, his lordship seemed initially shocked at the idea of going beyond British and Irish golfers, but eventually he told me he thought there was some merit in the idea and asked me to write him a letter formalizing my case that he could put before his fellow PGA officers. I did so, with a copy to Don Padgett, then the president of our PGA. The crux of my argument could be summed up in the sentence: "It is vital to widen the selection procedures if the Ryder Cup is to enjoy its past prestige."

In 1989, Michael Williams, one of Britain's leading golf writers, published an official history of the Ryder Cup. Here's what he had to say about the ensuing events:

> There was still some reluctance on the part of the British PGA to make a change, but, since their hand was being forced, there was one obvious road down which they were pointed. Not only had Severiano Ballesteros finished second in the 1976 Open championship at Royal Birkdale, but at the time of the 1977 Ryder Cup at Royal Lytham, he was about to become for the first time the leading money-winner on the PGA European Tour. . . . Furthermore, in 1976 and then at the end of 1977, Ballesteros partnered first Manuel Pinero and then Antonio Garrido to victory in the World Cup. As all three players were very much a part of the growing European family, it was only logical for them to be a part of the Ryder Cup as well. Certainly the other (European Tour) players were unanimous in their approval; nor was there any objection from Mrs. Joan Scarfe, daughter of Samuel Ryder who had donated the Cup.
>
> Accordingly, Ken Schofield, the executive director of the PGA European Tour, was summoned to Lord Derby's home, where it was arranged for Brian Huggett, as the most recent captain, and Peter

Butler, of the Ryder Cup committee, to complete the formalities at the 1978 Masters. . . . Nine months later, Don Padgett, president of the United States PGA, announced at The Greenbrier in West Virginia, where the 1979 match was to be played, that, at the instigation if not the insistence of the Americans, the Great Britain and Ireland side was to be extended to include continental Europeans, and that the team would subsequently be known as "Europe."

America won fairly easily at the Greenbrier, and again in 1981 at Walton Heath in England with perhaps its strongest-ever team: Ben Crenshaw, Ray Floyd, Hale Irwin, Tom Kite, Bruce Lietzke, Johnny Miller, Larry Nelson, Jack Nicklaus, Jerry Pate, Bill Rogers, Lee Trevino, and Tom Watson, under the captaincy of Dave Marr.

But by then Seve had captured his first Masters and British Open, and players like Nick Faldo and Sandy Lyle and Bernhard Langer and Ian Woosnam were on their way to similar heights. Here's how the combination of the broadened field of talent and Europe's fast-improving playing standards impacted the next seven Ryder Cups:

1983	PGA National GC, FL	USA 14½	Europe 13½
1985	The Belfry, England	Europe 16½	USA 11½
1987	Muirfield Village, OH	Europe 15	USA 13
1989	The Belfry, England	Europe 14	USA 14
1991	Kiawah Island, SC	USA 14½	Europe 13½
1993	The Belfry, England	USA 15	Europe 13
1995	Oak Hill, NY	Europe 14½	USA 13½

In little over a decade, then, with three wins to each side plus a tie and only a four-point differential in total scores, the Ryder Cup went from being almost a nonevent to one of golf's greatest competitive spectacles, as witness the latest thriller at Oak Hill. Indeed, many fans now rate it the game's single most exciting contest.

So long as we don't let media hype and fan partisanship overinfect the players on either side, I see nothing but good in its future, and remain proud of my contribution to its remarkable turnaround.

Stay With Proven Principles, Not "Methods"

I've never believed in "methods," and I've always been skeptical of teachers who try to make others swing the same way they themselves swing, or think they do.

If you videotaped a thousand good golfers then looked at them every which way in slow-motion, you wouldn't be able to find even two who swung exactly alike. What you would see is a lot of similarities, certainly at address, and probably at the top of the backswing, and definitely at impact. In other words, you'd identify some *fundamental principles* adhered to by just about everyone who could play a lick. But identical swings? . . . Exact replication? . . . Lots of fine golfers all indistinguishable from each other? That has never happened in the history of the game, and there's no way it ever will unless man finds a way to clone himself.

The only way to achieve your full potential at golf is to solidly grasp a few time-proven fundamentals or principles, then master them your own best individual way through trial and error in practice and play. Whatever anyone may tell you, whatever you may read or see on a screen, in golf there simply are no "secrets," no guarantees, no easy solutions.

Getting good at this game, then staying good, is a tough and lonely and endless journey, with lots of dead-ends and other frustrations to strain your body and stress your mind along the way. Which, of course, is why so few of the tens of thousands who set out on it get very far along it.

Why I Interlock

At one time or another I must have given the impression I adopted the interlocking grip because I had small hands, because I've read that about myself quite frequently over the years. Although interlocking instead of overlapping does sometimes work better for people with small or weak hands, the truth is that I used the interlock from the time I first discovered golf because it was the way my dad held the club. About a year after I got started at the game, Jack Grout had me try the overlapping or Vardon grip for a couple of days, but it did nothing for me and he quickly dropped the idea of me changing and it never resurfaced.

Understand Your Swing

A golfer never becomes a complete player, never achieves his full competitive potential, until he totally understands his own golf swing. The reason is that you have to be able to manage your swing in order to be able to manage the golf course. In my peak years I won as many tournaments hitting the ball poorly as I did hitting the ball well. That happened because I understood my swing sufficiently to be able to produce workable shots, *scoring* shots, even when they were less than the ideal. And because I had to work so much harder at them, I'm prouder of the good scoring rounds hitting the ball poorly than of the great rounds when everything was meshing perfectly.

How many players on tour truly understand their own swings? Not many, in my view. Arnold Palmer, Johnny Miller, Lee Trevino, Tom Watson, Raymond Floyd, and Hale Irwin would be tops in that area among my contemporaries, and among today's top performers probably Nick Faldo, Tom Lehman, Mark O'Meara, Bruce Lietzke, Phil Mickelson, and Tiger Woods.

On Power

I think probably the longest drive I ever hit in competition was in the 1964 Masters at the par-five fifteenth hole. I was making a charge and was pumped up. Although I felt like I'd caught the ball a little in the neck, when I got to it I had to decide between a 7- and 8-iron for my second shot. On a hole of 500 yards, that indicates a drive of at least 340 yards. (In the light of that shot, I was probably less surprised than most when Tiger Woods twice reached this hole with driver and 9-iron in the 1995 Masters.)

More important than the raw yardage, though, were the reasons I went for maximum distance. The most important was that, because of the wide fairway and minimal trouble to either side, my chances of making at least a par even if I sprayed the shot were still excellent, whereas if I hit both long and accurately I greatly improved my chance of a birdie or eagle. The other reason was that it's always easier, and thus safer, to go for extra distance when your adrenaline flow is high. That's because there's no need to force the shot, which makes you less prone to swing errors.

What this all boils down to is playing the percentages, which has always been my underlying strategy on every shot. As another example related to distance, I would never risk making a bad swing just to be able to hit one less club on an approach shot. However, if carrying the ball a little farther than usual enabled me to club down from a 5-iron to a wedge, or something of that order, then most times I would take the gamble.

The tendency of most golfers when they want to hit farther is to move everything quicker or harder than the one thing that must go faster, which is the clubhead. My way of protecting against that is to be a little less deliberate in setting up to minimize muscle tension, but then give myself a little more time with the swing itself—to be slow and smooth enough to complete all the moves that I know are necessary to produce a good pass.

Practicing Productively

Too many players never learn the difference between beating balls and practicing productively. You see guys hitting balls until their hands bleed, and all the time they are making the same mistakes, over and over and over again. Eventually they groove their errors to the point where they limit their scoring ability; they get stuck at a certain level.

Throughout my career I've used practice to try to learn, to improve, to advance myself. I've always had a specific goal when I practiced, drawn from what I was doing on the golf course. There was no need to try to groove anything, because my swing fundamentals essentially never changed from the time I first "grooved" them with Jack Grout in my late teens.

I never practice in the true sense of the word before I play. What I do is simply warm up to fully prepare myself for the upcoming round. The practice comes after the round when I can work to correct any flaws that surfaced or to ingrain the good moves I made on the course.

I made a habit very early on of giving every shot I hit in practice as much concentration and effort as those I played on the course. Once out of my teens, I never beat balls just for the sake of beating balls. There was always a specific objective, and also a strategy for attaining it, that I had carefully thought out before I got to the practice tee. When I couldn't attain that objective after a reasonable amount of trying, I would stop practicing and go do some more thinking. When I was satisfied I had achieved what I set out to do, I would quit while it was fresh in my mind.

The Actual Winning Is What's Fun

There is no question that the actual act of winning is the most fun, much more than the aftermath of "having won." Inevitably, after the winning is over and done with, the excitement and elation begin to subside. You're coming off such a high that there's nowhere to go but down, even if it's only a little way down. And I suppose it's because the actual act of winning is so enjoyable that I've kept on trying to repeat it for so many years.

The Intimidation Factor

There was a factor in my career that, to avoid sounding immodest, I talked little about over the years. But it was such a big contributor that I'd be remiss not to acknowledge it here. It was the degree to which my achievements intimidated other players.

J. C. Snead once said, "When you go head to head against Nicklaus, he knows he's going to beat you, you know he's going to beat you, and he knows you know he's going to beat you." That may be a little over the top, but there is no question that, coming down the stretch in my best years, I knew exactly how intimidating I was to most of the other players. And it gave me a huge competitive edge. I knew that if I kept the pressure on and didn't do anything stupid, I would often win.

This might sound like arrogance, but it really wasn't. I recognized that many of my opponents had physical skills equal or even superior to mine, but I also knew that few of them had the mental or emotional capability to use them as effectively as I generally could mine. Somebody might up and simply beat me, as Lee Trevino and Tom Watson did a number of times, but I was totally confident that I would not beat myself once I had gotten into a winning position.

The truth is that most players give tournaments away, particularly major championships. In at least a third of my majors wins, I was simply there to accept the gift. Often, I'd actually done the winning in the early part of the final round by scoring well enough to get the opposition either fearful or impatient. Then they would fail to make a move on me, allowing me to prevail if I could simply finish the tournament without making any dumb mistakes.

The biggest exceptions to this were the U.S. Opens of 1967 and 1980. And, of course, the Masters in 1986, when I won by shooting 30 on the back nine.

20

The 1986 Masters Tournament

The Most Fulfilling

THERE is one infallible way to tell when a golfer becomes a truly dominating force in the game. That's when all of the other players in a room look over at him when he walks in and say to themselves, "That's the man. That's the man I have to beat."

As 1978 marked the end of my ability to win on talent alone, I look back now on the 1980 season as the last in which I could consider myself "the man to beat."

Over the next five years, I managed to win all four matches in my last Ryder Cup outing in 1981, capture the Colonial the following year and the Chrysler Team Invitational with Johnny Miller early in 1983, then in the spring of 1984 win my second Memorial Tournament and, in the fall, the biggest check of my career, $240,000, in the Skins Game. Out of around eighty tournaments I played at home and abroad over that period, I also achieved thirteen seconds, three of them in major championships, and five thirds, bringing my career total of top-three finishes, amateur and professional, close to two hundred. But there is no ducking the fact that the Jack Nicklaus of the early 1980s was not the golfer of a decade earlier.

The near misses in the majors were particularly galling, because I believed then, and still do, that the Nicklaus of his man-to-beat years would have won each time. Those second places occurred, respectively, in the 1981 Masters, the 1982 U.S. Open, and the 1983 PGA Championship.

The Masters failure can be quickly disposed of. In the opening round I played tee to green as well as I ever had at Augusta but putted the new bent-grass greens poorly for a 70, then added a 65 the second day with an equally strong long game and a much hotter putter. That should have set me up to run away and hide. Instead, I had to work my tail off for a 75 on Saturday after hitting into water at twelve and thirteen, then lost a scrambling duel to Tom Watson on Sunday to tie with Johnny Miller two strokes back of Tom. Flying home that night, I figured out that I'd played the first forty-two holes in ten under par, and the next thirty in four over. It did not help my mood.

In the press session after I finished, someone suggested that luck had contributed heavily to Watson getting out of trouble as well as he managed to throughout the final round. I disagreed, and gave an example. Just after he had run an eagle putt well past the hole at fifteen, Tom saw me roll in a twenty-five-footer for birdie at sixteen to get back within striking distance. I pointed out that luck had nothing to do with the way he then stood up and knocked in his putt for birdie—just skill and nerve. Added to his previous Masters win and three British Opens, the victory gave him five majors and a total of thirty victories around the world over an eight-year period. Clearly, by the spring of 1982 it was beyond argument that Thomas Sturges Watson had replaced Jack William Nicklaus as "the man to beat."

There was certainly no change in that situation as, fourteen months later, I began the final round of the eighty-second U.S. Open at Pebble Beach three strokes adrift of Tom and the 1981 British Open champion, Bill Rogers. Despite feeling constantly close to taking advantage of the unusually easy conditions—little wind and relatively soft greens—all I had been able to do until then was grind along for three "okay" rounds of 74-70-71.

The theory of winning at Pebble Beach is that you beat up on the first seven holes, then hang on for dear life. When I opened Sunday with a sloppy bogey, followed by only a par at the second hole, a par five easily reachable in two, many of the locals must have written me off. But then began the run I'd been anticipating for three days: birdie at three from fifteen feet, at four from twenty-five feet, at the par-three fifth from two feet, at the par-five sixth with two putts off a 1-iron from a tight lie, and at that famous little out-in-the-ocean seventh hole from ten feet.

It was my hottest stretch ever in a U.S. Open, and its reward was a share of the lead with Rogers and Bruce Devlin. From that point I cooled considerably with a bogey off a weak second to number eight, pars at nine and ten, then a three-putt bogey from twenty feet at eleven. But I managed to slip a birdie at fifteen into a string of closing pars, for a 69 and a four-under-par total of 284, six strokes better than when I'd won the Open at Pebble Beach ten years previously.

The leader boards had kept me abreast of Rogers's and Devlin's slide soon after they turned for home. Following his outward 37, they also showed me the bare numbers of Watson's resurgence on the back nine that would bring him to the seventeenth tee tied with me. I discovered later that his par at ten had included a pitch from the beach and a twenty-five-foot putt, his birdie at eleven another long putt, his bogey at twelve a bunkered tee shot, and his birdie at fourteen a forty-five-foot snake about which Rogers, his playing partner, commented, "Human beings would have three-putted."

I was asked a number of times after that Open why I teed off with the 3-wood instead of the driver at the final hole, meaning I left myself no chance of going for the green in two and making a two-putt birdie that might have sewn things up for me. The answer is that, while you might think of taking a crack at Pebble's eighteenth green with a helping wind and the flagstick set back left, with the cup cut front right, as it was that day, the shot is just too dangerous. Ninety-nine percent of the time in my prior visits to Pebble Beach I'd played my second at eighteen to the vicinity of a sprinkler-head located eighty-four yards from the front of the green, leaving an easy pitch shot. With Tom still to play the always-difficult seventeenth hole, there was no way I was going to suddenly change a strategy that had won me an Amateur, an Open and three Crosby tournaments over the course.

As I came off the eighteenth green, I really felt I would win the championship, that this would be my fifth U.S. Open, so much so that I flung my ball to the crowd in a surge of elation. Then, as Jack Whitaker interviewed me for ABC while we watched Tom hit his tee shot long and left at the par-three seventeenth, I became even more upbeat about my chances. I figured it would require a miraculous shot to get the ball within even ten feet of the hole, meaning, particularly on so bumpy a green, that the odds favored a bogey, meaning in turn that Tom would have to birdie eighteen just to tie me.

Feeling so good about things, my attention then wandered from the television screen as Tom set up to chip, as a result of which I missed seeing his ball slam against the flagstick and drop in the hole. But the crowd roar brought me back to the screen fast, to watch Tom shove up his arms and leap in the air and race around the green with a big grin on his face. Incredulous that he could have holed out, I asked, "What did he do, hit the pin?" and someone replied, "No, he knocked it in." "Aw, c'mon," I said, still for a moment unable to believe it. But it had happened. The man of that time to beat had done the seemingly impossible, making a birdie two when a bogey four appeared almost certain. Which meant, of course, that instead of trailing me by a shot, he now led me by one.

As everyone could see on television when the camera moved in tight on Tom's ball in the endless replays, he had a perfect lie in the fluffy rough, and he took advantage of it to make the only play that would work for him at that moment, hitting the flagstick flush enough for the ball to fall straight in the hole. There is no question that it was one of the most sensational shots in the history of golf. I admit that it stunned me, but really it shouldn't have because I'd always known that what separates the great from the good players is their ability to visualize and will themselves into making superb shots when they most need them. For instance, I learned later that Tom's response to his caddie when Bruce Edwards offered some last-second encouragement was, "Get it close, hell, I'm going to make it."

Lee Trevino had done something similar at the seventeenth hole at Muirfield to cost me the 1972 British Open and a chance at the grand slam. Tom's shot not only cost me a record fifth U.S. Open but, as it proved, took most of the wind out my sails for the rest of that season. But what could I say then, or now, beyond, "That's golf"? As he came off the eighteenth green after birdieing there to increase his winning margin to two strokes, I told Tom, and meant it, that I was proud of him and happy for him. Then at the prize presentation I leaned over and said, affectionately, "You little s.o.b., I'm going to get you yet," and I meant that, too.

Sure, there was some luck in that shot, but over the years I had enjoyed at least as many lucky breaks against others as had gone against me. There was nothing to do but keep it in perspective, use it to inspire more work, to try harder next time. I'd played the best golf I was capable of that week, and another guy had played a little better. So be it. The sun would come up and the world would continue rotating. Life would go on and had to be lived.

This philosophical attitude became necessary again some fourteen months later when Hal Sutton led from start to finish in edging me by a stroke in the 1983 PGA at Riviera in Los Angeles.

I recall being asked after the third round of that championship what I figured I would have to shoot to win the next day. I told my questioner 65, the score I'd made in the second round, my reasoning being that Hal, with a six-stroke advantage starting out, would then have to break par to beat me, never an easy task for a golfer trying to win his first major. It was a close prediction.

Two weeks before that PGA, Sutton had blown a six-shot lead on the last day to lose a tournament in Virginia, which drove him to work harder on his game, he said, than ever before with his longtime teacher, Jimmy Ballard. After rounds of 65-66-72, followed by an outward 32 on Sunday, the effort appeared to be paying off magnificently, and the tournament to many folks probably seemed to be over. Then, out of the blue, Hal bogeyed the twelfth, thirteenth and fourteenth holes, allowing my birdies at fourteen and sixteen to pull me within a stroke. After it was all over, he told how, determined not to suffer another collapse, he gave himself a severe pep talk on the fifteenth tee that carried him to four straight pars, including an impeccable one at the fabulous but always hazardous eighteenth hole. After I congratulated him, he asked me how I'd kept my composure and my mind on what I was doing all those years coming down the stretch with a chance to win, with the whooping and hollering of the crowds adding to the distractions and the emotional pressure. I told him what I've always believed: that, because they are what you have worked so hard to achieve, you should welcome and enjoy such moments to the fullest.

Although most analysts decided it was my failure to birdie Riviera's long par-five seventeenth hole the last day that cost me that PGA, I believed then, and still do, that I lost it in the opening round. After what felt like a great drive at eighteen that Thursday, I found my ball a little farther right than was ideal, necessitating a slightly faded approach to get around a big eucalyptus tree that juts into the fairway. I've always controlled the amount I fade shots by how much at address I align my body left of target, along with the degree to which I open the clubface. In this instance, I got the face alignment of the 6-iron right but didn't open my body enough, causing the ball to start insufficiently left and catch a skinny little branch sticking out all by itself, resulting in a double-bogey six. The following morning a fine obituary of Jack Nicklaus, golfer, appeared in the *Los Angeles Times* under the byline of its famous columnist and his good friend Jim Murray. I still believe it was this colorful write-off that inspired me to a 65 the next day. Like my closing 66, it wasn't quite good enough, but Jim's witty and heartfelt resurrection of me in Monday's edition of the paper was some consolation.

You will sometimes hear it argued, especially by those who dislike what they perceive as its "elitism," that the Masters shouldn't be a major because it's not the championship of anything. The truth, of course, is that its founder, Bob Jones, would have agreed with that contention, in that he did not intend the event to be anything but an enjoyable outing for his friends. Indeed, his modesty was such that he insisted the inaugural playing be called the "Augusta National Invitation Tournament" and, in the years I knew him, always hated any reference to the event as a "championship" rather than a "tournament." As he invariably pointed out when such matters came up, it was the media that named his invention "The Masters," then later elected it a major.

For those reasons, as I have written, even though the Masters is my favorite *tournament,* I've always placed it fourth when pressured to rate the majors in terms of their importance, behind the U.S. Open, the British Open, and the PGA Championship, in that order.

I believe my majors record is a good indicator of the difficulty of the U.S. Open relative to the other three. I won six Masters and was in contention to the end at least half a dozen more times. I won three

British Opens and was second seven times and third twice. I won five PGA Championships and was right up there six or seven more times. In the U.S. Open I won four times and was second as an amateur in 1960 at Cherry Hills to Arnold Palmer, in 1968 at Oak Hill and in 1971 at Merion to Lee Trevino, and in 1982 to Tom Watson. Apart from those years, I either won or was out of contention. The reason for that, I believe, lies in the way the United States Golf Association set up U.S. Open courses during most of my best years. Narrow fairways bordered by inches-deep rough demand exceptional driving of the ball. My recollection is that when I drove well I was in contention, and when I didn't I wasn't. Driving well was important at the other three majors, too, but rarely to the extent it has been in our national championship during my time in the game.

In 1985, after finishing tied for sixth in the Masters, four strokes behind Bernhard Langer, weak driving more than any other factor caused me to miss the cut in the U.S. Open at Oakland Hills, with rounds of 76-73, for the first time in twenty-two years and only the second time as a professional. At Royal St. George's, I would also miss the cut for the first time in the British Open since first playing in the championship in 1962. In the PGA Championship at Cherry Hills, I finished tied for thirty-second, eleven strokes behind Hubert Green.

As the season progressed, these failures spurred me to yet again talk with my family about my future as a golfer. I had begun to wonder whether I was playing for the right reasons. I had told the world at age twenty-five that I'd be done at thirty-five, and at thirty-five I'd sworn I'd be long gone by the age of forty-five, and now here I was, forty-five years old, and still out there. Was I playing for my personal enjoyment, or because I believed I could still win, or to give something back to the game, or to try to extend my record for others to aim at, or for some combination of all of those reasons? If so, fine —they remained valid goals. What worried me was the suspicion that my continued playing was mostly an ego trip—that, after all the years of success, my psyche simply wouldn't let me stop.

There was no doubt about the family's feelings. As at the end of 1979, Barbara and the children all definitely wanted me to continue playing. When I mulled the matter over with friends, they felt the same way. So did everyone in my business world. Finishing second to

Greg Norman in the Canadian Open made it seem the right decision, but then, two weeks after that, came my failure in the British Open, and deep down the wondering began again. From then on, it would be a frequent visitor and ultimately an almost constant companion.

POORLY as I'd played throughout most of 1985, my early-season 1986 performance was worse.

My driving was nothing to write home about, but it was sensational compared with my iron play. Time and again I would stride up to the ball with an 8- or 9-iron in hand figuring how to best position it for a birdie putt, only to walk off the green with a bogey or worse. Out of seven tournaments I entered preceding the Masters, I missed the cut in three and could do no better than a tie for thirty-ninth in the other four. Flying up to Augusta for my customary on-site practice the week before the tournament, a statistic I happened across in a magazine painfully reflected the condition of my game: one hundred and sixtieth on the money list with $4,404.

By then, though, I was feeling better about my prospects than in many months.

Although Jack Grout was still mending from open-heart surgery, he had felt strong enough by early March to accompany Jackie down to Miami for a day to watch me play at Doral. Asked afterward for a diagnosis, my old teacher and friend minced no words: "Way too handsy."

The more I thought about this judgment, the more evident its truth became to me. Although at my best my hands and wrists played a key part in delivering the clubhead to the ball correctly, they did so reflexively, never through conscious direction. Accordingly, my sense of their role in the swing had always been one of passivity compared with the motion of my arms and the work of my lower body. This was a product of Jack's endlessly repeated doctrine of my youth: "reach for the sky" swinging back, and reach for it again swinging through. As a result once again of playing and practicing so much in Florida wind, where you're always wanting to knock the ball down, I had gradually regressed from that ideal to trying to hit the ball mostly with my hands and wrists. Jack pointed out that their forced and excessive cocking at the top virtually guaranteed an ill-timed transition from backswing to through-swing. Worse yet, when I somehow still managed to direct the club to the ball correctly in terms of path and face alignment, the violence of my hand and wrist action through impact frequently disrupted one or the other, or both.

With Jack's help, I began reaching for the sky again the Monday after Doral, and, although I missed the cut in New Orleans ten days later, I felt better about the way I struck the ball. Another missed cut followed at the Tournament Players Championship a week later, but by then even more light had appeared at the end of the tunnel. A change of the magnitude I was making required strong initial focus on the mechanics of the action, whereas I had always played my best relying on the feel deriving from sound mechanics. The Masters was two weeks away. To promote more feel, I began slowing the backswing to a point where I could gather myself more at the top, then use my hips and legs to pull me through the hitting area. Simultaneously, I worked at consciously keeping my head up as I began the swing to correct a career-long tendency to lower it at that point, with all kinds of unpleasant consequences. Yet more light glimmered at the tunnel's end. But the question remained: would I have exited the long, dark passage by the Thursday of Masters week?

Along with the improvement in my long game, I made a change in my chipping technique that would also pay off at Augusta. It arrived courtesy of Chi Chi Rodriguez via my son, Jackie.

Cheech had watched Jackie, by then a professional, struggling as he practiced short pitch shots at the Greater Milwaukee Open the previous September, then gone to him and offered help. They worked together after Jackie missed the cut, then on the weekend Chi Chi had come out an hour or so ahead of teeing off in the tournament for more sessions, telling Jackie when reminded he himself had to go and play that it only took him a few minutes to warm up and to stop worrying about him and concentrate on what he was being taught. This was typical of Chi Chi's warmheartedness and generosity, as was his invitation to Jackie to spend a week at his home in Puerto Rico that October and play in the big pro-am he hosts each year and work more intensively on his short game.

Until his sessions with Chi Chi, Jackie had suffered terribly with short pitch shots, chiefly as a result, as he sensed it, of being in his own way as he tried to make contact with the ball. In other words, by failing to clear his body he was unable to swing his arms freely past it, leaving him no alternative but to flip at the ball with his hands and wrists, causing all kinds of ugly shots, including even double hits.

Chi Chi's medicine was uncomplicated but highly effective. Its key ingredient was a change in Jackie's setup, taking him from square to the target line to open in his feet, knees, hips and shoulders, thereby preestablishing space for his arms to swing freely past his body without conscious or deliberate effort. With most of his weight set and remaining on his left side, Cheech then had Jackie swing the club back and through parallel to his body line, or from slightly out to in, but with the face looking directly at the target. The final basic he stressed was a firm-wristed action in which the clubhead never caught up with the back of the left hand until well after impact. To stop the ball quickly, you simply increased clubhead speed to generate more spin. To make the ball roll, you simply took a bigger and slower swing for a softer impact and minimal spin. In either case, the one thing you never forgot to do was accelerate the clubhead through the ball.

From being unable to even get the ball on the green half the time when he missed it by a few yards, Jackie by that winter had become such a fine short pitcher and chipper that, as we played and practiced together, I went from tentatively trying out what he was doing, to liking it, to adding it to my own arsenal of recovery shots. The pitching technique Phil Rodgers had taught me six years previously was still great when I needed extra-"soft" shots, but had caused me some problems with distance control. By the time of the Masters I had switched fully to Chi Chi/Jackie's method for routine chips and short pitches. It would not let me down.

As noted earlier, my good friend John Montgomery is an inveterate prankster, so I know it gave him much pleasure to tape to the refrigerator door of the house he and his wife Nancy, Pandel and Janice Savic, and Barbara and I shared for the 1986 Masters a column by Tom McCollister, of the *Atlanta Journal,* announcing the demise of Jack Nicklaus, golfer. According to this piece I was finished, washed up, kaput, the clubs were rusted out, the Bear was off hibernating somewhere, it was all over and done with, forget it, hang 'em up and go design golf courses or whatever.

Similar sentiments had been expressed enough times during my career for me to invariably just shrug them off, but, coinciding as it did with my upbeat attitude about my game, this one struck a nerve. "Finished, huh?" I said to myself. "All washed up, am I? Well, we'll see about that this week." To keep me wanting to make Mr. McCollister eat his words—ideally with Mr. Montgomery also swallowing a portion—I insisted on leaving the clipping on the door, then looked at it every time I visited the refrigerator. I had never needed external stimuli to spark my competitive drive, but maybe the arrival of this one was fortuitous, perhaps even an omen. At least it was a spur.

My first three rounds of the Augusta National that week were 74-71-69. I played about as well as I expected to from tee to green, and pitched or chipped nicely the few times I missed greens. Thus the progressively lower scores were mostly due to steadily improved putting. All spring I had used a new aluminum-headed, large-faced, offset, center-shafted putter that my equipment manufacturer of the time had developed. I had not recently putted particularly well with it, but, as the club felt progressively better and better in my hands, I went from putting poorly the first day to okay the second on dry and crusty greens, then pretty well on Saturday. Someone asked me in the press session after that third-round 69 about when I had last broken 70, and I responded that it was so long ago I couldn't remember, which was the truth.

After fifty-four holes I thus stood at two under par. The bad news about the number was that it left me four strokes back of Greg Norman. But there was also some good news. Even though the list included Seve Ballesteros, Bernhard Langer, Tom Kite and Tom Watson, there were only seven players between Norman and me. The natural tendency when trailing going into the final round of a tournament is to focus mostly or entirely on stroke deficit in evaluating one's chances and deciding strategy. I'd learned a long time ago that an equally important factor is the number of players needing to be overtaken. That evening, weighing how I was by now playing and putting against the number of golfers ahead of me, I felt good about my chances.

A short time before this Masters, Barbara's mother, Helen Bash, had passed away in Columbus, where the funeral service was conducted by the Reverend Dr. William Smith, who had given the benediction at our Memorial Tournament ceremonies since the event began. Bill's son, Craig, a great fan of mine, had always wanted me to wear yellow golf shirts because he believed the color brought me luck. Craig had died two years previously of cancer at the age of thirteen, and Barbara thought it would be nice if I wore a yellow shirt in his memory one day at the Masters. We both thought fondly of Craig and his parents as I slipped it on that Sunday morning.

BACK then, our second son, Steve, was employed by Executive Sports, the tournament management/marketing organization created and run by John Montgomery that would later become part of Golden Bear International. Soon after breakfast Sunday morning Steve called from Hattiesburg, Mississippi, where he was working the event for PGA Tour members not qualified for the Masters. "Well, Pops," he asked me after we'd talked a while, "what's it going to take?" I told him I believed 66 would earn me a tie and 65 would win. "That's the number I've been thinking of," said Steve. "Go shoot it."

By the time I stood where my drive had finished amid the pine trees off to the right of the eighth fairway around three o'clock that afternoon, the possibility of doing so seemed pretty remote. After comfortably parring the first hole, I'd birdied the second with a nice pitch and putt after pushing my drive into the trees on the right, but then three-putted the tough par-three fourth hole after my 2-iron tee shot landed just short of the cup and trickled forty feet back down the green. At the par-three sixth I felt I'd given away another shot when I missed the putt after knocking a 5-iron four feet past the hole. And then came a stroke of good fortune that refired my sense that this might still be my day. Certainly, without it, this book would have been a chapter shorter.

Had I been in the lead, or closer to it, I would have punched an iron shot back to the eighth fairway through about a six-foot opening between a couple of large trees about twenty feet ahead of me. As things stood, I felt I had to begin putting better numbers on the board right then if I was going to get in the hunt. This was a par-five hole where I'd always looked for birdies or better, and my yardage checks confirmed I was within 3-wood distance of the green. Studying the gap, I figured that if could keep the ball down and fade it slightly while still striking it solidly, I might just get home. I pulled the 3-wood from the bag, set up extra carefully, made what felt like a good swing, but pushed the ball slightly. About a foot to the right of the tree forming the right side of the gap I was aiming at stood another fat pine. My ball shot through that little aperture, missed a couple more trees that could have deflected it anywhere, and finished just to the right of the green, from where I pitched to about ten feet and two-putted for par. It was a tremendous gamble followed by a huge piece of luck, and I still get cold shivers whenever it comes to mind.

Periodically after Angelo Argea stopped caddying for me in the late 1970s, one of my sons would volunteer to take the bag, particularly in the majors. Jackie was looping for me this time, and, as we walked down the ninth fairway after a good tee shot, he said, "Well, Dad, what do you think?" At that point I was even par for the round and, although not sure by how many strokes, still well behind probably half a dozen players. "Jackie," I told him, "I have to get myself in gear right now if I'm going to have any chance at all. We really need a birdie here. If we can get off this hole and through this nine under par, then we might make something happen."

Because of its precipitous back-to-front slope, Augusta National's ninth green is one of the trickiest to putt of perhaps the trickiest eighteen putting surfaces in golf. My pitching-wedge approach had left me about eleven feet above and to the right of the hole. "Looks like the left edge," Jackie told me after we'd surveyed the putt a while. "How about two inches on the right?" I asked him, reflecting what I thought I saw. But Jackie has great vision and his read gave me a little different feeling about the line, telling me to play for a little less break and go for the top of the cup.

With the decision made, I'd walked over and was beginning to set up to the ball when a huge roar came from the direction of the eighth green. "Aha," I told myself as I backed off, "that's either Kite or Ballesteros making eagle." Then, almost before I could get back to my putt again, along came another enormous yell from the same direction. "Aha," I told myself, "that's the other guy also making eagle." And, indeed, it turned out that both players had done just that by holing pitch shots, Tom from about fifty yards and Seve from eighty.

The hullabaloo naturally had stirred up the huge gallery around the ninth green. To settle things down, I turned to the folks nearest me and said, "Okay, now, let's see if we can make that same kind of noise here." People laughed and applauded, and when I got back over the ball I found myself more relaxed and very positive about both the line and speed of the putt. I made a good stroke and watched the ball roll dead in the heart of the hole for a birdie three.

I was off and running.

I REALLY should have hit a 3-wood instead of the driver off the tenth tee, and got another break when the gallery blocked the ball from going far enough right to tangle with the trees separating the tenth hole from the eighteenth. I followed up with a nice 4-iron to about twenty-five feet, and felt even more comfortable over the putt than I had the one at nine. The ball dropped cleanly in the center of the cup. Birdie, birdie.

The eleventh hole, the beginning of Augusta National's famed and feared Amen Corner, becomes more dangerous the shorter the drive you hit, due to the pond tightly fronting the green. I crushed my tee shot, leaving me with only an 8-iron second that stopped about twenty-five feet past the pin. Sandy Lyle, my playing partner, was on the same line, and after he moved his ball over one putter-head length I decided to roll mine just inside his marker coin. It was a perfect read. Beginning to get very excited, Jackie jumped high in the air from a standing start as the ball disappeared in the hole. Birdie, birdie, birdie. Three under par for the day, five under for the tournament.

The fans had been extremely gracious to me all through the week, invariably applauding as I came up to each green. Now as I walked onto the twelfth tee, I received an incredible ovation from the thousands of people gathered in the wooded area that forms the peak of Amen Corner. Few of them, I imagined, had expected this rally by the old guy, but it was clear how much they appreciated it and wanted it to continue.

If I needed any further charging up, it was the twelfth hole that provided it. The wind seemed to have come up a little, meaning that the club I probably needed to hit was the 6-iron. But I had a problem with that—namely, that if I aimed over the center of the front bunker to be sure of not going right and down into Rae's Creek off the green's steep frontal banking, but pulled the ball left or hit it a little strong, I would end up either in the back bunker or facing a very difficult chip from the bank behind the green. Eventually I decided on a firm 7-iron, and had begun swinging it when the wind came up again, causing me—for fear of going right and getting wet—to pull the shot a fraction. Finishing as it did on the back fringe, it wasn't that terrible a shot, but after I hit a pretty good chip that took a bad bounce, then an even better putt that caught a spike mark, the bogey I walked off with made me mad. "Come on, Jack," I told myself, "don't do what you did yesterday after you birdied twelve and became defensive. The only way you're going to win this thing at this stage is by being aggressive. Go for it, fella."

The pep talk seemed to work immediately, because at thirteen I drew an extremely solid 3-wood tighter even than I'd planned around the dogleg elbow. This left me a 3-iron to the green that I would like to have faded in, but had to draw because of a little branch sticking out from the trees that line the entire left side of the hole. The ball stopped about thirty feet past the pin, from where I two-putted for my fourth birdie in five holes. A glance at the scoreboard as I walked to the fourteenth tee showed me that the contenders by that point had been reduced to four: Ballesteros at seven under par, Kite at six under, Norman at five under after double-bogeying ten, and myself also at five under.

At the fourteenth hole I hit a 3-wood off the tee, then played a little 6-iron that looked great in the air but ran just over the green into the back fringe, leaving an awkward chip. Using the recently learned Chi Chi/Jackie technique, I rolled it down perfectly for a tap-in par.

Pretty much since turning for home there had been a consciousness at the back of my mind that, whatever the other holes brought, I would have to eagle the par-five fifteenth if I was going to win this Masters. Doing so obviously necessitated a fine drive, and I hit one, absolutely nailing the ball into the light breeze, leaving myself 202 yards to the hole. As we finished assessing the shot, I turned to Jackie and said, "How far do you think a three would go here?"—meaning, of course, with the 4-iron already in my hands, score, not club. "A long way—just hit it solid," he replied, and I did, the ball never leaving the flag and landing just short of the hole, then rolling down about twelve feet to its left.

After we got down to the green and began our surveying, I suddenly remembered that I'd had a similar putt for eagle in an early round in 1975, but hadn't hit it hard enough. As I finished aligning myself over the ball for about six inches of break, I switched focus totally to distance, telling myself, "Let's make sure we get this ball to the hole, just hit it hard enough." *Plunk*. Eagle three, five under for the day, seven under for the tournament. "Whoops," I said to myself, "here we go."

Although I don't remember registering what must have been the huge roar when the ball dropped, as I was walking after my tee shot on fifteen Seve was holing a putt of about eight feet for an eagle three at thirteen. Glancing at the scoreboard to the right of the fifteenth green as I headed to the sixteenth tee, I saw that he was now the only player ahead of me, and by only two strokes. The thought that went through my mind was, "Well, he still has some golf ahead of him."

The club I most like to hit at Augusta National's par-three sixteenth hole is the 6-iron. On that day, with 179 yards to the cup and the breeze in my face, I knew as soon as I stepped on the tee that it had to be the five, and a solid one too. "Put it up in the air" was my last thought before swinging, and I guess I did so just about perfectly, because, although the bunker short of the green prevented me from seeing the ball soon after it began rolling, the ever-louder crowd reaction told me it was going to finish very close. Later, of course, I saw on videotape that the ball had missed the hole by about half an inch, before trickling about two and half feet past and left. It was a tricky little putt, though, and Jackie and I took all the time we needed deciding how much from left to right the ball would break. When it fell in the heart of the hole, I was glad I hadn't putted before we reached total agreement. Six under for the day, eight under for the tournament. And now, for the first time, absolutely certain that I could win myself a sixth Masters. So much so, in fact, that as we walked to the seventeenth tee, I told Jackie, "Hey, I haven't had this much fun in six years."

As I was beginning to address the ball with the driver at seventeen, a big gallery reaction from the direction of the fifteenth fairway caused me to back off. It was a strange sound: loud, but somehow more like a moan than the roar Masters galleries famously let loose when a contender does something dramatic. I told myself Seve had either holed out from somewhere off the green at fifteen or hit into the water, and I would have liked to have known which before I teed off. But unduly delaying play is against the rules, so I got on with my business, which was to drive up the left side of the fairway to set up the best angle to the green. I made what felt like a good swing, but pulled the shot a little too far in that direction. As I then walked to the side of the tee, someone in the crowd announced that Seve had hit his second shot at fifteen into the lake fronting the green. Later, seeing a replay on television, it seemed to me that he just quit on the swing, perhaps because he was uncertain whether the 4-iron he was using was the correct club. Whatever, he ended up with a bogey six.

When I got to my ball, I found it in light rough midway between a couple of pine trees, with the branches of one of them necessitating that I knock the approach down a little bit. The distance was 125 yards, which normally would have me reaching for the 9-iron. With so much adrenaline flowing, I decided on the pitching wedge and played exactly the shot I'd visualized, a crisp semipunch that stopped the ball about ten feet left of the pin. As on the previous hole, the putt was a difficult one to read, resulting in much conferring between caddie and player. Jackie said left edge. Remembering that putts here, perhaps influenced by Rae's Creek, always seemed to break more right than they appeared to, I figured just outside right. That's what we went with, and the ball broke beautifully dead into the center of the cup.

Miraculously, stunningly, at nine under par I now led the 1986 Masters.

From my birdie putt at nine to the one I'd just made to get in that position, I had played the most aggressive golf of my career in a major championship since my make-or-break final round at the 1972 British Open. Walking to the eighteenth tee, I decided on a strategy change. "You've had an incredible run to get where you are," I told myself, "so don't go and screw it up now by trying to cap yourself with a birdie at eighteen. Just go ahead and play the hole intelligently. If you make birdie, great, but par will be just fine."

That translated into a 3-wood from the tee, which I hit solidly into ideal position just to the right of the bunkers guarding the left side of the fairway. Throughout most of my career, the cup on Masters Sundays had been cut in the lower tier of the two-level green directly behind the front left bunker. This time it was located in the right rear segment of the upper tier. The math indicated I had 179 yards uphill into a slight breeze. The club I'd wanted to hit walking up to the ball was the 5-iron, and that's the one I quickly decided on and pulled. The swing I made with it was one of my best of the day, but, as the shot reached its apex, I felt the wind hit me in the face and knew the ball would finish short of the green's upper tier. It actually flew farther than I figured, landing about two thirds of the way up the green, but then rolled back down about forty feet short of the cup.

I will never forget the ovation we received on our walk up to the green that day. It was deafening, stunning, unbelievable in every way. Tears kept coming to my eyes and I had to tell myself a number of times to hold back on the emotions, that I still had some golf to play. But, as at Muirfield in 1972 and St. Andrews in 1978 and Baltusrol in 1980, it was awfully hard to do.

Getting down in two from forty feet on Augusta National's huge and difficult eighteenth green was far from the position I wanted to be in, but it was what I had to deal with to possibly win a sixth Masters. As I went about doing so, I kept telling myself, "Don't leave yourself a second putt, don't leave yourself a second putt." And, most fortunately, I did not, closing out a back nine of 30 and a round of 65 with a tap-in of about four inches, a distance I've generally been able to handle.

The affection Jackie and I then showed each other seems to have become one of sport's most indelible moments, and it will surely remain one of my most cherished memories through all of my remaining days. Jackie simply could not have been more helpful or supportive in the way he handled the mechanics of an always stressful and grueling task, nor in the timeliness and insight and sincerity of his encouragement. It was just a wonderful experience to have one of the people I care most deeply about share by far the most fulfilling achievement of my career. And what made it even more wonderful was that Jackie also enjoyed it so much. "I was so proud of him," he would tell the press later that evening. "Finally, when he putted out on eighteen, I told him, 'Dad, I loved seeing you play today.' It was the thrill of my life. I mean, that was just awesome."

From the scorers' tent we were taken to Bob Jones's cabin over by the tenth tee to watch the eight players behind us finish the tournament on television. By the time we got there, Watson and Nakajima, the pair immediately behind Lyle and me, had putted out, and Ballesteros and Kite were coming up the eighteenth fairway. With the wind knocked out of his sails on fifteen, Seve had three-putted at seventeen to drop to seven under par. But Tom was still at minus eight, meaning he could tie me with a birdie. Ideally positioned off the tee, he hit an approach that landed on the front of the green's upper tier, then ran to within about twelve feet of the cup. As I watched his putt after about six feet of roll I thought he had made it, but at the last second the ball swerved to the left and stopped on the lip. His score was 67, which in many years would have won the Masters for a golfer in contention starting the final round.

As the putt missed, someone in the room said, "OK, that's it, it's all over." "No it isn't," I quickly replied, "you've still got Norman." Donnie Hammond and Bernhard Langer, the next-to-last pair, were no longer a factor, and neither was Nick Price, Norman's playing partner. But Greg had surged to nine under par with four straight birdies from the fourteenth through the seventeenth, the last of which I'd seen on television. If he parred eighteen, we would be tied. After mostly sitting since I arrived at the cabin, and aware that my back was beginning to stiffen, I got up and started walking around while still looking at the screen. Greg might birdie to win outright, but the odds were favoring a playoff. If it came, I wanted to be as ready for it as possible.

Greg's tee shot at eighteen split the fairway, but was far enough back to indicate he'd hit the 3-wood. I figured he would play either the 4- or 5-iron, and it transpired that he went with the former. I could tell from the way he almost lost his balance that the swing wasn't a good one, and the ball flew into the gallery well right of the green. Long experience told me that he needed a miracle to birdie from there, but I continued pacing because he could still par the hole. He made a good attempt at about the only shot that would work for him, pitch-and-running the ball to the back of the green about fifteen feet above the cup. Considering how he'd putted the previous four holes, I felt there was a pretty good chance he'd make this one, but as soon as the ball started rolling it was apparent that he'd pulled it slightly.

Amazingly, stunningly, I had played the last ten holes of the Augusta National in birdie-birdie-birdie-bogey-birdie-par-eagle-birdie-birdie-par, and it had won me a sixth Masters.

• • •

I WOULD have been on top of the world for a long time after that victory without any of what followed it, but the reaction of hundreds and hundreds of people, from close friends to complete strangers, and from everywhere golf is played, with calls, telegrams, cablegrams, cards, letters, flowers—even champagne—simply would not let me down from my high for weeks and weeks afterward.

We stopped counting the pieces of mail when they reached five thousand. Mountains of them arrived each morning at the house and office for many days, some addressed just "Jack Nicklaus, Florida, America," and each of them seemingly even nicer than the previous one. Most of them mentioned Jackie's and my moment of affection after I putted out on eighteen—it really seemed to have touched a lot of hearts. I've never been a great reader of anything, but I read every single one of those telegrams, cablegrams, cards, and letters. Perhaps the one that sticks in mind the most was the telegram from Arnold Palmer: "That was fantastic! Congratulations. Do you think there's any chance for a fifty-six-year-old?" Lee and Claudia Trevino, Gary and Vivienne Player, Hale and Sally Irwin, and Tom and Jeanne Weiskopf, among others of my peers, sent beautiful letters.

IN his *New Yorker* report, Herbert Warren Wind, to my mind golf's top historian as well as a superb writer, described my 1986 Masters victory as "nothing less than the most important accomplishment in golf since Bobby Jones' Grand Slam in 1930." Another writer described my performance over the last ten holes as "the greatest stretch of competitive golf ever played." A number of articles said again what had been said about me numerous times over the years, which was that I had dominated golf for a longer period of time, and with greater certainty, than anyone in the game's history.

Asked for an assessment of my career after that win, here's what my collaborator on this book wrote:

> There have been prettier swingers of the club than Jack Nicklaus. There may have been better ball-strikers than Jack Nicklaus. There have definitely been better short-game exponents than Jack Nicklaus. Other golfers have putted as well as Jack Nicklaus. There may have

been golfers as dedicated and fiercely competitive as Jack Nicklaus. But no individual has been able to develop and combine and sustain all of the complex physical skills and the immense mental and emotional resources the game demands at its highest level as well as Jack Nicklaus has for as long as he has.

It is for others to judge whether that and all the other wonderful compliments that followed my final major championship victory are true.

To end this story, all I want to say is that no golfer ever had more fun or enjoyed more fulfillment from trying to be the best at the greatest game of all than Jack Nicklaus.

Appendix: Jack Nicklaus's Tournament Records

Single asterisks (*) indicate wins, double asterisks (**) indicate top-three finishes. Major championships are in **bold** type.

THE AMATEUR YEARS

1950

* Scioto C.C. Juvenile Championship, Scioto C.C., Columbus, Ohio
  Winner, 61-60–121 (18 holes).

1951

* Scioto C.C. Juvenile Championship, Scioto C.C., Columbus, Ohio
  Winner, 90-84–174 (36 holes).

Columbus District Junior Golf League Championship, Army Course, Columbus, Ohio
Qualified with 81; eliminated in first round.

1952

* Columbus District Junior Golf League Championship, 10 courses around Columbus, Ohio
  Youngest member of Scioto C.C. team champions with 10–0 record.

1953

* Ohio State Junior Championship, Class B (13–15 years), Sylvania C.C., Toledo, Ohio
  Winner, 82-83–165.
* Columbus Junior Match-Play Championship Class B (13–15 years), Groveport C.C., Columbus, Ohio
  Won final, 1 up.
* Columbus Junior Stroke-Play Championship Class B (13–15 years), Ohio State University Gray Course, Columbus, Ohio
  Winner in sudden-death playoff following rounds of 77-76-74-73-72.

U.S. Junior Amateur Championship, Southern Hills C.C., Tulsa, Okla.
Eliminated in fourth round, 5 and 4.
Columbus Amateur Championship, Columbus C.C., Columbus, Ohio
Eliminated in second round, 2 and 1.

1954

* Tri-State (Ohio/Indiana/Kentucky) High School Championship, Potter's Park G.C., Hamilton, Ohio
Medalist, 68; member of winning team.
* Columbus Junior Stroke-Play Championship Class B (13–15 years), Groveport C.C., Columbus, Ohio
Winner, 70-69–139.
* Columbus Junior Match-Play Championship Class B (13–15 years), Scioto C.C., Columbus, Ohio
Won final, 6 and 5.
U.S. Junior Amateur Championship, Los Angeles C.C., North Course, Los Angeles, Calif.
Eliminated in second round, 4 and 3.
* Ohio State Junior Championship, Brookside C.C., Columbus, Ohio
Winner, 74-85–159.
* Scioto C.C. Junior Championship, Scioto C.C., Columbus, Ohio
Winner over 38 holes in sudden death; holed in one for the first time in second round.
Columbus District Amateur Championship, York Temple G.C., Columbus, Ohio
Eliminated in quarterfinal, 2 and 1.
Ohio State Amateur Championship, Sylvania C.C., Toledo, Ohio
Eliminated in first round, 1 down (Arnold Palmer won title).

1955

* Ohio Jaycees Championship, Elks C.C., Portsmouth, Ohio
Winner, 67-68–135.
* Columbus Junior Match-Play Championship Class A, Ohio State University Gray Course, Columbus, Ohio
Won final, 6 and 5.
* Columbus Junior Stroke-Play Championship Class A, York Temple C.C., Columbus, Ohio
Winner, 71-72-73–216.
* Ohio State Junior Championship Class B (13–15 years), Springfield C.C., Springfield, Ohio
Winner, 72-73–145.
Columbus District Amateur Championship Class A, Scioto C.C., Columbus, Ohio
Eliminated in semifinal, 3 and 2.
National Jaycees Championship (18 and under), Columbus C.C., Columbus, Ga.
Medalist (tie), 144 for two rounds; thirteenth, 293 for four rounds.
Ohio State Amateur Championship, Zanesville C.C., Zanesville, Ohio
Medalist; eliminated in first round.

U.S. Junior Amateur Championship, Purdue University South Course, Lafayette, Ind.
Eliminated in quarterfinals, 4 and 2.

U.S. Amateur Championship, C.C. of Virginia James River Course, Richmond, Va.
Qualified for a national championship for first time; eliminated in first round, 1 down.

1956

Tri-State (Ohio/Indiana/Kentucky) High School Championship, Potter's Park G.C., Hamilton, Ohio
Medalist, 67.

* Ohio High School State Championship, Ohio State University Scarlet Course, Columbus, Ohio
Winner, 73.

* Columbus Amateur Match-play Championship, Winding Hollow C.C., Columbus, Ohio
Won final, 5 and 4.

* Columbus Junior Match-play Championship, Brookside C.C., Columbus, Ohio
Won final, 2 up.

Exhibition Match, Urbana C.C., Urbana, Ohio
Sam Snead 68, Jack Nicklaus 72.

* Ohio State Open Championship, Marietta C.C., Marietta, Ohio
Winner, 76-70-64-72–282.

* Ohio Jaycees Championship, Findlay C.C., Findlay, Ohio
Winner, 72-70–142.

* Scioto C.C. Father/Son Championship, Scioto C.C., Columbus, Ohio
Winners, 151 (Charlie Nicklaus 77, Jack Nicklaus 74).

** National Jaycees Championship, Edgewood Municipal G.C., Fargo, N. Dak.
Defeated in playoff, 69–71.

U.S. Junior Amateur Championship, Taconic Club, Williamstown, Mass.
Eliminated in semifinal, 1 down.

Ohio State Amateur Championship, Westbrook G.C., Manfield, Ohio
Medalist; eliminated in first round, 2 and 1.

Sunnehanna Amateur Invitational, Sunnehanna C.C., Johnstown, Pa.
Fifth, 286 for four rounds.

U.S. Open Championship, Oak Hill C.C. East Course, Rochester, N.Y.
Second alternate after qualifying round; missed championship proper.

U.S. Amateur Championship, Knollwood Club, Lake Forest, Ill.
Eliminated in third round, 3 and 2.

1957

* Tri-State (Ohio/Indiana/Kentucky) High School Championship, Potter's Park G.C., Hamilton, Ohio
Medalist; led winning Upper Arlington team.

* Ohio High School State Championship, Ohio State University Scarlet Course, Columbus, Ohio
Winner, 72-76–148.

★ Ohio Jaycees Championship, Sharon Woods G.C., Cincinnati, Ohio
Winner, 75-71–146.

★ Ohio High School Central District Championship, Ohio State University Gray Course, Columbus, Ohio
Winner, 69.

★ National Jaycees Championship, Ohio State University Scarlet Course, Columbus, Ohio
Winner, 71-76-74-73–294.

U.S. Junior Amateur Championship, Manor C.C., Rockville, Md.
Eliminated in third round, 4 and 3.

U.S. Open Championship, Inverness Club, Toledo, Ohio
Qualified for first time with 68-71–139 at Cloverbrook C.C., Cincinnati, Ohio; missed cut, 80-80–160.

U.S. Amateur Championship, The Country Club, Brookline, Mass.
Eliminated in fourth round, 3 and 2.

★ Greater Columbus High School Golf League Championship, Ohio State University Scarlet Course, Columbus, Ohio
Medalist, 74; member of winning team.

1958

★ Trans-Mississippi Amateur Championship, Prairie Dunes G.C., Hutchinson, Kans.
Won final, 9 and 8.

★ Queen City Open Championship, Kenwood G.C., Cincinnati, Ohio
Winner, 70-67–137.

Colonial Invitational, Colonial C.C., Memphis, Tenn.
Medalist, 71-71–142.

Rubber City Open, Firestone C.C., Akron, Ohio
Twelfth; low amateur, 67-66-76-68–277 (first PGA Tour event).

U.S. Open Championship, Southern Hills C.C., Tulsa, Okla.
Medalist in regional qualifying; forty-first (tie), 79-75-73-77–304.

U.S. Amateur Championship, Olympic Club, San Francisco, Calif.
Eliminated in second round, 1 down.

1959

Masters Tournament, Augusta National G.C., Augusta, Ga.
Missed cut by one stroke with 76-74–150.

★ North and South Amateur Championship, Pinehurst, N.C.
Won final, 1 up.

★ Trans-Mississippi Amateur Championship, Woodhill C.C., Wayzata, Minn.
Won final, 3 and 2.

U.S. Open, Winged Foot G.C., Mamaroneck, N.Y.
Qualified with 67-75–142 at Cloverbrook C.C., Cincinnati, Ohio; missed cut, 77-77–154.

Gleneagles-Chicago Open, Gleneagles C.C., Lemont, Ill.
Twenty-sixth (tie), 67-69-76-73–285 (PGA Tour event).

Motor City Open, Meadowbrook C.C., Northville, Mich.
Forty-fifth (tie), 75-74-72-71–292 (PGA Tour event).

Buick Open, Warwick Hills G. & C.C., Grand Blanc, Mich.
Twelfth (tie), 76-70-70-72–288 (PGA Tour event).

★ U.S. Amateur Championship, Broadmoor G.C., Colorado Springs, Colo.
Winner, 1 up in final (first national title).

INTERNATIONAL

★ Walker Cup Match, The Honourable Company of Edinburgh Golfers, Muirfield, Scotland
Won foursome, partnered by Ward Wettlaufer, 2 and 1; won single, 5 and 4, in U.S. victory over Great Britain and Ireland, 9 points to 3.

★ Royal St. George's Challenge Cup, Royal St. George's G.C., Sandwich, England
Winner, 76-73–149.

British Amateur Championship, Royal St. George's G.C., Sandwich, England
Eliminated in quarterfinals, 4 and 3.

1960

★ International Four-Ball, Orange Brook G.C., Hollywood, Fla.
Winner with Deane Beman, 266.

Masters Tournament, Augusta National G.C., Augusta, Ga.
Thirteenth (tie); low amateur, 75-71-72-75–293.

★ Colonial Invitational, Colonial C.C., Memphis, Tenn.
Won final, 4 and 2.

★ NCAA Big Ten Conference Championship, Michigan State University G.C., East Lansing, Mich.
Member of winning team (Ohio State); runner-up for individual title, 284–282.

★★ U.S. Open Championship, Cherry Hills C.C., Englewood, Colo.
Second; low amateur, 71-71-69-71–282.

NCAA Championship, Broadmoor G.C., Colorado Springs, Colo.
Eliminated in third round, 4 and 3.

U.S. Amateur Championship, St. Louis C.C., Clayton, Mo.
Eliminated in fourth round, 5 and 3.

INTERNATIONAL

★ World Amateur Team Championship, Merion G.C., Ardmore, Pa.
Led 42-stroke U.S. team victory; won individual title, 66-67-68-68–269.

★ Americas Cup, Ottawa Hunt Club, Ottawa, Canada
Won two singles matches; lost two foursomes, partnered by Deane Beman in U.S. victory over Canada and Mexico (U.S. 21.5, Canada 20, Mexico 12.5).

1961

★ Western Amateur Championship, New Orleans C.C., New Orleans, La.
Won final, 4 and 3.

Masters Tournament, Augusta National G.C., Augusta, Ga.
Seventh (tie), 70-75-70-72–287.

Colonial National Invitation, Colonial C.C., Ft. Worth, Tex.
Thirty-eighth (tie), 75-74-76-72–297 (PGA Tour event).

U.S. Open Championship, Oakland Hills C.C., Birmingham, Mich.
Fourth (tie); low amateur, 75-69-70-70–284.

★ NCAA Big Ten Conference Championship, Indiana University G.C., Bloomington, Ind.
Winner in individual competition, 68-70-73-72–283; member of winning team (Ohio State).

★ NCAA Individual Championship, Purdue University G.C., West Lafayette, Ind.
Won final, 5 and 3.

Buick Open, Warwick Hills G. & C.C., Grand Blanc, Mich.
Twenty-fourth (tie), 74-72-72-74–292 (PGA Tour event).

American Golf Classic, Firestone C.C., Akron, Ohio
Fifty-fifth (tie), 76-73-74-76–299 (PGA Tour event).

★ **U.S. Amateur Championship, Pebble Beach G.L., Monterey, Calif.**
Won final, 8 and 6.

INTERNATIONAL

★ Walker Cup Match, Seattle G.C., Seattle, Wash.
Won foursome with Deane Beman, 6 and 5; won single, 6 and 4, in U.S. victory over Great Britain and Ireland, 11 points to 1.

★ Americas Cup Match, Club Campestre Monterrey, Monterrey City, Mexico
Won one and halved one singles match; won one and halved one foursomes match, partnered by Dudley Wysong, in U.S. victory over Canada and Mexico (U.S. 29, Canada 14, Mexico 11).

THE PROFESSIONAL YEARS

The following are official championships and tournaments of major golf organizations in which Jack Nicklaus competed as a professional, together with a number of notable events not officially recognized in terms of prize money won. Additionally, he has participated throughout his career in invitational or limited-field contests for charitable causes, promotional endeavors, and entertainment purposes too numerous to itemize here.

1962

U.S.A.

Los Angeles Open, Rancho Municipal G.C., Los Angeles, Calif.
Fiftieth (tie), 74-70-72-73–289.

San Diego Open, Mission Valley C.C., San Diego, Calif.
Fifteenth (tie), 72-69-74-67–282.

Bing Crosby National Pro-Am, Pebble Beach G.L., Monterey Peninsula C.C., Cypress Point G.C., Monterey Peninsula, Calif.
Twenty-third (tie), 71-77-72-76–296.

Lucky International Open, Harding Park G.C., San Francisco, Calif.
Forty-seventh (tie), 71-73-73-73–290.

Palm Springs Golf Classic, Thunderbird C.C., Tamarisk C.C., Indian Wells C.C., Bermuda Dunes C.C., El Dorado C.C., Coachella Valley, Calif.
Thirty-second (tie), 71-71-73-65-75–355.

★★ Phoenix Open, Phoenix C.C., Phoenix, Ariz.
Second (tie), 69-73-68-71–281.

Greater New Orleans Open, City Park G.C., New Orleans, La.
Seventeenth (tie), 71-80-70-71–292.
Baton Rouge Open, Baton Rouge C.C., Baton Rouge, La.
Ninth (tie), 72-68-69-71–280.
Pensacola Open, Pensacola C.C., Pensacola, Fla.
Sixteenth (tie), 71-71-74-64–280.
** Doral Open, Doral C.C., Miami, Fla.
Third, 69-74-69-73–285.
Masters Tournament, Augusta National G.C., Augusta, Ga.
Fourteenth (tie), 74-75-70-72–291.
Greater Greensboro Open, Sedgefield C.C., Greensboro, N.C.
Seventh (tie), 70-72-74-70–286.
** Houston Classic, Memorial Park C.C., Houston, Tex.
Second (tie), 68-70-68-72–278.
** Waco Turner Open, Turner Lodge & C.C., Burneyville, Okla.
Third (tie), 71-73-70-71–285.
Colonial National Invitation, Colonial C.C., Ft. Worth, Tex.
Fourth, 69-71-74-69–283.
"500" Festival Open, Speedway G.C., Indianapolis, Ind.
Twenty-ninth (tie), 73-66-69-69–277.
** Thunderbird Classic, Upper Montclair C.C., Upper Montclair, N.J.
Second, 69-73-65-70–277.
*** U.S. Open Championship, Oakmont C.C., Oakmont, Pa.**
Winner in playoff, 72-70-72-69–283 and 71.
Western Open, Medinah C.C., Medinah, Ill.
Eighth (tie), 70-73-73-75–291.
**** PGA Championship, Aronimink G.C., Newtown Square, Pa.**
Third (tie), 71-74-69-67–281.
** American Golf Classic, Firestone C.C., Akron, Ohio
Third (tie), 72-70-71-71–284.
* World Series of Golf (made-for-TV match between season's major championship winners), Firestone C.C., Akron, Ohio
Winner, 66-69–135.
Dallas Open, Oak Cliff C.C., Dallas, Tex.
Fifth (tie), 72-71-68-72–283.
* Seattle World's Fair Pro-Am, Broadmoor C.C., Seattle, Wash.
Winner, 67-65-65-68–265.
* Portland Open, Columbia-Edgewater C.C., Portland, Ore.
Winner, 64-69-67-69–269.

INTERNATIONAL

Piccadilly Tournament, Hillside G.C., Southport, England
Forty-third, 79-71-70-78–298.
British Open Championship, Troon G.C., Troon, Scotland
Thirty-second (tie), 80-72-74-79–305.
Canadian Open Championship, Laval sur le Lac G.C., Montreal, Quebec, Canada
Fifth (tie), 70-75-68-71–284.
Australian Open Championship, Royal Adelaide G.C., Brisbane, Australia
Fifth, 74-70-71-71–286.

Wills Masters, The Lakes G.C., Sydney, Australia
Fifth.

1963

U.S.A.

Los Angeles Open, Rancho Municipal G.C., Los Angeles, Calif.
Twenty-fourth (tie), 71-74-68-67–280.

** Bing Crosby National Pro-Am, Pebble Beach G.L., Monterey Peninsula C.C., Cypress Point G.C., Monterey Peninsula, Calif.
Second (tie), 71-69-76-70–286.

Lucky International Open, Harding Park, G.C., San Francisco, Calif.
Missed cut, 76-73–149.

* Palm Springs Golf Classic, Thunderbird C.C., Tamarisk C.C., Indian Wells C.C., Bermuda Dunes C.C., El Dorado C.C., Coachella Valley, Calif.
Winner in playoff, 69-66-67-71-72–345 and 65.

** Phoenix Open, Arizona C.C., Phoenix, Ariz.
Third (tie), 67-70-67-71–275.

Greater New Orleans Open, Lakewood C.C., New Orleans, La.
Eighth (tie), 74-73-69-72–288.

Doral Open, Doral C.C., Miami, Fla.
Ninth (tie), 73-73-72-73–291.

* **Masters Tournament, Augusta National G.C., Augusta, Ga.**
Winner, 74-66-74-72–286.

Houston Classic, Memorial Park C.C., Houston, Tex.
Fourth, 65-69-68-71–273.

* Tournament of Champions, Desert Inn, Las Vegas, Nev.
Winner, 64-68-72-69–273.

** Colonial National Invitation, Colonial C.C., Ft. Worth, Tex.
Third, 71-69-74-70–284.

Memphis Open, Colonial C.C., Memphis, Tenn.
Eleventh, 67-73-70-68–278.

Thunderbird Classic, Westchester C.C., Harrison, N.Y.
Twenty-first (tie), 69-72-71-72–284.

U.S. Open Championship, The Country Club, Brookline, Mass.
Missed cut, 76-77–153.

Cleveland Open, Beechmont C.C., Cleveland, Ohio
Seventh, 68-68-69-70–275.

* **PGA Championship, Dallas A.C., Dallas, Tex.**
Winner, 69-73-69-68–279.

** Western Open, Beverely C.C., Chicago, Ill.
Second (tie), 69-74-71-66–280.

Insurance City Open, Wethersfield C.C., Wethersfield, Conn.
Fifth (tie), 73-67-67-71–278.

American Golf Classic, Firestone C.C., Akron, Ohio
Fifth (tie), 70-70-71-72–283.

* World Series of Golf (made-for-TV match between season's major-championship winners), Firestone C.C., Akron, Ohio
Winner, 70-70–140.

Seattle Open, Inglewood C.C., Seattle, Wash.
Missed cut, 77-72–149.
Portland Open, Columbia-Edgewater G.C., Portland, Ore.
Tenth (tie), 72-67-68-70–277.
Whitemarsh Open, Whitemarsh Valley C.C., Chestnut Hill, Pa.
Eighteenth (tie), 71-77-74-67–289.
* Sahara Invitational, Paradise Valley C.C., Las Vegas, Nev.
Winner, 75-66-66-69–276.
Cajun Classic Open, Oakbourne C.C., Lafayette, La.
Fifth (tie), 69-72-69-69–279.

INTERNATIONAL

**** British Open Championship. Royal Lytham & St. Annes G.C., Lytham St. Annes, England**
Third, 71-67-70-70–278.
* Canada Cup, St. Nom la Breteche G.C., Paris, France
Winner of team title, partnered by Arnold Palmer, 482; winner in individual competition, 67-72-66-32–237. (Event restricted by weather to 63 holes.)
** Wills Masters, The Lakes G.C., Sydney, Australia
Second, 74-77-64-72–287.

1964

U.S.A.

Bing Crosby National Pro-Am, Pebble Beach G.L., Monterey Peninsula C.C., Cypress Point G.C., Monterey Peninsula, Calif.
Missed cut, 75-70-77–222.
Lucky International Open, Harding Park G.C., San Francisco, Calif.
Twelfth (tie), 74-72-66-68–280.
Palm Springs Golf Classic, Indian Wells C.C., Bermuda Dunes C.C., El Dorado C.C., La Quinta C.C., Coachella Valley, Calif.
Twentieth (tie), 73-72-69-72-74–360.
* Phoenix Open, Phoenix C.C., Phoenix, Ariz.
Winner, 71-66-68-66–271.
** Greater New Orleans Open, Lakewood C.C., New Orleans, La.
Second (tie), 70-70-72-72–284.
St. Petersburg Open, Lakewood C.C., St. Petersburg, Fla.
Fourth (tie), 71-69-68-70–278.
** Doral Open, Doral C.C., Miami, Fla.
Second, 70-66-73-69–278.
Greater Greensboro Open, Sedgefield C.C., Greensboro, N.C.
Fourth, 70-69-67-73–279.
**** Masters Tournament, Augusta National G.C., Augusta, Ga.**
Second (tie), 71-73-71-67–282.
** Houston Classic, Sharpstown C.C., Houston, Tex.
Second, 76-66-66-71–279.
* Tournament of Champions, Desert Inn C.C., Las Vegas, Nev.
Winner, 68-73-65-73–279.
Colonial National Invitation, Colonial C.C., Ft. Worth, Tex.
Twenty-first (tie), 76-72-71-73–292.

Memphis Open, Colonial C.C., Memphis, Tenn.
Twelfth (tie), 72-70-66-66–274.
"500" Festival Open, Speedway C.C., Indianapolis, Ind.
Eighteenth (tie), 72-69-68-71–280.
Thunderbird Classic, Westchester C.C., Harrison, N.Y.
Eleventh (tie), 73-69-68-72–282.
U.S. Open Championship, Congressional C.C., Washington, D.C.
Twenty-third (tie), 72-73-77-73–295.
** Cleveland Open, Highland Park C.C., Cleveland, Ohio
Third (tie), 68-65-69-70–272.
* Whitemarsh Open, Whitemarsh C.C., Chestnut Hill, Pa.
Winner, 69-70-70-67–276.
**** PGA Championship, Columbus C.C., Columbus, Ohio**
Second (tie), 67-73-70-64–274.
** Western Open, Tam O'Shanter C.C., Niles, Ill.
Third (tie), 72-71-65-67–275.
American Golf Classic, Firestone, C.C., Akron, Ohio
Fourth, 73-69-70-73–285.
Carling World Open, Oakland Hills C.C., Birmingham, Mich.
Eleventh (tie), 73-72-70-71–286.
* Portland Open, Portland G.C., Portland, Ore.
Winner, 68-72-68-67–275.
** Sahara Invitational, Paradise C.C., Las Vegas, Nev.
Third (tie), 70-71-69-67–277.
** Cajun Classic, Oakbourne C.C., Lafayette, La.
Second (tie), 68-71-72-71–282.

INTERNATIONAL

**** British Open Championship, Old Course, St. Andrews, Scotland**
Second, 76-74-66-68–284.
Canadian Open Championship. Pine Grove C.C., St. Luc, Quebec, Canada
Fifth (tie), 70-72-71-69–282.
Piccadilly World Match-play, Wentworth G.C., Virginia Water, England
Eliminated in first round.
* Canada Cup, Royal Kaanapali G.C., Maui, Hawaii
Winner of team title, partnered by Arnold Palmer, 554; winner in individual competition, 72-69-65-70–276.
* Australian Open Championship, The Lakes G.C., Sydney, Australia
Winner, 75-71-74-67–287.

1965

U.S.A.

** Bing Crosby National Pro-Am, Pebble Beach G.L., Monterey Peninsula C.C., Cypress Point G.C., Monterey Peninsula, Calif.
Third (tie), 72-68-77-71–288.
Bob Hope Desert Classic, Indian Wells C.C., Bermuda Dunes C.C., El Dorado C.C., La Quinta C.C., Coachella Valley, Calif.
Fourth (tie), 71-71-69-72-69–352.
Phoenix Open, Arizona C.C., Phoenix, Ariz.
Eighth (tie), 70-69-70-71–280.

** Pensacola Open, Pensacola C.C., Pensacola, Fla.
Second, 68-71-67-71–277.

Doral Open, Doral C.C., Miami, Fla.
Fifth (tie), 70-73-69-70–282.

** Jacksonville Open, Selva Marina C.C., Jacksonville, Fla.
Second (tie), 72-69-73-72–286.

*** Masters Tournament, Augusta National G.C., Augusta, Ga.**
Winner, 67-71-64-69–271.

Tournament of Champions, Desert Inn C.C., Las Vegas, Nev.
Eleventh, 74-71-67-78–290.

* Memphis Open, Colonial C.C., Memphis, Tenn.
Winner, 67-68-71-65–271.

Buick Open, Warwick Hills C.C., Grand Blanc, Mich.
Fourth, 70-71-70-73–284.

U.S. Open Championship, Bellerive C.C., St. Louis, Mo.
Thirty-first (tie), 78-72-73-76–299.

St. Paul Open, Keller G.C., St. Paul, Minn.
Fifth (tie), 70-69-69-68–276.

** National Challenge Cup, Lakewood C.C., Rockville, Md.
Second, 72-76-66-66–280.

* Thunderbird Classic, Westchester C.C., Harrison, N.Y.
Winner, 67-66-69-68–270.

* Philadelphia Golf Classic, Whitemarsh C.C., Chestnut Hill, Pa.
Winner, 71-65-73-68–277.

**** PGA Championship, Laurel Valley C.C., Ligonier, Pa.**
Second (tie), 69-70-72-71–282.

Carling World Open, Pleasant Valley C.C., Sutton, Mass.
Thirty-eighth (tie), 74-73-74-70–291.

American Golf Classic, Firestone C.C., Akron, Ohio
Fifty-second (tie), 80-69-79-75–303.

** World Series of Golf (made-for-TV match between season's major championship winners), Firestone C.C., Akron, Ohio
Second, 71-71–142.

* Portland Open, Portland G.C., Portland, Ore.
Winner, 69-68-68-68–273.

Sahara Invitational, Paradise Valley C.C., Las Vegas, Nev.
Sixth (tie), 71-67-70-68—276.

** Cajun Classic, Oakbourne C.C., Lafayette, La.
Third (tie), 69-67-71-69–276.

PGA National Team Championship, PGA National G.C., Palm Beach Gardens, Fla.
Seventh, partnered by Arnold Palmer, 67-66-65-68–266.

INTERNATIONAL

British Open Championship, Royal Birkdale G.C., Southport, England
Twelfth (tie), 73-71-77-73–294.

** Canadian Open Championship, Mississaugua G. & C.C., Rexdale, Ontario, Canada
Second, 69-66-72-67–274.

** Australian Open Championship, Kooyonga G.C., Adelaide, Australia
Second, 66-63-70-71–270.

1966

U.S.A.

Bing Crosby National Pro-Am, Pebble Beach G.L., Monterey Peninsula C.C., Cypress Point G.C., Monterey Peninsula, Calif.
Twenty-fourth (tie), 73-71-75-76–295.

Doral Open, Doral C.C., Miami, Fla.
Fourteenth (tie), 77-66-70-70–283.

** Florida Citrus Open, Rio Pinar C.C., Orlando, Fla.
Second (tie), 70-73-68-70–281.

Jacksonville Open, Selva Marina C.C., Jacksonville, Fla.
Eighth (tie), 70-72-71-67–280.

* **Masters Tournament, Augusta National G.C., Augusta, Ga.**
Winner in playoff, 68-76-72-72–288 and 70.

Tournament of Champions, Desert Inn C.C., Las Vegas, Nev.
Fifth (tie), 76-71-69-72–288.

** Greater New Orleans Open, Lakewood C.C., New Orleans, La.
Third, (tie), 68-70-70-71–279.

** Oklahoma City Open, Quail Creek C.C., Oklahoma City, Okla.
Third, 73-70-65-71–279.

Memphis Open, Colonial C.C., Memphis, Tenn.
Fourth (tie), 72-64-68-68–272.

** **U.S. Open Championship, Olympic Club, San Francisco, Calif.**
Third, 71-71-69-74–285.

PGA Championship, Firestone, C.C., Akron, Ohio
Twenty-second (tie), 75-71-75-71–292.

Cleveland Open, Lakewood C.C., Cleveland, Ohio
Thirteenth (tie), 74-66-68-70–278.

** Thunderbird Classic, Upper Montclair C.C., Clifton, N.J.
Second, 71-72-66-70–279.

** Philadelphia Golf Classic, Whitemarsh C.C., Chestnut Hill, Pa.
Second, 72-70-70-67–279.

** World Series of Golf (made-for-TV match between season's major-championship winners), Firestone C.C., Akron, Ohio
Third, 70-73–143.

Portland Open, Columbia-Edgewater C.C., Portland, Ore.
Sixth (tie), 72-72-65-70–279.

* Sahara Invitational, Paradise Valley C.C., Las Vegas, Nev.
Winner, 71-77-68-66–282.

Houston Champions International, Champions G.C., Houston, Tex.
Nineteenth (tie), 69-71-70-74–284.

* PGA National Team Championship, PGA National G.C., Palm Beach Gardens, Fla.
Winner, partnered by Arnold Palmer, 63-66-63-64–256.

INTERNATIONAL

*** British Open Championship, Honourable Company of Edinburgh Golfers, Muirfield, Scotland**
Winner, 70-67-75-70–282.

Canadian Open Championship. Shaughnessey G.C., Vancouver, British Columbia, Canada
Twenty-seventh (tie), 73-72-72-75–292.

** Piccadilly World Match-play, Wentworth G.C., Virginia Water, England
Defeated in 36-hole final, 6 and 4.

* World Cup (formerly Canada Cup), Yomiuri C.C., Tokyo, Japan
Winner of team title, partnered by Arnold Palmer, 548; third in individual competition, 69-68-67-69–273.

1967

U.S.A.

* Bing Crosby National Pro-Am, Pebble Beach G.L., Cypress Point G.C., Spyglass Hill G.C., Monterey Peninsula, Calif.
Winner, 69-73-74-68–284.

Los Angeles Open, Rancho Municipal G.C., Los Angeles, Calif.
Fifty-first (tie), 69-74-72-71–286.

Bob Hope Desert Classic, Indian Wells C.C., Bermuda Dunes C.C., El Dorado C.C., La Quinta C.C., Coachella Valley, Calif.
Fourth (tie), 75-70-67-71-72–355.

Doral Open, Doral C.C., Miami, Fla.
Fourth, 68-71-66-72–277.

Florida Citrus Open, Rio Pinar C.C., Orlando, Fla.
Seventh (tie), 71-69-69-69–278.

Pensacola Open, Pensacola C.C., Pensacola, Fla.
Thirty-first (tie), 71-69-70-67–277.

Masters Tournament, Augusta National G.C., Augusta, Ga.
Missed cut, 72-79–151.

Tournament of Champions, Desert Inn C.C., Las Vegas, Nev.
Fourth (tie), 68-68-75-73–284.

Houston Champions International, Champions G.C., Houston, Tex.
Thirty-seventh (tie), 77-71-72-71–291.

** Greater New Orleans Open, Lakewood C.C., New Orleans, La.
Second, 70-68-69-71—278.

Colonial National Invitation, Colonial C.C., Ft. Worth, Tex.
Eighth (tie), 72-71-72-70–285.

Memphis Open, Colonial C.C., Memphis, Tenn.
Twentieth (tie), 77-67-67-69-280.

*** U.S. Open Championship, Baltusrol, Springfield, N.J.**
Winner, 71-67-72-65–275.

Cleveland Open, Aurora C.C., Aurora, Ohio
Twenty-sixth (tie), 72-69-69-72–282.

**** PGA Championship, Columbine C.C., Denver, Colo.**
Third (tie), 67-75-69-71–282.

* Western Open, Beverely C.C., Chicago, Ill.
Winner, 72-68-65-69–274.

** American Golf Classic, Firestone C.C., Akron, Ohio
Third (tie), 70-69-70-71–280.

* World Series of Golf (made-for-TV match between season's major-championship winners), Firestone C.C., Akron, Ohio
Winner, 74-70–144.

* Westchester Classic, Westchester C.C., Harrison, N.Y.
Winner, 67-69-65-71–272.

** Thunderbird Classic, Upper Montclair C.C., Clifton, N.J.
Second (tie), 73-70-69-72–284.

* Sahara Invitational, Paradise Valley C.C., Las Vegas, Nev.
Winner, 68-69-62-71—270.

INTERNATIONAL

** Canadian Open Championship, Montreal Municipal G.C., Montreal, Quebec, Canada
Third (tie), 69-72-70-69–280.

**** British Open Championship, Royal Liverpool G.C., Hoylake, England**
Second, 71-69-71-69–280.

World Cup, Club de Golf Mexico, Mexico City, Mexico
Winner of team title, partnered by Arnold Palmer, 557; second in individual competition, 72-71-69-69–281.

1968

U.S.A.

Bing Crosby National Pro-Am, Pebble Beach G.L., Cypress Point G.C., Spyglass Hill G.C., Monterey Peninsula, Calif.
Eighth, 71-75-70-73–289.

Andy Williams San Diego Open, Torrey Pines C.C., San Diego, Calif.
Fifth, 67-69-69-72–277.

Phoenix Open, Phoenix C.C., Phoenix, Ariz.
Missed cut, 75-71–146.

Doral Open, Doral C.C., Miami, Fla.
Seventeenth (tie), 72-74-70-70–286.

** Florida Citrus Open, Rio Pinar C.C., Orlando, Fla.
Third, 67-68-73-68–276.

Jacksonville Open, Deerwood C.C., Jacksonville, Fla.
Twenty-third (tie), 74-68-70-68–280.

Masters Tournament, Augusta National G.C., Augusta, Ga.
Fifth (tie), 69-71-74-67–281.

Byron Nelson Golf Classic, Preston Trail G.C., Dallas, Tex.
Tenth, 73-67-70-69–279.

Houston Champions International, Champions G.C., Houston, Tex.
Fourth, 65-69-72-72–278.

Greater New Orleans Open, Lakewood C.C., New Orleans, La.
Thirteenth (tie), 71-71-71-68–281.

Memphis Open, Colonial C.C., Memphis, Tenn.
Seventeenth (tie), 71-65-69-70–275.

Atlanta Classic, Atlanta C.C., Atlanta, Ga.
Sixteenth (tie), 69-73-75-71–288.

**** U.S. Open Championship, Oak Hill C.C., Rochester, N.Y.**
Second, 72-70-70-67–279.

PGA Championship, Pecan Valley C.C., San Antonio, Tex.
Missed cut, 71-79–150.

* Western Open, Olympia Fields C.C., Olympia Fields, Ill.
Winner, 65-72-65-71–273.

* American Golf Classic, Firestone C.C., Akron, Ohio
Winner, 70-69-72-69–280.

** Westchester Classic, Westchester C.C., Harrison, N.Y.
Second (tie), 67-68-72-66–273.

Philadelphia Golf Classic, Whitemarsh Valley C.C., Chestnut Hill, Pa.
Fourth (tie), 73-69-66-70–278.

Thunderbird Classic, Upper Montclair C.C., Clifton, N.J.
Fifth (tie), 73-69-70-71–283.

Sahara Invitational, Paradise Valley C.C., Las Vegas, Nev.
Twelfth (tie), 67-70-68-74–279.

INTERNATIONAL

** Canadian Open Championship, St. George's G. & C.C., Toronto, Ontario, Canada
Second, 73-68-68-67–276.

**** British Open Championship, Carnoustie G.L., Carnoustie, Scotland**
Second (tie), 76-69-73-73–291.

* Australian Open Championship, Lake Karrinyup G.C., Perth, Australia
Winner, 71-64-68-67–270.

** Australian PGA Championship, Metropolitan G.C., Melbourne, Australia
Second, 71-67-72-72–282.

1969

U.S.A.

Bing Crosby National Pro-Am, Pebble Beach G.L., Cypress Point G.C., Spyglass Hill G.C., Monterey Peninsula, Calif.
Sixth, 71-73-73-70–287.

* Andy Williams San Diego Open, Torrey Pines C.C., San Diego, Calif.
Winner, 68-72-71-73–284.

Bob Hope Desert Classic, Indian Wells C.C., Bermuda Dunes C.C., El Dorado C.C., La Quinta C.C., Coachella Valley, Calif.
Thirteenth (tie), 72-71-74-68-69–354.

Doral Open, Doral C.C., Miami, Fla.
Fourth (tie), 72-71-64-72–279.

Florida Citrus Open, Rio Pinar C.C., Orlando, Fla.
Tenth (tie), 70-71-71-71–283.

Greater Jacksonville Open, Deerwood Club, Jacksonville, Fla.
Twenty-eighth (tie), 69-72-70-75–286.

National Airlines Open, C.C. of Miami, Miami, Fla.
Missed cut, 73-75–148.

Masters Tournament, Augusta National G.C., Augusta, Ga.
Twenty-fourth (tie), 68-75-72-76–291.

Western Open, Midlothian C.C., Midlothian, Ill.
Thirty-sixth (tie), 71-72-75-73–291.

U.S. Open Championship, Champions G.C., Houston, Tex.
Twenty-fifth (tie), 74-67-75-73–289.

Cleveland Open, Aurora C.C., Aurora, Ohio
Fifty-second (tie), 73-68-74-74–289.

American Golf Classic, Firestone C.C., Akron, Ohio
Sixth (tie), 66-66-71-75–278.

Westchester Classic, Westchester C.C., Harrison, N.Y.
Twelfth (tie), 71-73-69-70–283.

PGA Championship, NCR G.C., Dayton, Ohio
Eleventh (tie), 70-68-74-71–283.

Greater Hartford Open, Wethersfield C.C., Wethersfield, Conn.
Seventh, 68-68-69-68–273.

* Sahara Invitational, Paradise Valley C.C., Las Vegas, Nev.
Winner, 69-68-70-65–272.

* Kaiser Invitational, Silverado C.C., Napa, Calif.
Winner, 66-67-69-71–273.

** Hawaiian Open, Waialae C.C., Honolulu, Hawaii
Second, 63-71-74-70–278.

Heritage Golf Classic, Harbour Town Links, Hilton Head Island, S.C.
Sixth (tie), 71-72-71-75–289.

INTERNATIONAL

British Open Championship, Royal Lytham & St. Annes G.C., Lytham, England
Sixth (tie), 75-70-68-72–285.

Ryder Cup Match, Royal Birkdale G.C., Southport, England
Won foursome, partnered by Dan Sikes, 1 up; lost four-ball, partnered by Dan Sikes, 1 down; lost single, 4 and 3; halved single in U.S. tie with Great Britain and Ireland, 16 points each.

1970

U.S.A.

** Bing Crosby National Pro-Am, Pebble Beach G.L., Cypress Point G.C., Spyglass Hill G.C., Monterey Peninsula, Calif.
Second, 70-72-72-65–279.

** Andy Williams San Diego Open, Torrey Pines C.C., San Diego, Calif.
Third, 65-68-70-73–276.

Florida Citrus Invitational, Rio Pinar C.C., Orlando, Fla.
Nineteenth (tie), 69-70-71-70–280.

Greater Jacksonville Open, Hidden Hills C.C., Jacksonville, Fla.
Fifth (tie), 70-71-72-70–283.

Masters Tournament, Augusta National G.C., Augusta, Ga.
Eighth (tie), 71-75-69-69–284.

Tournament of Champions, La Costa C.C., Carlsbad, Calif.
Seventh (tie), 71-69-72-74–286.

* Byron Nelson Golf Classic, Preston Trail G.C., Dallas, Tex.
Winner, 67-68-68-71–274.

Colonial National Invitation, Colonial C.C., Ft. Worth, Tex.
Seventeenth (tie), 71-70-69-73–283.

Atlanta Classic, Atlanta C.C., Atlanta, Ga.
Seventh (tie), 69-69-68-72–278.

Kemper Open, Quail Hollow C.C., Charlotte, N.C.
Missed cut.

** Western Open, Beverly C.C., Chicago, Ill.
Third (tie), 72-70-67-69–278.

U.S. Open Championship, Hazeltine National G.C., Chaska, Minn.
Fifty-first (tie), 81-72-75-76–304.

Philadelphia Golf Classic, Whitemarsh Valley C.C., Chestnut Hill, Pa.
74, withdrew.

* National Team Championship, Laurel Valley C.C., Ligonier, Pa.
Winner, partnered by Arnold Palmer, 61-67-64-67–259.

** Westchester Classic, Westchester C.C., Harrison, N.Y.
Second (tie), 72-67-67-68–274.

** American Golf Classic, Firestone C.C., Akron, Ohio
Second (tie), 73-67-69-69–278.

PGA Championship, Southern Hills C.C., Tulsa, Okla.
Sixth (tie), 68-76-73-66–283.

* World Series of Golf (made-for-TV match between season's major-championship winners), Firestone C.C., Akron, Ohio
Winner, 66-70–136.

Dow Jones Open, Upper Montclair C.C., Clifton, N.J.
Twelfth (tie), 73-68-69-74–284.

Kaiser International Open, Silverado C.C., Napa, Calif.
Missed cut.

Sahara Invitational, Paradise Valley C.C., Las Vegas, Nev.
Forty-third (tie),76-69-70-71–286.

Heritage Classic, Harbour Town G.L., Hilton Head Island, S.C.
Seventeenth (tie), 75-71-72-73–291.

INTERNATIONAL

*** British Open Championship, Old Course, St. Andrews, Scotland**
Winner in playoff, 68-71-71-73–283 and 72.

* Piccadilly World Match-play, Wentworth G.C., Virginia Water, England
Won final, 2 and 1.

1971

U.S.A.

Bing Crosby National Pro-Am, Pebble Beach G.L., Cypress Point G.C., Spyglass Hill G.C., Monterey Peninsula, Calif.
Thirty-fourth (tie), 72-75-69-76–292.

** Andy Williams San Diego Open, San Diego, Calif.
Third (tie), 69-71-71-66–277.

Hawaiian Open, Waialae C.C., Honolulu, Hawaii
Forty-sixth (tie), 70-74-70-73–287.

★ **PGA Championship, PGA National, Palm Beach Gardens, Fla.**
Winner, 69-69-70-73–281.
Doral-Eastern Open, Doral C.C., Miami, Fla.
Ninth (tie), 74-68-67-73–282.
Greater Jacksonville Open, Hidden Hills C.C., Jacksonville, Fla.
Ninth (tie), 71-75-72-69–287.
★★ **Masters Tournament, Augusta National G.C., Augusta, Ga.**
Second (tie), 70-71-68-72–281.
★ Tournament of Champions, La Costa C.C., Carlsbad, Calif.
Winner, 69-71-69-70–279.
★ Byron Nelson Golf Classic, Preston Trail G.C., Dallas, Tex.
Winner, 69-71-68-66–274.
★★ Atlanta Classic, Atlanta C.C., Atlanta, Ga.
Second, 67-68-70-70–275.
★★ **U.S. Open Championship, Merion G.C., Ardmore, Pa.**
Second, 69-72-68-71–280.
Westchester Classic, Westchester C.C., Harrison, N.Y.
Ninth (tie), 72-69-72-67–280.
★ National Team Championship, Laurel Valley C.C., Ligonier, Pa.
Winner (with Arnold Palmer), 62-64-65-66–257.
American Golf Classic, Firestone C.C., Akron, Ohio
Fourth, 73-68-69-70–280.
★★ 1VB-Philadelphia Classic, Whitemarsh Valley C.C., Chestnut Hill, Pa.
Third, 66-73-70-67–276.
U.S. Match-play Championship, C.C. of North Carolina, Pinehurst, N.C.
Eliminated in first round.
★★ World Series of Golf (made-for-TV match between season's major-championship winners), Firestone C.C., Akron, Ohio
Second, 71-71–142.
★★ Heritage Classic, Harbour Town G.L., Hilton Head Island, S.C.
Third (tie), 71-69-71-70–281.
★ Walt Disney World Open, Lake Buena Vista, Fla.
Winner, 67-68-70-68–273.

INTERNATIONAL

British Open Championship, Royal Birkdale G.C., Southport, England
Fifth (tie), 71-71-72-69–283.
★ Ryder Cup Match, Old Warson C.C., St. Louis, Mo.
Lost foursome, partnered by Dave Stockton, 1 down; won foursome, partnered by J.C. Snead, 5 and 3; won four-ball, partnered by Gene Littler, 2 and 1; won four-ball, partnered by Arnold Palmer, 1 up; won single, 3 and 2; won single, 5 and 3, in U.S. victory over Great Britain and Ireland, 18.5 points to 13.5 points.
★★ Piccadilly World Match-play, Wentworth G.C., Virginia Water, England
Defeated in final, 5 and 4.
★ Australian Open Championship, Royal Hobart G.C., Tasmania, Australia
Winner, 68-65-66-70–269.
★ Dunlop International, Manly G.C., Manly, Australia
Winner, 69-62-73-70–274.

★ World Cup, PGA National G.C., Palm Beach Gardens, Fla.
Winner of team title, partnered by Lee Trevino, 558; winner in individual competition, 68-69-63-71–271.

1972

U.S.A.

★ Bing Crosby National Pro-Am, Pebble Beach G.L., Cypress Point G.C., Spyglass Hill G.C., Monterey Peninsula, Calif.
Winner, 66-74-71-73–284.

Andy Williams San Diego Open, Torrey Pines C.C., San Diego, Calif.
Thirty-second (tie), 73-68-72-72–285.

Hawaiian Open, Waialae C.C., Honolulu, Hawaii
Forty-fourth (tie), 70-71-73-71–285.

Bob Hope Desert Classic, Bermuda Dunes C.C., Indian Wells C.C., Eldorado C.C., La Quinta C.C., Coachella Valley, Calif.
Tenth (tie), 70-72-68-71-70–351.

★★ Jackie Gleason's Inverrary Classic, Inverrary G. & C.C., Lauderhill, Fla.
Second, 73-68-71-67–279.

★ Doral-Eastern Open, Doral C.C., Miami, Fla.
Winner, 71-71-64-70–276.

Florida Citrus Open, Rio Pinar C.C., Orlando, Fla.
Tenth (tie), 70-72-70-69–281.

★★ Greater New Orleans Open, Lakewood C.C., New Orleans, La.
Second (tie), 66-70-71-73–280.

★ Masters Tournament, Augusta National G.C., Augusta, Ga.
Winner, 68-71-73-74–286.

★★ Tournament of Champions, La Costa C.C., Carlsbad, Calif.
Second, 70-71-67-72–280.

Byron Nelson Golf Classic, Preston Trail G.C., Dallas, Tex.
Twenty-ninth (tie), 69-71-73-71–284.

Atlanta Golf Classic, Atlanta C.C., Atlanta, Ga.
Eighteenth (tie), 70-64-75-76–285.

★ U.S. Open Championship, Pebble Beach G.L., Monterey Peninsula, Calif.
Winner, 71-73-72-74–290.

PGA Championship, Oakland Hills C.C., Birmingham, Mich.
Thirteenth (tie), 72-75-68-72–287.

★ Westchester Classic, Westchester C.C., Harrison, N.Y.
Winner, 65-67-70-68–270.

★ U.S. Match-play Championship, C.C. of North Carolina, Pinehurst, N.C.
Won final, 2 and 1.

★★ World Series of Golf (made-for-TV match between season's major-championship winners), Firestone C.C., Akron, Ohio
Second, 75-69–144.

Kaiser International, Silverado C.C., Napa, Calif.
Ninth (tie), 69-71-69-72–281.

Sahara Invitational, Paradise Valley C.C., Las Vegas, Nev.
Fifth (tie), 66-69-73-68–276.

* Walt Disney World Open, Lake Buena Vista, Fla.
Winner, 68-68-67-64–267.

INTERNATIONAL

**** British Open Championship, Honourable Company of Edinburgh Golfers, Muirfield, Scotland**
Second, 70-72-71-66–279.

1973

U.S.A.

Glen Campbell Los Angeles Open, Riviera C.C., Pacific Palisades, Calif.
Sixth, 69-70-71-70–280.

* Bing Crosby National Pro-Am, Pebble Beach G.L., Cypress Point G.C., Spyglass Hill G.C., Monterey Peninsula, Calif.
Winner, 71-69-71-71–282.

** Bob Hope Desert Classic, Bermuda Dunes C.C., Indian Wells C.C., Tamarisk C.C., La Quinta C.C., Coachella Valley, Calif.
Second (tie), 64-70-71-68-72–345.

Jackie Gleason's Inverrary Classic, Inverrary G. & C.C., Lauderhill, Fla.
Sixth (tie), 73-69-70-71–283.

Doral-Eastern Open, Doral C.C., Miami, Fla.
Sixteenth (tie), 69-74-73-69–285.

Greater Jacksonville Open, Deerwood C.C., Jacksonville, Fla.
Twenty-sixth (tie), 69-73-75-71–288.

* Greater New Orleans Open, Lakewood C.C., New Orleans, La.
Winner, 68-72-71-69–280.

**** Masters Tournament, Augusta National G.C., Augusta, Ga.**
Third (tie), 69-77-73-66–285.

* Tournament of Champions, La Costa C.C., Carlsbad, Calif.
Winner, 70-70-68-68–276.

* Atlanta Golf Classic, Atlanta C.C., Atlanta, Ga.
Winner, 67-66-66-73–272.

1VB-Philadelphia Golf Classic, Whitemarsh Valley C.C., Chestnut Hill, Pa.
Fifth (tie), 73-70-70-67–280.

U.S. Open Championship, Oakmont C.C., Oakmont, Pa.
Fourth (tie), 71-69-74-68–282.

American Golf Classic, Firestone, C.C., Akron, Ohio
Ninth (tie), 69-70-73-68–280.

*** PGA Championship, Canterbury C.C., Cleveland, Ohio**
Winner, 72-68-68-69–277.

U.S. Professional Match-play Championship, MacGregor Downs C.C., Cary, N.C.
Eliminated in quarterfinals.

** World Series of Golf (made-for-TV match between season's major-championship winners), Firestone C.C., Akron, Ohio
Third, 71-69–140.

* Ohio King's Island Open, Jack Nicklaus Golf Center, Mason, Ohio
Winner, 68-69-62-72–271.

* Walt Disney World Open, Lake Buena Vista, Fla.
  Winner, 70-71-67-67–275

INTERNATIONAL

British Open Championship, Troon G.C., Troon, Scotland
  Fourth, 69-70-76-65–280.

* Ryder Cup Match, Honourable Company of Edinburgh Golfers, Muirfield, Scotland
  Won foursome, partnered by Arnold Palmer, 6 and 5; lost four-ball, partnered by Arnold Palmer, 1 down; won foursome, partnered by Tom Weiskopf, 1 up; won four-ball, partnered by Tom Weiskopf, 3 and 2; tied single; won single, 1 up, in U.S. victory over Great Britain and Ireland, 19 points to 13 points.

* World Cup, Nueva Andalucia G.C., Marbella, Spain
  Won team title partnered by Johnny Miller, 558; third (tie) in individual competition, 69-68-73-71–281.

1974

U.S.A.

Bing Crosby National Pro-Am, Pebble Beach G.L., Cypress Point G.C., Spyglass Hill G.C., Monterey Peninsula, Calif.
  Twenty-fourth (tie), 74-73-71–218.

* Hawaiian Open, Waialae C.C., Honolulu, Hawaii
  Winner, 65-67-69-70–271.

Glen Campbell Los Angeles Open, Riviera C.C., Pacific Palisades, Calif.
  Eleventh (tie), 66-73-71-75–285.

Jackie Gleason's Inverrary Classic, Inverrary G. & C.C., Lauderhill, Fla.
  Fourth (tie), 74-73-69-65–281.

Doral-Eastern Open, Doral C.C., Miami, Fla.
  Fourteenth (tie), 71-72-66-70–279.

Greater New Orleans Open, Lakewood C.C., New Orleans, La.
  Sixth (tie), 66-71-70-70–277.

Masters Tournament, Augusta National G.C., Augusta, Ga.
  Fourth (tie), 69-71-72-69–281.

Tournament of Champions, La Costa C.C., Carlsbad, Calif.
  Ninth (tie), 72-71-69-75–287.

** Colonial National Invitation, Colonial C.C., Ft. Worth, Tex.
  Second, 71-69-69-68–277.

Kemper Open, Quail Hollow C.C., Charlotte, N.C.
  Fifteenth (tie), 70-69-69-70–278.

U.S. Open Championship, Winged Foot G.C., Mamaroneck, N.Y.
  Tenth (tie), 75-74-76-69–294.

**** PGA Championship, Tanglewood G.C., Clemmons, N.C.**
  Second, 69-69-70-69–277.

Westchester Classic, Westchester C.C., Harrison, N.Y.
  Fifth (tie), 68-69-68-70–275.

* Tournament Players Championship, Atlanta C.C., Atlanta, Ga.
  Winner, 66-71-68-67–272.

** World Open, Pinehurst No. 2, Pinehurst, N.C.
  Second (tie), 68-71-70-72–281.

Ohio King's Island Open, Jack Nicklaus Golf Center, Mason, Ohio
Seventh (tie), 71-71-69-73–284.
National Team Championship, Walt Disney World, Lake Buena Vista, Fla.
Fourteenth (tie), partnered by Tom Weiskopf, 67-64-64-66–261.

INTERNATIONAL

**** British Open Championship, Royal Lytham & St. Annes G.C., Lytham St. Annes, England**
Third, 74-72-70-71–287.
Canadian Open Championship, Mississaugua G. & C.C., Rexdale, Ontario, Canada
Thirteenth (tie), 70-65-72-70–277.
Dunlop Phoenix Tournament, Phoenix C.C., Miyazaki, Japan
Thirteenth (tie), 70-73-71-75–289.

1975

U.S.A.

Bing Crosby National Pro-Am, Pebble Beach G.L., Cypress Point G.C., Spyglass Hill G.C., Monterey Peninsula, Calif.
Sixth (tie), 71-74-72-72–289.
Hawaiian Open, Waialae C.C., Honolulu, Hawaii
Fourteenth (tie), 68-74-70-69–281.
** Glen Campbell Los Angeles Open, Riviera C.C., Pacific Palisades, Calif.
Third, 69-75-71-65–280.
** Jackie Gleason's Inverrary Classic, Inverrary G. & C.C., Lauderhill, Fla.
Third, 67-69-66-73–275.
* Doral-Eastern Open, Doral C.C., Miami, Fla.
Winner, 69-70-69-68–276.
* Heritage Classic, Harbour Town G.L., Hilton Head Island, S.C.
Winner, 66-63-74-68–271.
*** Masters Tournament, Augusta National G.C., Augusta, Ga.**
Winner, 68-67-73-68–276.
MONY Tournament of Champions, La Costa C.C., Carlsbad, Calif.
Ninth (tie), 70-72-71-74–287.
** Danny Thomas Memphis Classic, Colonial C.C., Memphis, Tenn.
Third (tie), 66-70-73-68–277.
Atlanta Classic, Atlanta C.C., Atlanta, Ga.
Fourth (tie), 68-73-67-69–277.
U.S. Open Championship, Medinah C.C., Medinah, Ill.
Seventh (tie), 72-70-75-72–289.
*** PGA Championship, Firestone C.C., Akron, Ohio**
Winner, 70-68-67-71–276.
Tournament Players Championship, Colonial C.C., Ft. Worth, Tex.
Eighteenth (tie), 67-75-70-75–287.
* World Open, Pinehurst No. 2, Pinehurst, N.C.
Winner, 70-71-70-69–280.
Kaiser International, Silverado C.C., Napa, Calif.
Sixth, 72-67-69-69–277.

INTERNATIONAL

** Canadian Open Championship, Royal Montreal G.C., Montreal, Quebec, Canada
Second, 65-71-70-68–274.

**** British Open Championship, Carnoustie G.C., Carnoustie, Scotland**
Third (tie), 69-71-68-72–280.

* Ryder Cup Match, Laurel Valley G.C., Ligonier, Pa.
Won foursome, partnered by Tom Weiskopf, 5 and 4; tied four-ball, partnered by Bob Murphy; won four-ball, partnered by J.C. Snead, 4 and 2; lost single, 1 down; lost single, 1 down, in U.S. victory over Great Britain and Ireland, 21 points to 11 points.

* Australian Open Championship, Australian G.C., Sydney, Australia
Winner, 67-70-70-72–279.

1976

U.S.A.

Bing Crosby National Pro-Am, Pebble Beach G.L., Cypress Point G.C., Spyglass Hill G.C., Monterey Peninsula, Calif.
Eighteenth (tie), 67-72-70-82–291.

Bob Hope Desert Classic, Bermuda Dunes C.C., Indian Wells C.C., Eldorado C.C., La Quinta C.C., Coachella Valley, Calif.
Seventh (tie), 69-70-72-69-72–352.

* Tournament Players Championship, Inverrary G. & C.C., Lauderhill, Fla.
Winner, 66-70-68-65–269.

** Doral-Eastern Open, Doral C.C., Miami, Fla.
Second (tie), 69-71-68-68–276.

Heritage Classic, Harbour Town G.L., Hilton Head Island, S.C.
Eleventh (tie), 72-69-68-73–282.

**** Masters Tournament, Augusta National G.C., Augusta, Ga.**
Third (tie), 67-69-73-73–282.

Greater New Orleans Open, Lakewood C.C., New Orleans, La.
Fourth (tie), 68-67-74-69–278.

Byron Nelson Golf Classic, Preston Trail G.C., Dallas, Tex.
Eighth (tie), 71-68-71-71–281.

Memorial Tournament, Muirfield Village G.C., Dublin, Ohio
Eighth (tie), 71-75-73-73–292.

U.S. Open Championship, Atlanta A.C., Duluth, Ga.
Eleventh (tie), 74-70-75-68–287.

American Express Westchester Classic, Westchester C.C., Harrison, N.Y.
Twenty-third (tie), 70-73-69-68–280.

PGA Championship, Congressional C.C., Bethesda, Md.
Fourth (tie), 71-69-69-74–283.

* World Series of Golf, Firestone C.C., Akron, Ohio
Winner, 68-70-69-68–275.

World Open, Pinehurst No. 2, Pinehurst, N.C.
Missed cut, 72-74–146.

Ohio King's Island Open, Jack Nicklaus Golf Center, Mason, Ohio
Sixth (tie), 71-69-69-67–276.

INTERNATIONAL

** Canadian Open Championship, Essex G. & C.C., Windsor, Ontario, Canada
Second, 67-67-72-65–271.

**** British Open Championship, Royal Birkdale G.C., Southport, England**
Second (tie), 74-70-72-69–285.

* Australian Open Championship, Australian G.C., Sydney, Australia
Winner, 72-71-72-71–286.

Dunlop Phoenix Tournament, Phoenix C.C., Miyazaki, Japan
Thirty-seventh (tie), 76-67-76-75–294.

1977

U.S.A.

Bing Crosby National Pro-Am, Pebble Beach G.L., Cypress Point G.C., Monterey Peninsula C.C., Monterey Peninsula, Calif.
Eleventh, 69-69-70-73–281.

Hawaiian Open, Waialea C.C., Honolulu, Hawaii
Missed cut, 73-72–145.

* Jackie Gleason's Inverrary Classic, Inverrary G. & C.C., Lauderhill, Fla.
Winner, 70-66-69-70–275.

Doral-Eastern Open, Doral C.C., Miami, Fla.
Eleventh (tie), 72-70-70-71–283.

Tournament Players Championship, Sawgrass, Ponte Vedra, Fla.
Fifth (tie), 73-74-72-74–293.

Heritage Classic, Harbour Town G.L., Hilton Head Island, S.C.
Seventh (tie), 68-72-70-70–280.

**** Masters Tournament, Augusta National G.C., Augusta, Ga.**
Second, 72-70-70-66–278.

* MONY Tournament of Champions, La Costa C.C., Carlsbad, Calif.
Winner, 71-69-70-71–281.

Houston Open, Woodlands, C.C., Houston, Tex.
Sixth (tie), 69-75-67-71–282.

* Memorial Tournament, Muirfield Village G.C., Dublin, Ohio
Winner, 72-68-70-71–281.

Atlanta Classic, Atlanta C.C., Atlanta, Ga.
Fifth, 70-73-67-68–278.

U.S. Open Championship, Southern Hills C.C., Tulsa, Okla.
Tenth (tie), 74-68-71-72–285.

** Pleasant Valley Classic, Pleasant Valley C.C., Sutton, Mass.
Second, 68-67-70-67–272.

**** PGA Championship, Pebble Beach G.L., Monterey Peninsula, Calif.**
Third, 69-71-70-73–283.

American Express Westchester Classic, Westchester C.C., Harrison, N.Y.
Eighth (tie), 71-74-68-66–279.

World Series of Golf, Firestone C.C., Akron, Ohio
Fifth (tie), 69-73-68-68–278.
Ohio King's Island Open, Jack Nicklaus Golf Center, Mason, Ohio
Missed cut, 73-72–145.

INTERNATIONAL

Canadian Open Championship, Glen Abbey G.C., Oakville, Ontario, Canada
Fourth (tie), 68-70-74-74–286.
** **British Open Championship, Turnberry G.L., Turnberry, Scotland**
Second, 68-70-65-66–269.
* Ryder Cup Match, Royal Lytham & St. Annes, Lytham St. Annes, England
Won foursome, partnered by Tom Watson, 5 and 4; lost four-ball, partnered by Raymond Floyd, 1 down; lost single, 1 down, in U.S. victory over Great Britain and Ireland, 12.5 points to 7.5 points.
Australian Open Championship, Australian G.C., Sydney, Australia
Fourteenth (tie), 77-67-72-80–296.

1978

U.S.A.

Bing Crosby National Pro-Am, Pebble Beach G.L., Cypress Point G.C., Spyglass Hill G.C., Monterey Peninsula, Calif.
Twenty-ninth (tie), 77-74-66-73–290.
** Glen Campbell Los Angeles Open, Riviera C.C., Pacific Palisades Calif.
Second, 72-66-70-72–280.
* Jackie Gleason's Inverrary Classic, Inverrary G. & C.C., Lauderhill, Fla.
Winner, 70-75-66-65–276.
** Doral-Eastern Open, Doral C.C., Miami, Fla.
Second, 67-69-72-65–273.
* Tournament Players Championship, Sawgrass, Ponte Vedra, Fla.
Winner, 70-71-73-75–289.
Masters Tournament, Augusta National G.C., Augusta, Ga.
Seventh, 72-73-69-67–281.
MONY Tournament of Champions, La Costa, Carlsbad, Calif.
Fifteenth (tie), 72-69-73-77–291.
Memorial Tournament, Muirfield Village G.C., Dublin, Ohio
Fourth (tie), 67-76-71-74–288.
Atlanta Classic, Atlanta C.C., Atlanta, Ga.
Missed cut, 73-74–147.
U.S. Open Championship, Cherry Hills C.C., Denver, Colo.
Sixth (tie), 73-69-74-73–289.
* 1VB Philadelphia Classic, Whitemarsh Valley C.C., Chestnut Hill, Pa.
Winner, 66-64-72-68–270.
PGA Championship, Oakmont C.C., Oakmont, Pa.
Missed cut, 79-74–153.
American Express Westchester Classic, Westchester C.C., Harrison, N.Y.
Tenth (tie), 67-69-71-72–279.
World Series of Golf, Firestone C.C., Akron, Ohio
Seventh, 72-76-70-67–285.

INTERNATIONAL

Canadian Open Championship, Glen Abbey G.C., Oakville, Ontario, Canada
Fifteenth (tie), 73-72-72-72–289.

*** British Open Championship, Old Course, St. Andrews, Scotland**
Winner, 71-72-69-69–281.

* Australian Open Championship, Australian G.C., Sydney, Australia
Winner, 73-66-74-71–284.

1979

U.S.A.

Bob Hope Desert Classic, Bermuda Dunes C.C., Indian Wells C.C., Tamarisk C.C., La Quinta C.C., Coachella Valley, Calif.
Eleventh (tie), 71-69-69-72-69–350.

Bay Hill Citrus Classic, Bay Hill Club, Orlando, Fla.
Thirtieth (tie), 68-70-72-78–288.

Jackie Gleason's Inverrary Classic, Inverrary G. & C.C., Lauderhill, Fla.
Sixty-sixth (tie), 74-72-73-75–294.

Doral-Eastern Open, Doral C.C., Miami, Fla.
Fifty-third (tie), 73-74-75-72–294.

Tournament Players Championship, Sawgrass, Ponte Vedra, Fla.
Thirty-third (tie), 67-73-82-78–300.

Masters Tournament, Augusta National G.C., Augusta, Ga.
Fourth, 69-71-72-69–281.

MONY Tournament of Champions, La Costa, Carlsbad, Calif.
Fifteenth (tie), 72-72-77-73–294.

Memorial Tournament, Muirfield Village G.C., Dublin, Ohio
Twenty-seventh (tie), 73-73-74-79–299.

U.S. Open Championship, Inverness C.C., Toledo, Ohio
Ninth (tie), 74-77-72-68–291.

** 1VB-Philadelphia Classic, Whitemarsh C.C., Chestnut Hill, Pa.
Third (tie), 72-70-67-65–274.

PGA Championship, Oakland Hills C.C., Birmingham, Mich.
Sixty-fifth (tie), 73-72-78-71–294.

INTERNATIONAL

Canadian Open Championship, Glen Abbey G.C., Oakville, Ontario, Canada
Twenty-second (tie), 70-75-71-77–293.

**** British Open Championship, Royal Lytham & St. Annes, Lytham St. Annes, England**
Second (tie), 72-69-73-72–286.

1980

U.S.A.

Bing Crosby National Pro-Am, Pebble Beach G.L., Cypress Point G.C., Spyglass Hill G.C., Monterey Peninsula, Calif.
Eleventh (tie), 69-76-66-73–284.

Glen Campbell Los Angeles Open, Riviera C.C., Pacific Palisades, Calif.
Sixteenth (tie), 73-70-69-71–283.
Jackie Gleason's Inverrary Classic, Inverrary G. and C.C., Lauderhill, Fla.
Fifty-third (tie), 69-76-72-73–290.
** Doral-Eastern Open, Doral C.C., Miami, Fla.
Second, 72-67-71-69–279.
Tournament Players Championship, Sawgrass, Ponte Vedra, Fla.
Fourteenth (tie), 69-73-69-73–284.
Masters Tournament, Augusta National G.C., Augusta, Ga.
Thirty-third (tie), 74-71-73-73–291.
Byron Nelson Classic, Preston Trail G.C., Dallas, Tex.
Forty-third (tie), 70-74-74-71–289.
Memorial Tournament, Muirfield Village G.C., Dublin, Ohio
Twentieth (tie), 71-73-71-73–288.
Atlanta Classic, Atlanta C.C., Atlanta, Ga.
Missed cut, 78-67–145.
*** U.S. Open Championship, Baltusrol G.C., Springfield, N.J.**
Winner, 63-71-70-68–272.
*** PGA Championship, Oak Hill C.C., Rochester, N.Y.**
Winner, 70-69-66-69–274.
World Series of Golf, Firestone C.C., Akron, Ohio
Withdrew injured, 68-72-71–211.

INTERNATIONAL

Canadian Open Championship, Royal Montreal G.C., Quebec, Canada
Thirteenth (tie), 71-68-70-73–282.
British Open Championship, Honourable Company of Edinburgh Golfers, Muirfield, Scotland
Fourth (tie), 73-67-71-69–280.

1981

U.S.A.

Bob Hope Desert Classic, Bermuda Dunes C.C., Indian Wells C.C., Eldorado C.C., La Quinta C.C., Coachella Valley, Calif.
Twenty-eighth (tie), 68-67-74-71-69–349.
Bing Crosby National Pro-Am, Pebble Beach G.L., Cypress Point G.C., Spyglass Hill G.C., Monterey Peninsula, Calif.
Eleventh (tie), 71-68-72–211.
Glen Campbell Los Angeles Open, Riviera C.C., Pacific Palisades, Calif.
Fifteenth (tie), 71-70-67-70–278.
** American Motors Inverrary Classic, Inverrary G. & C.C., Lauderhill, Fla.
Second, 65-73-69-68–275.
Doral-Eastern Open, Doral C.C., Miami, Fla.
Missed cut, 74-73–147.
Tournament Players Championship, Sawgrass, Ponte Vedra, Fla.
Twenty-ninth (tie), 75-68-74-76–293.
**** Masters Tournament, Augusta National G.C., Augusta, Ga.**
Second (tie), 70-65-75-72–282.

MONY Tournament of Champions, La Costa C.C., Carlsbad, Calif.
Eleventh (tie), 72-69-74-71–286.
Memorial Tournament, Muirfield Village G.C., Dublin, Ohio
Twelfth (tie), 71-71-74-72–288.
Atlanta Classic, Atlanta C.C., Atlanta, Ga.
Ninth (tie), 68-72-69-72–281.
U.S. Open Championship, Merion C.C., Ardmore, Pa.
Sixth (tie), 69-68-71-72–280.
Western Open, Butler National C.C., Oak Brook, Ill.
Seventh, 75-72-70-69–286.
PGA Championship, Atlanta A.C., Atlanta, Ga.
Fourth (tie), 71-68-71-69–279.
World Series of Golf, Firestone C.C., Akron, Ohio
Tenth (tie), 71-67-71-74–283.
Hall of Fame Tournament, Pinehurst No. 2, Pinehurst, N.C.
Twenty-fifth (tie), 67-71-71-75–284.

INTERNATIONAL

** Canadian Open, Glen Abbey G.C., Oakville, Ontario, Canada
Second (tie), 70-70-70-71–281.
British Open Championship, Royal St. George's G.C., Sandwich, England
Twenty-third (tie), 83-66-71-70–290.

1982

U.S.A.

** Wickes–Andy Williams San Diego Open, Torrey Pines G.C., San Diego, Calif.
Second, 69-68-70-64–271.
** Bing Crosby National Pro-Am, Pebble Beach G.L., Cypress Point G.C., Spyglass Hill G.C., Monterey Peninsula, Calif.
Third (tie), 69-70-71-70–280.
Doral-Eastern Open, Doral C.C., Miami, Fla.
Eleventh (tie), 67-71-72-74–284.
** Bay Hill Classic, Bay Hill Club, Orlando, Fla.
Second (tie), 69-67-67-75–278.
Honda Inverrary Classic, Inverrary G. & C.C., Lauderhill, Fla.
Missed cut, 73-71–144.
Tournament Players Championship, Tournament Players Club at Sawgrass, Ponto Vedra, Fla.
Missed cut, 73-78–151.
Masters Tournament, Augusta National G.C., Augusta, Ga.
Fifteenth (tie), 69-77-71-75–292.
USF&G Classic, Lakewood C.C., New Orleans, La.
Sixty-seventh (tie), 71-76–147.
* Colonial National Invitation, Colonial C.C., Ft. Worth, Tex.
Winner, 66-70-70-67–273.

Memorial Tournament, Muirfield Village G.C., Dublin, Ohio
Eleventh (tie), 74-68-72-72–286.
** Kemper Open, Congressional C.C., Bethesda, Md.
Third (tie), 72-65-72-74–283.
**** U.S. Open Championship, Pebble Beach G.L., Monterey Peninsula, Calif.**
Second, 74-70-71-69–284.
PGA Championship, Southern Hills C.C., Tulsa, Okla.
Sixteenth (tie), 74-70-72-67–283.
World Series of Golf, Firestone C.C., Akron, Ohio
Sixth (tie), 71-75-72-67–285.

INTERNATIONAL

Canadian Open Championship, Glen Abbey G.C., Oakville, Ontario, Canada
Missed cut, 73-73–146.
British Open Championship, Royal Troon G.C., Troon, Scotland
Tenth (tie), 77-70-72-69–288.

1983

U.S.A.

Bob Hope Desert Classic, Bermuda Dunes C.C., Indian Wells C.C., Tamarisk C.C., La Quinta C.C., Coachella Valley, Calif.
Twenty-fifth (tie), 72-68-69-69-71–349.
Bing Crosby National Pro-Am, Pebble Beach G.L., Cypress Point G.C., Spyglass Hill G.C., Monterey Peninsula, Calif.
Sixth, 71-71-66-72–280.
Doral-Eastern Open, Doral C.C., Miami, Fla.
Eighth (tie), 70-70-69-71–280.
** Honda Inverrary Classic, Inverrary G. & C.C., Lauderhill, Fla.
Second, 72-72-70-66–280.
Bay Hill Classic, Bay Hill Club, Orlando, Fla.
Fifth (tie), 72-72-73-70–287.
Tournament Players Championship, Tournament Players Club at Sawgrass, Ponte Vedra, Fla.
Nineteenth (tie), 73-76-68-74–291.
Masters Tournament, Augusta National G.C., Augusta, Ga.
73 (withdrew injured).
MONY Tournament of Champions, La Costa C.C., Carlsbad, Calif.
Tenth (tie), 65-72-77-73–287.
Byron Nelson Golf Classic, Preston Trail G.C., Dallas, Tex.
Twenty-third (tie), 69-74-70-69–282.
Colonial National Invitation, Colonial C.C., Ft. Worth, Tex.
Twenty-eighth (tie), 66-75-74-69–284.
Memorial Tournament, Muirfield Village G.C., Dublin, Ohio
Thirty-third (tie), 76-72-70-73–291.
U.S. Open Championship, Oakmont C.C., Oakmont, Pa.
Forty-third (tie), 73-74-77-76–300.
**** PGA Championship, Riviera C.C., Pacific Palisades, Calif.**
Second, 73-65-71-66–275.

** World Series of Golf, Firestone C.C., Akron, Ohio
Second, 67-73-69-65–274.

* Chrysler Team Championship, Boca West, Boca Raton, Fla.
Winner, partnered by Johnny Miller, 61-65-65–191.

INTERNATIONAL

British Open Championship, Royal Birkdale G.C., Southport, England
Twenty-ninth (tie), 71-72-72-70–285.

** Canadian Open Championship, Glen Abbey G.C., Oakville, Ontario, Canada
Third, 73-68-70-67–278.

1984

U.S.A.

Bing Crosby National Pro-Am, Pebble Beach G.L., Cypress Point G.C., Spyglass Hill G.C., Monterey Peninsula, Calif.
Seventeenth (tie), 72-73-71-70–286.

** Los Angeles Open, Riviera C.C., Pacific Palisades, Calif.
Third, 73-71-70-69–283.

Honda Classic, Tournament Players Club at Eagle Trace, Coral Springs, Fla.
Nineteenth (tie), 77-70-70-71–288.

** Doral-Eastern Open, Doral C.C., Miami, Fla.
Second, 67-69-70-68–274.

Bay Hill Classic, Bay Hill Club, Orlando, Fla.
Ninth (tie), 69-72-73-66–280.

Tournament Players Championship, Tournament Players Club at Sawgrass, Ponte Vedra, Fla.
Thirty-third (tie), 78-70-75-69–292.

Masters Tournament, Augusta National G.C., Augusta, Ga.
Eighteenth (tie), 73-73-70-70–286.

* Memorial Tournament, Muirfield Village G.C., Dublin, Ohio
Winner, 69-70-71-70–280.

U.S. Open Championship, Winged Foot G.C., Mamaroneck, N.Y.
Twenty-first (tie), 71-71-70-77–289.

PGA Championship, Shoal Creek G.C., Birmingham, Ala.
Twenty-fifth (tie), 77-70-71-69–287.

NEC World Series of Golf, Firestone C.C., Akron, Ohio
Tenth, 72-73-69-66–280.

Southern Open, Green Island C.C., Columbus, Ga.
Eleventh (tie), 70-68-70-66–274.

Chrysler Team Championship, Boca West, Boca Raton, Fla.
Twelfth (tie), partnered by Johnny Miller, 62-66-69-66–263.

INTERNATIONAL

** Canadian Open Championship, Glen Abbey C.C., Oakville, Ontario, Canada
Second, 73-69-69-69–280.

British Open Championship, Old Course, St. Andrews, Scotland
Thirty-first (tie), 76-72-68-72–288.

1985

U.S.A.

Bob Hope Desert Classic, Bermuda Dunes C.C., Indian Wells C.C., Tamarisk C.C., La Quinta C.C., Coachella Valley, Calif.
Fifty-third (tie), 71-69-72-71-71–354.
Los Angeles Open, Riviera C.C., Pacific Palisades, Calif.
Seventeenth (tie), 67-71-70-71–279.
Bing Crosby National Pro-Am, Pebble Beach G.L., Cypress Point G.C., Spyglass Hill G.C., Monterey Penninsula, Calif.
Fifteenth (tie), 76-72-73-67–288.
** Doral-Eastern Open, Doral C.C., Miami, Fla.
Third (tie), 76-68-69-74-287.
Honda Classic, Tournament Players Club at Eagle Trace, Coral Springs, Fla.
Twenty seventh (tie), 70-68-73-73–284.
USF&G Classic, Lakewood C.C., New Orleans, La.
Thirty-fifth (tie), 68-72-74–214.
Tournament Players Championship, Tournament Players Club at Sawgrass, Ponte Vedra, Fla.
Seventeenth (tie), 71-70-71-76–288.
Masters Tournament, Augusta National G.C., Augusta, Ga.
Sixth (tie), 71-74-72-69–286.
MONY Tournament of Champions, La Costa, Carlsbad, Calif.
Twenty-first (tie), 74-72-72-74–292.
Memorial Tournament, Muirfield Village G.C., Dublin, Ohio
Fifty-fourth (tie), 71-76-74-78–299.
U.S. Open Championship, Oakland Hills C.C., Birmingham, Mich.
Missed cut, 76-73–149.
Western Open, Butler National G.C., Oak Brook, Ill.
Sixty-first (tie), 76-72-74-76–298.
PGA Championship, Cherry Hills C.C., Denver, Colo.
Thirty-second (tie), 66-75-74-74–289.
** Greater Milwaukee Open, Tuckaway C.C., Franklin, Wisc.
Second, 70-69-67-71–277.
Chrysler Team Championship, Boca West, Boca Raton, Fla.
Twenty-third (tie), partnered by Johnny Miller, 65-65-70-66–266.

INTERNATIONAL

** Canadian Open Championship, Glen Abbey C.C., Oakville, Ontario, Canada
Second (tie), 70-73-66-72–281.
British Open Championship, Royal St. George's G.C., Sandwich, England
Missed cut, 77-75–152.

1986

U.S.A.

Phoenix Open, Phoenix C.C., Phoenix, Ariz,
Sixtieth (tie), 72-69-69-72–282.
AT&T National Pro-Am, Pebble Beach G.L., Cypress Point G.C., Spyglass Hill G.C., Monterey Peninsula, Calif.
Missed cut, 73-80-74–227.
Hawaiian Open, Waialae C.C., Honolulu, Hawaii
Thirty-ninth (tie), 70-69-71-74–284.
Honda Classic, Tournament Players Club at Eagle Trace, Coral Springs, Fla.
Missed cut, 73-76–149.
Doral-Eastern Open, Doral C.C., Miami, Fla.
Forty-seventh (tie), 70-70-73-75–288.
Tournament Players Championship, Tournament Players Club at Sawgrass, Ponte Vedra, Fla.
74-73 (withdrew injured).
*** Masters Tournament, Augusta National G.C., Augusta, Ga.**
Winner, 74-71-69-65–279.
Houston Open, Tournament Players Club at Woodlands, Houston, Tex.
Forty-second (tie), 72-73-72-73–290.
Memorial Tournament, Muirfield Village G.C., Dublin, Ohio
Fifth (tie), 66-70-72-69–277.
U.S. Open Championship, Shinnecock Hills G.C., Southampton, N.Y.
Eighth (tie), 77-72-67-68–284.
PGA Championship, Inverness Club, Toledo, Ohio
Sixteenth (tie), 70-68-72-75–285.
The International, Castle Pines C.C., Castle Rock, Colo.
Twenty-third (tie).
NEC World Series of Golf, Firestone C.C., Akron, Ohio
Ninth (tie), 71-69-69-73–282.
Chrysler Team Championship, Boca West R. & C., Broken Sound C.C., Boca Raton, Fla.
Fourth (tie), partnered by Jack Nicklaus II, 65-63-63-65–256.

INTERNATIONAL

Canadian Open Championship, Glen Abbey G.C., Oakville, Ontario, Canada
Sixteenth (tie), 74-69-70-74–287.
British Open Championship, Turnberry G.L., Turnberry, Scotland
Forty-sixth (tie), 78-73-76-71–298.
Suntory International Open, Narashino C.C., Chiba Prefecture, Japan
Twenty-third (tie), 71-74-72-67–284.

1987

U.S.A.

AT&T National Pro-Am, Pebble Beach G.L., Cypress Point G.C., Spyglass Hill G.C., Monterey Peninsula, Calif.
Fifteenth (tie), 72-72-70-71–285.

Doral-Ryder Open, Doral C.C., Miami, Fla.
Twenty-second (tie), 69-74-73-70–286.
Honda Classic, Tournament Players Club at Eagle Trace, Coral Springs, Fla.
Seventy-first, 74-77-73-76–300.
Tournament Players Championship, Tournament Players Club at Sawgrass, Ponte Vedra, Fla.
Missed cut, 70-74–144.
Masters Tournament, Augusta National G.C., Augusta, Ga.
Seventh (tie), 74-72-73-70–289.
Memorial Tournament, Muirfield Village G.C., Dublin, Ohio
Sixty-sixth (tie), 73-73-72-75–293.
Manufacturers Hanover Westchester Classic, Westchester C.C., Harrison, N.Y.
Missed cut, 77-76–153.
U.S. Open Championship, Olympic Club, San Francisco, Calif.
Forty-sixth (tie), 70-68-76-77–291.
PGA Championship, PGA National, Palm Beach Gardens, Fla.
Twenty-fourth (tie), 76-73-74-73–296.
The International, Castle Pines G.C., Castle Rock, Colo.
Thirty-sixth (tie).
Izuzu Kapalua International, Kapalua Resort, Maui, Hawaii
Thirty-sixth (tie), 73-70-75-71–289.
Chrysler Team Championship, Palm Beach Polo Club, Wellington Club, Greenview Cove C.C., West Palm Beach, Fla.
Missed cut, partnered by Jack Nicklaus II, 64-66-70–200.

INTERNATIONAL

Canadian Open Championship, Glen Abbey G.C., Oakville, Ontario, Canada
Twenty-fourth (tie), 72-70-72-73–287.
British Open Championship, Honourable Company of Edinburgh Golfers, Muirfield, Scotland
Seventy-second (tie), 74-71-81-76–302.

1988

U.S.A.

AT&T National Pro-Am, Pebble Beach G.L., Cypress Point G.C., Spyglass Hill G.C., Monterey Peninsula, Calif.
Sixty-fourth (tie), 73-73-73–219.
Doral-Ryder Open, Doral C.C., Miami, Fla.
Twenty-fourth (tie), 68-69-71-75–283.
Players Championship, Tournament Players Club at Sawgrass, Ponte Vedra, Fla.
Missed cut, 73-74–147.
Masters Tournament, Augusta National G.C., Augusta, Ga.
Twenty-first (tie), 75-73-72-72–292.
Memorial Tournament, Muirfield Village G.C., Dublin, Ohio
Missed cut, 74-76–150.
U.S. Open Championship, The Country Club, Brookline, Mass.
Missed cut, 74-73–147.

PGA Championship, Oak Tree G.C., Edmond, Okla.
Missed cut, 72-79–151.
The International, Castle Pines G.C., Castle Rock, Colo.
Thirty-fourth (tie).

INTERNATIONAL

British Open Championship, Royal Lytham & St. Annes G.C., Lytham St. Annes, England
Twenty-fifth (tie), 75-70-75-68–288.
Canadian Open Championship, Glen Abbey G.C., Oakville, Ontario, Canada
Thirty-eighth (tie), 68-74-76-67–285.

1989

U.S.A.

AT&T National Pro-Am, Pebble Beach G.L., Cypress Point G.C., Spyglass Hill G.C., Monterey Peninsula, Calif.
Forty-fifth (tie), 69-69-80-71–289.
Doral-Ryder Open, Doral C.C., Miami, Fla.
Missed cut, 78-76–154.
Players Championship, Tournament Players Club at Sawgrass, Ponte Vedra, Fla.
Twenty-ninth (tie), 71-72-68-78–289.
USG&G Classic, English Turn G. & C.C., New Orleans, La.
Twenty-fifth (tie), 73-69-70-72–284.
Masters Tournament, Augusta National G.C., Augusta, Ga.
Eighteenth (tie), 73-74-73-71–291.
Memorial Tournament, Muirfield Village G.C., Dublin, Ohio
Sixty-seventh, 72-78-77-75–302.
U.S. Open Championship, Oak Hill C.C., Rochester, N.Y.
Forty-third (tie), 67-74-74-75–290.
PGA Championship, Kemper Lakes G.C., Hawthorn Woods, Ill.
Twenty-seventh (tie), 68-72-73-72–285.
The International, Castle Pines, G.C., Castle Rock, Colo.
Ninth.
Ronald McDonald Children's Charities Invitational, Sherwood C.C., Thousand Oaks, Calif.
Fourth (tie), partnered by Greg Norman, 74-65-58–197.

INTERNATIONAL

Canadian Open Championship, Glen Abbey G.C., Oakville, Ontario, Canada
Tenth (tie), 68-69-69-70–276.
British Open Championship, Royal Troon G.C., Troon, Scotland
Thirtieth (tie), 74-71-71-70–286.

1990

U.S.A.—PGA TOUR

AT&T National Pro-Am, Pebble Beach G.L., Cypress Point G.C., Spyglass Hill G.C., Monterey Peninsula, Calif.
Sixty-first, 72-71-78-78–299.

Doral-Ryder Open, Coral C.C., Miami, Fla.
Sixty-eight (tie), 68-72-75-74–289.
Players Championship, Tournament Players Club at Sawgrass, Ponte Vedra, Fla.
Missed cut, 75-78–153.
Masters Tournament, Augusta National G.C., Augusta, Ga.
Sixth, 72-70-69-74–285.
USF&G Classic, English Turn G. & C.C., New Orleans, La.
78 (withdrew injured).
Memorial Tournament, Muirfield Village G.C., Dublin, Ohio
Twenty-sixth (tie), 78-73-73–224.
U.S. Open Championship, Medinah C.C., Medinah, Ill.
Thirty-third (tie), 71-74-68-76–289.
PGA Championship, Shoal Creek G.C., Birmingham, Ala.
Missed cut, 78-74–152.
The International, Castle Pines G.C., Castle Rock, Colo.
Fifty-fourth (tie).
Ronald McDonald Children's Charities Invitational, Sherwood C.C., Thousand Oaks, Calif.
Ninth, partnered by Greg Norman, 65-70-62–197.
Sazale Classic, Binks Forest G.C., Wellington, Fla.
Missed cut.

U.S.A.—SENIOR TOUR

* The Tradition, G.C. at Desert Mountain, Scottsdale, Ariz.
Winner, 71-67-68–206.
** PGA Seniors Championship, PGA National, Palm Beach Gardens, Fla.
Third (tie), 68-78-67-72–285.
* Mazda Senior Tournament Players Championship, Dearborn C.C., Dearborn, Mich.
Winner, 65-68-64-64–261.
** U.S. Senior Open Championship, Ridgewood C.C., Paramus, N.J.
Second, 71-69-67-70–277.

INTERNATIONAL

British Open Championship, Old Course, St. Andrews, Scotland
Sixty-third (tie), 71-70-77-71–289.

1991

U.S.A.—PGA TOUR

AT&T National Pro-Am, Pebble Beach G.L., Spyglass Hill G.C., Poppy Hills G.C., Monterey Peninsula, Calif.
Missed cut, 70-77-75–222.
Doral-Ryder Open, Doral C.C., Miami, Fla.
Fifth (tie), 71-63-75-70–279.
USF&G Classic, English Turn G. & C.C., New Orleans, La.
Fourteenth (tie), 68-69-74-71–282.
Masters Tournament, Augusta National G.C., Augusta, Ga.
Thirty-fifth (tie), 68-72-72-76–288.

Memorial Tournament, Muirfield Village G.C., Dublin, Ohio
Fifteenth (tie), 71-68-69-74–282.

U.S. Open Championship, Hazeltine National G.C., Chaska, Minn.
Forty-sixth (tie), 70-76-77-74–297.

PGA Championship, Crooked Stick G.C., Carmel, Ind.
Twenty-third (tie), 71-72-73-71–287.

** Shark Shootout, Sherwood C.C., Thousand Oaks, Calif.
Second, partnered by Greg Norman, 68-66-59–193.

U.S.A.—SENIOR TOUR

* The Tradition, G.C. at Desert Mountain, Scottsdale, Ariz.
Winner, 71-73-66-67–277.

* PGA Seniors Championship, PGA National, Palm Beach Gardens, Fla.
Winner, 66-66-69-70–271.

Mazda Senior Players Championship, Tournament Players Club at Michigan, Dearborn, Mich.
Twenty-second (tie), 77-70-69-73–289.

Kroger Senior Classic, Jack Nicklaus Sports Center, Mason, Ohio
Seventh (tie), 71-66-70–207.

* U.S. Senior Open Championship, Oakland Hills C.C., Birmingham, Mich.
Winner, 72-69-70-71–282.

INTERNATIONAL

British Open Championship, Royal Birkdale G.C., Southport, England
Forty-third (tie), 70-75-69-71–285.

Canadian Open Championship, Glen Abbey G.C., Oakville, Ontario, Canada
Twenty-seventh (tie), 74-68-74-67–283.

1992

U.S.A.—PGA TOUR

AT&T National Pro-Am, Pebble Beach G.L., Spyglass Hill G.C., Poppy Hills G.C., Monterey Peninsula, Calif.
Missed cut, 76-73-70–219.

Doral-Ryder Open, Doral C.C., Miami, Fla.
Missed cut, 71-75–146.

Honda Classic, Weston Hills G. & C.C., Ft. Lauderdale, Fla.
Twenty-ninth (tie), 70-70-69-72–281.

Masters Tournament, Augusta National G.C., Augusta, Ga.
Forty-second (tie), 69-75-69-74–287.

Memorial Tournament, Muirfield Village G.C., Dublin, Ohio
Forty-eighth (tie), 74-69-70-71–284.

U.S. Open Championship, Pebble Beach G.L., Monterey Peninsula, Calif.
Missed cut, 77-74–151.

PGA Championship, Bellerive C.C., St. Louis, Mo.
Missed cut, 72-78–150.

The International, Castle Pines G.C., Castle Rock, Colo.
Missed cut.

U.S.A.—SENIOR TOUR

** The Tradition, G.C. at Desert Mountain, Scottsdale, Ariz.
Second, 65-72-69-69–275.

PGA Seniors Championship, PGA National, Palm Beach Gardens, Fla.
Tenth (tie), 73-68-74-76–291.

** U.S. Senior Open Championship, Saucon Valley C.C., Bethlehem, Pa.
Third (tie), 70-68-75-67–280.

Nationwide Championship, C.C. of the South, Alpharetta, Ga.
Thirty-ninth (tie), 73-75–148.

INTERNATIONAL

British Open Championship, Honourable Company of Edinburgh Golfers, Muirfield, Scotland
Missed cut, 75-73–148.

1993

U.S.A.—PGA TOUR

AT&T National Pro-Am, Pebble Beach G.L., Spyglass Hill G.C., Poppy Hills G.C., Monterey Peninsula, Calif.
Missed cut, 73-76-72–221.

Doral-Ryder Open, Doral C.C., Miami, Fla.
Tenth (tie), 69-68-67-73–277.

Honda Classic, Weston Hills G. & C.C., Ft. Lauderdale, Fla.
Missed cut, 73-80–153.

Nestlé Invitational, Bay Hill Club, Orlando, Fla.
Missed cut, 72-78–150.

Masters Tournament, Augusta National G.C., Augusta, Ga.
Twenty-seventh (tie), 67-75-76-71–289.

Memorial Tournament, Muirfield Village G.C., Dublin, Ohio
Seventy-second, 70-75-81-72–298.

U.S. Open Championship, Baltusrol G.C., Springfield, N.J.
Seventy-second (tie), 70-72-76-71–289.

PGA Championship, Inverness Club, Toledo, Ohio
Missed cut, 71-73–144.

The International, Castle Pines G.C., Castle Rock, Colo.
Missed cut.

U.S.A.—SENIOR TOUR

The Tradition, G.C. at Desert Mountain, Scottsdale, Ariz.
Ninth (tie), 72-69-70-67–278.

PGA Seniors Championship, PGA National, Palm Beach Gardens, Fla.
Ninth (tie), 69-71-73-71–284.

Bell Atlantic Classic, Chester Valley G.C., Malvern, Pa.
Twenty-eighth (tie), 72-71-75–218.

Ford Senior Players Championship, Tournament Players Club at Michigan, Dearborn, Mich.
Twenty-second (tie), 67-75-78-71–291.

★ U.S. Senior Open Championship, Cherry Hills G.C., Denver, Colo.
Winner, 68-73-67-70–278.

Nationwide Championship, C.C. of the South, Alpharetta, Ga.
Sixteenth (tie), 68-73-72–213.

INTERNATIONAL

British Open Championship, Royal St. George's G.C., Sandwich, England
Missed cut, 69-75–144.

Canadian Open Championship, Glen Abbey G.C., Oakville, Ontario, Canada
Missed cut, 76-73–149.

1994

U.S.A.—PGA TOUR

AT&T National Pro-Am, Pebble Beach G.L., Spyglass Hill G.C., Poppy Hills G.C., Monterey Peninsula, Calif.
Missed cut, 74-73-73–220.

Nissan Los Angeles Open, Riviera C.C., Pacific Palisades, Calif.
Missed cut, 73-77–150.

Doral-Ryder Open, Doral C.C., Miami, Fla.
Missed cut, 80-73–153.

Nestlé Invitational, Bay Hill Club, Orlando, Fla.
Missed cut, 75-77–152.

Masters Tournament, Augusta National G.C., Augusta, Ga.
Missed cut, 78-74–152.

Memorial Tournament, Muirfield Village G.C., Dublin, Ohio
Missed cut, 75-77–152.

U.S. Open Championship, Oakmont G.C., Oakmont, Pa.
Twenty-eighth (tie), 69-70-77-76–292.

PGA Championship, Southern Hills C.C., Tulsa, Okla.
Missed cut, 79-71–150.

Lincoln-Mercury Kapalua International, Kapalua Resort, Maui, Hawaii
Thirty-first (tie), 69-71-76-78–294.

U.S.A.—SENIOR TOUR

★ Mercedes Championships, La Costa C.C., Carlsbad, Calif.
Winner, 73-69-69-68–279.

The Tradition, G.C. at Desert Mountain, Scottsdale, Ariz.
Fourth (tie), 70-71-69-68–278.

PGA Seniors Championship, PGA National, Palm Beach Gardens, Fla.
Ninth, 71-71-72-72–286.

Ford Senior Players Championship, Tournament Players Club at Michigan, Dearborn, Mich.
Sixth (tie), 68-72-73-67–280.

U.S. Senior Open Championship, Pinehurst No. 2, Pinehurst, N.C.
Seventh (tie), 69-68-70-72–279.

Northville Long Island Classic, Meadow Brook C., Jericho, N.Y.
Thirtieth (tie), 70-74-72–216.

Diners Club Matches, PGA West, La Quinta, Calif.
Defeated in final at 19th hole in sudden-death playoff, partnered by Arnold Palmer.

INTERNATIONAL

British Open Championship, Turnberry G.L., Turnberry, Scotland
Missed cut, 72-73–145.
Dunlop Phoenix Tournament, Phoenix C.C., Miyazaki, Japan
Twenty-eighth (tie), 70-71-70–211.

1995

U.S.A.—PGA TOUR

AT&T National Pro-Am, Pebble Beach G.L., Spyglass Hill G.C., Poppy Hills G.C., Monterey Peninsula, Calif.
Sixth (tie), 71-70-67-70–278.
Doral-Ryder Open, Doral C.C., Miami, Fla.
Missed cut, 77-67–144.
Nestlé Invitational, Bay Hill Club, Orlando, Fla.
Missed cut, 79-78–157.
Players Championship, Tournament Players Club at Sawgrass, Ponte Vedra, Fla.
Missed cut, 76-79–155.
Masters Tournament, Augusta National G.C., Augusta, Ga.
Thirty-fifth (tie), 67-78-70-75–290.
Memorial Tournament, Muirfield Village G.C., Dublin, Ohio
Missed cut, 78-75–153.
U.S. Open Championship, Shinnecock Hills G.C., Southampton, N.Y.
Missed cut, 71-81–152.
PGA Championship, Riviera C.C., Pacific Palisades, Calif.
Sixty-seventh (tie), 69-71-71-76–287.

U.S.A—SENIOR TOUR

Senior Tournament of Champions, Hyatt Dorado Beach, Puerto Rico
Ninth, 75-72-68–215.
GTE Suncoast Classic, Tournament Players Club of Tampa Bay, Lutz, Fla.
Fifth (tie), 69-70-68–207.
* The Tradition, G.C. at Desert Mountain, Scottsdale, Ariz.
Winner, 69-71-69-67–276.
PGA Seniors Championship, PGA National, Palm Beach Gardens, Fla.
Eighth, 76-66-68-74–284.
** Bell Atlantic Classic, Chester Valley G.C., Malvern, Pa.
Third, 72-69-68–209.
** U.S. Senior Open Championship, Congressional C.C., Bethesda, Md.,
Second, 71-71-70-67–279.
** Ford Senior Players Championship, Tournament Players Club at Michigan, Dearborn, Mich.
Second, 71-68-66-67–272.
Diners Club Matches, PGA West, La Quinta, Calif.
Defeated in first round, partnered by Arnold Palmer.

INTERNATIONAL

British Open Championship, Old Course, St. Andrews, Scotland
Seventy-ninth (tie), 78-70-77-71–296.

1996

U.S.A.—PGA TOUR

AT&T National Pro-Am, Pebble Beach G.L., Spyglass Hill G.C., Poppy Hills G.C., Monterey Peninsula, Calif.
71-72 (tournament flooded out).

Doral-Ryder Open, Doral C.C., Miami, Fla.
Missed cut, 72-75–147.

Masters Tournament, Augusta National G.C., Augusta, Ga.
Forty-first (tie), 70-73-76-78–297.

Memorial Tournament, Muirfield Village G.C., Dublin, Ohio
Missed cut, 77-75–152.

U.S. Open Championship, Oakland Hills C.C., Bloomfield Hills, Mich.
Twenty-seventh (tie), 72-74-69-72–287.

PGA Championship, Valhalla G.C., Louisville, Ky.
Missed cut, 77-69–146.

Office Depot Father-Son Challenge, Windsor Club, Vero Beach, Fla.
Sixth, partnered by Gary Nicklaus, 65-67–132.

U.S.A.—SENIOR TOUR

Puerto Rico Senior Tournament of Champions, Hyatt Dorado Beach, Puerto Rico
Seventh (tie), 70-72-68–210.

* GTE, Suncoast Classic, Tournament Players Club of Tampa Bay, Lutz, Fla.
Winner, 76-68-67–211.

** Legends of Golf, PGA West, La Quinta, Calif.
Second (tie, with Gary Player), 66-69-65–200.

* The Tradition, G.C. at Desert Mountain, Scottsdale, Ariz.
Winner, 68-74-65-65–272.

PGA Seniors Championship, PGA National, Palm Beach Gardens, Fla.
Twenty-second (tie), 77-72-74-70–293.

U.S. Senior Open Championship, Canterbury G.C., Beechwood, Ohio
Sixteenth, 77-72-68-73–290.

Ford Senior Players Championship, Tournament Players Club at Michigan, Dearborn, Mich.
Twenty-fourth (tie), 74-70-72-71–287.

Northville Long Island Classic, Meadowbrook C., Jericho, N.Y.
Twelfth (tie), 69-70-71–210.

INTERNATIONAL

British Open Championship, Royal Lytham & St. Annes G.C., Lytham St. Annes, England
Forty-fourth (tie), 69-66-77-73–285.

Dunlop Phoenix Tournament, Phoenix C.C., Miyazaki, Japan
Missed cut.

Index

Photo Credits

1,2: from author's collection
3,9,20,38: © Wide World Photos
4,5,8,10,12,31: Bill Foley
6: © Ed Leppert Photographs
7: Dick Davis/Rocky Mountain News
11: © Henri Dauman, 1965, NYC
13: © Life Magazine
14,15,19,29,33,35,39,40,41,43,44,45: © Associated Press
17: Charles M. Pugh, Jr.
18,22,48,52: Brian Morgan
25: Davidoff Studios
26: Jerry Tobias
28: John Wettermann
30: Chuck Brenkus
34: © Time, Inc.
36: H.W. Neale
37: © Sports Illustrated/Walter Iooss
42: Ray Matjasic
47: Ruffin Beckwith
49: Hal Brown
55: © Sports Illustrated

The author and publisher have endeavored to trace the copyright proprietors and the identities of the photographers responsible for the photographs in this book. Readers with information with respect to those identities are requested to furnish it to the author and publisher. Acknowledgement, if appropriate, will be made in future printings, if any, of this book.